Impressionists on Paper

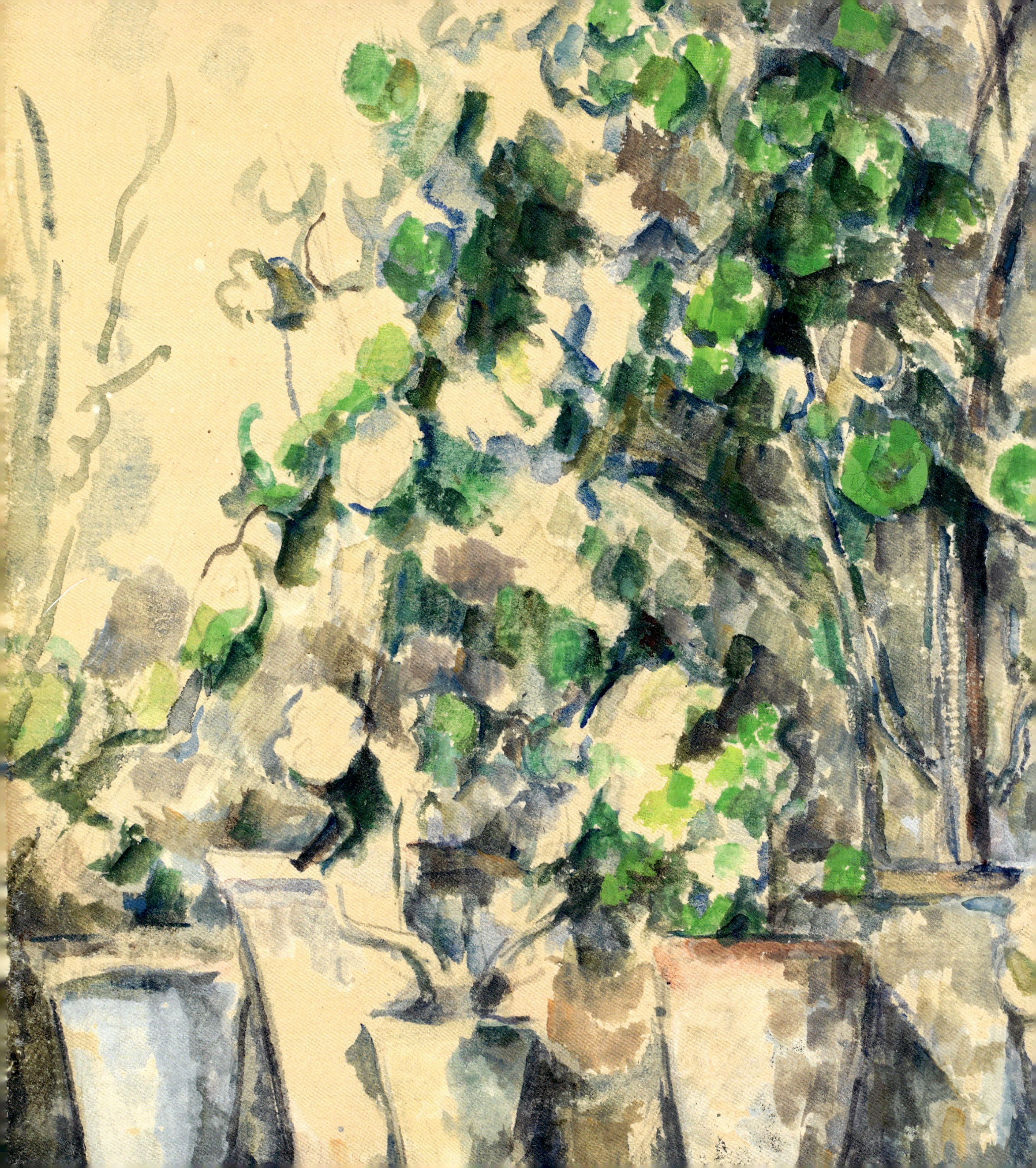

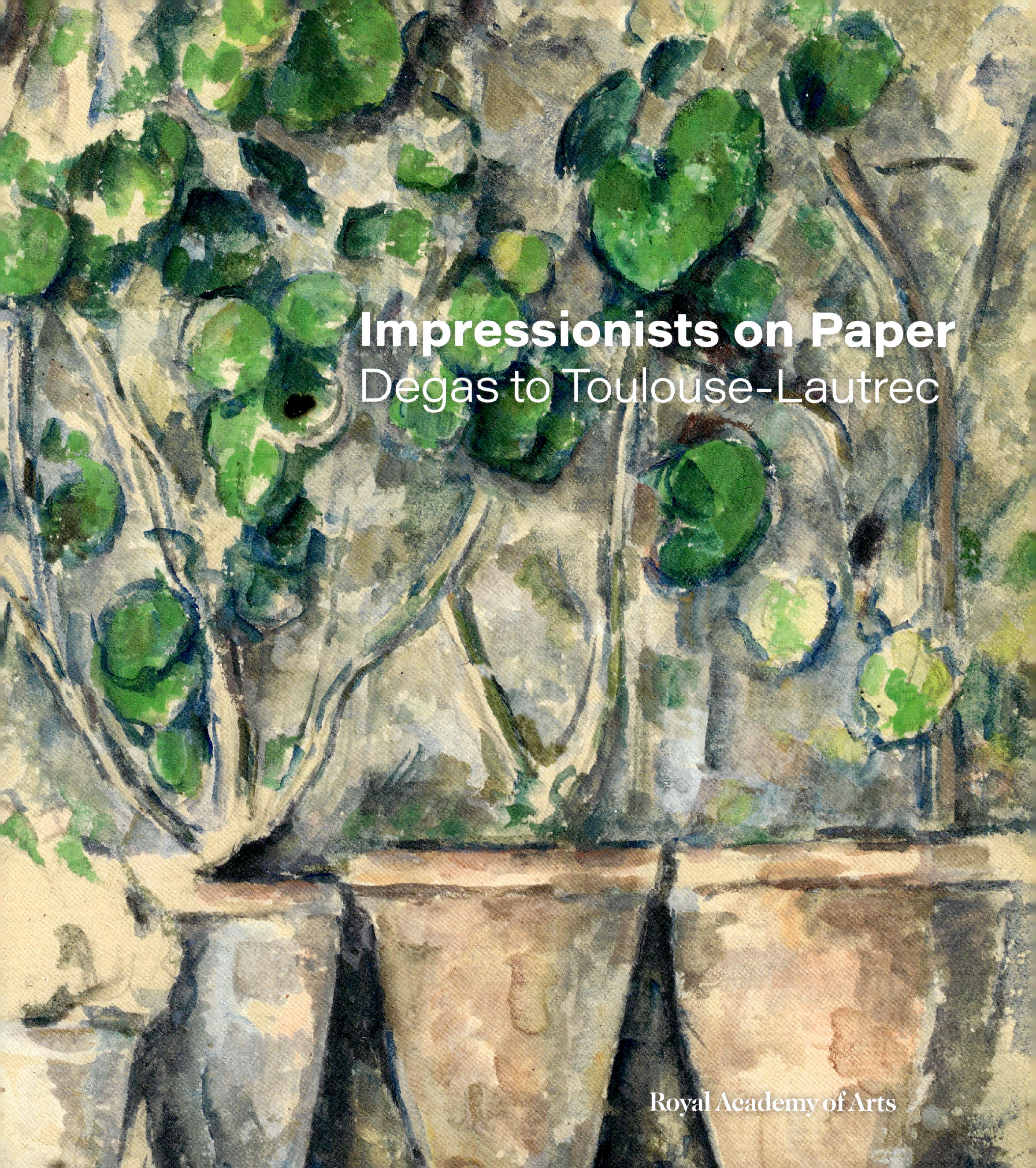
Impressionists on Paper
Degas to Toulouse-Lautrec
Royal Academy of Arts

First published on the occasion of the exhibition
Impressionists on Paper: Degas to Toulouse-Lautrec

Royal Academy of Arts, London
25 November 2023 – 10 March 2024

Supported by

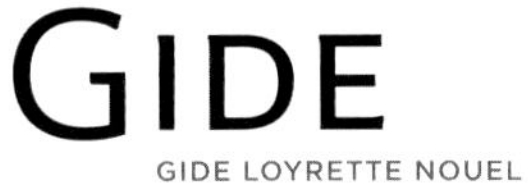

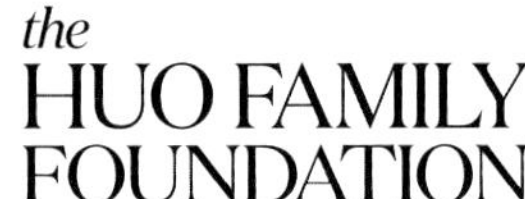

with additional support from

Kathryn Uhde

This exhibition has been made possible as a result of the Government Indemnity Scheme. The Royal Academy of Arts would like to thank HM Government for providing indemnity and the Department for Culture, Media & Sport and Arts Council England for arranging the indemnity.

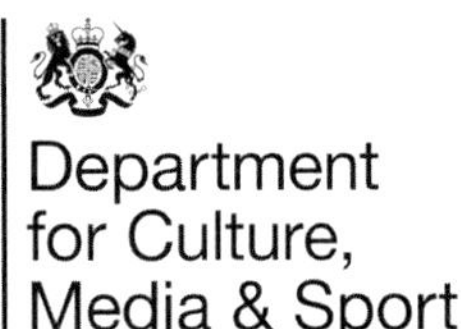

DIRECTOR OF EXHIBITIONS
Andrea Tarsia

EXHIBITION CURATORS
Ann Dumas
Christopher Lloyd
with Sylvie Broussine
Rhiannon Hope

EXHIBITION ORGANISATION
Joanna Weston
Stephanie Bush
with Helena Cooper

PHOTOGRAPHIC AND COPYRIGHT CO-ORDINATION
Susana Vázquez Fernández

EXHIBITION CATALOGUE
Royal Academy Publications
Florence Dassonville, Production and Distribution Co-ordinator
Carola Krueger, Production and Distribution Manager
Peter Sawbridge, Head of Publishing and Editorial Director

Translation from the French (Leïla Jarbouai): Caroline Beamish
Copy-editing and proofreading: Kate Bell
Design: Kathrin Jacobsen
Colour origination and print: Gomer Press, Wales

British Library Cataloguing-in-Publication Data
A catalogue record for this book is available from the British Library

ISBN 978-1-912520-97-8

Distributed outside the United States and Canada by ACC Art Books Ltd, Riverside House, Dock Lane, Melton, Woodbridge, IP12 1PE

Distributed in the United States and Canada by ARTBOOK | D.A.P., 75 Broad Street, Suite 630, New York, NY 10004

EDITORIAL NOTE
Dimensions of all works of art are given in centimetres, height before width.

ILLUSTRATIONS
Cover: detail of cat. 9
Edgar Degas, *Dancer Yawning (Dancer Stretching)*, 1873. *Essence* (diluted oil paint) on prepared green paperboard, 53 x 45 cm. Private collection

Pages 2–3: detail of cat. 32
Page 6: detail of cat. 10
Page 9: detail of cat. 64
Pages 10–11: detail of cat. 52
Pages 54–55: detail of cat. 3
Pages 76–77: detail of cat. 40
Pages 112–13: detail of cat. 77

Contents

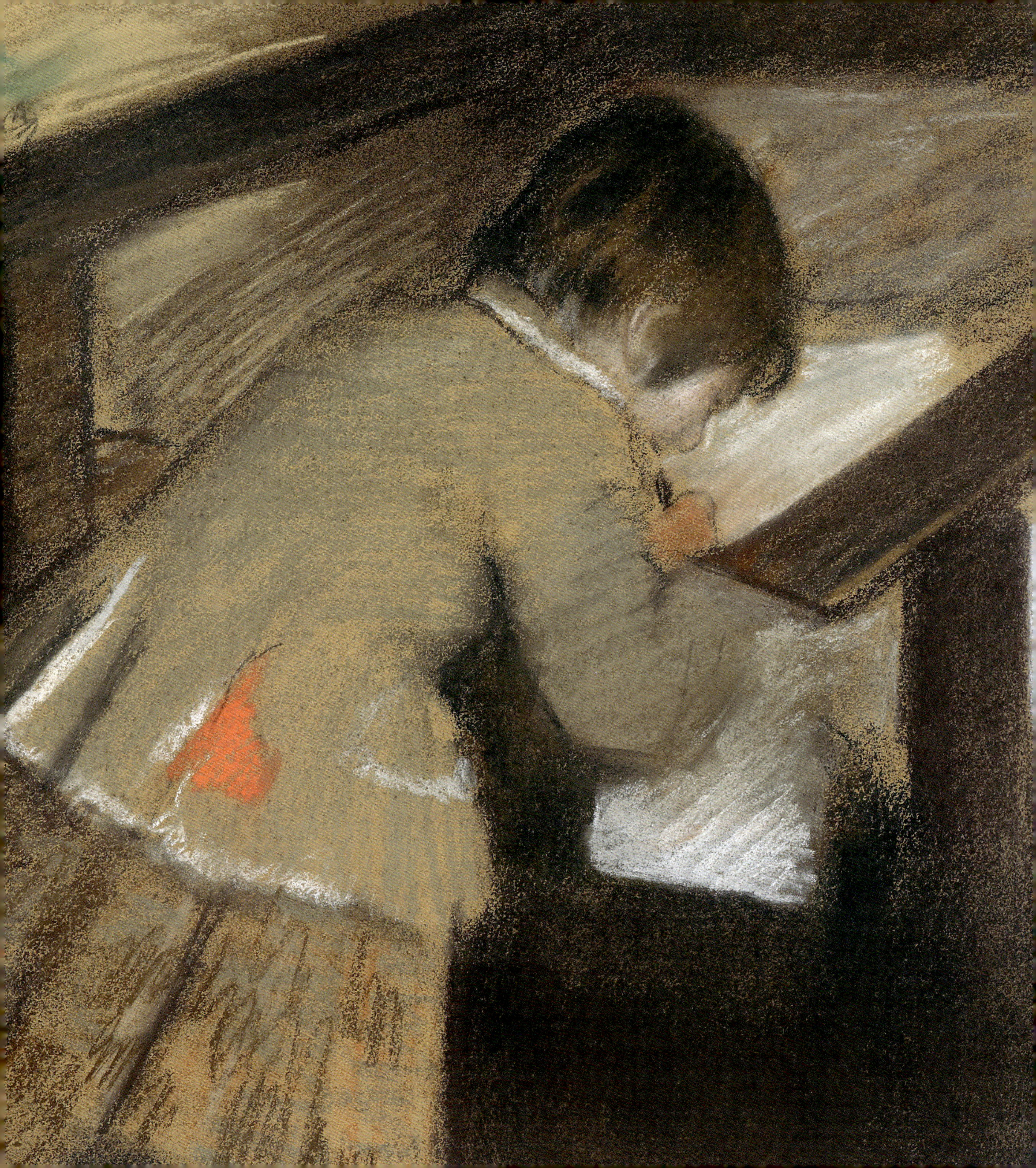

President's Foreword

In late nineteenth-century France, Impressionist and Post-Impressionist artists transformed the status of works on paper. No longer perceived as merely preparatory, their drawings, pastels, watercolours, temperas and gouaches increasingly claimed a shared aesthetic with their oil paintings and became autonomous works of art. In depicting contemporary subjects and scenes from everyday life, these pioneering artists challenged traditional attitudes to drawing and constantly strove for innovation. They cultivated a more relaxed approach to media, supports and techniques, thanks in part to the significant improvements being made to artists' materials at the time. For the first time in the history of European art, spontaneity and a lack of finish – those hallmarks of modernity – were evident in works on paper.

This exhibition examines the crucial shift. Curated by Christopher Lloyd, former Surveyor of the Queen's Pictures, and Ann Dumas, Curator at the Royal Academy, with Sylvie Broussine and Rhiannon Hope, the show is the latest in a long tradition of displays of Impressionist art at the Royal Academy. We thank the curators for their thoughtful and skilful selection, and for their insightful contributions to this accompanying catalogue. We are also immensely grateful to Leïla Jarbouai and Harriet K. Stratis for enriching the catalogue with their expert knowledge.

The exhibition would not have been possible without the remarkable generosity of our many lenders across Britain and Europe, to whom we are sincerely thankful. We owe a special debt of gratitude to all our lenders, in particular the Ashmolean Museum, the British Museum, David Lachenmann, the Musée d'Orsay, and Stephen Ongpin Fine Art for their invaluable support. Loans have also come from many individuals who wish to remain anonymous, and to them we are similarly grateful.

We would like to thank Axel Rüger, Secretary and Chief Executive, Andrea Tarsia, Director of Exhibitions, and Adrian Locke, Chief Curator, for programming the exhibition and for their support throughout, and the many staff at the Royal Academy who have contributed to the success of this exhibition. We extend our gratitude to Joanna Weston, Stephanie Bush and Helena Cooper, who expertly managed the organisation of the exhibition, and to Susana Vázquez Fernández, who oversaw the photographic rights. Our thanks are also due to Natalia de Wilde for her elegant design of both the exhibition and its graphics, to Sanford Lighting Design and to the Royal Academy's publishing team for producing this beautiful catalogue.

We are especially grateful to our generous supporters Gide Loyrette Nouel, the Huo Family Foundation, and Kathryn Uhde, without whom this exhibition would not have been possible.

Although no less radical than those in their oil paintings, the innovations made by Impressionist and Post-Impressionist artists in their drawings are still relatively unknown. We hope that this exhibition and its accompanying book will reveal how these artists, while working on paper, challenged tradition, embraced experimentation and modernity, and ultimately broke ground for their successors.

Rebecca Salter PRA
President, Royal Academy of Arts

Acknowledgements

The Royal Academy acknowledges with gratitude the assistance of the following individuals in the making of this exhibition and its catalogue: Hélène Alexander, Jennifer Alexander, Francesca Antognazza, Jacqui Austin, László Baán, Melanie Baldwin, Maria Balshaw, Beatrice Bertram, Kinga Bódi, Kata Bodor, Katalin Borbély-Roberts, Alesa Boyle, Jamilla Briggs, Tarn Brown, Carol Burnier, Philippe Büttner, Laurence des Cars, Daisy Cartwright, Dennis Cate, Hubert Cavaniol, Eleanor Chant, Hugo Chapman, Taz Chappell, Delphine Charpentier, Oronzo Cilli, Renske Cohen Tervaert, Elise Comberti, Omar Cucciniello, Ana Debenedetti, Sam Dorman, Duncan Dornan, Caroline Ellerby, Patrick Elliott, Agnès Faure, Anna Ferrari, Gabriele Finaldi, Hartwig Fischer, Fonds de Dotation Jean-Louis Forain, Frances Fowle, Matthew Gale, Becky Gee, Christina Gernon, Veronica Ghizzi, Lukas Gloor, Emilie Gordenker, Ketty Gottardo, Paul Greenhalgh, Vivien Hamilton, Colin Harrison, Ailsa Hendry, Jill Holmen, Arthur Holmes, Imogen Holmes-Roe, Wobke Hooites, Alistair Hudson, Tristram Hunt, Hervé Irien, Hannah Kauffman, Bettina Kaufmann, Teresa Krasny, Dienke van der Kuijl, David Lachenmann, Samantha Lackey, Belén Lasheras Díaz, Sir John Leighton, Annick Lemoine, Christophe Leribault, Chloe Le Tissier, Henry Little, Rosalind McKever, Daniele Mancini, Karin Marti, Simon Martin, Géraldine Masson, Renato Miracco, H.S.H. The Prince of Monaco, Jane Munro, Hannah Murray, Liberté Nuti, Stephen Ongpin, Guillaume Parage, Lisette Pelsers, Roberta Piccinelli, Isolde Pludermacher, Catherine Porteous, Laura Reeves, Beatrice Reymond, Christopher Riopelle, Robert Ritter, Mélanie Rivault, Clara Roca, Fleur Roos Rosa de Carvalho, Elena Saggers, Samantha Saward, Ilenia Scerra, Santa Scommegna, Christian Selvatico, Karen Serres, Olivia Sherman, Pippa Stephenson-Sit, Karen Stewart, Rebecca Storr, Alexander Sturgis, Luke Syson, Sophie Szynaka, Anna Testar, Richard Thomson, Florence Valdès-Forain, Ernst Vegelin van Claerbergen, Marije Vellekoop, Sarah Vowles, Natalia de Wilde, Liz Wilkinson, Ghislaine Wood, Paola Zatti, and others who wish to remain anonymous.

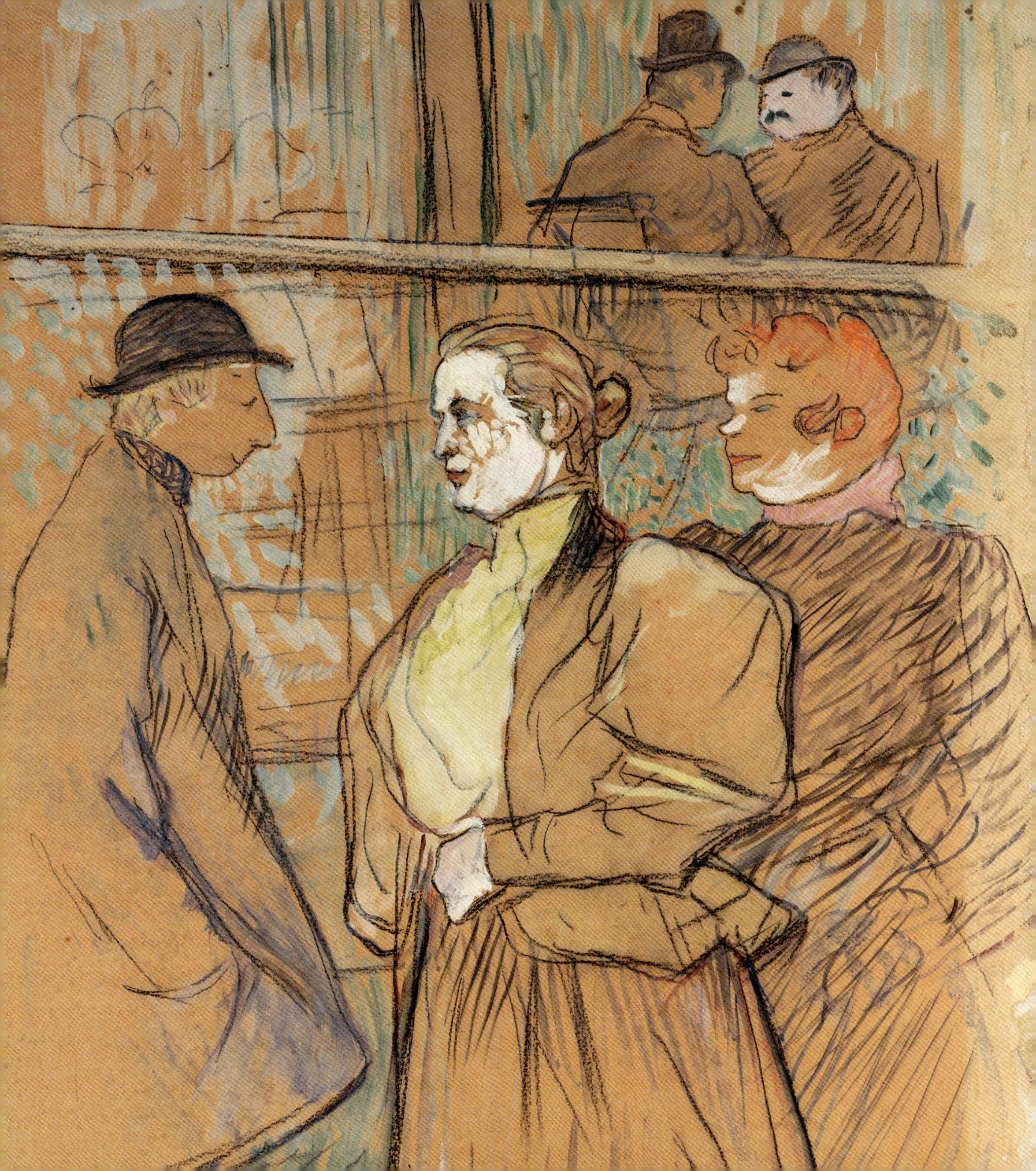

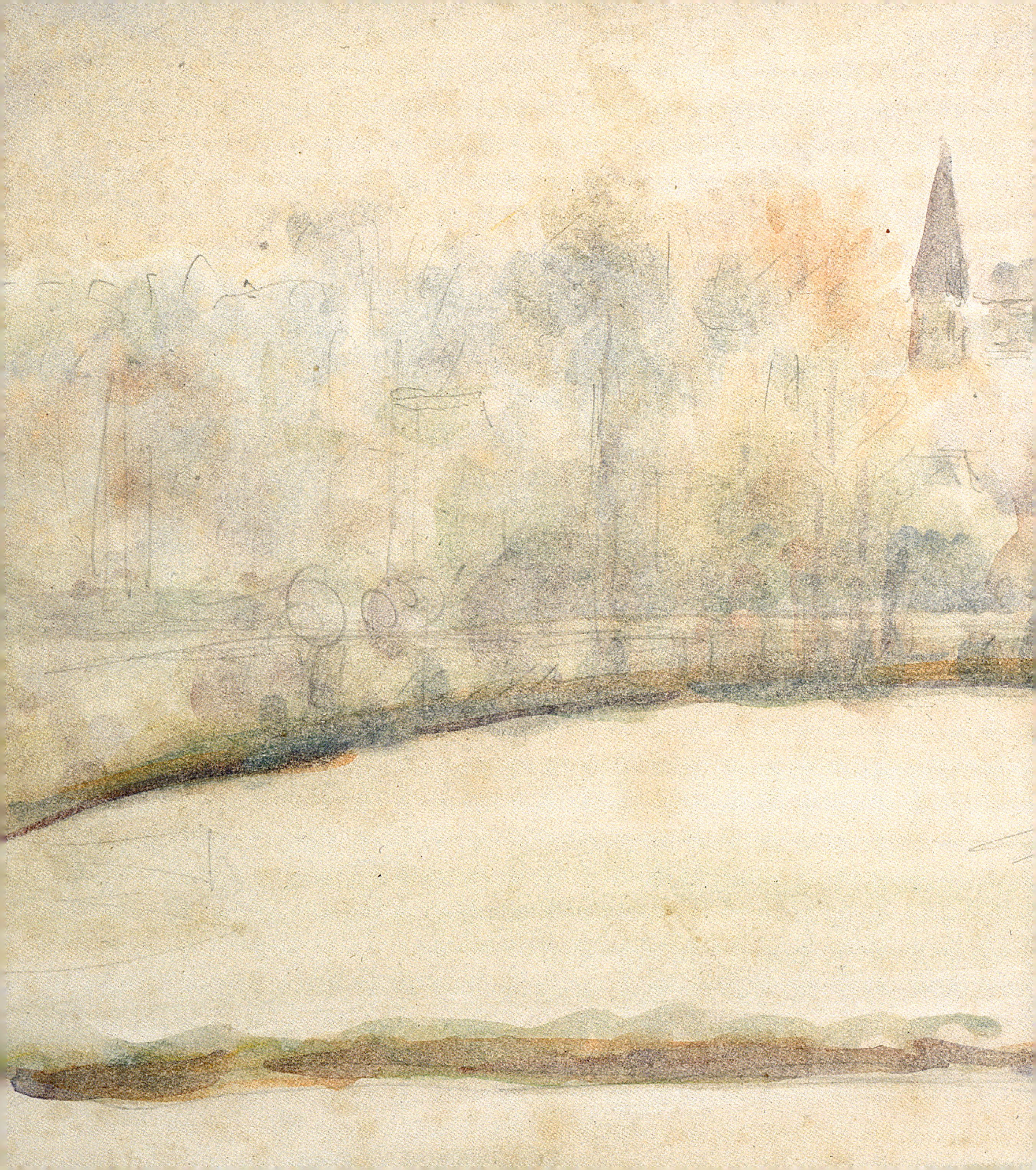

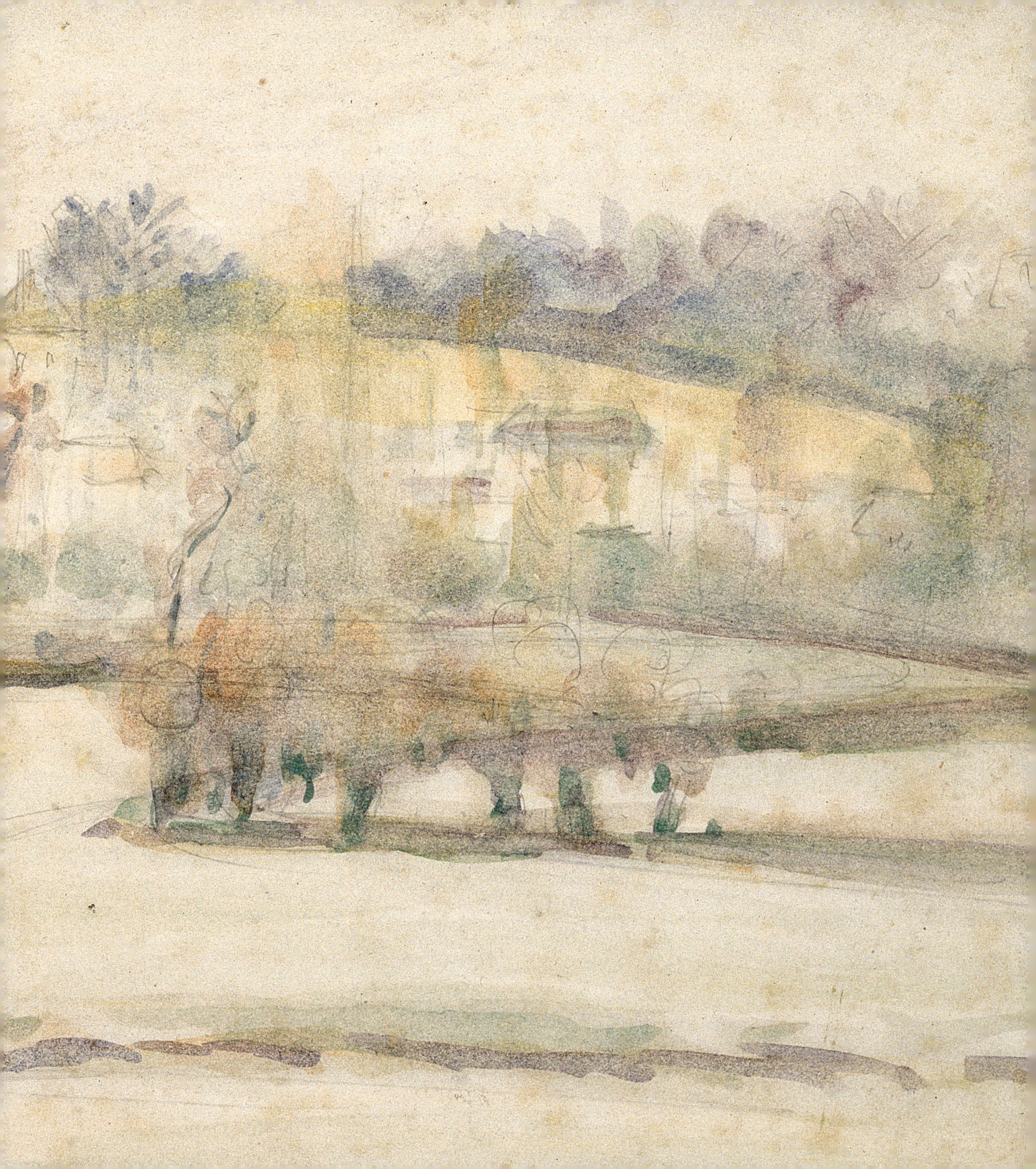

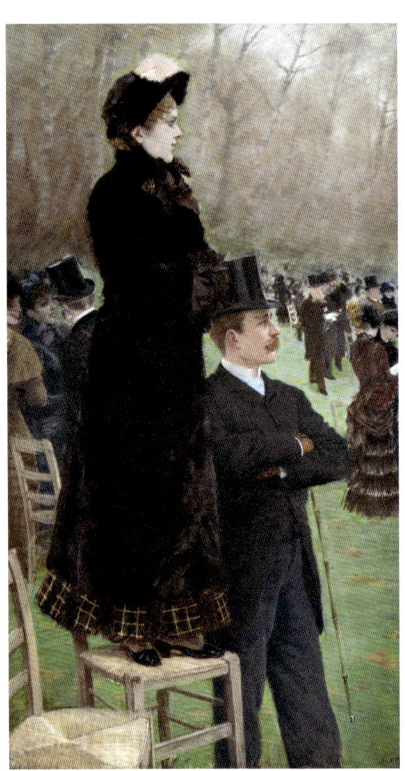
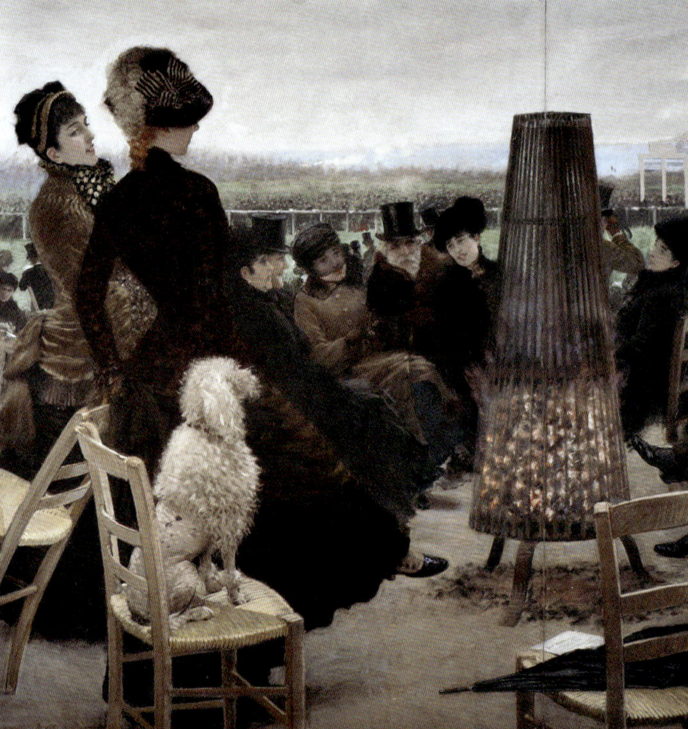
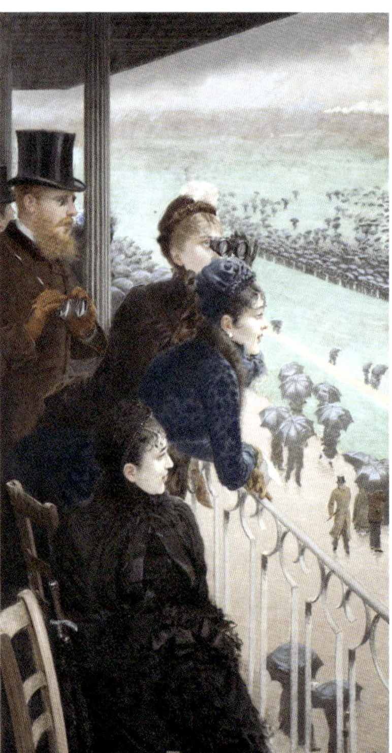

Fig. 1 Giuseppe de Nittis, *The Races in the Bois de Boulogne,* 1881. Pastel on canvas, triptych (left wing: 196 x 106 cm; centre: 196 x 191 cm; right wing: 196 x 106 cm). Galleria Nazionale d'Arte Moderna, Rome, 143 G5799

'Drawing is a struggle between nature and the artist, in which the artist will triumph the more easily as he has a better understanding of the intentions of nature. For him it is not a matter of copying, but of interpreting in a simpler and more luminous language.'
CHARLES BAUDELAIRE, 1846[1]

'Drawing is not what one sees but what one can make others see'
EDGAR DEGAS[2]

Impressionists on Paper: Degas to Toulouse-Lautrec

CHRISTOPHER LLOYD

The eight Impressionist exhibitions held in Paris between 1874 and 1886 created a watershed in art. They became focal points for avant-garde artists keen to overthrow the theoretical and practical constraints imposed by the French state on the pursuit of art. The Impressionists (known at the time also as 'indépendants' or 'intransigeants') were in essence a loose association of artists who found themselves in the vanguard because of their concern to pursue new developments in art. Not all of them were so well known, or their work so easily recalled, as those of their number who are so admired today, such as Edouard Manet, Edgar Degas, Claude Monet, Pierre-Auguste Renoir, Camille Pissarro, Paul Gauguin, Mary Cassatt, Berthe Morisot, Alfred Sisley, Paul Cézanne, Georges Seurat, Vincent van Gogh, Odilon Redon and Henri de Toulouse-Lautrec. All those who contributed to the eight exhibitions, however, objected to the limitations of the traditional training methods offered by the state and the restrictions placed by the authorities on artists over the choice of specific subjects – historical, mythological or scriptural – to fulfil public expectations. They deplored the jury system that controlled the annual exhibitions at the Salon, which was the only official outlet for their work, and they objected to the awards given on those same occasions, which served as a stepping stone to critical and financial success.

The Impressionists instead chose to depict contemporary scenes (fig. 1). For this to be done with the greatest possible authenticity, however, they believed it necessary to record the light, colour and atmosphere of everyday life by direct observation rather than to rely on rigid rules or received opinions learned from the past. Impressionism, like the various movements that followed it in France and Belgium towards the end of the nineteenth century, questioned the belief in justification by tradition and wanted rather to demonstrate how artists could best depict the present. The freedoms these artists established, both stylistically and politically, were to have wide-ranging consequences for the development of art not only in Europe but subsequently also in America.

During the second half of the nineteenth century dutiful art critics had two types of exhibition to review in Paris: firstly, the overcrowded Salon held in the Palais de l'Industrie on the Avenue des Champs-Elysées with thousands of items on display, which the novelist and critic Joris-Karl Huysmans likened in 1879 to a 'Stock Exchange in oils'[3] and in 1880 to a 'warehouse of the State';[4] and, secondly, the much smaller exhibitions such as those organised by the Impressionists, which were mounted in private premises lent or hired for the occasion. Reactions to the eight Impressionist exhibitions varied from the farcical to the rarefied. Some critics excoriated and lampooned what was on display, encouraging their readers to laugh and jeer; others sought to explain and to elucidate, although occasionally with some difficulty. The Impressionists' critical reception was not aided by the factions that arose among them as to how, if at all, they should be defined as a group, or whether figurative painters or landscapists should take precedence at any one exhibition. Such uncertainties resulted in several avant-garde artists who participated in the Impressionist exhibitions, notably Manet, Monet, Renoir and Sisley, continuing to submit their paintings to the Salon in the hope of increasing sales of their work.

The catalogues of the eight Impressionist exhibitions reveal that paintings in oil on canvas were by no means alone on the walls of the various spaces. Some sculpture was shown, but this was greatly surpassed by the number of works on paper – both drawings in various media and prints.[5] The fact that drawings executed in watercolour, pastel, tempera and gouache were hung alongside paintings, as opposed to being restricted to separate areas, as was usual at the Salon, suggests that the Impressionists attached particular significance to their graphic work. It also implies that their drawings in whatever medium had parity with their paintings. This new emphasis was acknowledged by many critics. Whereas like artists from the Renaissance onwards they continued to use drawings as part of their preparatory process, the Impressionists denied the traditional hierarchical differences between painting and drawing. As Huysmans expressed it in his review of the sixth Impressionist exhibition (1881):

> *Watercolour has a spontaneity, a freshness, a spicy brilliance inaccessible to oil ... and pastel has a bloom, a velvety smoothness, like a delicate freedom or a dying grace, that neither watercolour nor oil can touch. It is thus simply a question for the painter to choose among these various processes whichever seems to be the best adapted to the subject he wants to treat.*[6]

As Huysmans suggests, the looser, more spontaneous effects obtained by the Impressionists in their drawings matched their artistic ambitions just as much as their paintings did and, furthermore, did so in a way that was relatively easier to accomplish. Rather than being hidebound by tradition, the Impressionists adopted a far more relaxed approach to their selection of techniques and choice of materials, which often resulted in unusual combinations of media, varied supports, surprising changes of format, and freer – even unorthodox – methods of application. There is always an air of experimentation about Impressionist works on paper. Indeed, the graphic work of these artists, who produced some of the finest drawings in European art, is best described as a re-evaluation of tested systems, which gave rise to new and challenging ways of making images that anticipated modern art.

The Impressionists' intrinsic belief in the art of drawing was not without foundation. The earlier history of French painting had been punctuated by the names of famous draughtsmen: Jean and François Clouet (father and son) in the sixteenth century; Nicolas Poussin and Claude Lorrain in the seventeenth; Antoine Watteau, François Boucher and Jean-Honoré Fragonard in the eighteenth; with Jean-Baptiste Greuze and Pierre-Paul Prud'hon ushering in the nineteenth. The most influential body in French art was the longstanding Académie de Peinture et de Sculpture, a royal foundation established in 1648 with an outpost in Rome known as the Académie de France that was set up in 1666. It controlled the training of artists, monitored commissions and measured artistic success continuously. Its influence and practices extended well beyond the city boundaries of Paris into the regions. Denounced at the time of the Revolution but later reinstated as the Académie des Beaux-Arts, the institution continued to hold sway into the nineteenth century, exercising its authority through the Ecole des Beaux-Arts in Paris and by the promotion of the Salon exhibitions, which it alone organised until 1881.

The basis of the teaching at the Ecole des Beaux-Arts was that, although art may be defined as the imitation of nature, it should at the same time be subordinate to an overriding principle or 'idea' apparent in both its subject and its execution. The completion of a work of art, therefore, involved the mind as much as the eye or the hand so that, correspondingly, the appeal to the viewer lay not just in the senses but in the intellect. To enable this to happen, artists had to be taught how to rationalise what they observed in nature and this could only be done through a set of rules. In short, innate talent had to be directed and focused.

The objectives of the Ecole des Beaux-Arts were achieved by encouraging aspiring young artists to begin by copying approved works of art, first of all from prints or drawings and then from plaster casts usually made after antique sculpture. Once the requisite skills in the art of copying had been mastered, the student-artist could progress to working from living models. These often highly finished drawings made at the final stage were known as *académies*. Students were also encouraged to attend lectures on anatomy and consult technical manuals. Teaching was undertaken by successful Salon artists such as Alexandre Cabanel, Isidore Pils and Jean-Léon Gérôme, who often also taught those preparing for the rigours of the entrance examination. Reforms carried out at the Ecole des Beaux-Arts in 1863 brought about a more open-minded approach to teaching and provided better facilities, but the main objective remained unchanged. Such a curriculum created artists, it was thought, who were well disciplined, respectful of tradition and capable of equating correctness in drawing with moral rectitude.

This was the dilemma faced by the Impressionists at the outset of their careers in the 1850s and 1860s. Degas, Renoir, Gustave Caillebotte, Jean-Louis Forain and Seurat all persevered with the Ecole des Beaux-Arts with varying degrees of commitment, whereas Cézanne and Toulouse-Lautrec failed to gain admission. Others attended the studios of successful Salon artists operating within the orbit of the Ecole des Beaux-Arts but usually only for short periods: Manet was with Thomas Couture; Monet, Renoir and Sisley with Charles Gleyre; Cassatt, Redon and Jean-François Raffaëlli with Gérôme; Seurat with Henri Lehmann; Van Gogh (cat. 27) and Toulouse-Lautrec with Fernand Cormon. For access to life models there were private studios, such as the Académie Suisse or the Académie Julian, which were not expensive to attend and offered no official teaching. There the models were encouraged to strike informal poses and a more liberal attitude to materials pervaded, with less emphasis on finish (cat. 16).

The Impressionists also accepted the significance of making copies of earlier works of art as a way of improving their technical skills and discovering new sources of inspiration. During the 1850s Manet travelled extensively in Europe and Degas widely in Italy specifically for this purpose. They could also register as copyists at the Musée du Louvre, the Bibliothèque Nationale or the Musée de Sculpture Comparée (Palais du Trocadéro), and inspect the contents of the short-lived Musée des Copies (1873). Further sources were to be found in publications, particularly Charles Blanc's *Histoire des peintres de toutes les écoles*, issued in fourteen volumes between 1861 and 1884. Numerous popular journals, such as *Le Magasin pittoresque*, were also liberally illustrated with relevant material. Notable is the fact that both Degas and Cézanne continued to make copies throughout their careers.

Another advocate for change was Horace Lecoq de Boisbaudran, author of *L'Education de la mémoire pittoresque* (1848). He taught at the Ecole Royale Gratuite de Dessin (known as the Petite Ecole) and proposed that models should be posed in the open air and that drawings (including copies) should be made from memory. These practices stimulated acute visual analysis and economy of style.

Degas informed Georges Jeanniot: 'It is very good to copy what one sees; it is much better to draw what you can't see any more but in your memory. It is a transformation in which imagination and memory work together. You only reproduce what struck you, that is to say the necessary. That way your memories and your fantasy are freed from the tyranny of nature.'[7] Most of the Impressionists were aware of Lecoq de Boisbaudran's ideas and benefited from them when devising compositions that were first observed in everyday life before being developed in the studio.

Time and again the Impressionists referred to the art of the past not just for inspiration, but as a signpost to the future. Their movement was never a renunciation of the past; rather, it was a reinterpretation of it, prompting their exploration of other ways of producing art. Thus, Manet in his portraits in pastel evokes comparison with a well-established French tradition dating from as early as the sixteenth century; Degas reinvents poses from classical art in his treatment of the female nude at her toilette (cat. 43); Renoir emulates eighteenth-century French masters in his use of sanguine, as well as revering antiquity and early Italian art (cat. 68); Cézanne looks to Peter Paul Rubens for his bathers and to Poussin for his landscapes; Van Gogh remained conscious of his predecessors in Dutch seventeenth-century landscape painting and particularly Rembrandt (cat. 38); Toulouse-Lautrec looked at sporting art before turning to popular illustration (cat. 58). The past for the Impressionists, therefore, was not an altar at which one worshipped, but more a tomb for raiding. A vivid example of this is the interest that many avant-garde artists took in the fan, which had a long history as a fashion accessory (fig. 2). Degas (cat. 18), Giuseppe de Nittis, Pissarro, Morisot, Forain (cat. 44) and Gauguin (cats 49, 59) all turned their attention to the fan from the late 1870s, sometimes adapting existing compositions to suit the unusual format and frequently choosing tempera, gouache or watercolour over oil as their favoured media. Fans still served a utilitarian purpose in late nineteenth-century France, but the influence of Japanese art then current encouraged a renewal of interest in them aesthetically, to the extent that they often featured in the Impressionist exhibitions. Indeed, Pissarro showed twelve examples in the fourth exhibition of 1879.

The Impressionists initially found inspiration in the work of artists active in France during the first half of the nineteenth century. Held in the greatest esteem, for example, were Jean-Auguste-Dominique Ingres and Eugène Delacroix, who are conveniently, although not necessarily correctly, referred to as the main representatives respectively of Neoclassicism and Romanticism. Stylistically, Ingres looked back to Florentine Renaissance artists and Raphael in particular, whereas Delacroix sought out Venetian Renaissance artists and Rubens. Both painted scenes inspired by history and literature, and undertook official decorative schemes and commissions for portraiture. The effect of their work on viewers, however, is contrasting: Ingres becalms and bemuses, whereas Delacroix terrifies and electrifies. Yet, paradoxically, in life

Fig. 2 Mary Cassatt, *In the Loge*, c. 1879. Pastel and gold metallic paint on canvas, 64.9 x 80.6 cm. Philadelphia Museum of Art. Gift of Mrs. Sargent McKean, 1950, 1950-52-1

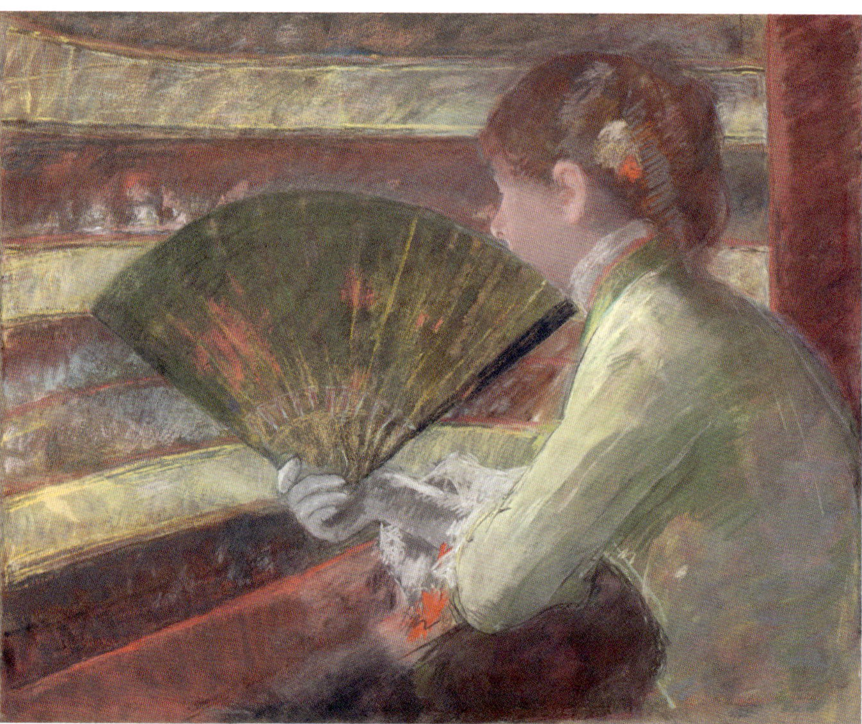

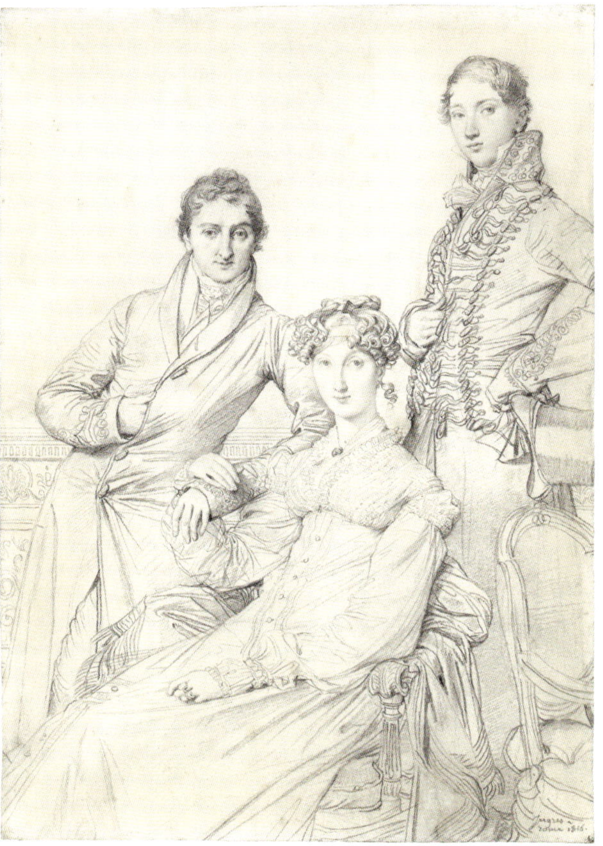

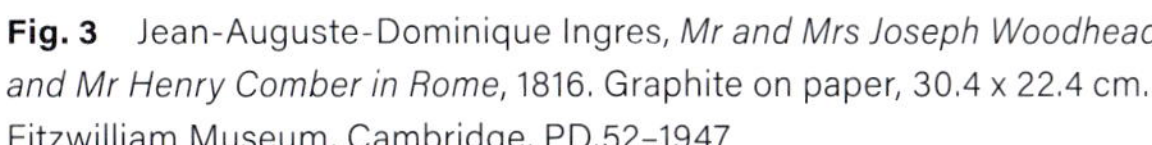

Fig. 3 Jean-Auguste-Dominique Ingres, *Mr and Mrs Joseph Woodhead and Mr Henry Comber in Rome*, 1816. Graphite on paper, 30.4 x 22.4 cm. Fitzwilliam Museum, Cambridge, PD.52–1947

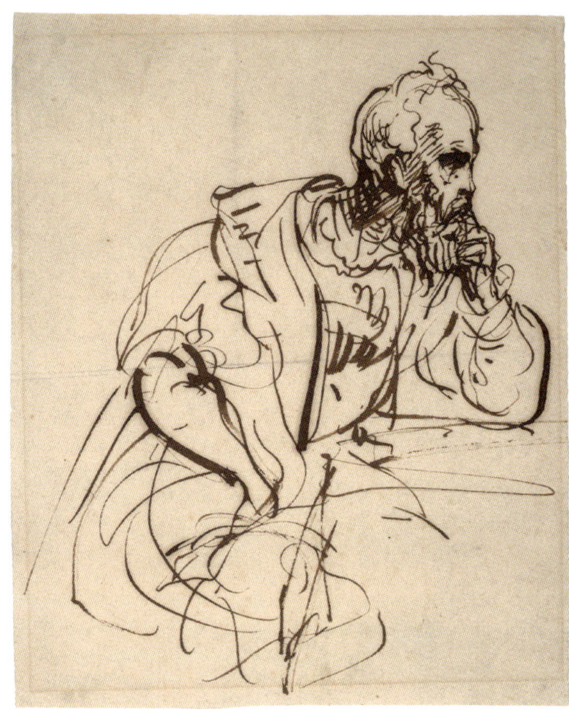

Fig. 4 Eugène Delacroix, *Study for 'The Two Foscari'*, c. 1847. Pen and ink on paper, 21.6 x 18 cm. Albertina, Vienna, 30711

Ingres, who on the surface seemed so austere, rational and conformist, was a man of deep emotions and remarkable sensuality; Delacroix, on the other hand, who appeared so vital, impulsive and neurotic, was often calculating, sardonic and reclusive. Charles Baudelaire described paintings by Ingres as 'the result of an excessive attentiveness and they demand an equal attentiveness to be understood. Born of suffering, they beget suffering,'[8] whereas he thought Delacroix 'a volcanic crater artistically concealed behind bouquets of flowers'.[9] Contemporaries regarded the stolid Ingres as bourgeois and the dandified Delacroix as aristocratic. Ingres made portentous statements that were endlessly quoted, but Delacroix confined his outlook on the world to his journal.

Both Ingres and Delacroix drew compulsively, but in different ways. Ingres courted purity of line, using pencil to good effect in his preparatory studies and particularly in his portraits (fig. 3). Delacroix liked the pen, which he handled frenetically like a rapier (fig. 4), and owing to his love of colour was sympathetic to other types of media, such as chalk, pastel and watercolour (fig. 5). Few artists could draw with the precision of Ingres or believed so ardently in the ultimate purpose of drawing, which he described as 'the probity of art'.[10] Baudelaire wrote that Ingres had 'a relentless and searching talent', and saw Delacroix as someone who enjoyed 'covering paper with dreams, ideas, or figures half-glimpsed amid the random accidents of life'.[11] In their drawings Ingres was as economical with line as Delacroix was prodigal: the former was stimulated by the known and the latter by the unexpected. With his clear outlines Ingres aimed for precision, whereas in Delacroix the endless swirling lines resemble the motion of the sea.

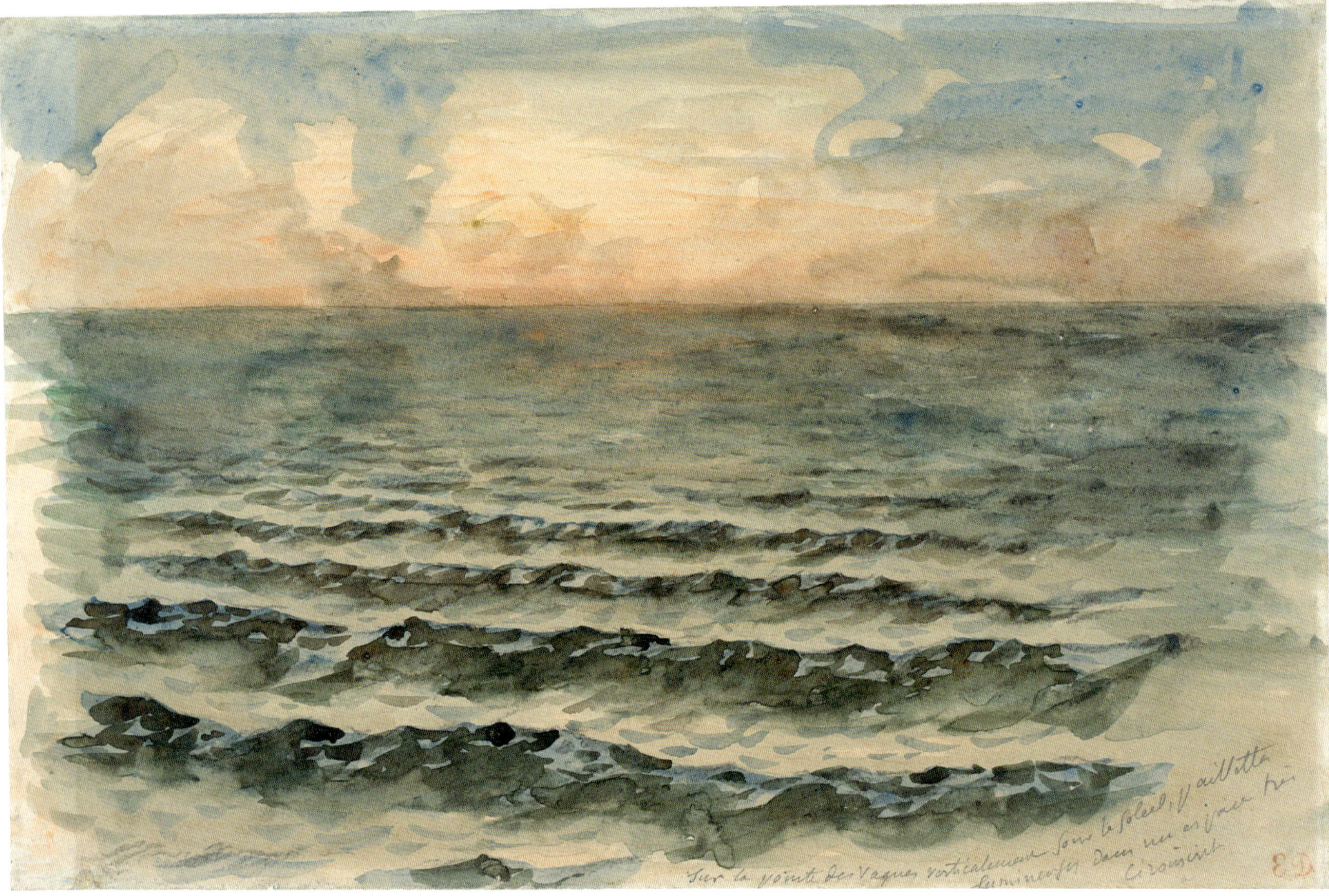

Fig. 5 Eugène Delacroix, *The Sea at Dieppe*, c. 1854. Watercolour over graphite on paper, 22.8 x 35.2 cm. Albertina, Vienna, 24099

It should be no surprise that Degas revered Ingres, while Renoir and Cézanne honoured Delacroix.

The appeal of Ingres and Delacroix for the Impressionists lay not just in their technical brilliance or the variety of their work, but in the fact that it transcended time. Although both artists were trained within the academic system, they were able to move beyond it and establish their own individuality as artists, which often involved them in disagreements with the authorities. Their work was readily available for inspection in exhibitions, public buildings and museums, as well as in public sales. Above all, their combined output was all-embracing and their approach open-minded.

A more enigmatic, but just as influential, figure was Pierre Puvis de Chavannes. His appeal was more to the younger Impressionists, particularly Seurat, Paul Signac and Van Gogh, but even more so for the Symbolists and the Nabis towards the very end of the century (fig. 6). He combined an awareness of Ingres and of Delacroix to form a style that was also derived from his knowledge of early Italian Renaissance fresco cycles. Older Impressionists, such as Pissarro, were at first wary of Puvis de Chavannes's success with the official authorities, but respectful of his technical skills, especially on a large scale. In a letter drafted in 1890 Van Gogh wrote: 'I am increasingly beginning to feel that one may consider Puvis de Chavannes as having the importance of *Delacroix*, anyway that he has equal worth with the people whose genius attains a thus-far-and-no-further, forever consoling.'[12] In fact, it was virtually impossible to avoid seeing paintings by Puvis de Chavannes for he carried out some of the most significant public decorative schemes of late nineteenth-century France, in Amiens, Lyons, Paris and Marseilles. All are on a huge scale with clearly organised, rather flat compositions and carefully modelled figures set against idealised landscapes. Their slow rhythms, calm gestures and extensive patches of light-toned colour appealed to artists engaged in developing Impressionism. The allegorical subjects he favoured are inspired by literary, mainly classical, sources. Even when his figures are active there is a mood of reverie so that Puvis de Chavannes succeeds in creating a timeless world populated by sylph-like figures becalmed on the sun-drenched shores of a blue Mediterranean. He was a dreamer, but with both feet on the ground. This is all far removed from Impressionism, but it was generally recognised that here was an artist who was engaging with the past in order to address the present. It was Seurat, in his large canvases *Bathers at Asnières* (1884; National Gallery, London) and *A Sunday on La Grande Jatte – 1884* (*c.* 1884–86; Art Institute of Chicago), who translated the visual language of Puvis de Chavannes into the modern idiom (see cats 22, 23, 24).

Two figurative artists from the mid-nineteenth century who engaged the attention of the Impressionists but in more contemporaneous ways were Constantin Guys and Honoré Daumier. Both were prolific, and specialised in observing scenes from everyday life. They were essentially illustrators and their output was widely published in popular journals.

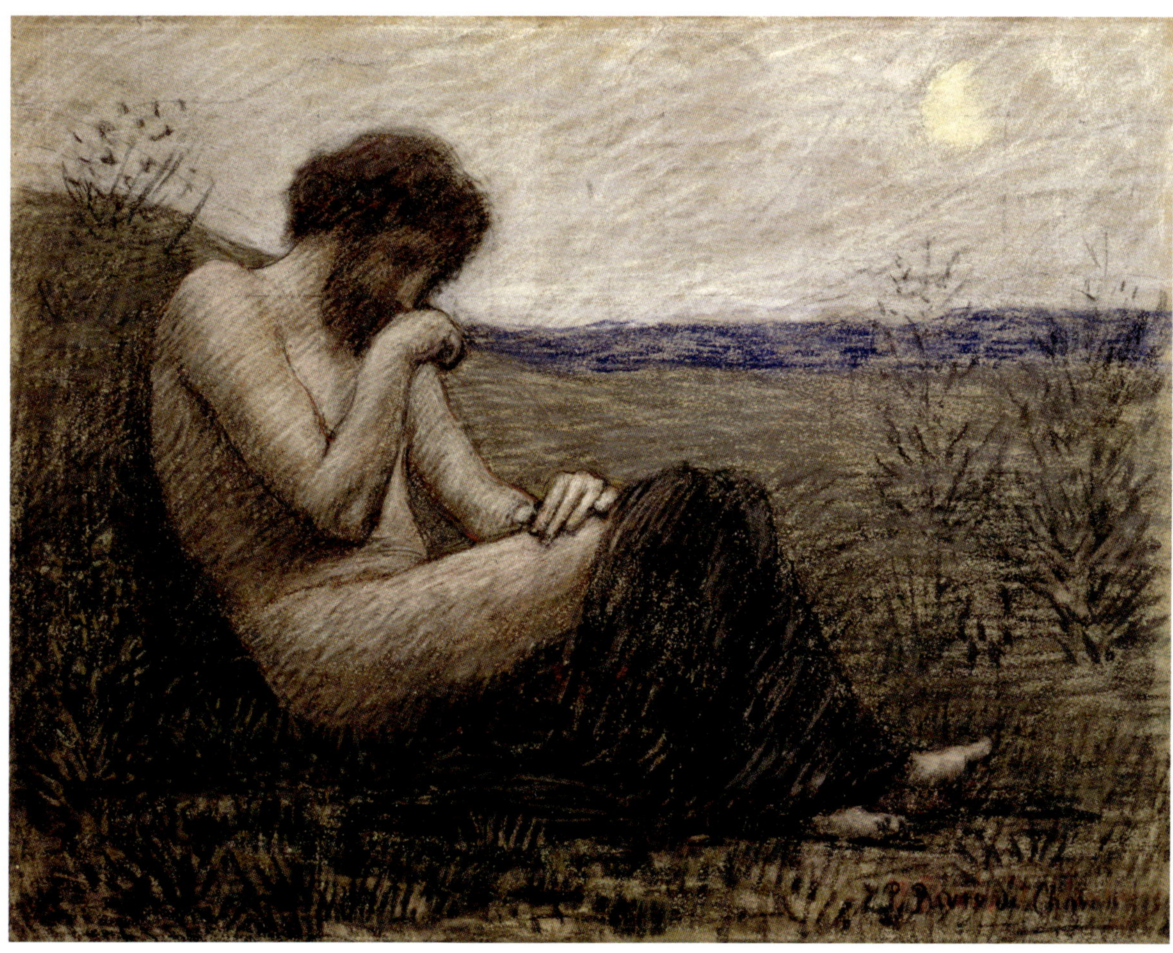

Fig. 6 Pierre Puvis de Chavannes, *Solitude*, *c.* 1880–85. Pastel on paper, 32 x 41.3 cm. Whitworth Art Gallery, Manchester, D22.1921

Such images needed to be instantly legible and the content immediately recognisable in order to be appreciated by readers caught up in life's turmoil. Significantly, Baudelaire nominated Guys, who was by no means regarded as an artist of the first rank, as the perfect example of what a modern artist should be. In his famous essay published in *Le Figaro* in 1863 entitled 'The Painter of Modern Life', Baudelaire described Guys ('Monsieur G') as spending his days and nights observing life on the boulevards, in the restaurants and cafés and in the parks, but then at the 'equivocal hour when the curtains of heaven are drawn and cities light up' he withdraws into his studio and begins 'skirmishing with his pencil, his pen, his brush, splashing his glass of water up to the ceiling, wiping his pen on his shirt, in a ferment of violent activity, as though afraid that the image might escape him, cantankerous though alone, elbowing himself on'.[13]

Guys depicts the world in a state of flux (fig. 7). He observes at random and takes everything on its own terms without passing moral judgement. He travelled extensively as an official illustrator and correspondent for the *Illustrated London News* for which journal he reported on the Crimean War (1853–56) before being employed by *Le Figaro*. He was active until an advanced age, but had to withdraw from life after being run over by a carriage. His pen-and-wash drawings seem spontaneous by virtue of their vitality. There is no attempt at a grand statement or a pompous theme and he enters politics only by implication. He celebrates the Parisian world as it is. Outside, there is a sense of perpetual motion: horses, carriages, pedestrians, military parades and crowds. Inside, there is a sense of claustrophobia: theatre, salon, brothel. As Baudelaire expressed it, 'His interest is the whole world; he wants to know, understand and appreciate everything that happens on the surface of our globe.'[14]

Guys is fascinated by the world of fashion and he loves materials and textures. He observes very closely how clothes are worn and is also very conscious of social distinctions. Manners and decorum, glances and expressions, just as much as dress or appearance, dictate the poses and gestures in his shrewdly chosen and deftly executed compositions. These sometimes involve nondescript or clandestine settings where social boundaries are blurred and morality is threatened. Guys might be accused of being a narrow artist on account of his limited themes, but there is an animated, almost cinematic quality to his image-making that gives it great energy. And, in the end, the variety of his drawings is no less than what Baudelaire termed 'the acrid or heady bouquet of the wine of life'.[15] The ways in which Guys

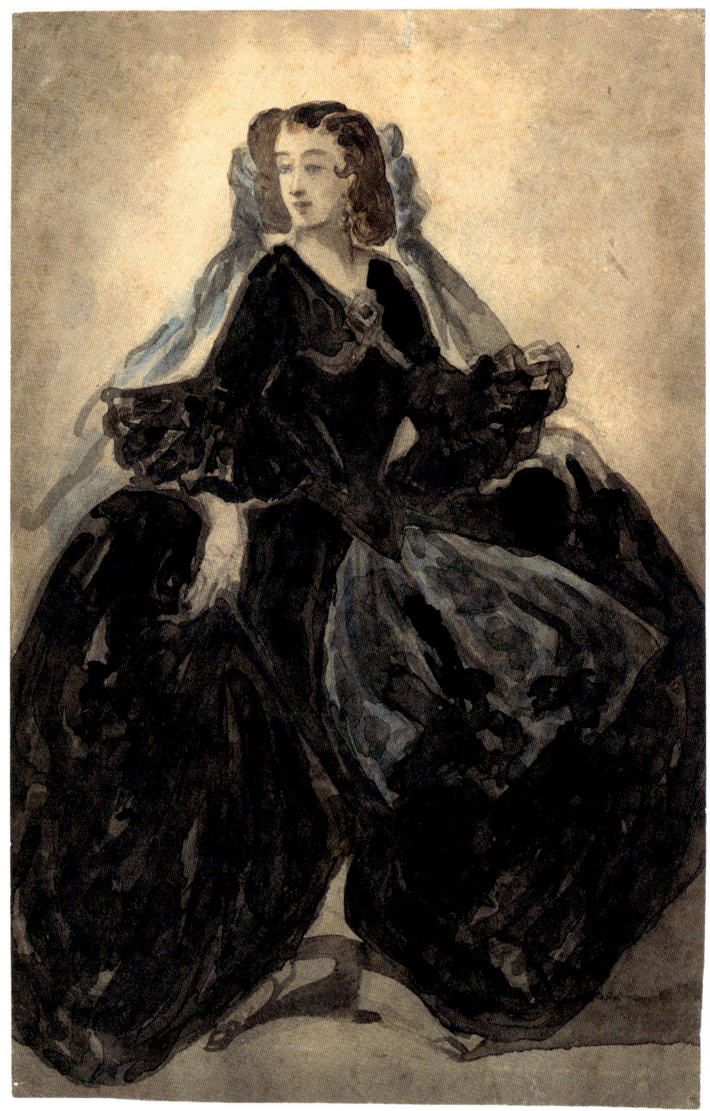

Fig. 7 Constantin Guys, *Standing Lady in Black Robe with Blue Veil*, *c.* 1855–63. Pen and ink with watercolour on paper, 36.7 x 23.8 cm. Collection Museum Boijmans Van Beuningen, Rotterdam, F.11.109

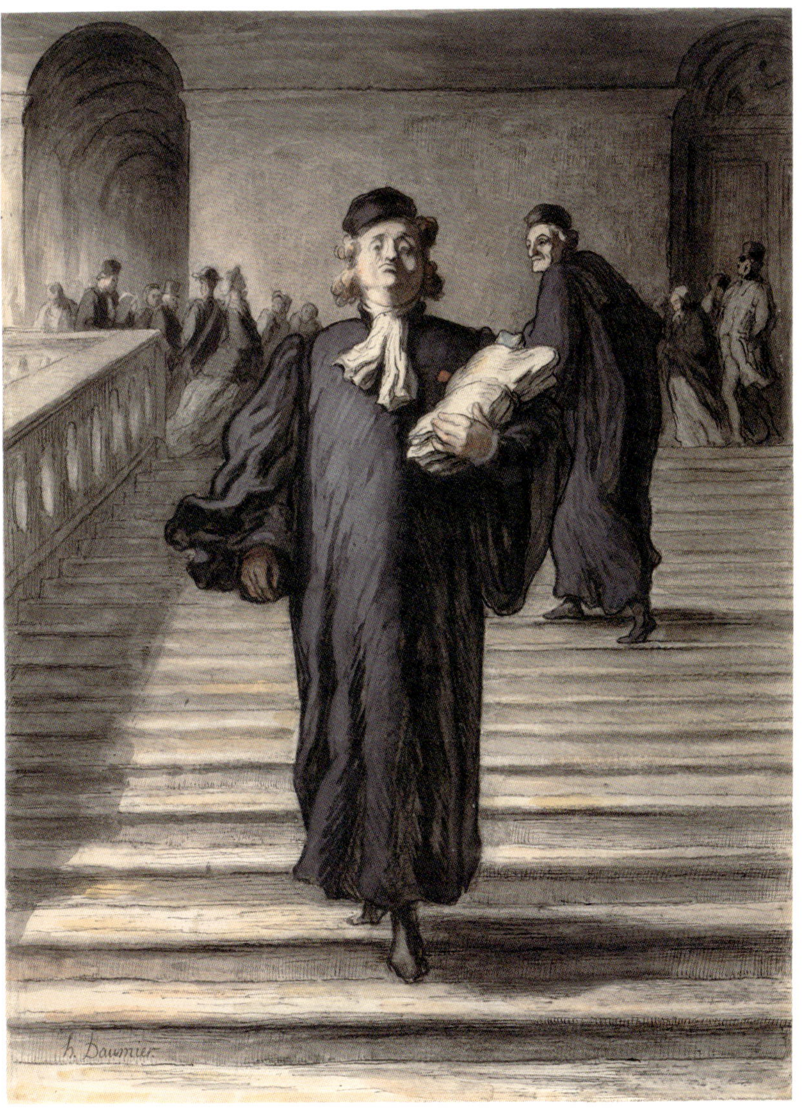

Fig. 8 Honoré Daumier, *The Grand Staircase of the Palace of Justice*, *c*. 1864. Charcoal, Conté crayon, watercolour, pen and ink, wash on paper, 35.9 x 26.7 cm. The Baltimore Museum of Art: The George A. Lucas Collection, BMA 1996.48.18685

looked at the world and recorded it are one of the roots of Impressionism as reflected in the work of Manet in particular (cat. 14). Younger artists, such as Raffaëlli, Forain (cats 44, 45), de Nittis (cat. 30), Henry Somm and, more distantly, Toulouse-Lautrec (cat. 57), however, were his true epigones.

Daumier was a more complete artist than Guys. He made paintings, drawings and sculpture, but he was trained in the art of lithography and produced thousands of illustrations for popular journals such as *La Caricature* and *Le Charivari*. Many of these were based on finished drawings in mixed media incorporating pen, ink and wash highlighted in watercolour or gouache. The style, irrespective of the content or source, is intensely lyrical and flamboyant with rococo flourishes. Like all caricaturists, Daumier exaggerated, partly as a result of working so quickly from memory (fig. 8). In another famous essay entitled 'Some French Caricaturists', published in *L'Artiste* in 1858, Baudelaire declared that 'what distinguishes Daumier is his sureness of touch. He draws as the great masters drew. His drawing is abundant and easy – it is a sustained improvisation; and yet it never descends to the "chic".'[16]

Nothing is sacred and no-one is spared in Daumier's art, especially right-wing politicians and the bourgeoisie. He was a committed Republican who inveighed fiercely against the restoration of any form of monarchical government in France. The poet Paul Valéry, who was married to Morisot's niece, wrote that Daumier's work exposes 'phantoms, demons, damned souls, monsters of greed, pride, egoism, or stupidity, in the mud and the streets of the Paris of his day, at the Palace of Justice, in trains or bedrooms, in the porter's lodge or at the grocer's, on the throne or the bench; and who can endow capital sins, vices, madnesses, with their true anatomy, their essential attitudes and expressions.'[17] Daumier had society at his mercy, but he was not repaid by wealth or honours and died, like Guys, in distressed circumstances.

The Impressionists combined an examination of urban life in Paris, including the suburbs, with exploration of the surrounding countryside. This accorded with their instinct to paint directly in front of the motif, which was an aspiration open to individual interpretation as careers developed and fresh stylistic initiatives were sought. During the 1860s the Impressionists showed an interest in the work of the artists of the Barbizon School, who were active in the area of the Forest of Fontainebleau some 35 miles to the southeast of the capital. The terrain was varied, with woods and clearings studded with outcrops of rock and scattered boulders. Villages such as Barbizon, Marlotte and Chailly were well known to Monet, Pissarro and Sisley, who painted several early works there.

Artists of the Barbizon School painted and drew landscapes with related rural themes. Such interests ran counter to the teaching of the Ecole des Beaux-Arts, irrespective of the reputations of Poussin and Claude. The neoclassical theorist Pierre-Henri de Valenciennes had restored a degree of respectability to the art of landscape painting in France at the beginning of the nineteenth century, to the extent that it came to be accepted as an independent genre. Oil studies made *en plein air* as preparations for paintings were duly encouraged in the form of balanced and harmonious compositions with free brushwork and subtle tonal nuances. The more naturalistic results of such practices applied on a larger scale were to be the determining factors in the development of Impressionism.

Three of the Barbizon School artists were of particular significance in this respect. The oeuvre of Jean-Baptiste-Camille Corot included works on religious, mythological, literary and allegorical subjects, many of which were accepted for display at the Salon, but he was also an outstanding landscape painter. The drawings he made in Italy (1825–28, 1834, 1843) are delicately composed in contrast with his later, less topographical drawings, which are broadly handled in softer media. Corot particularly relished wide panoramas and filled them with a surprising amount of detail (fig. 9). The overall visual effect in both his landscape paintings and drawings can appear at first glance to be somewhat empty, but gradually there emerges a virtual lexicon of nature – gentle slopes, winding rivers, gnarled tree trunks and twisting branches with rustling leaves.

Charles-François Daubigny was equally well known to the Impressionists for his views of the banks of the quiet reaches of the Rivers Seine, Marne and Oise. During the Franco-Prussian War of 1870–71, like Monet and Pissarro, he took refuge in London, where these artists met the dealer Paul Durand-Ruel. Many of Daubigny's drawings are executed in black or occasionally red chalk. His topographical views of London and Paris are firmly handled, in contrast with his river views, which are expansive and poetic. He preferred the tranquillity of nature to the urban scene, spending hours painting and drawing on his specially designed boat (named *Le Botin*), a practice that Monet later adopted at Argenteuil.

Jean-François Millet, who won widespread fame during his lifetime with such paintings as *The Sower* (1850; Museum of Fine Arts, Boston), *The Angelus* (1855–57; Musée d'Orsay, Paris) and *The Gleaners* (1857; Musée d'Orsay, Paris), was undoubtedly of greater significance than either Corot or Daubigny for the Impressionists. His drawings were also much sought after. When Van Gogh saw the collection of Millet's work formed by Emile Gavet in the sale at the Hôtel Drouot in Paris (11–12 June 1875), which included 95 pastels, he wrote to his brother Theo: 'I felt something akin to:

Fig. 9 Jean-Baptiste-Camille Corot, *Woodland Scene with Rocks, Civita Castellana*, c. 1826/27. Graphite on paper, 31.1 x 38.9 cm. Musée du Louvre, Paris, RF 5220, Recto

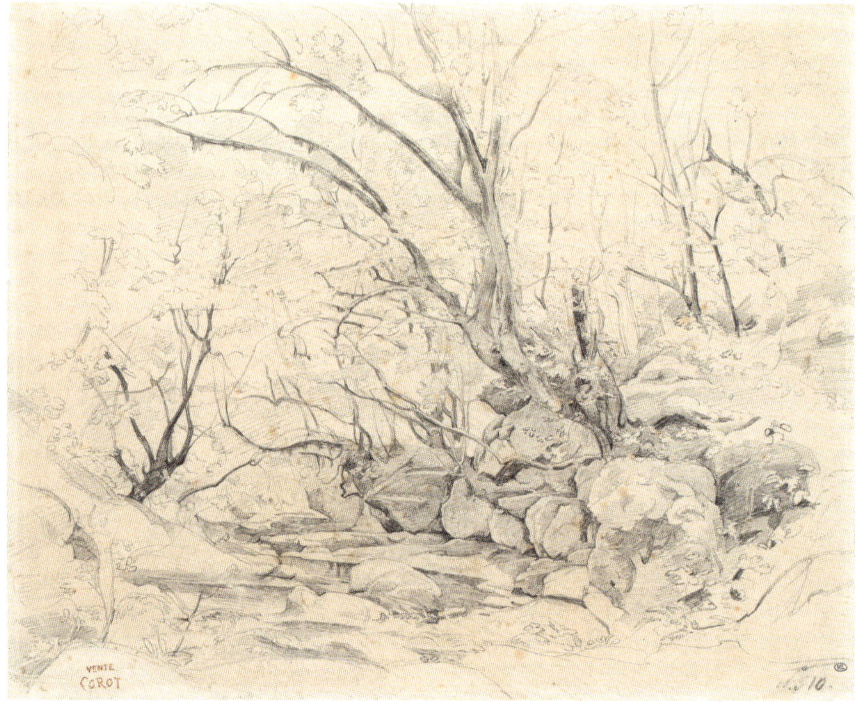

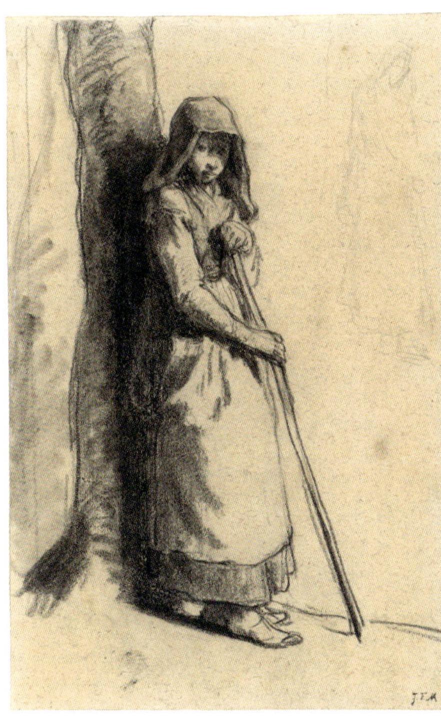

Fig. 10 Jean-François Millet, *Shepherdess Leaning Against a Tree (Study for 'Bergère au repos')*, 1849. Black crayon on brownish paper, 29.8 x 19.2 cm. Fitzwilliam Museum, Cambridge, PD.85-1961

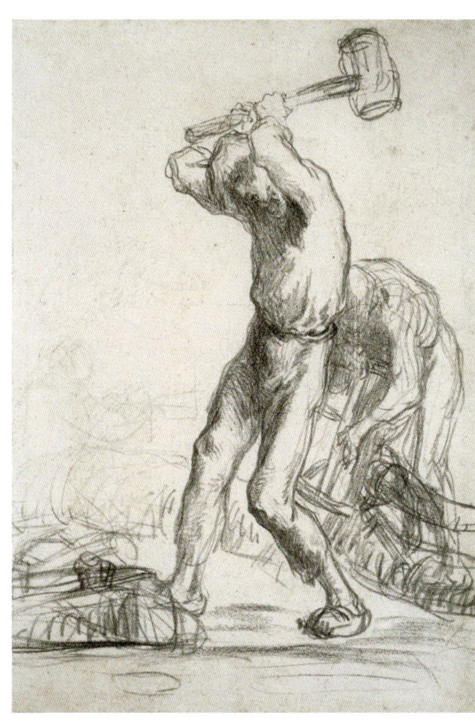

Fig. 11 Jean-François Millet, *Two Peasants Sawing and Splitting Wood*, *c.* 1850–51. Black chalk on laid paper, 39.8 x 27.9 cm. Ashmolean Museum, Oxford. Bequeathed by Percy Moore Turner, 1951, WA1951.23

Put off thy shoes from off thy feet, for the place whereon thou standest is holy ground.'[18]

Millet was born on the Normandy coast and had a traditional training at the Ecole des Beaux-Arts from 1837 to 1839. He was active in the village of Barbizon from 1849 when he began his examination of rural labour. His paintings showing peasant life in heroic terms were first seen as politically radical, but by the end of his life they had come to be regarded as nostalgic, or, as the anarchist Camille Pissarro phrased it, just a bit too 'biblical'.[19] Millet was well versed in the works of Michelangelo and Poussin, as well as French painting of the eighteenth century. He was also widely read in European literature (Homer, Virgil, Shakespeare, Milton, Hugo, Chateaubriand, La Fontaine). Such terms of reference set his art apart in its embrace of themes of universal significance.

However, there is nothing esoteric about Millet's drawings. His versatility, technique and powers of observation made him the outstanding draughtsman of mid-nineteenth-century France. His figure studies were normally drawn in black chalk with strong contours and confident modelling. Most of the figures are given natural poses as witnessed by the artist in the fields, with dramatic foreshortening and unusual viewpoints. When standing they are statuesque and majestic (fig. 10), but when working their repeated outlines often suggest the rhythms of the action itself, so committed is the artist to his task (fig. 11). Pen and ink with some wash are combined for the landscape drawings, which are pithier in style with clever use made of the white of the paper. Of greatest importance are the finished works in black crayon and charcoal dating from the 1850s and done in the tenebrist style with subtle gradations of tone achieved by changing the pressure of the hand. This style lent itself particularly to Millet's penchant for twilight scenes (fig. 12). But even these fine drawings take second place to the pastels, which he began to produce during the second half of the 1860s. These are done on coloured papers (grey, blue, lilac, buff) and built up with several layers. Brief outlines of the compositions were delicately laid in first with black Conté crayon over which stronger

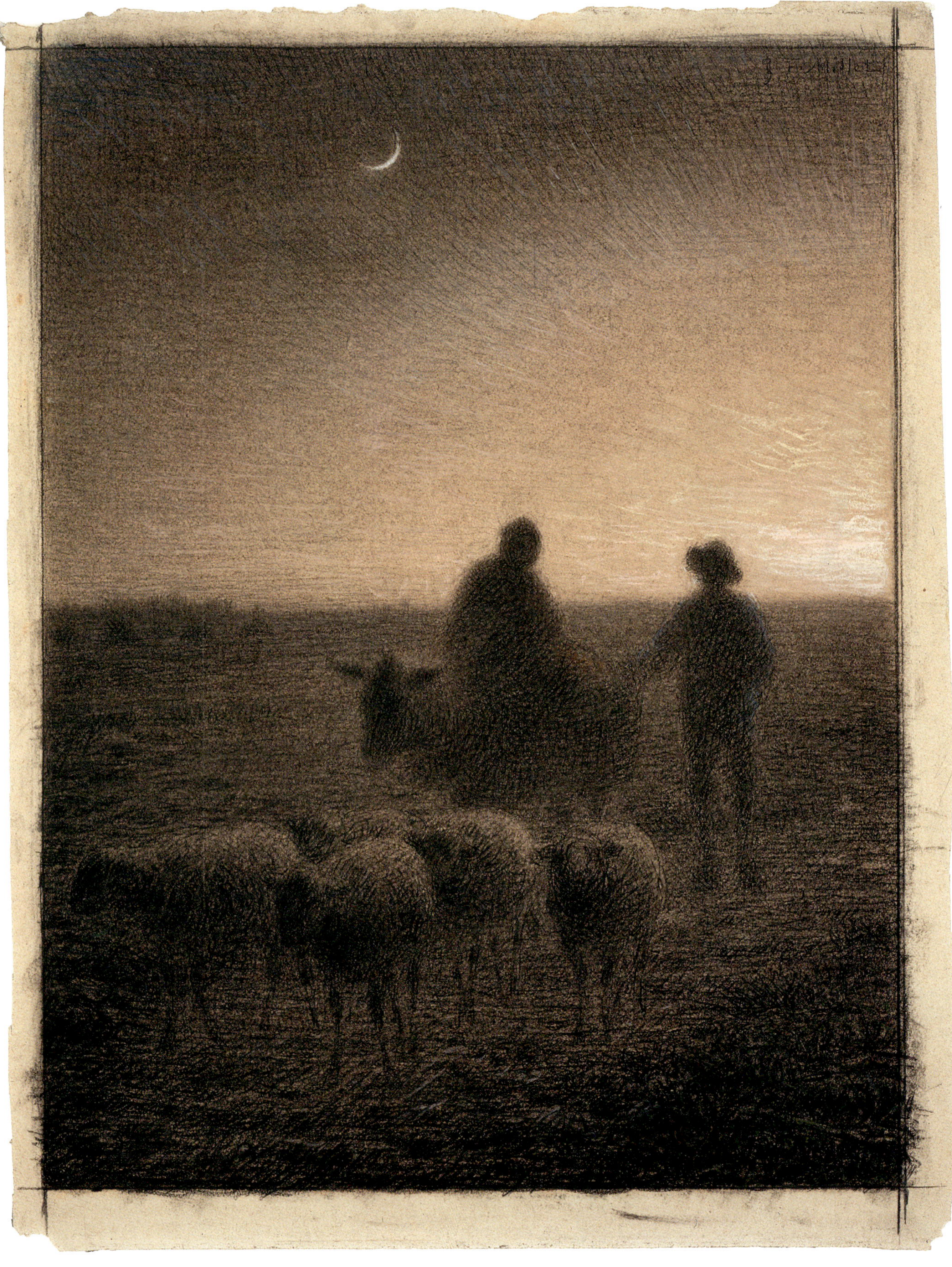

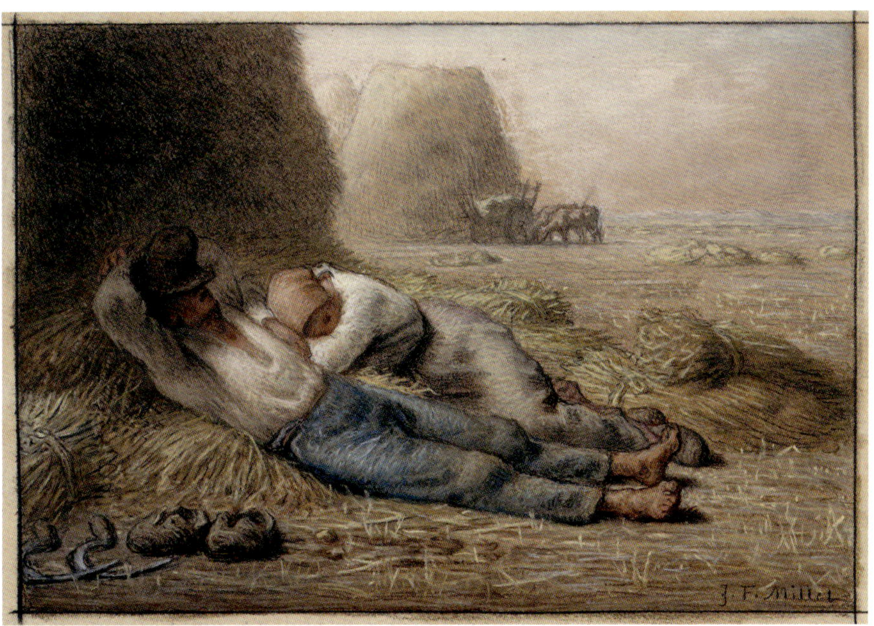

Fig. 13 Jean-François Millet, *Noonday Rest*, 1866. Pastel and black Conté crayon on buff wove paper, 29.2 x 41.9 cm. Museum of Fine Arts, Boston. Gift of Quincy Adams Shaw through Quincy Adams Shaw, Jr., and Mrs. Marian Shaw Haughton, 17.1511

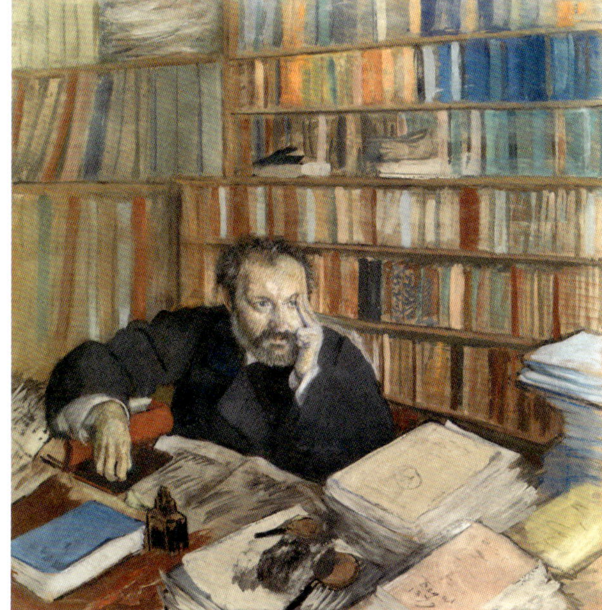

Fig. 14 Edgar Degas, *Portrait of Edmond Duranty*, 1879. Gouache heightened with pastel on linen, 100 x 100.4 cm. The Burrell Collection, Glasgow Life Museums, Glasgow. Gifted by Sir William and Lady Burrell to the City of Glasgow, 1944, 35.232

areas of modelling were applied in pastel. These were then highlighted in the final stages with more intense colours (fig. 13). Sometimes coloured crayons, watercolour or gouache were added to the mix for more dramatic results. The pastels are in many ways the summation of Millet's art and in their evolving technical skill they proved to be a catalyst for younger artists posing fresh questions and searching for new solutions.

The second Impressionist exhibition held in 1876 was marked by the publication of a pamphlet entitled *La Nouvelle Peinture* (*The New Painting, Concerning the Group of Artists Exhibiting at the Durand-Ruel Galleries*). It was written by Edmond Duranty, a novelist and critic who was a close friend of Degas (fig. 14). The text is the first considered defence of avant-garde painting, which the writer defines as 'trying to create from scratch a wholly modern art, an art imbued with our surroundings, our sentiments, and the things of our age'.[20] This, Duranty maintains, can be achieved by 'A new method of colour, of drawing, and a gamut of original points of view'.[21] He then explains, 'The new painters have tried to render the walk, movement, and hustle and bustle of passers-by, just as they have tried to render the trembling of leaves, the shimmer of water, and the vibration of sun-drenched air – just as they have managed to capture the hazy atmosphere of a grey day along with the iridescent play of sunshine.'[22] The teaching at the Ecole des Beaux-Arts is summarily dismissed: 'Farewell to the human body treated like a vase, with an eye for a decorative curve. Farewell to the uniform monotony of bone structure, to the anatomical model beneath the nude. What we need

Fig. 12 Jean-François Millet, *Twilight*, *c.* 1859–63. Black Conté crayon and pastel on buff wove paper, 50.5 x 38.9 cm. Museum of Fine Arts, Boston. Gift of Quincy Adams Shaw through Quincy Adams Shaw, Jr., and Mrs. Marian Shaw Haughton. 17.1518

are the special characteristics of the modern individual – in his clothing, in social situations, at home, or on the street.'[23] He then lists some of the characteristics that he believes the artist will be able to depict when his brush or pencil are 'infused with the essence of life'.[24]

Duranty stresses that such a new departure in art is only possible through 'a penetrating draughtsmanship, consonant with the character of modern beings and things'.[25] In other words, drawing is the key that opens the door to modernity and it is one of the reasons why Impressionist works on paper are so noteworthy. The great diversity of Impressionist art is a measure of the way in which it succeeds in the challenge of capturing 'the essence of life' that Duranty wanted artists to pursue. The spontaneity of drawing, as opposed to the more laborious process of making a finished painting, proved to be the ideal method of recording the restless activity of the modern world.

This change of emphasis in the hierarchy of art, whereby drawing achieved an equal status to painting, had implications for the future. Although it was still necessary to learn how to draw, the overthrow of the rigidity of the academic system created a feeling of *laissez-faire* in choices of technique, format and support. Even the most traditional task of making compositional drawings, together with related preparatory studies, which nearly all the Impressionists produced at most stages of their lives, was carried out with novel inflections. Degas, for example, who declared that all art is artifice, made numerous studies of ballet dancers and jockeys during the 1870s and 1880s before deciding on exactly which of the poses he had explored to include in his finished works (cats 8, 9, 20, 21). Some of these studies are particularly striking as the artist chose to execute them in *essence* (oil diluted with turpentine applied with a brush) on coloured papers (cats 8, 9). Towards the end of his life, when he was more confined to his studio, the use of tracing paper allowed him to transpose and even reverse poses before altering them in order to develop compositions in series. This practice was not just limited to dancers (cats 54, 69, 70), but included bathers and women at their toilette (cats 43, 55). Similarly, Pissarro (cat. 25), Van Gogh (cat. 37), Gauguin (cats 60, 67), Renoir (cat. 12) and even Toulouse-Lautrec (cat. 64) established a repertoire of figures for use in finished compositions. All such studies comprised poses that were usually observed in life and then, if necessary, re-created in the studio.

There is a similar variety in the landscape drawings made by the Impressionists, where the choice of medium was even more critical. Thus, Monet favours sombre-toned pastels for creating the strong contrasts in the stormy skies (cat. 35) and rugged coastline (cat. 36) of northern France, whereas for his representations of the bridges across the River Thames emerging from the mists of London he opts for lighter-toned pastels. Cézanne, on the other hand, suggests the sharper light and shimmering heat of Provence with touches of transparent watercolour surrounded by areas of untouched white paper (cats 48, 73). By extension, Pissarro working at Eragny-sur-Epte, his home in Normandy, finds watercolour the ideal medium for contrasting the cold of winter (cat. 52) with the heat of summer (cat. 51). Such technical sophistication, combined with freedom from the restrictions of earlier centuries, encouraged the opportunism and expansiveness of Impressionist drawing. Now the artist was free to select the appropriate medium suggested by a particular subject or motif rather than having to rely on received opinion or the rule book.

Given the wide range of drawings made by the Impressionists, three particular categories may be considered influential for the development of art in general. The first is the use of watercolour, a medium of which British eighteenth-century artists were considered to be the greatest exponents. In France watercolour remained for a long time the province mainly of topographical draughtsmen. An example is Baron Isidore Taylor's long-running project *Voyages pittoresques et romantiques dans l'ancienne France* (1820–78), which was undertaken at a time when French artists were beginning to appreciate the prominent role that watercolour was playing in the work of J. M. W. Turner, John

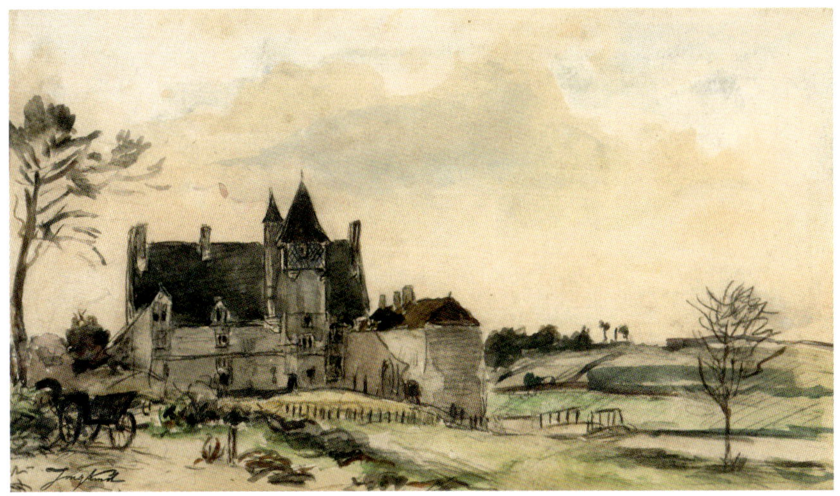

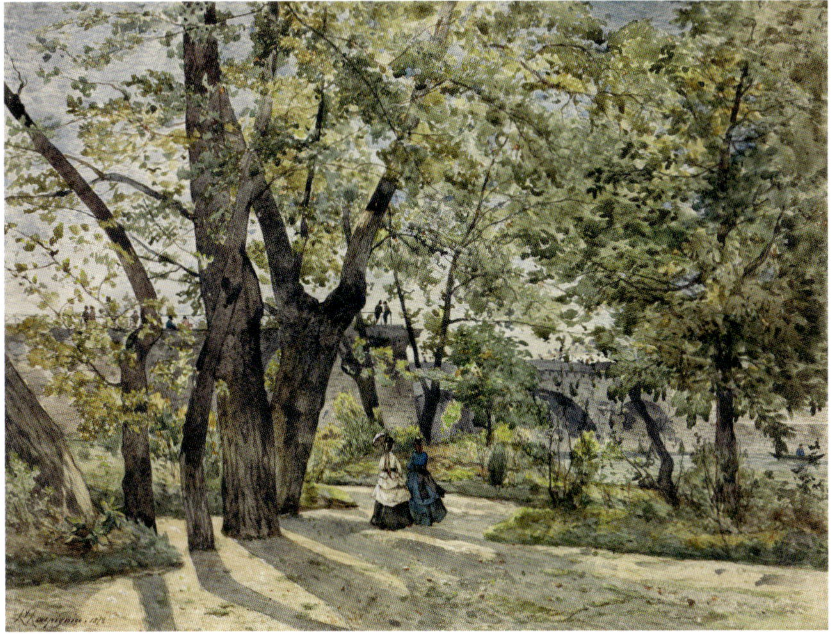

Fig. 15 Johan Barthold Jongkind, *Le Château de Villemenant*, 1872. Watercolour over traces of black chalk on paper, 26 x 45.5 cm. Musée du Louvre (Collection Musée d'Orsay), Paris, RF 35831, Recto

Fig. 16 Henri-Joseph Harpignies, *The Square of Vert Galant in Paris at the Tip of the Ile de la Cité*, 1872. Watercolour on paper, 51 x 68.8 cm. Szépművészeti Múzeum / Museum of Fine Arts, Budapest, 1950-4291

Constable, David Wilkie and Richard Parkes Bonington. A response came in France during the Romantic period in the work above all of Delacroix, but also that of Victor Hugo, Théodore Géricault, François-Marius Granet, Eugène Isabey and Paul Huet. Pissarro acknowledges this advance in a letter to his eldest son Lucien: 'Watercolour is not especially difficult, but I must warn you to steer clear of those pretty English watercolourists, so skilful and alas so weak, and so often too *truthful*... Think of the watercolours of Delacroix, Jongkind. Who else? Degas, Manet – with the rest it is a technique, though there are some who bring talent to it!'[26]

Among the French artists known to the Impressionists who brought talent to the art of watercolour were Johan Barthold Jongkind and Henri-Joseph Harpignies, both of whom were indirectly connected with the Barbizon School. Jongkind settled in France in 1846, although he retained his links with the Netherlands where he had been born. Travelling extensively throughout his career, he specialised in panoramic views overlaid with canopies of immense skies. His style is broad and he leaves obvious traces of the liquidity of the medium (fig. 15). Although he emphasises the horizontal in his watercolours, recession is often built up with carefully positioned patches of bolder colour. Signac, who was an outstanding watercolourist in his own right and who almost literally followed in the footsteps of Jongkind, wrote a monograph on the artist, which was published in 1927. Harpignies, by contrast, had a fussier style dominated by neatly balanced compositions often of peaceful scenes (fig. 16). His brushwork is precise and he enjoyed creating dappled effects bathed in a warm light. He seems to have relished the gentler seasons of spring and autumn over winter and summer.

Cognisant of the growing sympathy for watercolour and no doubt aware of its increasing success at the Salon and with dealers, nearly all the Impressionists chose to work in the medium at various intervals. Manet seems to have used it as much to record or amend his painted compositions in complicated ways as to prepare for them. Akin in technique to his watercolours are his brush drawings in dark ink, which were perhaps influenced by Japanese art and made specifically to capture fleeting moments, as well as for book illustrations. In these works, often drawn in sketchbooks, Manet captures the ephemeral with speed and confidence (cat. 14). By the end of his life, however, when increasingly unwell, he resorted to decorating his letters to friends with charming vignettes in watercolour of fruit, flowers and, amusingly, of different types of women's footwear espied under café tables. Watercolours by his sister-in-law, Berthe Morisot, were constantly praised when they were shown regularly at the Impressionist exhibitions for the variety in their execution and wide-ranging subject matter. Indeed, the brushwork of Morisot's stronger watercolours (cat. 31) is comparable with Manet's in its energy and confidence. Renoir applied watercolour diffidently, betraying his training as a porcelain painter, and only occasionally used it with total confidence in a few of his landscapes. Very different in purpose and style are Forain and Somm, who chose the medium for their work in more of a caricatural vein: the former to expose the hypocrisy of bourgeois life and the latter to illustrate the various social types and activities witnessed on the streets of Paris.[27] Raffaëlli, too, chose watercolour to reveal the hardships of those poor ragpickers, roadmen, tinkers and vagabonds living on the edge of the city and in the margins of society who were forever doomed to wander across the industrial wastelands of the suburbs of Paris as though auditioning for roles in Samuel Beckett's *Waiting for Godot*.[28]

Writing again in a letter to his son Lucien, Pissarro extols the virtue of watercolour: 'Remember that watercolours help the memory, and enable you to retain the fugitive effects – watercolours render so well the impalpable, the powerful, the delicate.'[29] This was written at a time when Cézanne was making his finest watercolours. As soon as they became better known, towards the very end of his life, these were to prove a decisive influence on modern artists. Cézanne used watercolour as a counterpart to his paintings of landscapes (cats 48, 71), bathers, portraits and still-lifes (cats 32, 50). His early style in the medium was fulsome and often elaborate, particularly while working under the overcast skies of northern France. From the mid-1880s, however, he began to rediscover the Provence of his childhood: the abandoned quarry at Bibémus, the unfinished Château Noir and above all Mont Sainte-Victoire (cat. 73). The intense Provençal light and the relentless heat caused Cézanne to rethink his style in watercolour. The object now was to record as directly as possible those sensations which he experienced in front of nature out in the sun or in his studio at Les Lauves on the outskirts of Aix-en-Provence. The technique he developed for this purpose was to place a few marks in pencil on the paper first, around which he then laid in carefully judged patches of colour, often in single touches or sometimes overlaid. These areas created an aerial rather than a mathematical perspective in which a sense of recession and a feeling of atmosphere are integrated. They also suggested forms even though the patches themselves are abstract. Those parts of the paper left blank remained key elements in the overall architectonic structure. The style is economical and very specific, being achieved only with intense concentration and through complete confidence in the medium. The viewer witnesses a high-wire performance governed not by self-confidence and bravura, but rather by a mixture of extreme caution and reckless daring. Occasionally, Cézanne misjudges, but when he succeeds his watercolours are some of the finest ever made.

Most critics writing about the Impressionist exhibitions commented on the watercolours on display. Some even noted how the fluidity of the brush stroke associated with the medium was comparable with the looser, more broken technique being used in the paintings. Armand Silvestre even went so far as to write, in his review of the sixth exhibition (1881), 'One might think that watercolour would have lent itself better than oils to this summary and rapid conception of renderings.'[30] Certainly this was true for any exploration of technique beyond Impressionism as reflected in the gradual move towards abstraction evident in some later works by Degas, Cézanne and Monet.

A second category of drawing that the Impressionists advanced was known as a *fusain*. These were made with charcoal, black Conté crayon or black chalk in a highly finished, dark tonal style. The *fusain* is essentially a tenebrist drawing dependent on the stark contrast between black and white. This type of drawing was already attracting attention during the 1860s and 1870s with special exhibitions mounted in galleries such as the Dudley Gallery in London and Durand-Ruel in Paris, in addition to the Salon. As a style it developed alongside a revival in printmaking, especially etching, aquatint and lithography. It was favoured by the Realists, particularly Gustave Courbet and François Bonvin, and also by Millet (fig. 12), before being taken up by the avant-garde. Certain artists, among them Auguste Allongé, Léon-Augustin Lhermitte, Maxime Lalanne and Henri Fantin-Latour, could be described as specialists in the technique. There were no limits to the subject matter of these drawings: landscape, topography, portraiture, still-life, illustration and ultimately fantasy. The skill lay in the delicate manipulation of the medium on good-quality laid paper. Gradation of tone came about not only through pressure of the hand, but also by rubbing with a stump, dampening with a sponge, scraping or even by smudging with the fingers.

A number of *fusains* were included in the Impressionist exhibitions. Most were contributed by Albert Lebourg to the fourth and fifth exhibitions (cat. 13), but Redon, Seurat and Signac produced examples for the last showing in 1886 and in so doing acknowledged the importance of such work for the avant-garde. Seurat, in fact, achieved the most sophisticated effects by alternating the silhouetting of a dark figure or object against a light background with the placement of luminous forms emerging out of dark backgrounds (cats 22, 23, 24). By varying the density of the dark passages he could introduce contrasting moods and dramatic effects. Signac was less committed to the art of the *fusain* (cat. 29) and rapidly became more enamoured of colour, as is evident from his book *D'Eugène Delacroix au Néo-Impressionnisme* (1899).

Whereas Seurat's images remain firmly within the world he saw about him, Redon, who confessed to being terrified when confronted by a blank sheet of paper, allowed his imagination free rein, so that he produced phantasmagoric compositions based on parts of the body, plants and animals. In some of these last drawings Redon anticipates Surrealism (cat. 39). The wide range of work produced by those artists who favoured the tenebrist style emphasises that apart from being an exercise in technical skill tenebrism encouraged attempts in new interpretations of traditional subject matter.

As significant as watercolour and the *fusain* for the Impressionists was their interest in pastel, tempera and gouache, which is the third category of drawing where great changes occurred. These media are more closely associated with artists working in earlier centuries and required supports other than paper. Once more, the Impressionists proved themselves to be versatile by opting for canvas, cardboard, millboard and even silk, and by experimenting with different types of paper. Dealers regarded works made in pastel, tempera or gouache as easier and less time-consuming for artists to make and therefore a means of increasing their turnover and potential sales. As he grew older, Degas found that pastel was less tiring than working in oils. But, even so, he liked to test the limits by enlarging and reducing compositions at will, often quite dramatically (cat. 55).

Gauguin and Toulouse-Lautrec were also experimental, mainly in answer to their circumstances. Owing to his tendency to be nomadic, Gauguin was often short of materials and so was forced to improvise. His paintings, drawings, carvings, ceramics and prints surprise by virtue of the ingenuity needed to create the actual works of art as much as by the images themselves (cat. 60). Anticipated to some degree by Manet, Gauguin also liked to push the boundaries of art in the sense that he enjoyed the ambivalence inherent in making zincographs, transfer drawings, *papiers collés* and prints of various types. Toulouse-Lautrec was an omnivorous artist whose output was enhanced by his extrovert behaviour. His immersion in the bohemian activities of Montmartre only intensified his wish to create art in a correspondingly varied and challenging way, and he did not limit himself to paintings and works on paper, but drew illustrations and designed posters. He developed a fluent linear style using *essence* and mixed media (cat. 57). Loosely hatched strokes were combined with tone as the basis for modelling (cat. 63). Revealing the support and allowing the underdrawing to show through meant that many of his works appear unfinished or even abandoned (cat. 64). Active at the very end of the nineteenth century, Toulouse-Lautrec absorbs many existing artistic practices but adapts them in novel ways that provided others with fresh opportunities. This is exemplified by the manner in which his Impressionist style elides with Art Nouveau.

Larger works in pastel, tempera or gouache are hybrids in that they are in effect a crossover between paintings and drawings. The Impressionists found these techniques a more appropriate means than oils of depicting the fluctuating contemporary scene, regardless of the fact that they form part of time-honoured artistic practices. Tempera, and by extension gouache, are media referred to in the fourteenth-century treatise on workshop practices entitled *Il Libro dell'arte* written by Cennino Cennini, which was translated into French by Victor-Louis Mottez in 1858 and published in a new edition with a preface by Renoir in 1910. Pastel, on the other hand, was principally associated with the eighteenth century where it reached a zenith in France with Jean-Baptiste Perronneau, Maurice-Quentin de La Tour and Jean-Baptiste-Siméon Chardin. The work of these artists and others active in the eighteenth century was reassessed by Edmond and Jules de Goncourt in *L'Art du dix-huitième siècle* (1859–75).

Following the example of Manet, nearly all the Impressionists worked in pastel, producing examples of the highest quality, but very much in their own stylistic idiom. A rallying call was issued by Baudelaire in his review of the Salon of 1859, in which he writes an intensely poetic evocation of the febrile pastels of sea and sky made by Eugène Boudin (cat. 3).[31] Several of the Impressionists responded during the 1860s and 1870s, including Degas (cat. 1), Monet, Armand Guillaumin (cats 2, 6) and Redon.

During the remainder of the nineteenth century, pastel became more popular with avant-garde artists and possibly as a result also with Salon artists such as Jacques-Emile Blanche (cat. 42), but of particular interest is the range of subjects for which it became the chosen medium: Guillaumin along the banks of the River Seine (cat. 34); Sisley at Saint-Mammès and Moret-sur-Loing (cat. 19); Degas (cats 1, 10, 20, 54, 55, 69), Renoir (cat. 12) and de Nittis (cat. 30) on the streets and in private spaces; Manet, Eva Gonzalès (cat. 11), Cassatt (cat. 62) and Morisot (cat. 33) for portraiture; Federico Zandomeneghi (cats 56, 61) for moments of intimacy; Forain at social gatherings (cat. 45); Raffaëlli in the industrial suburbs of Paris; Pissarro for rural scenes and local markets (cats 7, 26); Monet and Emile Schuffenecker along the Normandy coast (cats 35, 36, 46). In short, all kinds of places and all variety of life.

Degas was seen as a particularly fine exponent of pastel, forever experimenting with different methods of application. In his review of the fifth Impressionist exhibition (1880) Huysmans recognised the significance of the medium for this artist, 'No painter since Delacroix ... has understood the marriage and the adultery of colours like M. Degas; no one today has a drawing style so precise and so broad a touch for colouring so delicate.'[32] But according to Huysmans Degas's brilliance really lies in his willingness 'to borrow from all the vocabularies of painting, to combine various elements of oil and pigment, of watercolour and pastel, of tempera and gouache, to forge neologisms of colour, to break with the accepted arrangement of subjects.'[33] Nowhere is this more apparent than in the controversial *Suite de nuds de femmes se baignant, se lavant, se séchant, s'essuyant, se peignant ou se faisant peigner* (Suite of female nudes, bathing, washing, drying themselves, wiping themselves, combing themselves or being combed) that Degas included in the eighth exhibition of 1886 (fig. 17).

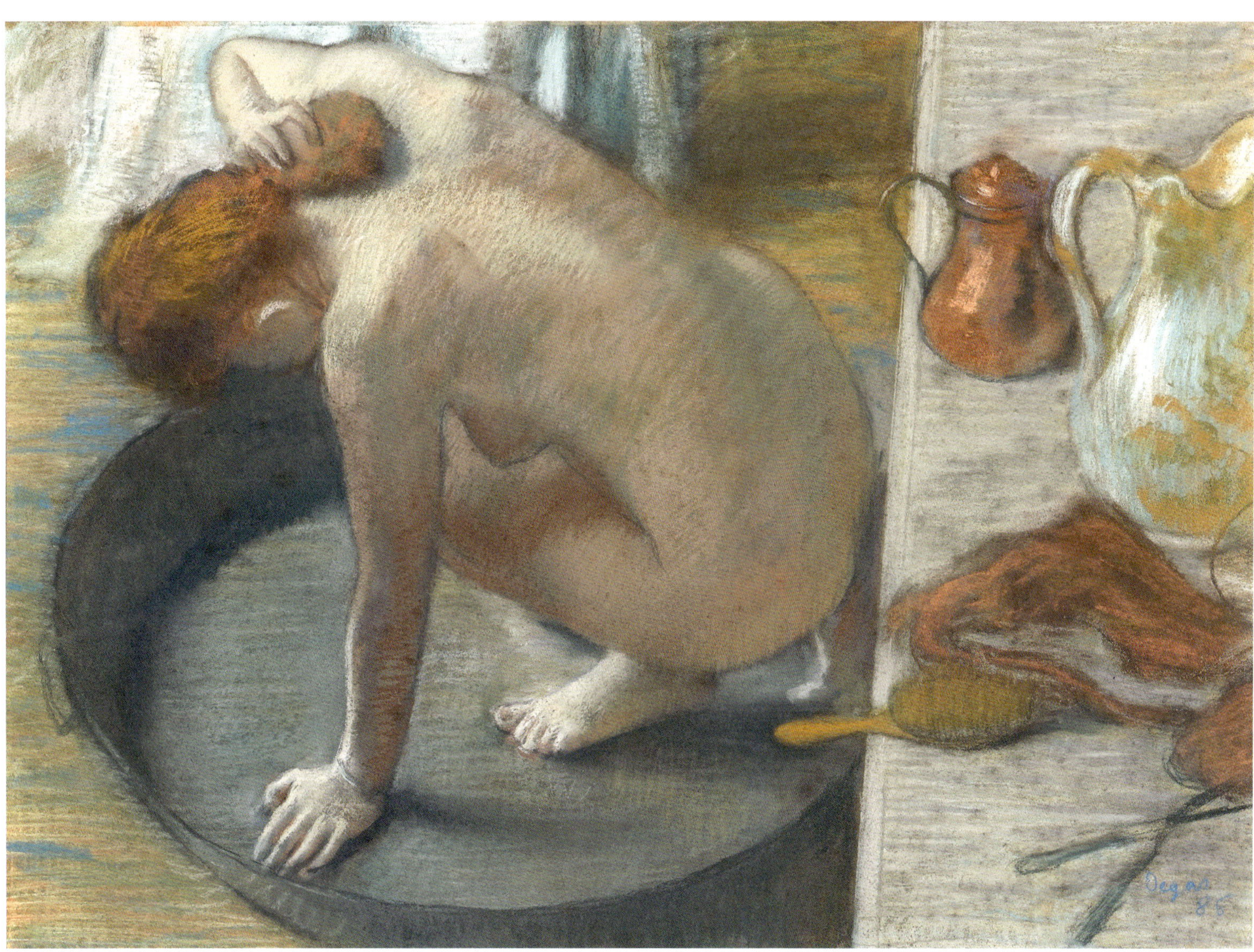

Fig. 17 Edgar Degas, *The Tub*, 1886. Pastel on cardboard, 60 x 83 cm. Musée d'Orsay, Paris. Bequest of Comte Isaac de Camondo, RF 4046

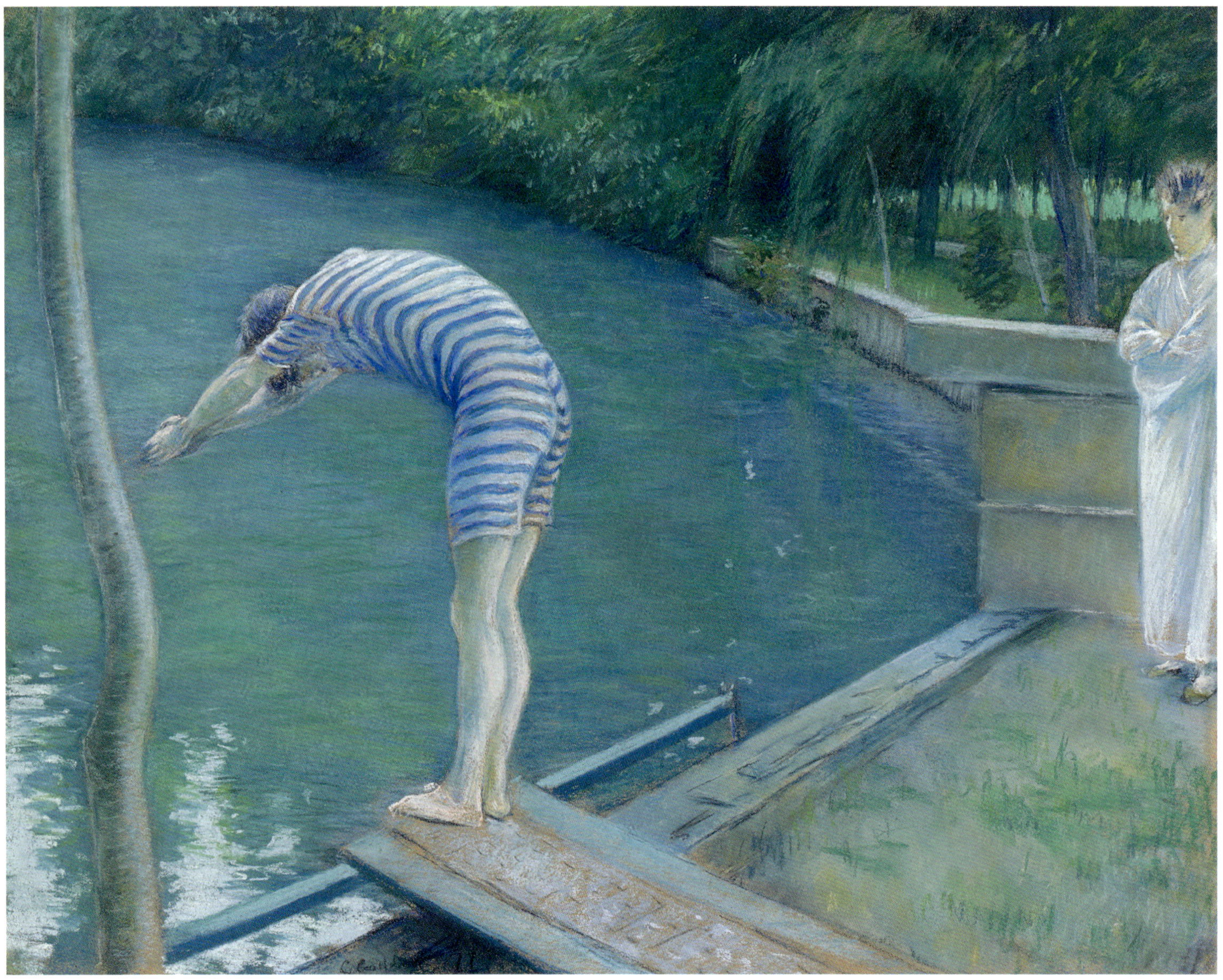

Fig. 18 Gustave Caillebotte, *The Swimmer*, 1877. Pastel on paper, 69 x 88.5 cm. Musée d'Orsay, Paris, 1946, RF 1946 34

Two other artists who extended the use of pastel into uncharted territory are Caillebotte and Redon: the former produced very few examples whereas the latter was prolific. The singular and challenging viewpoints of Caillebotte's paintings become even more enigmatic in his pastels (fig. 18), in which time is suspended, like a 'freeze-frame' in the cinema. Redon, meanwhile, explores worlds on the edge of time, or even beyond time through mythology, literature, world religions and mysticism (cats 66, 76, 77). As he wrote in his journal *A soi-même*: 'My drawings *inspire*, and are not definable. They determine nothing. They lead us, like music, into the ambiguous domain of the indeterminate.'[34] Redon's emphasis on an engagement with an inner vision was also independently explored by Gustave Moreau, who had known Degas in Italy during the late 1850s and towards the end of his life instructed artists such as Henri Matisse and Georges Rouault. It was not so much Moreau's preference for recondite or exotic subject matter as the willingness to abandon himself to the characteristics of the selected medium while also luxuriating in the purity and juxtaposition of colour that was subsequently embraced by the Abstract Expressionists (fig. 19).

* * *

The drawings made by the Impressionists eroded one of the traditional hierarchies of art. By standing up to the official authorities and breaking with prescriptive teaching practices the Impressionists were able to become more innovative. Not only were works on paper now autonomous, but they were also at the core of independent developments and ambitious experimentation. This advance freed drawing from its previously shackled status of being predominantly a preliminary exercise and instead allowed it to become an indisputable means of expression in its own right, which in turn could unleash new powers of interpretation. At the centre of this development is the artist's choice of a medium to fit a work's subject matter, which became an integral part of the creative process as significant as any technical accomplishment and as paramount as the final image itself.

Acknowledgement of the debt that modern artists owe to the Impressionists is apparent in the narrow sense by the ownership of their work. For example, Pablo Picasso owned a painting by Cézanne, a sanguine by Renoir and eleven monotypes by Degas, while Henri Matisse owned a painting by Cézanne and pen-and-ink drawings by Van Gogh. Among contemporary artists, Jasper Johns has an extensive collection of works on paper by Cézanne, and Jeff Koons a pastel by Manet. But, the real proof of the influence lies in the type of art produced during the twentieth century, nearly all of which could not have been undertaken without the advances made in painting and drawing by the Impressionists. The combination of line and colour in Degas, the tonal qualities of Seurat, the vigorous penwork of Van Gogh, the economy of Cézanne's watercolours, and the search for paradise underlying the imagery of Gauguin and Redon all open the door to modern art on both sides of the Atlantic Ocean. The liberties won by the Impressionists, coupled with their search for innovations, created the freedoms from which future generations of artists were to benefit. As Cézanne wrote in a letter to Roger Marx: 'In my opinion, one does not replace the past, one only adds a new link.'[35]

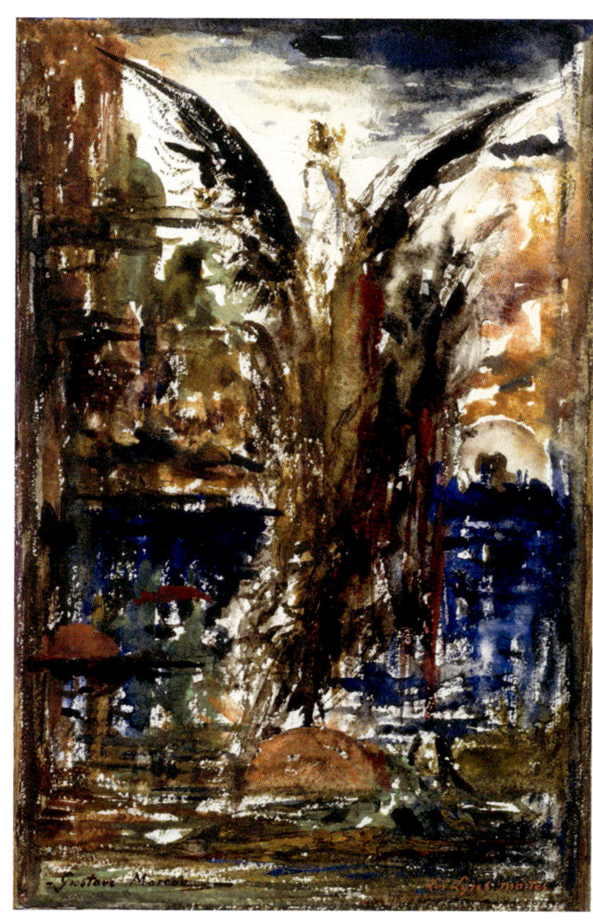

Fig. 19 Gustave Moreau, *Les Lyres mortes*, 1896. Watercolour on paper, 37.5 x 25 cm. Musée Gustave Moreau, Paris, Cat.346

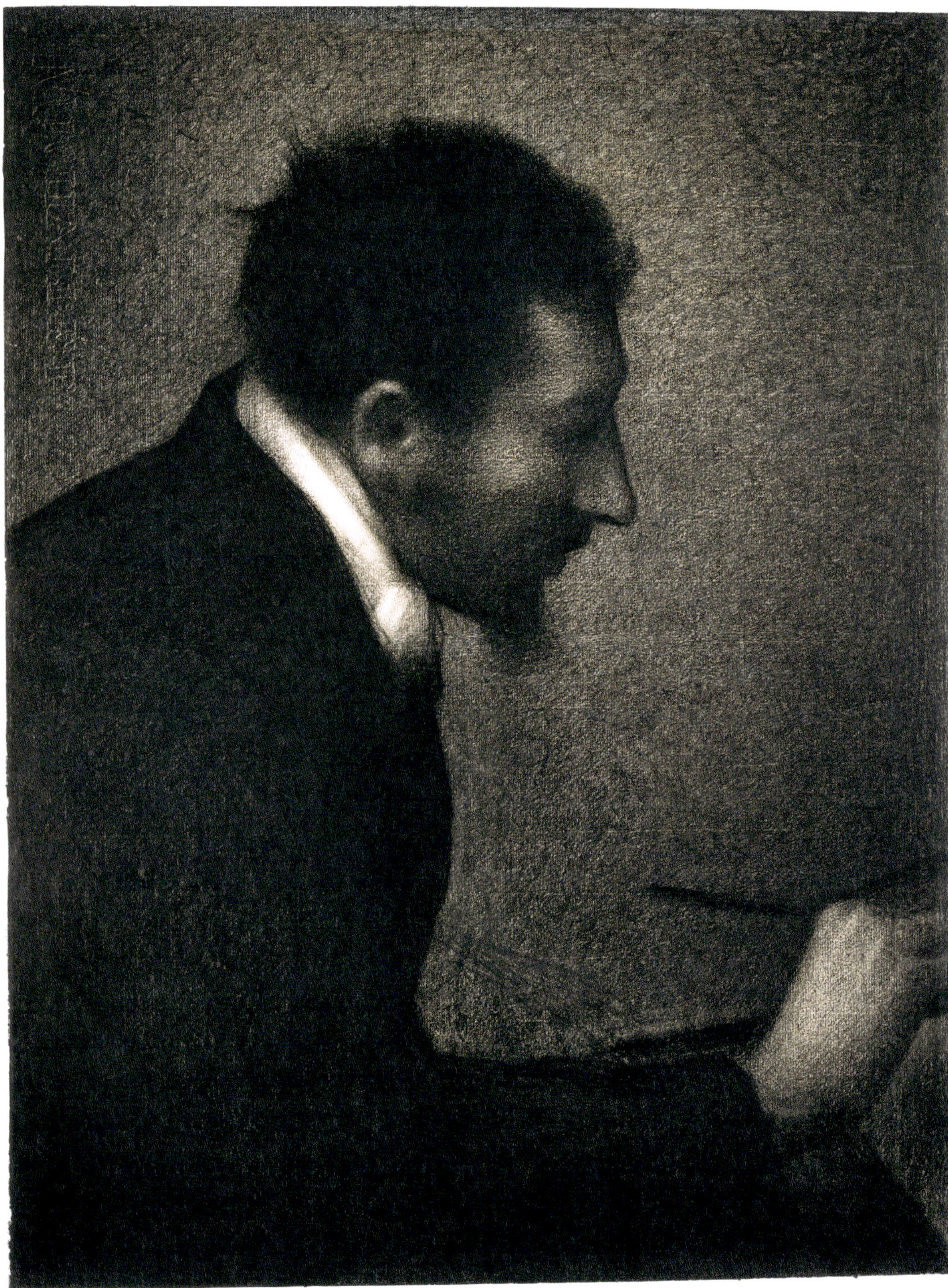

Fig. 20 Georges Seurat, *Portrait of Edmond Aman-Jean*, 1882–83. Conté crayon on paper, 62.2 x 47.5 cm. The Metropolitan Museum of Art, New York. Bequest of Stephen C. Clark, 1960, 61.101.16

The Rising Status of Drawing from the 1870s to the 1890s

LEÏLA JARBOUAI

Throughout the nineteenth century, drawing continued to play a utilitarian role in relation to the other arts: it was the foundation of artistic training, whether at the Ecole des Beaux-Arts, in private art schools or in public drawing schools. Even the Impressionists, who aspired to paint from life without preparatory drawings, resorted to drawing when concentrating on real places and objects. Unlike in earlier centuries, artists had abundant drawing materials at their disposal in 'the paper century'.[1] They armed themselves with notebooks and sketchbooks, which were very handy for sketching from the motif or making visual notes, providing a visual repertoire to be consulted when working on a more finished piece. During the second half of the century, as academic teaching came under fire, drawing took more and more varied and unexpected turns. Although academicians and avant-garde artists were at one in the vibrancy of their gestures and the subjects of their drawings, the value given to drawing in the artistic process – its status, its aims and the definition of the frontier between finished and *non finito* – illustrates the widening gulf between artists and artistic movements. During the second half of the century, thanks to its acceptance by the art world, drawing came to occupy an increasingly important position. This was due to the locations, styles and types of exhibitions in which drawings were shown, as well as to the relationships developing between dealers and collectors, and to the publications devoted specifically to drawing. The vast scale of this panorama means, of course, that only a few protagonists can be dealt with here.

The position of drawing in the Salon

Every year, the Paris Salon, the great French contemporary art fair, exhibited the largest number of drawings to be seen anywhere in France. Originally held at the Musée du Louvre, by the late nineteenth century the Salon had moved to the Palais des Champs-Elysées. More than 10,000 drawings were exhibited at the Salon between 1860 and 1881, the date when the annual Salon was renamed the Salon de la Société des Artistes Français. In 1864, within the painting section, a subsection devoted to drawing was created, which included drawings, watercolours and pastels as well as porcelain, enamel, stained glass, faience, miniatures and fans – in other words, everything apart from the great genres. The same jury judged these categories, and drawing was listed in the booklet accompanying the Salon alongside the decorative arts, where it was described as a subsection of painting. This new arrangement was a disadvantage for drawing, which was treated as a separate category but with no allocated jury, unlike other arts (painting, sculpture, architecture, engraving). At the Salon of 1870, drawing was included in the section of 'painting, drawing etc.' for the awards but it was set apart for the commentary, after painting. Drawings were described as follows: 'DRAWINGS: watercolours, pastels, miniatures, enamels, porcelain, faience, cartoons for stained glass'. At the Salon of 1870, this enormous category of 'drawings' comprised 1,237 objects (nos 2992 to 4229) out of a total of 5,434 entries. At the Salon of 1890, with the same grouping, they were 951 (nos 2481 to 3432) out of a total of 5,301. This minor decrease in quantity, which grew more pronounced in the 1890s, was related to developments in the regulations of the Salon: the number of drawings admitted was lower for reasons of space and because opportunities for draughtsmen to exhibit elsewhere had increased. The fact that drawings were part of the painting section made the allocation of awards for the category less easy; it was not until 1880 that a quota was introduced, and solely for lesser awards because the new quota system was not regarded as valid for first-class medals. In 1880, therefore, two second-class medals and two honourable mentions were set aside for 'drawings, pastels or watercolours'. This quota lasted only a year and proved too ineffectual to cope with the number of drawings exhibited.

At exhibitions, drawings had their own separate space, as did pastels and watercolours, which each had their own areas closer to the paintings. This did not satisfy artists who presented drawings: their work was not shown to best effect, which meant that they had to find other means of attracting attention to it and selling it. Edgar Degas, in 1870, wrote a letter to the Salon deploring the hanging of the drawings, giving his own strong recommendations in this regard: 'Use large and small screens, as the English did at the Exposition... Universelle, place the ejected drawings upon these and distribute them through the two big rooms known as the dumps or junkyards, or elsewhere... the drawings would be withdrawn from their desert and mixed in with the paintings, which is what they deserve...'[2] The word was out: at the Salon, drawings were in the 'desert'. Artists soon sought means of escaping the desert, away from the Salon: they formed groups in drawing rooms and societies, making exhibitions specifically dedicated to drawing.

Drawings in colour: societies of watercolourists and pastel artists

To make up for the lack of space afforded to drawings in the official Salon, privately organised exhibitions began to appear under the Third Republic. Artists wanted to exhibit their graphic work in better conditions and to improve their visibility. As Jean-Paul Bouillon writes: 'The multiplication and development of artists' societies in the second half of the nineteenth century is one of the defining features of French artistic life during that period.'[3]

During the 1870s, societies of artists began to appear that focused specifically on drawing, according to the simple principle of 'Unity is strength'. The Société des Aquarellistes Français was founded in 1878 and continued until 1896 (fig. 21). This earliest association of graphic artists was inspired by foreign models: in the United Kingdom, the Society of Painters in Water Colours had been set up in 1804 and obtained its own premises in 1823. The New Society of Painters in Water Colours was founded in 1831 and gained its own exhibition premises in 1883. Another society of watercolour painters was born in London, at the Dudley Gallery, in 1864. In Belgium, the Société Royale Belge

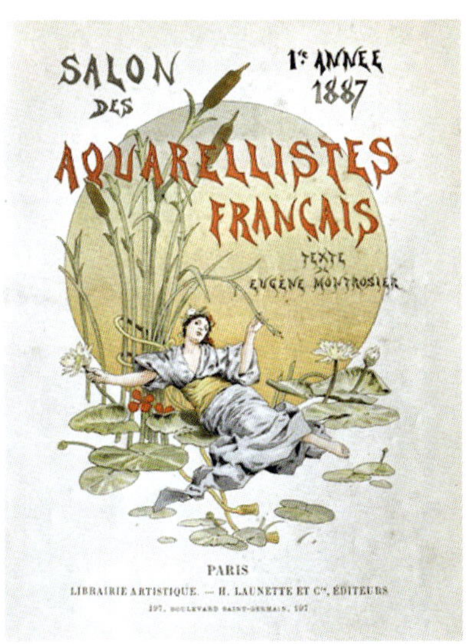

Fig. 21 Eugène Montrosier, *Salon des Aquarellistes Français*, première année, 1887. Librairie Artistique. H. Launette et Cie, Paris

LA NOUVELLE SALLE D'EXPOSITION DE M. GEORGES PETIT
8, Rue de Sèze.

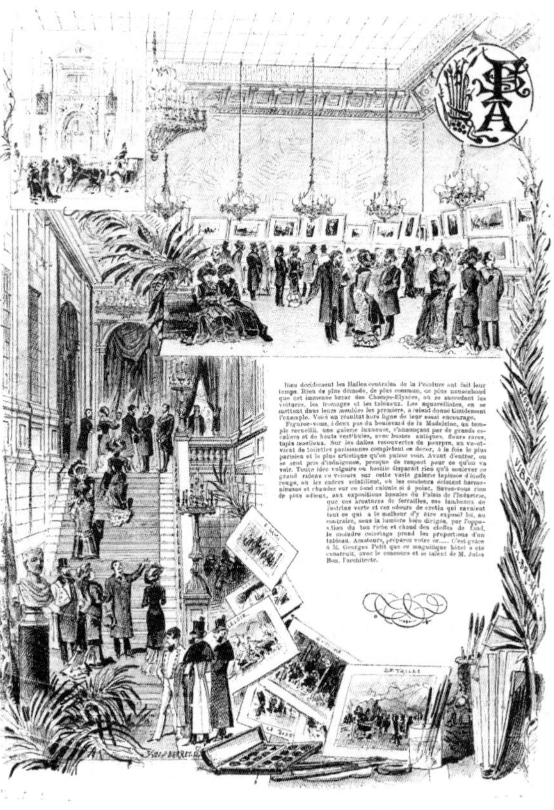

Fig. 22 Artist unknown, 'La Nouvelle Salle d'Exposition de M. Georges Petit, 8 Rue de Sèze', *La Vie parisienne*, 25 February 1882

d'Aquarellistes exhibited for the first time in 1856, extending the watercolour to include wash drawings (sepia, Indian ink). In France, members of the Société des Aquarellistes exhibited each year from 1879 at Paul Durand-Ruel, 16 Rue Lafitte, in Paris, then from 1882 at Georges Petit, Rue de Sèze, near the Madeleine (fig. 22); the two gallery owners were to play a major role in increasing the appreciation of drawing during the final 30 years of the nineteenth century. The Société des Aquarellistes witnessed major expansion during the years between 1870 and 1890: 123 works by 17 artists were exhibited in 1879, whereas 43 artists exhibited 213 works in 1892. The number of members also rose over the years. The association of French watercolour painters started when five artists who were friends – Jehan Georges Vibert, Etienne-Prosper Berne-Bellecour, Alexandre-Louis Leloir, Jules Worms and Eduardo Zamacois y Zabala, who all worked together at Montmorency in the Val d'Oise – got together. This association was restricted to a limited number of members; only they could exhibit their work, without restriction on the number of entries each. As Marie Leimbacher points out: 'although the society was established initially to foster the appreciation of one technique, it seems above all to have offered artists the opportunity to exhibit alongside the Salon since, from the first year, 1879, the Société d'Aquarellistes also organised exhibitions of oil paintings.'[4] Among its most famous members were Eugène Isabey, Jean-Paul Laurens, Eugène Lami, Henri-Joseph Harpignies, Gustave Doré, Pierre Puvis de Chavannes, Jacques-Emile Blanche, Emile Friant, Jules Bastien-Lepage, Henri Gervex, Jules-Ferdinand Jacquemart and Madeleine Lemaire. Members also exhibited annually at the Salon and many won medals. In addition to a catalogue of their exhibitions, they published illustrated collections of reviews, in partnership with the dealers Goupil & Cie and Knoedler. They were represented at the Exposition Universelle in 1889, with a special stand in the pavilion showcasing the arts and the graphic arts.

During the last two decades of the nineteenth century, another coloured technique, pastel, enjoyed a golden age. 'For the past few years, a movement in favour of pastel has emerged among artists,' declared the painter Rosa Bonheur in 1898; not wishing to 'remain a stranger to this trend', she confided on the subject of pastels to her friend and biographer Anna Klumpke, as 'it reminded me of the Old Masters I had admired in my youth, in the Louvre, even though I had never had a single lesson in this medium.'[5] In 1897 she exhibited four very large pastels at the Galerie Georges Petit. The vaporous technique serves to represent effects of moonlight, night and fog. This vision of the pastel, associating contemporary art with the Old Masters in the Louvre, chimes with the vision of the Société des Pastellistes Français, founded under the aegis of Paul-Albert Besnard. Roger Ballu, the critic and inspector general of the Beaux-Arts between 1883 and 1901, was president and the gallery owner Georges Petit executive vice-president.

The society was under the patronage of the Association des Artistes Peintres, Sculpteurs, Architectes, Graveurs et Dessinateurs, which had been founded by Baron Isidore Taylor in 1844. Ballu was a member. The members appear to have had the idea of creating the society after a visit to the exhibition 'Dessins du Siècle' at the Ecole des Beaux-Arts, where they may have seen pastels by Jean-François Millet. For its first exhibition, the society presented pastels by members and by deceased artists, such as the great pastel artists of the eighteenth century – Rosalba Carriera, Elisabeth Vigée Le Brun, Jean-Baptiste-Siméon Chardin, Maurice-Quentin de La Tour – and of the mid-nineteenth century, including Jean-François Millet and Constant Dutilleux. The effect was to combine a section of living artists with a retrospective section. Until 1928, when the society was dissolved, it concentrated on the work of living artists and of its members, sometimes opening its doors to foreigners such as Giovanni Boldini, admitted in 1891. The exhibitions took place at the Galerie Georges Petit, already home to the Société des Aquarellistes. Among the most regular exhibitors at the Société des Pastellistes Français were Besnard, Gervex (who succeeded him as president of the association) and Léon-Augustin Lhermitte. Besnard's fame encouraged purchases by the state and helped make mandatory the presence of pastel drawings in society drawing rooms. Unlike its role with watercolours, France led the way in pastels, preceding the United Kingdom, where in 1890 the British Pastel Society was created. Its members exhibited at the Grosvenor Gallery in London where, at its opening show in 1877, James Abbott McNeill Whistler exhibited *Nocturne in Black and Gold – The Falling Rocket* (1875; Detroit Institute of Arts). This was a turning point in Whistler's career, which gave rise to his famous libel suit against the art critic John Ruskin, who had accused the painter of 'flinging a pot of paint in the public's face'. Although Whistler won the suit, he had unintentionally provoked scandal by showing a painting that blurred the frontiers between the finished and the unfinished – an exhibited work that could be confused with a sketch.

Exhibitions in black and white

Concurrently with the emergence of colour through the recognition of watercolour and pastel as separate art categories, exhibitions solely devoted to black-and-white techniques began to develop. These followed the English example: exhibitions in black and white were held in London at the Dudley Gallery between 1872 and 1881. As Catherine Meneux has observed,[6] these shows fostered the revival of etching and the growing autonomy of press illustration. Such events were international and attracted many French artists, including Marie Cazin, Léopold Flameng, Henri Fantin-Latour, Alphonse Legros, Lhermitte and James Tissot. Following the English example, Paul Durand-Ruel organised the 'First French Exhibition of Work Executed in Black and White' in his gallery at Rue Le Peletier in 1876. Here were gathered the works of engravers, particularly etchers and some wood engravers, lithographers and charcoal artists. In all, 265 artists took part in the exhibition with 745 works, some of which had already been shown in the 'Black and White' exhibitions in London. Original drawings and works using reproductive techniques such as engraving were presented on the same level. Innovatory or at least experimental artists such as Henri Guérard, Legros, Lhermitte, Edouard Manet and Tissot rubbed shoulders with more traditional exponents.[7]

In 1881 a second exclusively black-and-white exhibition was held. This was in the galleries of the review *L'Art* and contained only original work. *L'Art* was an illustrated weekly magazine, somewhat luxurious, created in 1875 by Eugène Véron (and published until 1907) in association with the Librairie d'Art. It was copiously illustrated with reproductive and original engravings, mainly etchings. Neither of these two black-and-white exhibitions, one supported by a dealer, the other by a magazine, succeeded in arousing much interest with the public.

Nevertheless, a third attempt at grouping together black-and-white art in an exhibition saw the light of day in 1885, with the first real Salon du Dessin, embodied in the 'International Exhibition of Black and White' (fig. 23).

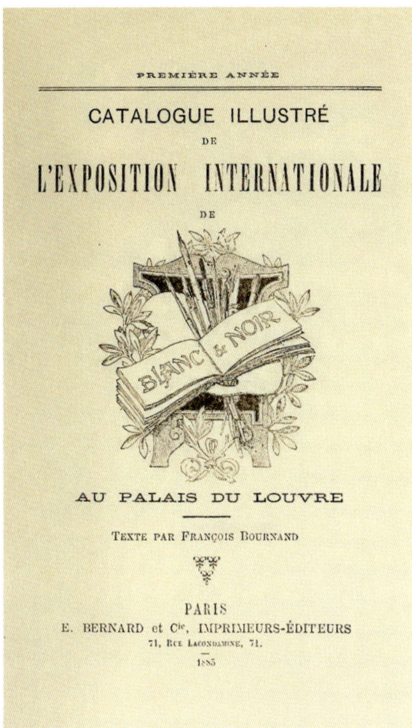

PREMIÈRE ANNÉE

CATALOGUE ILLUSTRÉ

DE

L'EXPOSITION INTERNATIONALE

DE

AU PALAIS DU LOUVRE

TEXTE PAR FRANÇOIS BOURNAND

PARIS

E. BERNARD et Cie, IMPRIMEURS-ÉDITEURS

71, RUE LACONDAMINE, 71.

1885

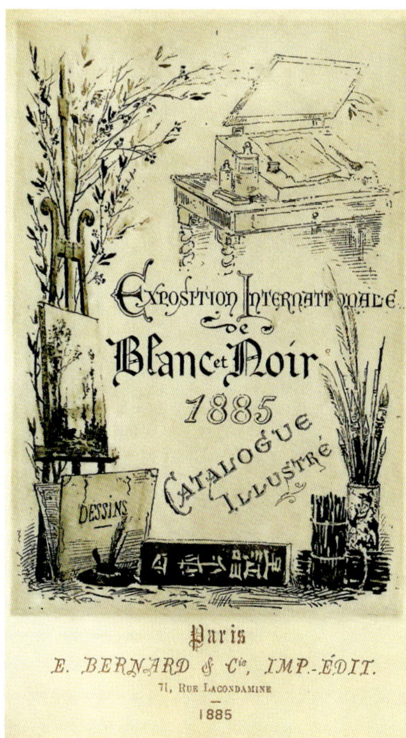

Exposition Internationale

de

Blanc et Noir

1885

Catalogue Illustré

Paris

E. BERNARD & Cie, IMP.-ÉDIT.

71, RUE LACONDAMINE

1885

Fig. 23 François Bournand, *Catalogue illustré de l'Exposition internationale de blanc & noir au Palais du Louvre*, 1885. E. Bernard & Cie, Paris

Six exhibitions of this nature were held between 1885 and 1892, supported by Ernest Bernard, the printer-publisher of *Paris-Salon*. From 1883 Bernard published *Le Dessin, revue des beaux-arts et de l'enseignement artistique*, whose editor was François Bournand, a teacher of art history. The magazine went through three iterations: *Le Fusain* (1880–81), *Le Dessin* (1883–87) and *Le Blanc et Noir*. Eugène Guillaume, director of Beaux-Arts in France from 1878 to 1879 and instigator of the reform that made the teaching of drawing mandatory in primary and secondary schools, presided over the 'Black and White' exhibition. Drawing was presented as fundamental to art and vital to the education of future generations. The exhibition was restricted to 'works executed in black and white only, such as: drawings in pencil, pen, charcoal, copper engravings, etchings, wood engravings, lithography'. It was run by an admissions panel and the works judged to be the best were rewarded. From 1886 the 'Black and White' exhibition accepted works in colour, watercolour and pastels, bowing to contemporary taste (fig. 24). A section embracing industrial art and instruction was added in 1888, with another section devoted to the illustrated press. The Salon never stopped adding to the range of work displayed, the decorative arts and Japanese art featuring in 1888 and a sculpture section making its appearance in 1892. This constant dilution heralded the Salon's demise.

The end of the frontiers: Impressionists and Independents

More noteworthy societies came into being during this period, none of them making any distinction between drawing and other categories and techniques. The Impressionist artists contributed to this breaking down of boundaries between the arts, thus modifying radically the status of drawing. They grouped together on 27 December 1873, forming an 'Anonymous co-operative society with variable personnel and capital of artist-painters, sculptors, engravers and lithographers for a period of ten years ... with the aim of: 1. Organising free exhibitions, without jury or honorific awards, where each of the associates can exhibit his or her work. 2. Selling the said work. 3. Publishing as soon as possible a journal relating exclusively to the arts.'[8] At the first of the Society's exhibitions, held at 35 Boulevard des Capucines (the photographer Nadar's house) from 15 April to 15 May 1874, the works were 'arranged by size', then positioned on a selective basis. There was no hierarchical distinction between the graphic arts and painting except that several works on paper were often grouped together under a single number, frequently at the end of the list and appended to the lists under individual artists' names. If we examine the works the most celebrated of the 'Impressionists' exhibited there in 1874, the important part played by drawing can be appreciated – assuming that the descriptions given genuinely correspond to the works on show. Eugène Boudin exhibited three paintings and six works on paper, six pastels and four watercolours. Félix Bracquemond only exhibited graphic work: one drawing and thirty-two etchings. Edgar Degas muddied the

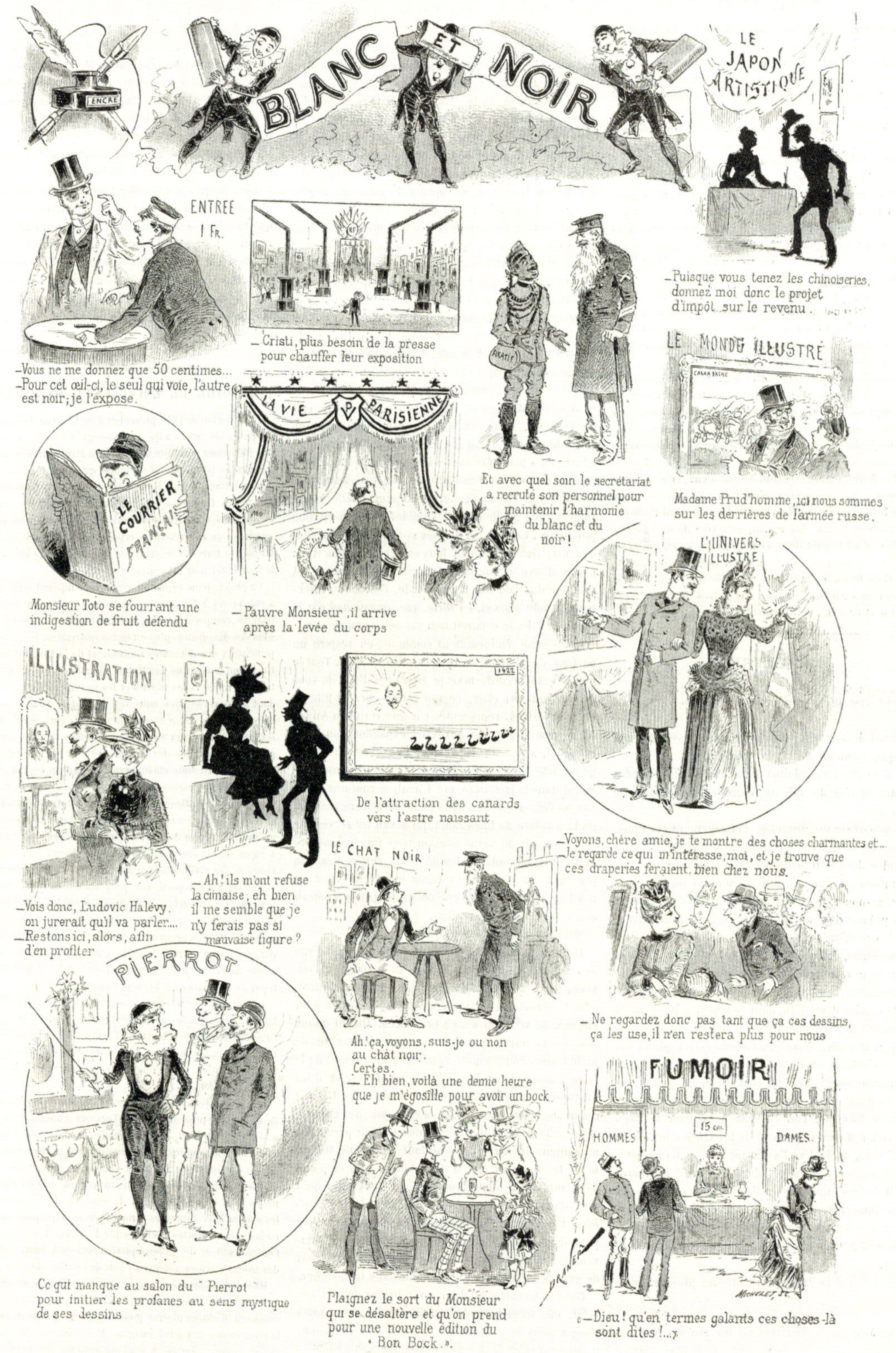

L'UNIVERS ILLUSTRÉ. 693

– Vous ne me donnez que 50 centimes...
– Pour cet œil-ci, le seul qui voie, l'autre est noir; je l'expose.

– Cristi, plus besoin de la presse pour chauffer leur exposition

– Puisque vous tenez les chinoiseries, donnez moi donc le projet d'impôt sur le revenu.

Et avec quel soin le secrétariat a recruté son personnel pour maintenir l'harmonie du blanc et du noir!

Madame Prud'homme, ici nous sommes sur les derrières de l'armée russe.

Monsieur Toto se fourrant une indigestion de fruit défendu

– Pauvre Monsieur, il arrive après la levée du corps

De l'attraction des canards vers l'astre naissant

– Vois donc, Ludovic Halévy, on jurerait qu'il va parler...
– Restons ici, alors, afin d'en profiter

– Ah! ils m'ont refusé la cimaise; eh bien il me semble que je n'y ferais pas si mauvaise figure?

– Voyons, chère amie, je te montre des choses charmantes et...
– Je regarde ce qui m'intéresse, moi, et je trouve que ces draperies feraient bien chez nous.

– Ne regardez donc pas tant que ça ces dessins, ça les use, il n'en restera plus pour nous

Ah! ça, voyons, suis-je ou non au chat noir.
Certes.
– Eh bien, voilà une demie heure que je m'égosille pour avoir un bock.

Ce qui manque au salon du "Pierrot" pour initier les profanes au sens mystique de ses dessins

Plaignez le sort du Monsieur qui se désaltère et qu'on prend pour une nouvelle édition du "Bon Bock."

« – Dieu! qu'en termes galants ces choses-là sont dites!... »

A L'EXPOSITION DE BLANC ET NOIR (PAVILLON DE LA VILLE DE PARIS). — (Dessin de Draner.)

distinction between techniques: mentioned in the catalogue are five 'drawings' out of his ten works on show, in other words, half, but we know that number 60, *Ballet Rehearsal on the Stage*, described as a drawing, is in fact a monochrome painting (fig. 25). The artist's decision to enter it as a drawing emphasises his wish to elevate the position of the category. His five drawings are characterised by the variety of their techniques and their status: monochrome painting, but also 'sketch', 'drawing with oil', 'pastel' and 'study'. Degas had already confused the issue in 1865 when he exhibited his *Scene of War in the Middle Ages* as a 'pastel', whereas it is in fact a painting in oils on paper glued to canvas. Even the most painterly of the Impressionists presented drawings: Claude Monet showed seven 'sketches' described as pastels, compared with only seven paintings.

Fig. 24 Draner (Jules Joseph-Georges Renard), 'A l'Exposition de Blanc et Noir (Pavillon de la Ville de Paris)', *L'Univers illustré*, 3 November 1888, p. 693. Bibliothèque Nationale de France, FOL-LC2-2956

Fig. 25 Edgar Degas, *Ballet Rehearsal on the Stage*, 1874. Oil on canvas, 65 x 81.5 cm. Musée d'Orsay, Paris. Bequest of Comte Isaac de Camondo, 1911, RF 1978

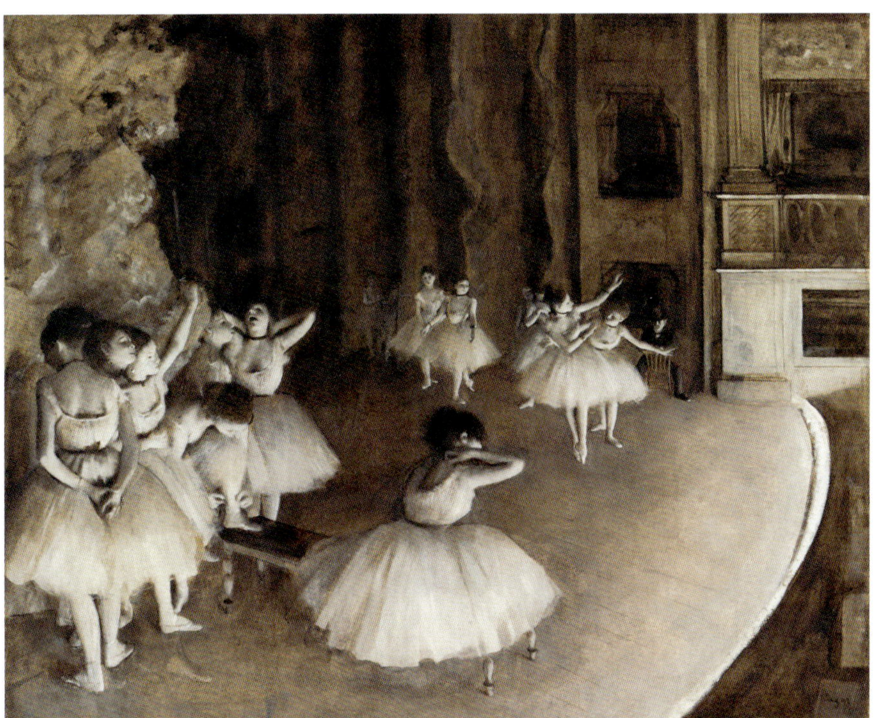

Pierre-Auguste Renoir exhibited one 'pastel' out of seven works, also all entitled 'sketch'. Berthe Morisot presented more graphic art than painting: two pastels and three watercolours, out of a total of nine works.

In 1886, at the eighth and final Impressionist exhibition, presented as an 'exhibition of painting', the part played by pastels is obviously greater. Degas exhibited only pastels, including the famous 'Suite of female nudes, bathing, washing, drying themselves, wiping themselves, combing themselves or being combed'. Federico Zandomeneghi exhibited eight pastels (and only four paintings). Of the seven works listed by Mary Cassatt, only one is listed as a 'pastel'. The new generation exhibited little graphic art (Paul Gauguin, Emile Schuffenecker, Georges Seurat, Paul Signac); Odilon Redon seems only to have shown paintings. Of the work presented by Marie Bracquemond, half were graphic pieces: a 'card, charcoal' and a watercolour; as for Morisot, she exhibited a 'series of drawings' and a 'series of watercolours', without more detail, plus a dozen paintings. Lucien Pissarro won fame with his wood engravings. Illustrations, gouaches, pen-and-ink drawings, etchings and fans joined the great variety of graphic art presented. Works on paper constituted one third of the work presented in the Impressionist exhibitions, the same proportion as in the official Salon.[9]

From 1884 another group of artists, some of whom had taken part in the later Impressionist exhibitions, began to question the hierarchical divisions between the arts, refusing to separate drawing from painting: the 'independent artists'. This progressive group rejected the idea of an admissions panel and prizes. They organised their Salon in huts in the courtyard of the Tuileries from 15 May to 30 June 1884. During the exhibition, Signac, Charles Angrand, Henri-Edmond Cross, Albert Dubois known as Dubois-Pillet, Redon and Schuffenecker officially established the Société des Artistes Indépendants. Among the first 'independent' artists, Seurat and Redon were to play the leading role in the revival and advance of the status of drawing.

Redon made his artistic debut in 1860 with charcoal drawings at the Société des Amis des Arts in Bordeaux.

He exhibited his first painting ten years later. His first entry to the Salon in Paris was an etching. His second exhibit at the Salon was a drawing after Leonardo da Vinci. His earliest one-man shows in Paris were exclusively graphic and were held in the premises of art journals: in 1881 he exhibited charcoal drawings at *La Vie moderne* and the following year, charcoal drawings and prints on the premises of *Le Gaulois*.

Seurat also chose to make his debut at the official Salon with a drawing, a work entitled *Broderie* (*Embroidery*). In the booklet to the Salon in 1883, no. 3189 is in fact a portrait of the painter Edmond Aman-Jean, a fine presentation drawing in Conté crayon and highly finished (fig. 20). The drawing was noticed by the critics, in particular by Roger Marx who adjudged it 'an excellent study of chiaroscuro, a praiseworthy piece, not like the work of a newcomer'.[10] The following year Seurat exhibited the pencil portrait of a friend at the Salon des Indépendants, presented as *Portrait of M. A. J., drawing*; he also presented a painting (*L'Ile de La Grande Jatte, study*) and '9 small sketches', the latter all under the same number.

The growing role of the critics

During the final quarter of the nineteenth century, the art world saw the withdrawal of the state from the organisation of the annual Salon – following the establishment of the Société des Artistes Français in 1881 – and the end of the Salon's monopoly; the role of the art critic became increasingly important. The law on press freedom of 29 July 1881 brought with it an unprecedented increase in the numbers of newspapers and journals. As the market developed within an 'open and competitive' system,[11] the critic became the 'indispensable partner of the artist as of the dealer'.[12] Théodore Duret, Edmond Duranty, Roger Marx, Gustave Geffroy, Charles Ephrussi, Gustave Kahn, Arsène Alexandre, Félix Fénéon and Albert Aurier were all art critics who also organised exhibitions; they were government officials in arts administration and also collectors, and often writers too – for example, Joris-Karl Huysmans, Octave Mirbeau and Remy de Gourmont all worked at writing the history of art as it was actually taking place, launching artists' careers as well as their own.

Duranty, a close friend of Gustave Courbet, Degas, Monet and Emile Zola, was a contributor to a variety of periodicals including *L'Artiste* (1870), *Les Beaux-Arts illustrés* (1877–80), the *Gazette des Beaux-Arts* and, from 1877, its supplement *La Chronique des arts et de la curiosité*. In *La Nouvelle Peinture* (1876, on the subject of the second Impressionist exhibition), he defends the 'pencil ... dipped in the sap of life', 'animated, expressive forms' against 'lines measured with a compass': 'drawing is such an individual means of expression, so indispensable that one cannot expect methods, processes or views. Drawing merges totally with its goal and remains the inseparable companion of the idea.'[13] Philippe Burty, another defender of the new painting and one of the founders of the *Gazette des Beaux-Arts*, also contributed to *La Chronique des arts et de la curiosité*, specialising in graphic art. He challenged the hierarchy that separated 'fine art' from the 'minor arts' and encouraged the revival of the original etching. He regarded Félix Bracquemond as 'the best of the draughtsmen of today'.[14]

Ephrussi was one of the first supporters of the Impressionist painters during his editorship of the *Gazette des Beaux-Arts*; he later became director and proprietor of the journal. In May 1879 he and Gustave Dreyfus organised an exhibition of Old Master drawings at the Ecole des Beaux-Arts, donating the takings to a fund set up to help young artists. He bought work by the Impressionists, including pastels by Morisot in 1876 – despite the fact that he specialised in Japanese prints and the drawings of Albrecht Dürer.[15] In 1895 Ephrussi invited Roger Marx (fig. 26) to contribute to the *Gazette des Beaux-Arts* and in 1902 Marx became editor of the journal. He was a champion of the so-called 'minor arts': decorative arts, medals and prints, in particular polychrome prints. He wrote reviews of exhibitions by watercolourists and pastel artists as well as of the first black-and-white exhibition, and wrote the foreword to the

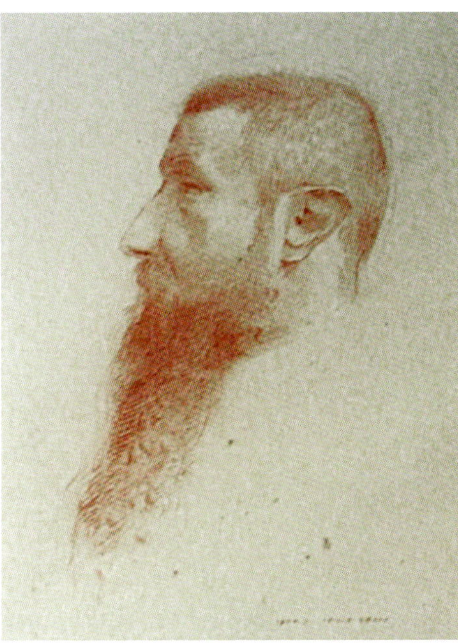

Fig. 26 Odilon Redon, *Portrait of Roger Marx*, 1904. Sanguine on grey paper laid down on card, in preparation for printing, 47 x 35.3 cm. Private collection, formerly in the sitter's collection

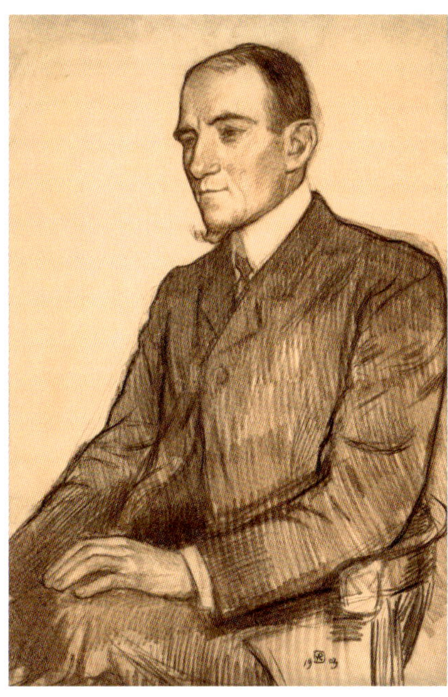

Fig. 27 Théo van Rysselberghe, *Portrait of Félix Fénéon*, 1903. Charcoal and sanguine on wove paper, 80 x 54 cm. Musée d'Orsay, Paris, 2022, RF MO AG 2022 5

albums *L'Estampe originale* and *Maîtres de l'affiche* (1895–1900). Marx was also heavily involved in museum administration: as Inspecteur des Beaux-Arts he organised, with Antonin Proust, the centenary exhibitions of French painting in 1889 and 1900.

'A new and unusual figure among art critics of the 1880s',[16] Fénéon (fig. 27) was the critic associated with the Neo-Impressionists, a term he invented, and the discoverer of Seurat. In 1886 he wrote a review of the eighth Impressionist exhibition in *La Vogue*, producing a new kind of language to analyse the pastels of Degas: 'human flesh breathes here with expressive life. The strokes of this cruel and sagacious observer elucidate, via the difficulties posed by crazily elliptical foreshortening, the mechanics of every movement.'[17] He was a close friend of the Natanson brothers (Alexandre, Thaddée and Louis-Alfred), who in 1891 took over *La Revue blanche*, the principal mouthpiece of the avant-garde in the 1890s, and supported the Nabis – who themselves accorded a central role to the art of drawing. The end of the century confirmed the importance of the art press as a means of promoting artists, taking over the baton from official recognition.

Through these various routes, sketched too hastily here, it can be seen how, during the final years of the nineteenth century, channels specific to drawing began to develop. Exhibitions by groups of artists, supported by galleries and publishers of reviews, contributed to this growing autonomy and the explosion of drawing as a technique. The phenomenon extended to the provinces, where art societies organised their own Salons with a section for drawings, or smaller Salons dedicated solely to graphic art. Although the Paris Salon remained a showcase for academic art, more experimental artists such as Degas, Redon and Seurat made their debut there with drawings. They soon left the Salon for arenas that offered more flexibility and fewer artistic hierarchies. For their first monographic exhibitions, Degas and Redon chose to exhibit solely graphic works. These artists contributed to the opening of the frontiers, renewing the art of drawing with experiments in monotype, pastel on monotype, pastel mixed with charcoal, etching, oil drawings, lithographs, chiaroscuro drawing with the new Conté crayons, charcoal on tracing, and so on. By the end of the century, drawing – the foundation of classical artistic training – had become a laboratory for modern ideas.

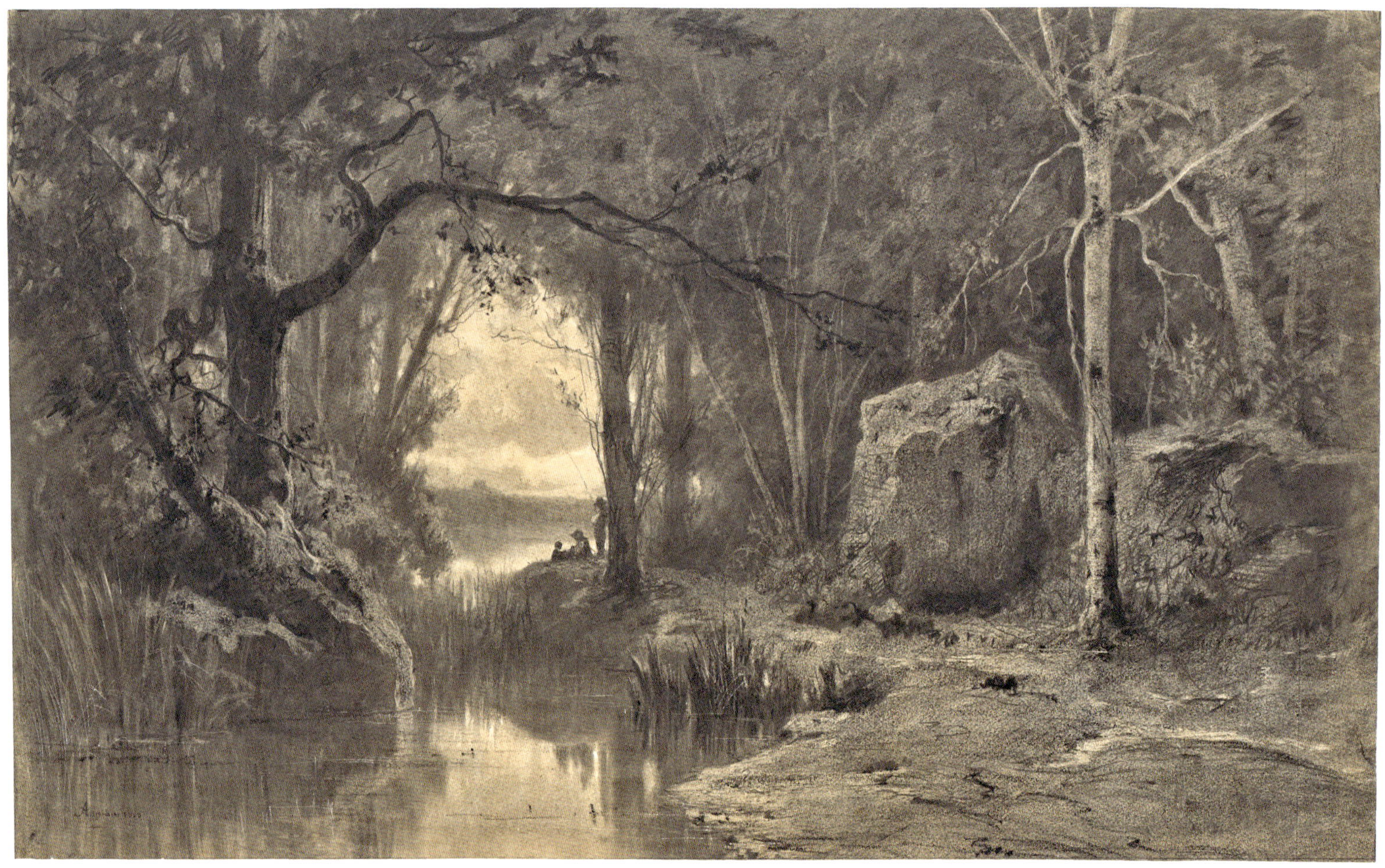

Fig. 28 Adolphe Appian, *Three Fishermen Along the Banks of a River at the Edge of a Forest*, 1868. Charcoal with stumping and scratching out and touches of white chalk on beige paper, 59.4 x 98.5 cm. The Cleveland Museum of Art, 2021.140

Reciprocal Invention: How Material Innovations Catalysed the Ascendance of Drawing in Nineteenth-century France

HARRIET K. STRATIS

Breaking with tradition, many artists working in France in the mid-nineteenth century eschewed the formal training of the Ecole des Beaux-Arts in favour of a new approach. Since the beginning of the century Neoclassicism had enjoyed the distinction of being the 'official' style endorsed by Napoleon I. As a result, academic draughtsmanship emphasised harmony, idealised proportions and restraint by prescribing the study of the human form and meticulous rendering from plaster casts or studies after the Old Masters. As Neoclassicism yielded to Romanticism, artists began to champion the immediacy of the drawn line. Drawings started to transcend the preparatory sketch and became more frequent submissions to the official Paris Salons and other critical bodies for formal consideration as independent works of art.[1] Established oil painters began to include drawings alongside their paintings in exhibitions, and by 1864, drawings were assigned a category of their own in the annual Salon (a practice that was to continue into the 1890s).

Although some important art-material innovations, such as wove paper, had gained favour across the Channel in the latter part of the eighteenth century, it was not until after the French Revolution (1789–99) and the Napoleonic Wars with England (1803–15) that trade resumed and these materials began to flood the French marketplace. As the demand for variety grew, natural black chalk was joined by a plethora of new, monochromatic drawing materials in the form of fabricated charcoals and chalks, Conté crayon and pastel.[2] By the 1850s, coincidental with artists' growing desire to suffuse their drawings with more colour, the first synthetic dyes were accidentally invented. In 1847 the German chemist Friedlieb Ferdinand Runge fixed the organic colourant logwood with chromium in an attempt to invent a writing ink that would not corrode steel pen nibs as rapidly as traditional iron-gall ink. In 1856 mauvine was happened upon by the British chemist William Henry Perkin, whose failed attempt to synthesise quinine resulted instead in the first aniline dye. Their discoveries precipitated the birth of dazzling, synthetic colourants with intense chroma and high tinting strength. The chromatic range and variety of the drawing materials made with them exploded in the shops of colourmen – the purveyors of fine artists' materials

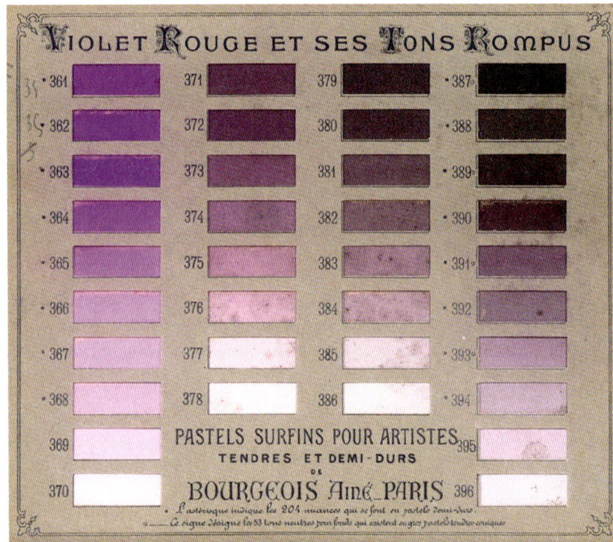

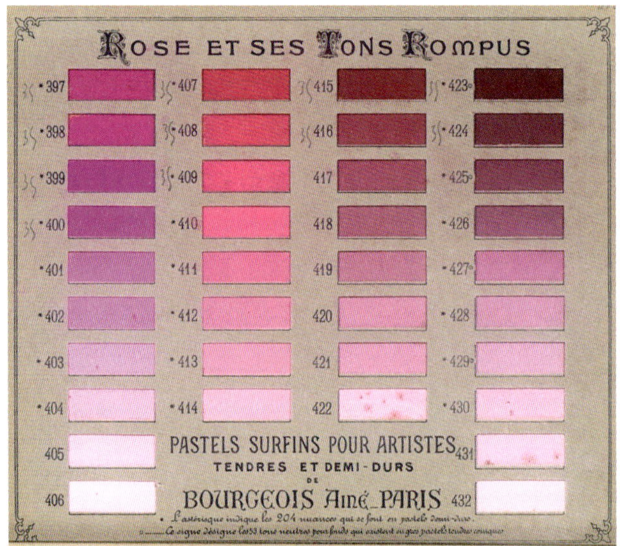

Fig. 29 Bourgeois Ainé, Paris, *Tons des pastels surfins pour artistes, tendres et demi-durs*, 1890–1920. Two of 16 unnumbered cards with 528 pastel samples. National Gallery of Art Library, Washington, David K. E. Bruce Fund

– dispersed throughout Paris and beyond. Imagine Edgar Degas's reaction when he first saw the bright pink, yellow, blue and green sheets of wove paper that he was to fill with dancers at work or in repose (cats 8, 9); or the possibilities presented by the magnificent range of sticks formulated by the esteemed pastel-makers Henri Roché and Gustave Sennelier (among others) that were enthusiastically adopted by Odilon Redon, who put their highly saturated, sometimes otherworldly colours to work in depicting religious or mythological subjects or the decorative ensembles that enveloped the sitters of his late portraits (cats 76, 77). The discovery of aniline and chrome-based dyes had an impact on everything from papers to writing inks, watercolours to pastels (fig. 29). Accoutrements for drawing and painting *en plein air*, such as portable charcoal and pastel sets and intricate watercolour boxes with cake and tube paints and miniaturised accessories, were invented to meet the needs of artists who sought to liberate themselves from the confines of the studio (fig. 30). Had the selection of artists' materials themselves remained stagnant, the drawings of the Impressionists and Post-Impressionists would have remained far more conventional. Their aesthetic innovations were certainly reliant upon industries that revolutionised the market.

And yet, the availability of these materials alone does not account for the artistic achievements that followed their introduction. Were it not for artists' willingness to experiment with them to discover attributes that could be beneficial to their own work, they would have remained on store shelves. Instead, artists begin to combine all manner of materials to realise their ambitions: pastel and opaque watercolour (gouache) were used together as, for example, in Paul Gauguin's *Landscape in Martinique* (cat. 49); even metallic paint was used in combination with oil and coloured chalks, as in Redon's *'The Golden Cell' (Profile of a Woman's Head)* (cat. 66). Henri de Toulouse-Lautrec and others mixed oil paint with solvent (most likely turpentine) after extracting much of its oil binder to make *essence*, a medium that was favoured for its matte surface qualities like those found in Toulouse-Lautrec's *Woman with a Black Boa* (cat. 57). Degas too used *essence* and achieved marvellous translucent effects with this matte medium by diluting it to varying consistencies with solvent, as is exemplified in his rendering of the gauzy tutu in *Dancer Seen from Behind* (cat. 8).

To understand better the climate that precipitated such movements as Synthetism and Fauvism, it is useful to return to an earlier moment in the century in which black media had assumed a prominent role in the making of drawings. The many varieties of black – from cool, blue-

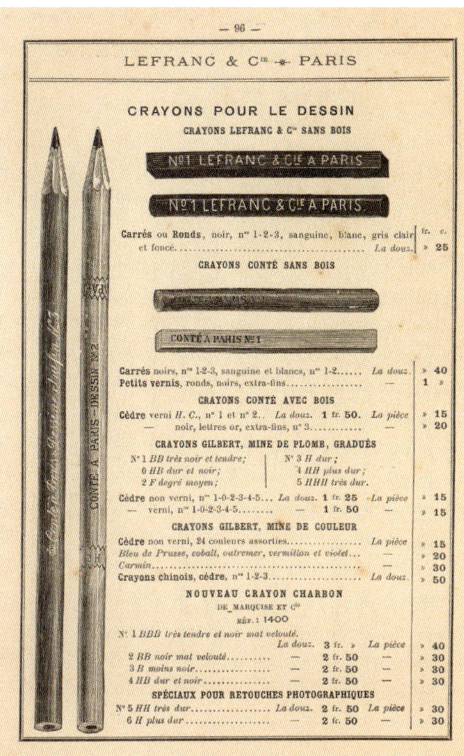

— 96 —

LEFRANC & Cie PARIS

CRAYONS POUR LE DESSIN

CRAYONS LEFRANC & Cie SANS BOIS

	fr. c.
Carrés ou **Ronds**, noir, nos 1-2-3, sanguine, blanc, gris clair et foncé .... *La douz.*	» 25

CRAYONS CONTÉ SANS BOIS

Carrés noirs, nos 1-2-3, sanguine et blancs, nos 1-2 ...... *La douz.*	» 40
Petits vernis, ronds, noirs, extra-fins .... —	1 »
CRAYONS CONTÉ AVEC BOIS	
Cèdre verni *H. C.*, no 1 et no 2.. *La douz.* **1 fr. 50.** *La pièce*	» 15
— noir, lettres or, extra-fins, no 3 .... —	» 20
CRAYONS GILBERT, MINE DE PLOMB, GRADUÉS	
No 1 *BB très noir et tendre;* 0 *HB dur et noir;* 2 *F degré moyen;* / No 3 *H dur;* 4 *HH plus dur;* 5 *HHH très dur.*	
Cèdre non verni, nos 1-0-2-3-4-5... *La douz.* **1 fr. 25** *La pièce*	» 15
— verni, nos 1-0-2-3-4-5 .... — **1 fr. 50** —	» 15
CRAYONS GILBERT, MINE DE COULEUR	
Cèdre non verni, 24 couleurs assorties .... *La pièce*	» 15
Bleu de Prusse, cobalt, outremer, vermillon et violet... —	» 20
Carmin .... —	» 30
Crayons chinois, cèdre, nos 1-2-3 .... *La douz.*	» 50
NOUVEAU CRAYON CHARBON DE MARQUISE ET Cie — RÉF. : 1400	
No 1 *BBB très tendre et noir mat velouté.* *La douz.* **3 fr. »** *La pièce*	» 40
2 *BB noir mat velouté* .... — **2 fr. 50** —	» 30
3 *B moins noir* .... — **2 fr. 50** —	» 30
4 *HB dur et noir* .... — **2 fr. 50** —	» 30
SPÉCIAUX POUR RETOUCHES PHOTOGRAPHIQUES	
No 5 *HH très dur* .... *La douz.* **2 fr. 50** *La pièce*	» 30
6 *H plus dur* .... — **2 fr. 50** —	» 30

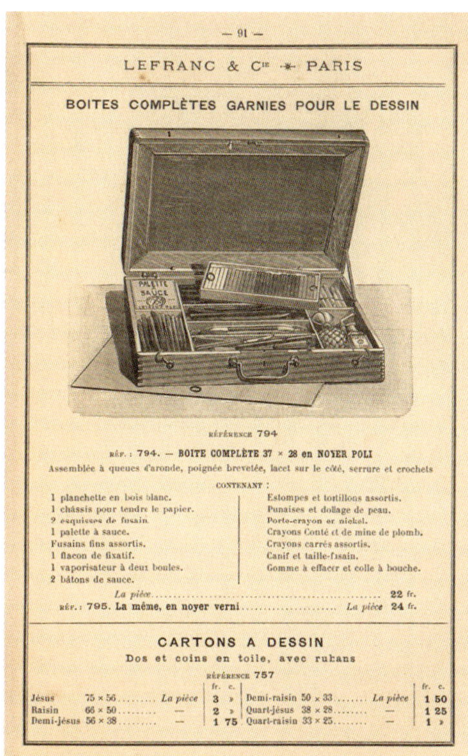

— 91 —

LEFRANC & Cie PARIS

BOITES COMPLÈTES GARNIES POUR LE DESSIN

RÉFÉRENCE 794

RÉF. : 794. — **BOITE COMPLÈTE 37 × 28 en NOYER POLI**

Assemblée à queues d'aronde, poignée brevetée, lacet sur le côté, serrure et crochets

CONTENANT :

1 planchette en bois blanc.	Estompes et tortillons assortis.
1 châssis pour tendre le papier.	Punaises et dollage de peau.
2 esquisses de fusain.	Porte-crayon en nickel.
1 palette à sauce.	Crayons Conté et de mine de plomb.
Fusains fins assortis.	Crayons carrés assortis.
1 flacon de fixatif.	Canif et taille-fusain.
1 vaporisateur à deux boules.	Gomme à effacer et colle à bouche.
2 bâtons de sauce.	

La pièce .... 22 fr.

RÉF. : 795. **La même, en noyer verni** .... *La pièce* 24 fr.

CARTONS A DESSIN

Dos et coins en toile, avec rubans

RÉFÉRENCE 757

		fr. c.			fr. c.
Jésus	75 × 56 .... *La pièce*	3 »	Demi-raisin	50 × 33 .... *La pièce*	1 50
Raisin	66 × 50 .... —	2 »	Quart-jésus	38 × 28 .... —	1 25
Demi-jésus	56 × 38 .... —	1 75	Quart-raisin	33 × 25 .... —	1 »

Fig. 30 A. Lefranc et Cie, Paris, *Fabrique de couleurs & vernis*, 1892. National Gallery of Art Library, Washington, David K. E. Bruce Fund

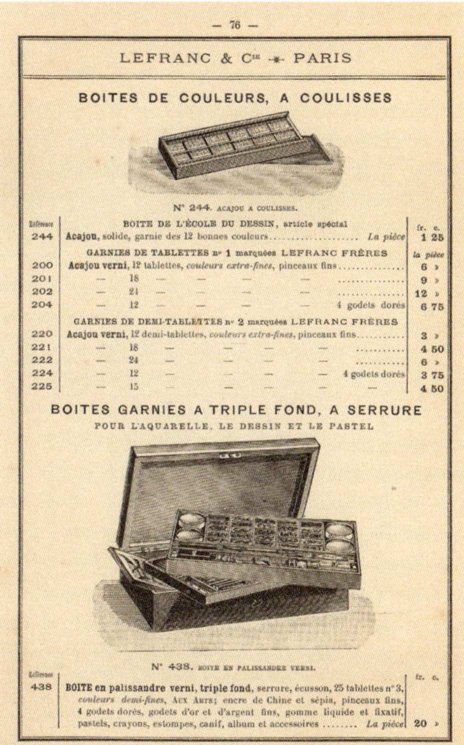

— 76 —

LEFRANC & Cie PARIS

BOITES DE COULEURS, A COULISSES

No 244. ACAJOU A COULISSES.

Référence		fr. c.
	BOITE DE L'ÉCOLE DU DESSIN, article spécial	
244	**Acajou**, solide, garnie des 12 bonnes couleurs .... *La pièce*	1 25
	GARNIES DE TABLETTES no 1 marquées LEFRANC FRÈRES	*la pièce*
200	**Acajou verni**, 12 tablettes, *couleurs extra-fines*, pinceaux fins	6 »
201	— 18 — — — —	9 »
202	— 24 — — — —	12 »
204	— 12 — — — — 4 godets dorés	6 75
	GARNIES DE DEMI-TABLETTES no 2 marquées LEFRANC FRÈRES	
220	**Acajou verni**, 12 demi-tablettes, *couleurs extra-fines*, pinceaux fins	3 »
221	— 18 — — — —	4 50
222	— 24 — — — —	6 »
224	— 12 — — — — 4 godets dorés	3 75
225	— 15 — — — — —	4 50

BOITES GARNIES A TRIPLE FOND, A SERRURE

POUR L'AQUARELLE, LE DESSIN ET LE PASTEL

No 438. BOITE EN PALISSANDRE VERNI.

Référence		fr. c.
438	**BOITE en palissandre verni, triple fond**, serrure, écusson, 25 tablettes no 3, *couleurs demi-fines*, AUX ARTS; encre de Chine et sépia, pinceaux fins, 4 godets dorés, godets d'or et d'argent fins, gomme liquide et fixatif, pastels, crayons, estompes, canif, album et accessoires .... *La pièce*	20 »

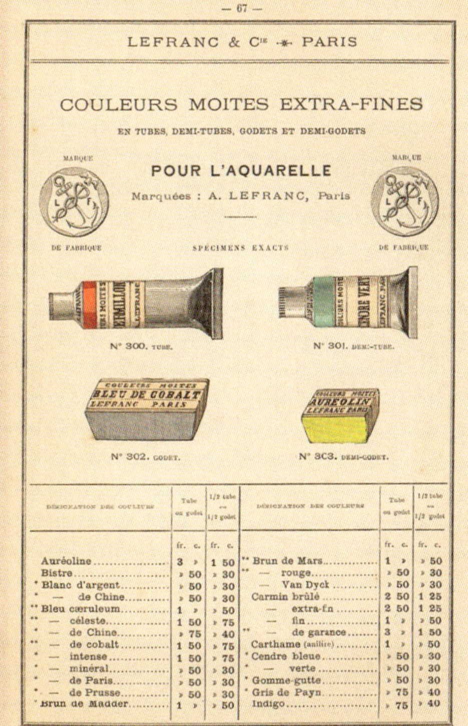

— 67 —

LEFRANC & Cie PARIS

COULEURS MOITES EXTRA-FINES

EN TUBES, DEMI-TUBES, GODETS ET DEMI-GODETS

MARQUE DE FABRIQUE

POUR L'AQUARELLE

Marquées : A. LEFRANC, Paris

SPÉCIMENS EXACTS

No 300. TUBE.

No 301. DEMI-TUBE.

No 302. GODET.

No 303. DEMI-GODET.

DÉSIGNATION DES COULEURS	Tube ou godet	1/2 tube ou 1/2 godet	DÉSIGNATION DES COULEURS	Tube ou godet	1/2 tube ou 1/2 godet
	fr. c.	fr. c.		fr. c.	fr. c.
Auréoline	3 »	1 50	** Brun de Mars	1 »	» 50
Bistre	» 50	» 30	** — rouge	» 50	» 30
* Blanc d'argent	» 50	» 30	— Van Dyck	» 50	» 30
* — de Chine	» 50	» 30	Carmin brûlé	2 50	1 25
** Bleu cæruleum	1 »	» 50	— extra-fin	2 50	1 25
** — céleste	1 50	» 75	— fin	1 »	» 50
* — de Chine	» 75	» 40	** — de garance	3 »	1 50
** — de cobalt	1 50	» 75	Carthame (aniline)	1 »	» 50
* — intense	1 50	» 75	* Cendre bleue	» 50	» 30
* — minéral	» 50	» 30	* — verte	» 50	» 30
* — de Paris	» 50	» 30	* Gomme-gutte	» 50	» 30
* — de Prusse	» 50	» 30	* Gris de Payn	» 75	» 40
* Brun de Madder	1 »	» 50	Indigo	» 75	» 40

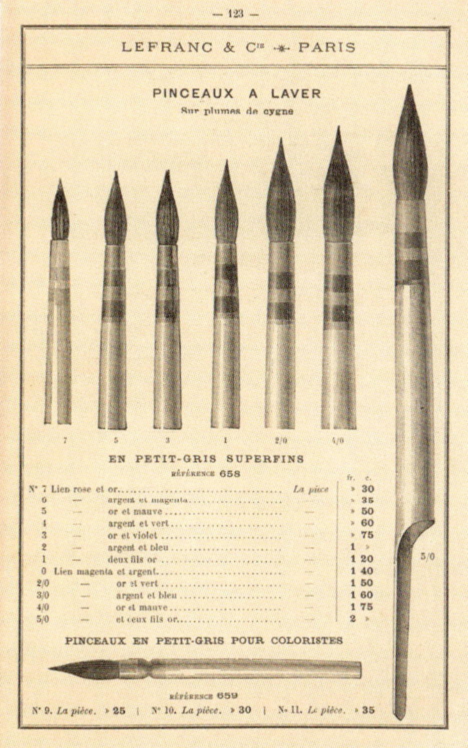

— 123 —

LEFRANC & Cie PARIS

PINCEAUX A LAVER

Sur plumes de cygne

EN PETIT-GRIS SUPERFINS

RÉFÉRENCE 658

		fr. c.
No 7	Lien rose et or .... *La pièce*	» 30
6	— argent et magenta .... —	» 35
5	— or et mauve .... —	» 50
4	— argent et vert .... —	» 60
3	— or et violet .... —	» 75
2	— argent et bleu .... —	1 »
1	— deux fils or .... —	1 20
0	Lien magenta et argent .... —	1 40
2/0	— or et vert .... —	1 50
3/0	— argent et bleu .... —	1 60
4/0	— or et mauve .... —	1 75
5/0	— et deux fils or .... —	2 »

PINCEAUX EN PETIT-GRIS POUR COLORISTES

RÉFÉRENCE 659

No 9. *La pièce.* » 25 | No 10. *La pièce.* » 30 | No 11. *La pièce.* » 35

black fabricated chalks to warm, brown-black charcoals manipulated by physical techniques like stumping and scraping, and altered chemically by the application of fixatives – resulted in drawings that display a broad, tonal 'colour' range. Drawing on variously coloured papers further enhanced this perception. To call these drawings simply achromatic or monochromatic would be misleading, even though the very exercise of using a range of blacks and greys was intended to hone drawing to its essence without the distraction of a more chromatic palette. This was informed in large part by the popularity of the colour theories expounded by Michel-Eugène Chevreul and Charles Blanc, and it was in Blanc's *Grammaire des arts du dessin*, published in 1867, that he addressed the relative merits of colour versus drawing in black media alone.[3] Among those artists working in Paris in the last decades of the nineteenth century, Blanc's words had a significant influence upon Gauguin, Georges Seurat, Paul Cézanne, Vincent van Gogh, and many others.[4]

The earliest drawings to be produced in a range of black tones are most often landscapes drawn by the *fusainistes*, those artists who embraced the use of black, friable media for rendering. Among them, Adolphe Appian is the most well known. His monumental landscapes, often measuring more than 100 cm (three feet) in length, are virtuoso studies in the handling and manipulation of charcoal (fig. 28). Using both natural vine and harder fabricated charcoal sticks, Appian drew on top of an overall base tone of powdered charcoal, sold in glass vials or tins marketed as 'sauce', that one could apply dry with a rag or wet with a wide brush after mixing the powder with water. The natural sticks produced soft grey lines, whereas the fabricated ones produced darker, finer and more emphatic lines. Artists were cognisant that drawing with the softer medium dispersed the particles into the interstices of the paper, while lines drawn with the harder medium remained on the high points of the paper and did not scatter. Fixatives held the powdery media in place so that it would not smudge or dislodge. Artists were well aware that many of the adhesives intended for this purpose often darkened their media and discoloured their papers. Fixative recipes included gum arabic, all manner of natural resins such as balsam and mastic, and even casein (a proteinaceous, milk-based material). Instructions for various methods of application were provided, from brush-applying them to the verso of a drawing or spray-applying them with an atomiser to the recto.

So popular was the medium that treatises were published on the materials and techniques of charcoal drawing and are often found among the pages of merchants' catalogues in which these materials were listed for sale (fig. 30).[5] The papermaker Berville even included the surname of one of the most well-known *fusainistes*, Maxime Lalanne, in their watermarks to denote laid papers made specifically for drawing with charcoal. Similarly, drawing papers with a more uniform, refined texture devoid of pronounced laid and chain lines, watermarked Ingres, were particularly well suited for use with graphite, and were so named to acknowledge the great graphite draughtsman Jean-Auguste-Dominique Ingres. In a further technological development, at the turn of the nineteenth century, wove papers began to be machine-made rather than made by hand, adding to the variety and increasing the size of individual sheets while also reducing their cost. The prominence of the Michallet watermark in so many of Seurat's drawings is perhaps tacit acknowledgement of the artist's reciprocal collaboration with his material (cats 23, 24). Despite the rich, velvety black surfaces that Seurat created by alternating applications of black Conté crayon with light spray-applications of a shellac fixative,[6] he made sure that the watermark remained visible to some degree whenever present in the paper.

In France, the search for new drawing materials began well before the drawing revival of mid-century. In 1797 Nicolas-Jacques Conté produced the first fabricated graphite pencil in France in response to the difficulty of procuring the purest graphite from English mines during wartime. Mixing powdered graphite mined in France with white clay and lampblack, the new product was of a lesser quality than the pure graphite from England. The white clay undermined the silvery lustre so characteristic of graphite, and the addition of lampblack made it difficult to erase.[7] Despite these drawbacks, the manufacturer boasted that he had created 'an infinite variety of pencils, of every possible black tint'.[8] Continued modification by Conté's successors resulted in the production of sticks that by 1817 had salt or sugar added to the graphite-black pigment-clay mixture to improve homogeneity. Shaped into rectangular sticks with flat sides, this newer iteration was also coated with varnish to prevent the black medium from adhering to an artist's fingers while drawing (fig. 30).[9] The shape provided versatility: artists could use the flat side of a stick for tonal work or its pointed tip for more linear applications. Seurat often used his Conté crayon sticks on their sides to deposit broad swathes of media on the high points of his laid papers to allow the distinctive laid and chain line pattern as well as the watermark to remain visible (cat. 24). When drawn across a sheet of paper, the resultant dark black lines have a lustrous quality and form striations visible under magnification that resemble wax crayon despite the absence of a binder.[10] Such an expansion in the range of monochromatic media alone was enough to inspire new techniques and, for some artists, to prompt distinct, and at times prolonged, periods of exploration. Notably, in the early decades of his career, Redon used a variety of black drawing materials including graphite, much to the exclusion of coloured media like pastel or watercolour. His resulting *noirs* were made using a range of warm and cool black media applied in multiple layers and secured with generous amounts of balsam fixative deliberately to impart a golden tone that sets them apart as a group.[11] Although he came to embrace colour later, writing in 1882 the artist asserted that a 'fundamental *grey* distinguishes all masters ... and is the soul of all colour'.[12]

As the revival of drawing in black media waned to some degree, the emergence of another revival of sorts was underway: that of pastel painting (fig. 31).[13] Blurring the distinction between painting in oils and painting in the dry manner (as pastel had come to be known in the eighteenth century), artists such as Eva Gonzalès (cat. 11) and Edouard Manet embraced the use of canvas as well as paper for their pastel portraits in much the same way that eighteenth-century practitioners had. In these works, pastel combined with opaque watercolour was applied onto matte, oil-paint

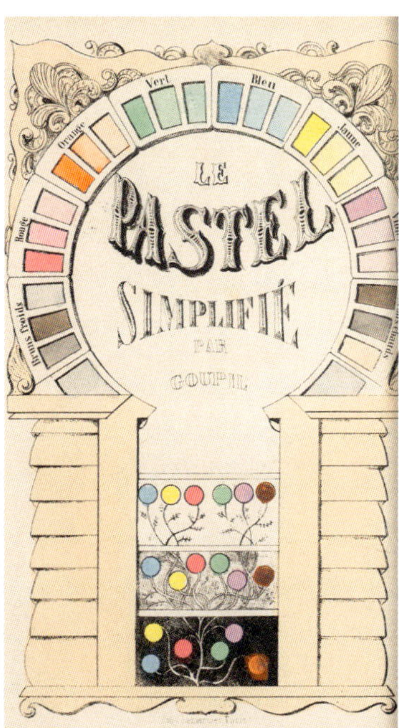

Fig. 31 Frédéric-Auguste-Antoine Goupil, *Le Pastel, simplifié et perfectionné*, 1864. Published by Desloges, Paris. National Gallery of Art Library, Washington, David K. E. Bruce Fund

grounds. Pastel could be applied by first wetting the tip of the stick to draw impasto strokes; it could be ground into a powder, mixed with a bit of medium and water and applied with a brush to form striated passages; and when used dry, various coloured pastels could be 'sweetened' by gently blending them with a leather stump or fingertip, a technique often used to establish the contours and shadows of facial features. Gonzalès and Manet used all these methods in their pastel portraits, as had pioneers of the medium a century before them. Rosalba Carriera, Jean-Etienne Liotard and Maurice Quentin de La Tour are notable exemplars revered by many nineteenth-century pastellists who were inspired by their achievements and emulated their techniques.[14]

As drawing in dry media gained prominence, all manner of aqueous media, including inks and opaque and translucent watercolours, continued to be used for drawing along with the less-familiar distemper (*détrempe*, powdered pigment mixed with warm glue) and *essence*, as noted above. Van Gogh often used a variety of inks (cats 28, 38), charcoal or chalk in a single drawing. Not only did he combine dry and aqueous media, he also used metal-nib and reed pens interchangeably in a single drawing to vary the visual appearance of his drawn lines. And although his carbon black inks remain unchanged, others derived from logwood have faded to various brown tones, significantly altering the way we perceive some of his drawings (fig. 32).[15] This phenomenon is not unique to Van Gogh's drawings; the brown tones ubiquitous in so many nineteenth-century drawings today are likely once to have been purple, magenta or red.[16]

Artistic ingenuity even extended to the use of shaped supports. For a time, fans were all the rage in art-making as well as fashion, and art-materials merchants seized upon the opportunity to provide arch-shaped supports in their shops. Inspired by Japanese prints and decorative screens, artists combined watercolour and ink washes with metallic paint on fan-shaped paper and even silk similar to that used for traditional Japanese scroll paintings (cats 18, 44). Mary Cassatt's pastel *In the Loge* (fig. 2) epitomises the fashionable Parisienne at the theatre clutching a fan that the artist rendered in a combination of pastel and gold-toned metallic paint on canvas, making it the focus of her composition. Gauguin revisited the form over several decades (cats 49,

Fig. 32 Vincent van Gogh, *Heath*, 1888. Pencil, reed pen and ink (faded from purple) on paper, 31.3 x 48.1 cm. Van Gogh Museum, Amsterdam (Vincent van Gogh Foundation), d0167V1962. The detail on the right shows the original colour of the purple ink that was preserved beneath the mount.

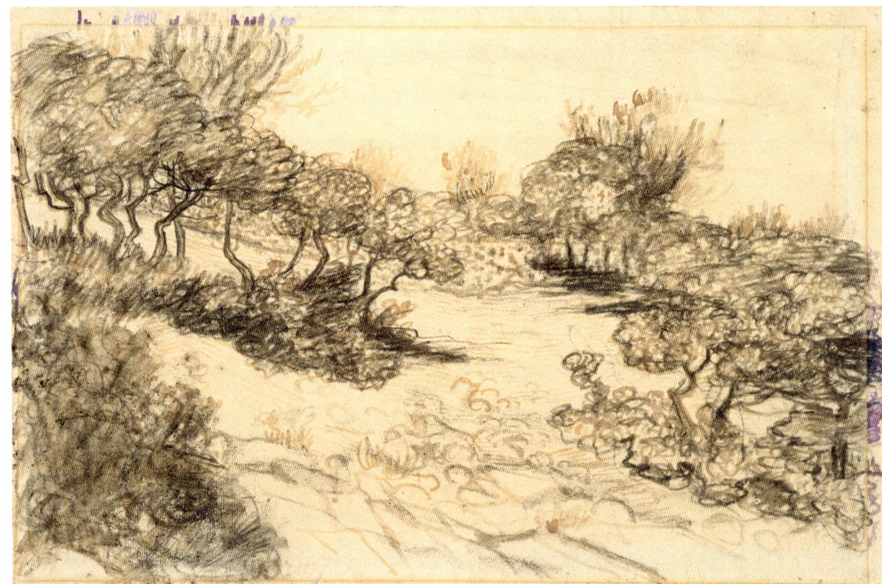

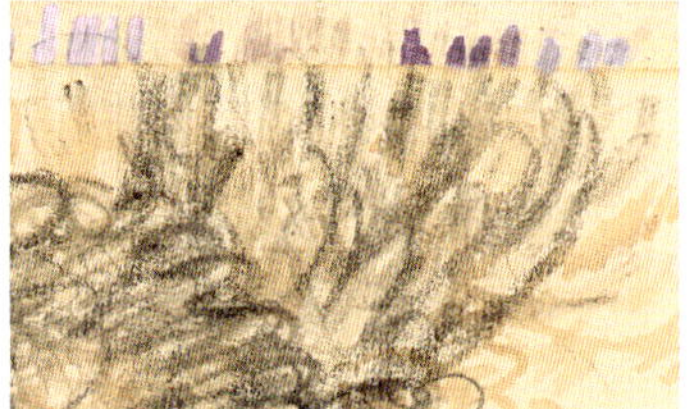

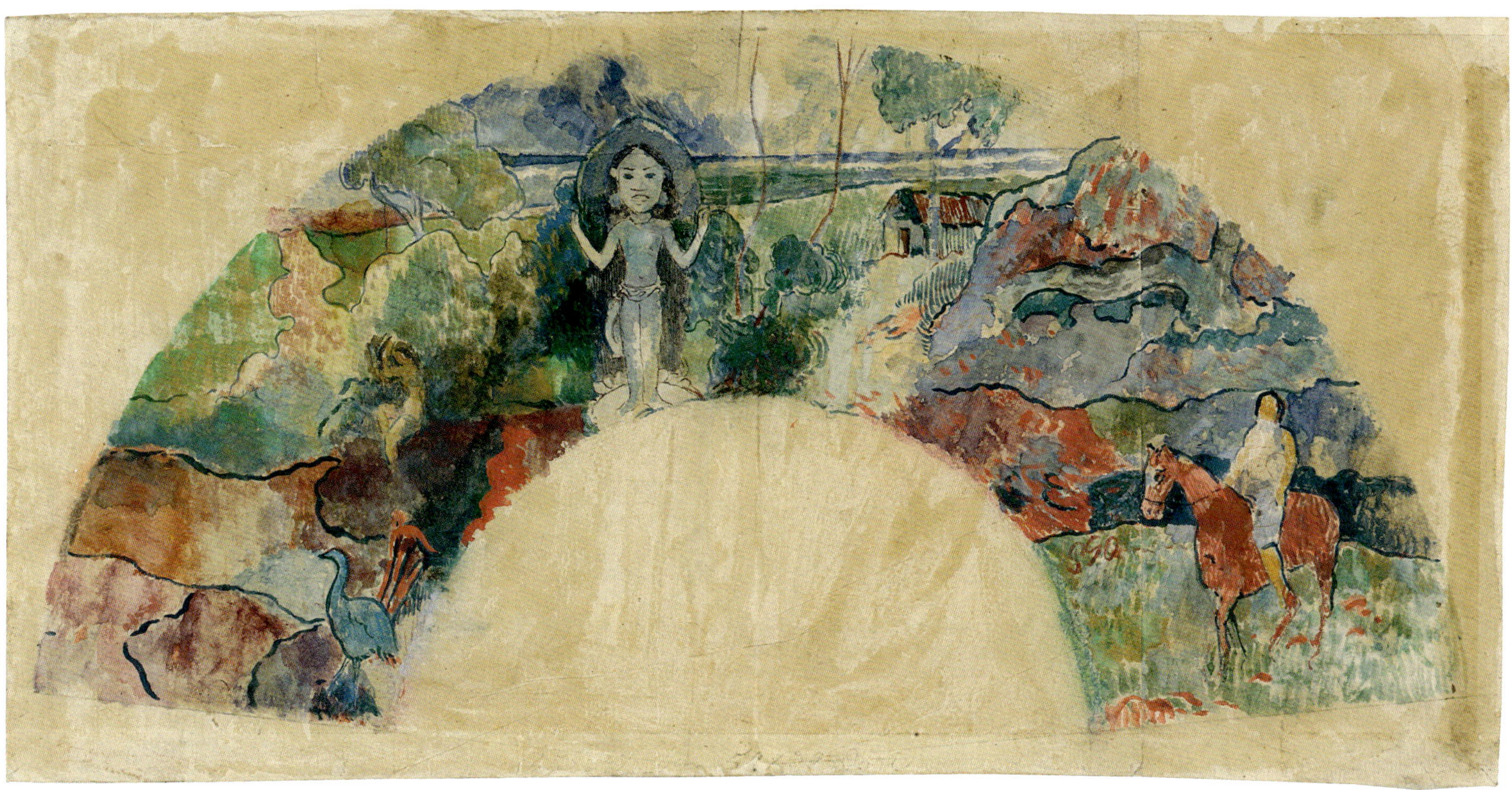

Fig. 33 Paul Gauguin, *Design for a Fan Featuring a Landscape and a Statue of the Goddess Hina*, 1900–03. Watercolour and gouache, with touches of pen and black ink, over traces of graphite, on cream Japanese paper (pieced), laid down on cream wove paper, 20.8 x 41.7 cm. The Art Institute of Chicago, 2002.225

59), each time introducing new subject matter; late in his career he even invoked a fan when reprising several major themes of his Tahitian paintings in watercolour (fig. 33).

As early as 1860 artists such as Degas, Armand Guillaumin and Eugène Boudin used landscape as the springboard to display sometimes audacious colour combinations in their striated pastel seascapes (cats 1, 2, 3). Working *en plein air* afforded them the opportunity to improvise, to capture quickly the nuances of changing light in a medium quite conducive to this. Among them, however, Degas soon abandoned the Impressionist landscape to move in a new and different direction. He was perhaps one of the greatest pastellists of the century, and over several decades he devised methods of application and manipulation that were unrivalled by his contemporaries. His innovations of the 1870s included the application of pastel over his monotypes printed in black ink, sometimes modifying compositions in the process (cat. 17). He produced 'pastellised' drawings in which pastel was used sparingly to add only the slightest touches of colour, as in *Two Dancers Resting* (cat. 20). In more formal drawings pastel was applied in one, two or three lightly fixed layers, covering the paper entirely so that the underlying sheet tone is only minimally visible, if at all (cat. 55). As his practice became more rigorous and inventive, he used fixative more generously, as in *Dancers on a Bench* (cat. 54), where darkened droplets of fixative are visible on the surface.[17] In many of his later works he intermittently fixed an increased number of pastel layers to form thick, textured impastos of colour, sometimes going so far that he undermined the works' structural stability; cracks have formed in the thick pastel layers over time. Very often he would bring unfinished drawings – mostly those on tracing paper – to a professional mounter who would adhere the fragile supports to larger, more rigid millboards and extend their working area with added strips of similar paper. A closer look at *Two Dancers* (cat. 69) is informative in this regard. Here the artist had two strips of paper added to extend the seated dancer's tutu on the left and to include the standing dancer's foot at bottom right. The work was left unfinished, and the difference in pastel application between the two campaigns provides a glimpse into Degas's working process (fig. 34).

The common aspirations of artists and chemists at the time merit comment, given that the success of the former was to some degree dependent upon the utility of the dyes and synthetic pigments for art-making purposes invented by the latter. As an offshoot of the textile industry, aniline dyes found their way into the hands of manufacturers of art materials. Having appropriated these industrial colourants, manufacturers devised recipes that took into consideration suitable working properties for application on paper, such as the hardness or softness of pastel sticks or the degree to which watercolour cakes wetted up when water was brushed onto them. In their recipes, amounts of clay fillers and binders were adjusted to provide the optimum cohesiveness and hardness in their pastel sticks. Modifiers such as honey were used with gum arabic in varying quantities to formulate watercolours with greater workability and more fluid dispersion of pigment particles. Most significantly, the manufacturers touted the novelty of the vibrant colours that they had made by adding new synthetic colourants to their formulations (fig. 29). As artists quickly became attuned to the aesthetic possibilities of these materials, so too did the public who encountered the drawings made with them.

However, with the rapid introduction of new art-making materials that had not been tested by time, artists and collectors became acutely aware of visual changes in their works of art within short periods; these could range from several months to several years. There is no doubt that the manufacturers themselves were equally aware of the instability of some of the watercolours, inks, pastels and coloured papers that they put on the market. It is interesting to note in this regard that Léon Monet, elder brother of Claude, was a colour chemist in the employ of the acclaimed Gobelins Manufactory, which was renowned for its tapestries. Based in Rouen, Léon was also an art collector on familiar terms with a number of Impressionist artists including Camille Pissarro and Pierre-Auguste Renoir. Léon would have been aware of the instability of some of the textile dyes that he had a hand in making, most likely sharing this information with the esteemed cadre of artists in his immediate circle.[18] And as artists became increasingly cognisant of the ephemeral nature of their materials on exposure to light as well as the chemical alteration that led to discolouration upon ageing, they placed responsibility squarely on the shoulders of the manufacturers of art materials.[19] Eventually, in response to criticism, the manufacturers – who created products based on demand with no standardised quality-control system yet in place – sought ways to better inform artists about potential colour change or fading in their art materials so that they could make more informed decisions about whether or not to use them.

Perhaps it was too little, too late. In numerous late nineteenth-century drawings colour shifts are significant. Several scientific investigations in recent decades have identified faded and altered colourants. With this information in hand, digital recolourisations, made to provide estimations of their original appearance in works of art, are now often used to illustrate an artist's intentions.[20] Such scientific input helps to quantify and contextualise the contemporary appearance of many nineteenth-century drawings that have altered with time. Scholars and the public know and love these works of art as they are and may be loath to think that an individual drawing as it exists today represents neither the artist's original intent nor the physical reality of what it once was. Although these findings are indeed revelatory, it may be disconcerting to accept this as part of the inevitable life of a drawing. Yet, although many nineteenth-century drawings are changed in some way, they remain as compelling today as they were more than a century ago.

Fig. 34 Detail of cat. 69, Edgar Degas, *Two Dancers*, *c.* 1891. Pastel on joined paper mounted on card laid down on board, 86.3 x 56.5 cm. Private collection, London

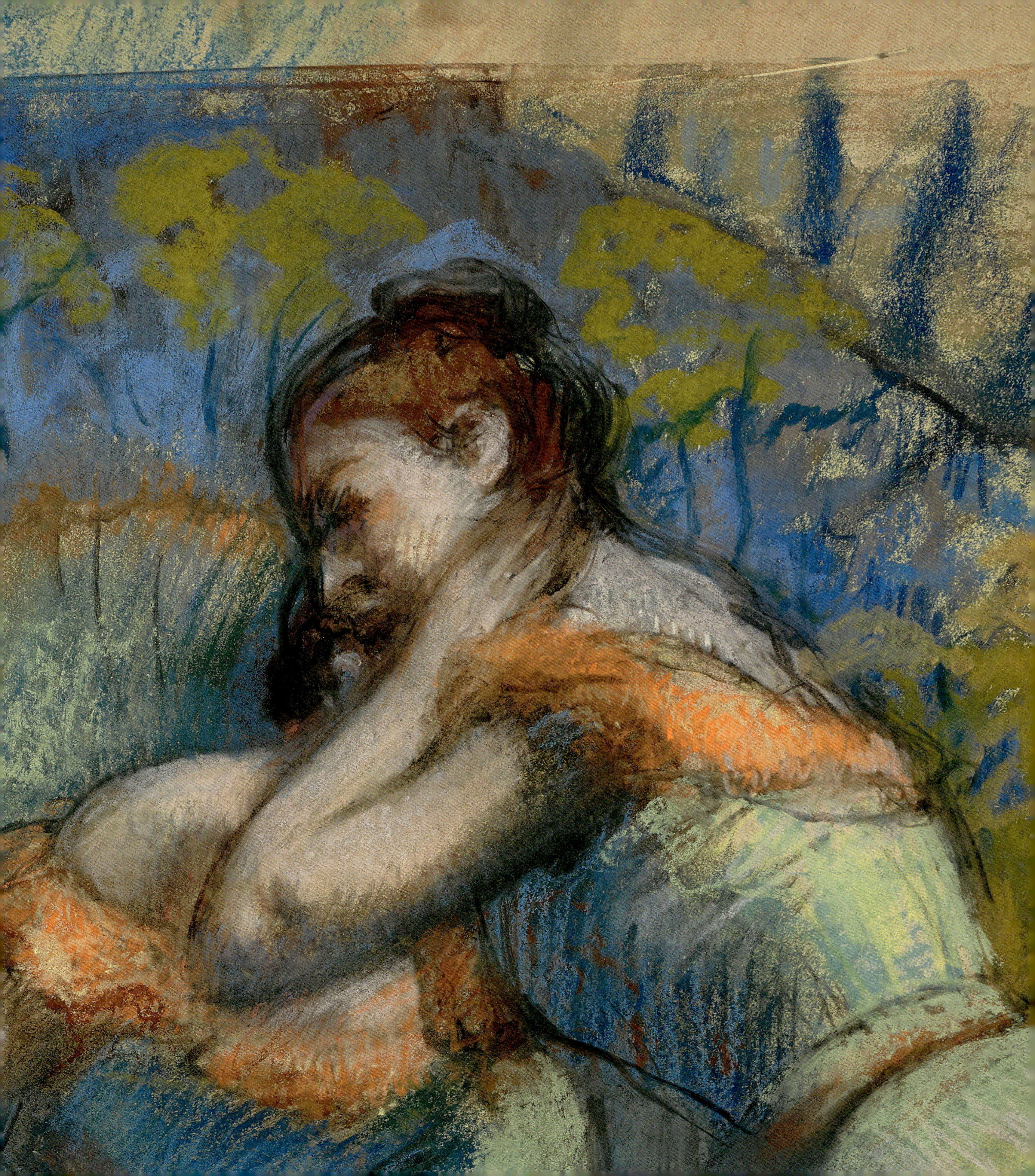

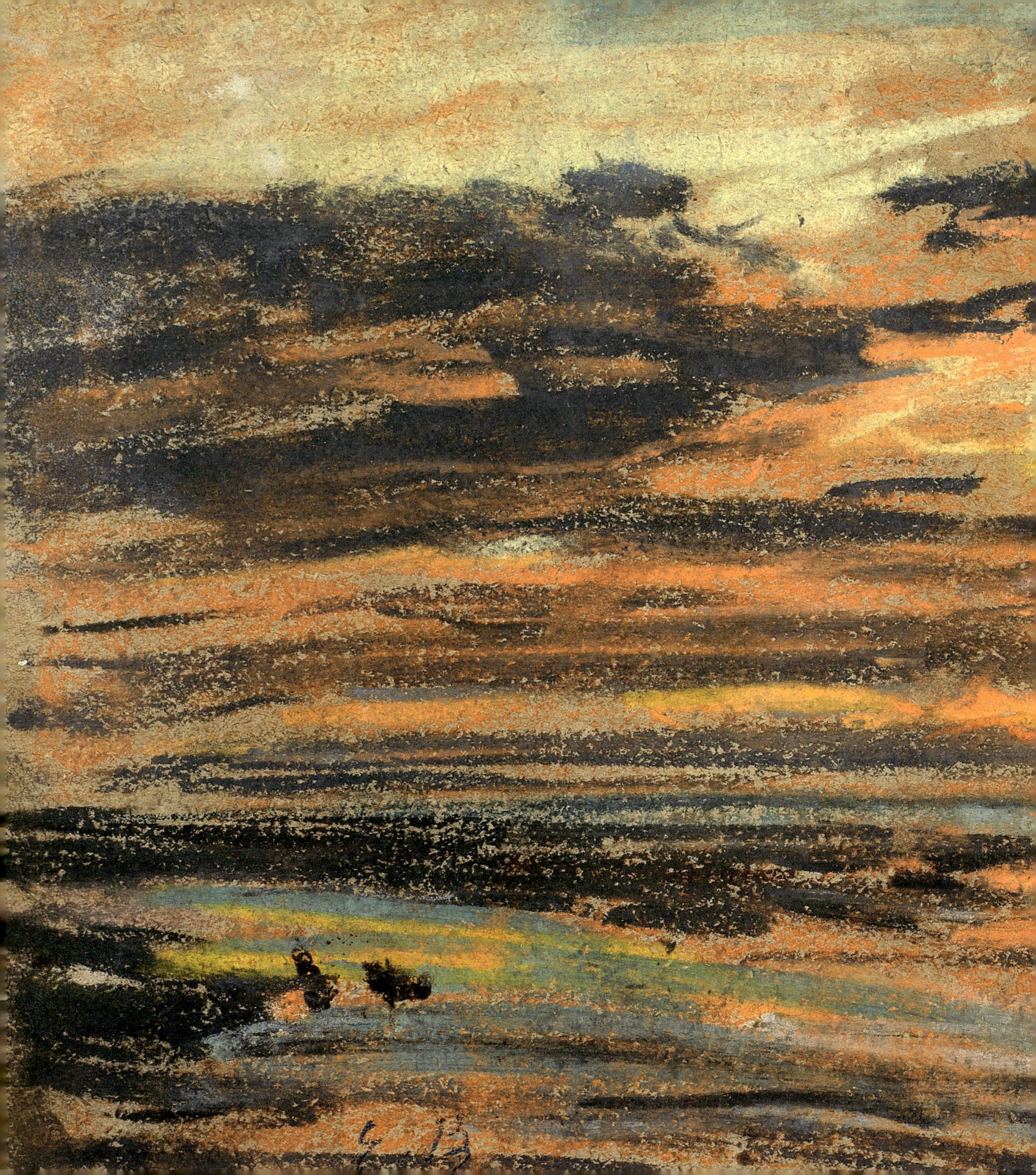

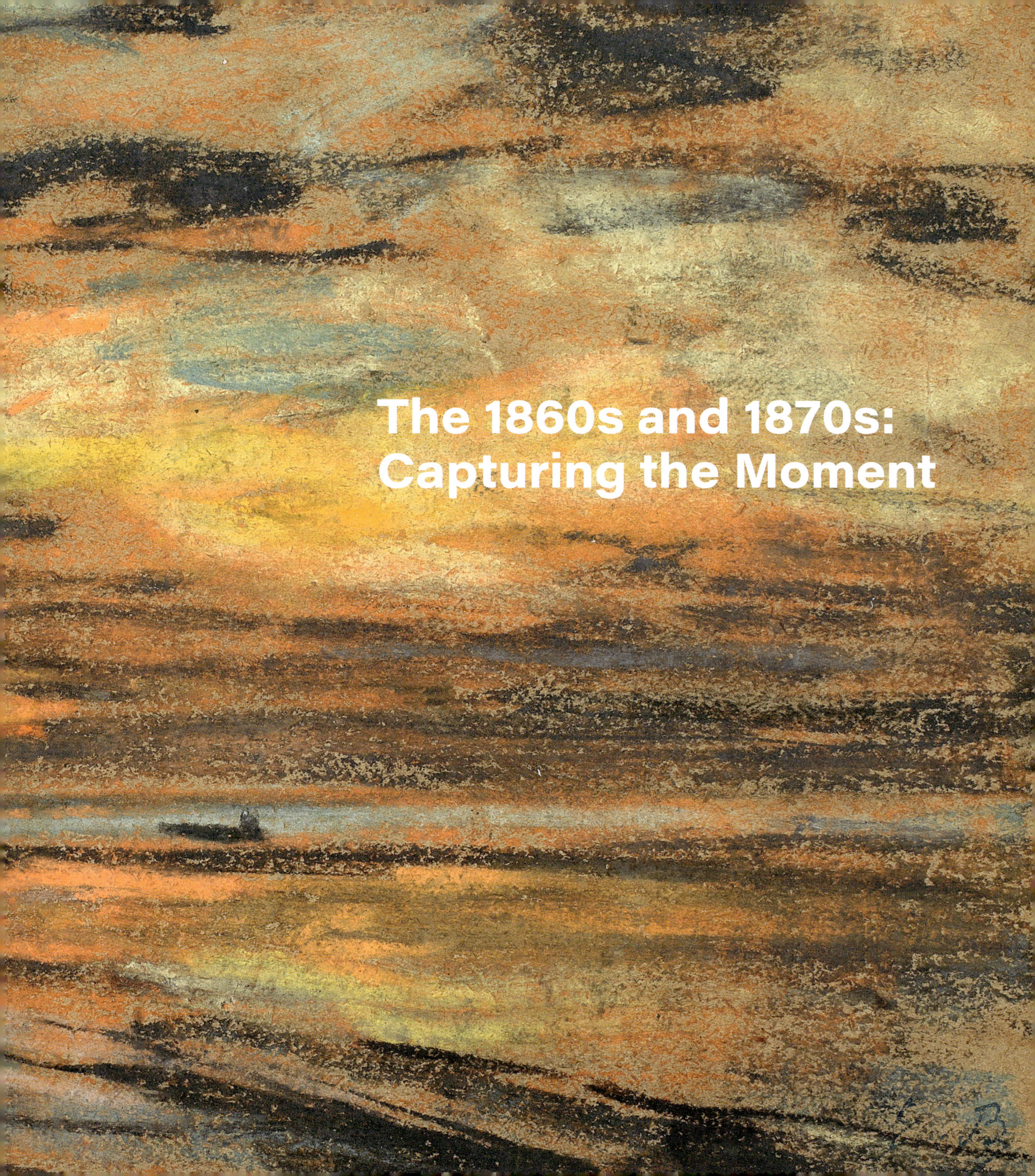

The 1860s and 1870s: Capturing the Moment

The avant-garde artists known as the Impressionists emerged in the late 1860s and early 1870s, and first exhibited in Paris as a group in 1874. All drew, and the style of their drawings, as with their paintings, was determined by their concern to depict scenes from everyday life, as opposed to subjects inspired by literature or the past. A quick, loose touch, vivid colour and daring viewpoints, together with a deliberate lack of finish, were their means of capturing the fugitive effects of nature as well as vignettes of modern life observed at home, in the café, in the theatre, at the races or on the street. Moreover, the portability of drawing materials – pencil, watercolour and pastel – greatly facilitated direct observation and the recording of scenes on the spot.

Eugène Boudin, a precursor of Impressionism, Edgar Degas and Armand Guillaumin all found in the increasingly popular medium of pastel an effective tool for capturing the luminosity of sea and sky (cats 1, 2, 3). Guillaumin's vibrant study of rocks and trees (cat. 6), complete with colour notations, gives an insight into his working methods. Eva Gonzalès's diaphanous study of a bride in silver, grey and white (cat. 11) recalls the delicacy of eighteenth-century pastels.

In *The Rue Mosnier in the Rain* (cat. 14) a few swift strokes of leadpoint and ink were all that it took for Edouard Manet to capture the movement of people and carriages. Degas, a passionate draughtsman, constantly experimented with a broad range of media, supports and formats. His enigmatic *Woman at a Window* (cat. 5) is executed in *essence* (oil paint diluted with turpentine), a medium he liked because of its freedom and its fusion of painting and drawing. The ballet, especially private moments behind the scenes, was central to Degas's programme of modernity. A dancer in the wings features in a fan painted with watercolour on silk (cat. 18), and his choice of coloured papers, pink or green, for informal studies of dancers (cats 8, 9) resulted in some of his most striking images.

Fashionable women appear frequently in the Impressionists' vision of the modern Parisian scene. In *Woman with a Veil* (cat. 12) Pierre-Auguste Renoir brilliantly exploits the density and texture of pastel and coloured chalk. Degas's elegant race-goer Lyda peers at the horses (or perhaps at us) through her field glasses (cat. 4) in an image highly appropriate for an artist renowned for his visual acuity.

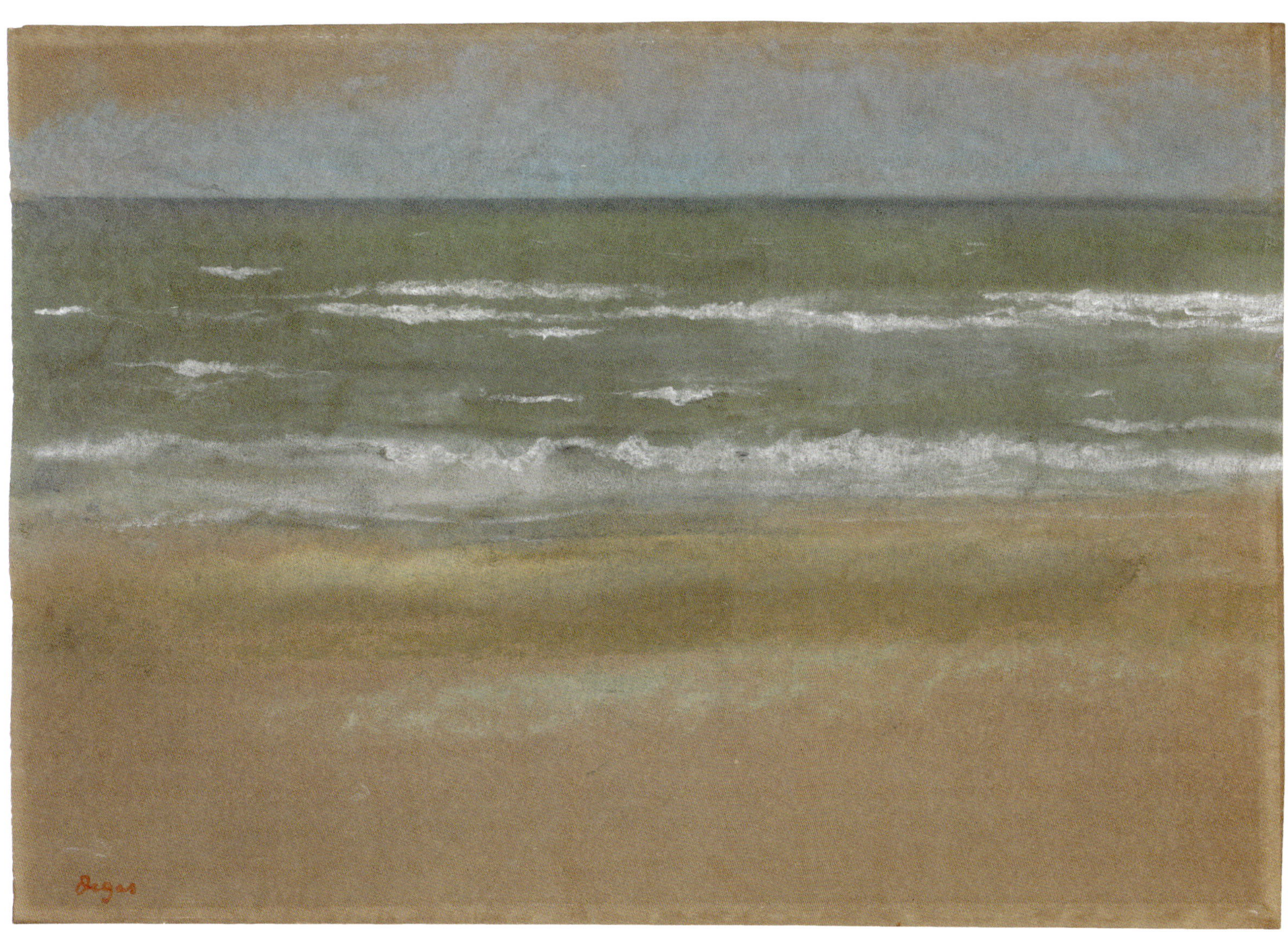

1

Edgar Degas (1834–1917)
Beach at Low Tide, 1869
Pastel on paper, 27.2 x 39.6 cm
Private collection, London

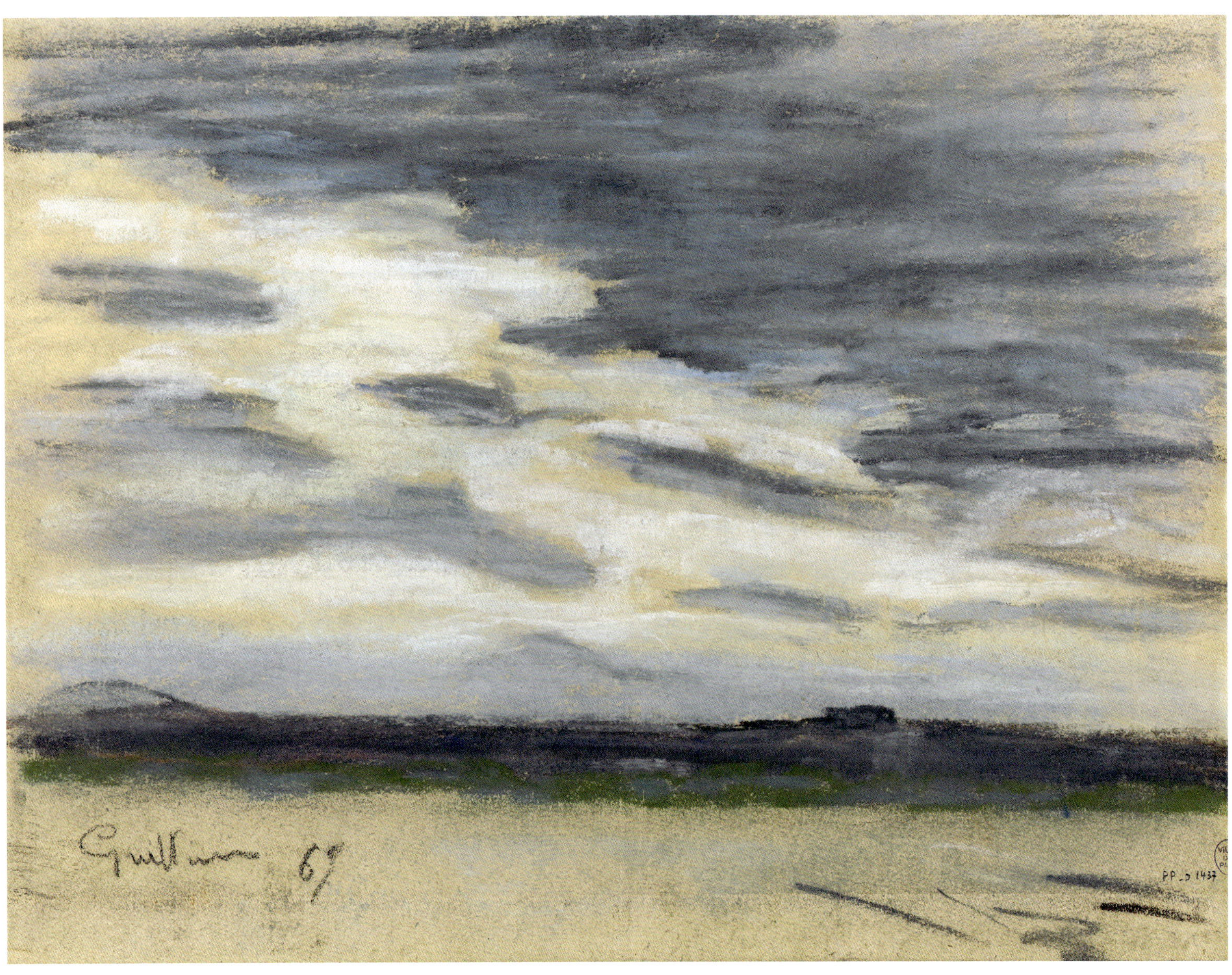

2

Armand Guillaumin (1841–1927)
Sky Study, 1869
Pastel on paper, 23.4 x 31.2 cm
Petit Palais, Musée des Beaux-Arts de la Ville de Paris.
Gifted by Armand Guillaumin, 1922, PPD1437

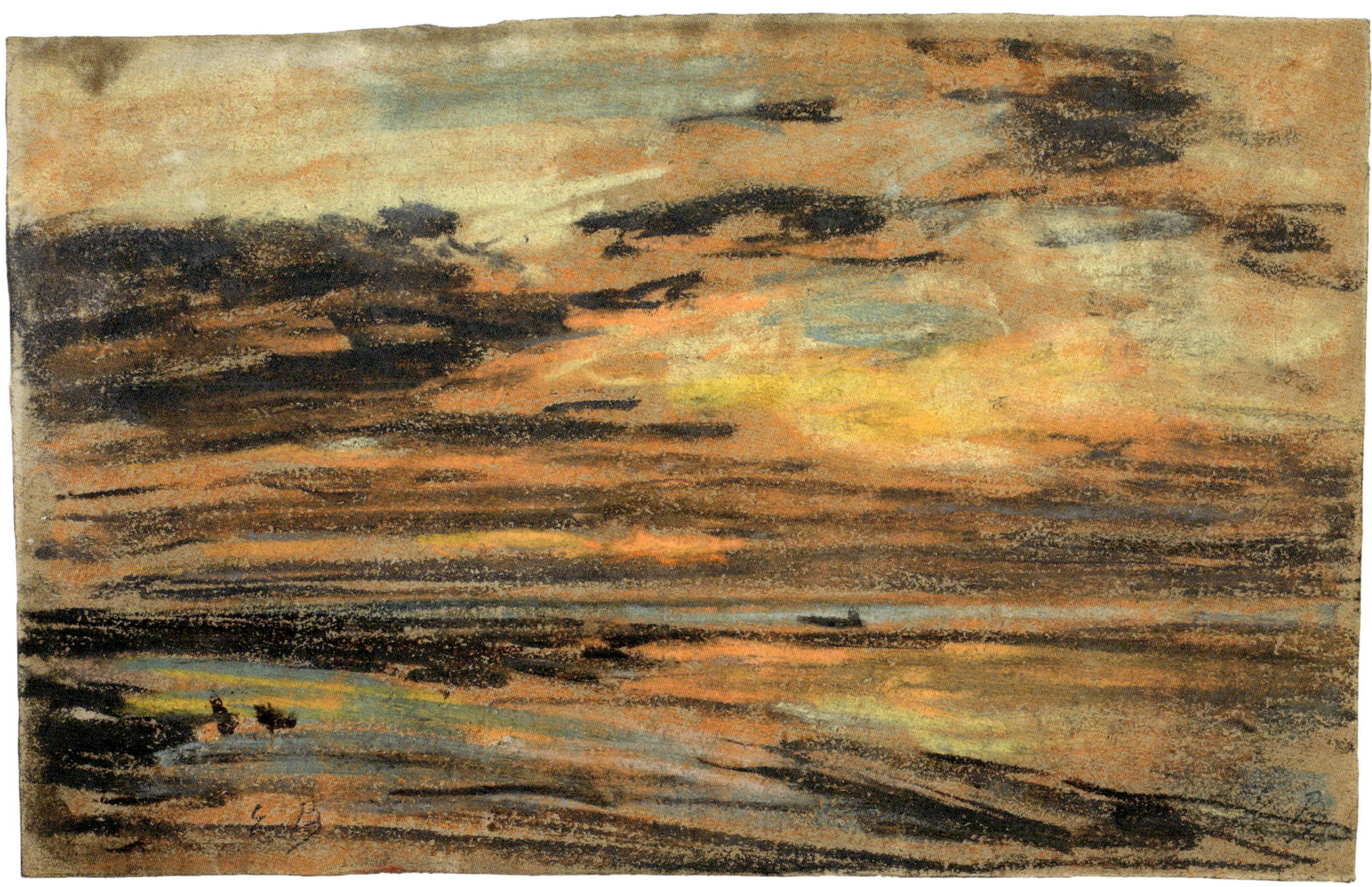

3

Eugène Boudin (1824–1898)
Sunset over the Sea, *c.* 1860–70
Pastel on buff paper, 17.7 x 29 cm
The Syndics of the Fitzwilliam Museum, University of Cambridge, 2380

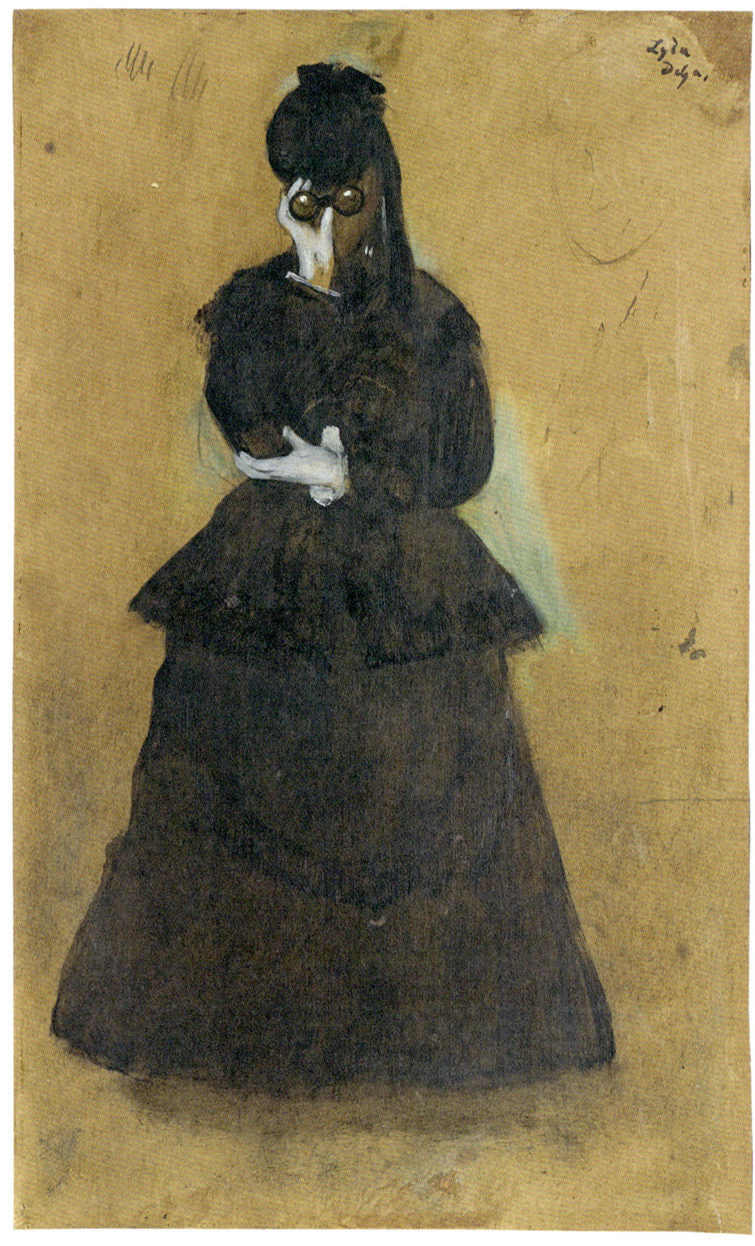

4

Edgar Degas (1834–1917)
Lyda, Woman with a Pair of Binoculars, *c.* 1866–68
Oil over graphite on paper, 35.3 x 22.3 cm
Collection of David Lachenmann

5

Edgar Degas (1834–1917)
Woman at a Window, 1870–71
Essence (diluted oil paint) on wove paper laid down on canvas, 61.2 x 45.7 cm
The Courtauld, London (Samuel Courtauld Trust), P.1932.SC.88

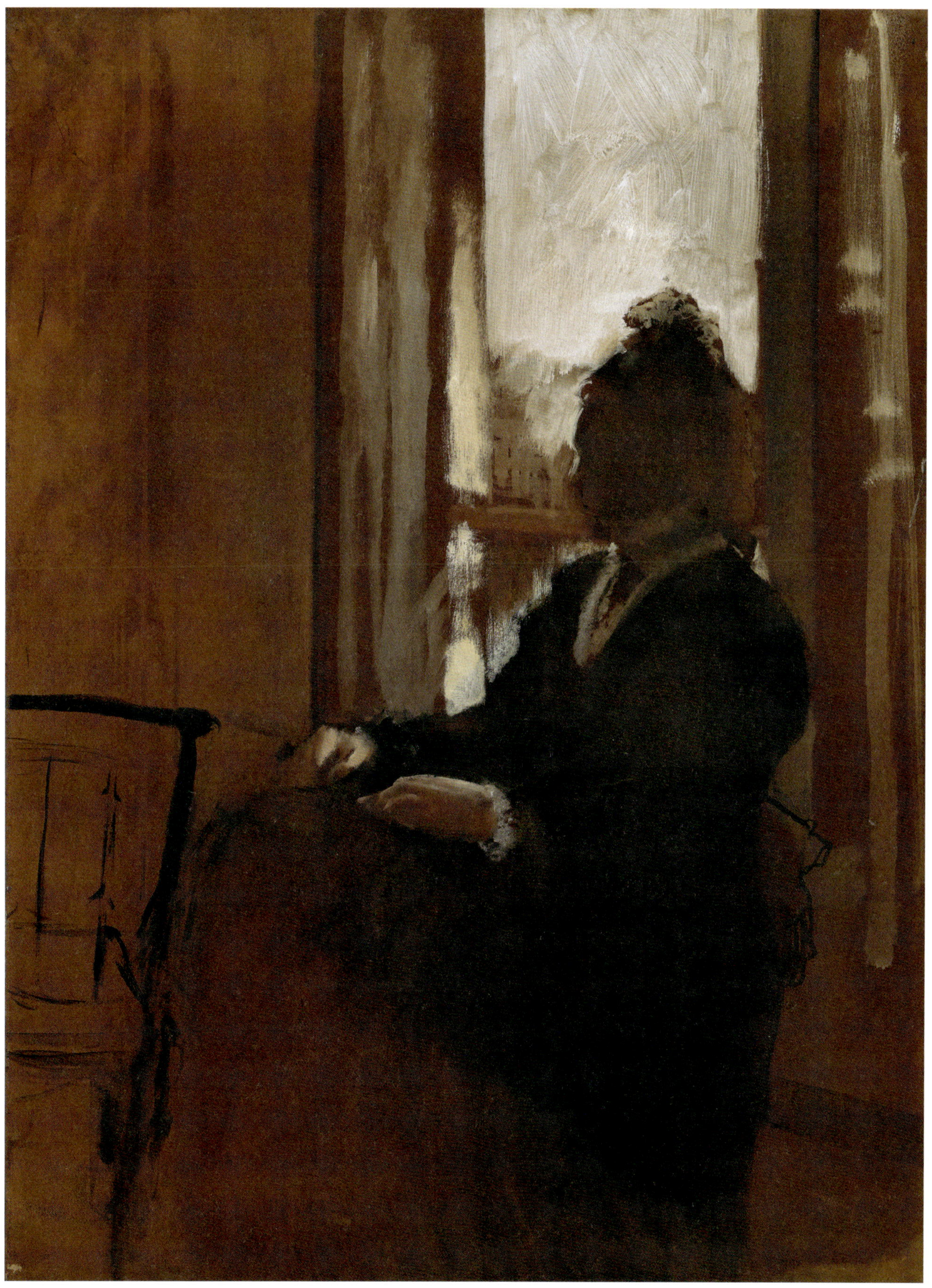

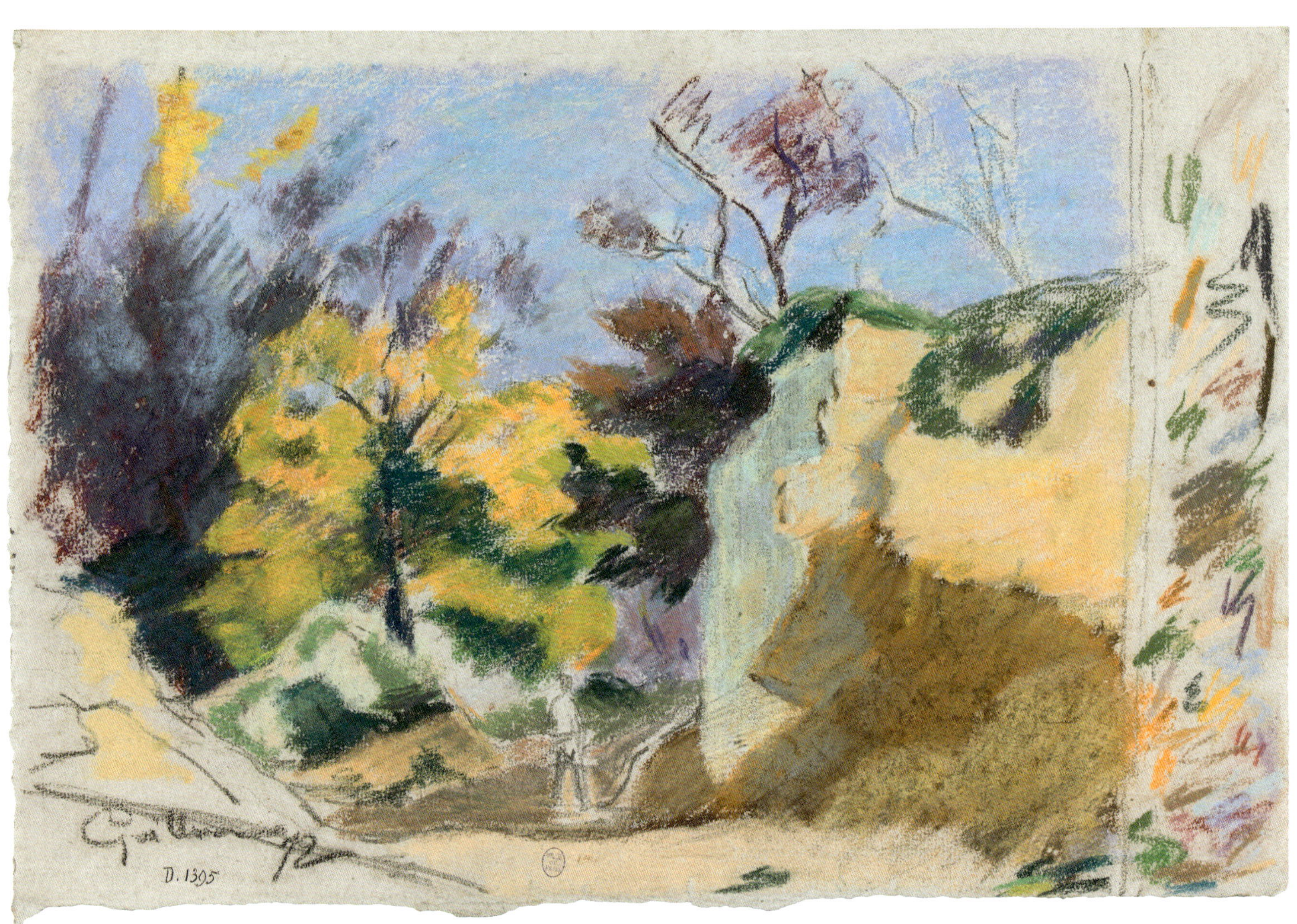

6

Armand Guillaumin (1841–1927)
Landscape with Trees and Rocks with Colour Tests, 1872
Pastel on laid paper, 25.9 x 39.2 cm
Petit Palais, Musée des Beaux-Arts de la Ville de Paris.
Gifted by Armand Guillaumin, 1922, PPD1395

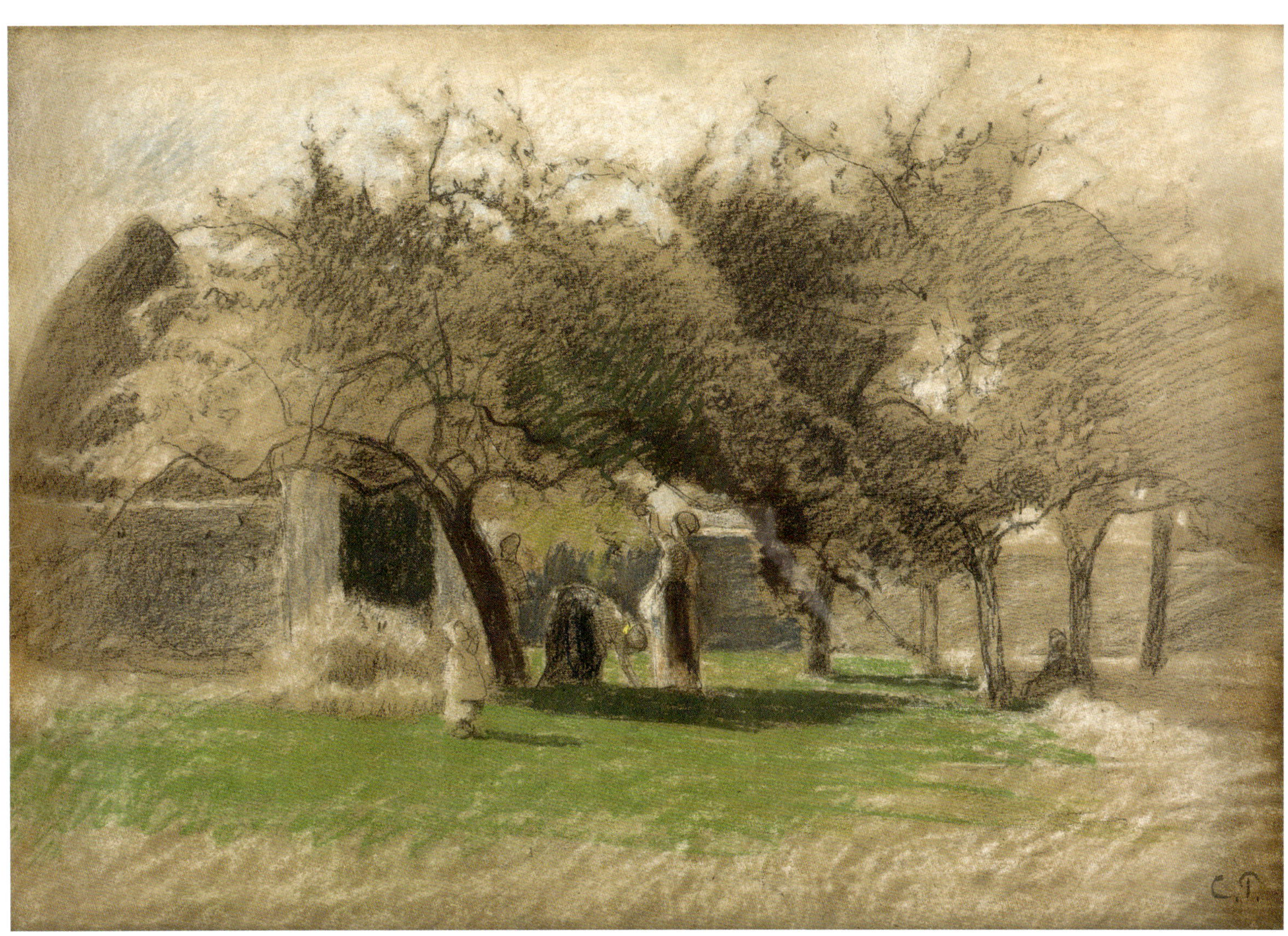

7

Camille Pissarro (1830–1903)
Apple Picking, 1870–75
Black and white chalk on buff paper, 38 x 53 cm
York Museums Trust (York Art Gallery), YORAG: R2027

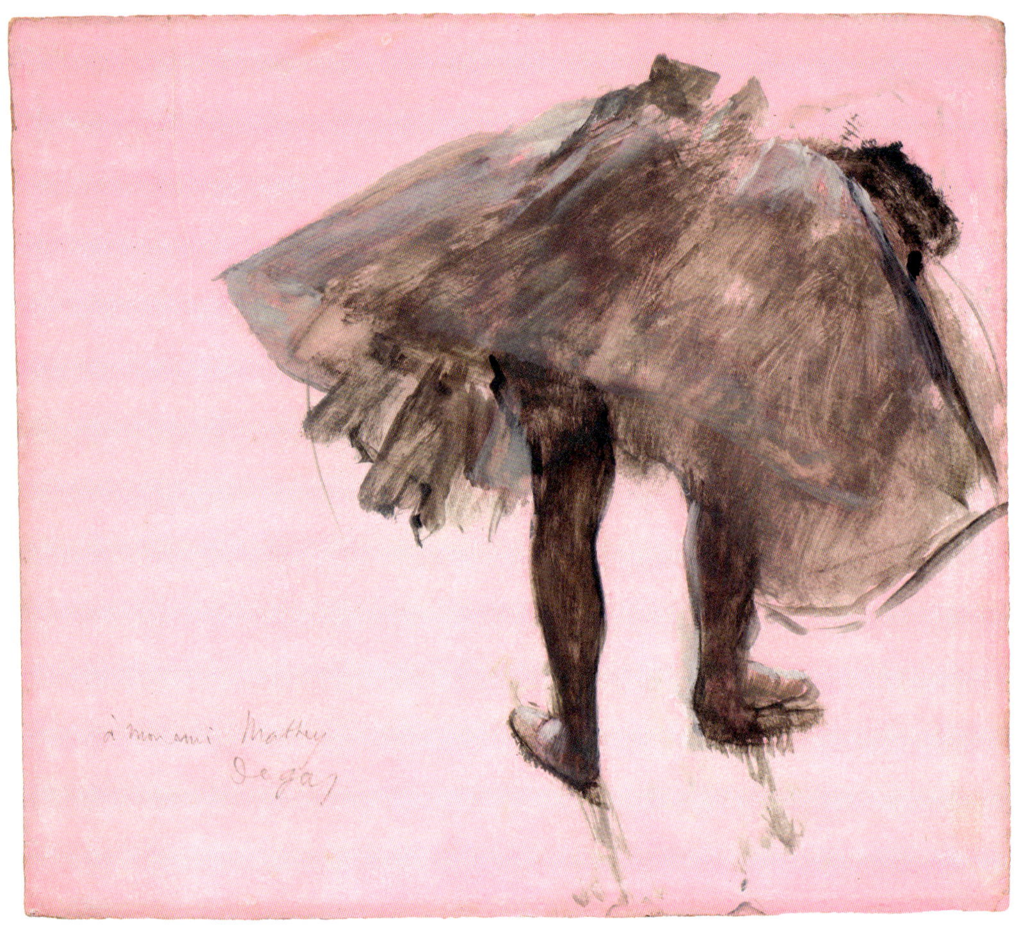

8

Edgar Degas (1834–1917)
Dancer Seen from Behind, c. 1873
Essence (diluted oil paint) on prepared pink paper, 28.4 x 32 cm
Collection of David Lachenmann

9

Edgar Degas (1834–1917)
Dancer Yawning (Dancer Stretching), 1873
Essence (diluted oil paint) on prepared green paperboard, 53 x 45 cm
Private collection

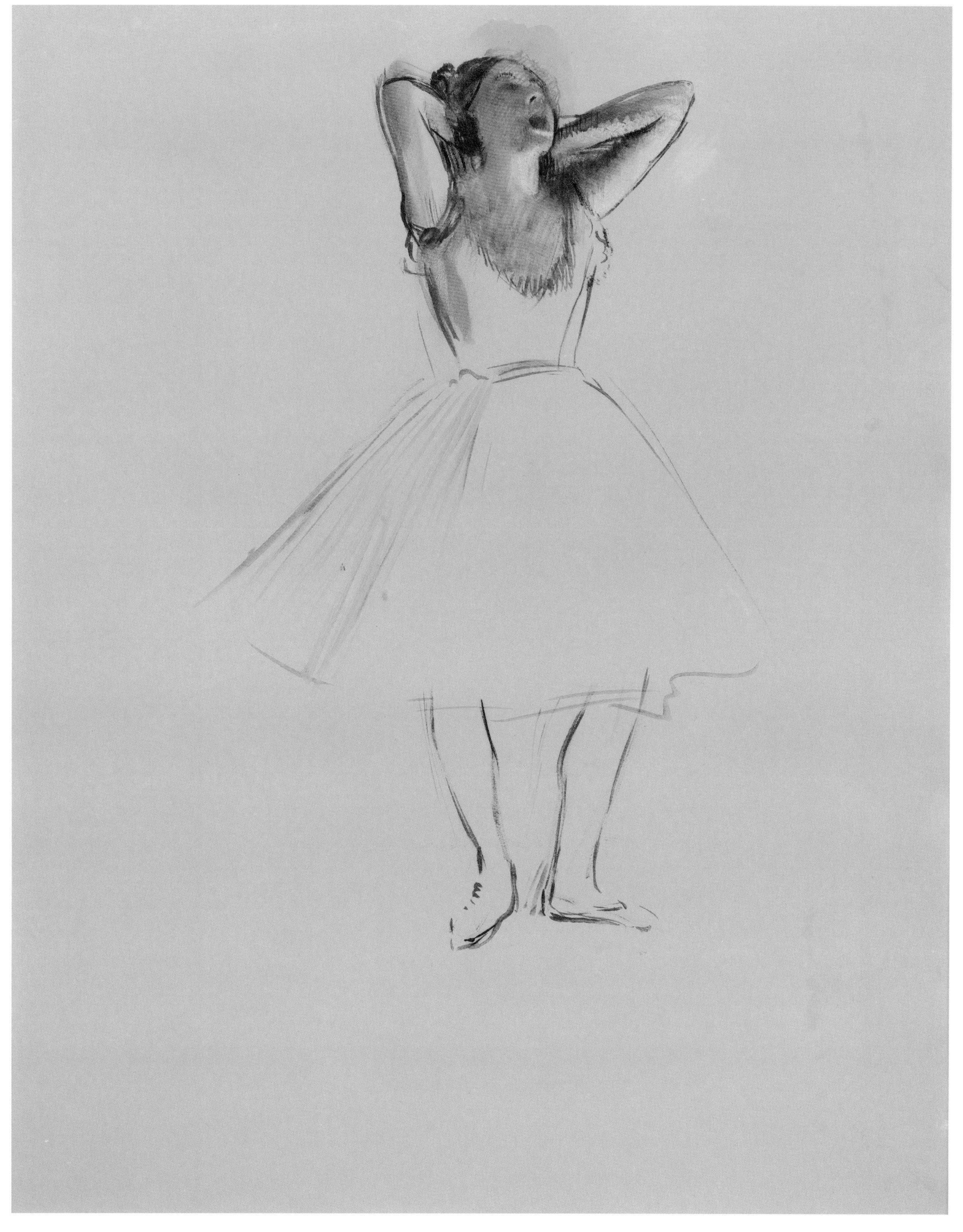

10

Edgar Degas (1834–1917)
Jacques de Nittis (Son of Giuseppe de Nittis), *c.* 1878–80
Pastel on laid paper, 60 x 48 cm
Private collection

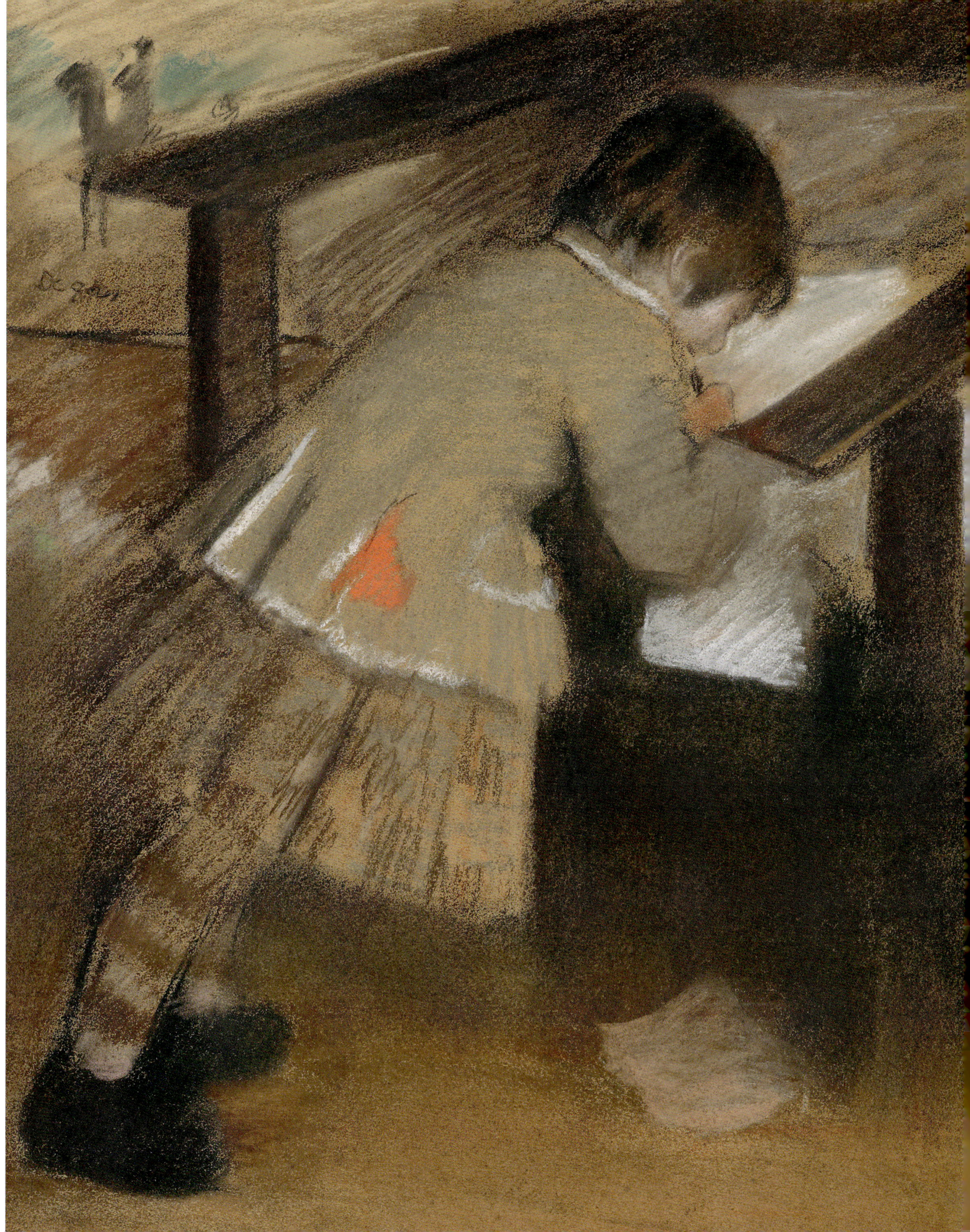
Degas

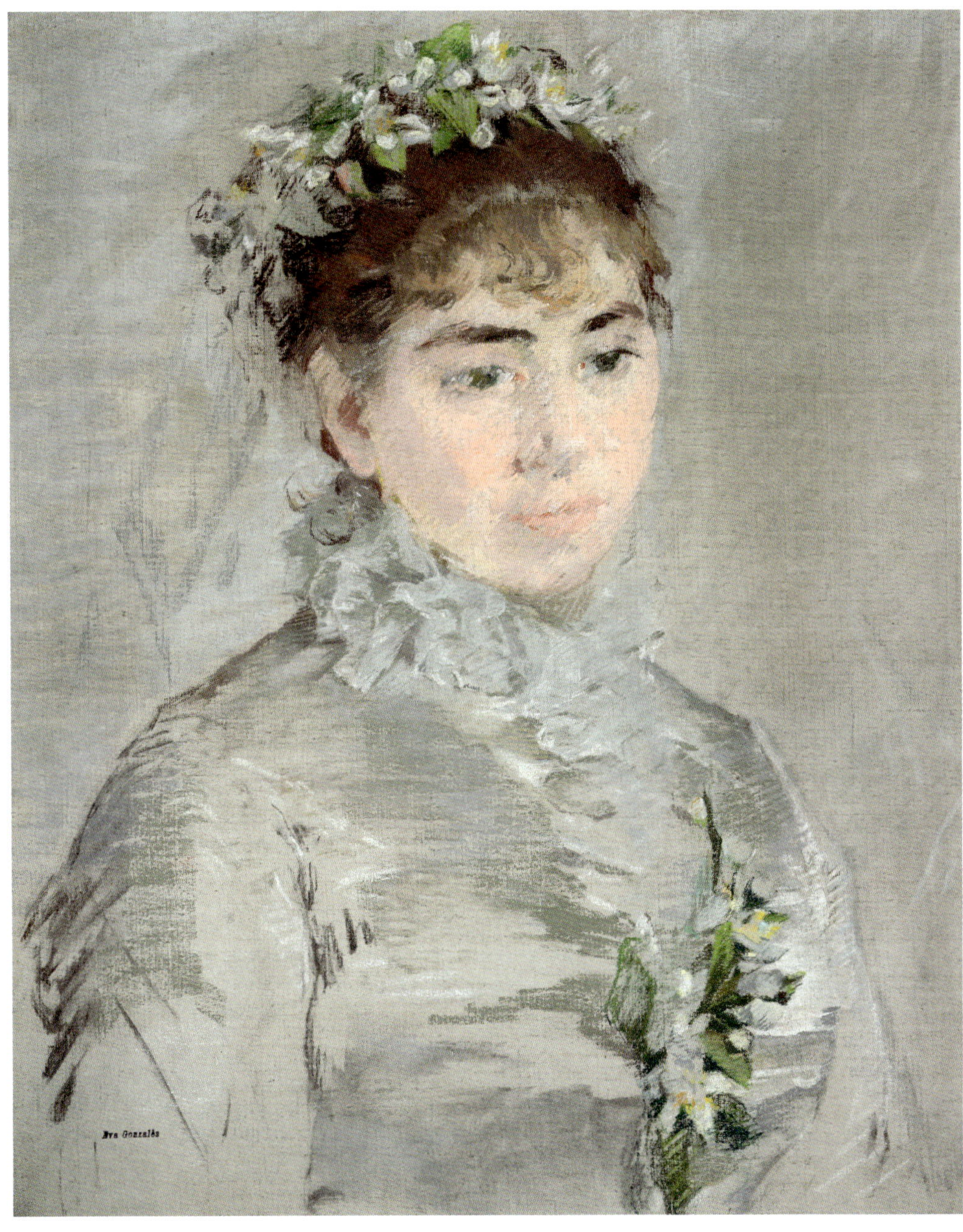

11

Eva Gonzalès (1849–1883)
The Bride, 1879
Pastel on canvas, 46.2 x 38.2 cm
Palais princier de Monaco

12

Pierre-Auguste Renoir (1841–1919)
Woman with a Veil, *c.* 1877–79
Pastel and coloured chalks on wove paper, 69.5 x 41.5 cm
Private collection. On long-term loan to The Courtauld Gallery, London, LD.1997.XX.10

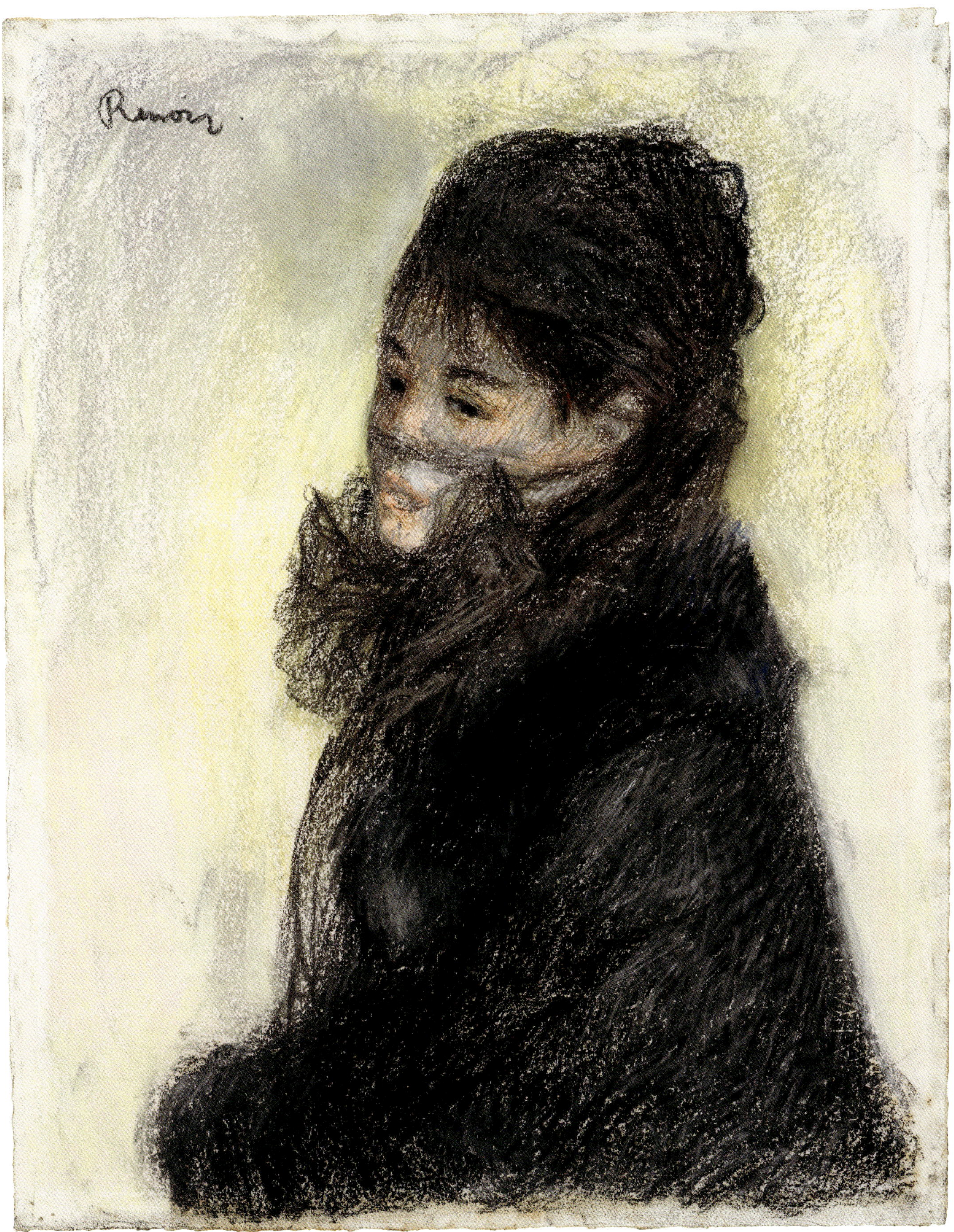
Renoir

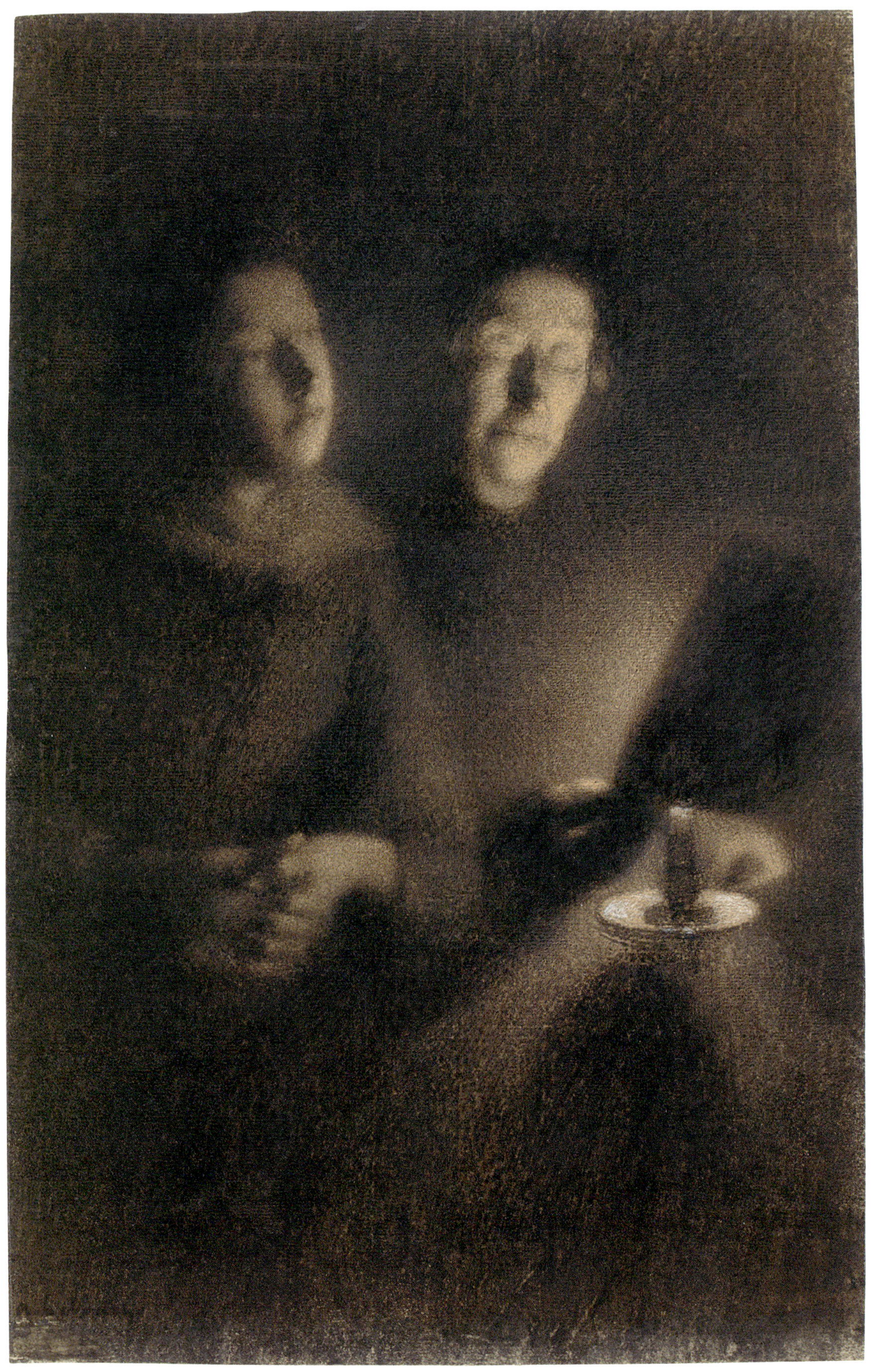

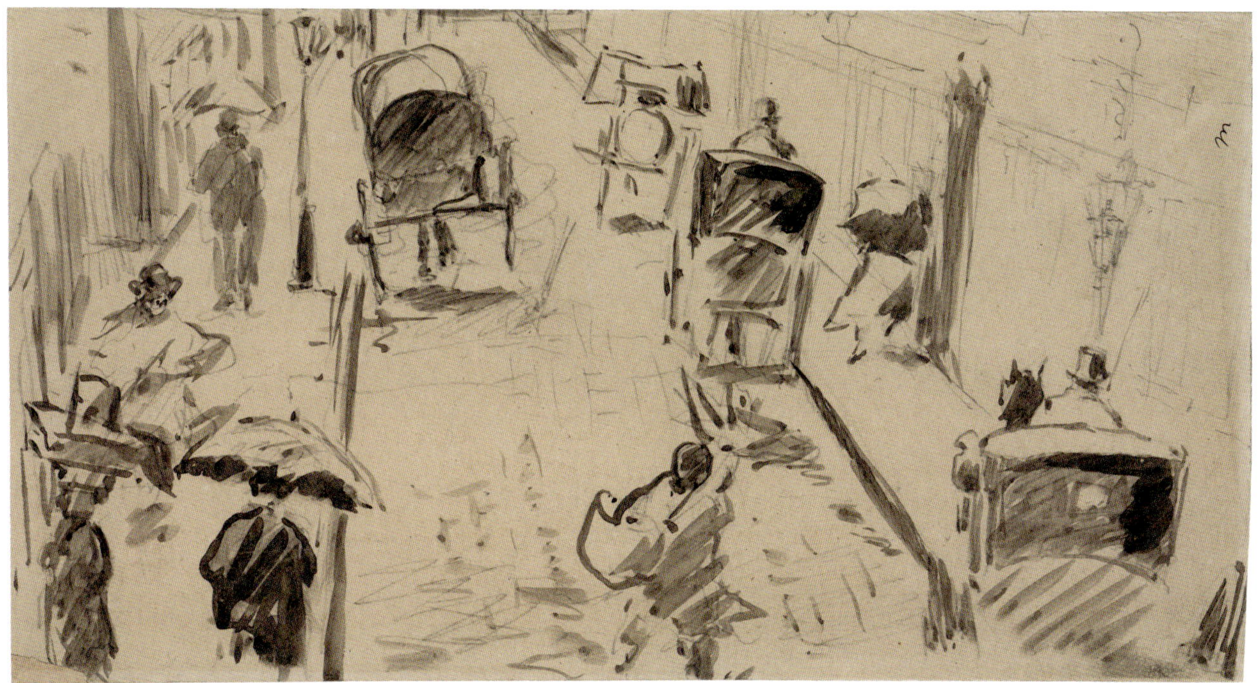

13

Albert Lebourg (1849–1928)
The Artist's Wife and Mother-in-law Reading a Letter by Candlelight, *c.* 1878–79
Charcoal and graphite, heightened with white, on buff paper, 43.5 x 28.3 cm
British Museum, London, 1978,1007.3

14

Edouard Manet (1832–1883)
The Rue Mosnier in the Rain, 1878
Leadpoint and ink wash on crayon paper mounted on cardboard, 19 x 36 cm
Szépművészeti Múzeum / Museum of Fine Arts, Budapest, 1935-2735

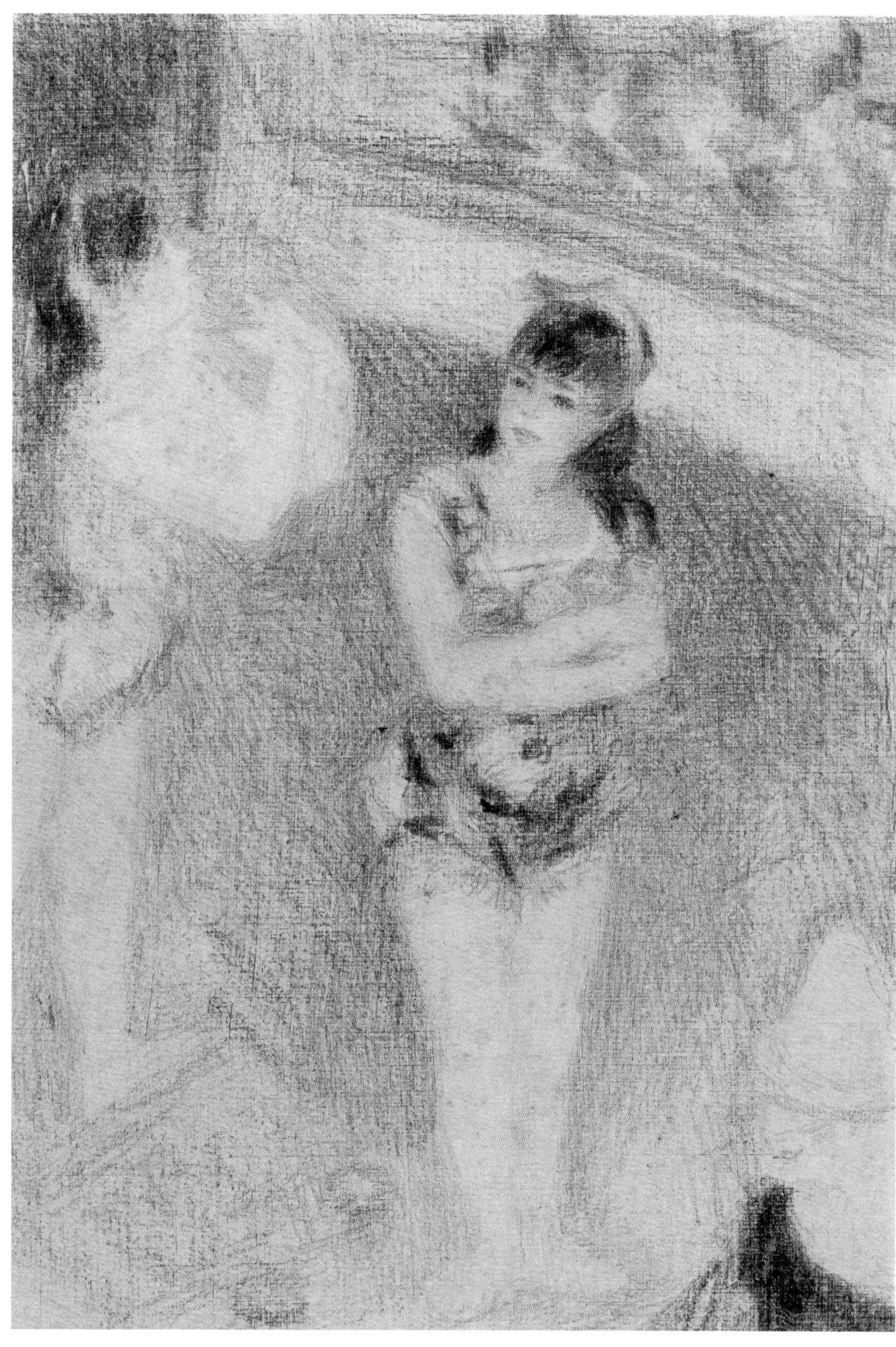

16

Paul Cézanne (1839–1906)
Academic Study of a Male Nude with His Right Hand Clenched Across His Chest, *c.* 1867–70
Black chalk and black crayon with trial touches of watercolour at upper right, on laid paper, 48.2 x 29.5 cm
The Ashmolean Museum, University of Oxford. Bequeathed by John Bryson, 1977, WA1977.24

15

Pierre-Auguste Renoir (1841–1919)
Study for Acrobats at the Cirque Fernando, *c.* 1879
Pencil and crayon on canvas, 29 x 20 cm
Private collection

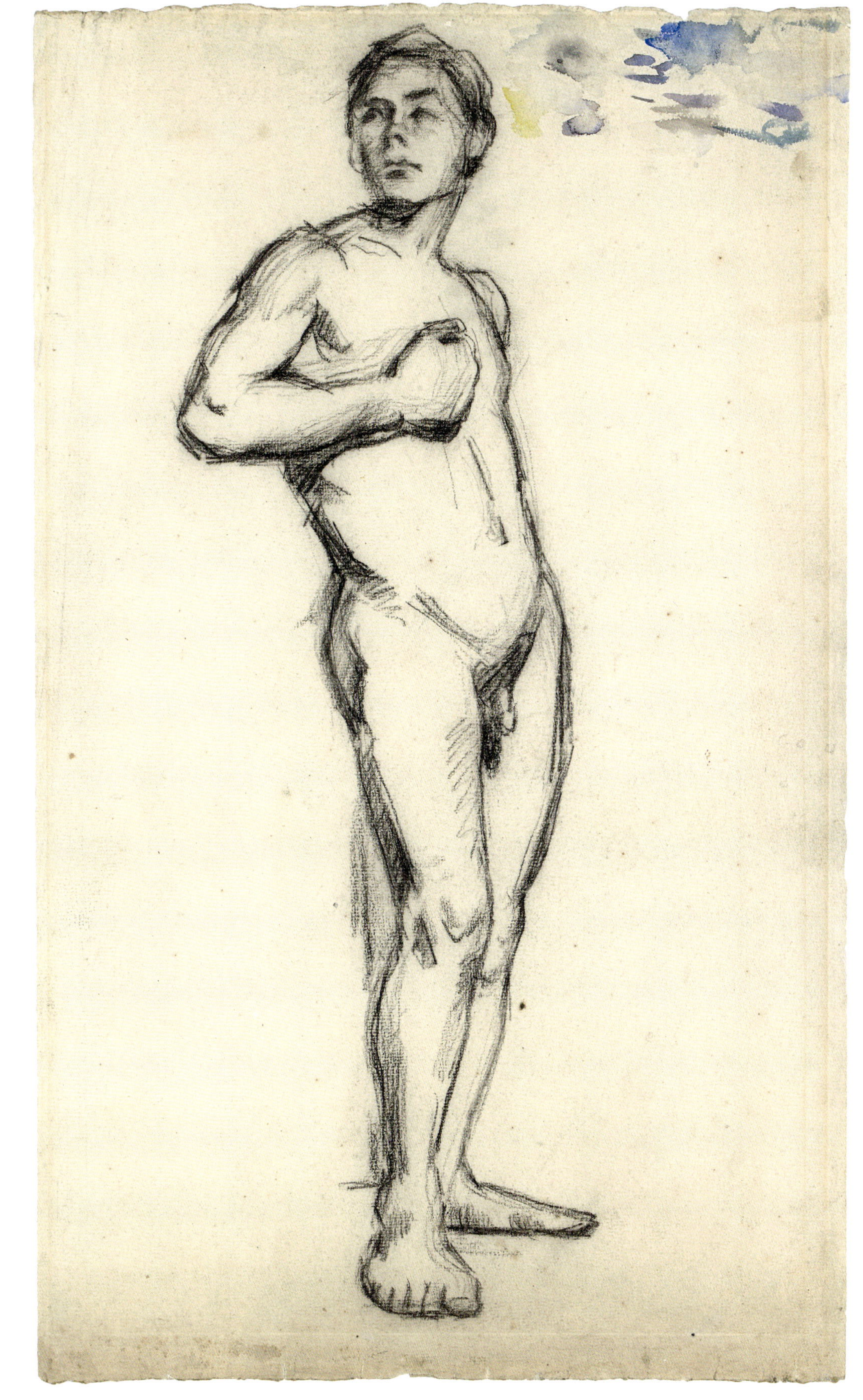

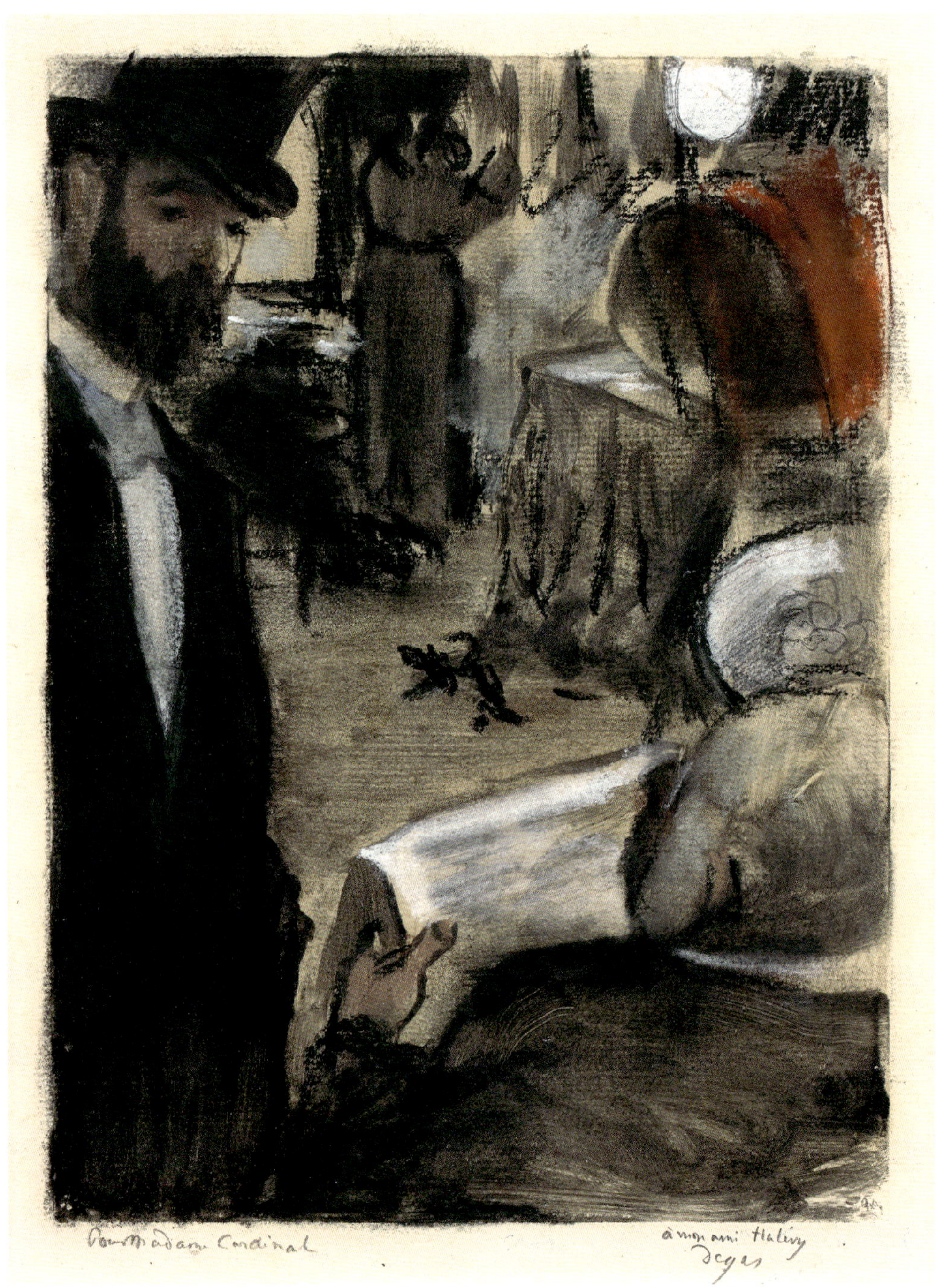

17

Edgar Degas (1834–1917)
Ludovic Halévy Finds Madame Cardinal in the Dressing Room, 1876–77
Pastel and graphite over monotype in black ink on paper, 26.7 x 22.9 cm
Collection of David Lachenmann

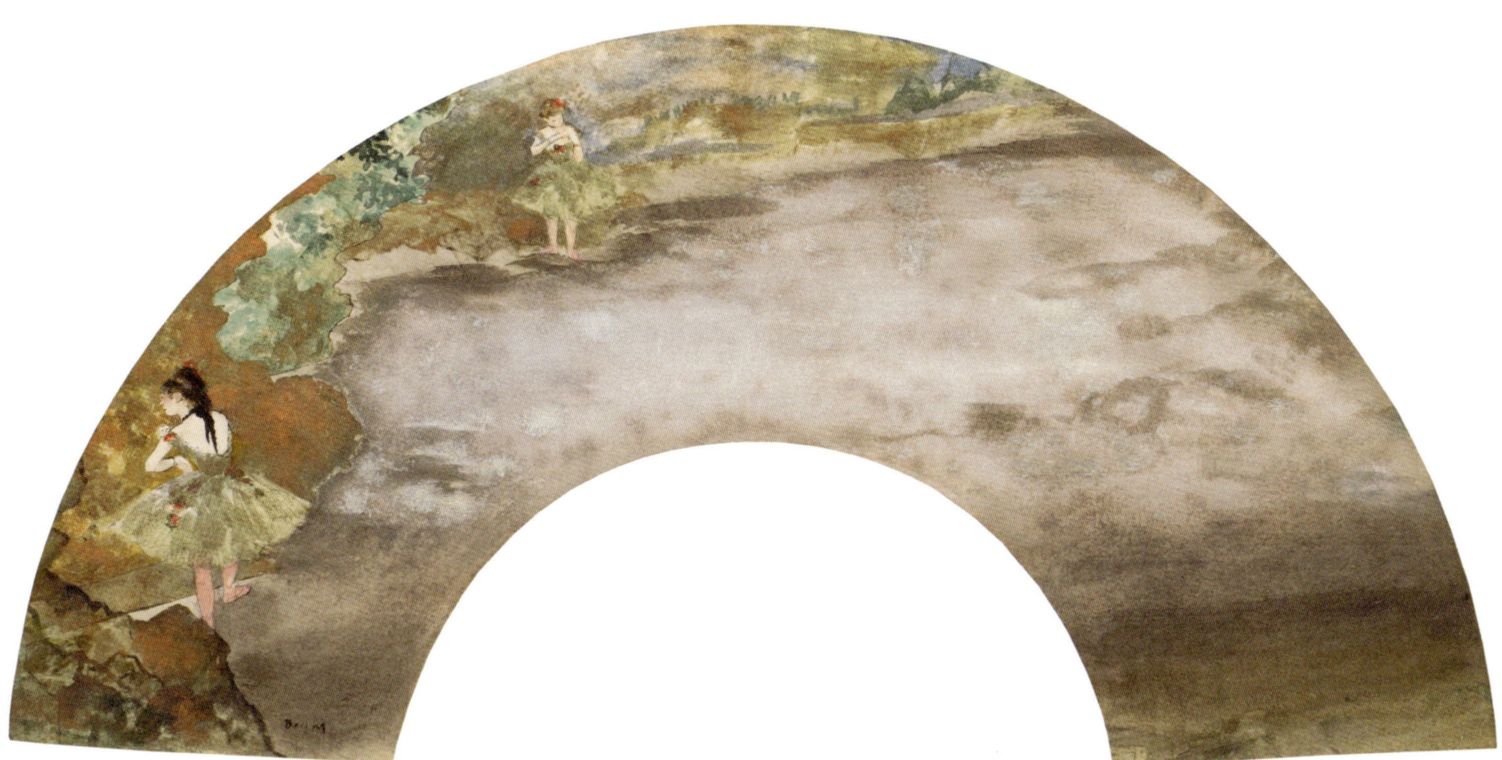

18

Edgar Degas (1834–1917)
Two Dancers, *c.* 1878–79
Watercolour heightened with gold and silver on silk laid on card, 28 x 57.8 cm
Private collection

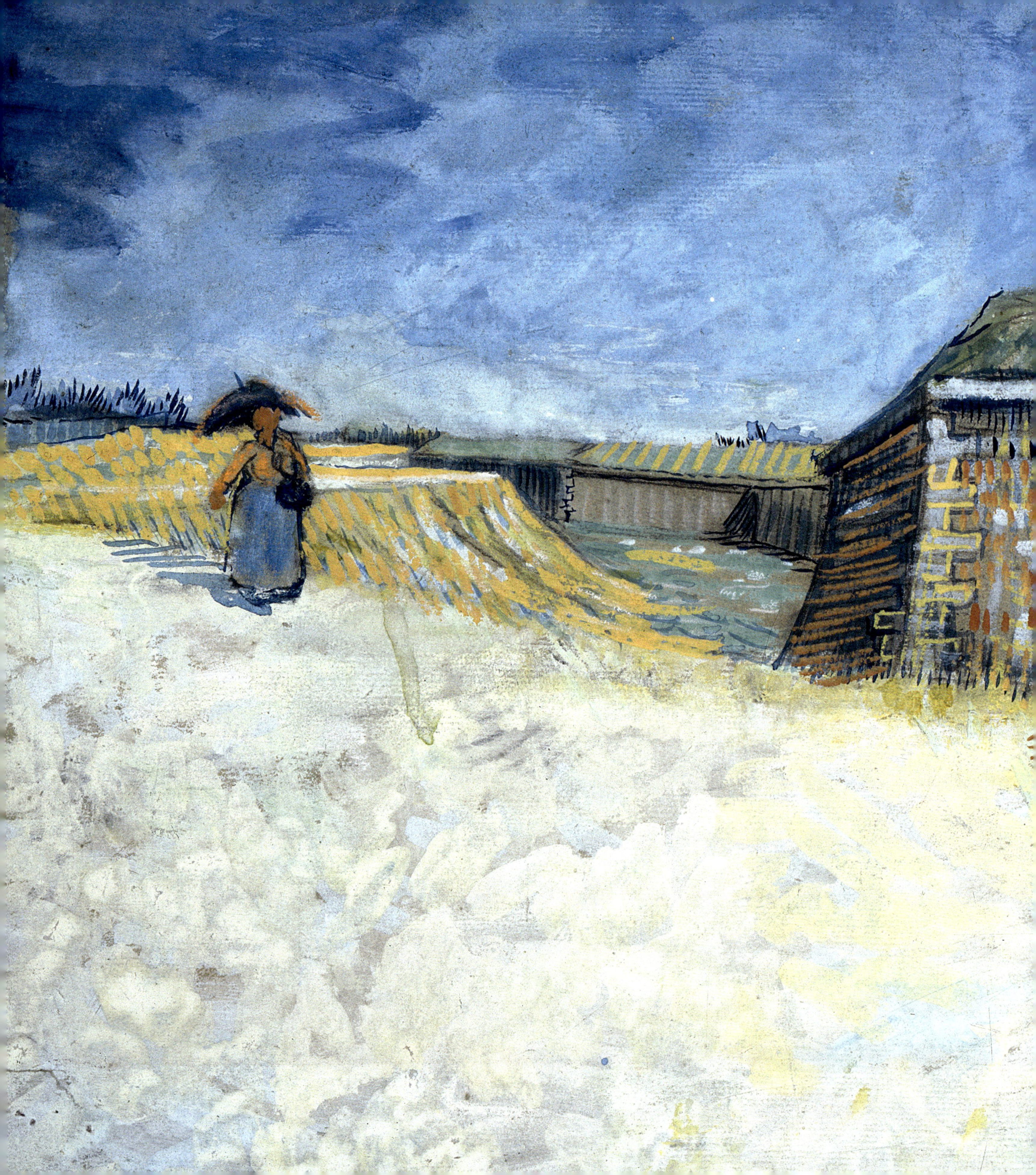

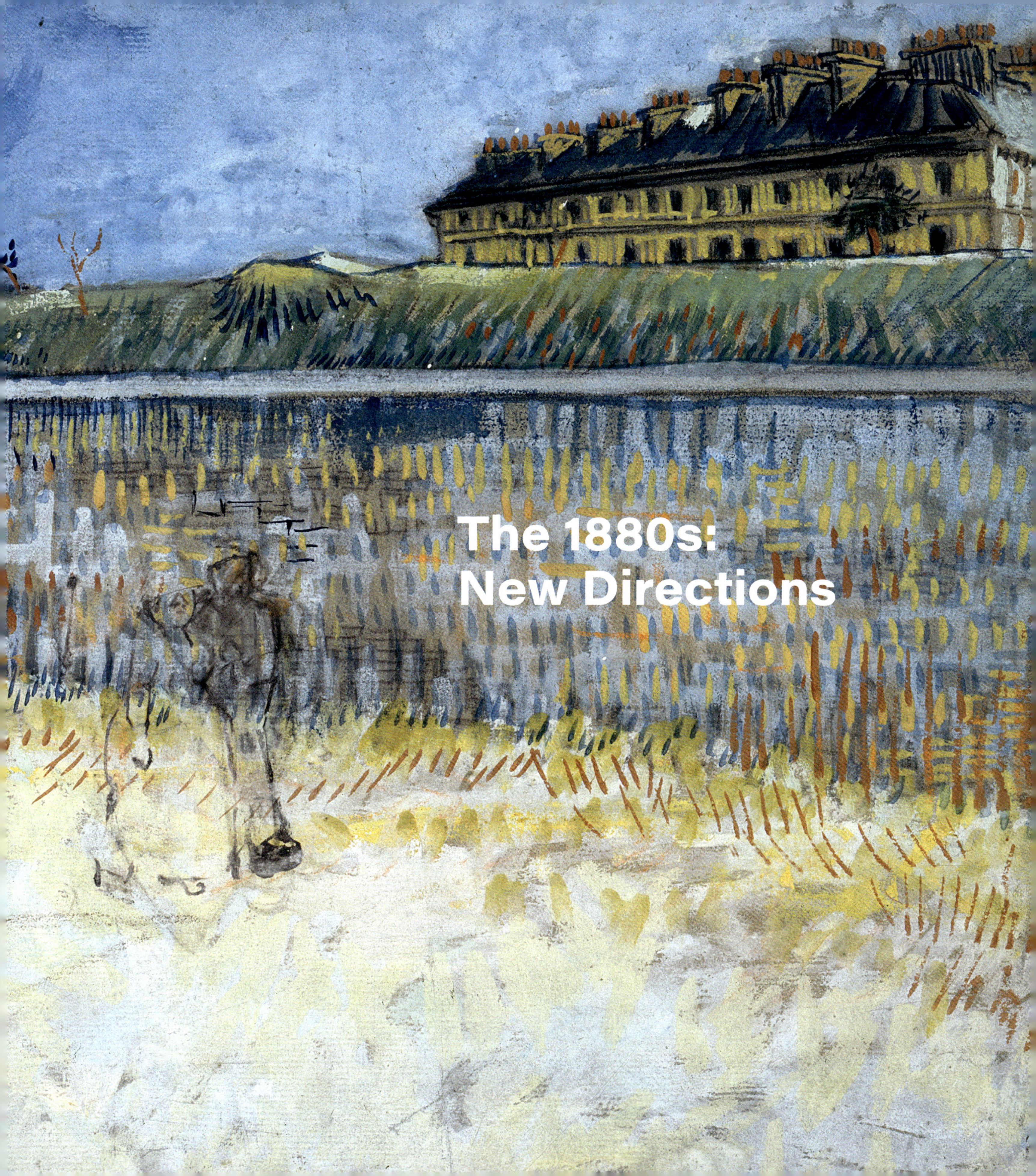

The 1880s: New Directions

The Impressionists held their last group exhibition in Paris in 1886. By then, several of them, dissatisfied with Impressionism's emphasis on the transient, had begun to seek new, personal directions in their work. Yet, for each the practice of drawing remained fundamental. Primarily known as a painter, Claude Monet also made pastels throughout his career. At Etretat on the Normandy coast, he used soft, moody tones to record the famous arched cliffs at various times of day (cats 35, 36).

Best known for his scenes of rural life, Camille Pissarro drew constantly in a variety of media. In his superb *The Market Stall* (cat. 26) he combines watercolour, tempera and black chalk in a fully realised composition in which figures and background are perfectly integrated. Here, materials generally associated with drawing are handled on a scale and with a panache that combine to create the impact of a painting.

Largely self-taught, Vincent van Gogh believed that drawing was 'the root of everything'. From the beginning of his artistic career, which lasted only a decade, he was a consummate and extremely original draughtsman, working in a broad range of graphic techniques. In the summer of 1885, while still in the Netherlands, he produced a series of powerful chalk drawings of peasants working in the fields (cat. 37). His unexpected, meticulous *Bust of a Young Warrior* (cat. 27) shows that even such a radical artist as Van Gogh could, on occasion, copy the art of the past to hone his technique. The superbly confident *Fortifications of Paris with Houses* (cat. 40) shows how he embraced colour after discovering Impressionism during the two years he spent in Paris in 1886–88, whereas in *Thistles by the Roadside* (cat. 41), produced in Arles in 1888, using graphite, ink and the pens he made himself by cutting roadside reeds with his penknife, we can appreciate his virtuosity and the range of marks that he achieved in his most distinctive drawings.

Watercolour was ideally suited to Berthe Morisot's fluent, luminous technique, as her evocation of a summer's day in the Bois de Boulogne (cat. 31) reveals. The supreme master of watercolour in late nineteenth-century French art was Paul Cézanne. The intensity of his gaze and his deeply contemplative approach resulted in such exquisitely nuanced images as *Flowerpots* (cat. 32).

Georges Seurat achieved the deepest, lustrous blacks with Conté crayon. Although he is best known for his pointillist paintings composed of small dots of colour, in his drawing he developed a unique and compelling style based on strong contrasts of black and white, with dark figures silhouetted against a penumbral light (cats 23, 24).

In Jacques-Emile Blanche's grand society portrait of Madame Henri Wallet (cat. 42) we see a more traditional artist absorbing avant-garde practice and, by working at scale in pastel, eroding the distinction between painting and drawing.

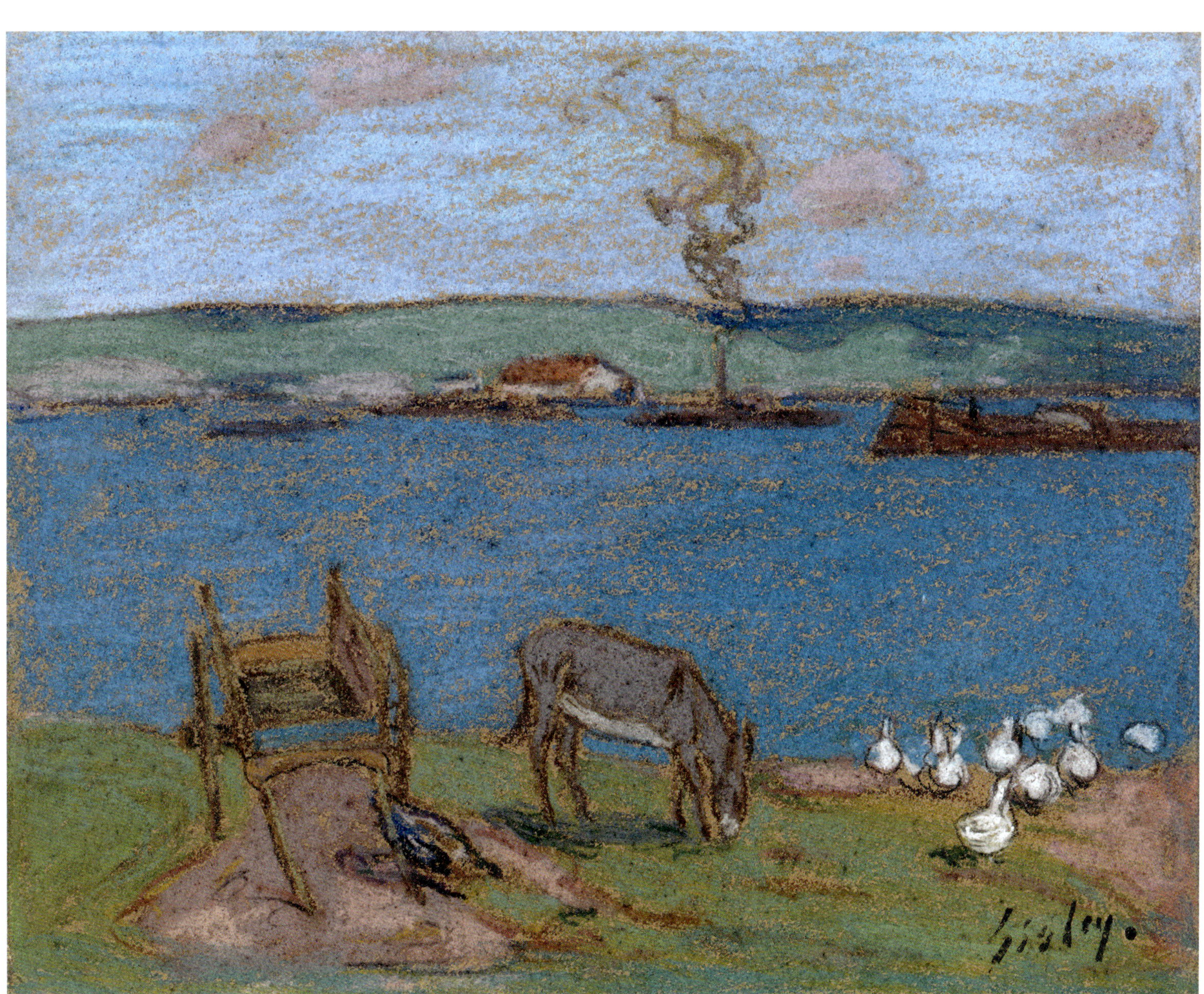

19

Alfred Sisley (1839–1899)
Landscape with a Donkey at Saint-Mammès, *c.* 1885–95
Pastel on wove paper, 26.7 x 33 cm
Lent by Glasgow Life Museums on behalf of Glasgow City Council: from the Burrell Collection with the approval of the Burrell Trustees, 35.624

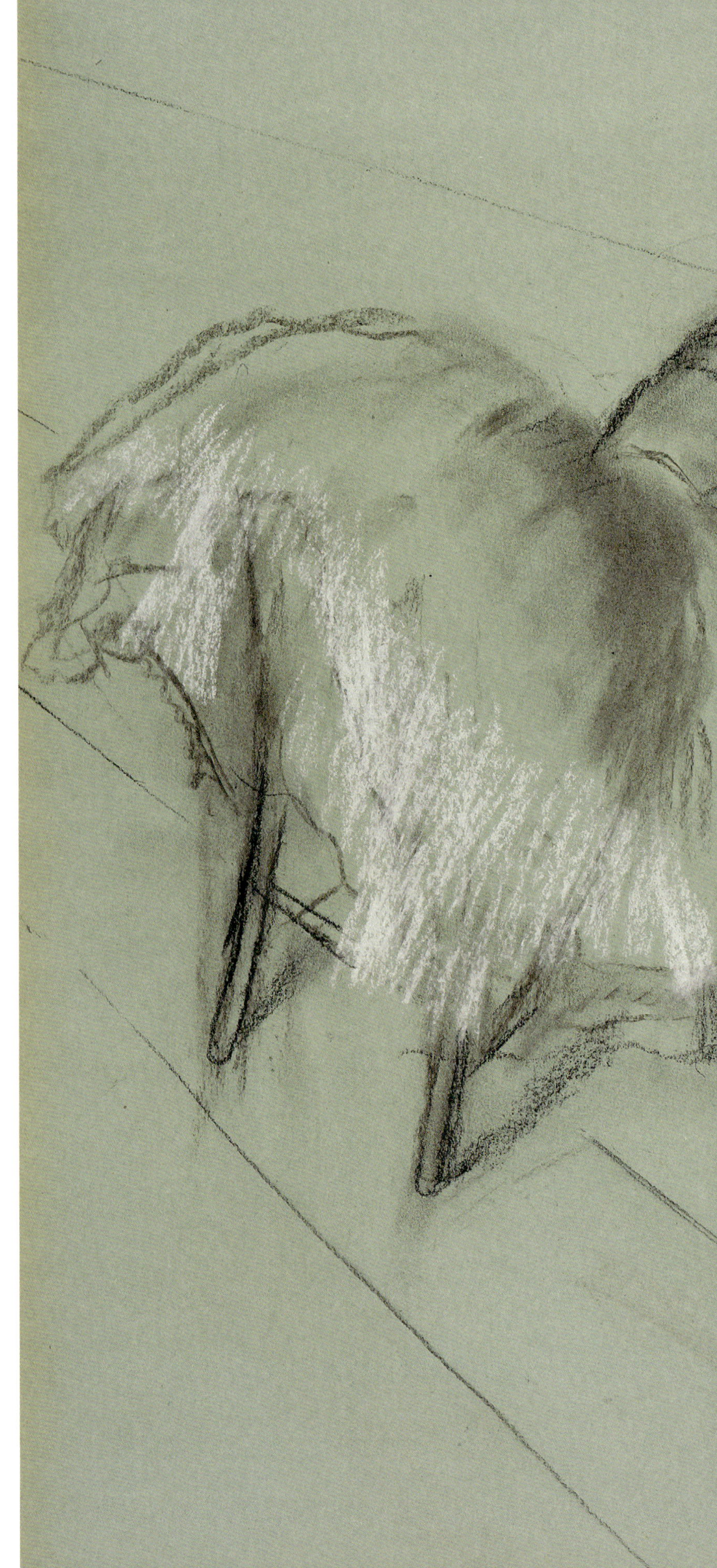

20

Edgar Degas (1834–1917)
Two Dancers Resting, *c.* 1880
Charcoal and pastel on green paper, 48.3 x 63.5 cm
Collection of David Lachenmann

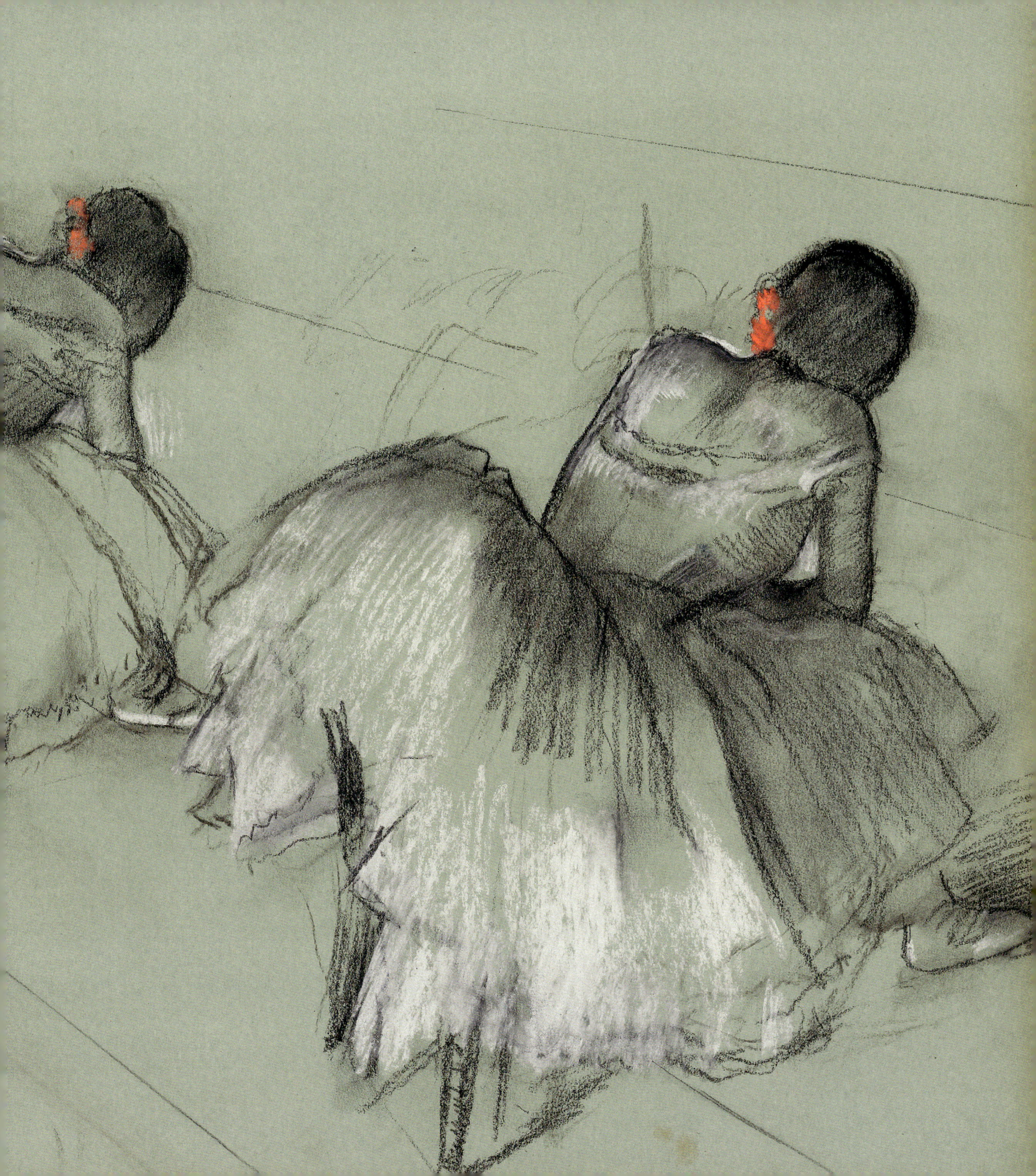

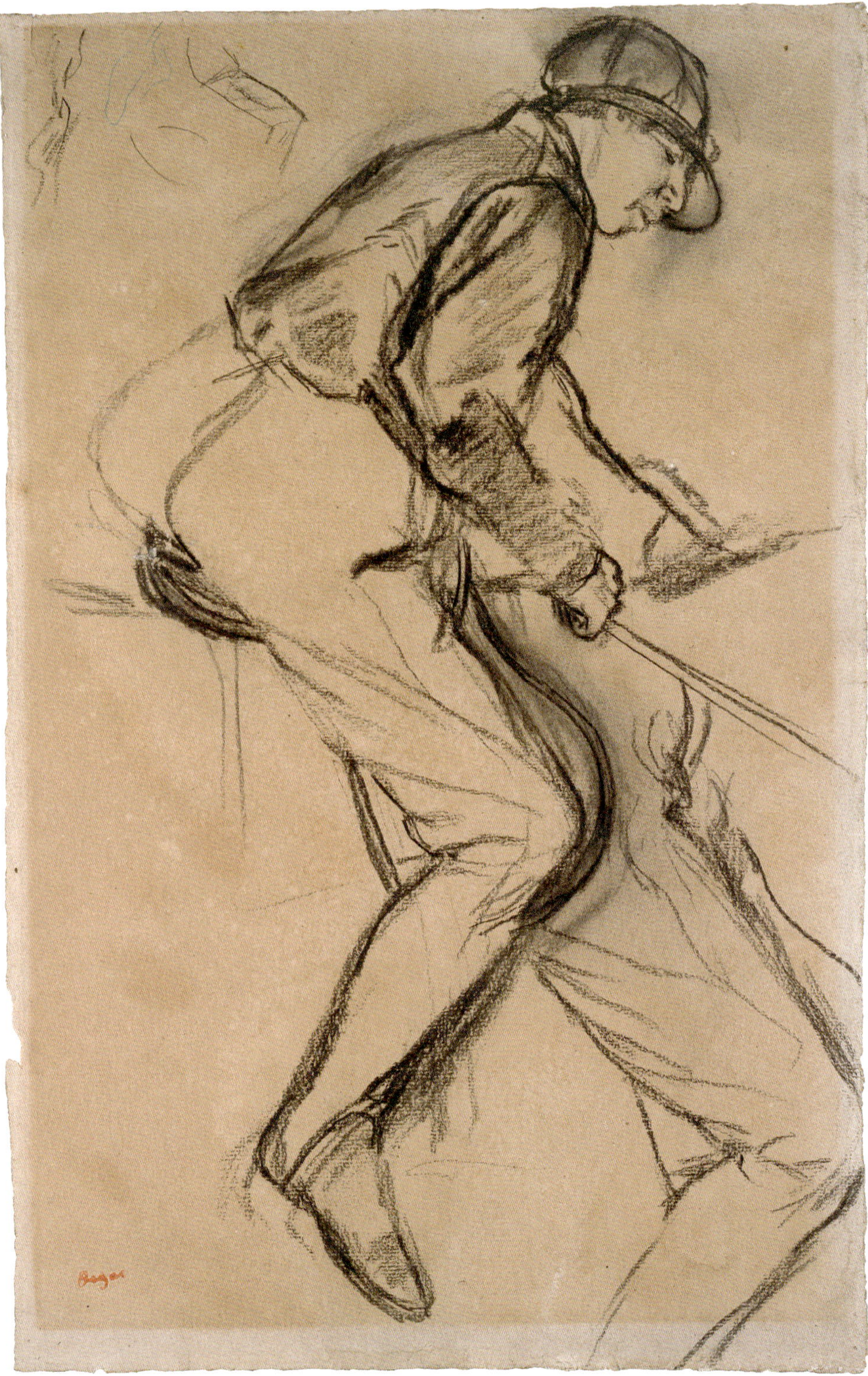

21

Edgar Degas (1834–1917)
A Seated Jockey, Facing Right, *c.* 1880–82
Charcoal, slightly rubbed, with some unrelated lines in blue pencil, on laid paper, 48 x 31 cm
The Ashmolean Museum, University of Oxford. Bequeathed by John Bryson, 1977, WA1977.27

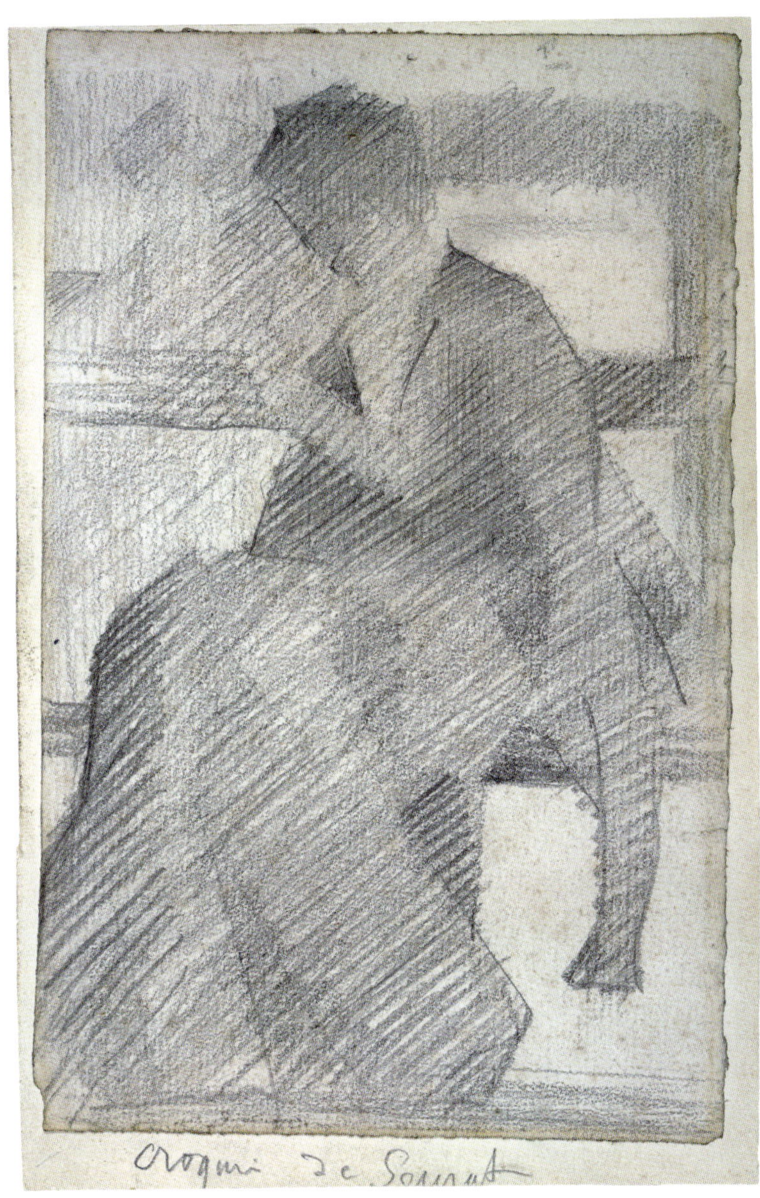

22

Georges Seurat (1859–1891)
Woman on a Bench, 1880
Graphite on paper, 16.5 x 10.4 cm
Sainsbury Centre, University of East Anglia, Norwich, UEA 4

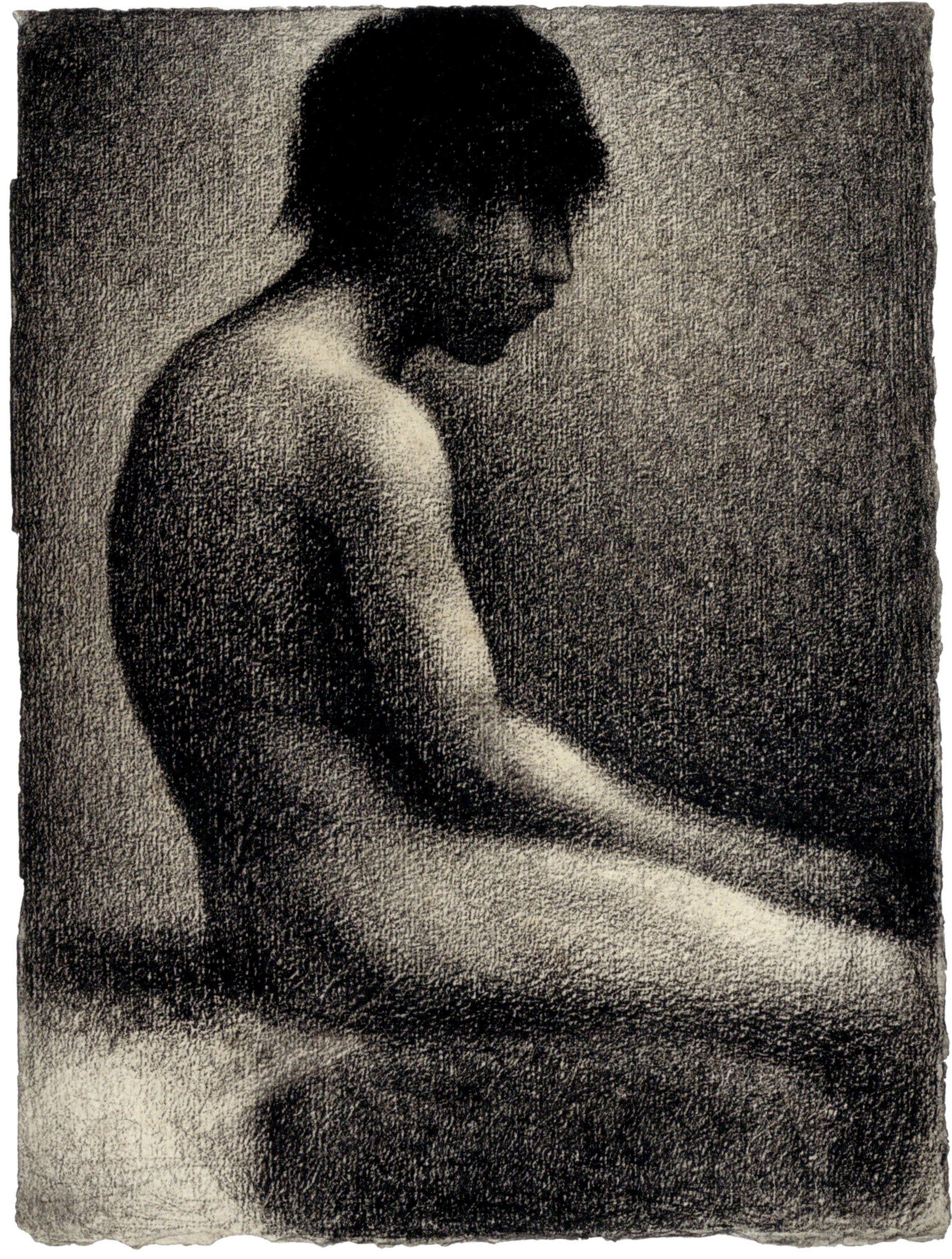

23

Georges Seurat (1859–1891)
Seated Youth, Study for 'Bathers at Asnières', 1883
Black Conté crayon on laid paper, 31.7 x 24.7 cm
National Galleries of Scotland. Purchased by
Private Treaty, 1982, D 5110

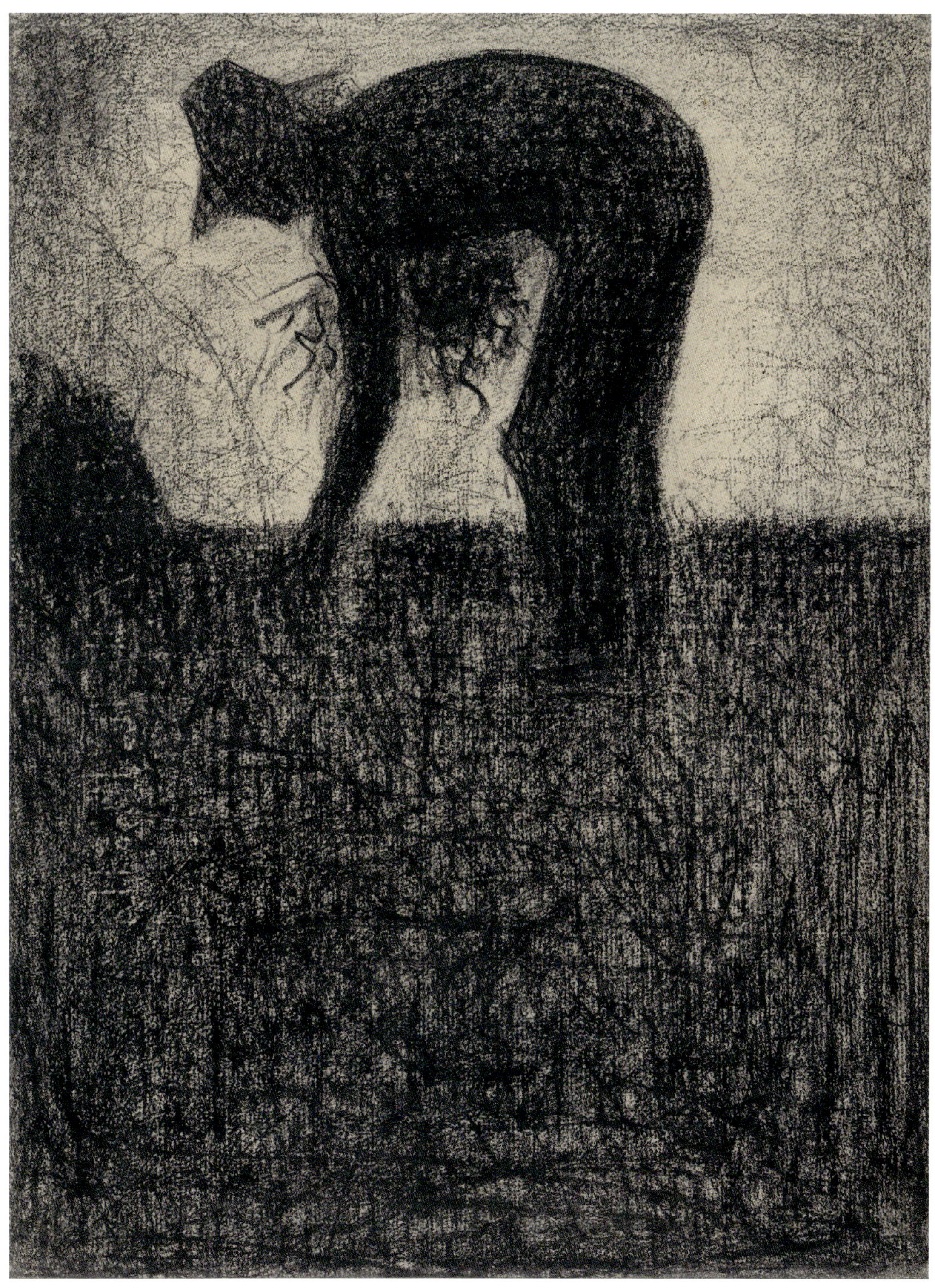

24

Georges Seurat (1859–1891)
The Gleaner, *c.* 1882
Black Conté crayon, over touches of graphite on paper, 32 x 24 cm
British Museum, London, 1949,0411.83
Bequeathed by Campbell Dodgson

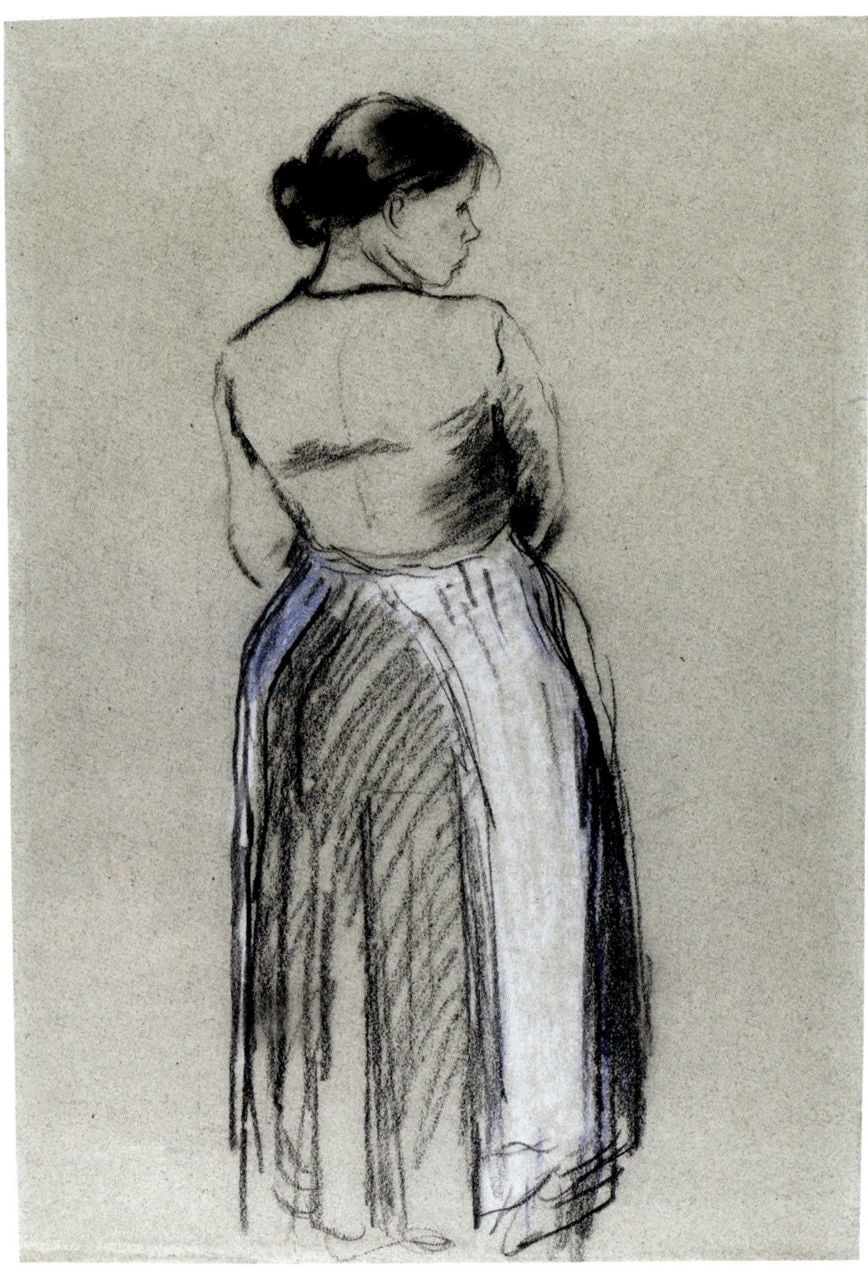

25

Camille Pissarro (1830–1903)
Young Female Peasant Standing in Three-quarters Profile Facing Right Seen from the Back, 1881
Black, blue and white chalks on paper, 44.5 x 31.3 cm
British Museum, London, 1920,0712.3
Purchased through the H.L. Florence Fund

26

Camille Pissarro (1830–1903)
The Market Stall, 1884
Tempera and watercolour over black chalk on board, 61 x 48.3 cm
Lent by Glasgow Life Museums on behalf of Glasgow City Council: from the Burrell Collection with the approval of the Burrell Trustees, 35.592

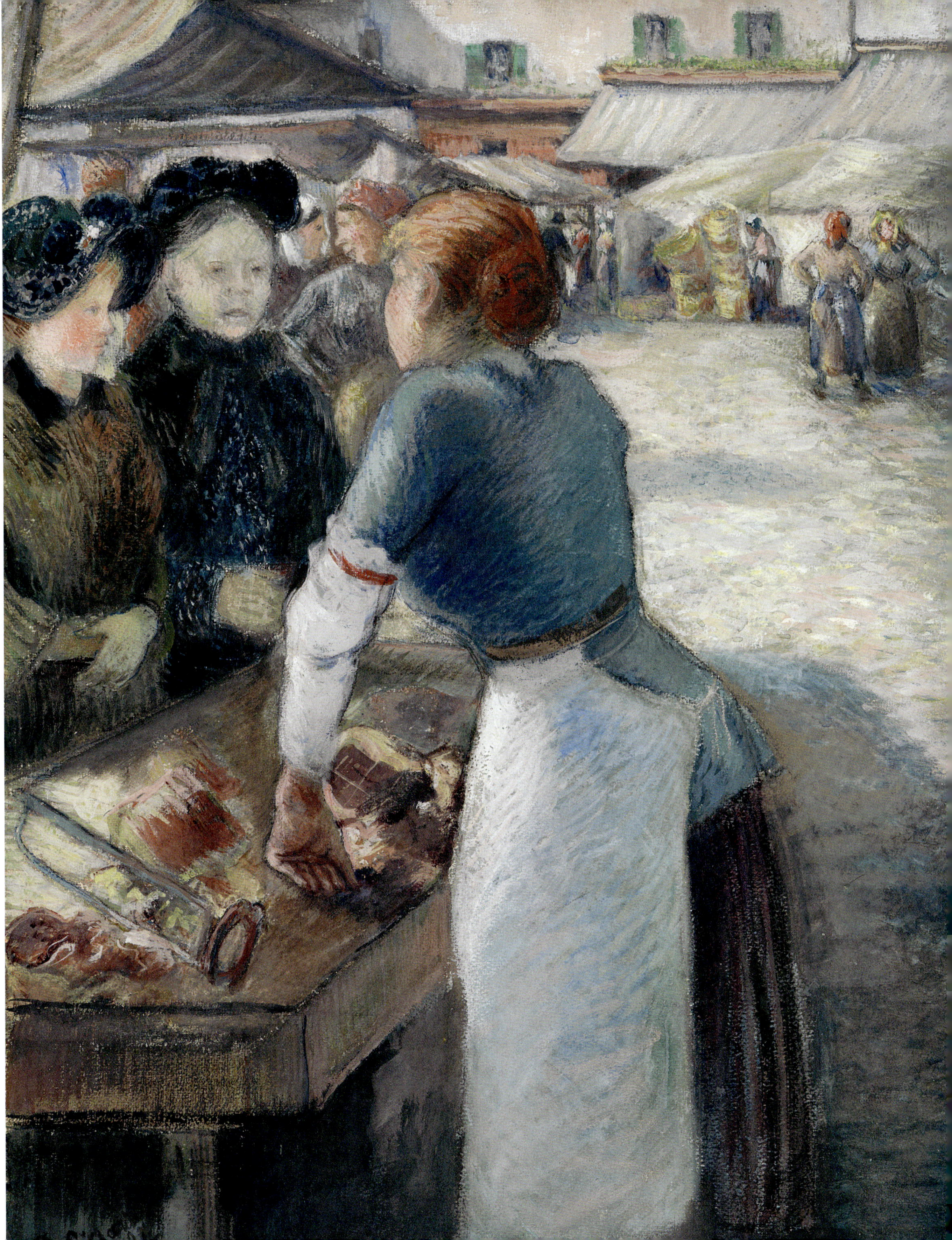

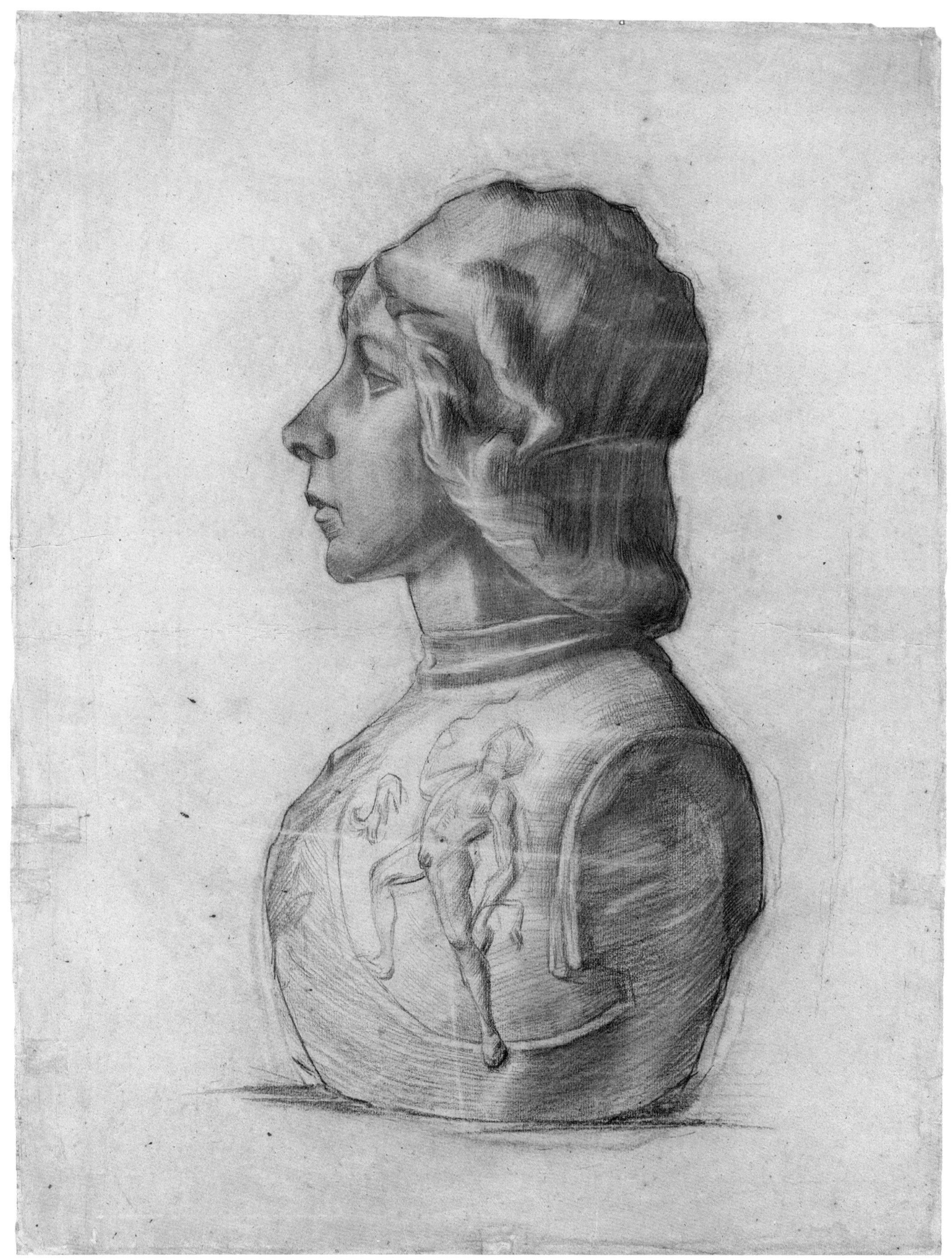

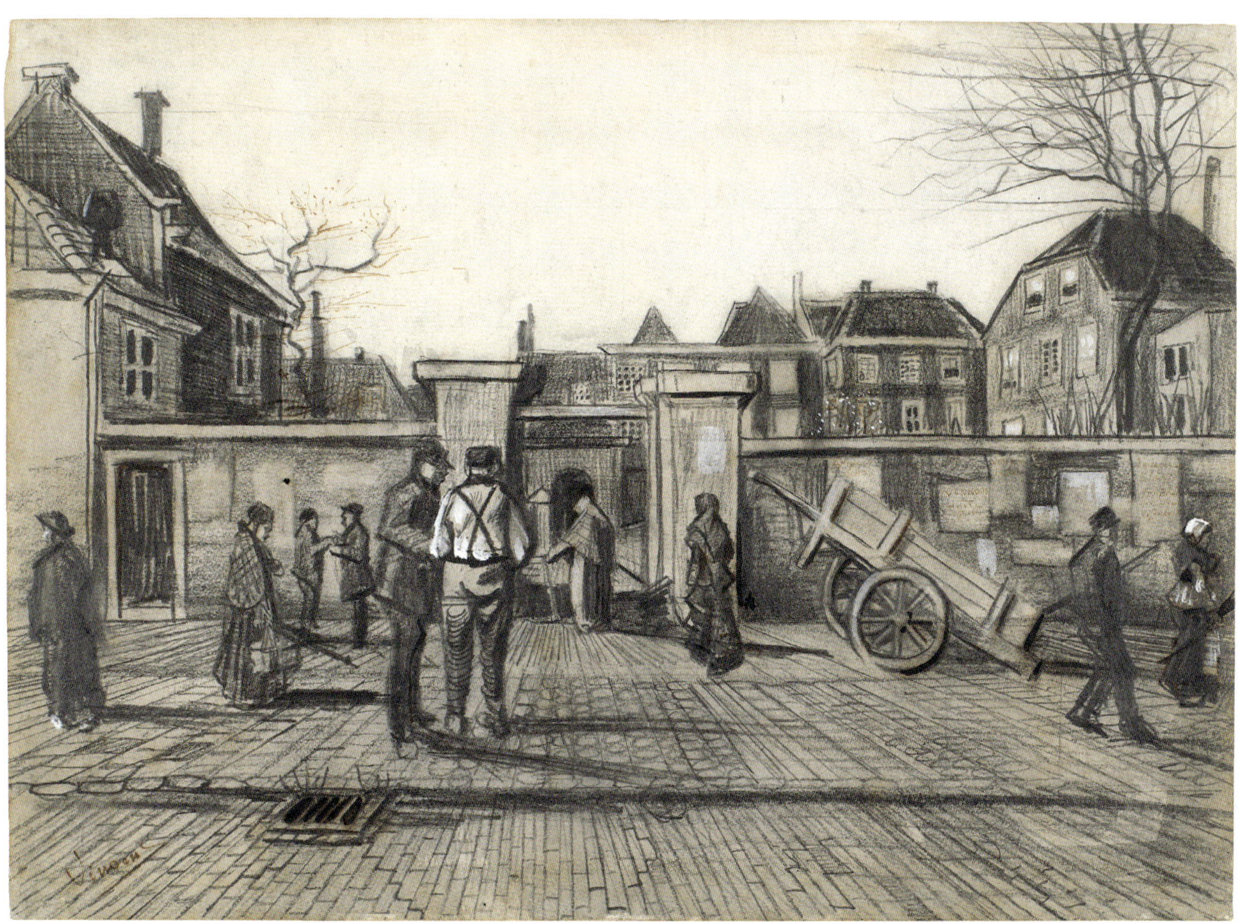

27

Vincent van Gogh (1853–1890)
Bust of a Young Warrior, 1886
Charcoal and black chalk on laid paper, 61.7 x 48.2 cm
Van Gogh Museum, Amsterdam (Vincent van Gogh Foundation), d0169V1962r

28

Vincent van Gogh (1853–1890)
The Entrance to the Pawn Bank, The Hague, 1882
Graphite, pen, brush and ink, watercolour and grey wash on laid paper, 23.9 x 33.7 cm
Van Gogh Museum, Amsterdam (Vincent van Gogh Foundation), d0374V1975

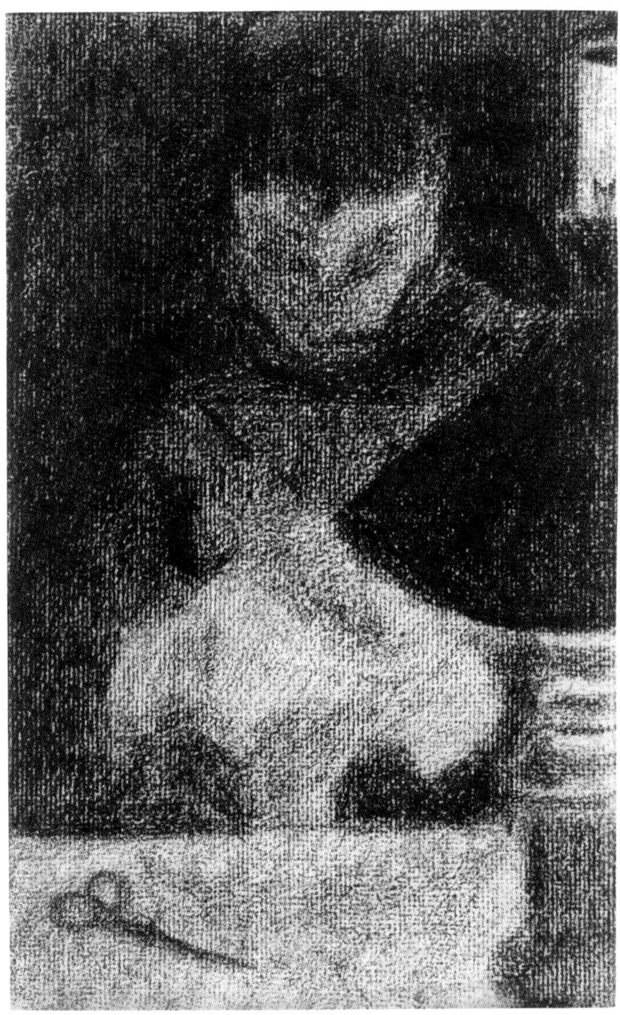

29

Paul Signac (1863–1935)
Woman Sewing (Study for 'The Milliners'), 1885
Black Conté crayon on paper, 25.8 x 16.4 cm
Private collection

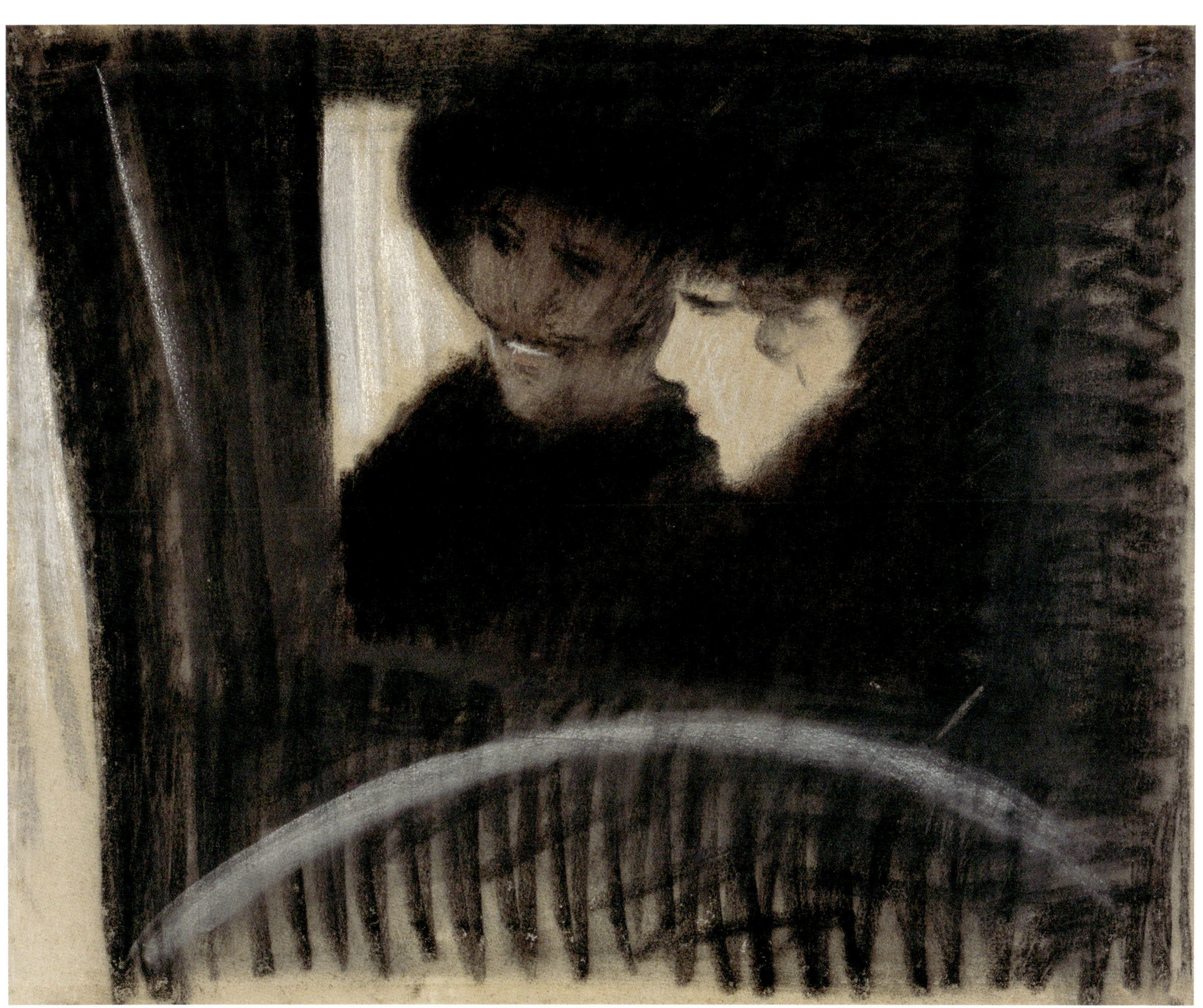

30

Giuseppe de Nittis (1846–1884)
In the Cab, 1880–83
Pastel on canvas, 60 x 73 cm
Pinacoteca Giuseppe de Nittis, Barletta, 924

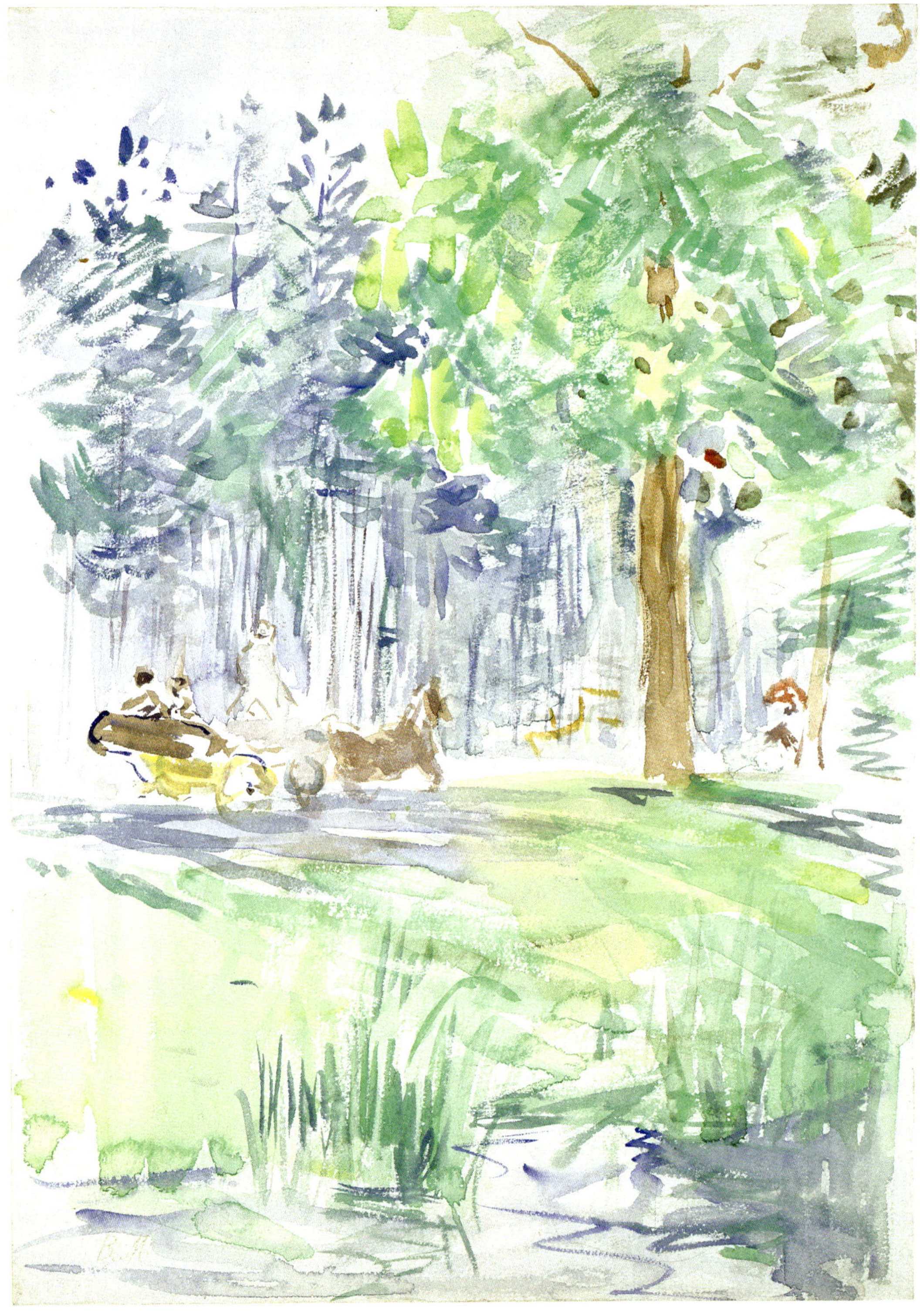

31

Berthe Morisot (1841–1895)
A Horse and Carriage in the Bois de Boulogne, after 1883
Watercolour on wove paper, 28.4 x 20.4 cm
The Ashmolean Museum, University of Oxford.
Bequeathed by Mrs Daisy Turner, 1959, WA1959.4.5

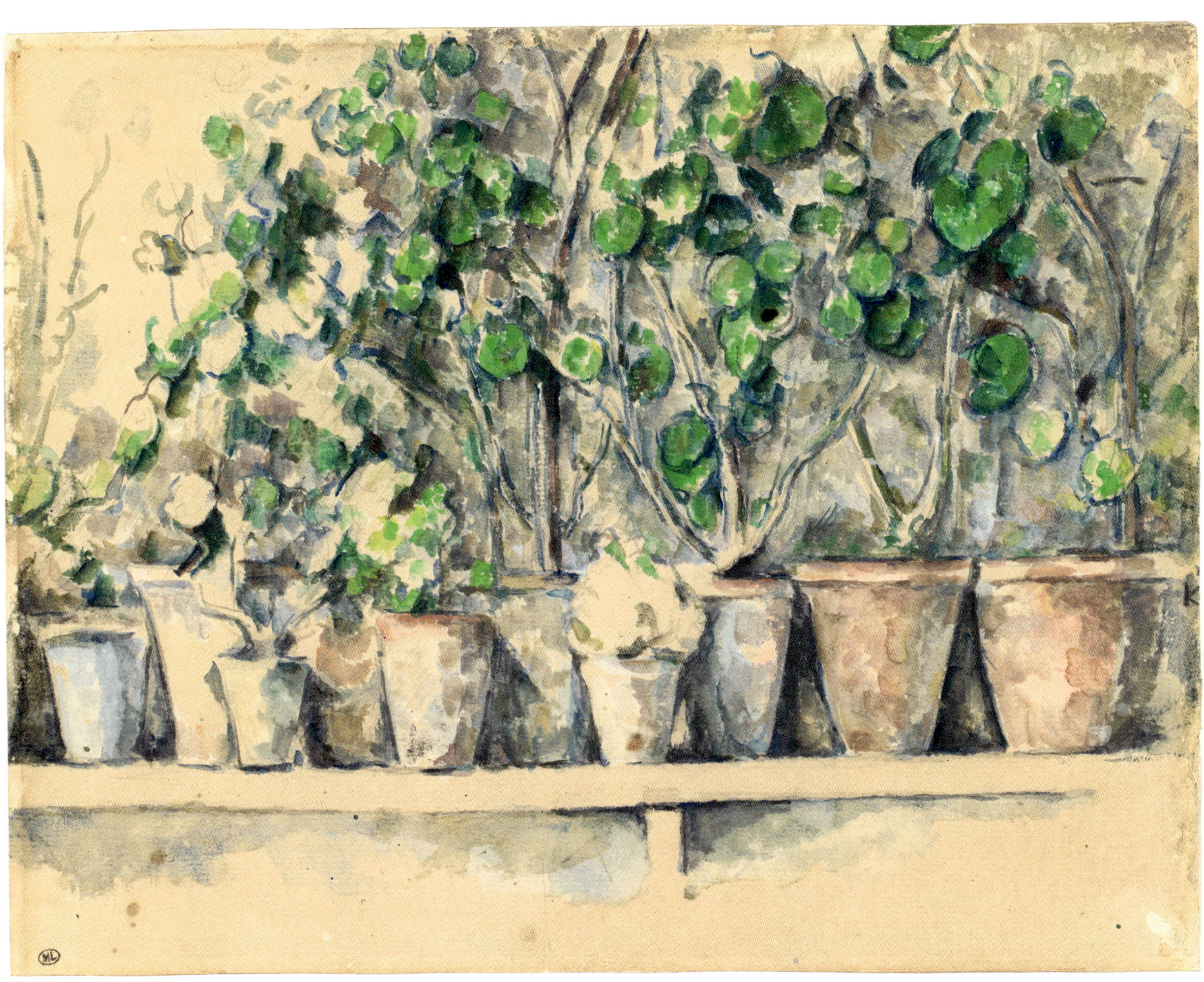

32

Paul Cézanne (1839–1906)
Flowerpots, *c.* 1885
Watercolour over graphite on
laid paper, 23.5 x 30.7 cm
Musée d'Orsay, Paris. Bequeathed by
Comte Isaac de Camondo, 1911, RF 4032

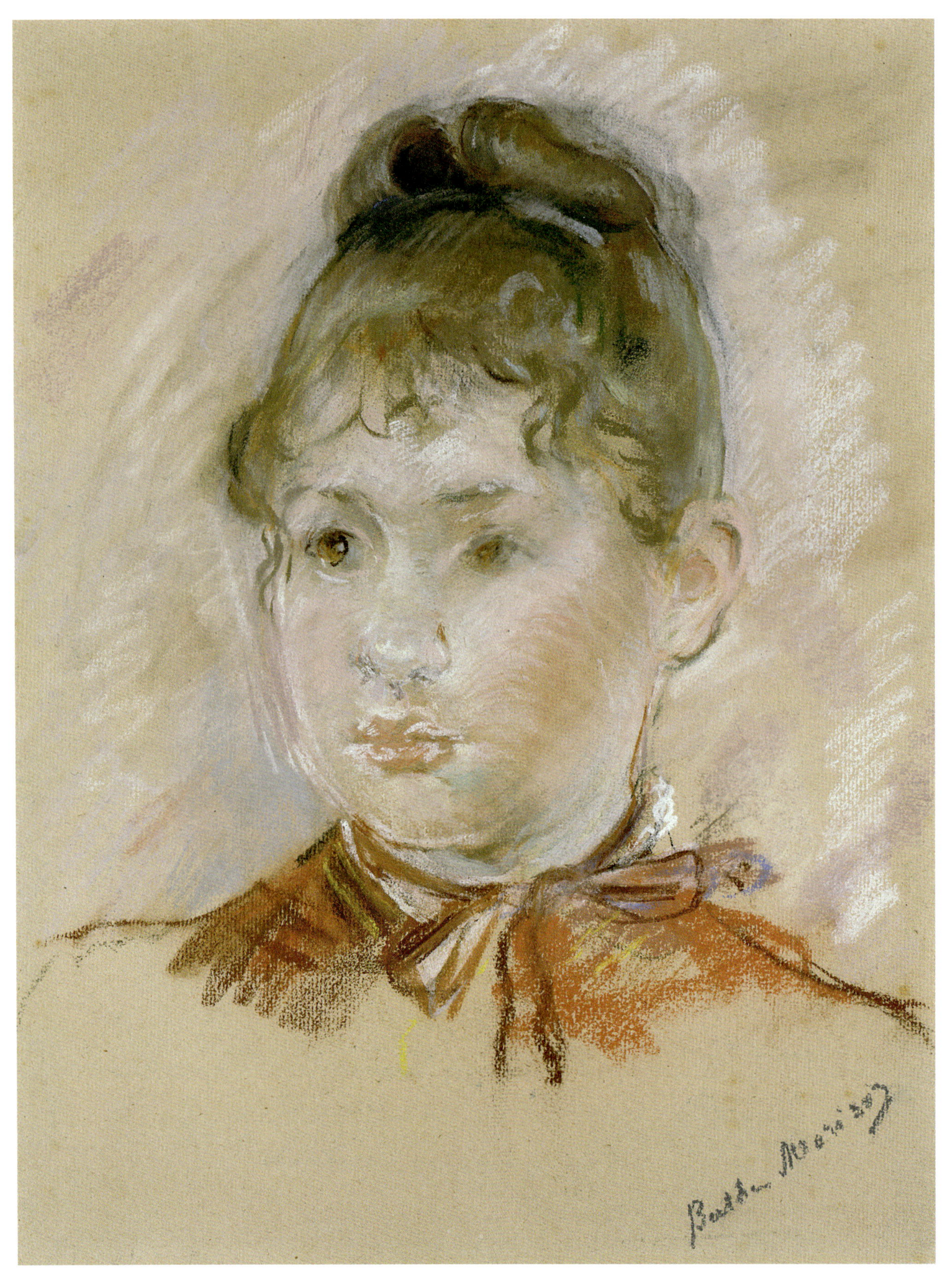

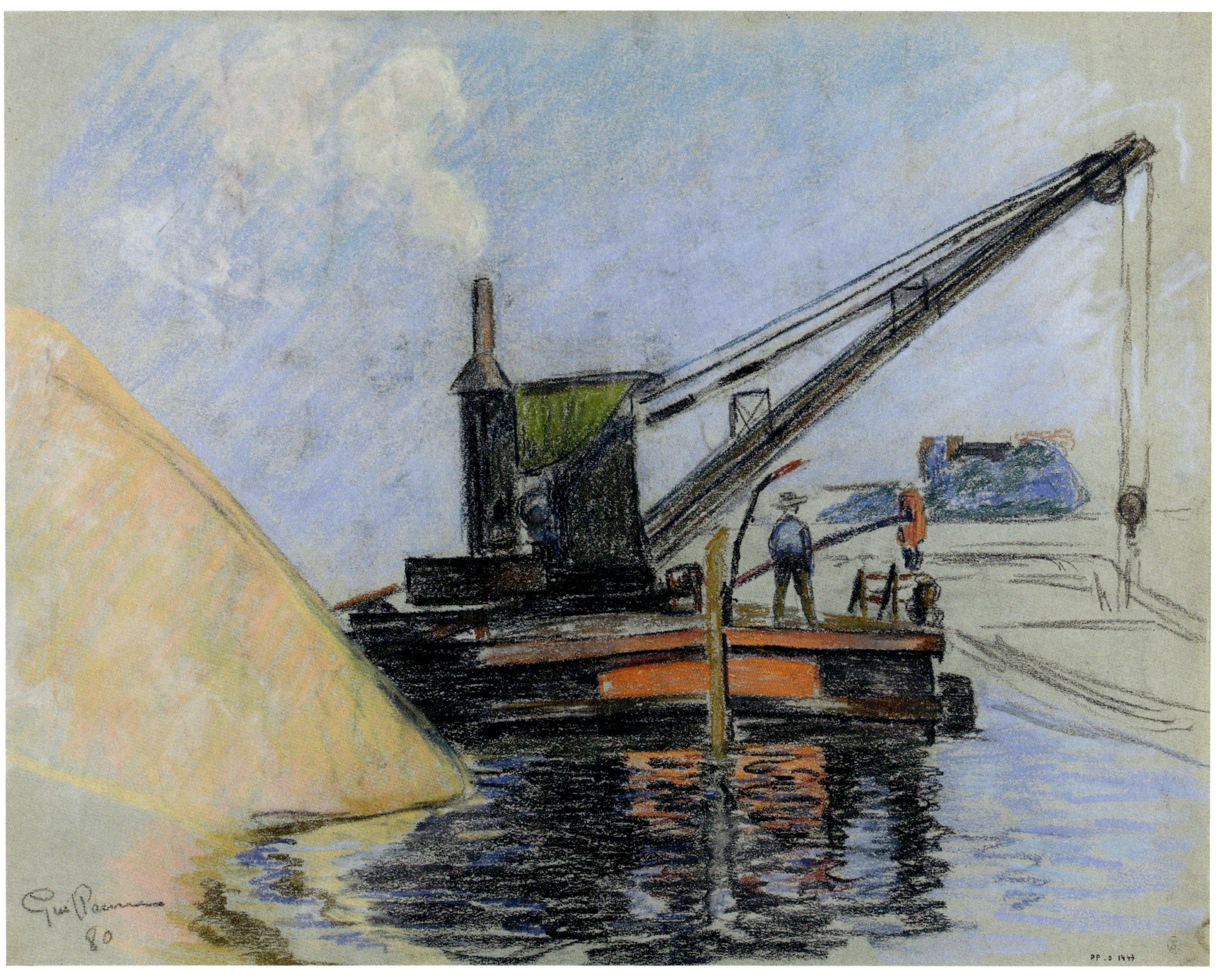

33

Berthe Morisot (1841–1895)
Portrait of Isabelle Lambert, 1885
Pastel on paper, 39 x 37 cm
Sainsbury Centre, University of East Anglia, Norwich, UEA 3

34

Armand Guillaumin (1841–1927)
Crane on the Seine, 1880
Pastel on paper, 49 x 63.5 cm
Petit Palais, Musée des Beaux-Arts de la Ville de Paris. Gifted by Armand Guillaumin, 1922, PPD1443

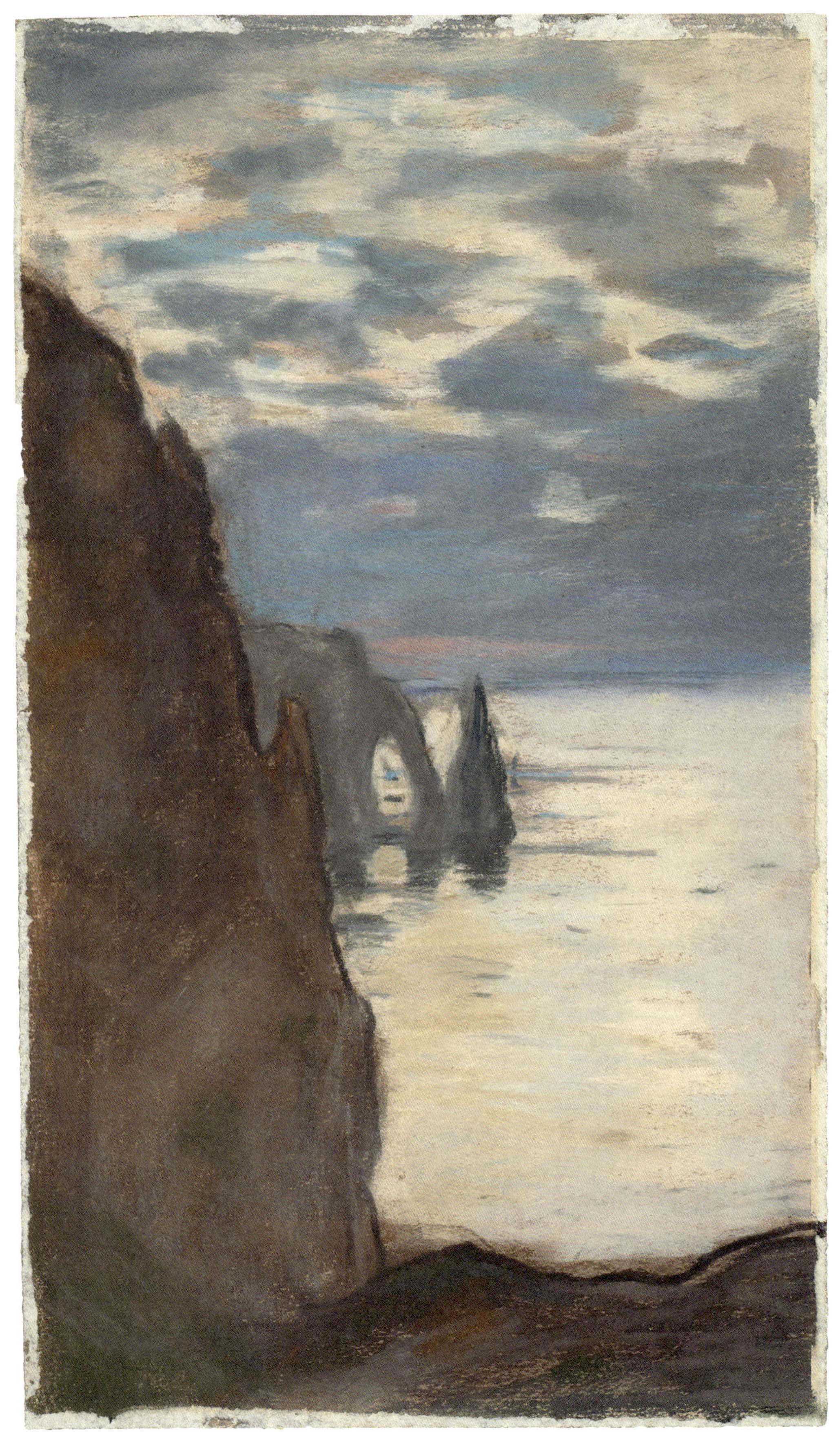

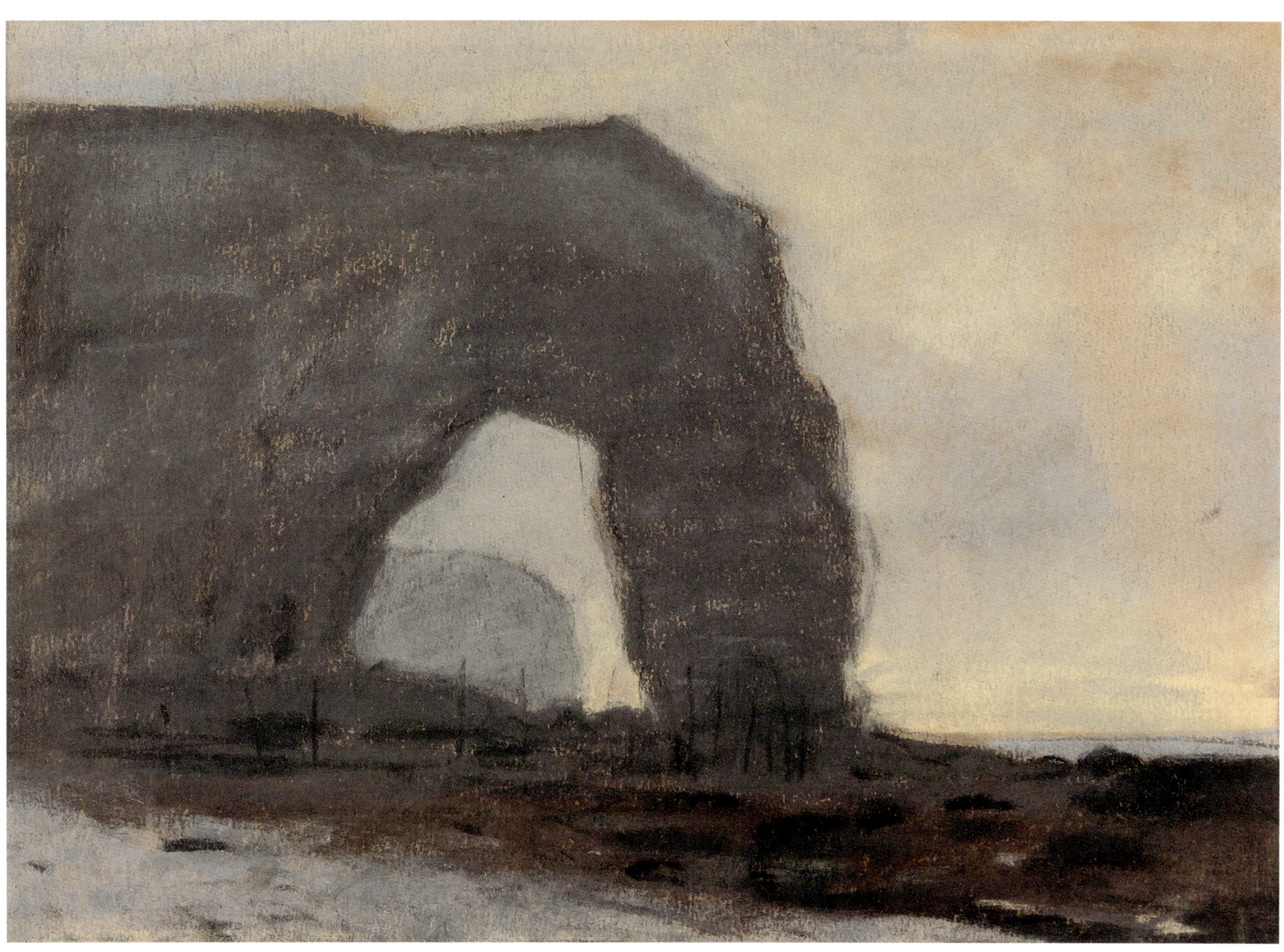

35

Claude Monet (1840–1926)
Cliffs at Etretat: The Needle Rock and Porte d'Aval, *c.* 1885
Pastel on wove paper, 39 x 23 cm
National Galleries of Scotland. Accepted in lieu of Inheritance Tax by HM Government from the estate of Miss Valerie Middleton and allocated to the Scottish National Gallery, 2016, D 5672

36

Claude Monet (1840–1926)
Cliffs at Etretat: The Manneporte at Low Tide, *c.* 1885
Pastel on paper, 24 x 34 cm
Private collection

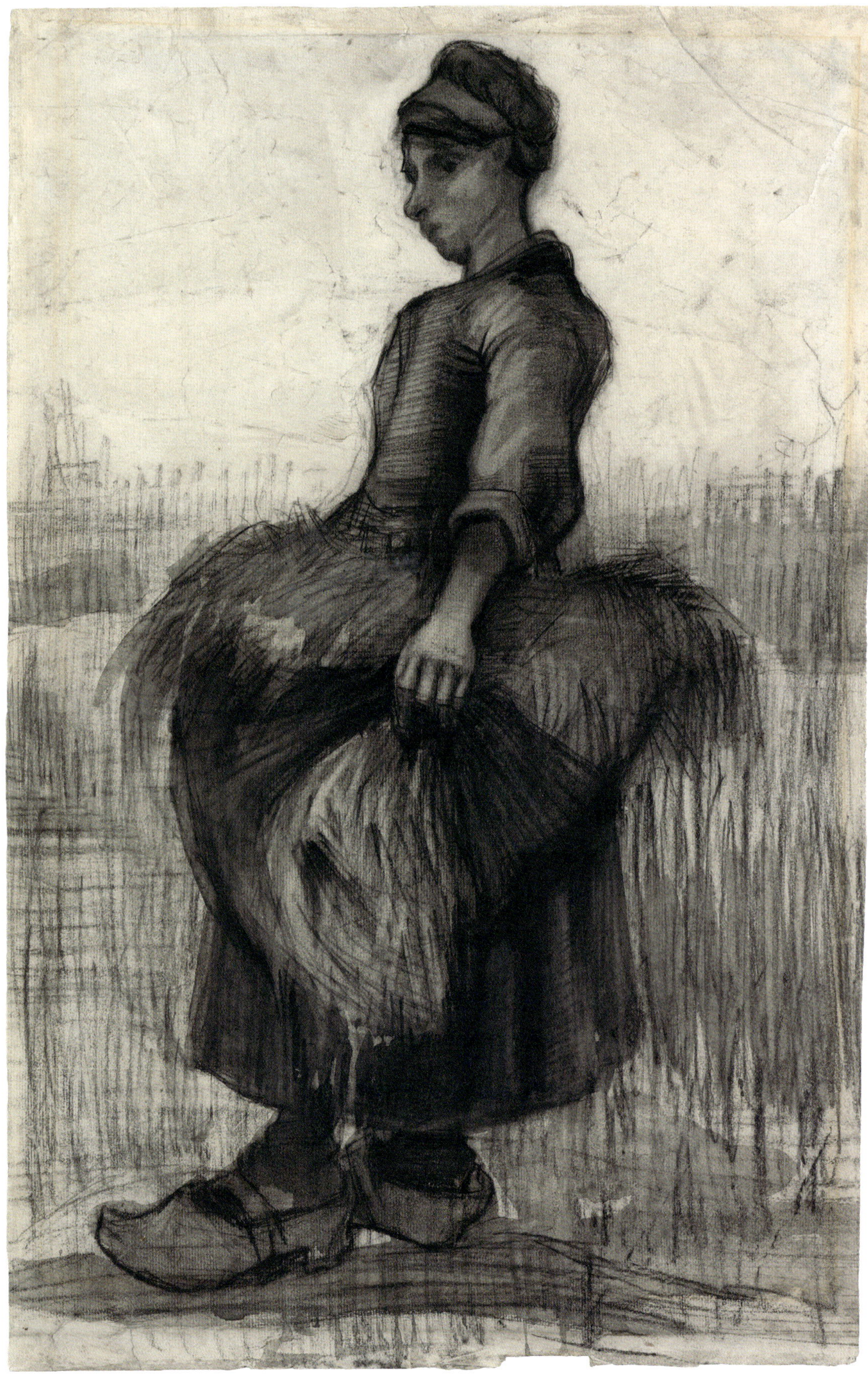

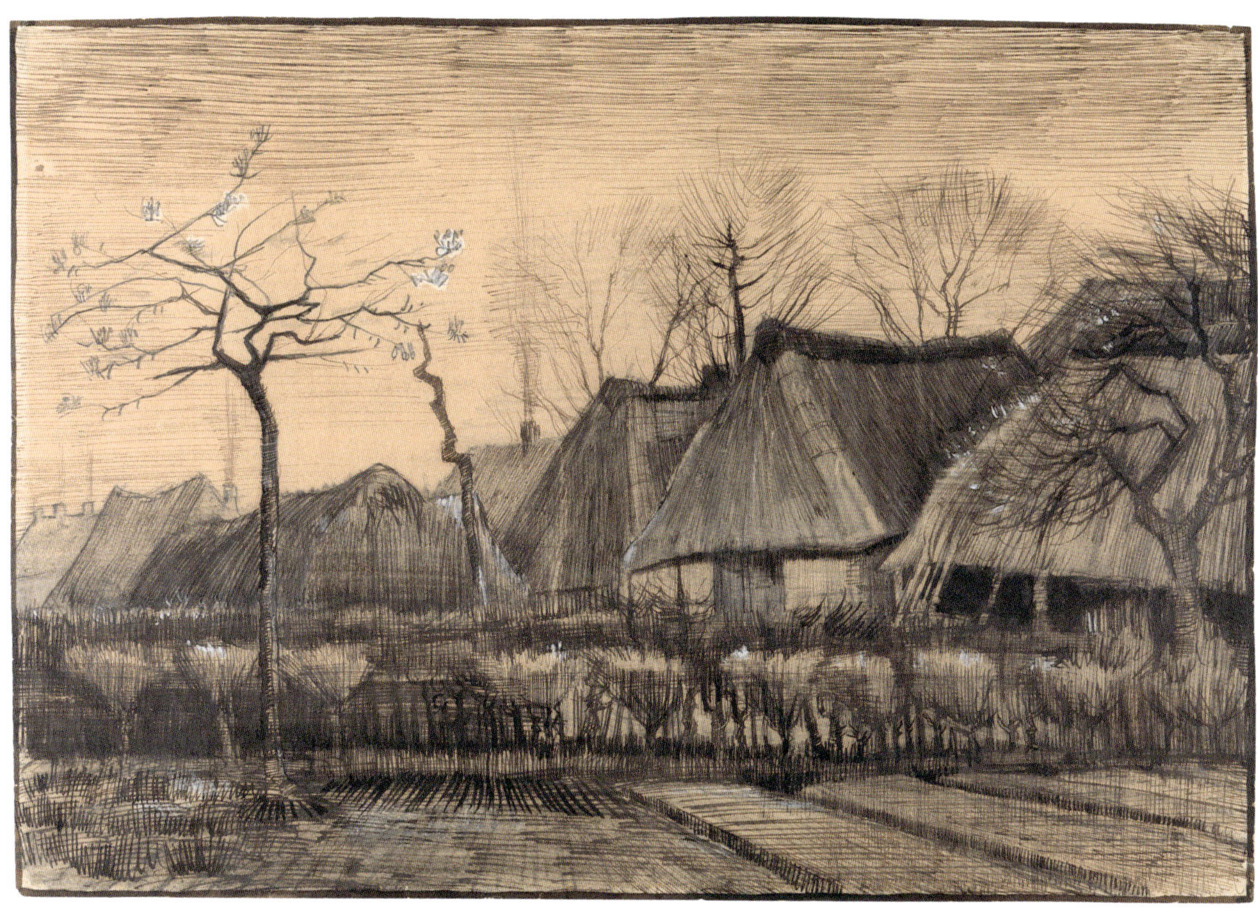

37

Vincent van Gogh (1853–1890)
Peasant Woman Carrying Wheat in Her Apron, July–August 1885
Black chalk, grey wash and gouache on laid paper, 58.2 x 38 cm
Kröller-Müller Museum, Otterlo, KM 112.766

38

Vincent van Gogh (1853–1890)
Thatched Roofs, 1884
Ink, graphite and gouache on paper, 30.5 x 44.8 cm
Tate: Bequeathed by C. Frank Stoop, 1933, N04715

39

Odilon Redon (1840–1916)
Two Human-headed Flowers in a Vase, 1880
Charcoal on paper on board, 44.2 x 32 cm
Private collection, Vienna

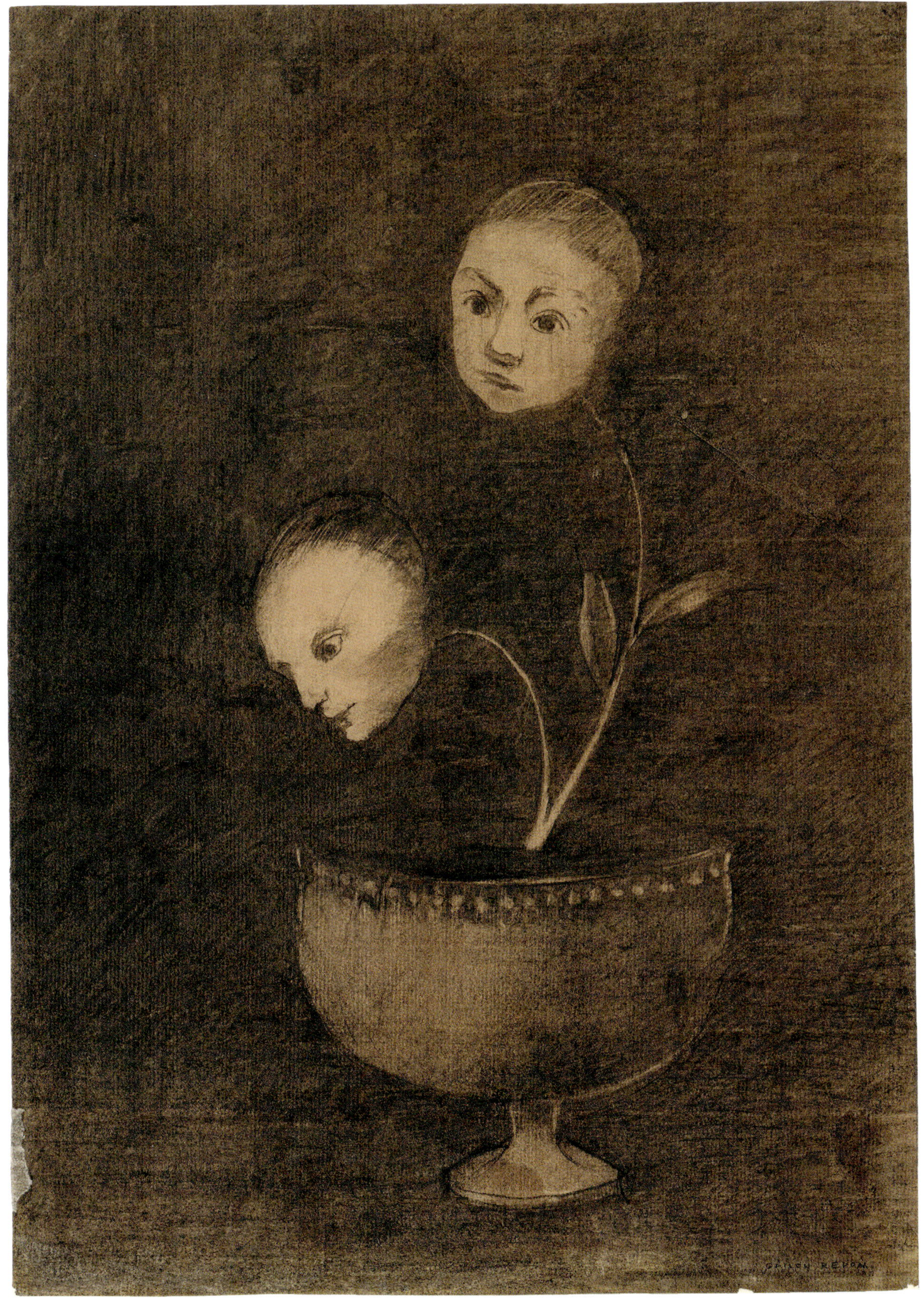

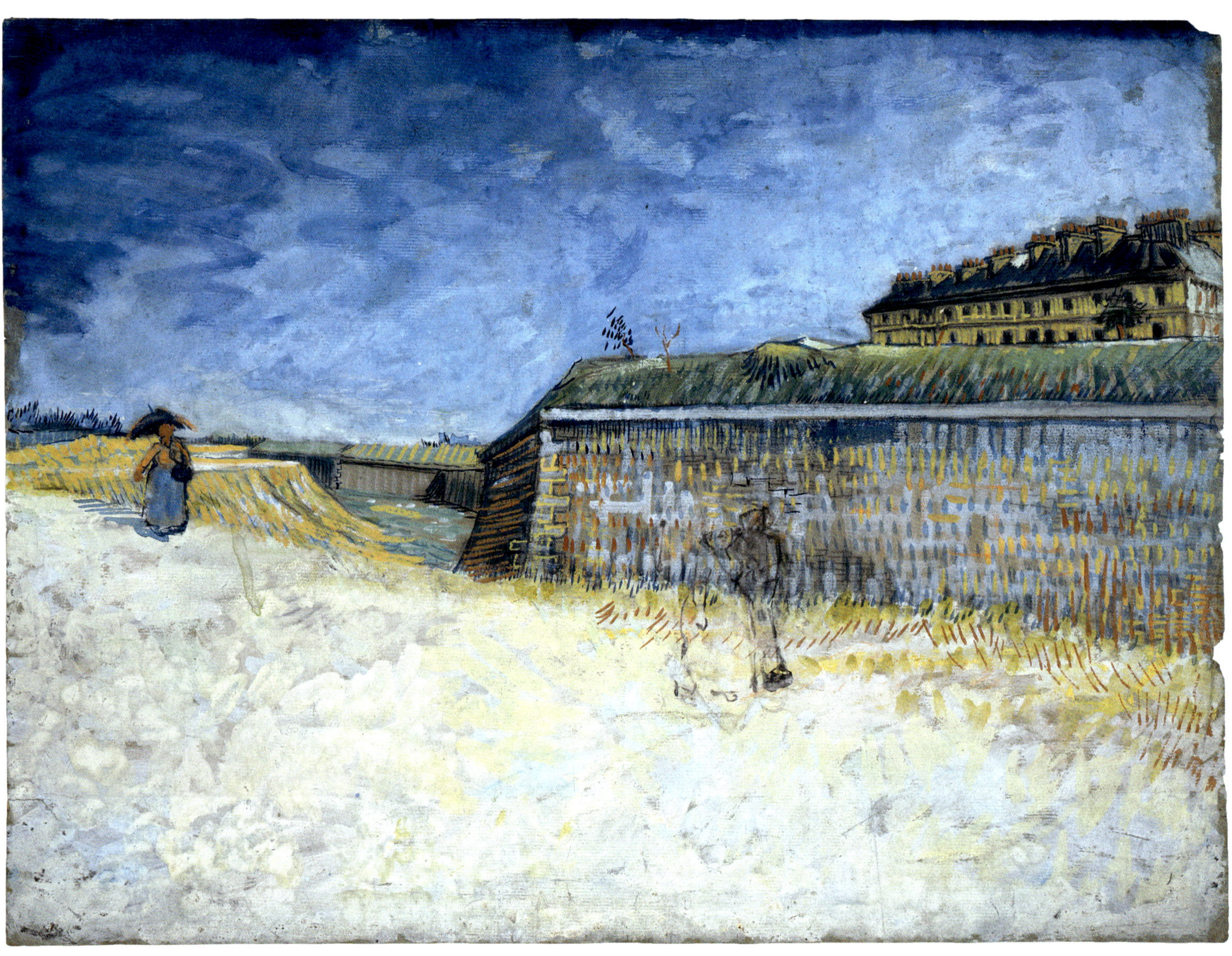

40

Vincent van Gogh (1853–1890)
The Fortifications of Paris with Houses, 1887
Graphite, black chalk, watercolour
and gouache on paper, 38.7 x 53.4 cm
The Whitworth, The University of Manchester, D.1927.4

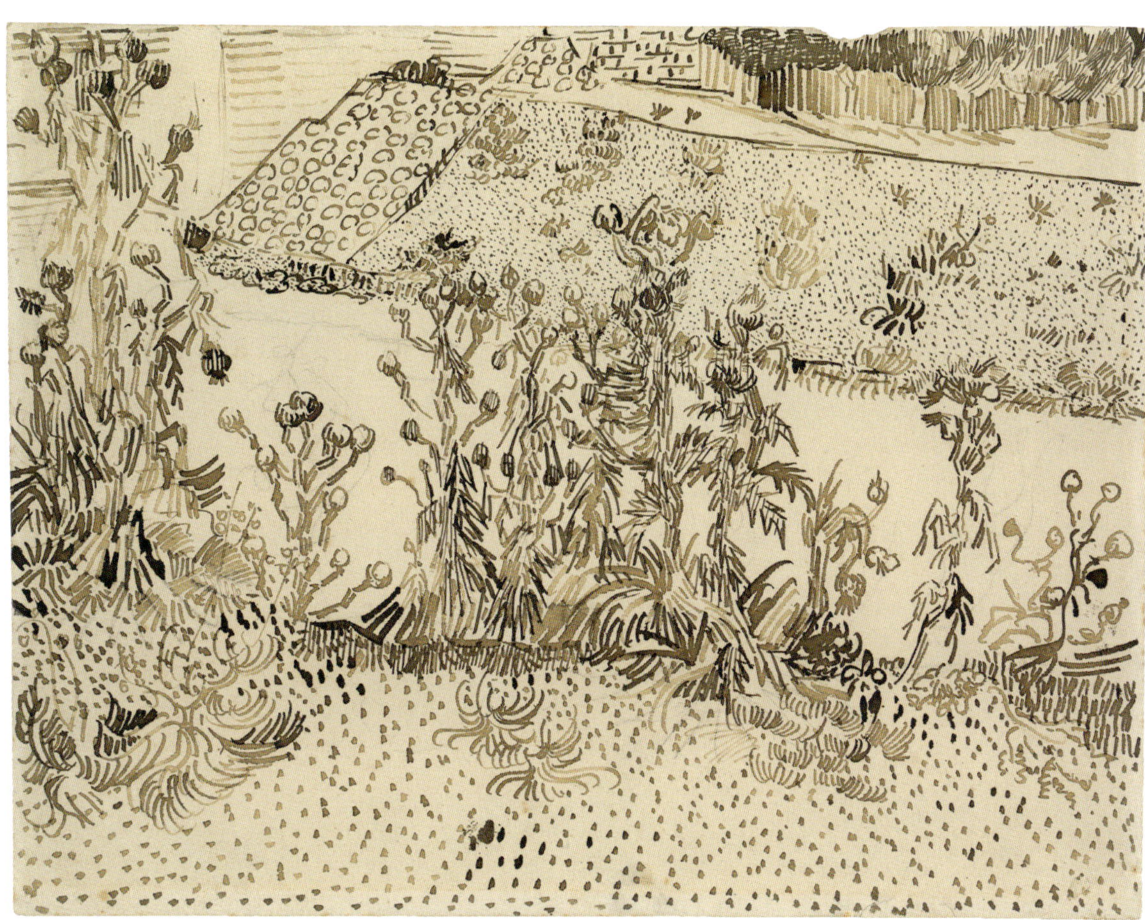

41

Vincent van Gogh (1853–1890)
Thistles by the Roadside, August 1888
Graphite, pen, reed pen and ink
on wove paper, 24.4 x 32 cm
Van Gogh Museum, Amsterdam
(Vincent van Gogh Foundation), d0422V1962

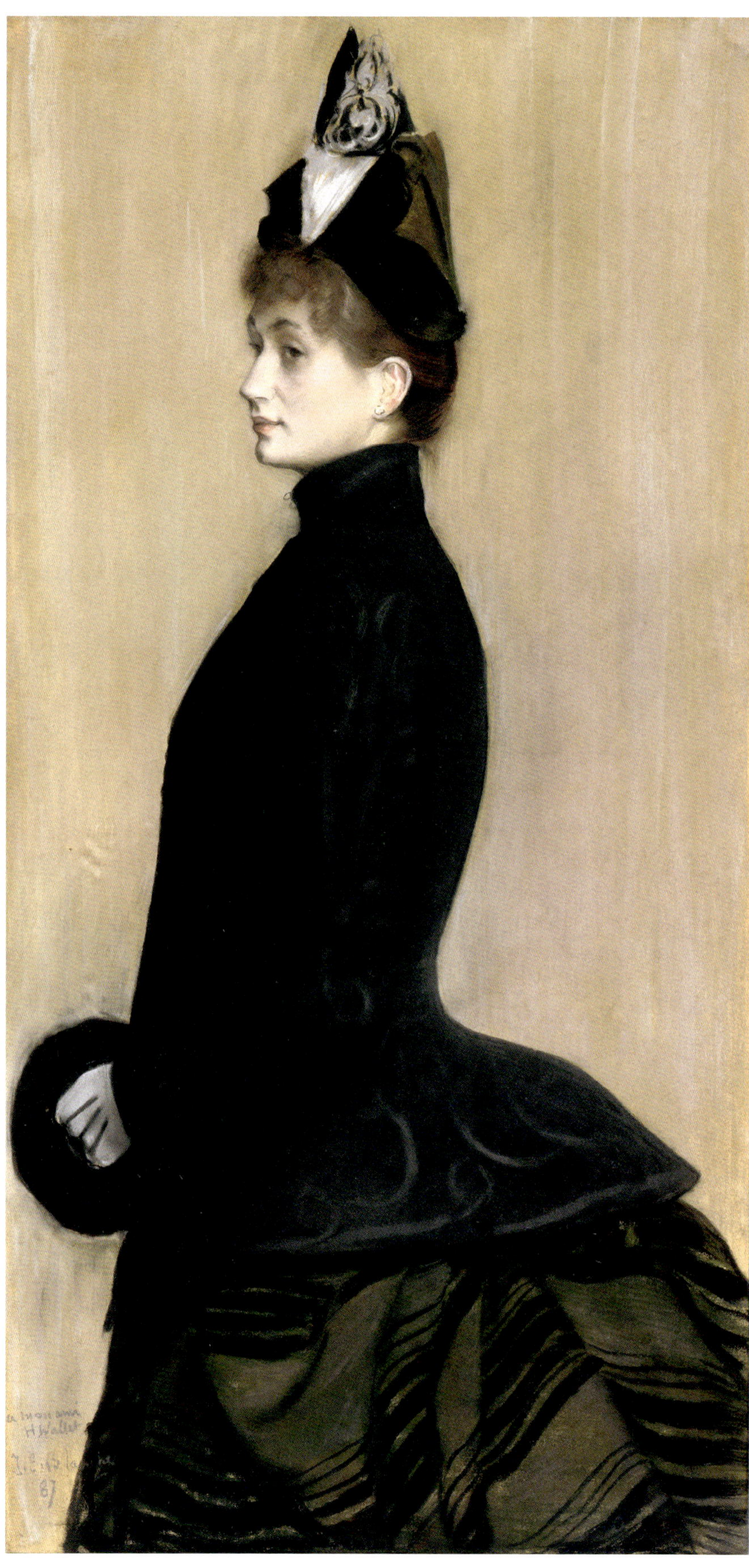

42

Jacques-Emile Blanche (1861–1942)
Portrait of Madame Henri Wallet, 1887
Pastel on canvas, 129 x 64 cm
Musée d'Orsay, Paris, RF 43327

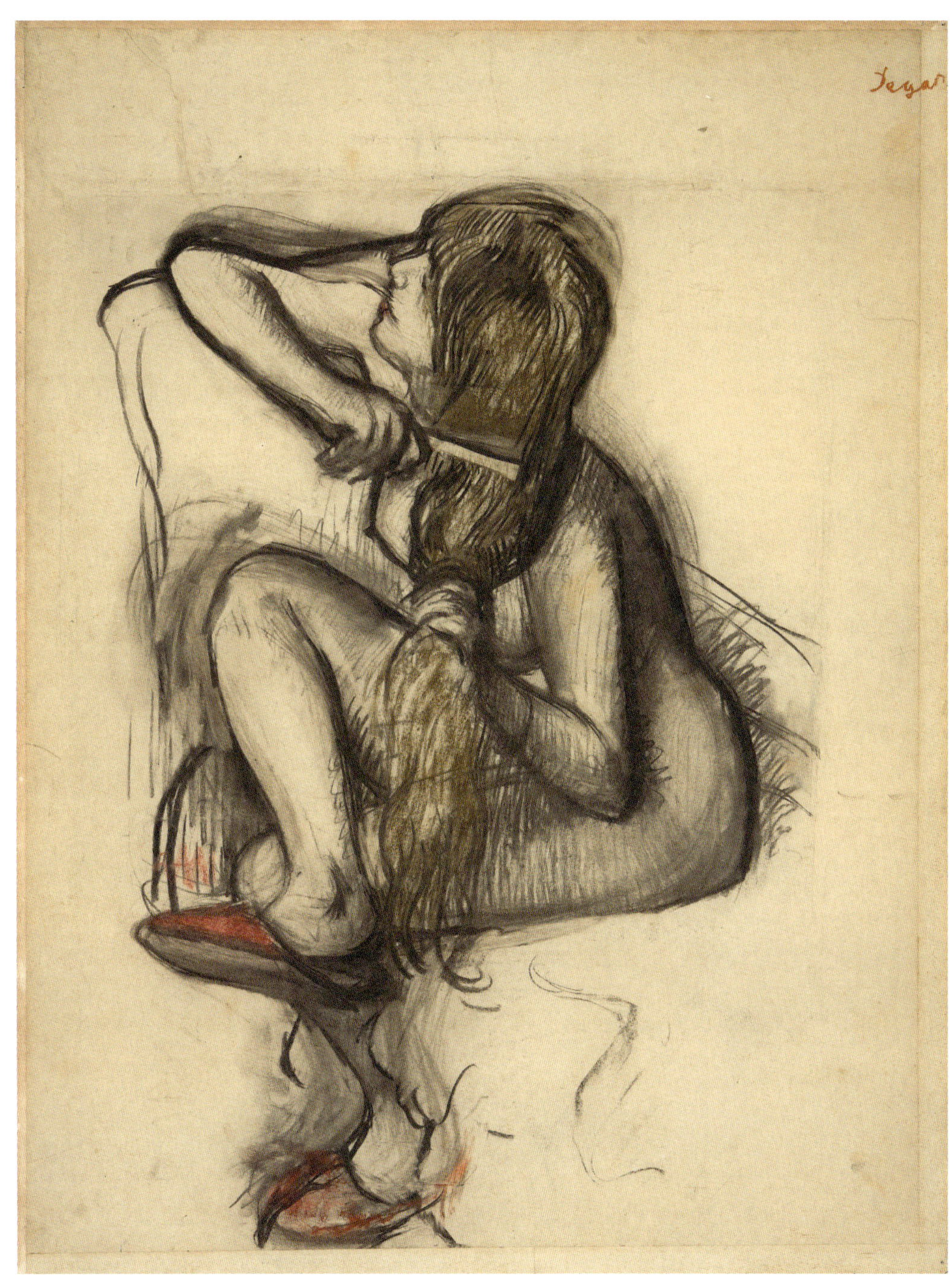

43

Edgar Degas (1834–1917)
Woman Combing Her Hair, *c.* 1887–90
Charcoal and red and brown chalk on tracing paper laid down on board, 109 x 83 cm
Pallant House Gallery, Chichester. Accepted by HM Government in Lieu of Inheritance Tax from the estate of Stephen Brod and allocated to Pallant House Gallery (2016), CHCPH 2892

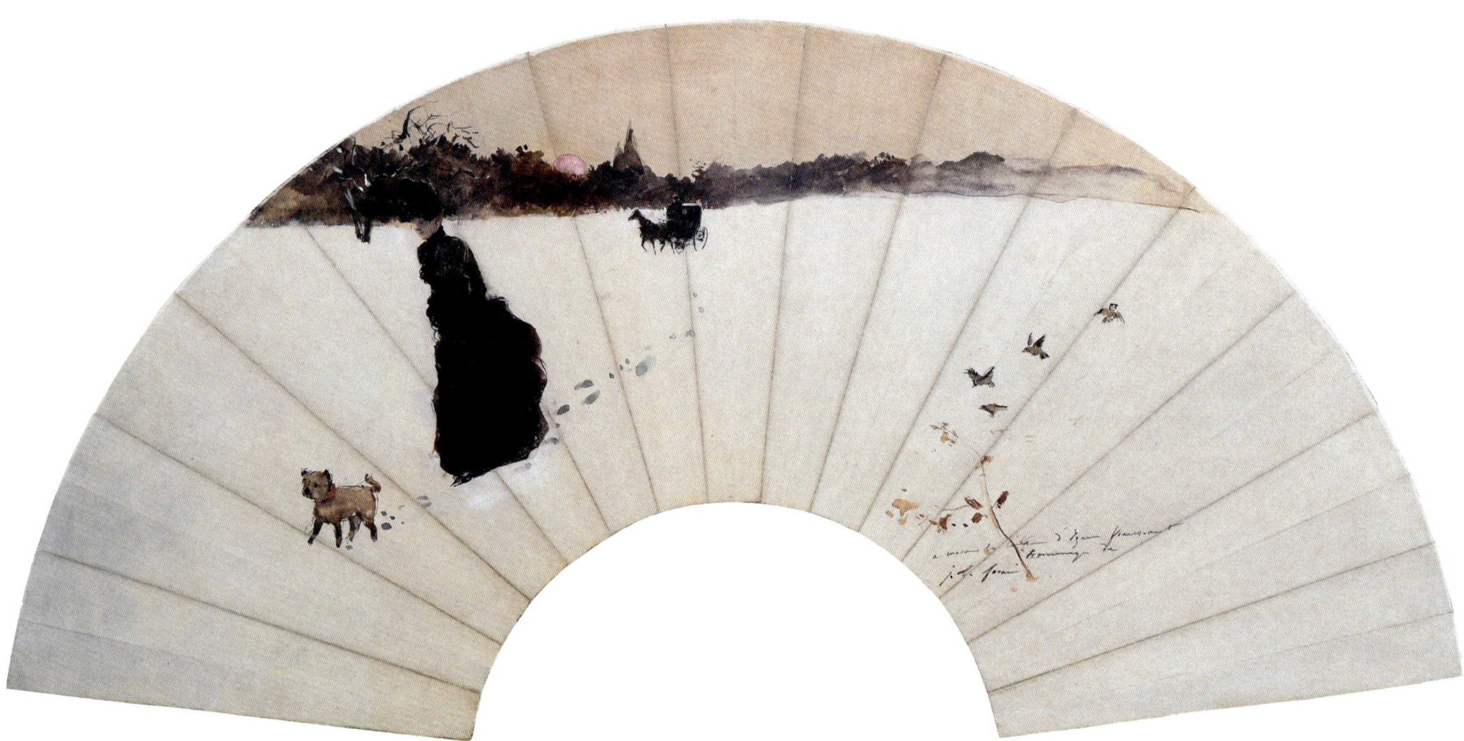

44

Jean-Louis Forain (1852–1931)
Walk in the Snow, *c.* 1885–88
Watercolour, ink wash and gouache highlights on paper, 20 x 62 cm
Private collection

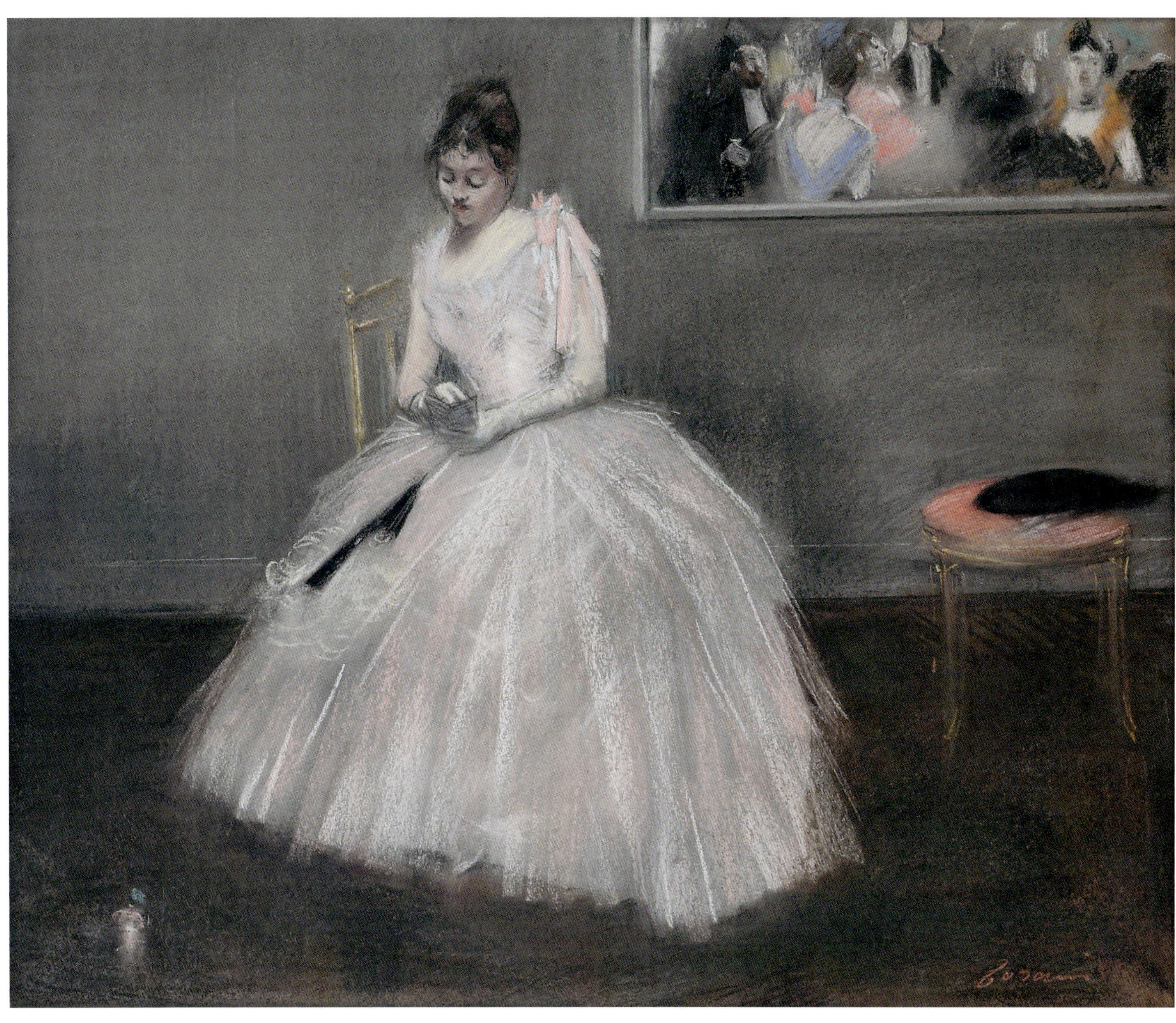

45

Jean-Louis Forain (1852–1931)
Dance Card, *c.* 1888
Pastel on paper mounted on canvas, 50 x 61 cm
Private collection

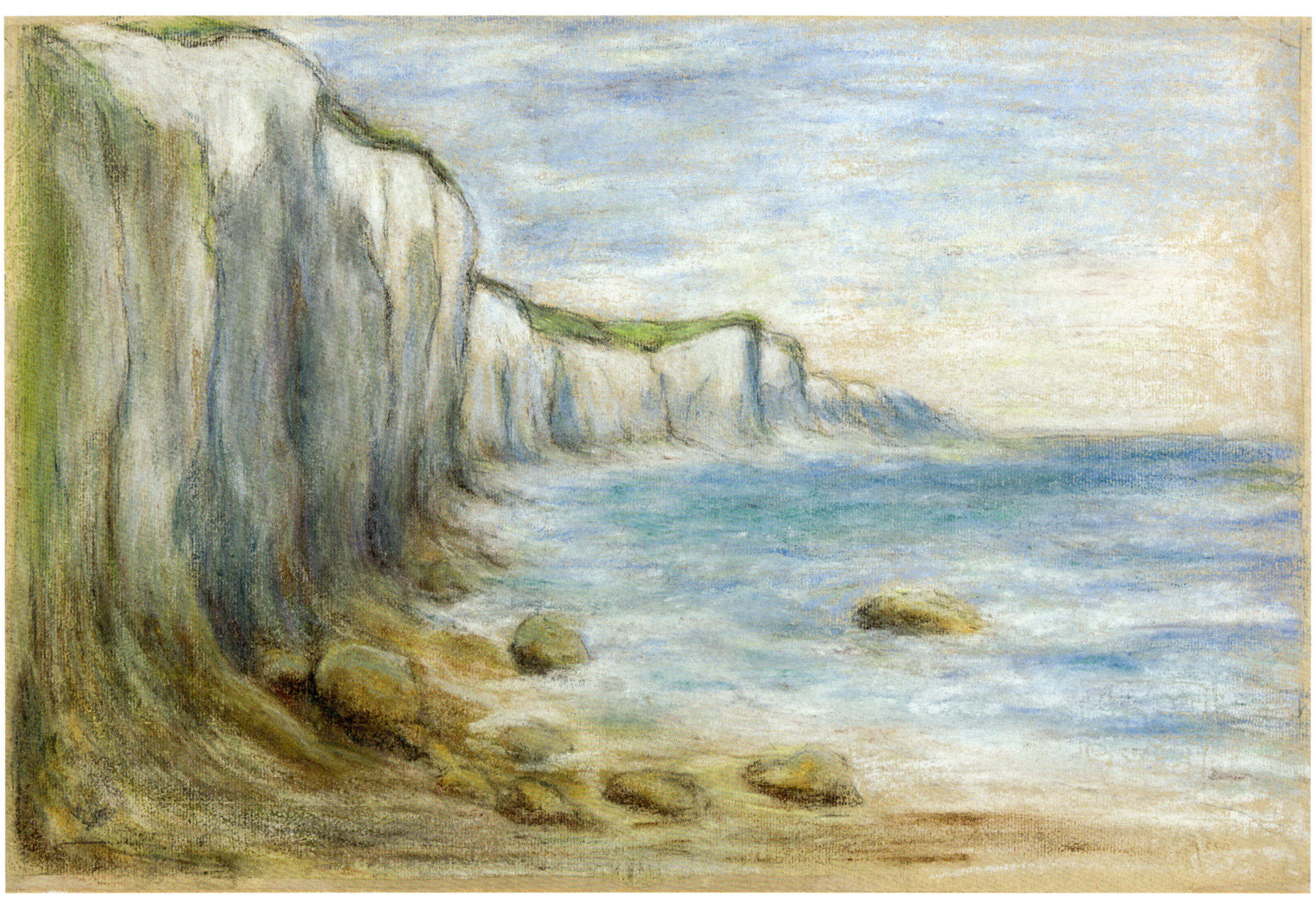

46

Emile Schuffenecker (1851–1934)
Coastal Cliffs, Normandy, *c*. 1880s–early 1890s
Pastel on paper, 30 x 45.7 cm
Stephen Ongpin Fine Art, London

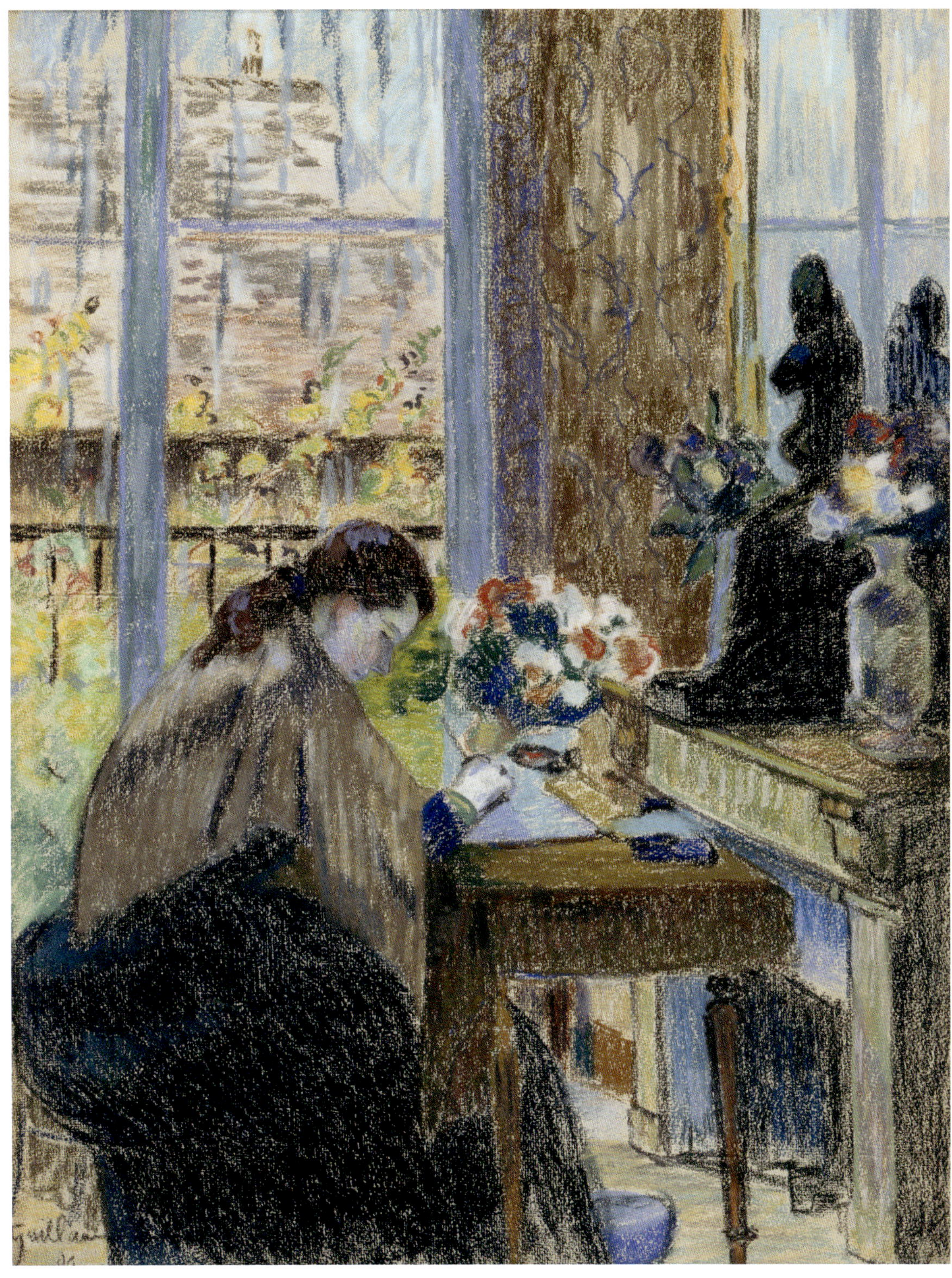

47

Armand Guillaumin (1841–1927)
Interior, 1889
Pastel on laid paper, 61.2 x 47.3 cm
Musée d'Orsay, Paris, RF 12298

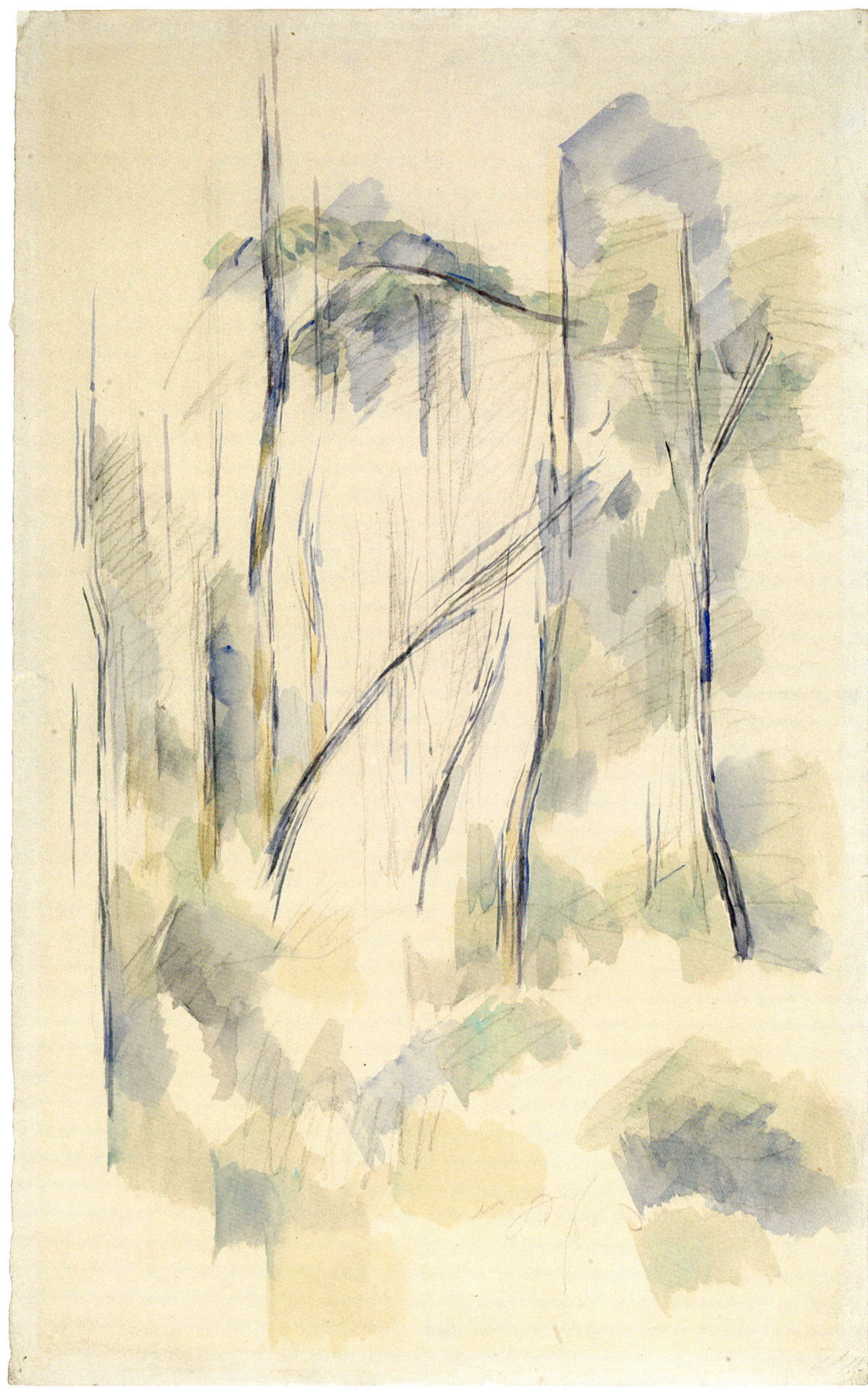

48

Paul Cézanne (1839–1906)
Study of Trees, *c.* 1888–90
Graphite and watercolour on wove paper, 49.5 x 32.1 cm
Victoria and Albert Museum, London.
Purchased with Art Fund support, P.6-1966

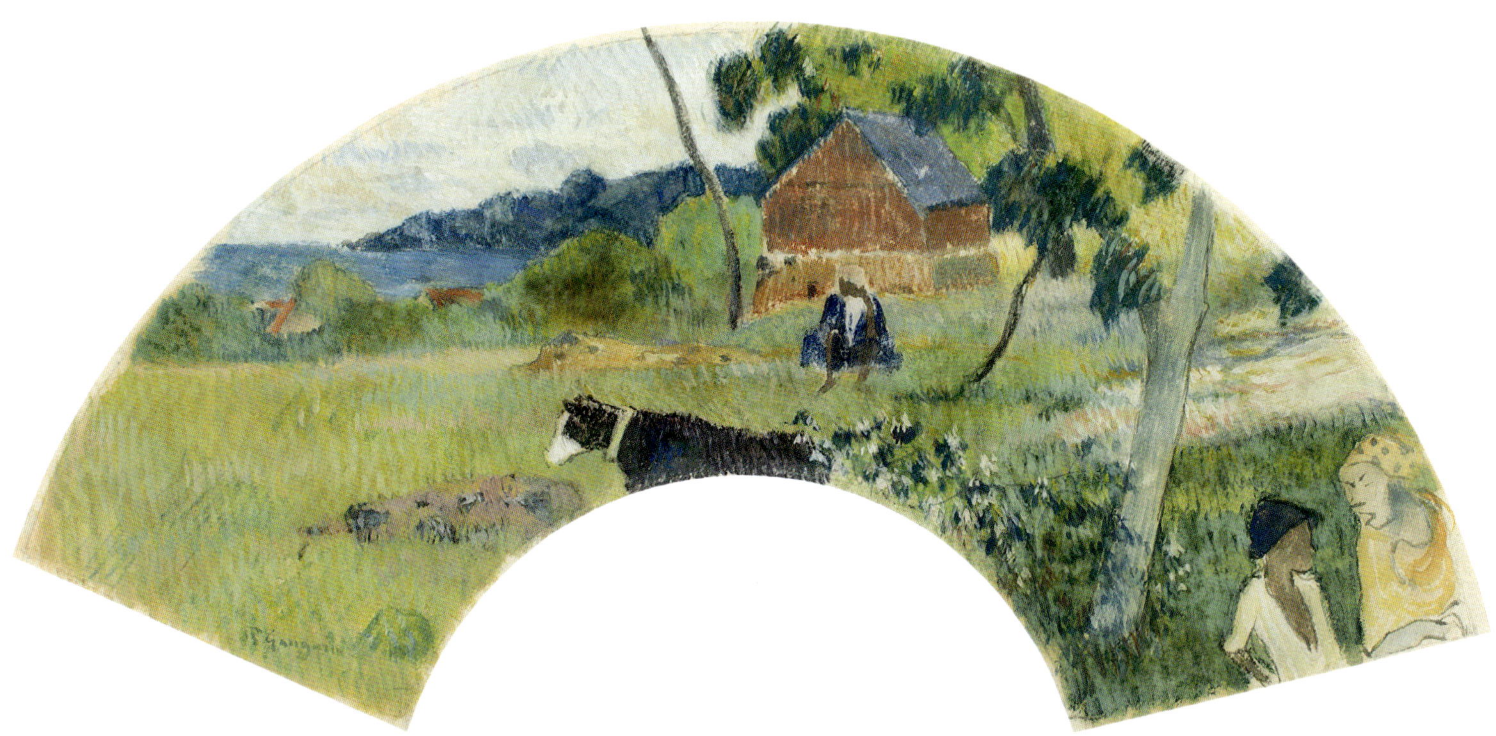

49

Paul Gauguin (1848–1903)
Landscape in Martinique, 1887
Watercolour, gouache and pastel on paper, 20 x 42 cm
The Fan Museum Trust Collection, London, LDFAN2006.16

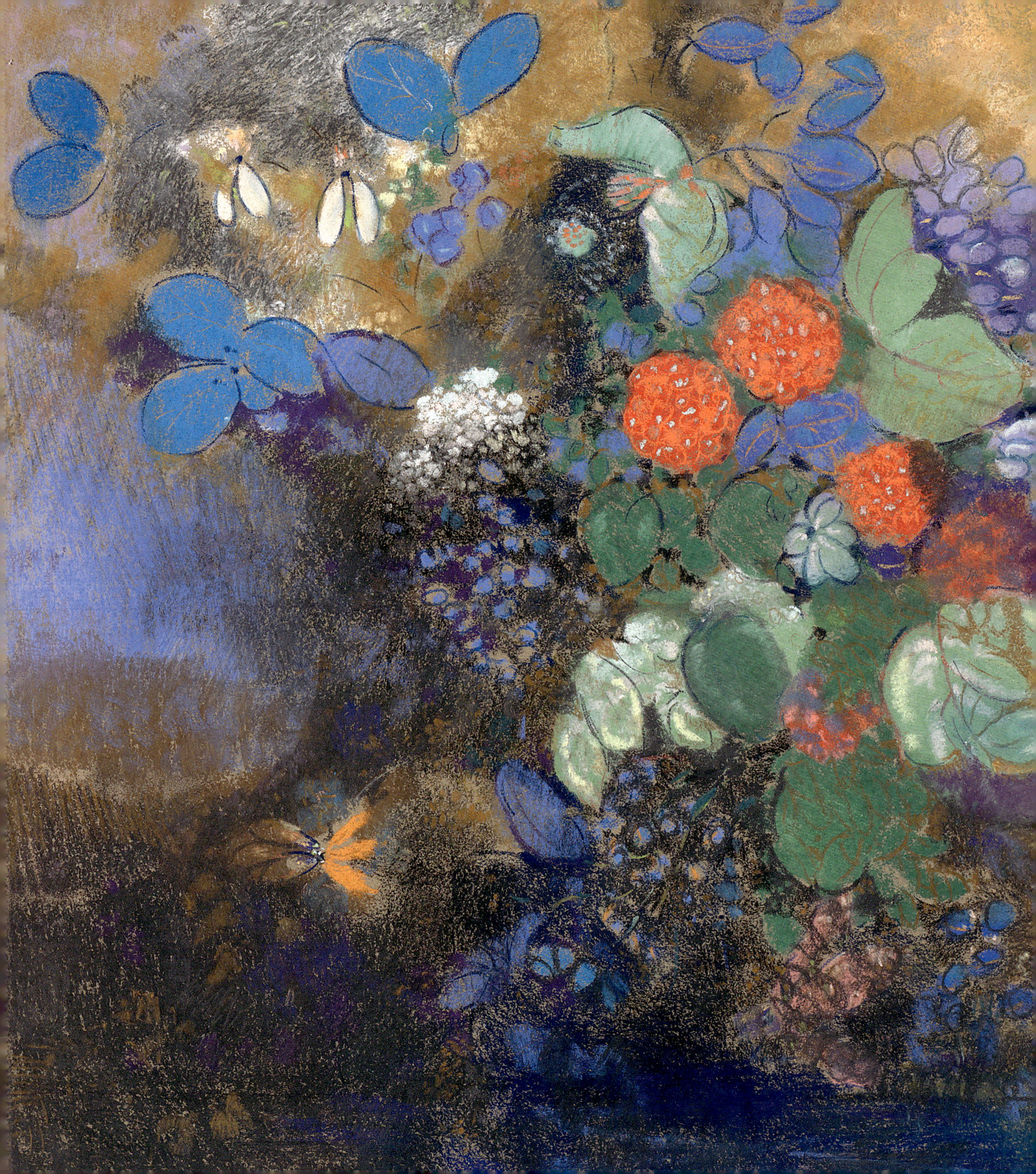

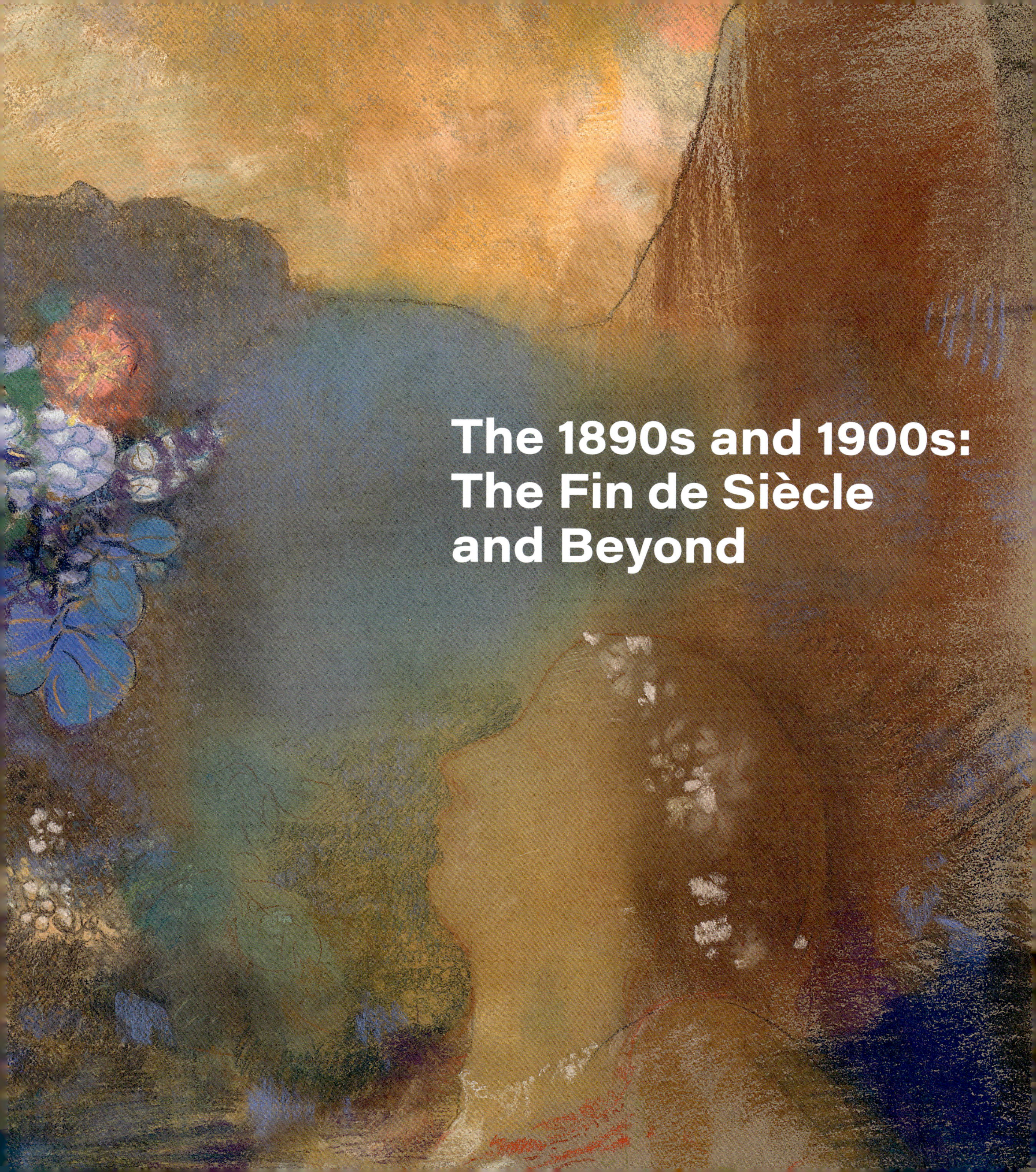

The 1890s and 1900s: The Fin de Siècle and Beyond

The last decade of the nineteenth century saw an ever-growing appreciation of works on paper. Exhibitions proliferated.

Many artists pursued the innovations of the previous decade, such as pointillism, a technique based on the application of small dots of pure colour to achieve an effect of shimmering light. Georges Seurat pioneered this style, which was pursued by several adherents, among them Hippolyte Petitjean (cat. 74).

The 1890s were the golden age of pastel. Degas, who excelled both as a draughtsman and a colourist, found in it the ideal medium in which to draw with colour, creating rich, chromatic effects by superimposing and fixing layers of powdery pigment. This is exemplified in *Dancers on a Bench* (cat. 54), one of his last and greatest renderings of a ballet scene, and in the classical subject of the female nude (cat. 55) that increasingly preoccupied him in his final years. Degas's remarkable achievements in pastel were echoed by other artists, notably his close friend the American Mary Cassatt (cat. 62) and the Italian Federico Zandomeneghi (cats 56, 61).

Like Degas, Paul Cézanne understood the fusion of line and colour, observing: 'Drawing and colour are not distinct from one another; gradually as one paints, one draws; the more harmonious the colours are, the more precise the drawing will be.' He focused on landscape and nature, evoking a timeless world in his exquisite late watercolours. In these deeply felt and meditative works, Cézanne, with great refinement, exploited the intrinsic properties of the medium (cats 71, 73). He often made his spare strokes of translucent colour more eloquent by leaving the paper around them blank.

Henri de Toulouse-Lautrec, a graphic artist of outstanding originality, created unforgettable images of the circus (cat. 58) and the urban underworld of Montmartre (cats 63, 64), as well as arresting portraits, such as that of a Montmartre *demi-mondaine* (cat. 57). Exceptionally inventive, he explored a variety of techniques often using humble cardboard as a support, partly because it was inexpensive but also because its absorbency permitted the matte surfaces he favoured to enhance his trenchant line and broad zones of bold colour.

Whereas Toulouse-Lautrec, like the Impressionists, drew inspiration from modern urban life, other artists of the 1890s rejected modernity, especially those involved with the literary movement Symbolism. Paul Gauguin conveyed the allure of the South Seas in a variety of graphic techniques (cats 59, 60, 75). Odilon Redon declared that his aim was to put 'the visible at the service of the invisible'. In his velvety black charcoal drawings, the 'noirs' (cat. 65), and later in such brilliantly colourful pastels as *Ophelia Among the Flowers* (cat. 77), he takes us into an esoteric, poetic world drawn from religion, literature, imagination and dreams.

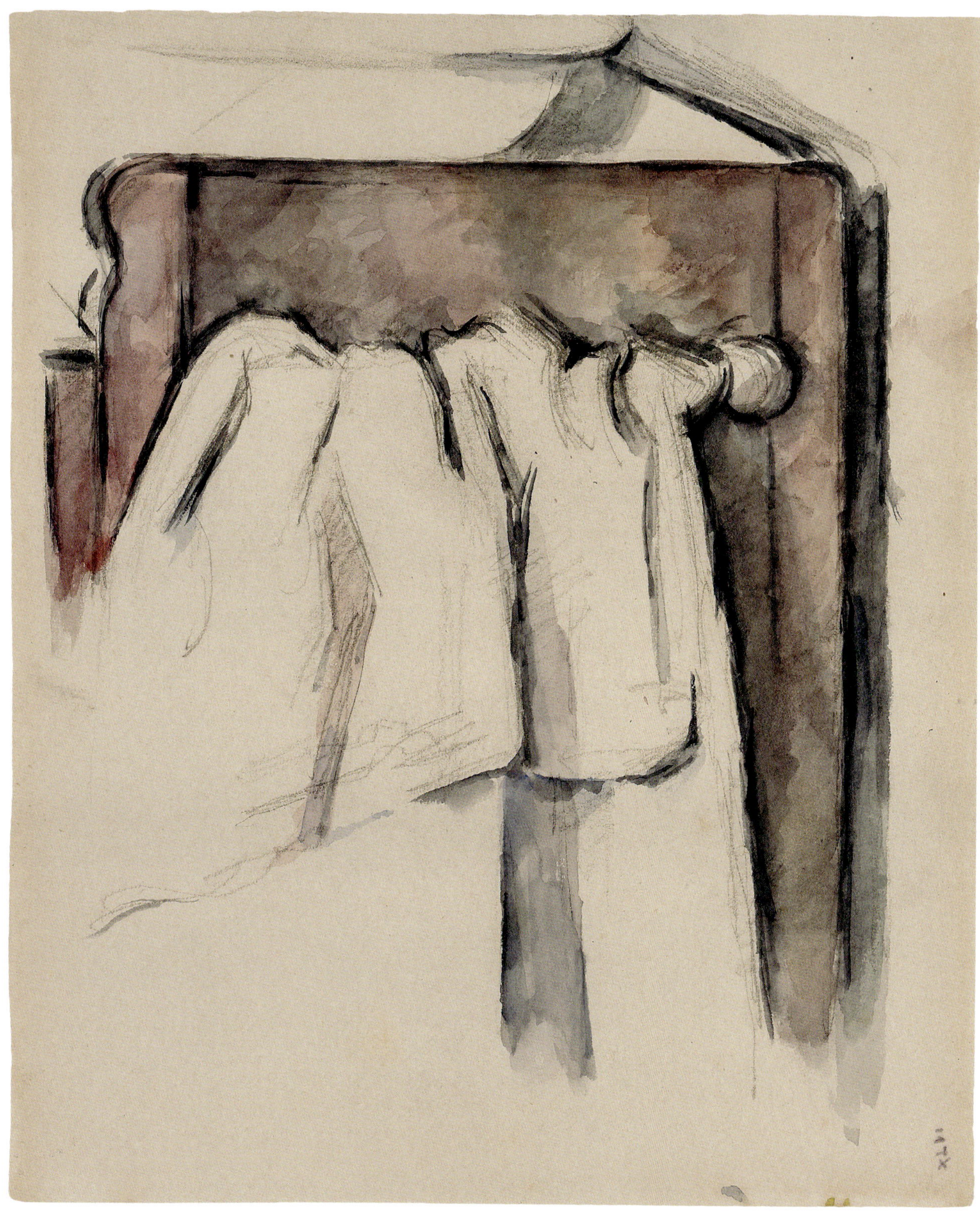

50

Paul Cézanne (1839–1906)
Dressing Table, *c.* 1890
Watercolour over graphite on paper, 25.6 x 21 cm
Collection of David Lachenmann

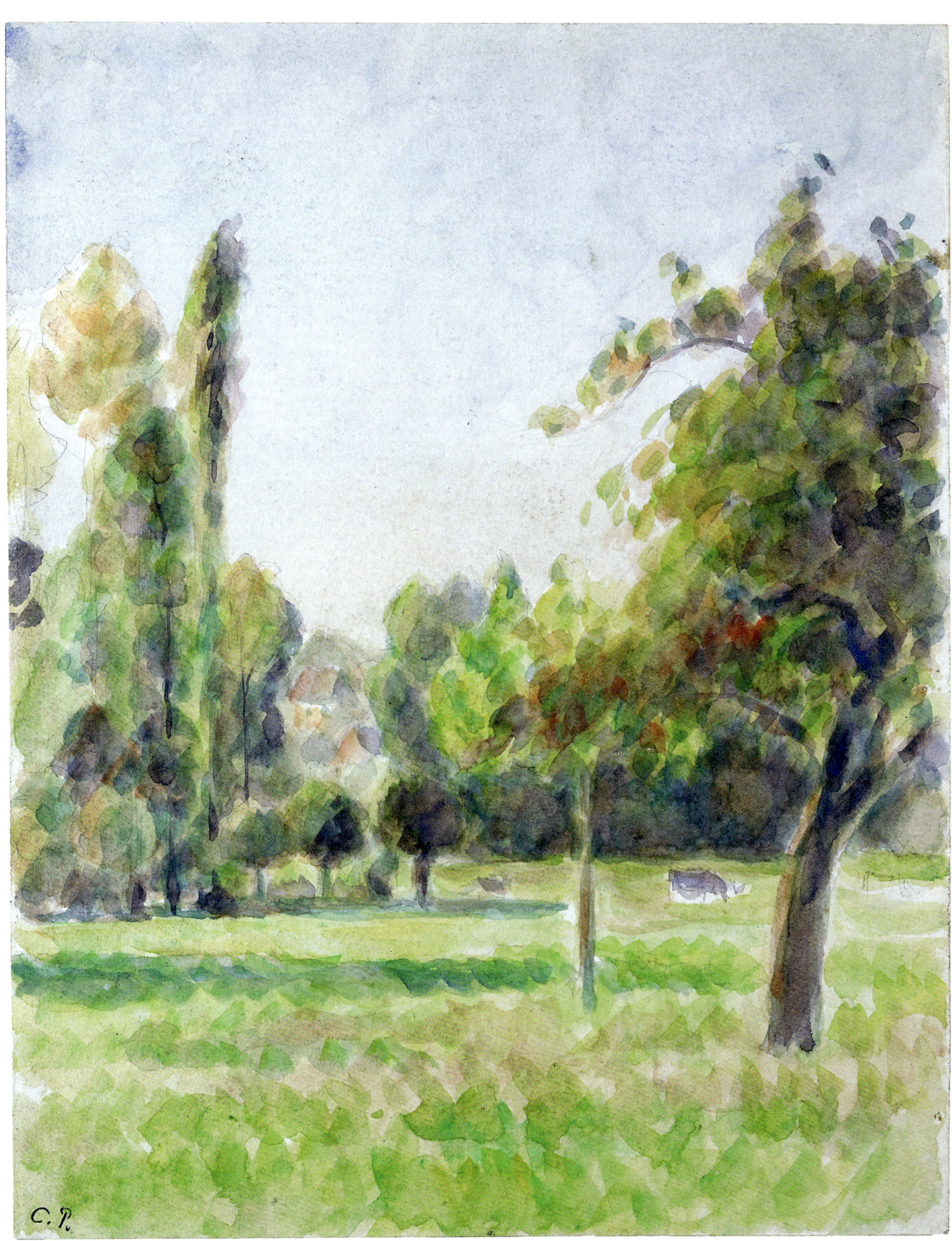

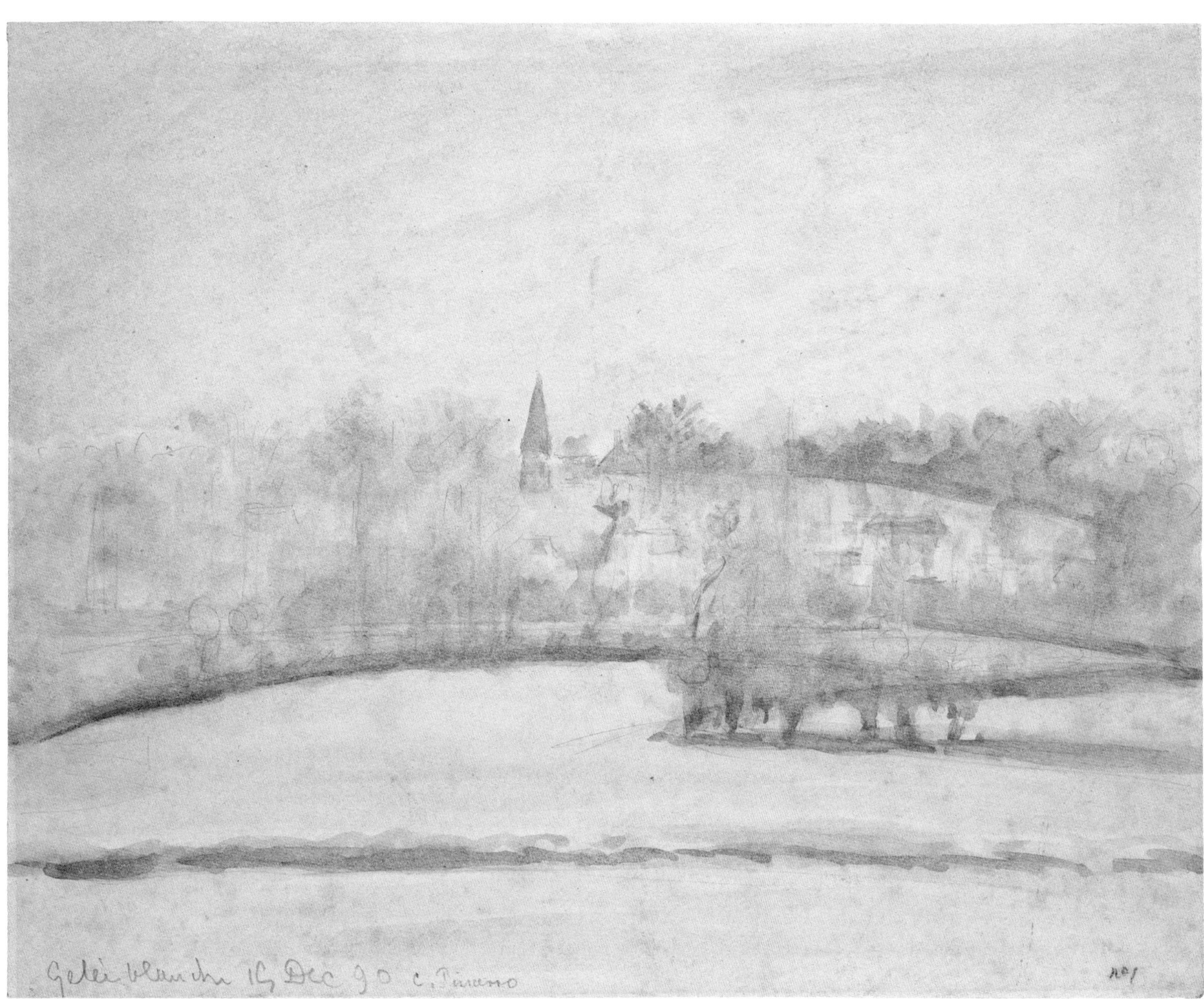

51

Camille Pissarro (1830–1903)
Study of the Orchard of the Artist's House at Eragny-sur-Epte, *c.* 1890
Watercolour over graphite on wove paper, 28.3 x 22.5 cm
The Ashmolean Museum, University of Oxford.
Presented by the Pissarro Family, 1952, WA1952.6.335

52

Camille Pissarro (1830–1903)
White Frost, 1890
Watercolour over graphite on wove paper, 20.8 x 26.3 cm
The Ashmolean Museum, University of Oxford.
Bequeathed by Frank Hindley Smith, 1939, WA1940.1.41

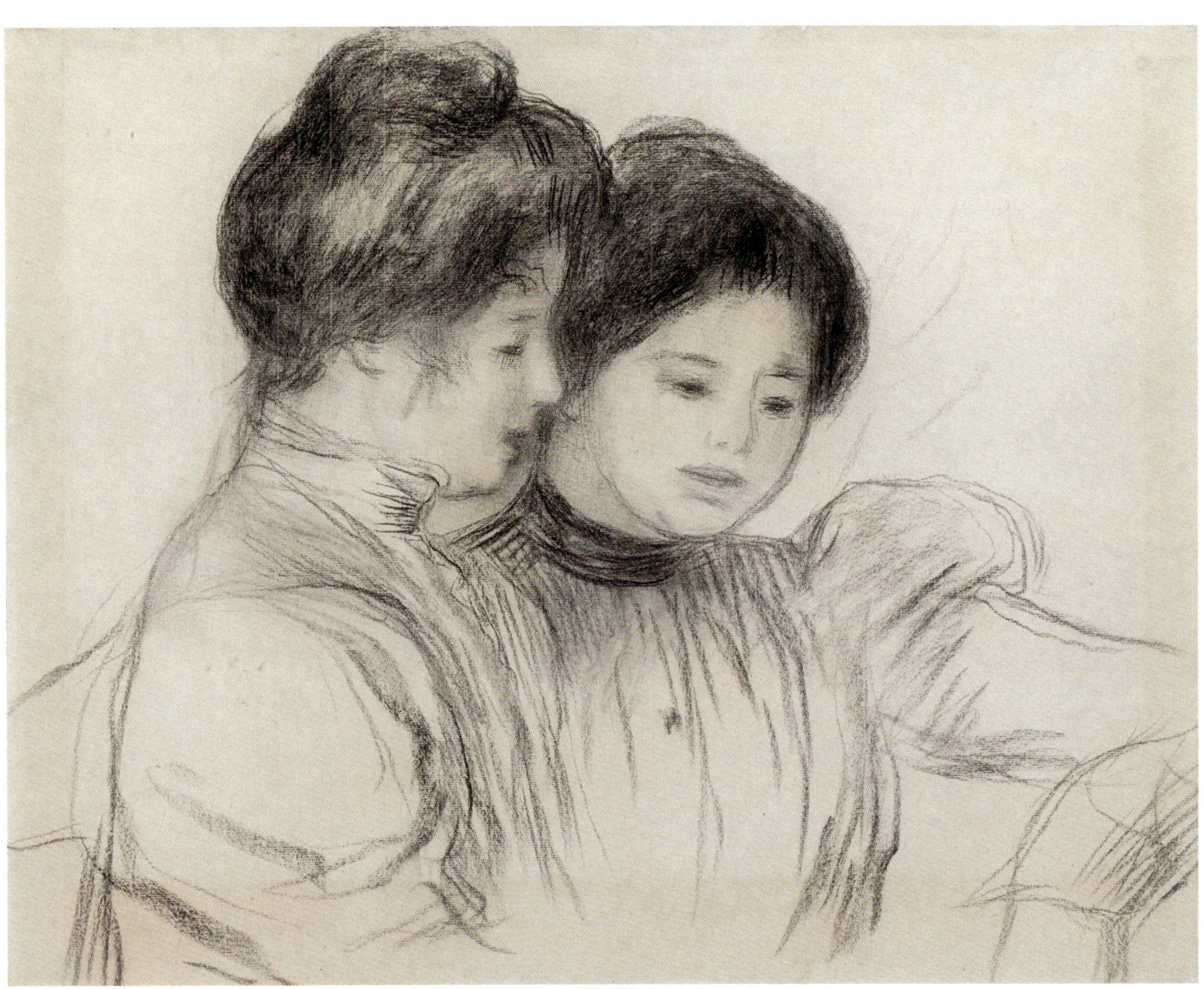

53

Pierre-Auguste Renoir (1841–1919)
Yvonne and Christine Lerolle at the Piano, c. 1890
Charcoal on laid paper, 48.5 x 63 cm
Private collection

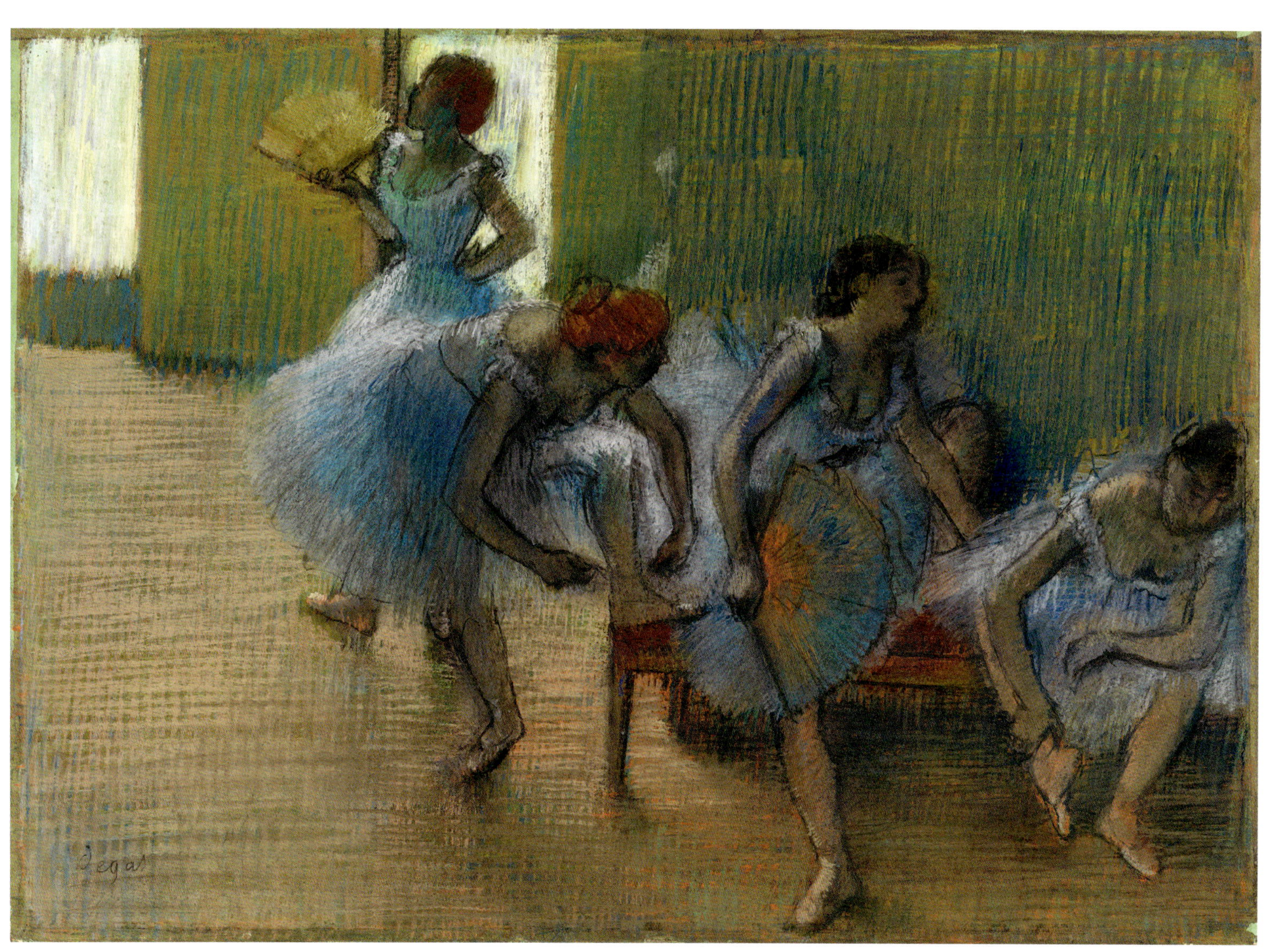

54

Edgar Degas (1834–1917)
Dancers on a Bench, c. 1898
Pastel on tracing paper, 53.7 x 75.6 cm
Lent by Glasgow Life Museums on behalf of Glasgow City Council, Bequeathed by William McInnes, 1944, 2441

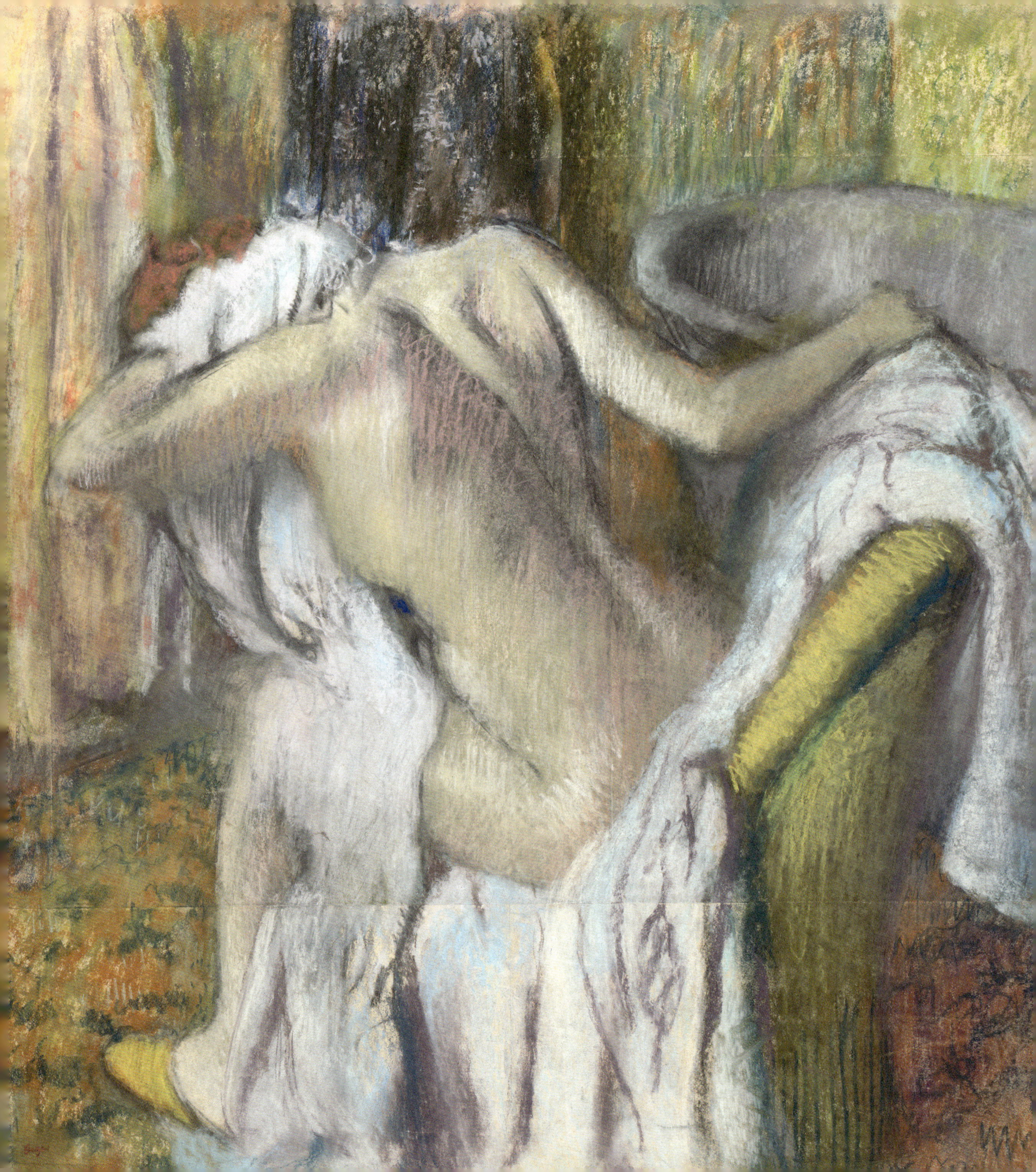

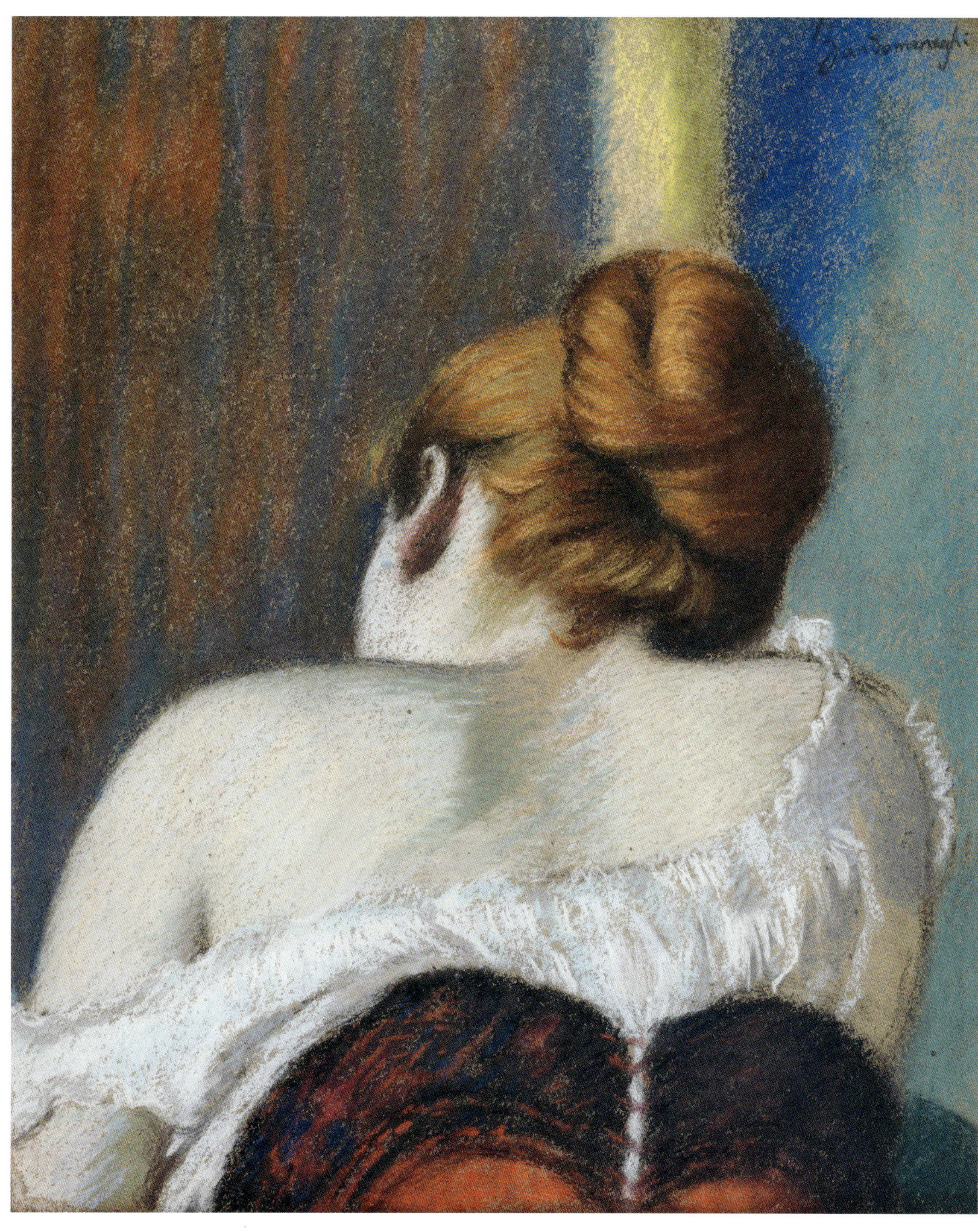

55

Edgar Degas (1834–1917)
After the Bath, Woman Drying Herself, c. 1890–95
Pastel on wove paper laid on millboard, 103.5 x 98.5 cm
The National Gallery, London. Bought, 1959, NG6295

56

Federico Zandomeneghi (1841–1917)
Study of a Woman from Behind, 1890–97
Pastel on cardboard, 48 x 38 cm
Galleria d'Arte Moderna, Milan, GAM 4870

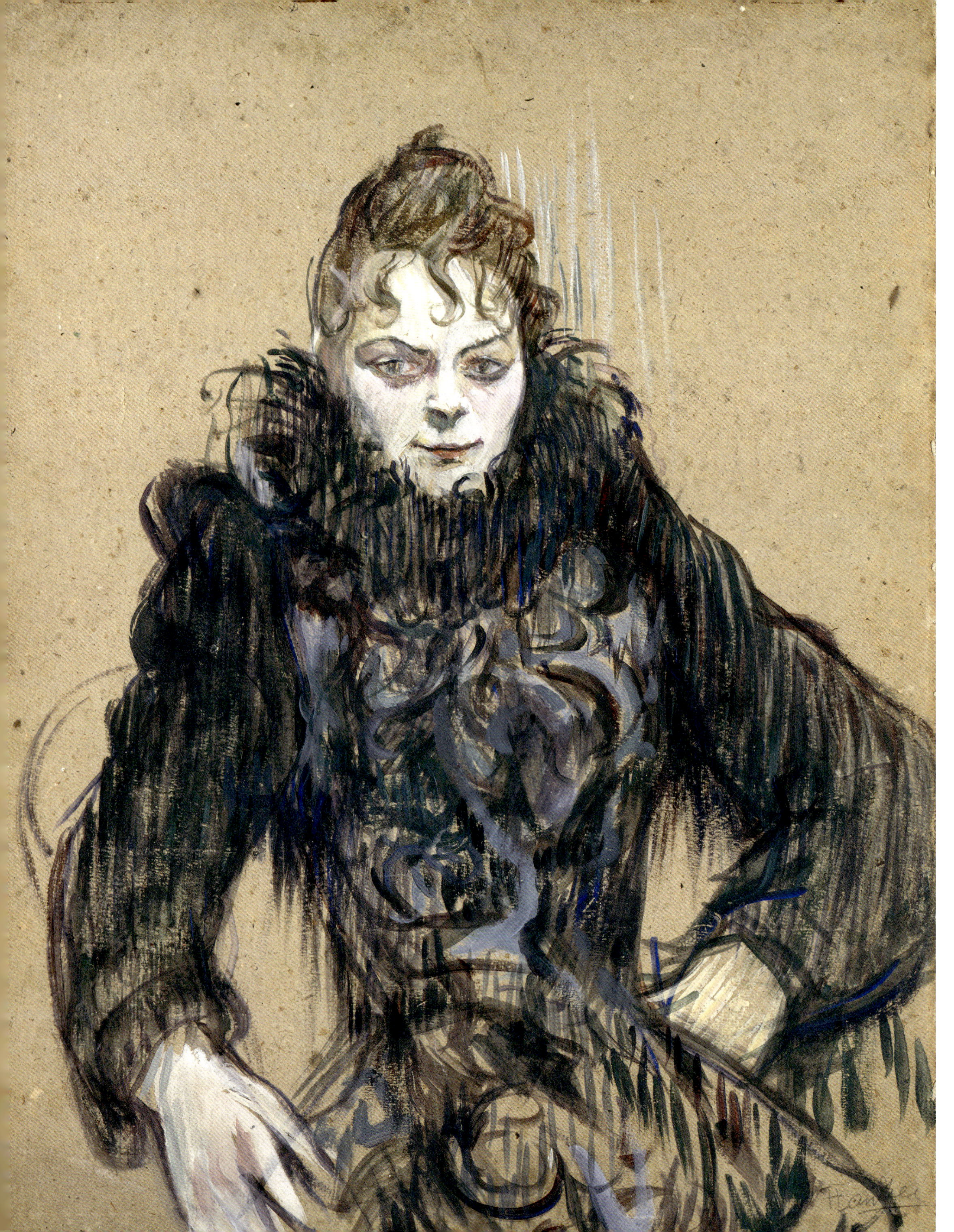

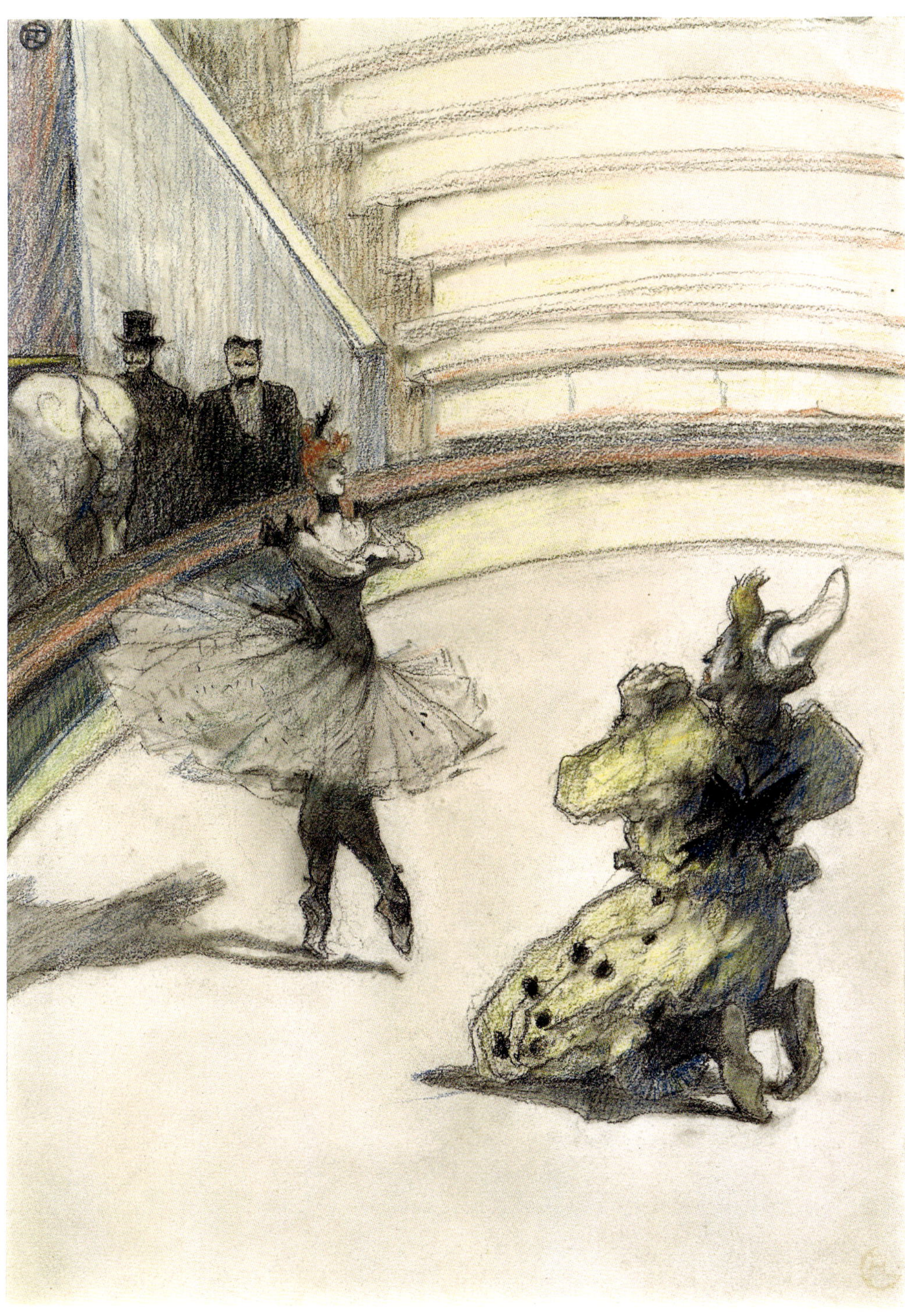

57

Henri de Toulouse-Lautrec (1864–1901)
Woman with a Black Boa, 1892
Essence (diluted oil paint) on cardboard, 50 x 40 cm
Musée d'Orsay, Paris. Gifted by the Comtesse Alphonse de Toulouse-Lautrec, mother of the artist, 1902, INV 20140

58

Henri de Toulouse-Lautrec (1864–1901)
At the Circus: The Encore, 1899
Black and coloured chalks on paper, 35.5 x 25 cm
Collection of David Lachenmann

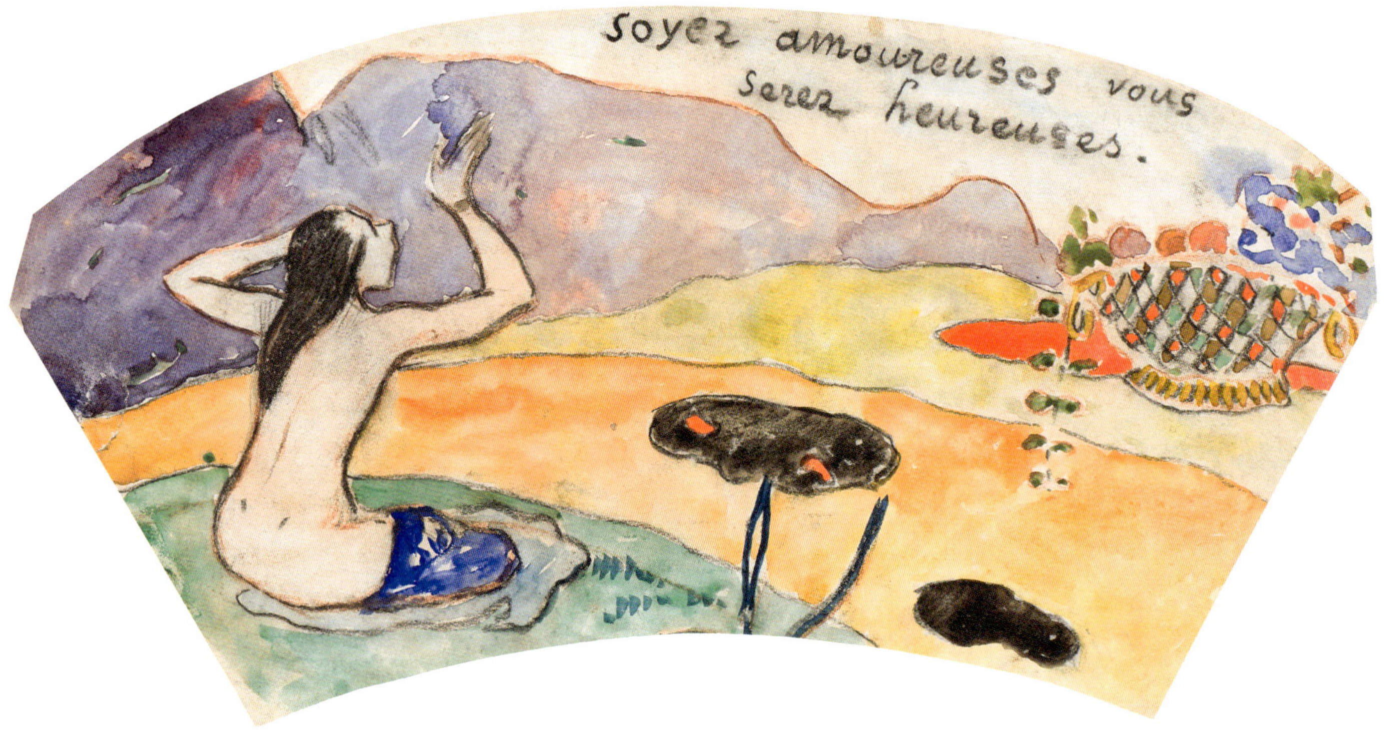

59

Paul Gauguin (1848–1903)
Soyez amoureuses vous serez heureuses
(Be In Love and You Will Be Happy), 1894
Watercolour and coloured
crayons on paper, 14 x 25.7 cm
Private collection

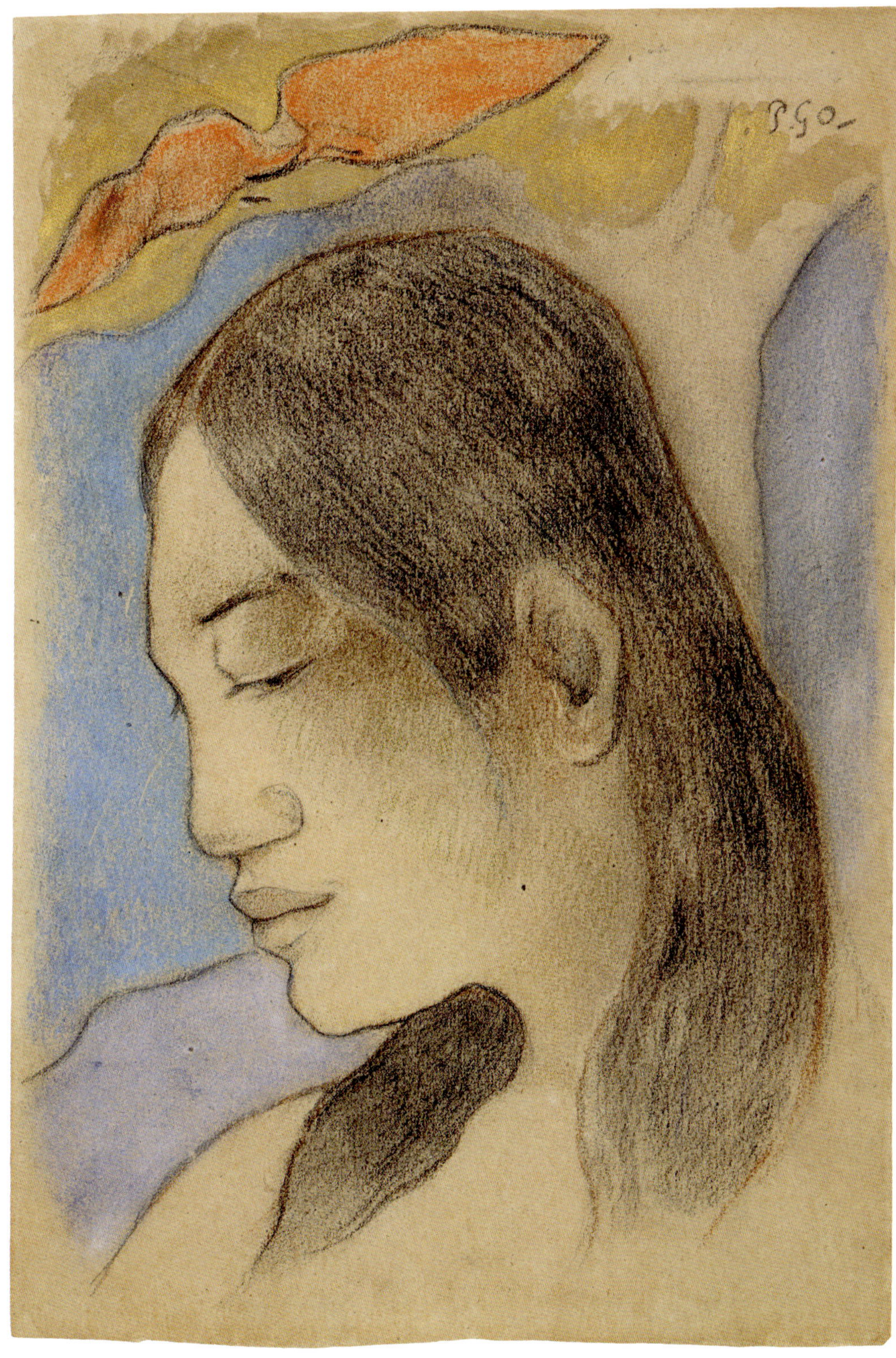

60

Paul Gauguin (1848–1903)
Head of a Tahitian Woman, 1892
Coloured chalks and pastel heightened with gold paint on wove paper, 31 x 21.2 cm
Private collection

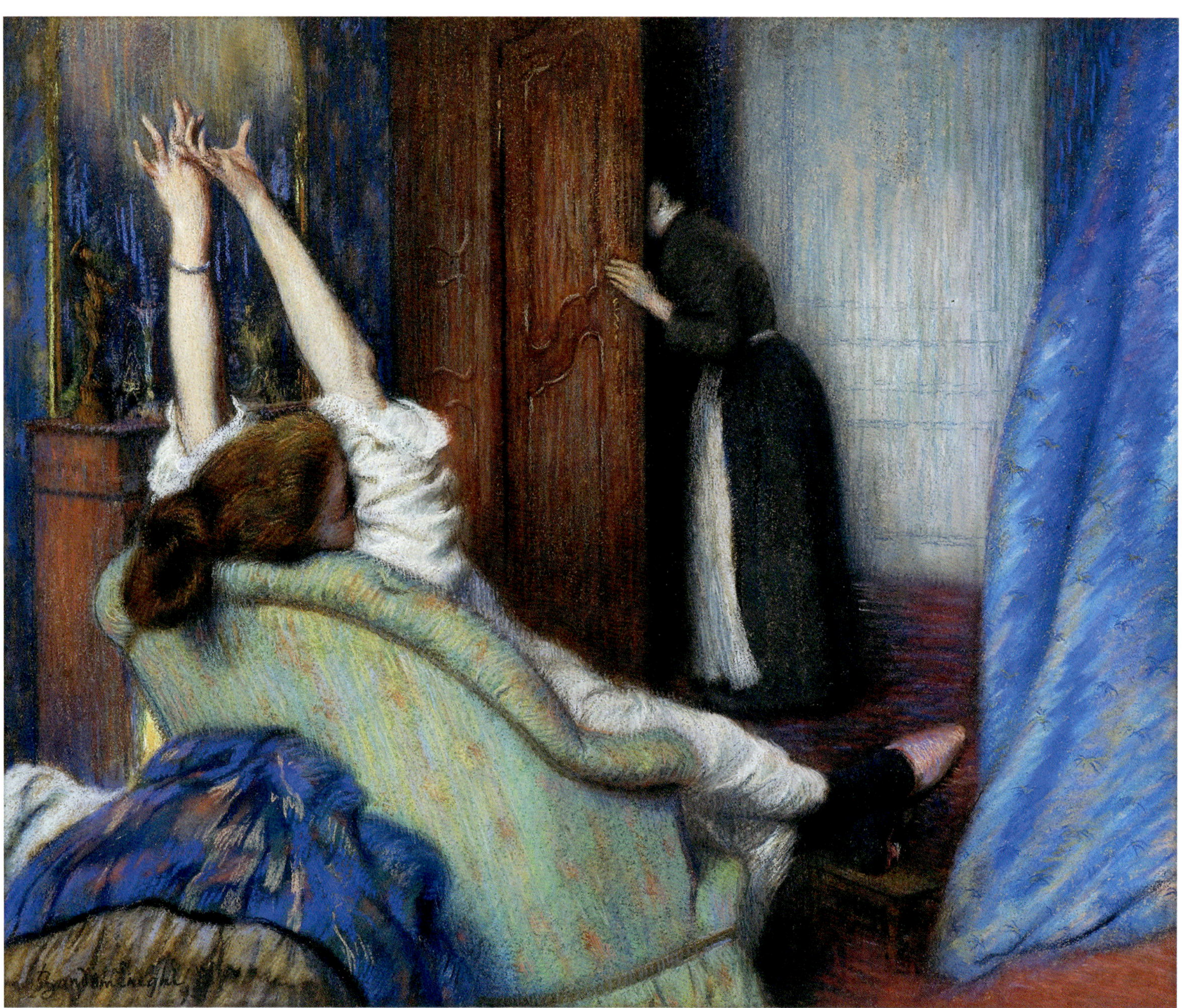

61

Federico Zandomeneghi (1841–1917)
Waking Up, 1895
Pastel on paper mounted on board, 60 x 73 cm
Musei Civici di Mantova, Mantua, 96210007

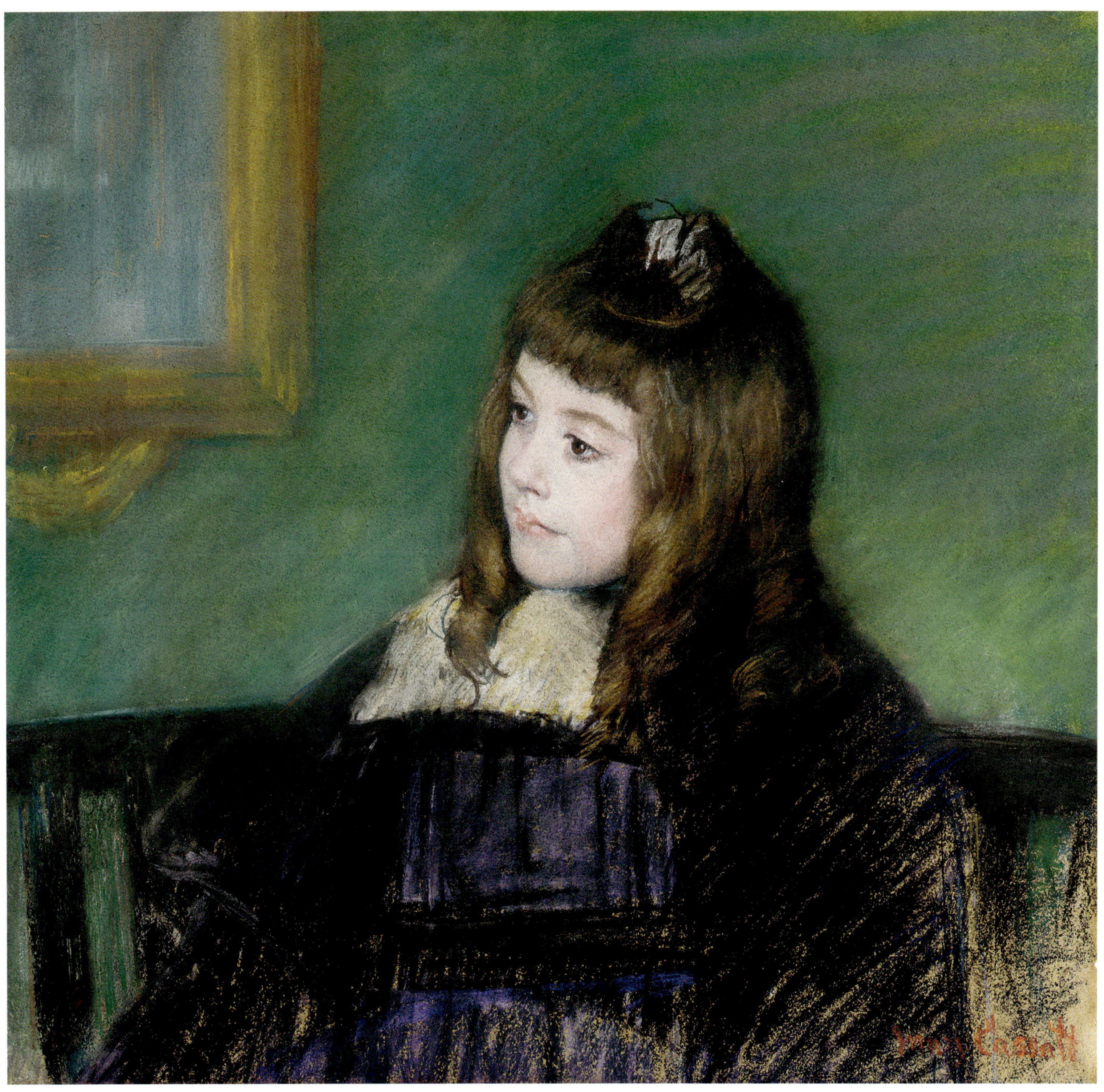

62

Mary Cassatt (1844–1926)
Portrait of Marie-Thérèse Gaillard, 1894
Pastel on paper, 51 x 54 cm
Private collection

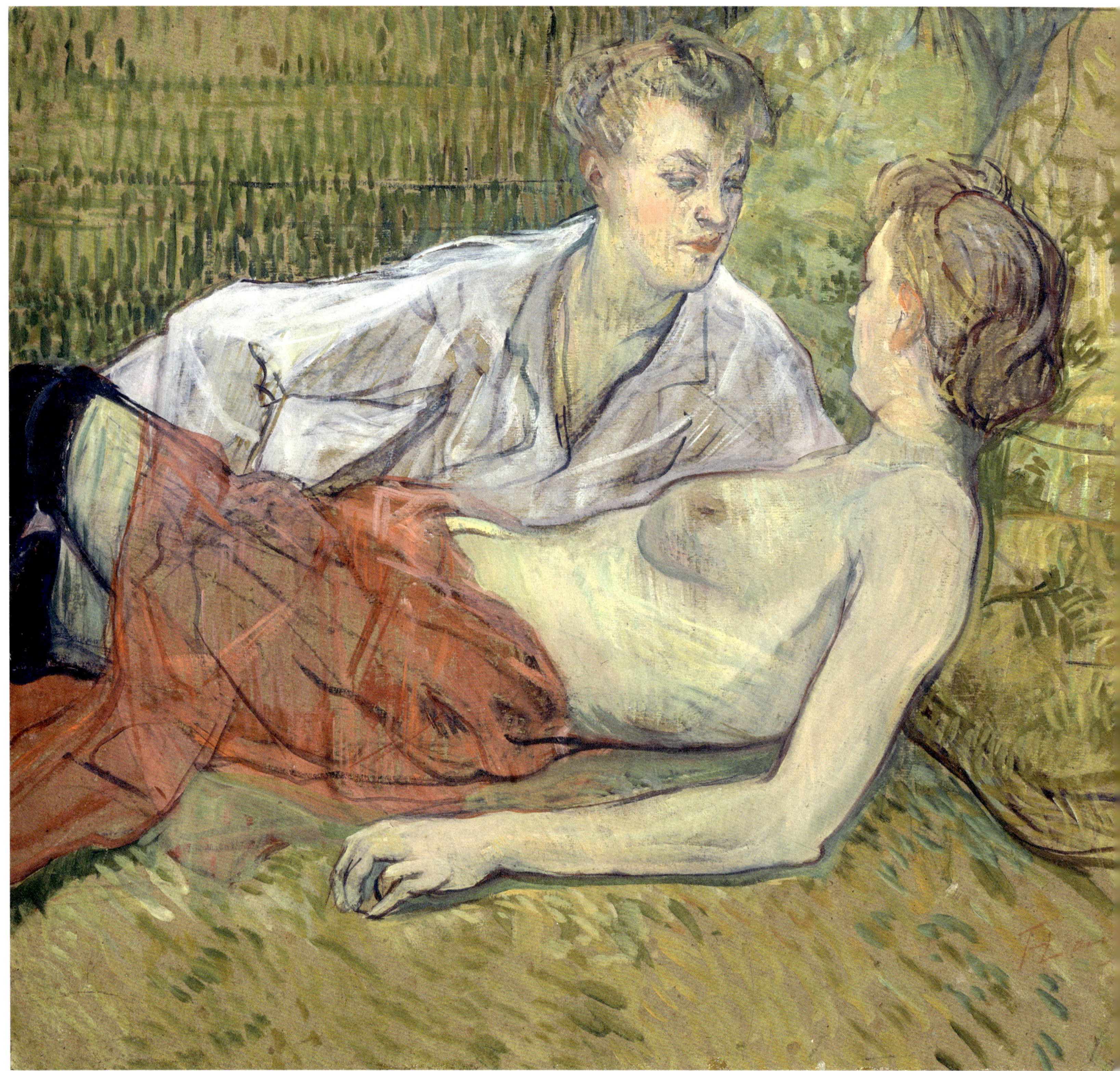

63

Henri de Toulouse-Lautrec (1864–1901)
Two Friends, 1895
Gouache on cardboard, 64.5 x 84 cm
Emil Bührle Collection, on long-term loan at Kunsthaus Zürich, BU/0106

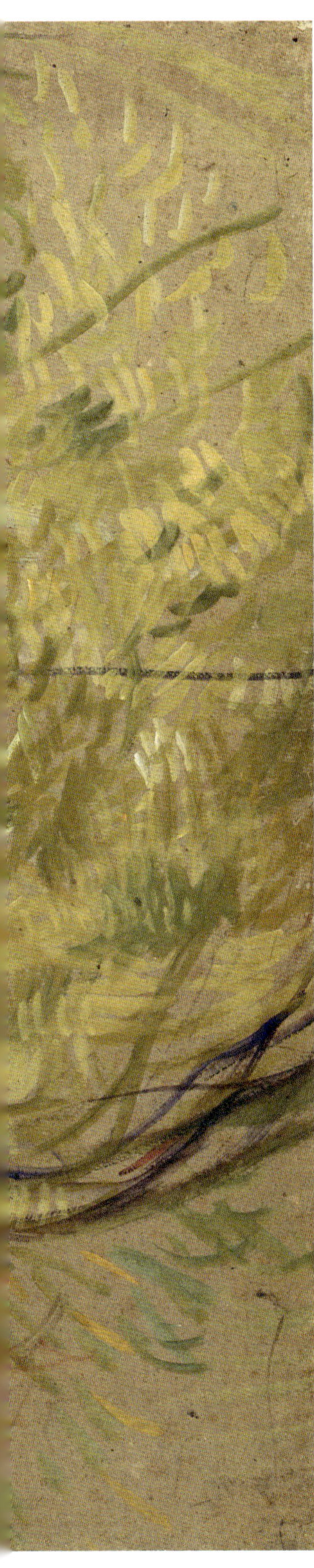

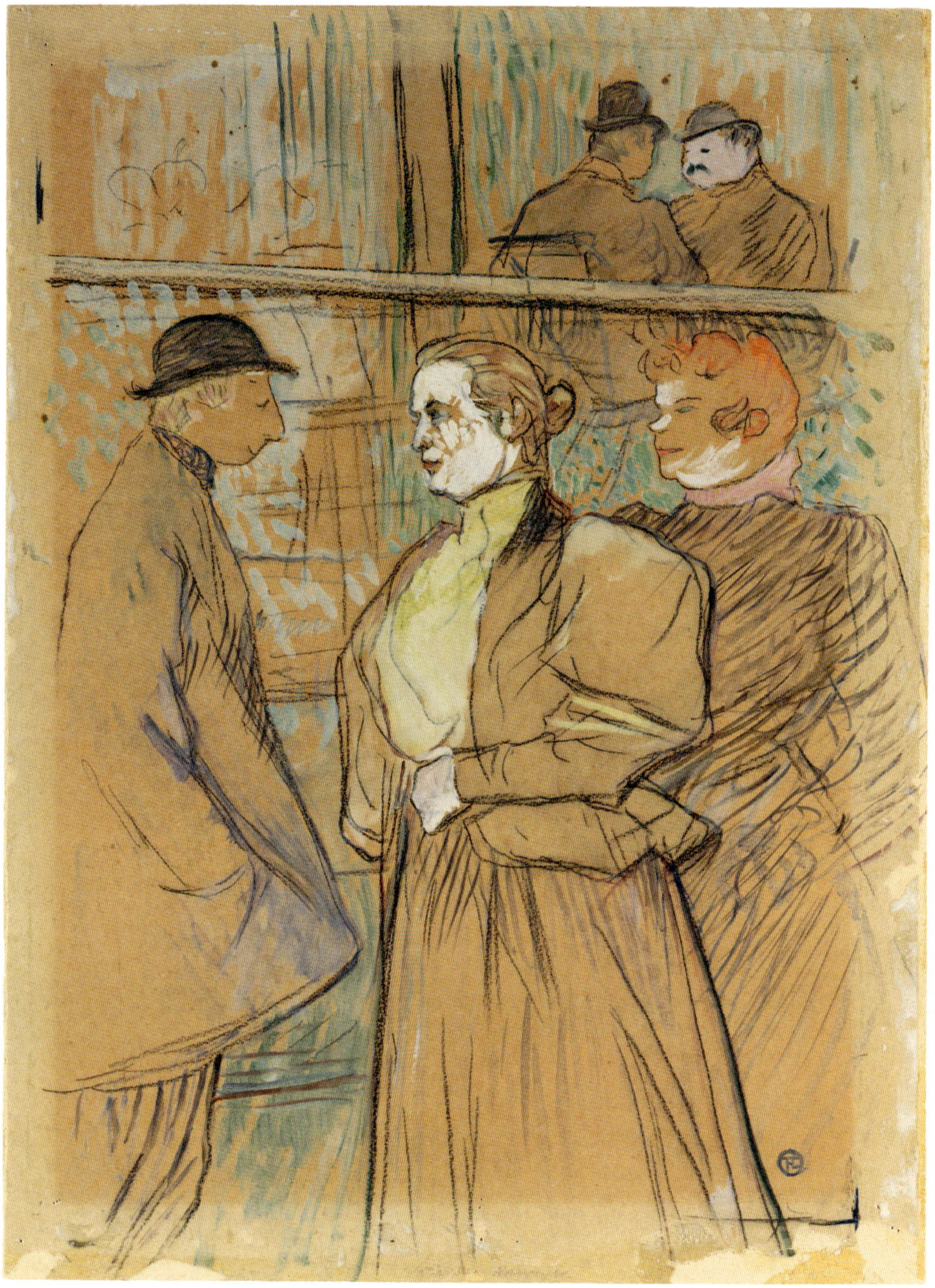

64

Henri de Toulouse-Lautrec (1864–1901)
In the Ballroom of the Moulin Rouge, 1895–96
Coloured crayons and tempera on paper mounted on cardboard, 56.4 x 42 cm
Szépművészeti Múzeum / Museum of Fine Arts, Budapest, 1935-2728

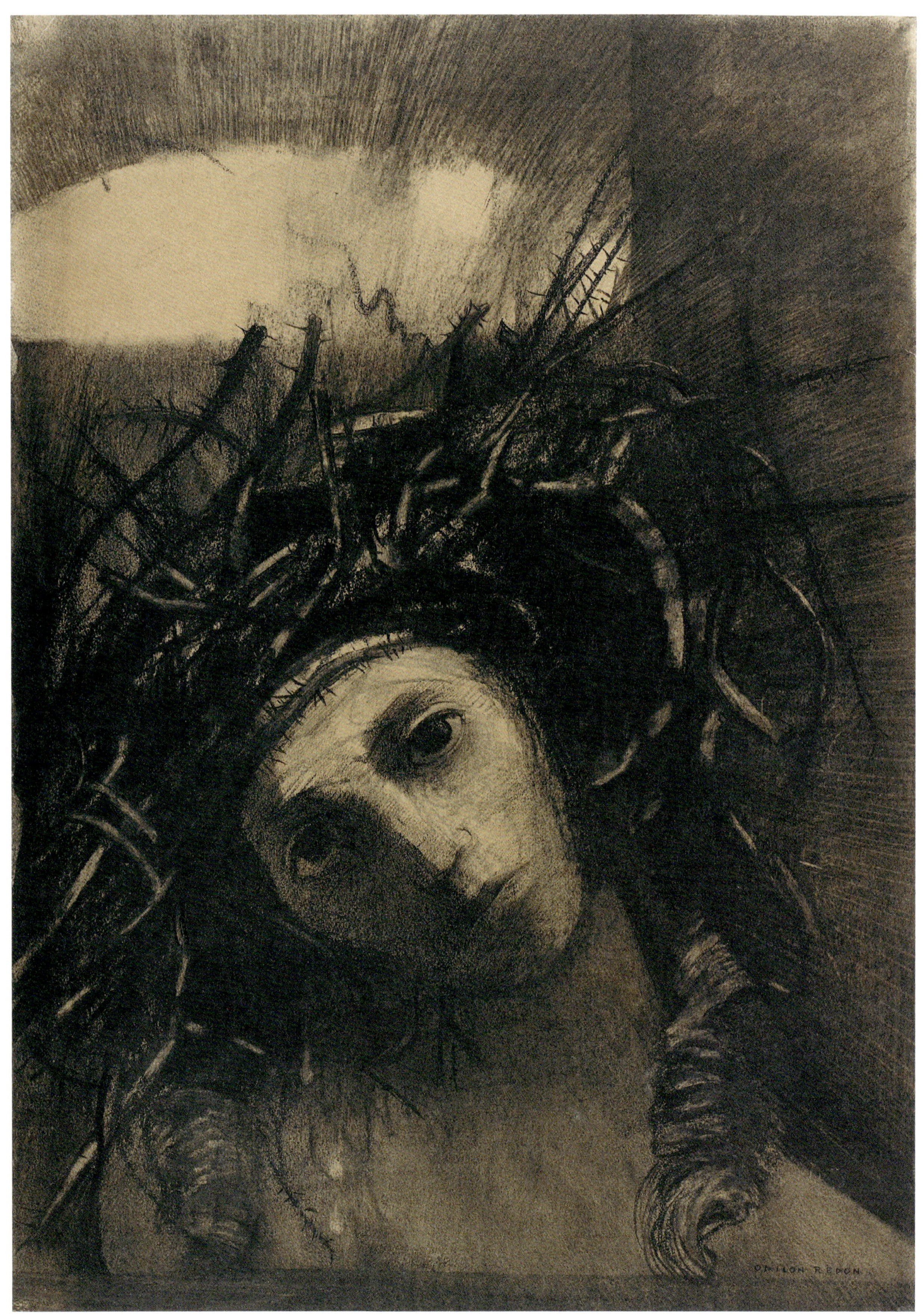
ODILON REDON

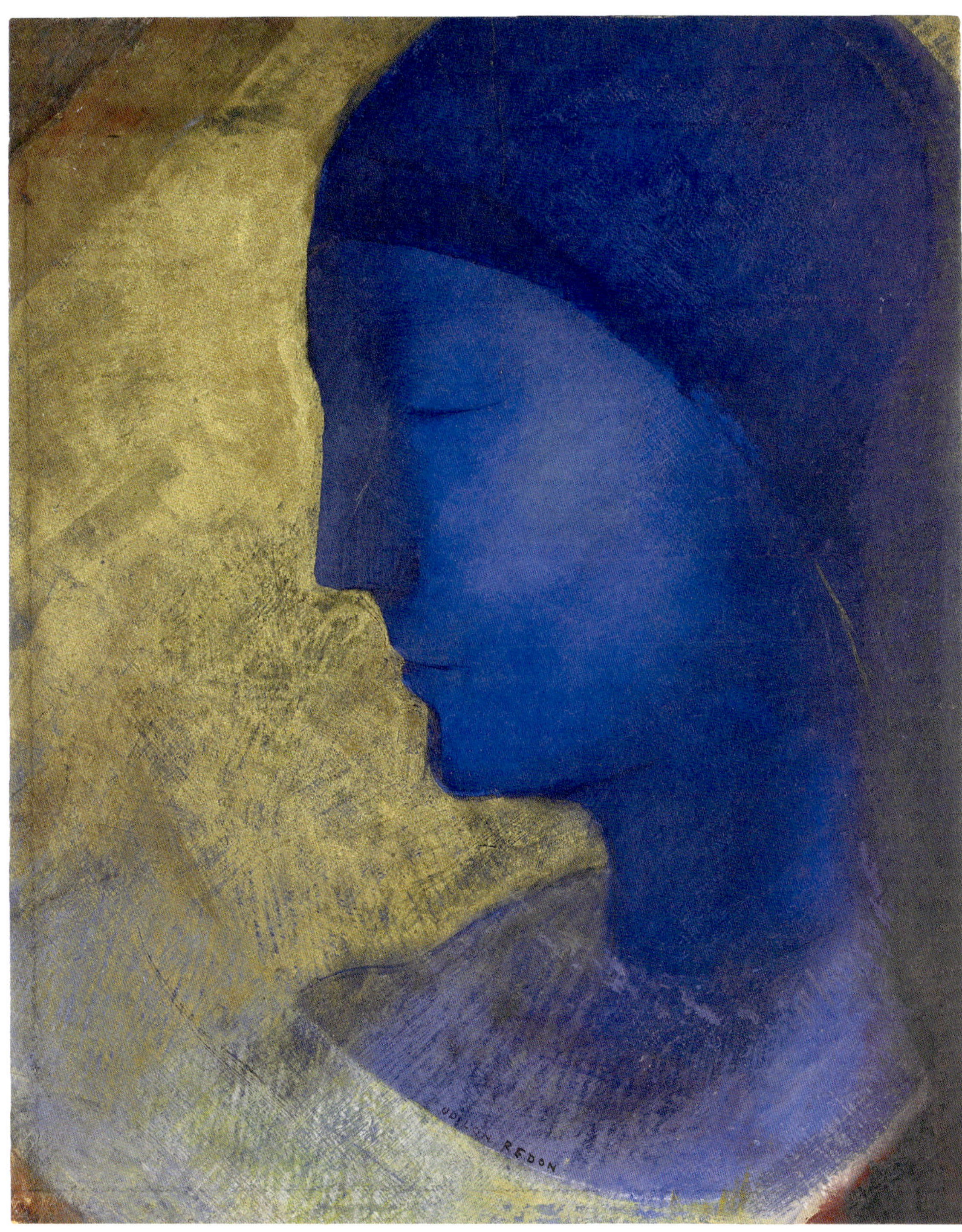

65

Odilon Redon (1840–1916)
Christ Crowned with Thorns, 1895
Charcoal, black pastel and black crayon, stumping, erasing, and incising on tan wove paper toned gold, 52.2 x 37.9 cm
British Museum, London, 1921,0411.1

66

Odilon Redon (1840–1916)
'The Golden Cell' (Profile of a Woman's Head), 1892
Oil and coloured chalks with gold on paper, 30.1 x 24.7 cm
British Museum, London, 1949,0411.80

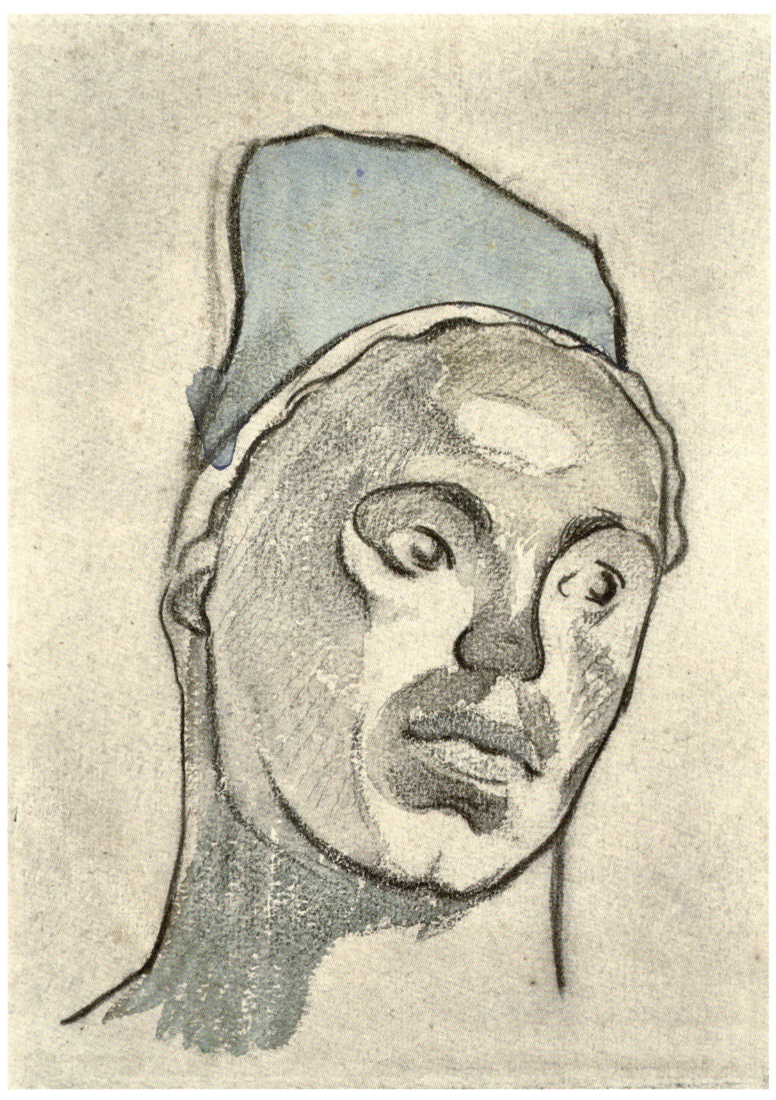

67

Paul Gauguin (1848–1903)
Head of a Breton Woman, 1894
Black chalk, charcoal and watercolour on buff paper, 26.8 x 19.9 cm
Private collection, London

68

Pierre-Auguste Renoir (1841–1919)
The Picnic, *c.* 1895
Sanguine and black chalk on paper, 42.3 x 31.5 cm
The Syndics of the Fitzwilliam Museum, University of Cambridge, PD.21-1964

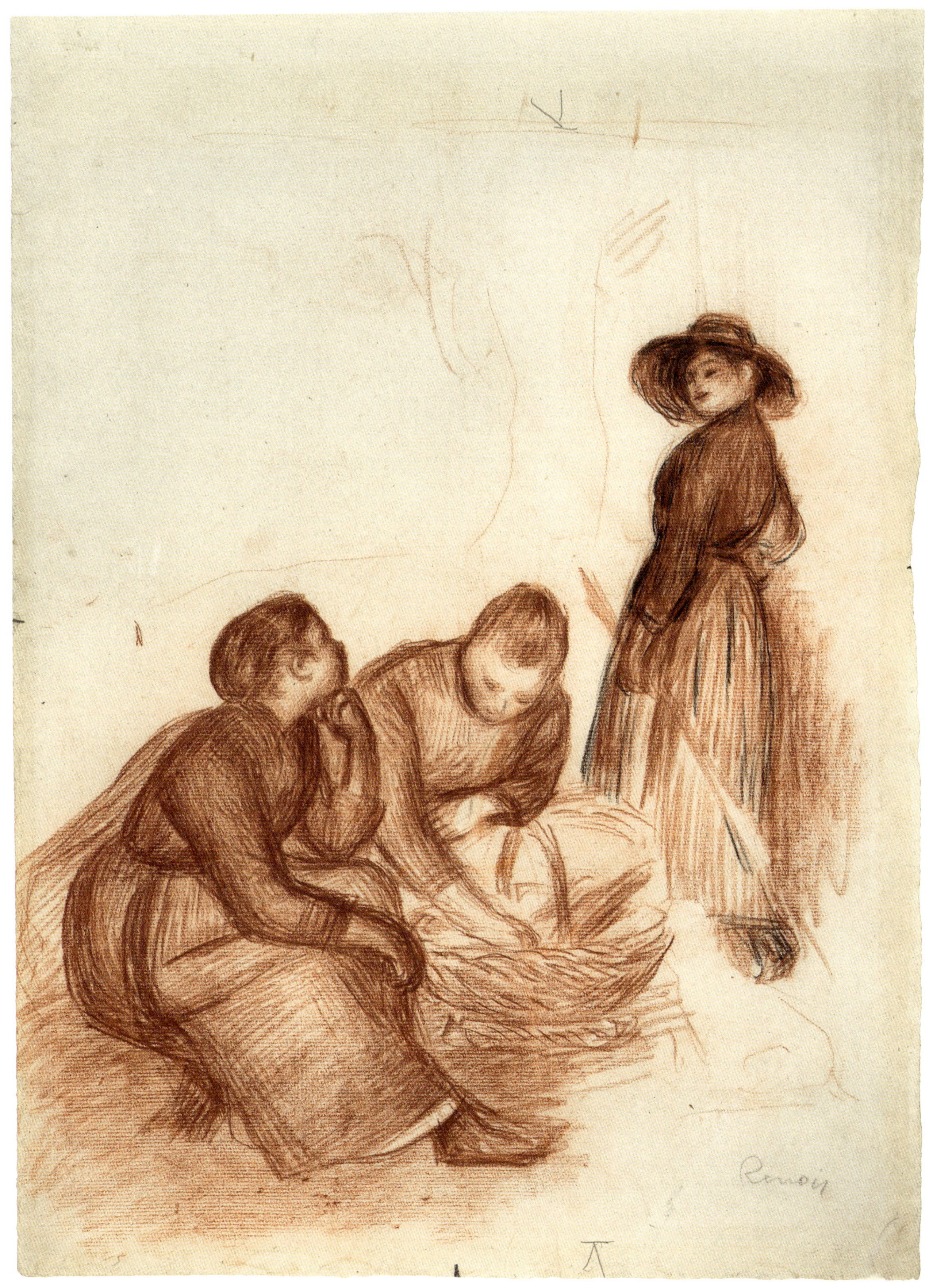

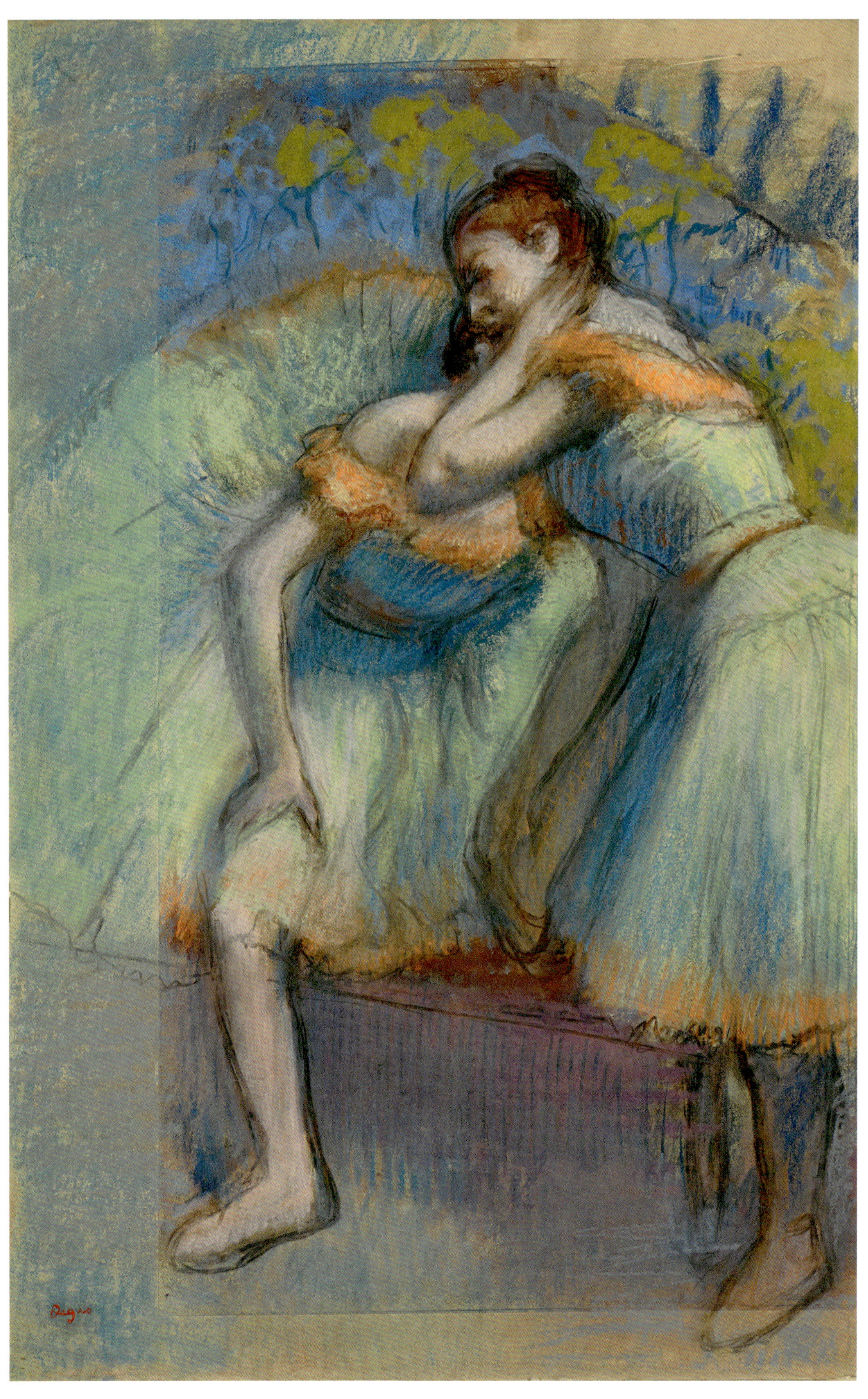
Degas

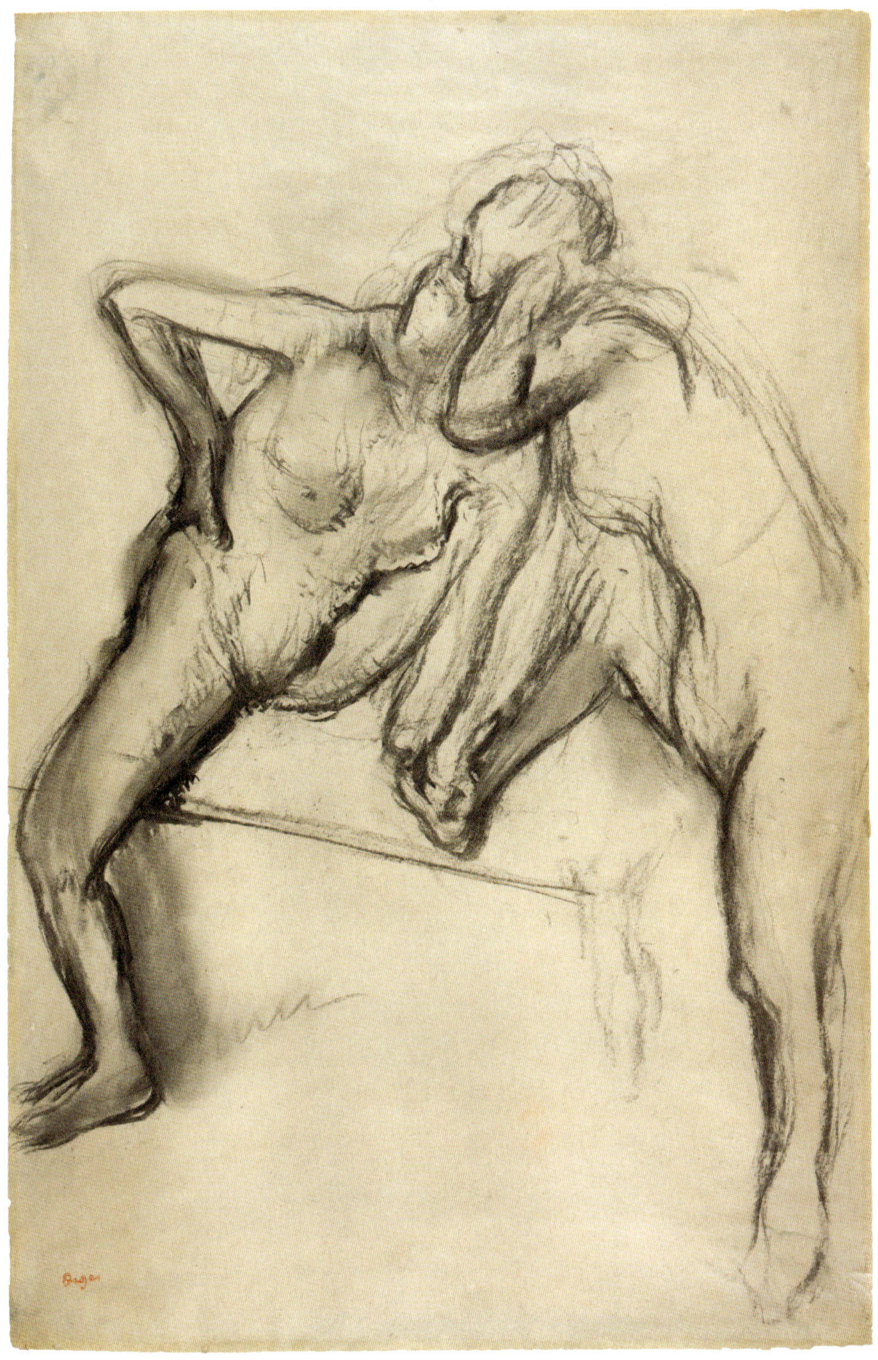

69

Edgar Degas (1834–1917)
Two Dancers, *c.* 1891
Pastel on joined paper mounted on card laid down on board, 86.3 x 56.5 cm
Private collection, London

70

Edgar Degas (1834–1917)
Study of Nudes, *c.* 1901
Black chalk on tracing paper, 75 x 49.2 cm
King's College, University of Cambridge, PDL.3065-034

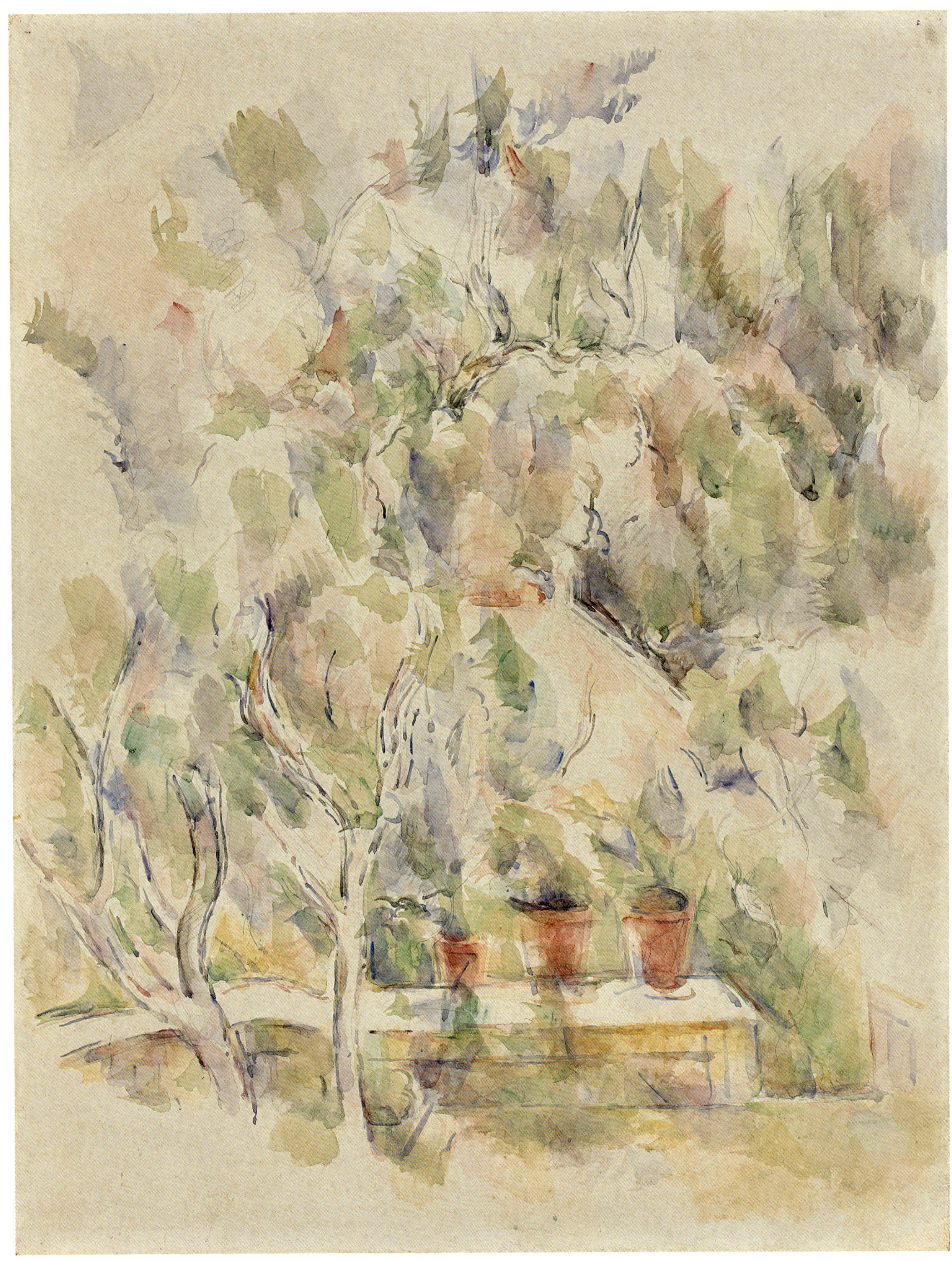

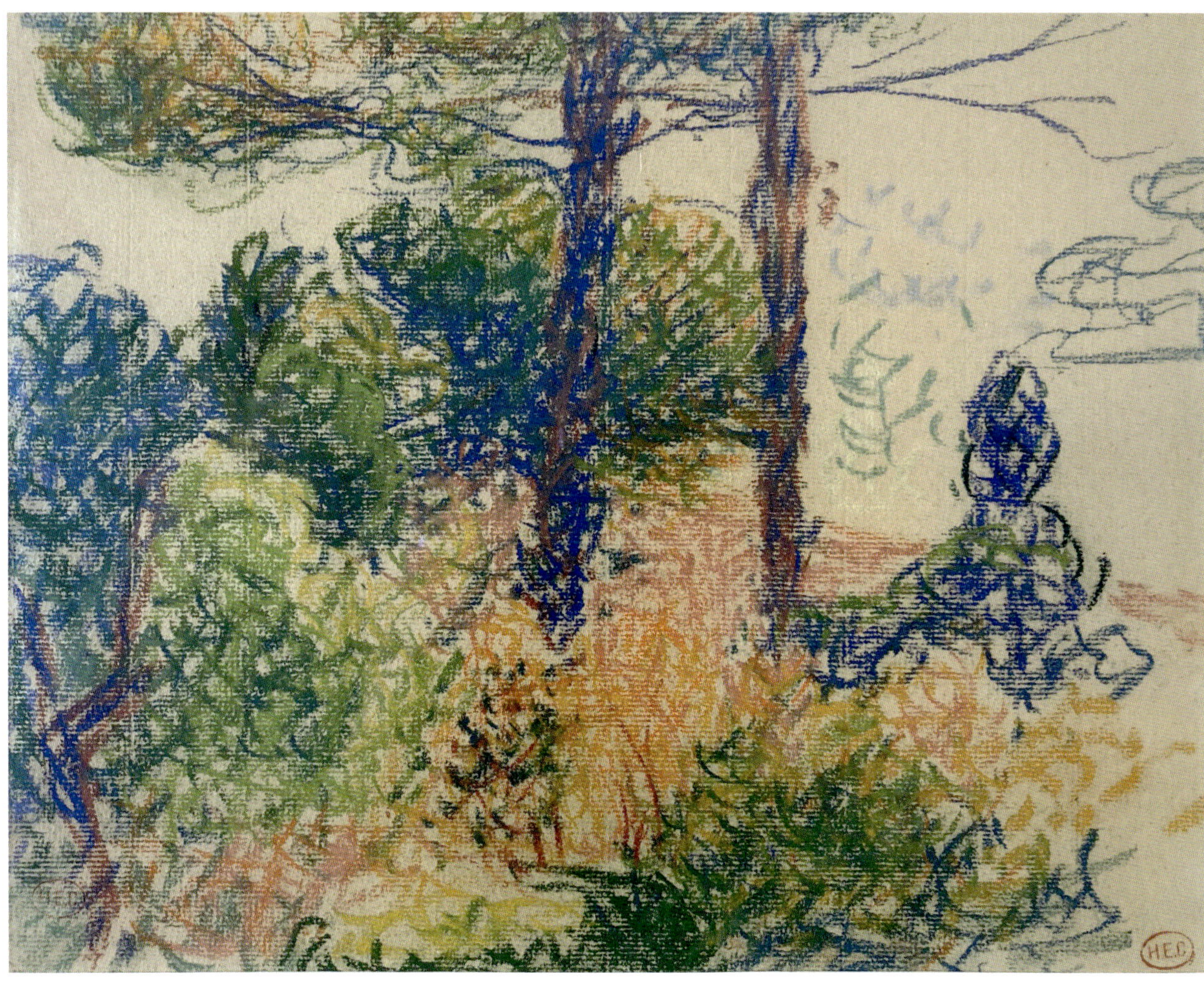

71

Paul Cézanne (1839–1906)
Flowerpots on the Terrace of the Artist's Studio at Les Lauves, *c.* 1902–06
Watercolour over graphite on paper, 60.7 x 47.8 cm
Collection of David Lachenmann

72

Henri-Edmond Cross (1856–1910)
Le Lavandou, *c.* 1898
Pastel on paper, 23 x 30 cm
Private collection

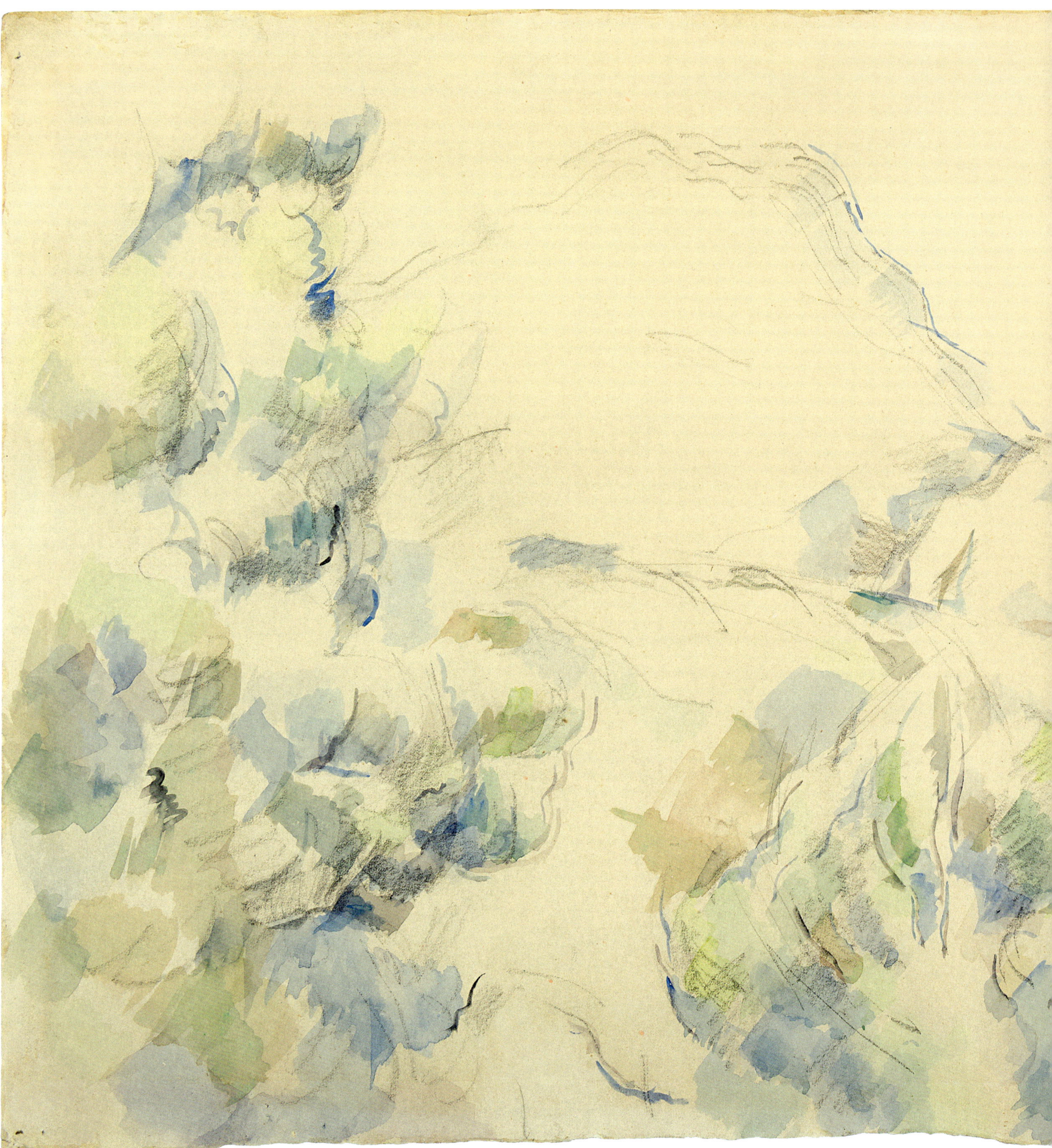

73

Paul Cézanne (1839–1906)
Landscape with La Montagne Sainte-Victoire, c. 1904–06
Watercolour and graphite on wove paper, 32.5 x 49.9 cm
Stephen Ongpin Fine Art, London

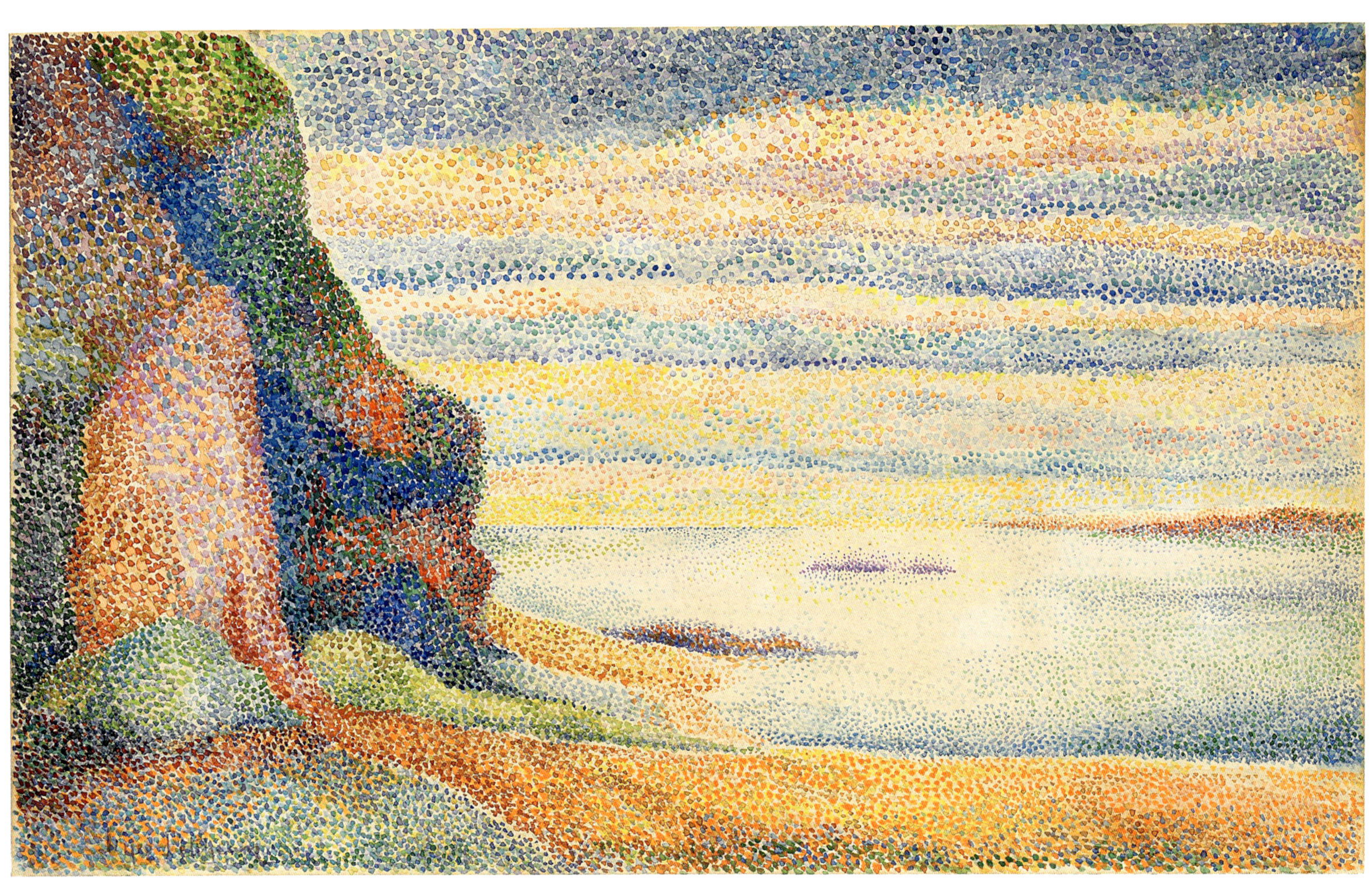

74

Hippolyte Petitjean (1854–1929)
Coastal Landscape with Cliffs, *c.* 1905
Watercolour on paper laid down
on board, 30.2 x 49.8 cm
Private collection, Paris

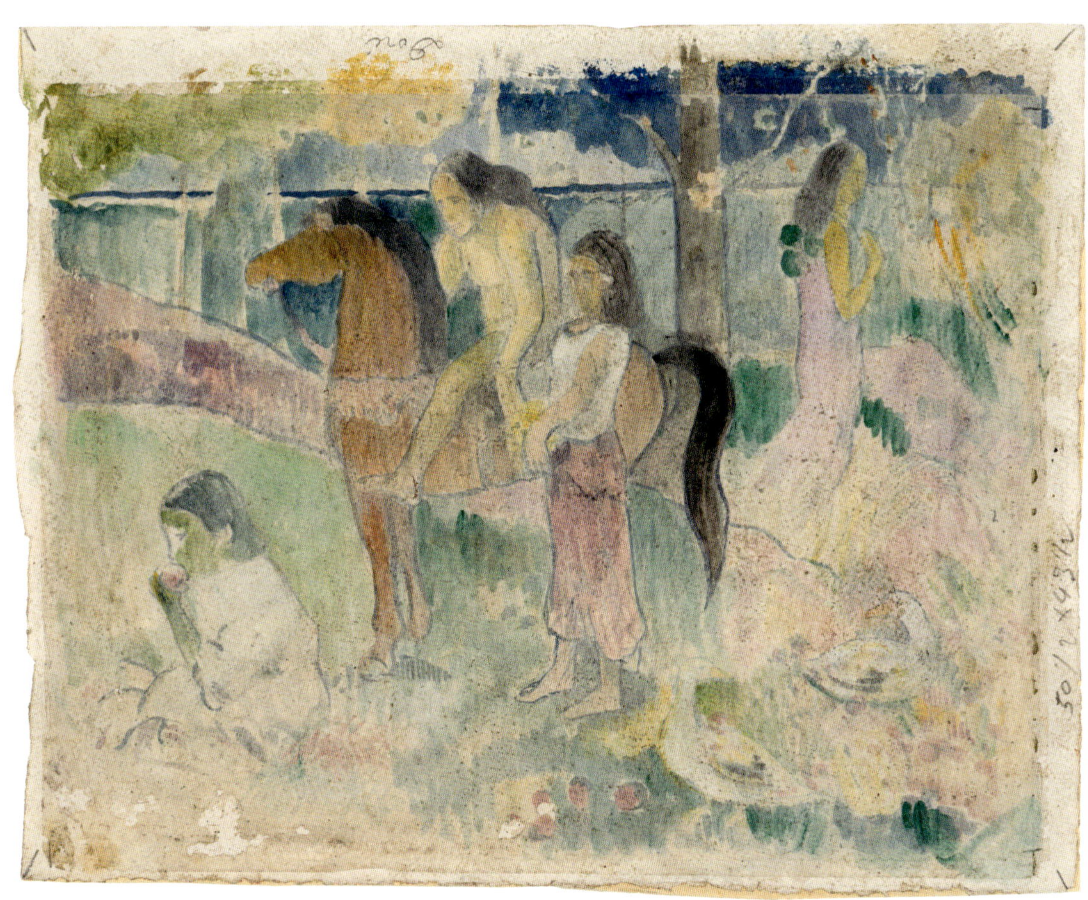

75

Paul Gauguin (1848–1903)
Tahitian Scene, 1896–98
Watercolour on Japan paper mounted
on laid paper, 25 x 32.5 cm
Szépművészeti Múzeum / Museum of Fine Arts,
Budapest, 1935-2716

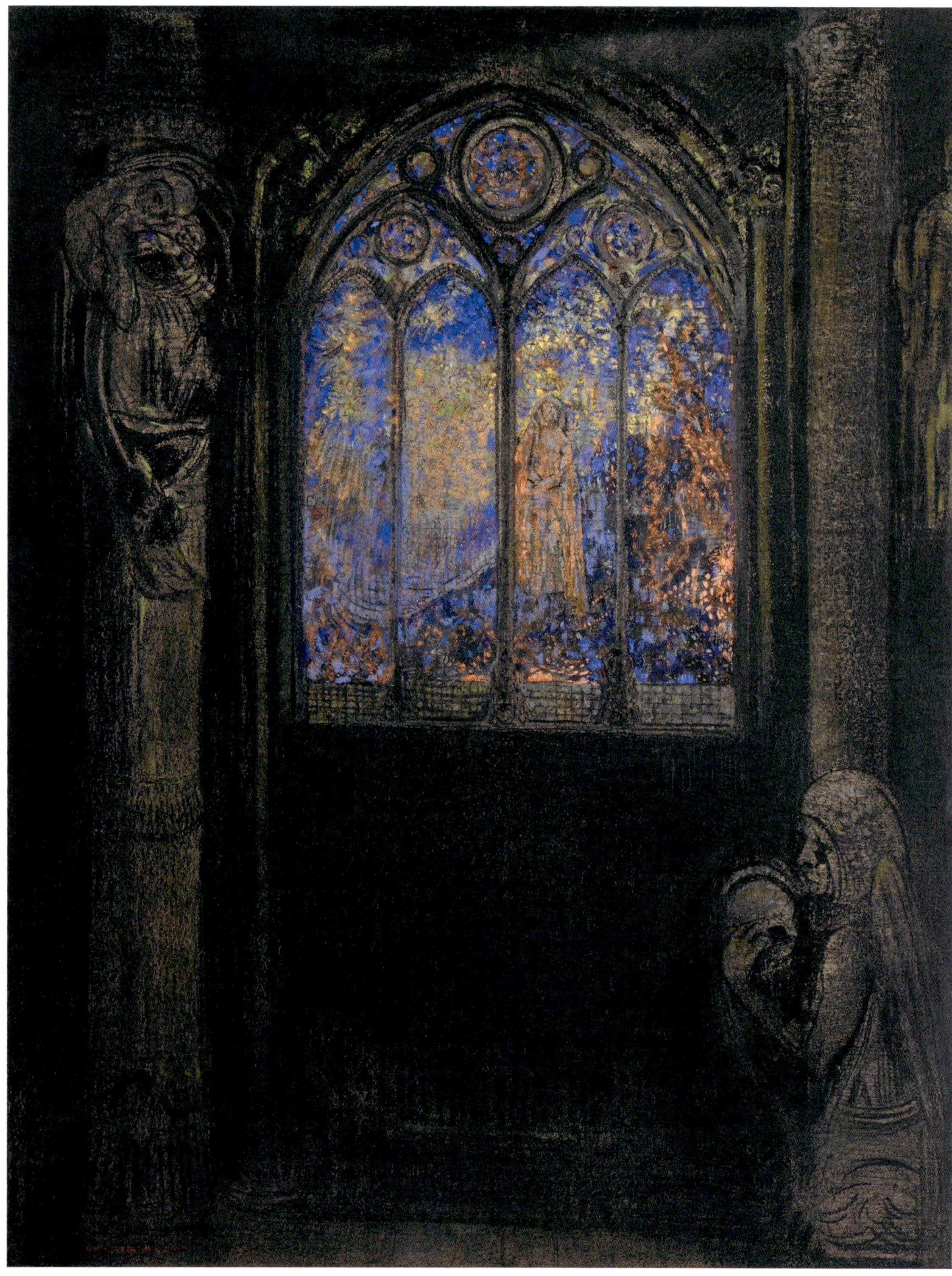

76

Odilon Redon (1840–1916)
Stained Glass Window, 1904
Charcoal and pastel on card, 87 x 68 cm
Musée d'Orsay, Paris, RF 36725

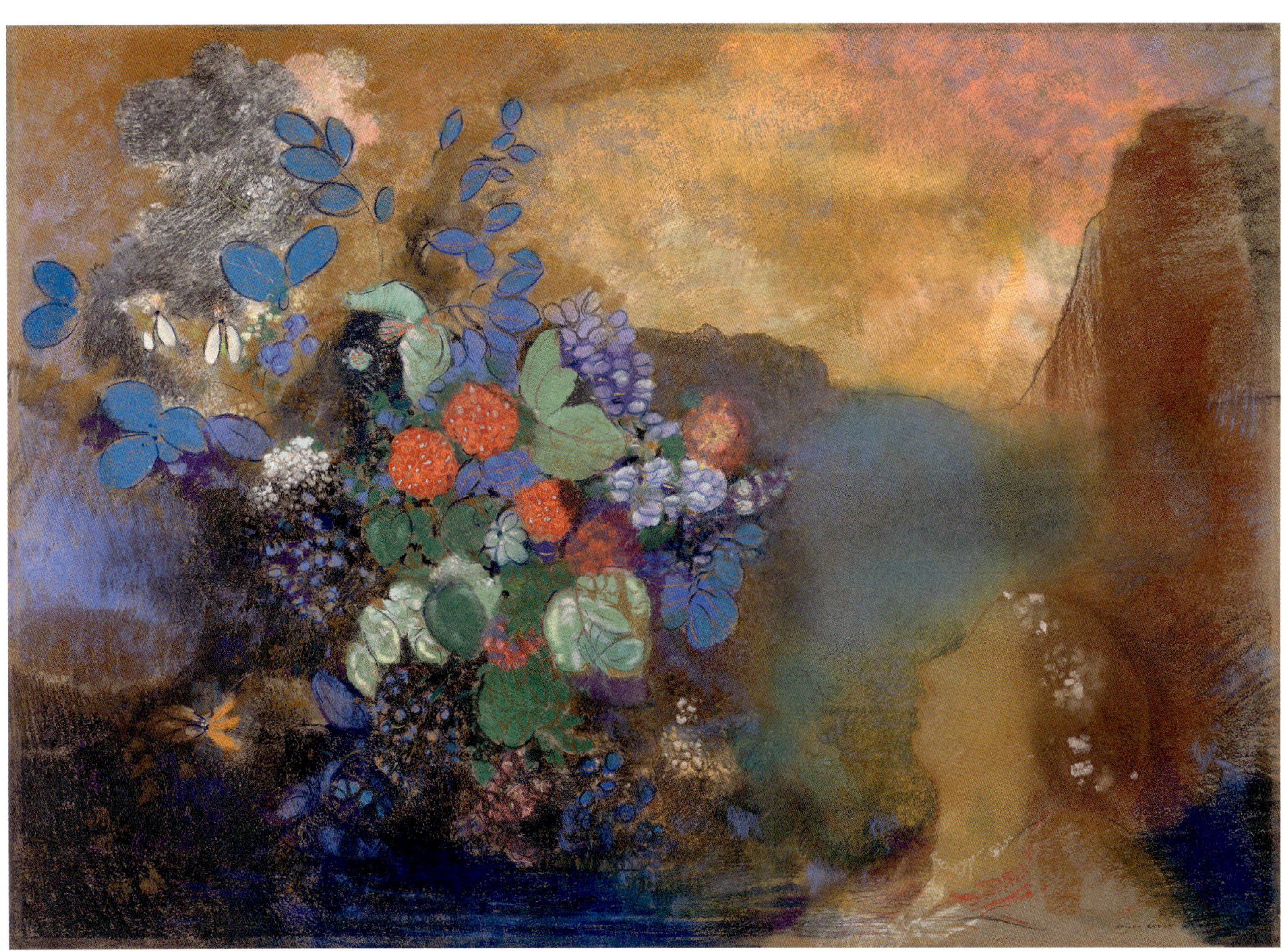

77

Odilon Redon (1840–1916)
Ophelia Among the Flowers, *c.* 1905–08
Pastel on paper, 64 x 91 cm
The National Gallery, London. Bought with a contribution from the Art Fund, 1977, NG6438

Endnotes

Impressionists on Paper: Degas to Toulouse-Lautrec

CHRISTOPHER LLOYD

1 Baudelaire 1965, p. 81.
2 Kendall 1987, p. 319.
3 Huysmans 2019, p. 31, in 'The Salon of 1879'.
4 Huysmans 2019, p. 31, in 'Exhibition of the Independents in 1880'.
5 DeWitte 2017, pp. 238–41. Although the percentages vary between the eight Impressionist exhibitions, DeWitte calculates that on average 20% of the works shown were drawings. The highest percentage was 22% in 1874 and the lowest 12% in 1876. For a different numerical breakdown, see Oxford, Manchester and Glasgow 1986, p. 50, n. 35. The display of drawings at the Salon is discussed in DeWitte 2015.
6 Huysmans 2019, p. 241, in 'Exhibition of the Independents in 1881'.
7 Kendall 1987, p. 299, in Georges Jeanniot, 'Souvenirs de Degas', *La Revue universelle*, 15 October 1933 and 1 November 1933.
8 Baudelaire 1964, p. 57, in 'The Salon of 1846'.
9 Baudelaire 1964, p. 57, in 'The Life and Work of Eugène Delacroix'.
10 Delaborde 1870, p. 123.
11 Baudelaire 1964, p. 62, in 'The Life and Work of Eugène Delacroix'.
12 Letter drafted on 25 May 1890, in Van Gogh 2009, vol. 5, p. 321, RM 21.
13 Baudelaire 1964, p. 11–12, in 'The Painter of Modern Life'.
14 Baudelaire 1964, p. 7.
15 Baudelaire 1964, p. 40.
16 Baudelaire 1964, p. 179, in 'Some French Caricaturists'.
17 Valéry 1989, p. 155, in 'Honoré Daumier'.
18 Letter dated 29 June 1875, in Van Gogh 2009, vol. 1, p. 6, no. 36.
19 Letter dated 2 May 1887, in Rewald 1980, p. 105. See further pp. 110–11 (letter dated 16 May 1887). For the French texts, see Bailly-Herzberg 1980–91, vol. 2, pp. 156–58, no. 419, and pp. 168–70, no. 424, respectively.
20 Washington and San Francisco 1986, p. 40.
21 Washington and San Francisco 1986, p. 42.
22 Washington and San Francisco 1986, p. 45.
23 Washington and San Francisco 1986, pp. 43–44.
24 Washington and San Francisco 1986, p. 44. 'Hands kept in pockets can be eloquent. The artist's pencil will be infused with the essence of life.'
25 Washington and San Francisco 1986, p. 41.
26 Letter dated 25 June 1883, in Rewald 1980, pp. 38–39. For the French text, see Bailly-Herzberg 1980–91, vol. 1, pp. 223–24, no. 164, where the date for this letter is correctly given as June 1883 and not July.
27 In his review of the eighth exhibition (1886) Octave Maus wrote of Forain: 'C'est le poête de la corruption en habit noir, du dandysme des boudoirs, de la haute vie masquant les vides du coeur' (Berson 1996, pp. 462–63). On the subject of the drawings by Somm shown at the fourth exhibition (1879), F. C. de Syène wrote: 'Il en est résulté un épanouissement de femmes moqueuses, de papillons soyeux, de cupidons pervers, d'oiseaux, de serpents, des spectres bizarres, de lunes croissants...' (Berson 1996, p. 243).
28 Raffaëlli exhibited at the fifth (1880) and sixth (1881) exhibitions. On both occasions leading critics such as Gustave Geffroy, Henry Hazard, Huysmans, Paul Mantz and Silvestre were profoundly moved by his examination of the plight of the dispossessed (see Berson 1996, pp. 257–374 for the relevant reviews).
29 Letter dated 13 May 1891, in Rewald 1980, pp. 169–71. For the French text see Bailly-Herzberg 1980–91, vol. 3, pp. 81–83, no. 661.
30 'On pouvait penser que l'aquarelle se serait mieux prêtée que l'huile à cette conception sommaire et rapide des rendus.' Berson 1996, pp. 364–65.
31 Baudelaire 1965, pp. 199–200, in 'The Salon of 1859'. 'In the end, all these clouds, with their fantastic and luminous forms; these ferments of gloom; these immensities of green and pink, suspended and added one upon another; these gaping furnaces; these firmaments of black or purple satin, crumpled, rolled or torn; these horizons in mourning, or streaming with molten metal – in short, all these depths and all these splendours rose to my brain like a heady drink or like the eloquence of opium.'
32 Huysmans 2019, p. 130, in 'Exhibition of the Independents in 1880'.
33 Huysmans 2019, p. 129.
34 Redon 1979, pp. 26–27.
35 Letter dated 23 January 1905, in Cézanne 2013, p. 350, no. 248.

The Rising Status of Drawing from the 1870s to the 1890s

LEILA JARBOUAI

1 Brettell 2012.
2 'A propos du Salon', *Paris-Journal*, 12 April 1870, p. 180, reproduced in Reff 1968.
3 Bouillon 1986.
4 Leimbacher 2007, p. 52.
5 Klumpke 1908, p. 88.
6 Méneux 2003.
7 Méneux 2003, p. 32.
8 *La Chronique des arts et de la curiosité*, supplement to the *Gazette des Beaux-Arts*, 17 January 1874, p. 19.
9 For a detailed analysis of the figures, see DeWitte 2017. My thanks to Christopher Lloyd for drawing my attention to this article.
10 Marx 1883.
11 Bouillon 2010, p. 197.
12 Bouillon 2010, p. 197.
13 Duranty 1876, p. 25.
14 Philippe Burty, 'Exposition des œuvres des Artistes Indépendants', *La République française*, 10 April 1880, p. 2, quoted in Bouillon 2010, p. 216.
15 Ephrussi wrote a book about Dürer in 1882: *Albert Dürer et ses dessins*.
16 Bouillon 2010, p. 280.
17 Félix Fénéon, 'Les Impressionistes', *La Vogue*, 13–20 June 1886, pp. 261–75, quoted in Bouillon 2010, p. 282.

Reciprocal Invention: How Material Innovations Catalysed the Ascendance of Drawing in Nineteenth-century France

HARRIET K. STRATIS

1 Stratis 1994, pp. 357–58.
2 See especially Mayhew 2016; Sullivan and Yocco 2016. Also Schenck 2005.
3 Blanc 1867; Chevreul 1860.
4 Druick 2007, p. 83.
5 See for example, Lalanne 1869; Allongé 1875; Robert 1876a; Robert 1876b.
6 Buchberg 2007, p. 37.
7 Mayhew 2023, pp. 44–45; Buchberg 2007, pp. 34–35; Mayhew 2016, pp. 130–31.
8 Buchberg 2007, p. 35.
9 Buchberg 2007, p. 35.
10 It was not until 2007 that scientific analysis of Seurat's drawings and vintage Conté crayons carried out at New York's Museum of Modern Art confirmed that wax was not used in the formulation of the popular sticks. See McGlinchey and Buchberg 2009, pp. 118–21.
11 Stratis 1994, p. 362.
12 Redon 1979, p. 129 (the italics are Redon's). Druick 2007, p. 83, p. 102, note 21.
13 Stratis 1994, p. 358.
14 For a definitive study on the subject, see Burns 2007.
15 See REassessing VIncent van GOgh (REVIGO) https://www.vangoghmuseum.nl/en/about/knowledge-and-research/completed-research-projects/revigo/research-results-revigo-drawings. Shelley and Centeno 2005, pp. 348–56.
16 See for example, Stratis 2016.
17 Stratis 2017, p. 40.
18 *Léon Monet. Brother of the Artist and Collector*, a recent exhibition at the Musée du Luxembourg, Paris (March–July 2023), provides new insights into the biography of the artist's brother as colour chemist and collector. See also Kalba 2017, pp. 81, 113.
19 'De l'influence de la lumière sur la conservation des couleurs', *La Chronique des arts et de la curiosité*, 2 February 1889, pp. 36–37. Russell and Abney 1888. See also Brommelle 1964.
20 See, for example, Stratis 2023, pp. 59–60; Fiedler et al. 2016.

Bibliography

Bibliographic Sources

Allongé 1875
Auguste Allongé, *Le Fusain*, Paris, 1875

Bailly-Herzberg 1980–91
Correspondance de Camille Pissarro, volume 1: 1865–85, volume 2: 1886–90, volume 3: 1891–94, volume 4: 1895–98, volume 5: 1899–1903, Janine Bailly-Herzberg (ed.), Paris and Saint-Ouen-l'Aumône, 1980–91

Baudelaire 1964
Charles Baudelaire, *The Painter of Modern Life and Other Essays*, Jonathan Mayne (trans. and ed.), London, 1964

Baudelaire 1965
Charles Baudelaire, *Art in Paris, 1845–1862: Salons and Other Exhibitions*, Jonathan Mayne (trans. and ed.), London, 1965

Berson 1996
Ruth Berson, *The New Painting, Impressionism 1874–1886. Documentation: Volume I. Reviews* and *Volume II. Exhibited Works*, San Francisco, 1996

Blanc 1867
Charles Blanc, *Grammaire des arts du dessin: Architecture, sculpture, peinture*, Paris, 1867

Bouillon 1986
Jean-Paul Bouillon, 'Sociétés d'artistes et institutions officielles dans la seconde moitié du XIXe siècle', *Romantisme*, 54, 1986, pp. 89–113

Bouillon 2010
Jean-Paul Bouillon, 'La Promenade du critique influent', in *Anthologie de la critique d'art en France, 1850–1900*, new edition, revised and published by Jean-Paul Bouillon and Catherine Meneux, Paris, 2010

Brettell 2012
Richard R. Brettell, 'The Paper Century: French Drawing in the 1800s', in *Color, Line, Light: French Drawings, Watercolors, and Pastels from Delacroix to Signac*, Margaret Morgan Grasselli and Andrew Robison (eds), exh. cat., National Gallery of Art, Washington, and Musée des Impressionnismes, Giverny, 2012, pp. 1–15

Brommelle 1964
N. S. Brommelle, 'The Russell and Abney Report on the Action of Light on Water Colours', *Studies in Conservation*, 9, 4, 1964, pp. 140–52, https://doi.org/10.2307/1505213

Buchberg 2007
Karl Buchberg, 'Seurat: Materials and Techniques', in *Georges Seurat: The Drawings*, Jodi Hauptman (ed.), exh. cat., The Museum of Modern Art, New York, 2007–08, pp. 30–41

Burns 2007
Thea Burns, *The Invention of Pastel Painting*, London, 2007

Cézanne 2013
The Letters of Paul Cézanne, Alex Danchev (ed. and trans.), London, 2013

Chevreul 1860
Michel-Eugène Chevreul, *The Principles of Harmony and Contrast of Colours, and Their Applications to the Arts, Including Painting, Interior Decoration, Tapestries, Carpets, Mosaics, Coloured Glazing, Paper-staining, Calico-printing, Letterpress Printing, Map-colouring, Dress, Landscape and Flower Gardening, Etc.*, Charles Martel (trans.), London, 1860

Delaborde 1870
Henri Delaborde, *Ingres: sa vie, ses travaux, sa doctrine*, Paris, 1870

DeWitte 2015
Debra J. DeWitte, 'The Exhibition of Drawings, Pastels and Watercolours in the French Salon: 1863–1881', *The Paris Fine Art Salon/Le Salon, 1791–1882*, 33, 2015, pp. 371–84

DeWitte 2017
Debra J. DeWitte, 'Drawings on View in State-funded Venues and Artists' Societies in Paris, 1860–90: A Data-driven Study', *Master Drawings*, 55:2, 2017, pp. 225–48

Druick 2007
Douglas Druick, 'Jasper Johns: Gray Matters', in *Jasper Johns: Gray*, James Rondeau and Douglas Druick (eds), exh. cat., The Art Institute of Chicago, 2007–08, pp. 80–107

Duranty 1876
Edmond Duranty, *La Nouvelle Peinture: à propos du groupe d'artistes qui exposent dans les galeries Durand-Ruel*, Paris, 1876; for an English translation see Washington and San Francisco 1986, pp. 37–47

Fiedler et al. 2016
Inge Fiedler et al., 'Materials, Intention, and Evolution: Van Gogh's Bedrooms', in *Van Gogh's Bedrooms*, Gloria Groom (ed.), exh. cat., The Art Institute of Chicago, 2016, pp. 68–103

Huysmans 2019
Joris-Karl Huysmans, *Modern Art (L'Art moderne)*, translated with an introduction and notes by Brendan King, Sawtry, 2019

Kalba 2017
Laura Anne Kalba, *Color in the Age of Impressionism: Commerce, Technology, and Art*, University Park, PA, 2017

Kendall 1987
Richard Kendall (ed.), *Degas by Himself: Drawings, Prints, Paintings, Writings*, London, 1987

Klumpke 1908
Anna Klumpke, *Rosa Bonheur. Sa vie, son œuvre*, Paris, 1908

Lalanne 1869
Maxime Lalanne, *Le Fusain*, Paris, 1869

Leimbacher 2007
Marie Leimbacher, *Les Arts graphiques dans les Salons parisiens de la deuxième moitié du XIXe siècle (1863–1892)*, MA thesis, Ecole du Louvre, 2007

McGlinchey and Buchberg 2009
Chris McGlinchey and Karl Buchberg, 'The Examination of Drawings by Georges Seurat Using Fourier Transform Infrared Micro-Spectroscopy (Micro-FTIR)', *e-Preservation Science*, 6, 2009, pp. 118–21

Marx 1883
Roger Marx, 'Le Salon VI', *Le Progrès artistique*, 15 June 1883

Mayhew 2016
Timothy David Mayhew, '*Dessin au fusain*: Nineteenth-century French Charcoal Drawing Materials and Techniques', in *Noir: The Romance of Black in Nineteenth-century French Drawings and Prints*, Lee Hendrix (ed.), exh. cat., J. Paul Getty Museum, Los Angeles, 2016, pp. 124–52

Mayhew 2023
Timothy David Mayhew, 'Traditional Nineteenth-century French Graphite Drawing Materials and Techniques', in *Nineteenth-century French Drawings*, Britany Salsbury (ed.), exh. cat., The Cleveland Museum of Art, 2023, pp. 42–51

Méneux 2003
Catherine Méneux, 'Les Salons en Noir et Blanc (1876–1892)', *Histoire de l'Art*, 52, June 2003, pp. 29–44

Oxford, Manchester and Glasgow 1986
Impressionist Drawings from British Public and Private Collections, Christopher Lloyd and Richard Thomson, exh. cat., Ashmolean Museum, Oxford, Manchester City Art Gallery, and Burrell Collection, Glasgow, 1986

Paris 2018
Gustave Moreau, Vers le Songe et l'abstrait, exh. cat., Musée Gustave Moreau, Paris, 2018–19

Redon 1979
Odilon Redon, *A soi-même. Journal (1867–1915): Notes sur la vie, l'art et les artistes*, Paris, 1979

Reff 1968
Theodore Reff, 'Some Unpublished Letters of Degas', *Art Bulletin*, 50, 1, 1968, pp. 87–88

Rewald 1980
Camille Pissarro, Letters to His Son Lucien, edited with the assistance of Lucien Pissarro by John Rewald, 4th edition, London, 1980

Robert 1876a
Karl Robert, *Le Pastel. Traite pratique et complet*, Paris, 1876

Robert 1876b
Karl Robert, *Le Fusain sans Maître*, Paris, 1876

Russell and Abney 1888
William James Russell and William de Wiveleslie Abney, *Report to the Science and Art Department of the Committee of Council on Education on the Action of Light on Water Colours: Presented to both Houses of Parliament by Command of Her Majesty*, London, 1888

Schenck 2005
Kimberly Schenck, 'Crayon, Paper, and Paint: An Examination of Nineteenth-century Drawing Materials' and 'Glossary', in *The Essence of Line: French Drawings from Ingres to Degas*, Jay Fisher et al., exh. cat., Baltimore Museum of Art, Walters Art Museum, Baltimore, and Birmingham Museum of Art, AL, 2005–06, pp. 56–85

Shelley and Centeno 2005
Marjorie Shelley and Silvia A. Centeno, 'Technical Studies: Observations on the Drawing Materials Used by Van Gogh in Provence', in *Vincent van Gogh: The Drawings*, Colta Ives, Susan Alyson Stein, Sjraar van Heugten and Marije Vellekoop (eds), exh. cat., Van Gogh Museum, Amsterdam, and The Metropolitan Museum of Art, New York, 2005, pp. 348–56

Stratis 1994
Harriet K. Stratis, 'Beneath the Surface: Redon's Methods and Materials', in *Odilon Redon: Prince of Dreams, 1840–1916*, Douglas Druick (ed.), exh. cat., The Art Institute of Chicago, Van Gogh Museum, Amsterdam, and Royal Academy of Arts, London, 1994, pp. 353–77

Stratis 2016
Harriet K. Stratis, with scientific analysis by Céline Daher, 'Gauguin, Cat. 37, *Sketch of Maori Woman and Child* (recto): Technical Study', in *Gauguin Paintings, Sculpture, and Graphic Works at the Art Institute of Chicago*, Gloria Groom and Genevieve Westerby (eds), The Art Institute of Chicago, 2016, paragraphs 5 and 6, https://publications.artic.edu/gauguin/reader/gauguinart/section/140275/technical_report_anchor/p-140275-5

Stratis 2017
Harriet K. Stratis, 'A Practised Touch: Edgar Degas and the Art of Pastel', in *Drawn in Colour: Degas from the Burrell Collection*, Christopher Riopelle (ed.), The National Gallery, London, 2017, pp. 32–43

Stratis 2023
Harriet K. Stratis, 'Unintended Outcomes: Recognising Change in Nineteenth-century French Drawings', in *Nineteenth-century French Drawings*, exh. cat., Britany Salsbury (ed.), The Cleveland Museum of Art, 2023, pp. 52–63

Sullivan and Yocco 2016
Michelle Sullivan and Nancy Yocco, 'A Closer Look: An Illustrated Glossary of Materials and Techniques Used in Nineteenth-century *Noir* Drawings', in *Noir: The Romance of Black in Nineteenth-century French Drawings and Prints*, Lee Hendrix (ed.), exh. cat., J. Paul Getty Museum, Los Angeles, 2016, pp. 153–56

Valéry 1989
Paul Valéry, *Degas, Manet, Morisot*, David Paul (trans.), Bollingen Series, XLV.12, Princeton, 1989

Van Gogh 2009
Vincent van Gogh, The Letters. The Complete Illustrated and Annotated Edition, Leo Jansen, Hans Luijten and Nienke Bakker (eds), 6 vols, London, 2009

Washington and San Francisco 1986
The New Painting. Impressionism 1874–1886, Charles S. Moffett, exh. cat., National Gallery of Art, Washington, and The Fine Arts Museums of San Francisco, 1986

Further Reading

The books listed below pertain specifically to the drawings made by the Impressionist and Post-Impressionist artists included in the present exhibition. The literature on the subject remains extremely random. In recent years most of the artists represented here have been the subject of important joint or monographic exhibitions, which have often included their drawings. Citations to the relevant catalogues can be found in the more recent titles listed below.

General
Christopher Lloyd and Richard Thomson, *Impressionist Drawings from British Public and Private Collections*, exh. cat., Ashmolean Museum, Oxford, Manchester City Art Gallery, and Burrell Collection, Glasgow, 1986
Nicholas Wadley, *Impressionist and Post-Impressionist Drawing*, London, 1991
Deanna Petherbridge, *The Primacy of Drawing: Histories and Theories of Practice*, New Haven and London, 2010
Christine Ekelhart and Christopher Lloyd, *Impressionism: Pastels, Watercolours, Drawings*, exh. cat., Milwaukee Art Museum, Milwaukee, and Albertina, Vienna, 2011
Louis-Antoine Prat, *Le Dessin français au XIXe siècle*, Paris, 2011
Christopher Lloyd, *Impressionist and Post-Impressionist Drawings*, London, 2019

Paul Cézanne
Adrien Chappuis, *The Drawings of Paul Cézanne: A Catalogue Raisonné*, 2 vols, London and Greenwich, CT, 1973
John Rewald, *Paul Cézanne: The Watercolours: A Catalogue Raisonné*, London and Boston, 1983
Matthew Sims, *Cézanne's Watercolours: Between Drawing and Painting*, New Haven and London, 2008
Christopher Lloyd, *Paul Cézanne: Drawings and Watercolours*, London, 2015

Edgar Degas
P.-A. Lemoisne, *Degas et son oeuvre*, 4 vols, Paris, 1946–49 with a Supplement by Philippe Brame, Theodore Reff and Arlene Reff, New York and London, 1984
Jean Sutherland Boggs and Anne Maheux, *Degas Pastels*, London and New York, 1992
Richard Kendall, *Degas: Beyond Impressionism*, exh. cat., The National Gallery, London, and The Art Institute of Chicago, 1996–97
Christopher Lloyd, *Edgar Degas: Drawings and Pastels*, London, 2014

Jean-Louis Forain
Florence Valdès-Forain, *Jean-Louis Forain (1852–1931): 'La Comédie Parisienne'*, exh. cat., Musée de la Ville de Paris (Petit Palais), Paris, and Dixon Gallery and Gardens, Memphis, 2011

Paul Gauguin
Ronald Pickvance, *The Drawings of Gauguin*, London and New York, 1970

Vincent van Gogh
Johannes van der Wolk, Ronald Pickvance and E. B. F. Pey, *Drawings: Vincent van Gogh*, exh. cat., Rijksmuseum Kröller-Müller, Otterlo, 1990
Sjraar van Heugten, Marije Vellekoop and Roelie Zwikker, *Van Gogh Museum: Vincent van Gogh Drawings*, 4 vols, Amsterdam and London, 1996–2007: vol. 1, *The Early Years, 1880–1883*; vol. 2, *Nuenen, 1883–1885*; vol. 3, *Antwerp and Paris, 1886–1888*; vol. 4, *Arles, Saint-Rémy, Auvers-sur-Oise, 1888–1890*
Sjraar van Heugten, *Van Gogh: The Master Draughtsman*, London, 2005
Colta Ives, Susan Alyson Stein and Sjraar van Heugten, *Vincent van Gogh: The Drawings*, exh. cat., Van Gogh Museum, Amsterdam, and The Metropolitan Museum of Art, New York, 2005
Teio Meedendorp, *Drawings and Prints by Vincent van Gogh in the Collection of the Kröller-Müller Museum*, Otterlo, 2007
Christopher Lloyd, *The Drawings of Vincent van Gogh*, London, 2023

Edouard Manet
Alain de Leiris, *The Drawings of Edouard Manet*, Berkeley and Los Angeles, 1969

Claude Monet
James A. Ganz and Richard Kendall, *The Unknown Monet: Pastels and Drawings*, exh. cat., Sterling and Francine Clark Art Institute, Williamstown, and Royal Academy of Arts, London, 2007

Camille Pissarro
Richard Brettell and Christopher Lloyd, *A Catalogue of Drawings by Camille Pissarro in the Ashmolean Museum, Oxford*, Oxford, 1980

Pierre-Auguste Renoir
John Rewald, *Renoir: Drawings*, New York, 1946

Georges Seurat
César M. de Hauke, *Seurat et son oeuvre*, 2 vols, Paris, 1961
Robert L. Herbert, *Seurat's Drawings*, London and New York, 1962
Jodi Hauptman (ed.), *Georges Seurat: The Drawings*, exh. cat., Museum of Modern Art, New York, 2007

Lenders to the Exhibition

Amsterdam
  Van Gogh Museum
    (Vincent van Gogh Foundation)
Barletta
  Pinacoteca Giuseppe de Nittis
Budapest
  Szépművészeti Múzeum /
    Museum of Fine Arts
Cambridge
  The Syndics of the Fitzwilliam Museum,
    University of Cambridge
  King's College, University of Cambridge
Chichester
  Pallant House Gallery
Edinburgh
  National Galleries of Scotland
Glasgow
  Glasgow Life Museums on behalf
    of Glasgow City Council
  Glasgow Life Museums on behalf
    of Glasgow City Council: from the
    Burrell Collection with the approval
    of the Burrell Trustees
Collection of David Lachenmann
London
  British Museum
  The Courtauld (Samuel Courtauld Trust)
  The Fan Museum Trust Collection
  The National Gallery
  Stephen Ongpin Fine Art
  Tate
  Victoria and Albert Museum
Manchester
  The Whitworth, The University
    of Manchester
Mantua
  Musei Civici di Mantova
Milan
  Galleria d'Arte Moderna
Monaco
  Collection of H.S.H. the Prince of Monaco
Norwich
  Sainsbury Centre, University of
    East Anglia
Otterlo
  Kröller-Müller Museum
Oxford
  Ashmolean Museum, University of
    Oxford
Paris
  Musée d'Orsay
  Petit Palais, Musée des Beaux-Arts de la
    Ville de Paris
York
  York Museums Trust (York Art Gallery)
Zurich
  Emil Bührle Collection, on long-term
    loan at Kunsthaus Zürich

and those who wish
to remain anonymous

Photographic Acknowledgements

All works are reproduced by kind permission of the owners. Every attempt has been made to trace the photographers and copyright holders. Specific acknowledgements are as follows:

Baltimore, © The Baltimore Museum of Art: The George A. Lucas Collection. Photography Mitro Hood: fig. 8
Boston, Museum of Fine Arts: figs 12, 13
Budapest, Szépművészeti Múzeum / Museum of Fine Arts, 2023: fig. 16, cats 14, 64, 75
Cambridge, © Fitzwilliam Museum, Cambridge: figs 3, 10, cats 3, 68
Cambridge, Reproduced with the permission of the Provost and Scholars of King's College, Cambridge: cat. 70
Chicago, The Art Institute of Chicago: fig. 33
Cleveland, The Cleveland Museum of Art: fig. 28
Photo Alex Fox (Roy Fox Fine Art Photography): cats 9, 15, 18, 59
Glasgow, © CSG CIC Glasgow Museums Collection: fig. 14, cats 19, 26, 54
London, © The Courtauld / Bridgeman Images: cats 5, 12
London, © The Fan Museum, Greenwich: cat. 49
London, © The National Gallery, London: cats 55, 77
London, © The Trustees of the British Museum: cats 13, 24, 25, 65, 66
London, © Victoria and Albert Museum, London: cat. 48
Manchester, © The Whitworth, The University of Manchester. Photography Michael Pollard: cat. 40; Bridgeman Images: fig. 6
Mantua, © Comune di Mantova – Musei Civici: cat. 61
Milan, © Comune di Milano – All Rights Reserved: cat. 56
Monaco, Photo Geoffroy Moufflet – Archives du palais de Monaco: cat. 11
New York, © 2007 Christie's Images Limited: cat. 62
New York, © The Metropolitan Museum of Art, Art Resource/Scala, Florence: fig. 20
Otterlo, © Collection Kröller-Müller Museum, Otterlo, The Netherlands. Photography Rik Klein Gotink: cat. 37
Oxford, © Ashmolean Museum, University of Oxford: fig. 11, cats 16, 21, 31, 51, 52
Paris, CCØ Paris Musées / Petit Palais, musée des Beaux-Arts de la Ville de Paris: cats 2, 6, 34
Paris, © RMN-Grand Palais (Musée d'Orsay). Photography Gérard Blot: fig. 15; Sophie Crépy: fig. 27; Adrien Didierjean: fig. 18; Hervé Lewandowski: fig. 17, cats 42, 47, 57, 76; Tony Querrec: cat. 32; Patrice Schmidt: fig. 25
Paris, © RMN-Grand Palais (Musée du Louvre). Photography Thierry Le Mage: fig. 9
Paris, © RMN-Grand Palais. Photography René-Gabriel Ojeda: fig. 19
Philadelphia, Museum of Art: fig. 2
Rome, Galleria Nazionale d'Arte Moderna: fig. 1
Rotterdam, © Collection Museum Boijmans Van Beuningen. Photography Studio Tromp: fig. 7
© Tate: cat. 38
Vienna, © The Albertina Museum, Vienna: figs 4, 5

Index

All references are to page numbers; those in **bold** type indicate catalogue plates, and those in *italic* type indicate essay illustrations

Benefactors of the Royal Academy of Arts

THE PRESIDENTS' CIRCLE
The Estate of the late
Annemarie Aschenagi
Blavatnik Family Foundation
Bloomberg Philanthropies
Mrs Linda Brownrigg
The Clore Duffield Foundation
Mervyn and Jeanne Davies
The Dorfman Foundation
Dunard Fund
Mrs Drue Heinz Hon DBE
Mr and Mrs Jungels-Winkler
Mrs Gabrielle Jungels-Winkler
David and Molly Lowell Borthwick
Ronald and Rita McAulay
The McLennan Family
Sir John Madejski OBE DL
The Mead Family Foundation
Mr and Mrs Robert Miller
The Monument Trust
National Lottery Heritage Fund
Julia and Hans Rausing
The Rothschild Foundation
Dame Jillian Sackler DBE
Jake and Hélène Marie Shafran
The Garfield Weston Foundation
The Maurice Wohl Charitable
Foundation
The Wolfson Foundation

MAJOR BENEFACTORS
The Band Trust
Ambassador Matthew Barzun
and Brooke Brown Barzun
Aryeh and Elana Bourkoff, LionTree
Sir Francis and the
Hon Lady Brooke
Mrs Linda Brownrigg
The Cadogan Charity
Sir Richard and Lady Carew Pole
Chenevière Travel Award
Adrian Cheng
Jeremy Coller Foundation
John and Gail Coombe
Sir Roger de Grey Memorial Fund
Lady Alison Deighton
Sir Harry Djanogly
The Eranda Rothschild Foundation
The Fidelity UK Foundation
The Foyle Foundation
J Paul Getty Jr Charitable Trust
Glenbevan Trust
Mrs Grete Goldhill
Horace W Goldsmith Foundation
Mr and Mrs Gounaris-Milner
Peter Greenham Fund
Mr and Mrs Jim Grover
The Alexis and Anne-Marie Habib
Foundation
Charles and Kaaren Hale
E Vincent Harris Fund
The Kirby Laing Foundation
Nicolette and Frederick Kwok
Lord Leverhulme's Charitable Trust
Christian Levett and Mougins
Museum of Classical Art
The Linbury Trust
Miss Rosemary Lomax Simpson
Mr William Loschert
Maintenance Fund
Philip and Valerie Marsden
The 29th May 1961 Charitable Trust
The Lord Mayor's Appeal
The Paul Mellon Estate
Milner Educational Trust
The Batia and Idan Ofer
Family Foundation
Christina Ong
Mr and Mrs James Paradise
The Estate of the late
Miss Constance-Anne Parker
J Heritage Peters
P F Charitable Trust
The late Mr John Porter
Ivor Rey Scholarship Fund
Sir Simon and Lady Robertson
Schools Portfolio Fund
The Schroder Foundation
Mr Sean Scully RA
Mr Richard S Sharp
Dasha Shenkman
William and Maureen Shenkman
The Estate of the late
Mrs Pauline Sitwell
Starr Fund
David and Deborah Stileman
The Swire Charitable Trust
The late Sir Anthony Tennant
and Lady Tennant
The Thompson Family
Charitable Trust
Patricia Turner Award
Vandaleur
Sir Siegmund Warburg's
Voluntary Settlement
The Welton Foundation
Mr W Galen Weston and the
Hon Mrs Hilary Weston

BENEFACTORS
Aldama Foundation
Lord and Lady Aldington
Mrs Allen-Huxley
Joan and Robin Alvarez
The Anson Charitable Trust
Artists Collecting Society
The Band Trust
Veronica and Lars Bane
Ms Linda Bennett and
Mr Philip Harley
Sir Win Bischoff
Charlotte Bonham-Carter
Charitable Trust
The William Brake Charitable Trust
The Deborah Loeb Brice
Foundation
The Consuelo and Anthony Brooke
Charitable Trust
Garvin and Steffanie Brown
Mr and Mrs John Burns
Ilaria Bulgari
Peter and Sally Cadbury
Carew Pole Charitable Trust
Dr Edmund Carter
Mr Richard Chang
Sir Trevor and Lady Susan Chinn
CHK Foundation
Mr and Mrs Jonathan Clarke
Mr Andrés Clase
The John S Cohen Foundation
Ms Elizabeth Crain Crankstart
Mr Michael Cowper
The Manny and Brigitta Davidson
Charitable Trust
Ina De and James Spicer
The Roger De Haan Charitable
Trust
Ron Dennis
The Gilbert and Eileen Edgar
Foundation
The John Ellerman Foundation
Mr Richard Elman
Epson
The Lord Faringdon Charitable
Trust
Mr and Mrs Stephen Fitzgerald
Mrs Jill Garcia
Mr and Mrs M Gee
Genesis Foundation
The Golden Bottle Trust
Nicholas and Judith Goodison's
Charitable Settlement
Antony Gormley and
Vicken Parsons
Mr Stephen Gosztony
The late Sir Ronald Grierson
Sir Nicholas Grimshaw CBE PPRA
Fiona and Peter Hare
Hauser & Wirth
Ms Katrin Henkel
Mr and Mrs Julian Heslop
Holbeck Charitable Trust
The Charles Michael Holloway
Charitable Trust
Mr and Mrs Jeremy Hosking
Huo Family Foundation (UK)
Harry Hyman and family
The Inchcape Foundation
Japanese Committee of Honour
of the Royal Academy of Arts
Chantal Joffe RA
Alistair D K Johnston CMG FCA
Mr Ivan Katzen
Mr Lagrange and Mr Burnough
Christopher Le Brun PPRA
and Charlotte Verity
The David Lean Foundation
Mr Nelson Leong
Mr and Mrs Mark Loveday
The Maccabaeans
Dr Lee MacCormick Edwards
Charitable Foundation
Mrs McAlpine
HRH Princess Marie-Chantal
of Greece
J P Marland Charitable Trust
The Rt Hon the Lord and
Lady Marland
The David Ellis Marlow Trust
The late Mr Minoru Mori Hon KBE
and Mrs Mori
Sir Michael Moritz
The Murray Family
Lady Alison Myners
Normanby Charitable Trust
Dr and Mrs Orentreich
Mr Charles Outhwaite
PF Charitable Trust
Stanley Picker Charitable Trust
The Pilgrim Trust
Mr and Mrs Maurice Pinto
The Earl and Countess of Plymouth
The Polonsky Foundation
Mrs Tineke Pugh
Red Butterfly Foundation
The Estate of the late Mr Ivor Rey
Peter Rippon
Sir Simon and Victoria,
Lady Robey OBE
Richard and Ruth Rogers
The Rose Foundation
Sir Paul and Lady Ruddock
The Basil Samuel Charitable Trust
Mrs Coral Samuel CBE
Edwina Sassoon
Guy Senior, in memory of
Brian and Mary Senior,
Friends of the RA
Louisa Service OBE
David and Sophie Shalit
Archie Sherman Charitable Trust
Mr Brian Smith
Mr Christopher Smith
Sir Paul and Lady Smith
The South Square Trust
Mr and Mrs Roger Staton
Sir Hugh and Lady Stevenson
The Nina and Roger Stewart
Charitable Trust
Mr John Studzinski
The late Sir David Tang KBE
Tavolozza Foundation
Tileyard London
Julian and Louisa Treger
Tresidor Investment Management
Celia Walker Art Foundation
Martin and Anja Weiss
Sian and Matthew Westerman
Chris Wilkinson OBE RA and
Diana Edmunds
Mr Peter Williams
Ivor and Caroline Windsor
The Harold Hyam Wingate
Foundation
Manuela and Iwan Wirth
The Lennox and Wyfold Foundation
Mr Yuzo Yagi
and those who wish
to remain anonymous

MAJOR BENEFACTORS TOWARDS REDEVELOPING THE RA SCHOOLS
The Band Trust
Adrian Cheng
Lady Alison Deighton
Dunard Fund
Christophe and Valérie
Jungels-Winkler
Nicolette and Frederick Kwok
The Mead Family Foundation
Milner Educational Trust
The Estate of the late
Miss Constance-Anne Parker
Julia and Hans Rausing
Jake and Hélène Marie Shafran
Sir Siegmund Warburg's
Voluntary Settlement
The Garfield Weston Foundation
The Wolfson Foundation

MAJOR BENEFACTORS OF THE RA SCHOOLS ENDOWMENT FUND
Chenevière Travel Award
Sir Roger de Grey Memorial
Fund
Dunard Fund
The Eranda Rothschild
Foundation
Peter Greenham Fund
E Vincent Harris Fund
J Heritage Peters Maintenance
Fund
Ronald and Rita McAulay
Ivor Rey Scholarship Fund
Schools Portfolio Fund
The Estate of the late
Mrs Pauline Sitwell
Starr Fund
Patricia Turner Award
Vandaleur
Mr and Mrs James Paradise

BENEFACTORS OF THE RA SCHOOLS
Artists Collecting Society
Charlotte Bonham-Carter
Charitable Trust
John S Cohen Foundation
Ron Dennis
Dreamchasing
Dunard Fund
The Gilbert and Eileen Edgar
Foundation
Epson
The Eranda Rothschild
Foundation
Peter Greenham Fund
The Charles Michael Holloway
Charitable Trust
Mr Nelson Leong
Leverhulme Trust
Mr and Mrs Mark Loveday
The Maccabaeans
Dr Lee MacCormick Edwards
Charitable Foundation
The Machin Foundation
The Normanby Charitable Trust
The Batia and Idan Ofer Family
Foundation
Andrés Olow Clase
Christina Ong
Stanley Picker Charitable Trust
Red Butterfly Foundation
The Estate of the late Mr Ivor Rey
Peter Rippon
Bianca Roden
The Rose Foundation
Archie Sherman Charitable Trust
The South Square Trust
Sir Paul and Lady Smith
The Stewarts Foundation
David and Deborah Stileman
The Adrian Swire Charitable
Trust
The Swire Charitable Trust
Tileyard London
Celia Walker Art Foundation
and those who wish
to remain anonymous

PATRONS

CHAIR OF RA PATRONS
Mr Matthew Langton

INTERNATIONAL CIRCLE
Mrs Niloufar Bakhtiar-Bakhtiari
Mr Lars Bane
Alexander and Ika Green
Ms Bella Kesoyan
Ms Ida Levine
Mr Sebastien Mazella di Bosco
Gaukhar Nurgalieva
Mr Thaddaeus Ropac
Antigone Theodorou &
Stefan Bollinger
Ms Chizuko Yashiro
Mr and Mrs Basil Zirinis
Ms Mercedes Zobel
and those who wish
to remain anonymous

PLATINUM PATRONS
Tim Ashley
Celia and Edward Atkin CBE
Paul Baines
Mr Christopher Bake
Alex Beard and Emma Vernetti
The Deborah Loeb Brice
Foundation
Ms Sue Butcher
Mrs Sophie Diedrichs-Cox
Mrs Willemien Downes
Hugo Eddis
Charles and Kaaren Hale
Mr Yan Huo
Mrs Elizabeth Lenz
Mr Nick Loup
Lady Alison Myners
Mrs Bianca Roden
Jake and Hélène Marie Shafran
Mrs Janet Winslow
and those who wish
to remain anonymous

GOLD PATRONS
Mr Stephen Allcock
Joan and Robin Alvarez
Ms Vanessa Aubry
Mrs Georgina Bennett
Sam and Rosie Berwick
Richard Bram and Monika
Machon
Molly Lowell Borthwick
Sir Francis Brooke Bt
Mr Thomas E Cantwell
Ms Lisa Carrodus
Margherita Castellani
Varun and Emma Chandra
Ms Natasha Cheung
Alexander Cicetti
Mr Andrés Clase
The Lady Renwick of Clifton
Maria Cristina Codognato
Vanessa Colomar de Enserro
Christopher and Alex Courage
Dr Juli Crocombe
Susan Elliott
Swag and Nupur Ganguly
Mrs Carol Gibson Jackson

Dr Chris and Mrs Marjorie Gibson-Smith
Amanda Gowing
Mr Stephen Griggs
Mr Jim Grover
Mr Joshua Harris
Rosalyn and Hugo Henderson
Dame Vivian Hunt
Mrs Josephine Jenno
Mr Kevin Kane
Sir and Lady Khalili
Ms Maxine Kohn
Sir Sydney Lipworth KC and Lady Lipworth CBE
Ms Olena Lutsenko
Mr Nicholas Maclean
Scott and Laura Malkin
Mr Stephen Marquardt
Louise Nathanson
Patrick and Bénédicte de Nonneville
Simon and Sabi North
Asta Paulauskaite
Paulo and Caroline Pereira
Mr Stuart Piercy
Mrs Ivetta Rabinovich
Ms Melanie Rademacher
Dianne Roberts
Sarah Ryan
Katrina Aleksa Ryemill
Mrs Oliwia Siemienczuk
Mr Richard Simmons CBE
Tim and Lynda Smith
Jane Spack
Mrs Raksha Sriram
Mr Michael Stiff
David and Deborah Stileman
Mr Robert Suss
Nesrin Tisdale
Kathryn Uhde
Miss M L Ulfane
Countess Cornelia Von Rittberg
Erica Wax
Mr Neil Westreich
Mr Peter Williams
Manuela and Iwan Wirth
David Yates and Yvonne Walcott Yates
Ms Catherine Walsh
Mr Robert John Yerbury
Mr Riccardo Zacconi
and those who wish to remain anonymous

SILVER PATRONS

Mrs Spindrift Al Swaidi
Ms Katherine Ashton-Young
Mila Askarova
Mrs Leslie Bacon
Mrs Ginny Battcock
Catherine Baxendale
Mr and Mrs Jonathan and Sarah Bayliss
Mrs J K M Bentley, Liveinart
Mr Bollinger
Ms Miel de Botton
Eleanor E Brass
Viscountess Bridgeman
Mrs Basia Briggs
Mrs Marcia Brocklebank
Mrs Charles Brown
Ms Debra Burt
Mrs Ann Chapman-Daniel
Sir Trevor and Lady Chinn
Mr John Clappier
Mrs Jane Clark
Rosalind Clayton
Sir Ronald and Lady Cohen
Andrew M Coppel, CBE and June V Coppel
Cathy Corbett
Edmund Coulthard
Mrs Caroline Cullinan
Monica and Knut Dahl
Mrs Georgina David
Mr Daniel Davies
Mrs Dominic Dowley
Mr and Mrs Jim Downing
Ms Noreen Doyle
Mrs Maurice Dwek
Mrs Samira Govers-El Hachioui
Mr and Mrs Jeff Eldredge
Mr David Fawkes
Mrs Stroma Finston
James Freedman
Virginia Gabbertas
Mr Stephen Garrett
Joanna George
Jacqueline and Jonathan Gestetner
Melanie and Piers Gibson
Caroline and Alan Gillespie
Mr Mark Glatman
Peter and Elizabeth Goulds, L.A. Louvre
John Gruzelier, Professor Emeritus
Mrs Margaret Guitar
Ms Han Guo
Ms Kim Habraken
Alex Haidas and Thalia Chryssikou
Mr Christopher Harrison
Sir John and Lady Hegarty
Sir Michael and Lady Heller
Mrs Katrin Henkel
Mrs Pat Heslop
Mr and Mrs Jonathan Hindle
Mrs Susan Hitchin
Anne Holmes-Drewry
Mr Philip Hudson
Mr and Mrs Jon Hunt
S Isern-Feliu
Mrs Caroline Jackson
Sir Martin and Lady Jacomb
Mr Tom Jacomb
Mrs Raymonde Jay
Fiona Johnstone
Mrs Marcelle Joseph
Dr Elisabeth Kehoe
Mrs Kit Kemp MBE
Paul and Susie Kempe
Miss Rebecca Kemsley
Simon and Emma Keswick
Mr Gerald Kidd
Mr and Mrs James Kirkman
Mrs Anna Kirrage
Mrs Latifa Kosta
Mrs Alkistis Koukouliou
Mrs Sybil Kretzmer
Mr Matthew Langton
Ms Isabella Lauder-Frost
Jessica Lavooy
Ms Patricia Lawrie
Mrs Anna Lee
Lady Lever of Manchester
Richard Burger and Rachel Lipson
Mr Jeremy and Dr Julie Llewelyn
Miss R Lomax-Simpson
Mr and Mrs Robin Lough
Mr George Maher
Olivier and Priscilla Malingue
Mr Richard Mansell-Jones
Mrs Janet Martin
Gillian McIntosh
Andrew and Judith McKinna
Itxaso Mediavilla-Murray
Ms Kimiya Minoukadeh
Victoria Miro
Shalini Misra
Simon Morris and Annalisa Burello
Mr Alan Morton
Mr Blair Morton
Mrs Alexandra Nash
Mrs Tessa Nicholson
Ms Minka Nyberg
Emma O'Donoghue
Flavia Ormond
Neil Osborn and Holly Smith
Sir Michael Palin
Maria N Peacock
Mr and Mrs D J Peacock
The Hon Julian Phillimore
Mr Adam and Mrs Michelle Plainer
Mary Pollock
Lady Purves
Mr William Ramsay
Ms Mouna Rebeiz
Peter Rice Esq
Erica Roberts
Kate de Rothschild Agius and Marcus Agius CBE
Miss Elaine Rowley
Sir Paul and Lady Ruddock
Mrs Janice Sacher
Ms Kim Samuel
Mrs Sirkka Sanderson
Mr Paul Sandilands
Mr Adrian Sassoon
Devinyl Schonfeld
Christina, Countess of Shaftesbury
Mr Robert N Shapiro
Mr David Shaw
Ms Elena Shchukina
Dr Shirley Sherwood OBE
Mrs Marianna E Simpson
Mr Martin Klosterfelde, Skarstedt Gallery
Mrs Jane Smith
Lady Henrietta St George
Mr Marc St John
Miss Sarah Straight
Mrs Ziona Strelitz
Ms Catherine Sutton
Mr Matt Symonds
Anne Elizabeth Tasca
Amy Thomson
Mr Anthony J Todd
Mrs Kirsten Tofte Jensen
Maria Toxavidi
Ms Roxane Vacca
Mrs Madhavi Vadera
Petri & Jolana Vainio
Tamara Varga
Mr Waqas Wajahat
Mrs Charlotte Warshaw
John and Carol Wates
The Duke and Duchess of Wellington
Ms Christine Westwood-Davis
Mrs Adriana Winters
Marek and Penny Wojciechowski
Mr and Mrs Maurice Wolridge
David Zwirner
and those who wish to remain anonymous

YOUNG PATRONS

Dr Ghadah W. Alharthi
Kalita Al Swaidi
Mr Eduardo Alves
Miss Aishwarya Anam
Yevheniya Bazhenova
Daniel Boehm
Mr Nicholas Bonsall
Mr Matthew Charlton
XiaoMeng Cheng
Mr George Clark
Sophie Dickson
Rebecca Dolan
Dr Brian Fu
Rebecca Glenapp
Miss Lucy von Goetz
Adam Gordon
Miss Lucinda Bellm, LAMB Gallery
Mrs Olivia Houlihan
Miss Amelia Hunton
Mr Phoebus Istavrioglu
Miss Minnie Kemp
Mr Callum Kempe
Ms Victoria Kleiner
Anna Kuchina
Ms Marianna Lemos
Miss Matilda Liu
Mrs Louisa Macmillan
Anna Maj Madsen
Mr Jean-David Malat
Patrick McCrae
Miss Yekaterina Munk
Mr Thomas Mustier
Miss Mimi Nguyen
Thomas de Noronha e Silva Tomei
Mrs Harriet O'Rourke
Danielle Petitti
Mr Gaudenz Probst
Ziba Sarikhani
Ms Julie Scotto
Fazilet Seçgin
Irene Sieberger
Lily Stone
Gigi Surel
The Honourable Clarence Tan
Ryan Sebastian Taylor
Mr Milan Tomic
Miss Ayse Unluturk
Ariana von der Heyde
Dimitrios Weedon-Topalopoulos
and those who wish to remain anonymous

PATRON DONORS

Geoffrey Ainsworth and Johanna Featherstone
The William Brake Foundation
The Breathe Project
Dr Bruce Horten
Mr D H Killick
The de Laszlo Foundation
The Michael and Nicola Sacher Charitable Trust
Melanie and Michael Sherwood Charitable Foundation
Mr and Mrs Anthony Williams
Ms Cynthia Wu
and those who wish to remain anonymous

TRUSTEES OF THE ROYAL ACADEMY TRUST

Registered Charity No. 1067270

HONORARY PRESIDENT

Pending confirmation

TRUSTEES

Lady Alison Myners (Chair)
Rob Suss (Deputy Chair)
President of the Royal Academy (ex officio)
Treasurer of the Royal Academy (ex officio)
Ms Clara Amfo
Mr Stefan Bollinger
Mr Aryeh Bourkoff
Mr Varun Chandra
Dr Adrian Cheng
Ms Melanie Clore
Lady Deighton
Sir Lloyd Dorfman CBE
Mr Pesh Framjee
Mr Stephen Gosztony
Lady Heywood
Mr Clive Humby OBE
Dame Vivian Hunt
Dame Carolyn McCall
Mr Scott Mead
Mrs Batia Ofer
Mrs Ina Sandmann
Mrs Sian Westerman
The Hon William Yerburgh

EMERITUS AND HONORARY TRUSTEES

Lord Aldington
Mrs Susan Burns
Sir James Butler CBE DL
Sir David Cannadine FBA
Sir Richard Carew Pole Bt OBE DL
Sir Trevor Chinn CVO
Mr John Coombe
Ms Elizabeth Crain
Lord Davies of Abersoch CBE
Ambassador Edward E Elson
Mr John Entwistle OBE
Mr Michael Gee
The Rt Hon the Earl of Gowrie PC
HRH Princess Marie-Chantal of Greece
C Hugh Hildesley
Mrs Anya Hindmarch CBE
Mrs Susan Ho
The Lady Lever of Manchester
Sir Sydney Lipworth QC
The Rt Hon Lord Luce GCVO DL
Mr Philip Marsden
Sir Keith Mills GBE DL
Mr Ludovic de Montille
Mrs Minori Mori
Mr John Raisman CBE
John Roberts Esq FRIBA
Sir Simon Robertson
Sir Evelyn de Rothschild
Mrs Maryam Sachs
The Hon Richard Sharp
Mr David Stileman
Mr Peter Williams

JAPANESE COMMITTEE OF HONOUR

Mr Hiroaki Fujii (Chair) and Mrs Fujii

CORPORATE MEMBERS

Mr Nobuyuki Idei (I Concept) and Mrs Idei
Mr Yoshitoshi Kitajima (Dai Nippon Printing Co Ltd) and Mrs Kitajima
Mr Shinzo Maeda and Mrs Maeda (Shiseido Co Ltd)
Mr Yoshihiko Miyauchi (ORIX Corporation) and Mrs Miyauchi
Mr Yuzaburo Mogi (Kikkoman Corporation) and Mrs Mogi
Mrs Minoru Mori (Mori Building Co Ltd)
Mr Takeo Obayashi (Obayashi Corporation) and Mrs Obayashi
Mr Nobutada Saji (Suntory Holding Co Ltd) and Mrs Saji
Mr Toichi Takenaka (Takenaka Corporation) and Mrs Takenaka
Mr Yuzo Yagi (Yagi Tsusho Ltd) and Mrs Yagi

PATRONS

Prof Tadao Ando Hon RA and Mrs Ando
HE Ambassador Hiroaki Fujii (Chair) and Mrs Fujii
Mr Shinji Fukukawa and Mrs Fukukawa
Prof Arata Isozaki Hon RA and Mrs Isozaki
Mr Hideo Morita and Mrs Morita
Mr Koichi Nezu and Mrs Nezu
Mr Yoji Shimizu and Mrs Shimizu
Mr Masayoshi Son and Mrs Son
Mr Jonathan Stone and Mrs Stone
Mrs Tadao Suzuki
Mr Hideya Taida Hon CBE and Mrs Taida
Mr Shuji Takashina and Mrs Takashina
Mr Tsuneharu Takeda and Mrs Takeda
Mr Hiroyasu Tomita and Mrs Tomita
Mrs Toshio Yamazaki

DIRECTOR
Mrs Yu Serizawa

SECRETARIAT
Mrs Yuko Tadano

CORPORATE MEMBERSHIP OF THE ROYAL ACADEMY OF ARTS
Launched in 1988, the Royal Academy's Corporate Membership Scheme offers company benefits for staff, clients and community partners and access to the Academy's facilities and resources. We thank all members for their valuable support and continued enthusiasm.

PREMIER
Allen & Overy
BNY Mellon
Charles Stanley
Convex UK Services Limited (Convex Group)
Evelyn Partners
EY
FTI Consulting
JM Finn & Co.
JTI
KPMG LLP
Rothschild & Co
Sotheby's
The Arts Club
Van Cleef & Arpels

CORPORATE
Bloomberg LP
Chanel
Christie's
Clifford Chance LLP
Edelman
Generation Investment Management LLP
Hakluyt & Company
HSBC
Lindsell Train
Marie Curie
Pictet
Rathbone Investment Management Ltd
Rolex
Santander
Sisk
Sky
Teneo
The Royal Society of Chemistry
Trowers & Hamlins
UBS
Value Retail
Weil Gotshal & Manges LLP

ASSOCIATE
Bank of America
Beaumont Nathan
Deutsche Bank AG
London Imperial College Healthcare Charity
Lazard
Morgan Stanley
SMBC Europe Ltd
The Boston Consulting Group UK LLP
The Cultivist

CORPORATE FOUNDING BENEFACTORS
BNY Mellon
Index Ventures
Newton Investment Management
Sisk
Sky

CORPORATE PARTNERS
AXA XL
Bloomberg Philanthropies
BNP Paribas
Burberry
Edwardian Hotels
Insight Investment
Viking

CORPORATE SUPPORTERS
Amathus
BNY Mellon, Anniversary Partner of the Royal Academy of Arts
Claridge's
Chrome Hearts
Natalia Cola Foundation
Fortnum & Mason
Gide Loyrette Nouel LLP
Hermès GB
House of Creed
Sean Kelly Gallery
L'ÉCOLE, School of Jewelry Arts, supported by Van Cleef & Arpels
Lia Rumma Gallery
Lisson Gallery
Louis Roederer
Stewarts
Tileyard London

BENEFACTORS OF THE RA LEARNING PROGRAMME
The Nicholas Bacon Charitable Trust
Jeanne and William Callanan
Capital Group
The Clore Duffield Foundation
Dunard Fund
Robin Hambro
The Margaret and Richard Merrell Foundation
Alexandra Nash
Peacock Charitable Trust
The Rothschild Foundation
Peter Storrs Charitable Trust
Lord Leonard and Lady Estelle Wolfson Foundation
Worshipful Company of Chartered Architects

BENEFACTORS OF THE RA EXHIBITION PROGRAMME
Art Mentor Foundation Lucerne
The Milton and Sally Avery Arts Foundation
Francis Bacon MB Art Foundation
Lars Bane
Blavatnik Family Foundation
Ivor Braka
Brooke Brown Barzun
Cockayne Grants for the Arts
The Daiwa Anglo Japanese Foundation
Dunard Fund
Dr Lee MacCormick Edwards Charitable Foundation
The Fanzhi Foundation for Art and Education
Ford Foundation
The Garcia Family Foundation
Genesis Foundation
The Great Britain Sasakawa Foundation
The International Music and Art Foundation
The Japan Foundation
Ömer Koç
Rosemary Lomax-Simpson
The Magic Trust
Scott and Laura Malkin
Cate Olson and Nash Robbins
Pro Helvetia
Tavolozza Foundation
The Terra Foundation for American Art
The Thompson Family Charitable Trust
Victoria Miro
Kathryn Uhde
Peter and Geraldine Williams
and those who wish to remain anonymous

RA BENEFACTORS
The Atlas Fund
CHK Foundation
Joseph Strong Frazer Trust

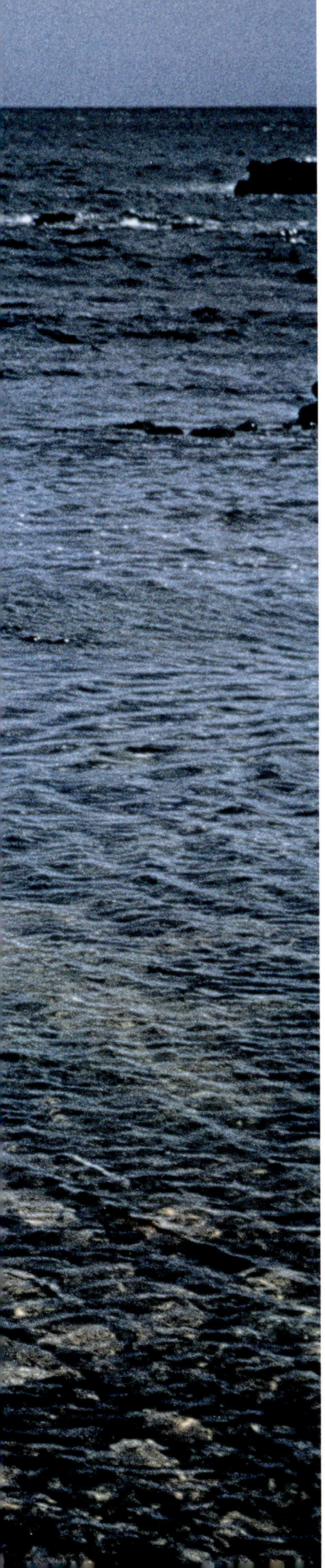

Fiona Pearson
with an essay by Sara Stevenson

Joan Eardley

National Galleries of Scotland
Edinburgh

First published by the Trustees of the National Galleries of Scotland to accompany the exhibition *Joan Eardley* held at the National Gallery Complex, Edinburgh, from 6 November 2007 to 13 January 2008.

Reprinted 2014, 2016, 2019, 2025

ISBN 978 1 906270 76 6

Designed and typeset in Mentor by Dalrymple
Printed on Magno Matt 170gsm by Gomer Press, UK

Front cover: Detail from *Summer Fields*, *c*.1961, Scottish National Gallery of Modern Art, Edinburgh [60]

Back cover: *Catterline in Winter*,
Scottish National Gallery of Modern Art, Edinburgh [51]

Half-title: *Black Sky with Blue Sea*, pastel on paper, 20.1 × 25.3cm
Scottish National Gallery of Modern Art, Edinburgh

Frontispiece: Eardley sketching on the shoreline at Catterline, *c*.1950s. Photo: Audrey Walker. Gracefield Art Centre, Dumfries

The proceeds from the sale of this book go towards supporting the National Galleries of Scotland.

National Galleries of Scotland is a charity registered in Scotland (No.SC003728)

www.nationalgalleries.org

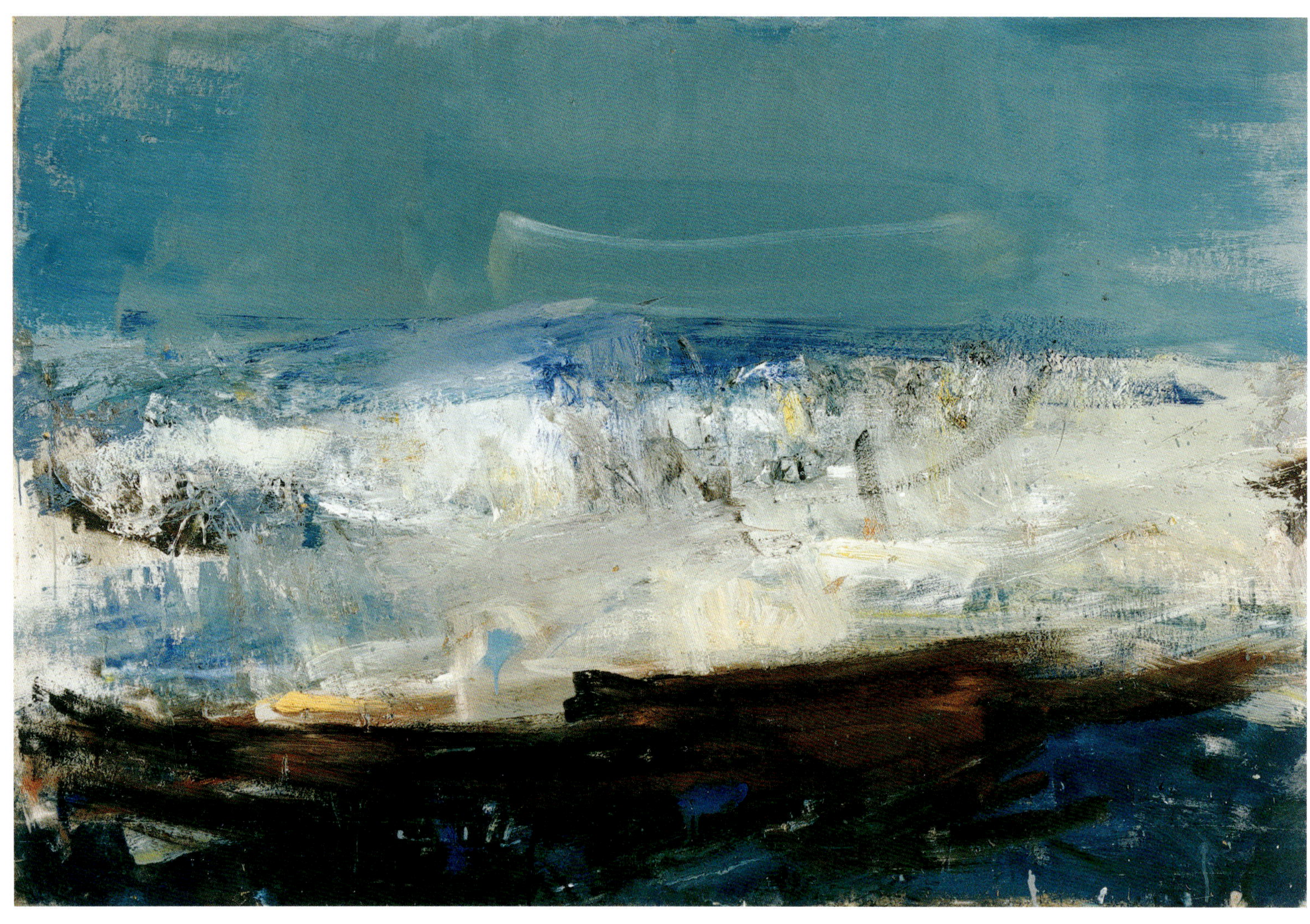

1 | ***Summer Sea*****, 1962**

Oil on board 122.2 × 183cm

Royal Scottish Academy, Edinburgh

Foreword

In the forty-four years since Joan Eardley's untimely death in 1963 there have been three major exhibitions of her work. The last was nearly twenty years ago. This retrospective exhibition organised by the National Galleries of Scotland is a welcome opportunity not only for a new generation to see the work of this much loved artist but also allows a re-assessment of her position in the postwar British art scene. Recent research into the battle between realism and abstraction has tended to polarise the two camps, but in Eardley one finds a genuine engagement with both approaches to modern art.

The exhibition includes works from both public and private collections across the United Kingdom. We are most grateful to all the lenders. However, the starting point for the exhibition was the generous gift of a group of Eardley's drawings, donated to the Scottish National Gallery of Modern Art by the artist's sister, Mrs Pat Black, in 1987. This extensive collection of drawings and also archival material has provided an invaluable basis for our studies.

The project has been curated by staff at the Scottish National Gallery of Modern Art, principally, Fiona Pearson, Senior Curator, working with Keith Hartley, the Acting Director and Patrick Elliott, the Chief Curator. Sara Stevenson, Chief Curator of the Scottish National Photography Collection at the Scottish National Portrait Gallery, has contributed an essay and many other colleagues have given invaluable help and support; we thank them all. Finally, we are extremely grateful to the Friends of the National Galleries of Scotland for their sponsorship of the exhibition, and William Zachs and Martin Adam for their contribution towards the cost of this book.

JOHN LEIGHTON
Director-General, National Galleries of Scotland

KEITH HARTLEY
Acting Director, Scottish National Gallery of Modern Art

Introduction

Who was Joan Eardley? Was she a painter of social realism working in parallel with the English Kitchen Sink School or was she Scotland's answer to the Cobra artists of continental Europe or America's Jackson Pollock and Willem de Kooning? Eardley was a strong, passionate painter who was totally engaged in depicting the life forces around her, everything from children to nature. She herself was a child of the Second World War and saw in Glasgow's shattered tenement street-life signs of richness among the decay. Eardley's deep love of humanity was manifest in images of the resilience of the human spirit among the poor, the old and the very young. Such was the impact of her paintings that she was perceived as a young member of the post-war British avant garde and her works were bought by galleries throughout Britain. Additionally, her landscape paintings, mostly of Catterline on the north-east coast of Scotland, saw Eardley using techniques in tune with Abstract Expressionism from America and Tachisme from Europe. This expressive abstraction drew praise in her lifetime, in London as well as Scotland. By the end of her short life Douglas Hall, then Keeper of the Scottish National Gallery of Modern Art, was stating that we had lost a painter of international stature.

This is the first major exhibition and re-assessment of Eardley for nearly twenty years. A new generation will be seeing her work. The last show at the Talbot Rice Art Centre, University of Edinburgh, coincided with a return to figurative art in the young Scottish art scene. Today, we hope to highlight the social realism of her work by showing how Eardley used photography. This book contains an insightful essay exploring this aspect of Eardley's work by Sara Stevenson, Chief Curator of the Scottish National Photography Collection at the Scottish National Portrait Gallery.

Within Scotland Eardley is one of the most popular painters of the twentieth century, reminding Scots of lost

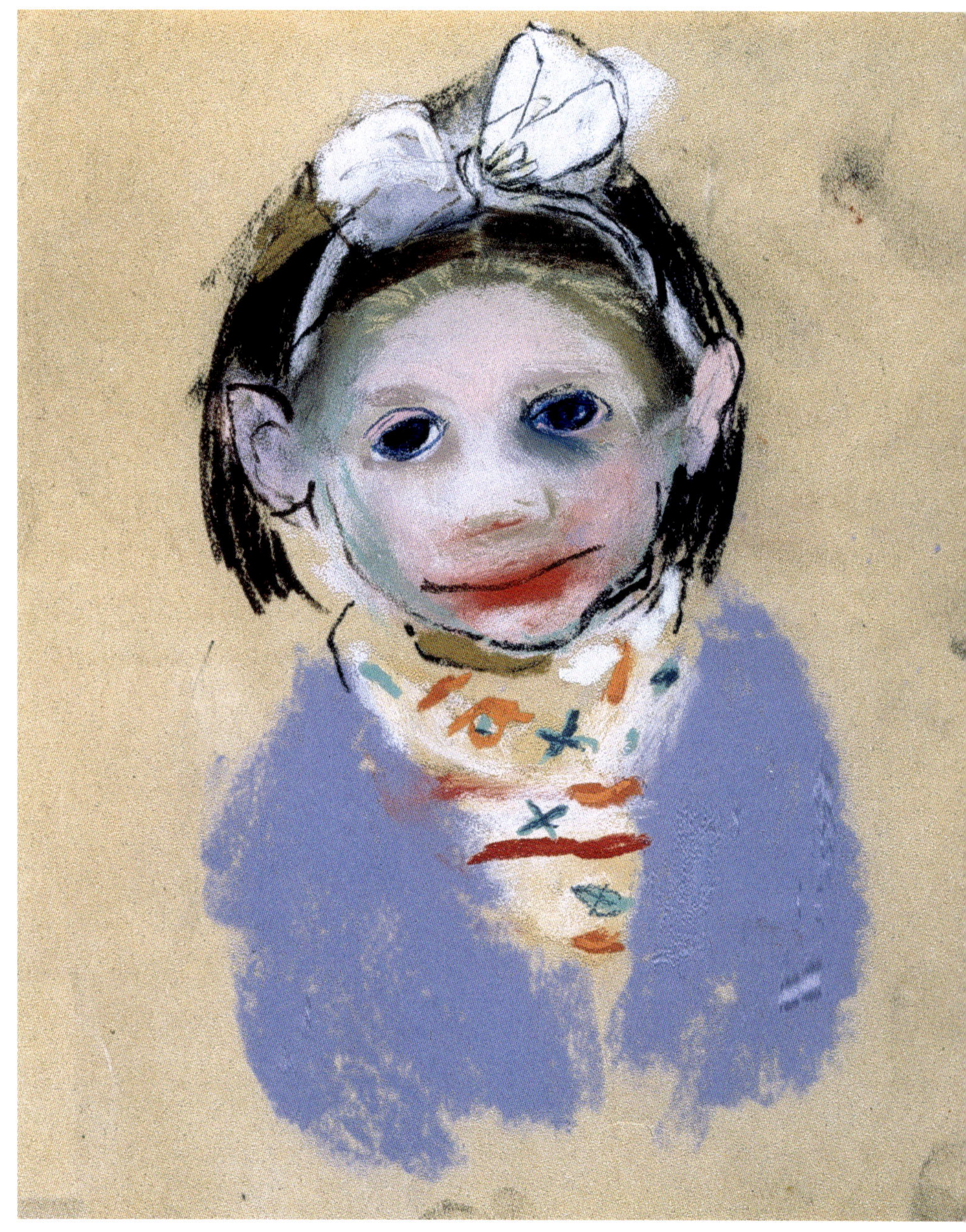

tenement communities and the wild natural beauty of the landscape. The childhood images speak strongly of kinship, with hands held, arms thrown around shoulders and direct gazes. Eardley's own photographs of the children also capture the almost adult self-awareness and stoicism of the small figures dressed in cast-off clothing. Eardley's life itself has been documented through the photographs of her friend, Audrey Walker. We see a physically strong figure with a keen eye and a ready smile. We can see her grinding her colours [93], standing in a studio filled with studies of children [27] and painting on the seashore at Catterline [**frontispiece**, 53]. We know through her letters to her friends and family that she had a strong sense of colour and form. Eardley was a sharp observer of life. Painting in town and country she celebrated the everyday and the ordinary.

Eardley's deep intuition and empathy with her subjects are expressed in her art. She is thought of primarily as a painter whose images evoke deep emotion. But Eardley was also a profound thinker who read philosophy and literature in order to engage with the meaning behind things. The freedom of Eardley's gestural paintwork in her landscapes is contained within very well thought-out compositions. The use in all her paintings of brilliant touches of colour in key positions shows her schooled eye for balance and dynamism.

But what was this woman painter's contribution to British art? In her expressive seascapes painted directly on the seashore and in her depictions of street urchins, Eardley was the natural successor of another well-loved Scottish artist of an earlier generation, William McTaggart. Her move towards abstraction in her seascapes was tempered by her need to stay grounded in reality. Eardley was very much engaged with such reality, be it the lives of the tenement children, peasants in Italy, the changing weather, or the light in the landscape. The postwar battle between realism and abstraction has been the subject of recent research. In Britain the St Ives painters such as Peter Lanyon and Patrick Heron were reaching out towards pure abstraction whilst in London the Kitchen Sink School of painters espoused social realism. Eardley, like another woman artist, Prunella Clough, moved freely between the two camps. Eardley said she was only looking at nature for her inspiration, that she was just trying to paint. Her friend Margot Sandeman has said that Eardley's triumph was that she had a genius for making paint into reality without changing the quality of the paint itself.

The purchase of Eardley's work by the Scottish National Gallery of Modern Art within Eardley's lifetime was part of a move by Douglas Hall to show the Scottish response to the art scene at home and abroad. Thus Eardley's works were purchased alongside classic pieces of modern art from Vuillard, Bonnard, Soutine and Klee to Jackson Pollock and Soulages; all artists with whom Eardley had an affinity. Now, forty-four years on from Eardley's death, we have a new awareness of the postwar British art scene. The contribution of Joan Eardley to Scottish art has never been questioned and she is a major figure in its history. However, the view of Eardley in the bigger picture has still to be established. It is to be hoped that this exhibition and book will help inform that debate.

2 | *Little Glasgow Girl*
Pastel on paper 49.5 × 34.9cm
Cyril Gerber Fine Art, Glasgow

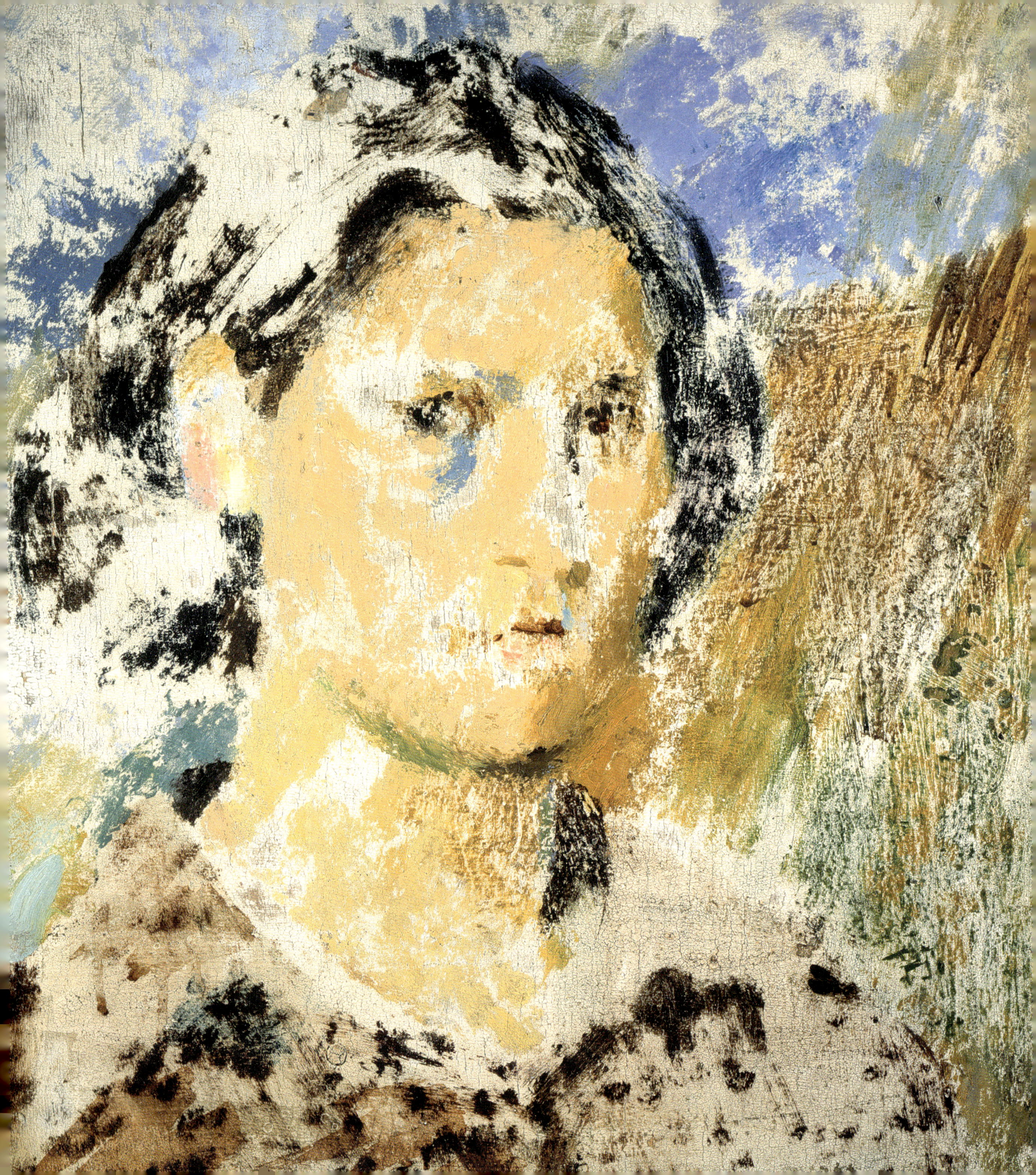

The Early Years

3 | ***Self-portrait*, 1943**
Oil on canvas 53.3 × 45.7cm
Scottish National Portrait Gallery, Edinburgh

Joan Kathleen Harding Eardley was born on 18 May 1921 at Bailing Hill Farm at Warnham in Sussex, the first child of Captain William Eardley and his wife Irene (née Morrison).[1] The couple had met during the First World War when Captain Eardley was stationed at Maryhill Barracks in Glasgow, and they married at the end of the war. He had been gassed in France and suffered from depression as a result. Following the failure of his dairy farm in Sussex, Captain Eardley found work with the Ministry of Agriculture. In 1926 Irene Eardley took her two daughters, Joan and Pat (born in 1922), to live in Blackheath in London with her mother Ellen and her sister Sybil Morrison. Joan and Pat went to Oakland House Primary School and then to St Helen's School, paid for by prosperous great-aunts, and there the art teacher Miss Waddland spotted Joan's talent [4]. Three years after this move, Eardley's father committed suicide; the nature of his death was not explained to Joan and Pat until much later. Although Joan inherited her father's tendency to depression, she thrived in the all-female household in Blackheath where her mother was a constant source of support in her quest to become an artist. Joan was also devoted to her grandmother and to her aunt Sybil, a leading light in the Peace Pledge Union, whose belief in women's rights exerted a lasting influence upon Joan.

Joan left St Helen's in the spring of 1938 and had two terms at the local art school in Blackheath. In the autumn of 1938 she enrolled at Goldsmiths College in London and also spent two terms there.

Glasgow School of Art

In 1939, the family moved away from London and returned to Scotland where they stayed with a relative in Auchterarder before moving to a house at 170 Drymen Road in the Glasgow suburb of Bearsden in January 1940. The timing of the move to Scotland meant that Joan Eardley entered Glasgow School of Art in the second term, in January 1940. Her fellow student, Margot Sandeman remembers Eardley arriving with a formal, permed hairstyle but recalled that Eardley soon relaxed and became her own down-to-earth self, uninterested in fashion and obsessed by her work.[2] Eardley and Sandeman [6], who also lived in Bearsden, soon began a lifelong friendship, a relationship which was to be the most important of Eardley's life. During the next two years Eardley completed the General Course at Glasgow School of Art. From 1942 to 1943 she took the diploma course in drawing and painting but her war work as a joiner's labourer meant that she was registered as an evening student specialising in life-drawing.[3]

In 1940 the Principal of Glasgow School of Art was the portrait painter William Oliphant Hutchison, while the Head of Painting was Hugh Adam Crawford. Ian Fleming taught History of Art. Hutchison left in 1943 and in his last Director's report, he singled out Eardley: 'The Painting School gave the impression of great liveliness, led by remarkably powerful and colourful work by a woman student.'[4] Eardley, in fact, had already come to wider notice. In May 1940, reviewing Glasgow School of Art's end-of-year exhibition the art critic of the *Glasgow Herald* noted: 'The most interesting picture is called 'Street Scene'. It is by a first year student and has a fine robust confidence about it. There is a sense of personality in the figure of a boy sitting straddle on a chair, playing with a dog, with the rest of the family in the background.'[5] Other early student works include *The Rush Hour* [12] a bustling street scene full of flying figures, and *Noah's Ark*, done in modern dress and bright colours. In both compositions the figures are simple and sturdy. It seems that Eardley was really striving to come to grips with movement and tone in *The Rush Hour* and formal composition and colour experiments in *Noah's Ark*.

In 1942 Eardley exhibited *Woman with a Shawl* with the Society of Scottish Artists in Edinburgh. It may be

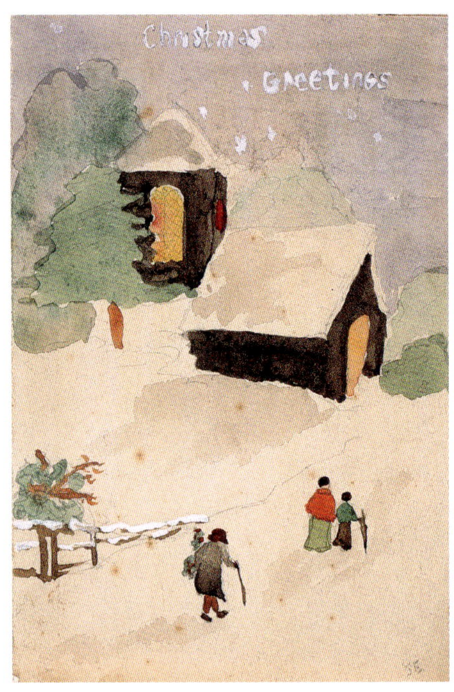

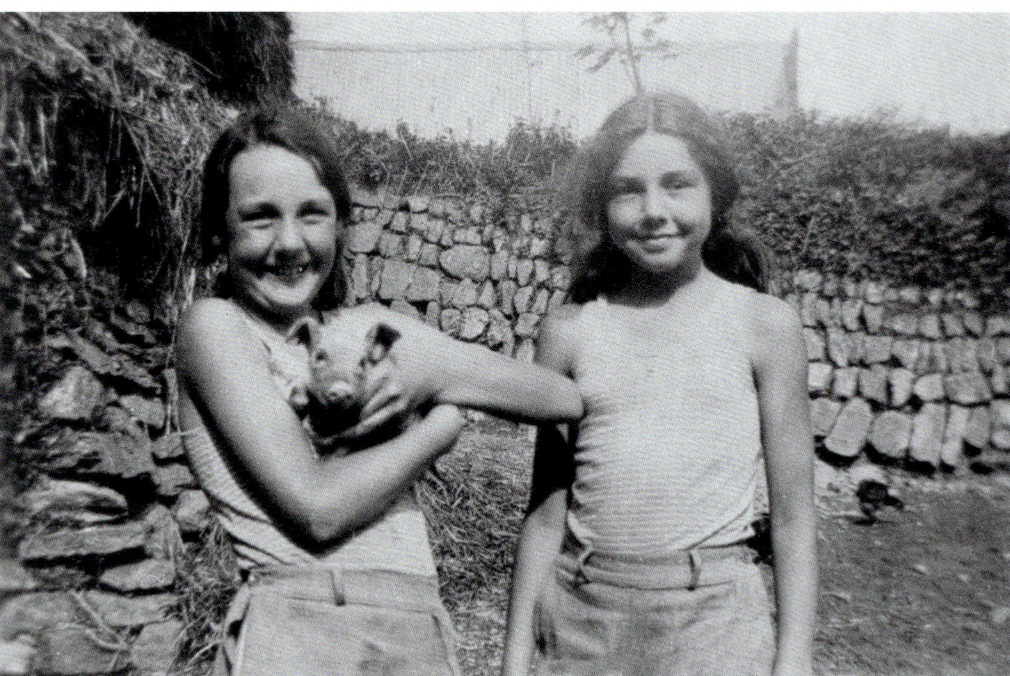

4 | **Joan Eardley, Christmas Greeting Calendar, c.1930**
Joan Eardley Archive, Scottish National Gallery of Modern Art, Edinburgh [GMA/A09]

5 | **Joan (left) and sister Pat with a piglet, c.1931**
Photographer unknown

one of the many studies she made on her trips to Arran with Margot Sandeman. On Arran, they rented a house called the Tabernacle [7] at Corrie from the redoubtable Mrs Kelso and her relative, Jeannie [8]. Eardley often portrayed them by the open range. The strange, traditional dress of Mrs Kelso and the naïve, couthy humour of Jeannie endeared them to Eardley, who, having been brought up with her grandmother, had a great affection for the elderly. The painting trips to Arran gave her the artistic companionship that she craved and Sandeman was to become the mainstay in Eardley's emotional life. It is interesting to note that it was Sandeman who first began to paint children, predating Eardley's works in this subject by several years. An important factor in Eardley's relationship with Sandeman was the correspondence started in the war years, when Sandeman worked at the Intelligence Centre at Bletchley Park in Buckinghamshire, and which continued until Eardley's death.

The only other close friend to share Eardley's inner life was Audrey Walker whom she met in 1952. Walker was a photographer and a gifted musician. She would document Eardley's life from this time in a remarkable series of photographs. Married to Sherriff Allan Walker and with a family to bring up, Walker would also become a sounding board for Eardley. Eardley came from a very close family where, however, emotional matters were not discussed and she in turn was private and reserved. In her diploma self-portrait [3], which won her the Sir James Guthrie Prize for portraiture in 1943, she gives little of herself away. It was painted on the back of a much more laboured self-portrait. According to Cordelia Oliver, a younger student and later Eardley's biographer, it was produced at great speed. From the partial image, Eardley's sparkling eyes stand out. It was purchased by her teacher Hugh Adam Crawford who paid her the extraordinary compliment of including it in the background of his own self-portrait.[6]

At this time Eardley was particularly influenced by Henry Moore and Stanley Spencer and there are several student life-drawings of heavy-limbed women made in direct homage to Moore. Among the private papers which she left at her death was a 1935 cutting about Moore's life-drawing and a *Picture Post* article from 1945. In 1940 Kenneth Clark had selected Stanley Spencer to work as a war artist and he would spend periods during the next six years painting at Lithgow's shipyard in Port Glasgow. Spencer also set one of his resurrection scenes in the town (Eardley owned a book about his resurrection paintings). Spencer's interest in depicting details of everyday life and ordinary working people may have influenced Eardley to celebrate the daily reality she saw around her. Her early drawings include a *Street Market* [14] showing the barrows in a Glasgow street; and among her many studies of street musicians is a strong figure in *Young Man Playing an Accordion* [9]. Eardley, like Spencer, was grounded in a love of humanity and a sense of kinship with the communities in which she lived. Above all, she was fascinated by Spencer's sense of detail. She later visited a Bond Street show of Spencer's work in order to study his paintings at first-hand. In these student days Eardley was also looking at artists as various as Braque, Rouault, Van Gogh, Vuillard, Blake, Rembrandt and Velázquez. Her painting *A Pot of Potatoes* [13] and the gritty strength of the working figures in *The Mixer Men* [15], which were exhibited at the Royal Glasgow Institute of Fine Arts Exhibition in 1944, were colourful, powerful works that paid homage to Van Gogh's studies of peasant life.[7]

In October 1943 Eardley enrolled at Jordanhill Teacher Training College but stayed only one term, considering herself unsuited for teaching art. She found war work as a joiner's labourer in a small boat-building firm called John A. Russell, near her home in Bearsden, and painted camouflage designs on landing craft. Little else is known of what Eardley did during this period, apart from her trips to Arran and her visits to Margot Sandeman at Bletchley Park, during which she helped her to set up a studio in nearby Stony Stratford.

Although staggering under the impact of war, there were many exciting developments on the Scottish art scene in the 1940s. In 1939 the Scottish Colourist, J. D. Fergusson, now resident in Glasgow with his wife, the dancer Margaret Morris, wrote his book *Modern Scottish Painting*, and in 1940 he formed the New Art Club. Morris became involved with the newly founded Scottish Ballet. In 1942, Fergusson, the painter Donald Bain and the sculptor George Innes founded the New Scottish Group. From 1940 to 1943 the Polish artist Josef Herman lived in Glasgow, and was soon joined by his fellow countryman Jankel Adler. Herman and Adler knew the European modernist artists whom most of the Scots had only read about. Herman later remembered Eardley's visits to his studio in 1940: 'Joan, though unbelievably shy, came frequently to my studio after this first meeting. She used to bring a home-made sketch book, very large and awkward to handle. From her early efforts it was difficult to perceive the fine artist she was to become.'[8] Eardley was obviously keen to learn and Herman's strong images of working people must have had an impact. She was also aware of Adler's work. In her correspondence with Sandeman, Eardley mentioned that fellow students at Glasgow School of Art (in particular Benjamin Crème) had fallen under Adler's influence.[9] Her predecessors at Glasgow School of Art, Robert Colquhoun and Robert MacBryde, were also influenced by Adler and his Picasso-esque way of painting.

During the war and in the immediate postwar years it was possible to see a surprising amount of new, continental art first-hand in Glasgow and Edinburgh.

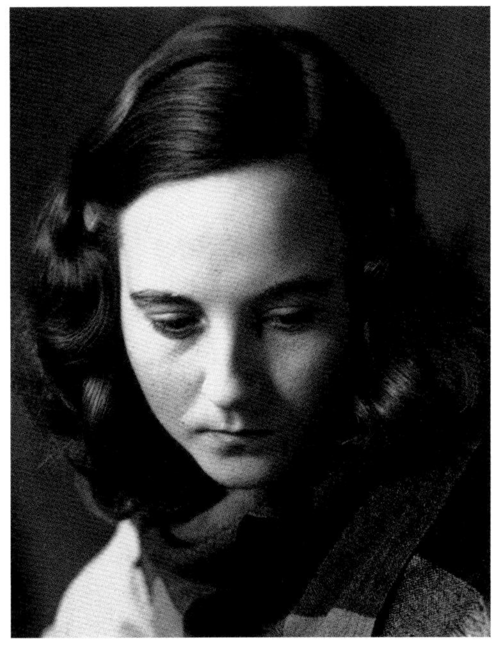

6 | Margot Sandeman, *c.*1940
Photo: Harold Fry of Thomas Annan & Sons, Glasgow
Private Collection

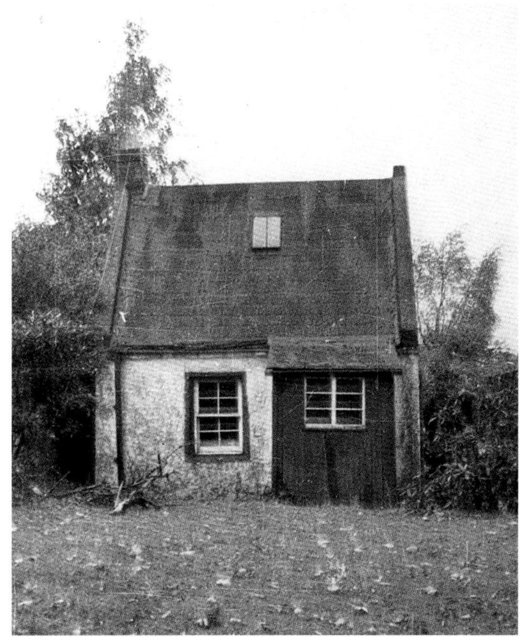

7 | The Tabernacle at Corrie on the Isle of Arran
Photo: Margot Sandeman
Scottish National Gallery of Modern Art, Edinburgh

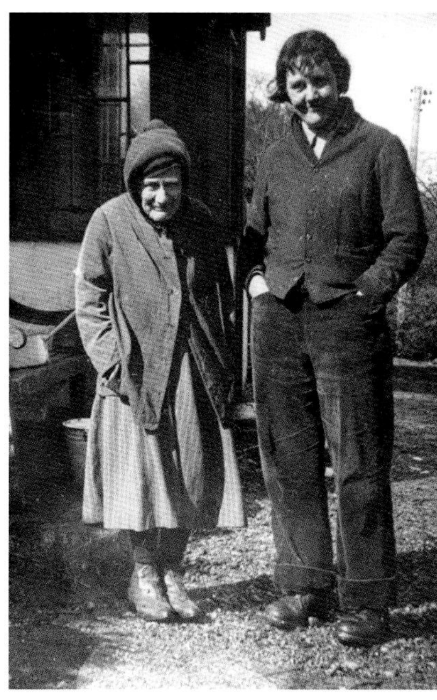

8 | Joan Eardley with Jeannie Kelso (left) at Corrie on the Isle of Arran, *c.*1940s
Photo: Margot Sandeman
Scottish National Gallery of Modern Art, Edinburgh

For example, Oskar Kokoschka's painting *Zrani* was presented by the Czechs to the National Galleries of Scotland in 1942. In the same year the Lithuanian sculptor Benno Schotz, who was Head of Sculpture at Glasgow School of Art, organised an exhibition of Jewish art at the Jewish Institute in Glasgow, which included work by Chagall, Modigliani, Zadkine, Bomberg, Soutine and others; in 1945 the work of Georges Rouault and other contemporary French artists was shown by the Society of Scottish Artists; and in 1946 there was a major Matisse and Picasso exhibition in Glasgow. The following year the Edinburgh International Festival was founded with the express purpose of enlivening and enriching the cultural life of Europe, Britain and Scotland in the aftermath of the Second World War.

Post-diploma Years

In 1946 Eardley went to Lincoln to execute a mural on the history of costume for Sincil Bank Secondary Modern Girls School (now part of a technical college). A friend of the Eardley family taught in Lincolnshire and the commission may have come through her. It is clear from the letters she sent to her mother that Eardley was dissatisfied with both the composition and the colour scheme of the murals.[10] She lodged with the headmistress Miss Joan Davis, whose energetic mind and strong personality appealed to Eardley. Miss Davis had a house full of books on modern artists such as Picasso, Degas, Van Gogh and Matisse. In letters to Margot Sandeman, Eardley wrote in emotional terms that Lincoln Cathedral was 'so beautiful that you feel happy and like crying all mixed up'.[11] She spoke also of working so hard, 'somehow with a real kind of feeling of purpose behind it all the time, & of a feeling of wanting to work and of interest and excitement and enjoyment … I hardly ever speak … being a kind of onlooker at everything. I've learnt a tremendous lot.'[12] She also described going to market in Lincoln and seeing the local women selling shrimps, mussels, apples, onions, and tulip bulbs.

Eardley enlisted the help of some of the pupils with the mural. Referring to two of them, girls aged about twelve, she wrote in a letter to her mother: 'I got them to do a whole two squares on their own of modern dresses. One of them did three women in day clothes and two children skipping about and the other did two women in evening clothes. I'm letting them do these completely on their own – painting and everything … I'm getting them to put on some of the backgrounds too. It's quite a job thinking out what I can give them to do each day – almost as bad as teaching!!'[13] Unfortunately, the murals have not survived and there seems to be no photographic record of them.

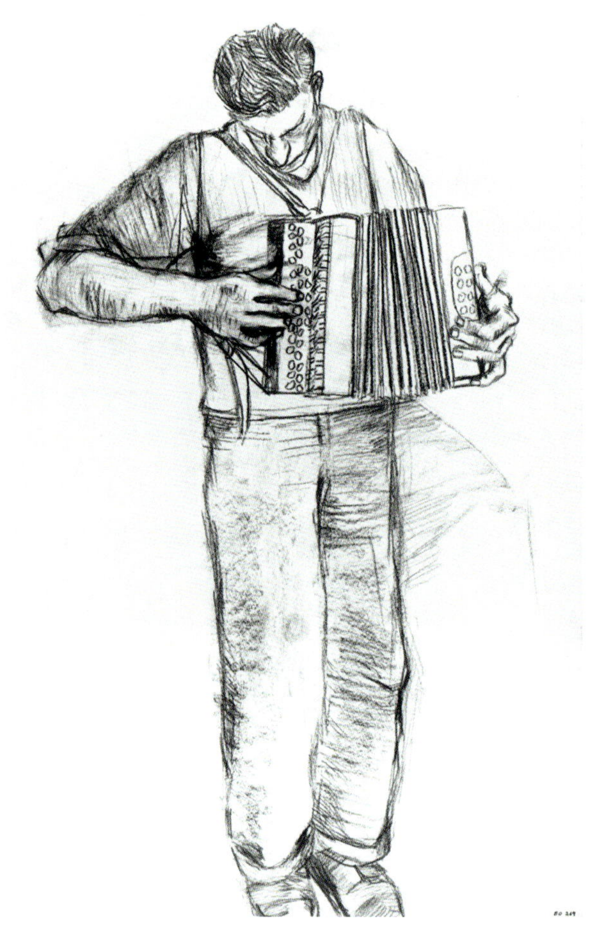

9 | Joan Eardley, *Young Man Playing an Accordion*, c.1940s
Black chalk on paper
66.2 × 42.2cm
Scottish National Gallery of Modern Art, Edinburgh

Among other works which may date from this time are three woodcuts, the oil of *Mrs Red Wallpaper*, the pen and ink *Bean Pickers Lincolnshire* and the pen and ink study, *Room at Swineshead*.

In a letter of January 1947, written in London, Eardley told Sandeman that Miss Davis had invited her back to help with a youth club, but it seems that this was not acted upon. Eardley was in London primarily to visit museums and galleries. She wrote to Sandeman, telling her that she had been exploring the Thames mudflats, had bought a book on Giotto and felt the tremendous freedom of being away from home: 'You seem to be able to understand all sorts of different things & somehow in a sort of a way amaze yourself in a way that belongs to you. And it is easier to let your mind be one track too and

I think you have to be a bit one track to be a painter.'[14] In the letter she noted that she had seen work by Keith Vaughan and Julian Trevelyan and mentioned an art school being set up by Adler, Colquhoun, MacBryde and Trevelyan.

Whilst in London she stayed partly in digs in Notting Hill, and partly with a family friend who lived in Blackheath, opposite the Eardley family's old house. She wrote to Sandeman about the difficulties she was encountering in her work: 'I think when I draw, I don't think whether it is paintable or drawable, but I just like the thing, and then do it, and then find out that it's not really a possible thing to do at all.'[15] She described drawing the fair at Blackheath and told Sandeman: 'I wish I could lift London up with me and take it back to Glasgow. There are some lovely old chestnut sellers with burning braziers that would be terrific for a composition ... I feel myself full of ideas and thoughts for work. Most terrific things – but I can see so much to learn, & in a way through seeing things that interest me so much in feeling & painting ... I really do feel much freshened up in my mind.' Eardley went to the Royal Academy to see an exhibition of paintings from the Royal Collection and commented in particular on a painting by the sixteenth-century Flemish painter Pieter Brueghel. She also mentioned buying a book on the French primitive painter Henri Rousseau.[16]

Hospitalfield

In London Eardley was elated by her new sense of freedom, but she also suffered bouts of depression. She wrote to Sandeman at length about her inability to produce work. In the winter of 1946, and still resident in Notting Hill, Eardley wrote to her mother, telling her that she was thinking of studying at the Patrick-Allan Fraser School of Art at Hospitalfield. The school, occupying a Victorian baronial house on the outskirts of Arbroath, had been set up in 1890 as a residential art school, and had later

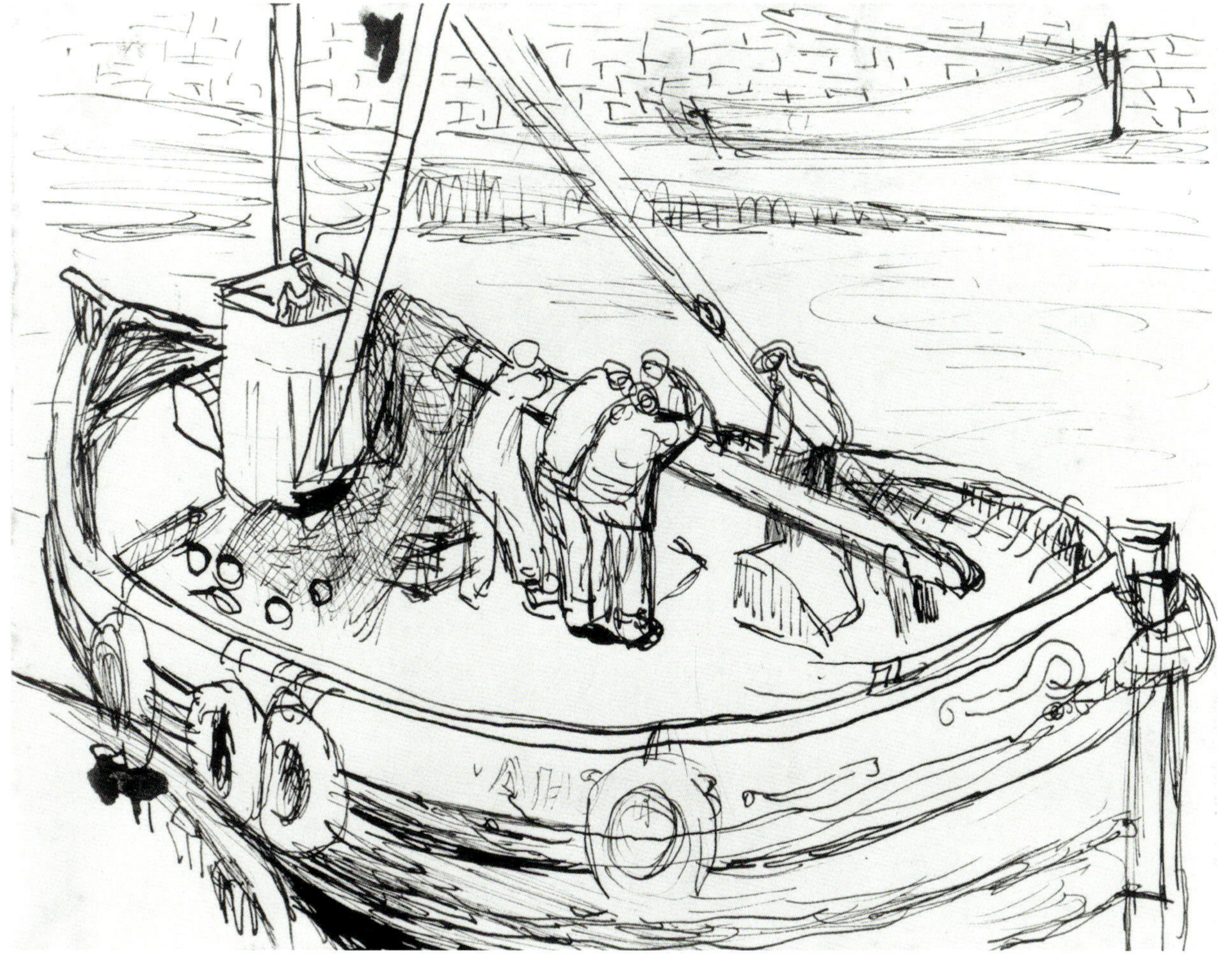

10 | **Joan Eardley,**
***Crew in a Fishing Boat in Arbroath Harbour*, 1947**
Black ink on paper
17.5 × 22.8cm
Scottish National Gallery of Modern Art, Edinburgh

become a post-graduate art school which, from 1938 to 1947, was run by the artist James Cowie. Eardley knew that Cowie's painstaking, linear approach was unlike her own, but she hoped that contact with a different style might be beneficial to her own work.

Eardley studied at Hospitalfield from April to September 1947. On fine days, she and the other students were sent out into the grounds of the school to draw; one of her letters was penned from a grain loft in the farm where she was left undisturbed apart from a daily visit from Cowie. When confined to the main building Eardley got into arguments with Cowie and described him in unflattering terms in a letter to her mother. However, she also acknowledged that she was learning a great deal from him. It has been suggested that Cowie's finely executed depictions of schoolgirls were an influence upon Eardley but the tenor of her letter to her mother suggests that it was Cowie's compositional skills that interested her, particularly with regard to landscape. Another letter to her mother includes an amusing description of Cowie and his wife, with little portrait sketches [11]. One of Eardley's criticisms of Cowie was that his work lacked feeling. In a letter to Margot Sandeman she wrote: 'I think I will have to be very strong to stand against Mr Cowie and I don't feel very strong just now – he asked me if I had changed my way of painting since I left the art school, and when I said yes, that I was trying to tighten it up a bit, he said "I'm very glad to hear it – this loose self-expression business is no good at all" and went into a whole long harangue of nonsense. Dash the horrid old man.'[17]

It was at Hospitalfield that Eardley met joiner and war veteran Angus Neil and in her correspondence with Sandeman she records the nervous tensions in the closed community: 'Precipices are everywhere … I'm in a bit of a state up and down and Angus is a bit mental anyway … And Mr and Mrs Cowie suspect everybody of everything that's immoral and each other – It's really very funny – I wouldn't have missed it.' Angus Neil and Eardley immediately formed a close bond. Following Eardley's departure from Hospitalfield they remained in close touch and when she took evening classes at Glasgow School of Art in 1950 he joined in and eventually took the diploma course part-time. His paintings of heads and boys are very similar to Eardley's contemporaneous paintings. Neil's biographer, Henry Guy, suspects that some of Neil's paintings have since been mistakenly ascribed to Eardley.[18]

At Hospitalfield, Eardley was desperate to paint a view inside the house. She was amazed to find that Cowie liked her palette-knife painting of the barn. However, as an exercise he made her copy it stroke for stroke in pastel. She found escape from Cowie by going down to Arbroath Harbour where she enjoyed the camaraderie of the fishermen [10]. One of her few surviving paintings from this period is *Fishing Boats, Arbroath*. Although she resented Cowie's manner, she realised that she could learn something from him: 'And anyway there's always *what* you paint which should govern the *way* you paint so that it doesn't really matter how you are taught.'[19]

In the autumn of 1947 Eardley registered for her post-diploma scholarship year at Glasgow School of Art. During this time she exhibited with the West of Scotland Artists' group at Skelmorlie, and in 1948 she showed with the Society of Scottish Artists and at Airdrie Library. A review of the SSA show remarks: 'In the first room an important place rightly goes to Miss Joan Eardley's painting of a strange but wholly convincing interior. Miss Eardley shows in Room 3 a still life and a drawing. All of them overflow with vigour and ingenuity. The paintings have a richness of colour and pattern, along with a powerfully acute execution, that is quite exceptional in a young painter.'[20] The works *The Mixer Men* [15], *Stackyard* and *Shipwright's Workshop* were exhibited together with landscapes from Arran, Greenwich, Hospitalfield, St Abb's Head and Lincolnshire.

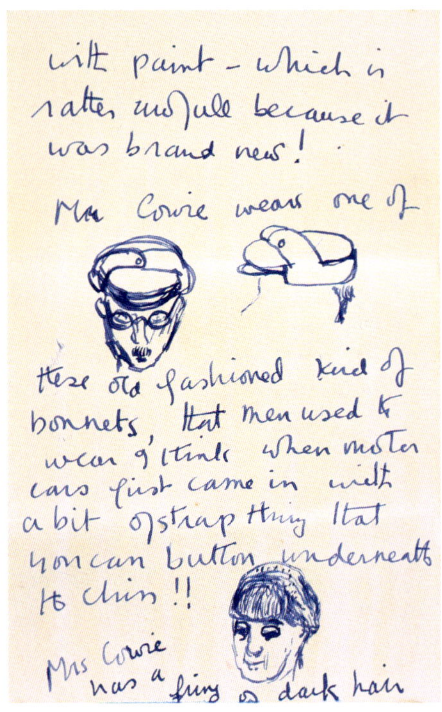
with paint – which is rather awful because it was brand new!
Mr Cowie wears one of these old fashioned kind of bonnets, that men used to wear I think when motor cars first came in with a bit of strap thing that you can button underneath the chin!!
Mrs Cowie has a fuzz of dark hair

11 | Joan Eardley, illustrated letter showing the heads of James Cowie and his wife, 1947
Joan Eardley Archive, Scottish National Gallery of Modern Art, Edinburgh [GMA/A09]

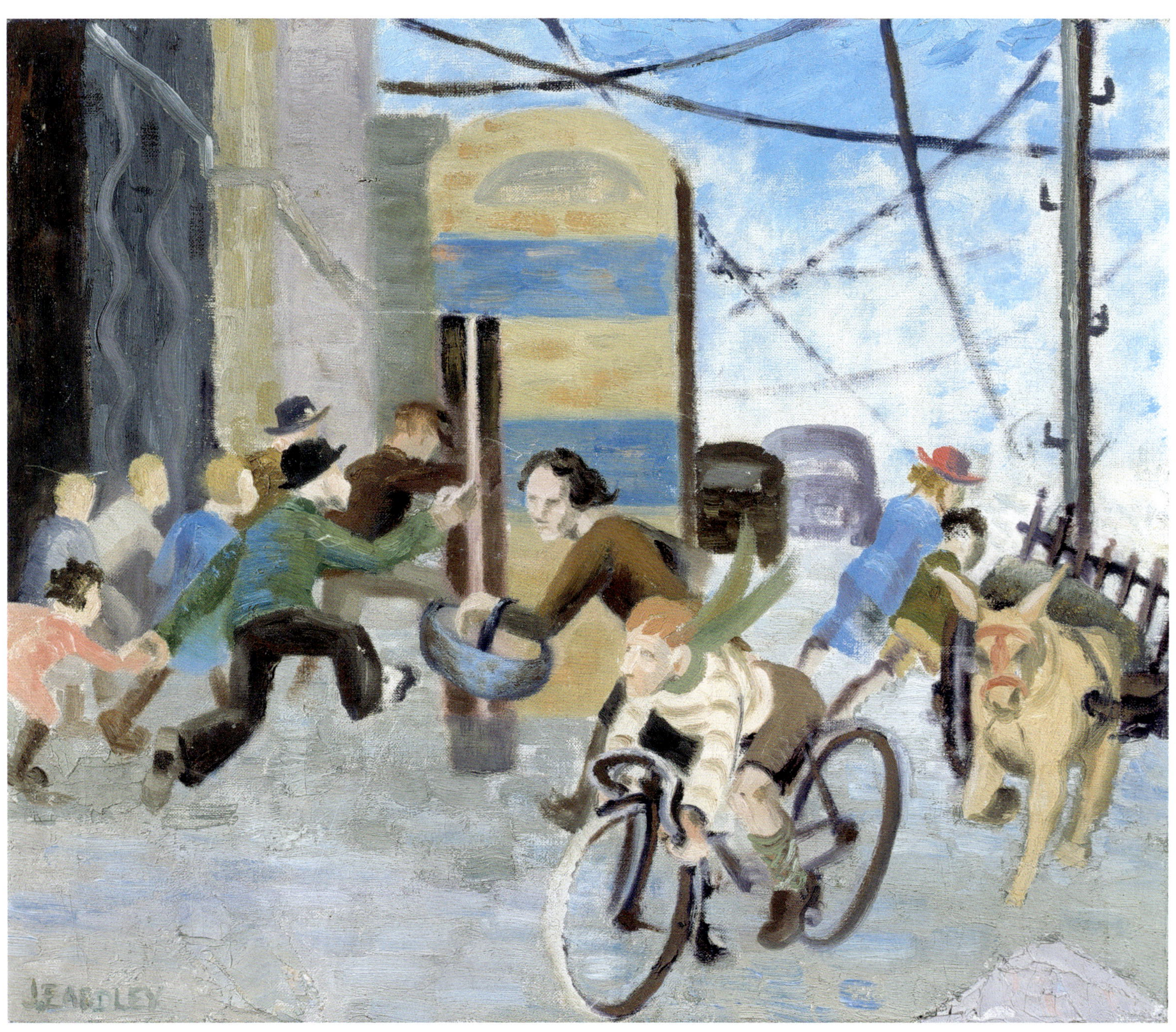

12 | *The Rush Hour*, c.1938
Oil on canvas 51 × 61cm
Cyril Gerber Fine Art, Glasgow

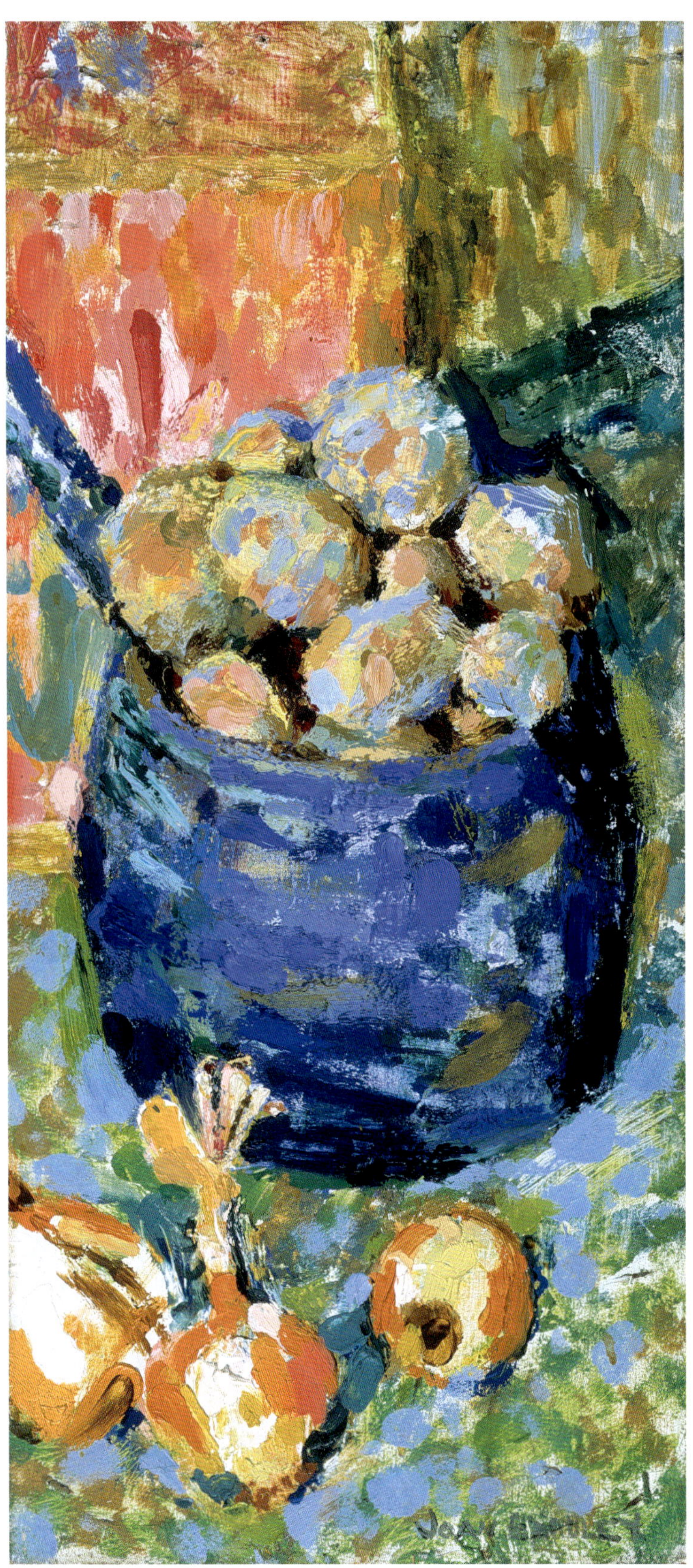

13 | ***A Pot of Potatoes***, 1944
Oil on board 63 × 29cm
Private Collection

14 | ***Street Market***, c.1940s
Mixed media on paper 63.5 × 53.5cm
Cyril Gerber Fine Art, Glasgow

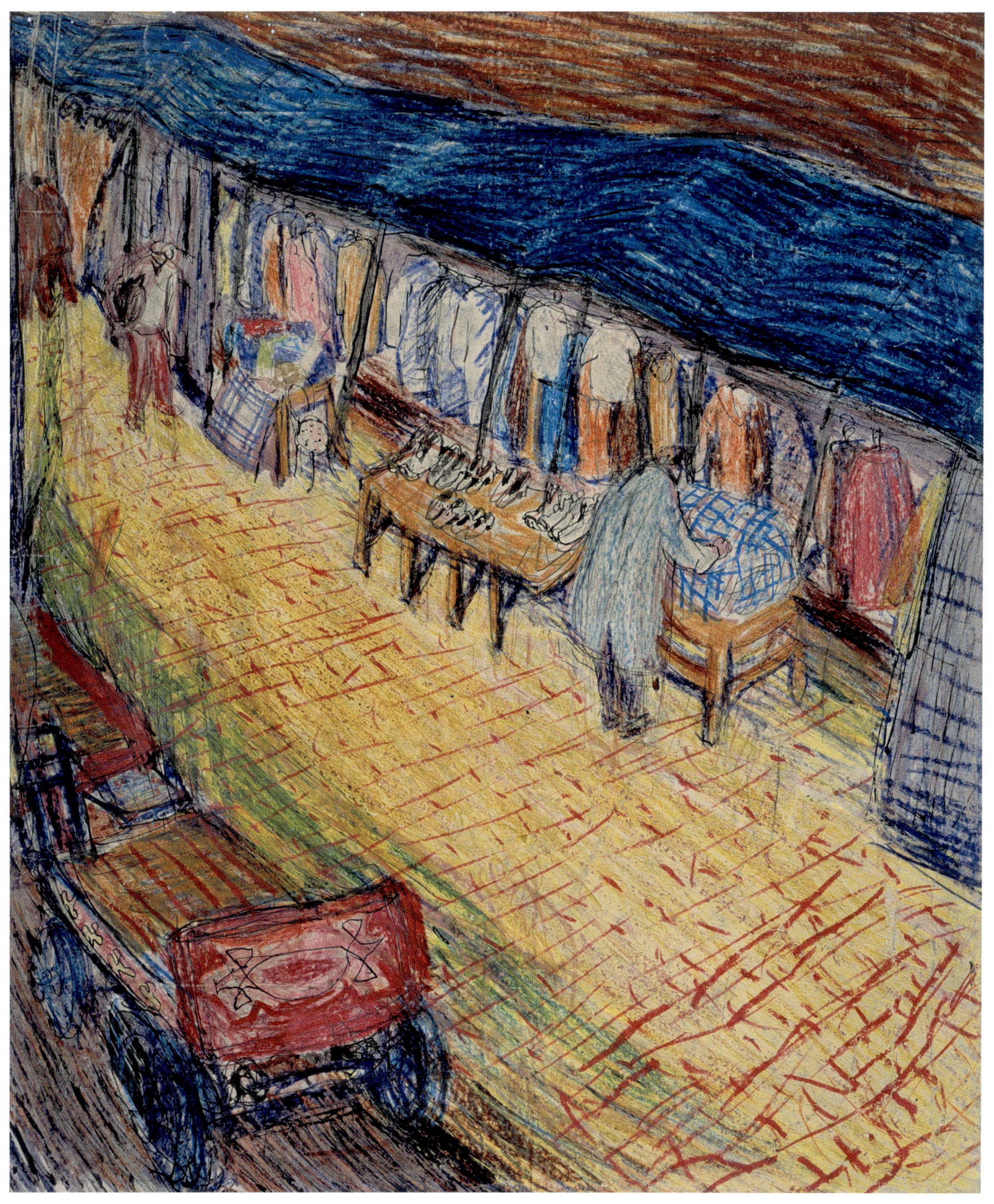

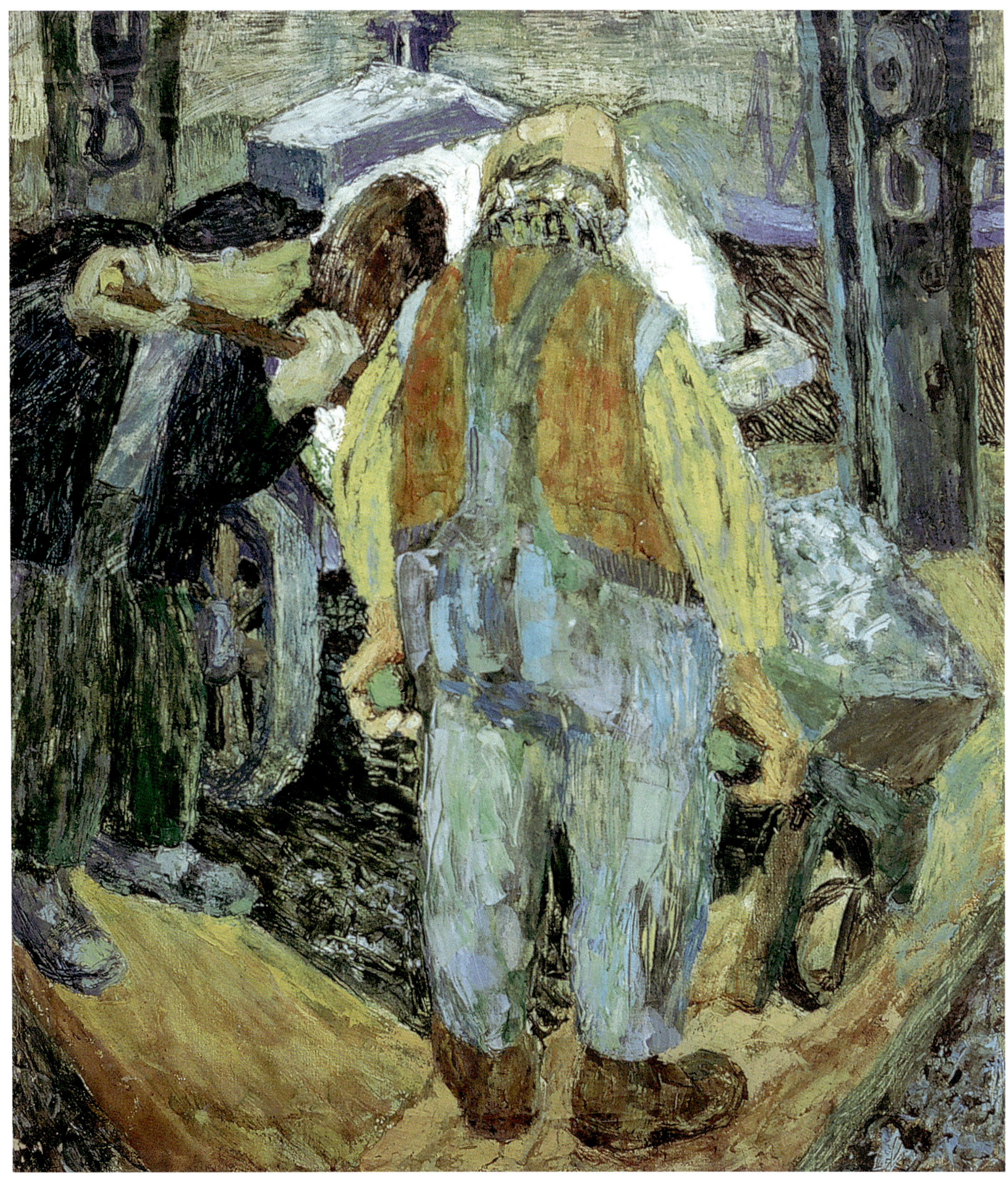

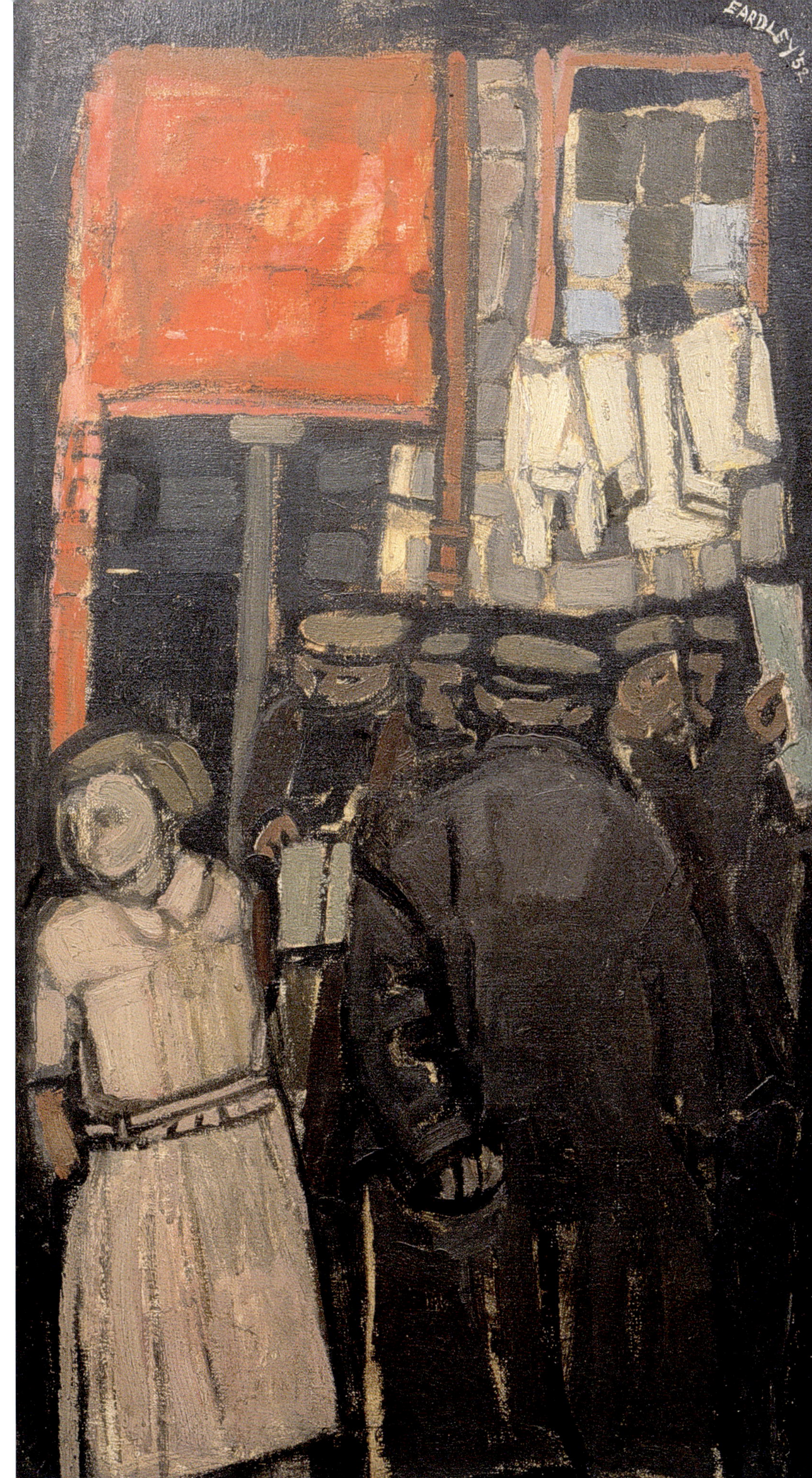

15 | *The Mixer Men*, 1944
Oil on canvas 88 × 77cm
Private Collection

16 | ***Back Street Bookie***, 1952
Oil on canvas 107 × 59cm
University of Edinburgh
Fine Art Collections

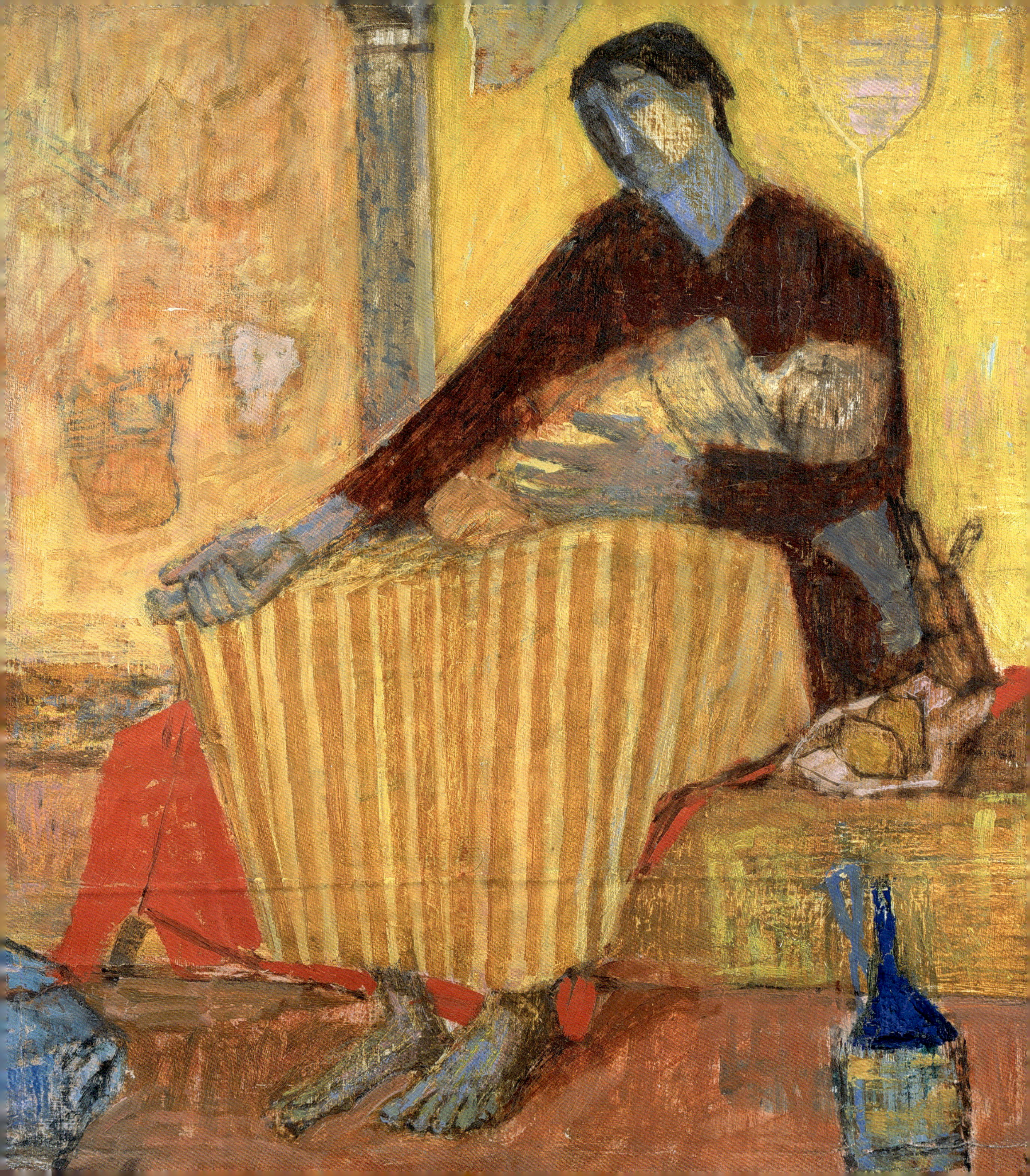

Italy and France

17 | ***Venetian Beggar Woman No.2***, 1948–9
Oil on canvas 83 × 75cm
Cyril Gerber Fine Art Glasgow

In the summer of 1948 Eardley won a Carnegie scholarship from the Royal Scottish Academy, and a travelling scholarship from Glasgow School of Art. On 27 September 1948 she set off by boat and train for Florence. Throughout the journey she worried about practical details concerning money and clothes [18].[21] But, in her descriptions of the people and places and her wish to paint, there is a certainty and self-confidence which made her shun the fashionable and material comforts of Italy; instead, she went in search of the primitive. She wrote of the sandy shore of the Arno with workmen digging channels, children playing, boys fishing and old ladies bringing their hens down to forage in the rubbish.[22]

In Florence Eardley looked at frescoes by Giotto in Santa Croce, Fra Angelico in San Marco and above all those by Masaccio in the Brancacci Chapel at Santa Maria del Carmine. In a sketchbook full of drawings and notes Eardley wrote: 'The stone wall in particular with its bulging massive blocks of stone is what one is familiar with from having walked by almost these very walls in Florence to reach the church of the Carmine where the Masaccios are. And as one walks by them again now these impenetrable prison like walls of stone seem to be Masaccio forever after – they become a painting of Masaccio and the maimed and crippled beggars who loll against them – hands outstretched asking for alms seems only to be again Masaccio … suddenly time is as if nothing is lost. And we realize that in the same way that all individual single people in all nations today are the same and have the same thoughts and worries and fears – so in the same way in a direction going down instead of across – time has not changed the individual; Masaccio saw what we see now and painted what he saw – the beggars, the poor people of Florence … also Cézanne and Van Gogh pink houses olive trees etc and we see them now almost as though they might have been painted only yesterday.'[23] She also commented: 'In Italy and in Paris too one realizes all the time how the great painters of these countries painted only always the simple everyday things that were around them.'[24] She herself chose to portray the poor, the peasants, the elderly, and the beggars. She drew the view from her lodging looking across the Piazza ss. Annunziata to Brunelleschi's Hospital [21], the market stalls, tiled roofs and the Ponte Vecchio, but she was keen to get out of Florence and explore.

On a visit to Assisi, Eardley was led on a round of churches and monasteries by an indefatigable Cambridge history undergraduate. Her written descriptions of Giotto's frescoes, the town, the people and the weather are made in terms of colours, and she berated herself for having only chalks, her painting materials having been left in Florence. She wrote to Sandeman of the backstreet workshops, the olive trees, the beggars, and the cobbler who invited her in to draw. Eardley decided that the church at Assisi was the most beautiful she had ever seen. Ill-health meant cycle rides for fresh air outside Florence where she was befriended by the local farmers and peasants [20].[25] The peasant custom of putting beaded bridles on the oxen led to a vivid chalk study, *A Pair of Oxen* [24].

Eardley seems to have struck up friendships despite the language barrier. Her landlady in Florence insisted on making sewing repairs to Eardley's skirt [19]. She loved the sense of community she found in Italy, particularly in the small seaside town of Forte dei Marmi, which she visited in November 1948. She sat on the beach and drew the fishermen and their boats. The work *Fishing Nets Hung up to Dry*, with its strong black outlines, owes much to Van Gogh. It was the first time she had tackled such a scene, a subject that was to fascinate her for the next fifteen years and which reached its apogee in works such as *Salmon Net Posts* [57]. Eardley also drew the children she met on the beach and nearby farms. In her letters home, she said that her rapid sketches of people meant more to her than her landscape paintings.[26] In her letters Eardley commented upon the strange contrast between the quarries and the rubbish dumps and the beauty of the farmhouses and the cypress trees. She not only observed the juxtaposition of the old and the new as tourism made inroads into the area, but also discovered the wrecked bridges and bullet-scarred houses left by the war. At last she began to paint. She described the clean, pure colours, 'pale pink, pale blue and yellowy and white right into the distance.' The heads of the peasant people fascinated her: 'I certainly find in the country people, and the country and the poor people in the towns and the way of life which is for these people still so primitive, something which interests me as a painter.'[27] She loved the fact that craftsmen, working with primitive tools, were still used to provide articles for everyday use and commented that, 'There is great poverty but I feel that in spite of the poverty they are perhaps living fuller lives than those who work for steady wages mass producing a part of a whole which they have never seen in the industrial corners of our own cities.'[28] However, she also remarked that she was looking forward to going to Paris to see contemporary painting because she had seen none at all in Florence.

So, in due course, Eardley headed north to Paris to see the public collections and contemporary exhibitions. She visited galleries, studios and, on Christmas day, distant relations who lived in the suburbs. She loved the print shops selling cheap reproductions of art. In a letter to Sandeman she said she dreaded the bohemian, arty crowd in Paris but once there, and having met fellow student Bill Henry, she was stimulated by seeing other people's work. She loved the fair along the Boulevard de Clichy in Montmartre, the Rodin Museum and a show at the Petit Palais of masterpieces from the Alte Pinakothek in Munich ('terrific Rembrandts, wonderful El Greco' she wrote). She also visited commercial galleries, seeing works by Modigliani and Utrillo. Eardley was struck by the dilemma of young artists in Paris: 'they are forced to paint *à la* Rouault or Picasso or Braque – these painters' works are all around them. And there is no doubt in my mind that they are great painters – but their work is so individual – so much a style evolved for themselves – that one cannot copy their works, because in using their style one gets left with that alone – & nature – or the idea which nature gives you – is forgotten. If one has an idea (an inspiration) this evolves for you a means of execution. And this means of execution then becomes your own – it is unlike anyone else.'[29] She also wrote of the need 'to leave one's mind completely open to all things political & social as well as plastic & visual'.[30]

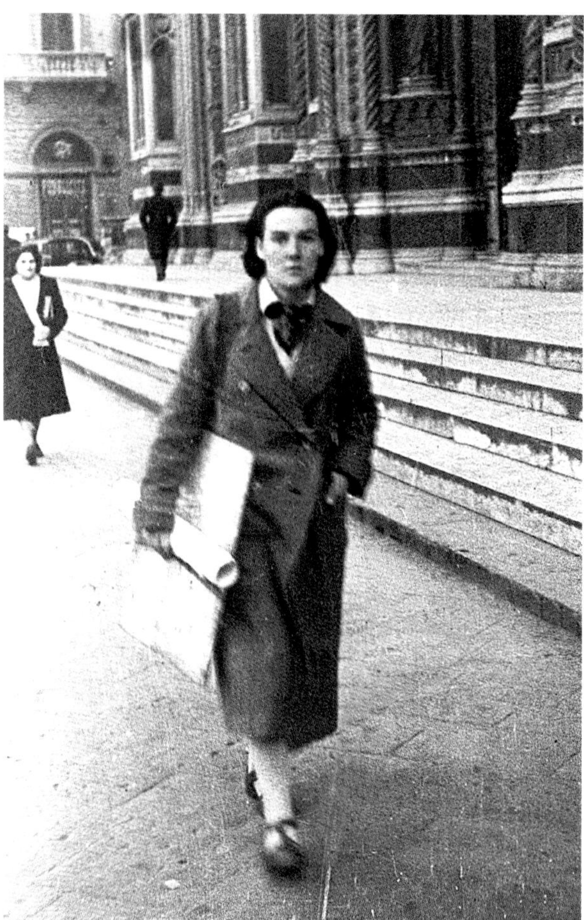

18 | Joan Eardley in Italy
Photographer unknown
Joan Eardley Archive, Scottish National Gallery of Modern Art, Edinburgh [GMA/A09]

OPPOSITE

19 | Joan Eardley, *Old Italian Woman Sewing*, c.1948–9
Black chalk on paper
29.2 × 49.8cm
Scottish National Gallery of Modern Art, Edinburgh

20 | Joan Eardley, *Italian Peasant Seated on the Ground*, c.1948–9
Black chalk on paper
52.6 × 48.7cm
Scottish National Gallery of Modern Art, Edinburgh

21 | Joan Eardley, *Piazza ss. Annunziata, Florence*, 1948
Pastel on tinted paper
48.3 × 61.5cm
Private Collection

During the final months of her travelling scholarship, Eardley headed back to Italy, leaving for Venice on the night train on 23 January 1949. There she became ill with flu and had to travel on to Florence to find English speakers and see a doctor. This was a period of some distress, when she felt vulnerable and unable to cope. It was perhaps because of this experience that Eardley never again travelled abroad alone. But by 4 February she was back in Venice. Ten days later she was in Arezzo to see Piero della Francesca's frescoes; then she travelled backwards and forwards between Florence, Ravenna and Venice. In Venice she stayed with two elderly ladies on the top floor of a building on the waterfront near the Piazza San Marco. She sketched the buildings and worked them into more resolved compositions in her room. A drawing sent with one of her letters shows two large compositions pinned to the walls and a large drawing on the floor, held

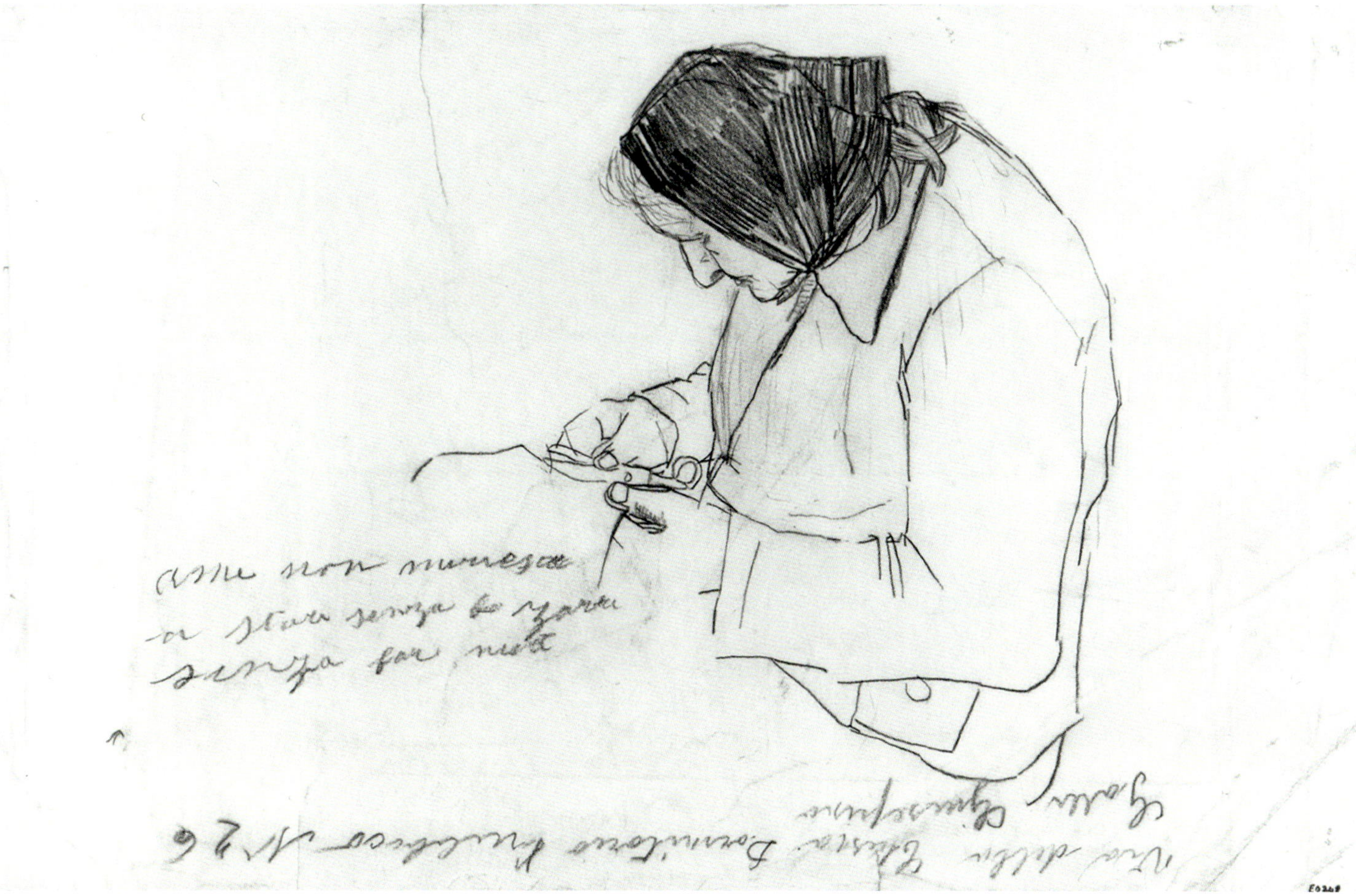

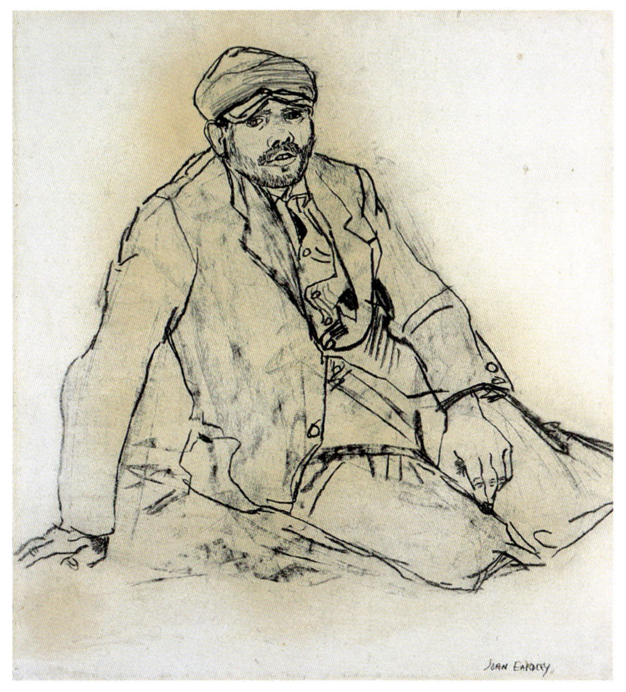

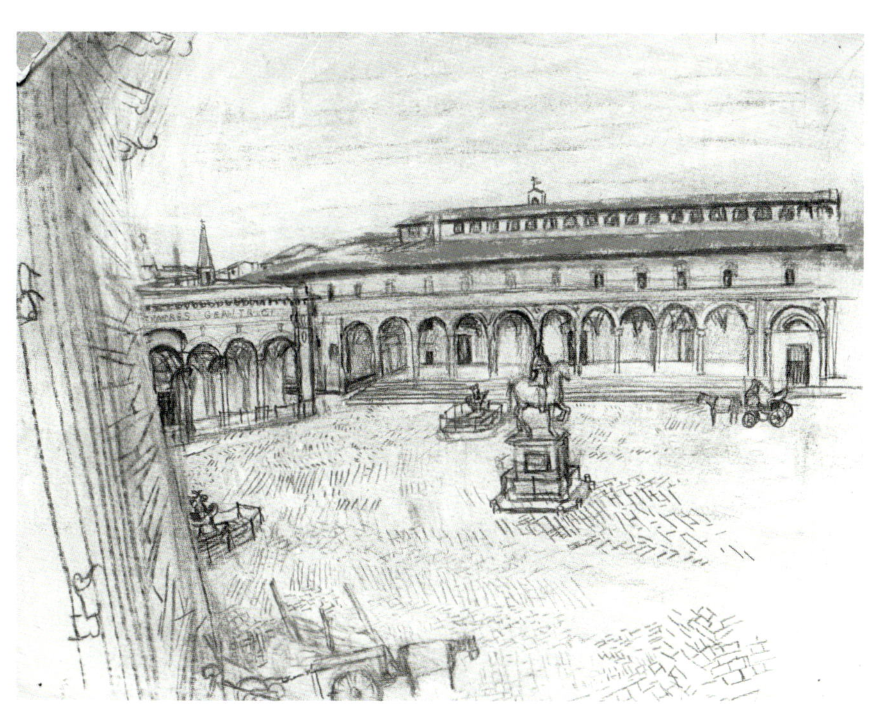

down by shoes and rolls of papers [22]. Although many of the drawings she produced on her trip were fragments, she did execute a beautiful finished painting, *Old Woman Praying in St Mark's, Venice* [23], which was exhibited at the Glasgow School of Art exhibition in 1949. She was still in Venice in March 1949, making trips out to the island of Torcello on the Lagoon. On the boat to Torcello she met fellow art student, Bronwen Pulsford. They went together to Ravenna, and then up the Brenta Canal and by train to Padua. While in Forte dei Marmi, in an unexplained moment, Eardley had thrown all of her paintings, except one, into the sea. But now back in Venice, she painted a number of works, including *Beggars in Venice* [25] and *Venetian Beggar Woman, No. 2* [17]. These, and the study for the latter, show her love of the disenfranchised in the city. She returned to Glasgow in the spring of 1949 with a good number of drawings and a small number of rolled-up oils on canvas.

In the autumn of 1949 Eardley exhibited her scholarship works at Glasgow School of Art, in what was effectively her first solo exhibition. Reviewing the show, which was called *Drawings of Italy*, the correspondent of the *Glasgow Herald* noted: 'Miss Eardley, who has been working in France and Italy for several months, was notable among the immediate post-graduate generation of the School of Art for the strength and selective quality in her drawings. Her talents have considerably matured in the course of her travels, and one or two of the sketches in this show are of quite exceptional quality. Among the most outstanding are a charcoal study of an old peasant woman sewing, wrapped in a ruckled shawl, her knobbly fingers drawing the eye irresistibly.'[31] Among the forty-three drawings there were seventeen depicting people from the street, fields and lodgings, and eleven architectural studies, while the remainder were set in the countryside or by the sea. Eardley also exhibited with the Society of Scottish Artists at the Royal Scottish Academy in Edinburgh. Under the heading 'Good Show!', *The Scotsman*'s art critic commented: 'Miss Joan Eardley and Miss Margot Sandeman more than maintain the exciting promise of their first appearances with the SSA. Both are quite fearless and convinced exponents of highly individual outlooks, both express themselves in terms of powerful and original design ... Miss Eardley displays a virility that few young male painters could match.'[32] The *Glasgow Herald* also singled out Eardley's works.[33]

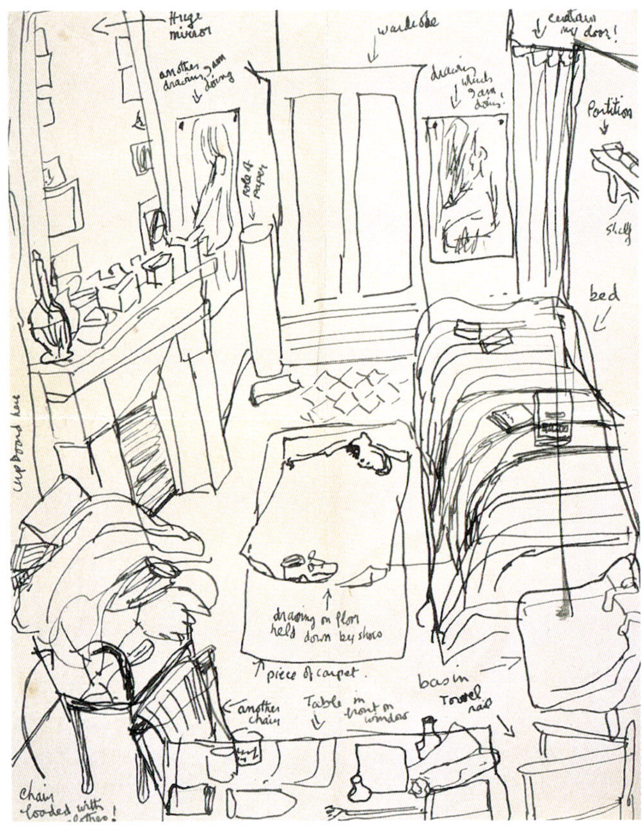

22 | Illustrated letter showing the interior of Eardley's room in Venice, c.1948–9
Joan Eardley Archive, Scottish National Gallery of Modern Art, Edinburgh [GMA/A09]

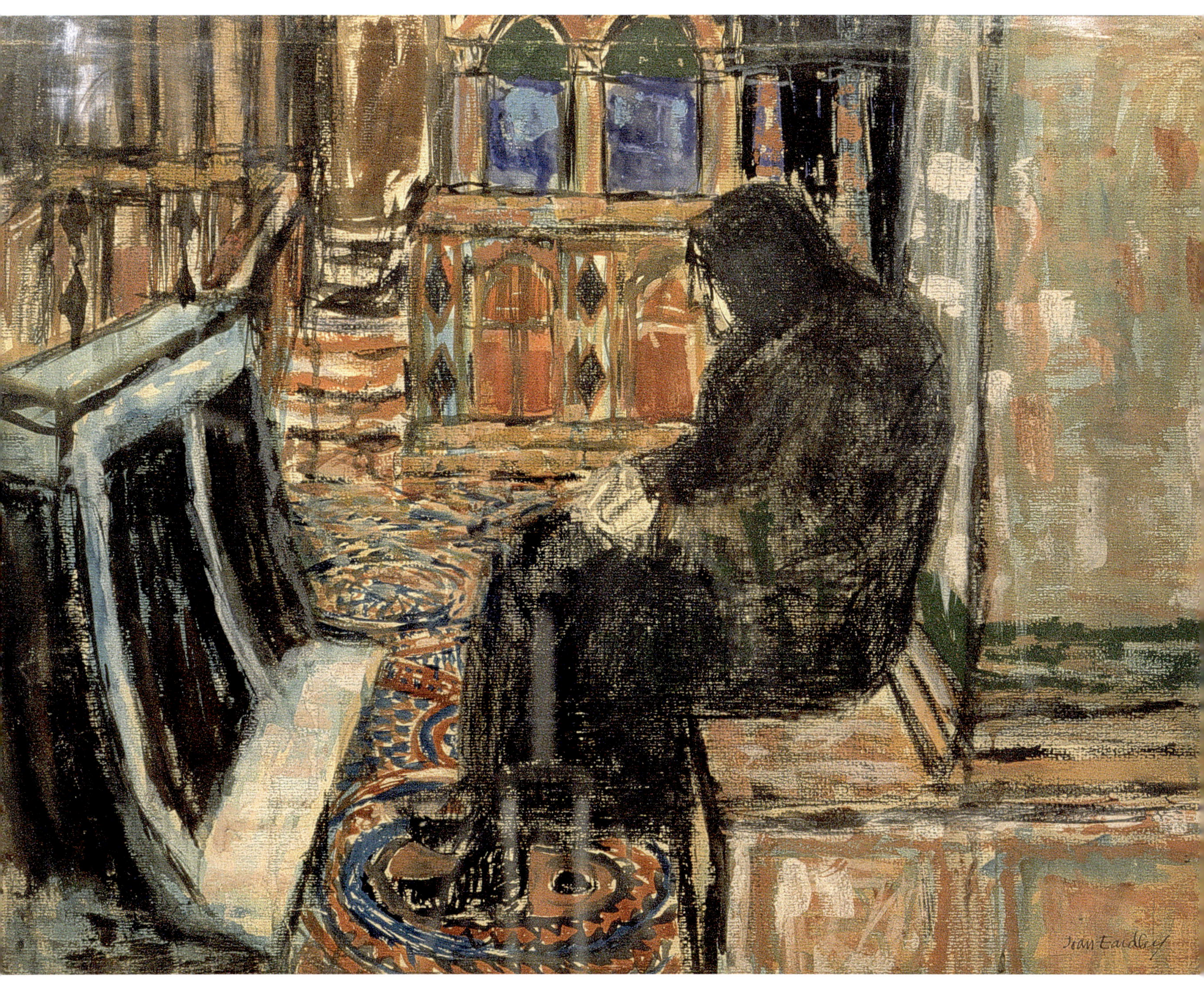

23 | ***Old Woman Praying in St Mark's, Venice***, 1948-9
Pastel and gouache on paper 54 × 72.5cm
University of Edinburgh Fine Art Collections

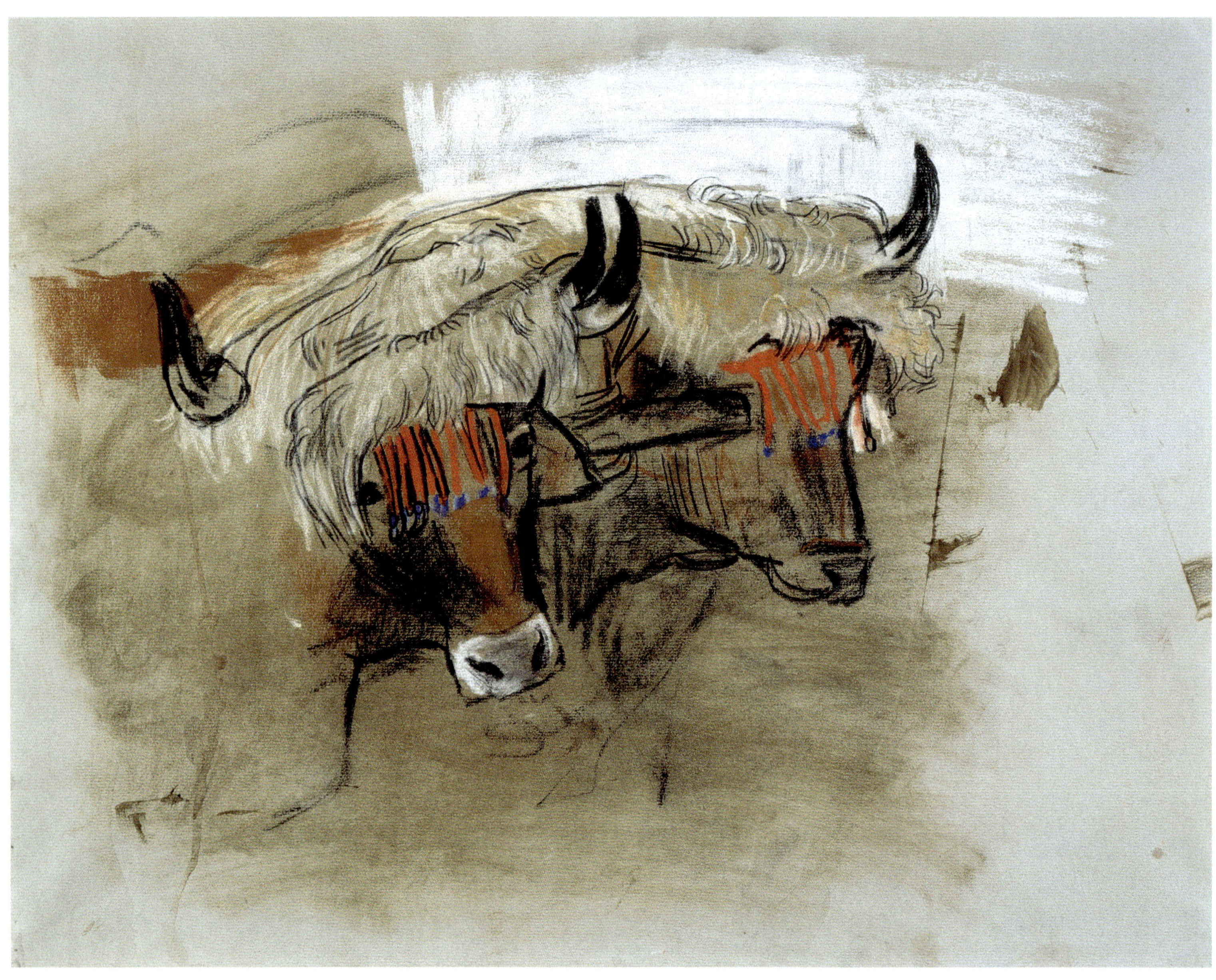

24 | *A Pair of Oxen*, 1948-9
Pastel on paper 48 × 38.6cm
Scottish National Gallery of Modern Art, Edinburgh

25 | *Beggars in Venice*, 1948-9
Oil on canvas 92.7 × 99.7cm
Private collection

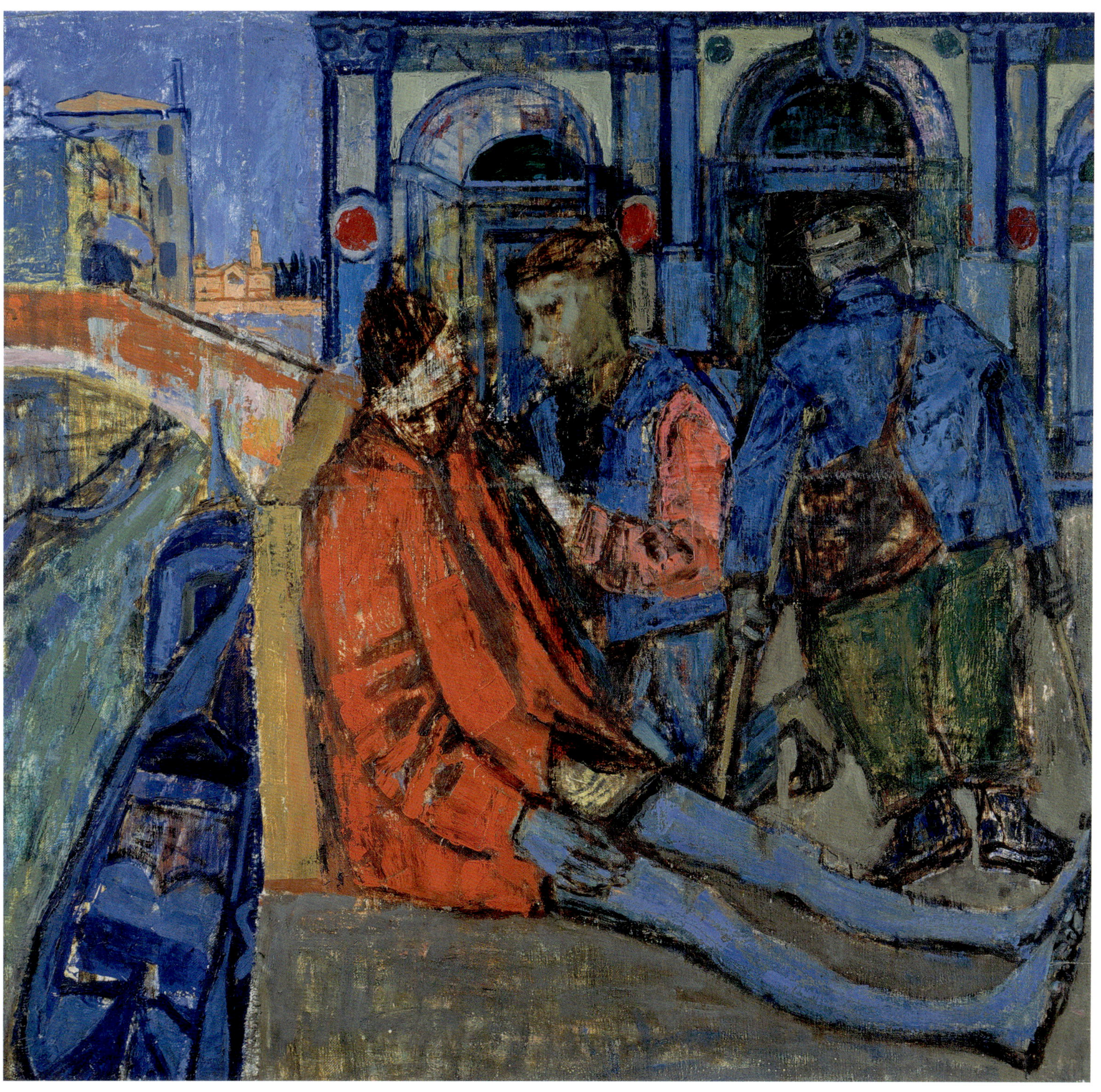

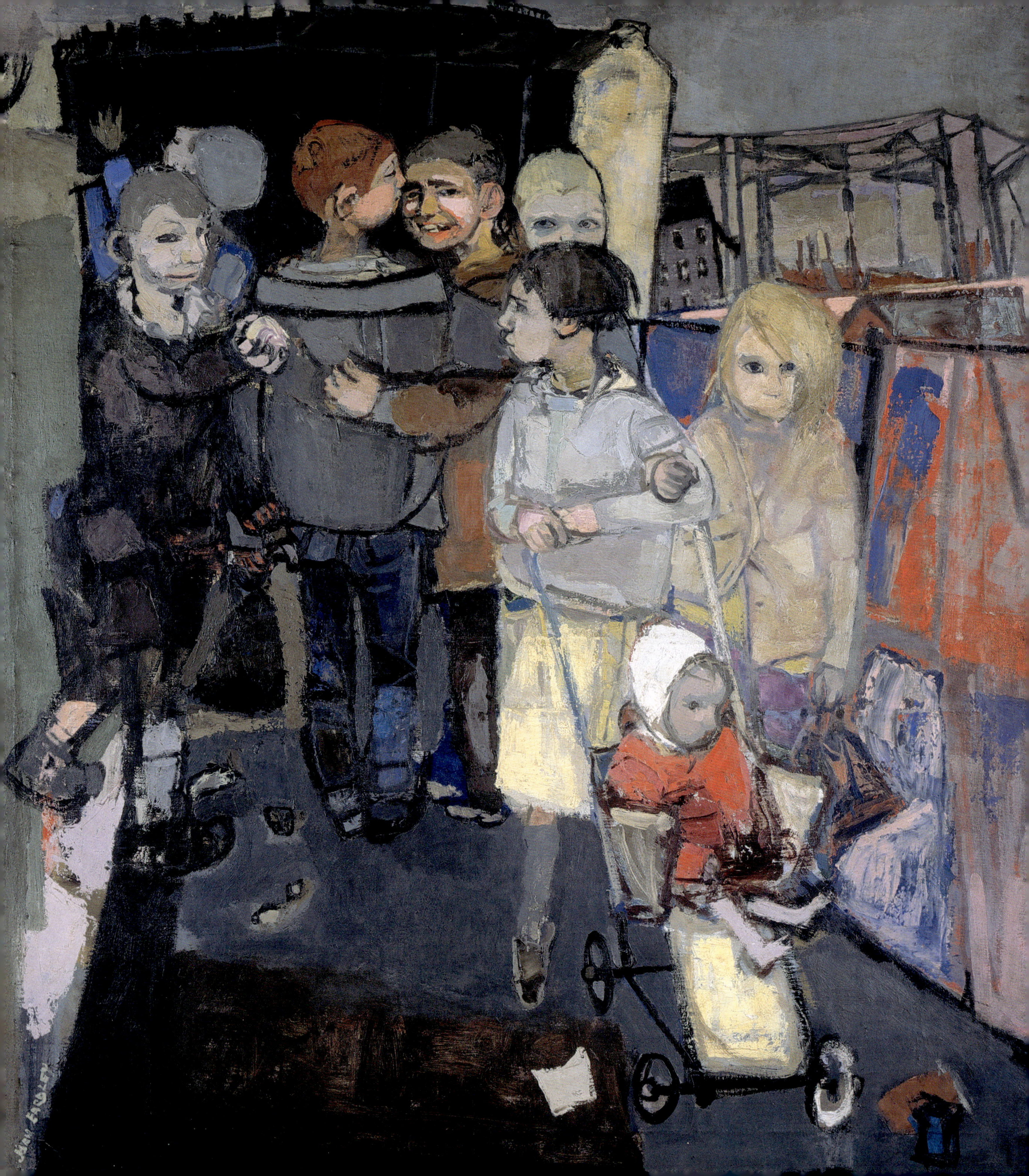

Glasgow and Childhood

26 | ***Children, Port Glasgow*, 1955**
Oil on canvas 135 × 123.2cm
Private Collection

On her return to Scotland Eardley rented a studio in the centre of Glasgow at 21 Cochrane Street, close to the City Chambers. The attic studio, reached by a steep set of stairs, was four storeys up. The building was shared by several manufacturers, including the bookbinder James Forsyth, whose invoice paper Eardley sometimes used for sketches.[34] Her friend Angus Neil lived and worked around the corner in Montrose Street. Eardley now set to work making chalk drawings of the local children. On some of these drawings she used the blue distemper with which she had painted the studio walls; in others she rubbed the paper with red chalk to give a warm background tone. She used scraps of paper, often extending the work with extra sheets and paperclips. She even did some of her chalk drawings of children on sandpaper. The brightly coloured oil composition, *Street Kids* [35] shows three children seated on the pavement kerb, one rapt in the contents of a comic, another holding an apple and the third gazing out of the picture, his spindly legs ending in t-bar sandals. In 2002 this painting was included in the catalogue *Transition: The London Art Scene in the Fifties* as the author, Martin Harrison, was keen to show Eardley in the context of painters such as John Bratby, Peter Blake, and the American painter Bernard Perlinn, all of whom depicted urban childhood in their work.

In her ideas about children and humour Eardley was greatly influenced by Paul Klee and Pablo Picasso. In America Ben Shahn was drawing urban children in a direct manner and with a keen, socially engaged edge. His work, like Stanley Spencer's, was made widely available through the illustrated series *Modern Painters*, published by Penguin in the postwar years. Eardley was a keen reader of *The Listener*, which ran lengthy articles on contemporary art by Patrick Heron, David Sylvester and Herbert Read, and left-wing journals such as the *New Statesman*.[35] She was also a regular reader of *Picture Post*, which on 31 January 1948 carried a now celebrated article, 'The Forgotten Gorbals', featuring photographs of children by Bert Hardy and Bill Brandt. Eardley herself was never without a camera after she had moved to her second studio at 204 St James Road [27, 28], which was also in Townhead and just north of the City Chambers. Some of Eardley's drawings and oils such as *Three Children at a Tenement Window* [37] and *Children at the Window* [42] are closely based on her photographs [30].

In the early 1960s Eardley recorded a taped interview, and spoke of her enthusiasm for the back streets of Glasgow and the children who played there: 'The community feeling is rapidly disappearing in Glasgow ... I do feel that there is still a little bit left. I try still to paint Glasgow so long as there is this family group quality. I've known about half a dozen families well I suppose during the period of time I've worked in Glasgow ... about ten years or more and at the present moment a family by the name of Samson [41, 43, 75]. I have been painting them for seven years ... there are a large number of them, twelve, so I've always had a certain number of children from this family of any age I choose ... some children I don't like ... most of them I get on with ... some interest me much more as characters ... these ones I encourage - they don't need much encouragement - they don't pose - they come up and say "will you paint me?" There are always knocks at the door - the ones I want - I try to get them to stand still - it's not possible to get a child to stay still ... I watch them moving about and do the best I can ... the Samsons - they amuse me - they are full of what's gone on today - whose broken into what shop and whose flung a pie in whose face - it goes on and on. They just let out all their life and energy ... and I just watch them and I do try and think about them in painterly terms ... all the bits of red and bits of colour and they wear each other's clothes - never the same thing twice running ... even that doesn't matter ... they are Glasgow - this richness that

Glasgow has - I hope it will always have - a living thing, intense quality - you can't ever know what you are going to do but as long as Glasgow has this I'll always want to paint. Whenever I come back I get a new feeling - chiefly the back streets - I always feel the same - I want to paint them differently - but the same thing - you can't stop observing, things are happening all the time - you are recognising them in your mind.'[36]

This sense of kinship between the figures is one of the most striking features of Eardley's paintings of children. It is pronounced in works such as *Street Kids* [35], *Some of the Samson Family* [43], the *Children and Chalked Wall* series [77, 78] and *Glasgow Back Street with Children Playing* [44]. The compositions of two children in close support of each other such as, *Brother and Sister* and *Glasgow Children* [39] are poignant reminders of the absences of parents in the children's lives. The riotous energy of groups of children is expressed in the vivid *Glasgow Kids, A Saturday Matinee Picture Queue* [49] and the tensions between the sexes in *Children, Port Glasgow* [26]. The latter is a *tour de force* compositionally with the teenage boys at the rear turning to jeer at the two girls with the pushchair containing the baby who has lost its shoes. In the background are gaunt tenement blocks and the great jibs of the cranes in the shipbuilding yards. The dejected figure of the little blond girl is set against coloured panels suggestive of advertisement hoardings.

Eardley also painted a series of long, rectangular panels of children playing in streets of boarded-up shops and bomb damage using photographs she had taken herself. In documenting these environments she was aided by Audrey Walker, whose arresting photographs of graffiti and street decay helped Eardley when she was painting in her studio [31A-C]. Some of the street scenes are grey in tonality, others bright red as if to reflect the red sandstone tenements. *Glasgow Close* realistically captures the colours of a stair close. The oil paintings of *Children Playing* [38], *Children in a Glasgow Back Street* [50], *Rottenrow* [36] and *Skipping* were concurrent with the work of the childhood folklorists, Peter and Iona Opie and, the filmmaker, James Ritchie who were recording children's play rhymes and customs at that time. Eardley was not alone in realising that this was a vanishing world.[37]

Eardley's works were not devoted exclusively to children. Paintings such as *Back Street Bookie* [16] record adult street life in a twilight scene. The drawings of *Swing Park, Port Glasgow* [32] and *Street Market* [14] evoke the gritty reality of life in Glasgow. One of Eardley's friends from her student days, the painter Dorothy Steel, lived in Gourock and introduced her to nearby Port Glasgow. Steel also painted tenement scenes and small domestic still lifes of basic household items, something Eardley had done since visiting Arran in the 1940s. Indeed, while on holiday with Steel in rural France in 1951, Eardley painted the view of the scullery with the lavatory door. The relationship with Steel was fraught and in letters to Sandeman, Eardley worried that they might not be friends by the end of the holiday.[38] Eventually Eardley acknowledged that Steel was probably nicer towards her than she was towards Steel. Sandeman records that most of Eardley's friendships invariably went through difficult periods. Although Steel invited Eardley to stay in France on a permanent basis, Eardley declined, saying that she would miss her tenements, her 'wee boys' and Angus Neil.[39]

Eardley had a difficult character, and she knew it. She suffered from depression throughout her life. In a student notebook used in Italy she noted: 'If you want experience and understanding of beauty then envy me now - but if you want happiness then don't envy me because

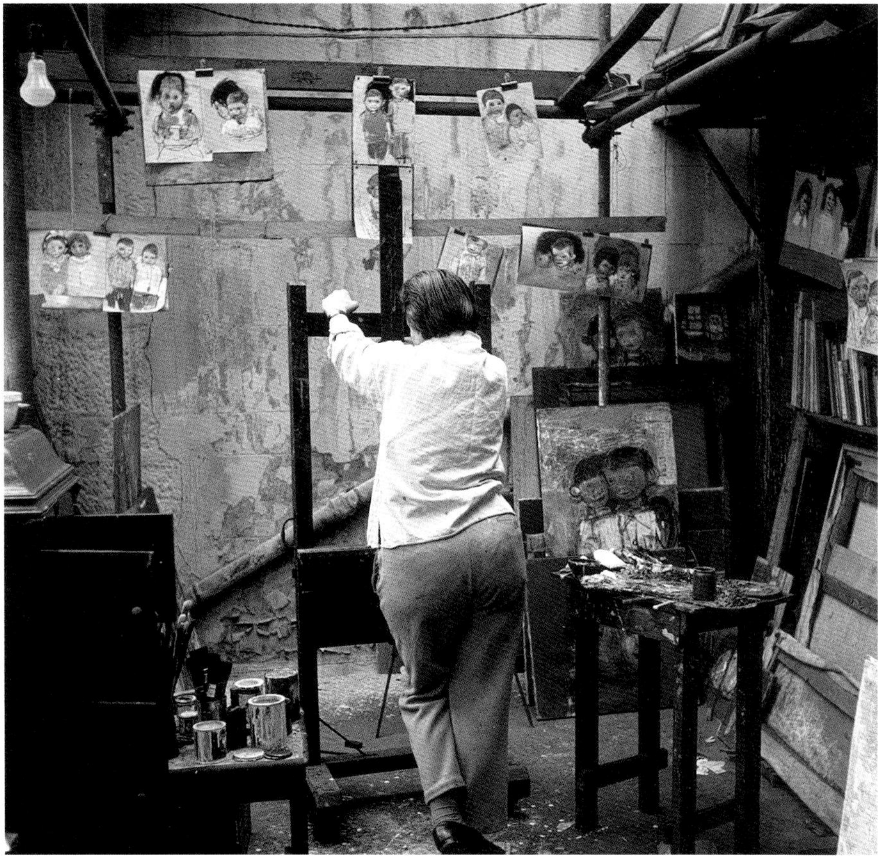

27 | Eardley in her studio at 204 St James Road, Townhead in Glasgow with chalk sketches of children c.1950s
Photo: Audrey Walker
Joan Eardley Archive, Scottish National Gallery of Modern Art, Edinburgh [GMA/A09]

28 | Glass-fronted studio used by Eardley on the second floor of a tenement on the corner of McAslin Street and St James Road Townhead in Glasgow
Photo: Audrey Walker
Scottish National Gallery of Modern Art, Edinburgh

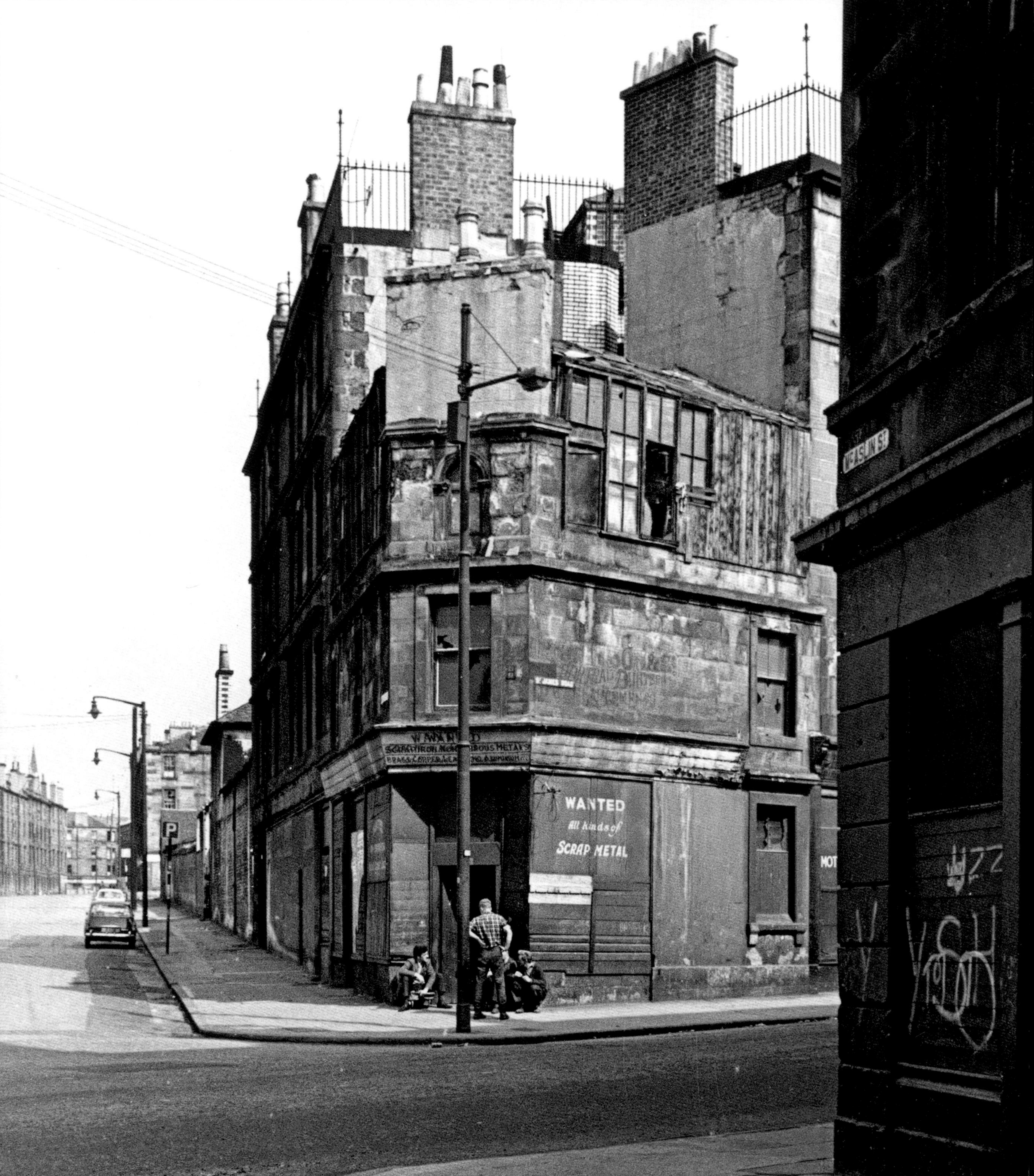
WANTED
All kinds of
SCRAP METAL
P

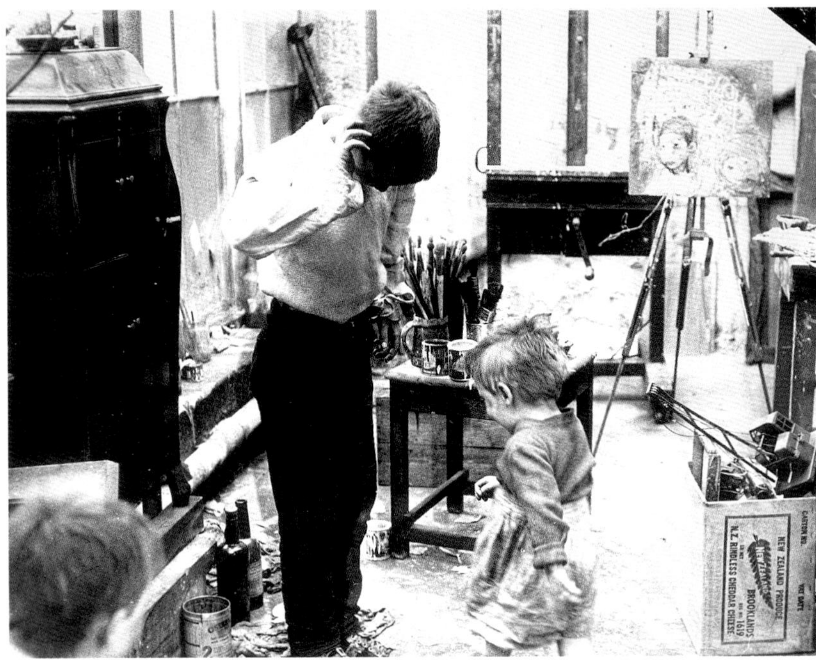

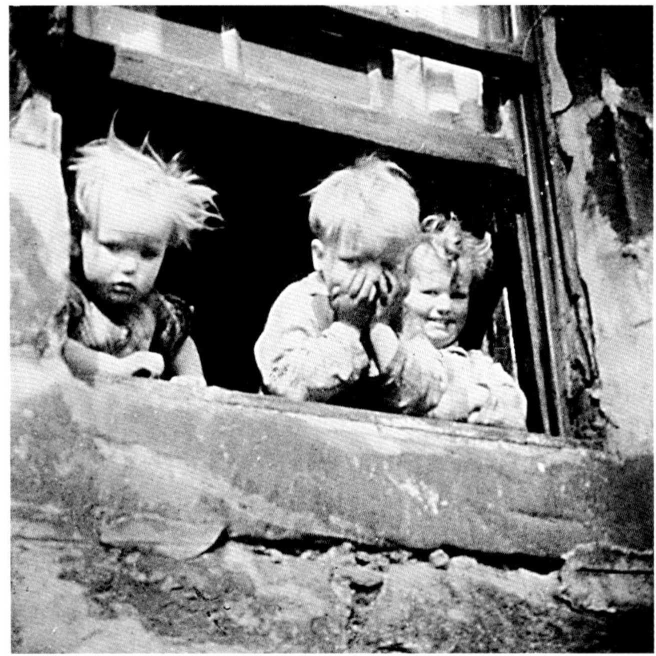

these things don't bring happiness.'[40] Furthermore, from the mid-1950s due to a slipped disc, she had to contend with back pain for the rest of her life and painted wearing a neck brace.

Eardley was very fond of Angus Neil. He had developed mental health problems after the war, and, although Eardley had no illusions about his temperamental and sometimes untrustworthy nature, they were close companions. He often posed for her. In *A Glasgow Lodging* he is shown as a lonely figure swamped in an army greatcoat by the fire, while in *The Table* [33] he is in a kitchen lit by strong shafts of colour. Sandeman recalls that when Angus took money or crossed other boundaries, Eardley would literally come to blows with him.[41] But Neil was a very patient model. In *Sleeping Nude* [34], which was likened at the time to a Belsen victim, the sombre grey palette-knife technique recalls that of Nicolas de Staël, whose work was shown in Edinburgh in 1954. Eardley was subjected to 'shock horror' headlines in the tabloid press on showing this work. One newspaper printed her address, whereupon various men turned up volunteering to pose for her. Eardley never again painted a male nude. Ironically, it was Angus Neil who protected Eardley from unwelcome attention when she went sketching in some of the roughest areas of Glasgow. He also helped with difficult joinery tasks and offered a barrier to the outside world by the very fact of his existence as a male friend.

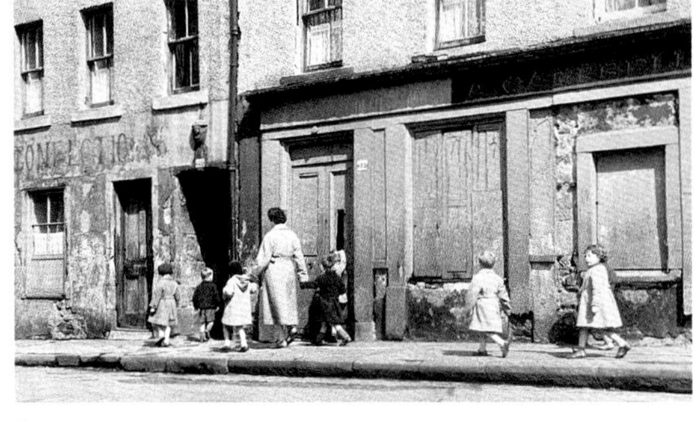

A

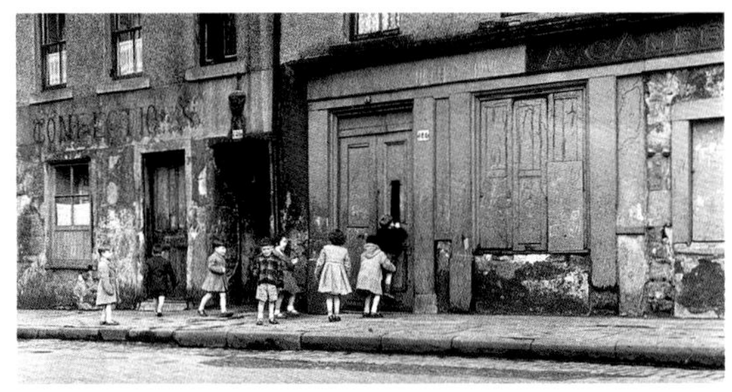

B

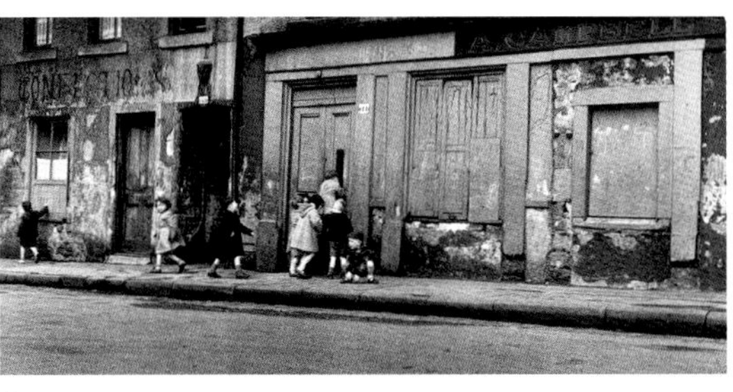

C

29 | Children in Eardley's studio with a painting of Brian and Pat Samson in the background
Photo: Audrey Walker
Gracefield Art Centre, Dumfries

30 | Photograph of children at a window, used by Joan Eardley as source material for her paintings
Photo: Joan Eardley
Joan Eardley Archive, Scottish National Gallery of Modern Art, Edinburgh [GMA/A09]

31A–C | Street scenes, Rottenrow, Glasgow, showing children exploring a bomb-damaged building
Photo: Audrey Walker post 1952
Joan Eardley Archive, Scottish National Gallery of Modern Art, Edinburgh [GMA/A09]

Eardley's view of impoverished tenement life was seen south of the border in London in 1954 when she exhibited at a group show at The Parsons Gallery in Grosvenor Street. A press photograph shows Eardley hanging pictures of Angus Neil alongside her vivid head studies of boys [45-7, 90]. A notice in the *Glasgow Herald* described how Eardley's work was 'concerned with scenes and people of working-class Glasgow, the back streets and tenements in the neighbourhood of her studio … they are social documents literal enough to please the most exacting realist … her portraits of children … a combination of skill, acute observation and sympathetic truth'.[42] During the early years of the war thousands of children had been evacuated from Glasgow and the terrible blitz on Clydebank in March 1941 had, besides killing many children and civilians, left much of the population homeless. In the postwar rebuilding of Glasgow new areas of housing such as Castlemilk provided hitherto unknown modern facilities for working-class families and Basil Spence's tower blocks in the Gorbals were a brave new world until the reality of leaking roofs, damp, and broken lifts would lead to disillusion in the sixties. In this push to modernise Glasgow, the city councillors were not always keen to see Eardley's depictions of the urban underclass.

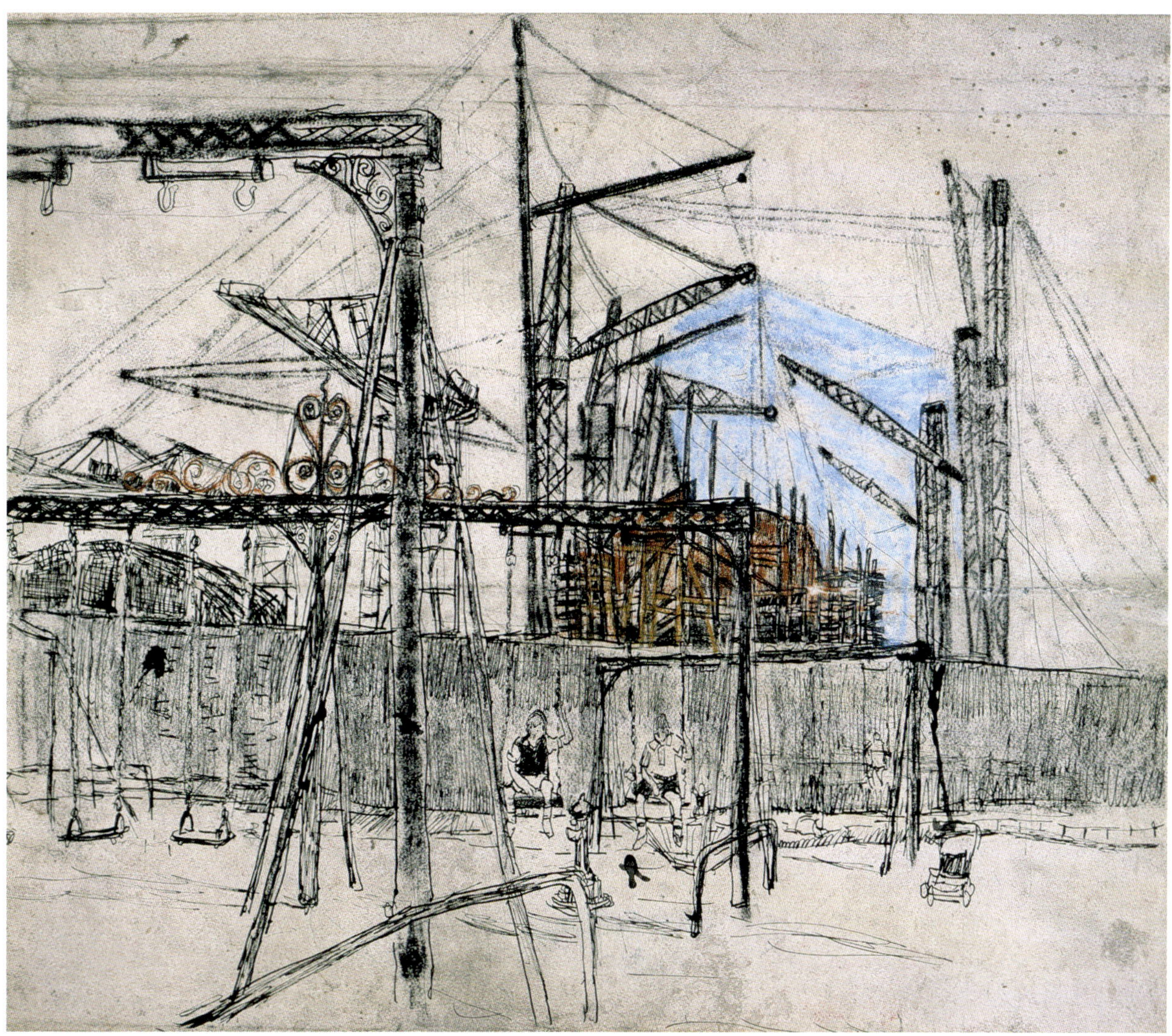

32 | ***Swing Park, Port Glasgow*, 1950**
Pen, ink, and chalk on paper
39.4 × 47.6cm
The Eardley Family

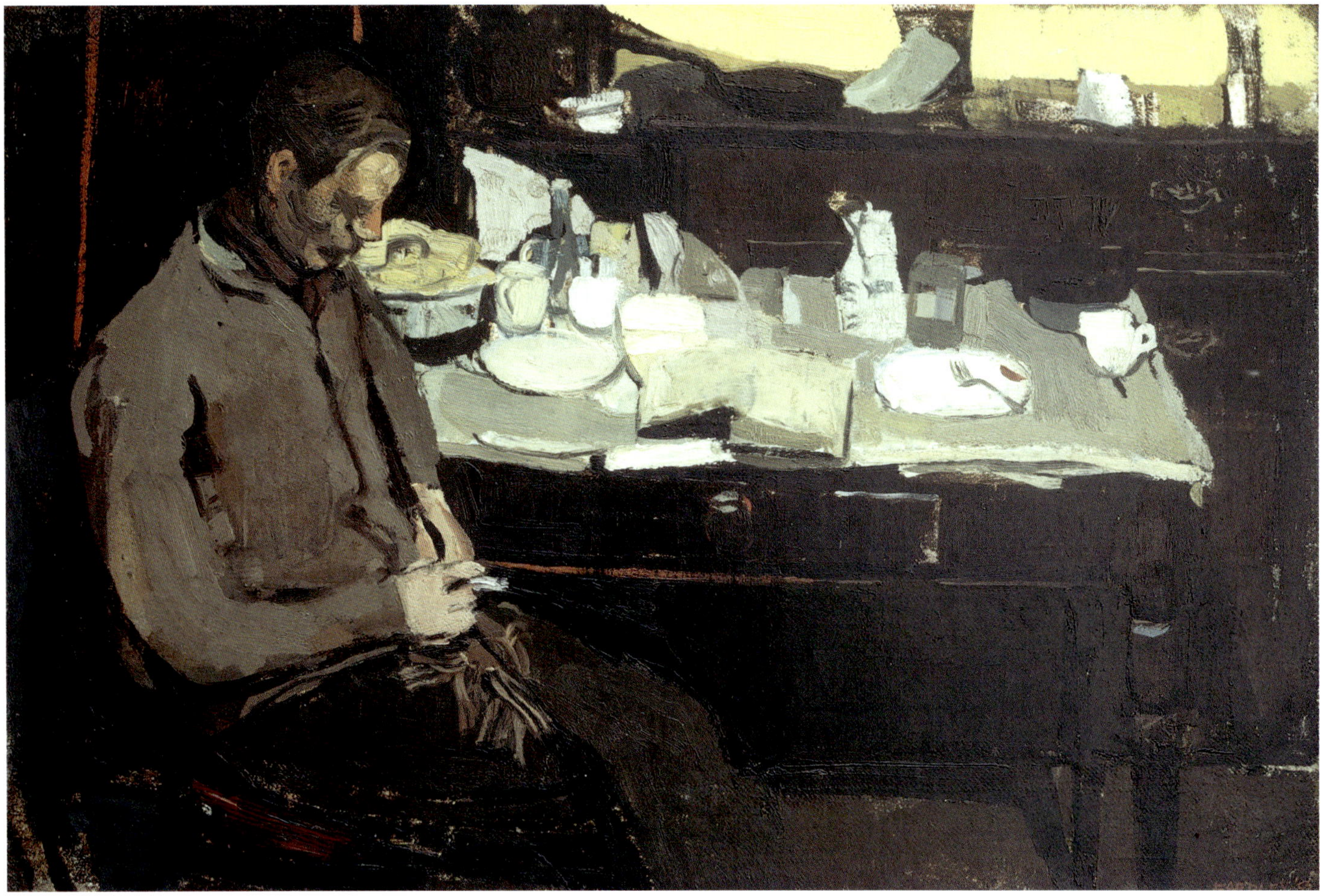

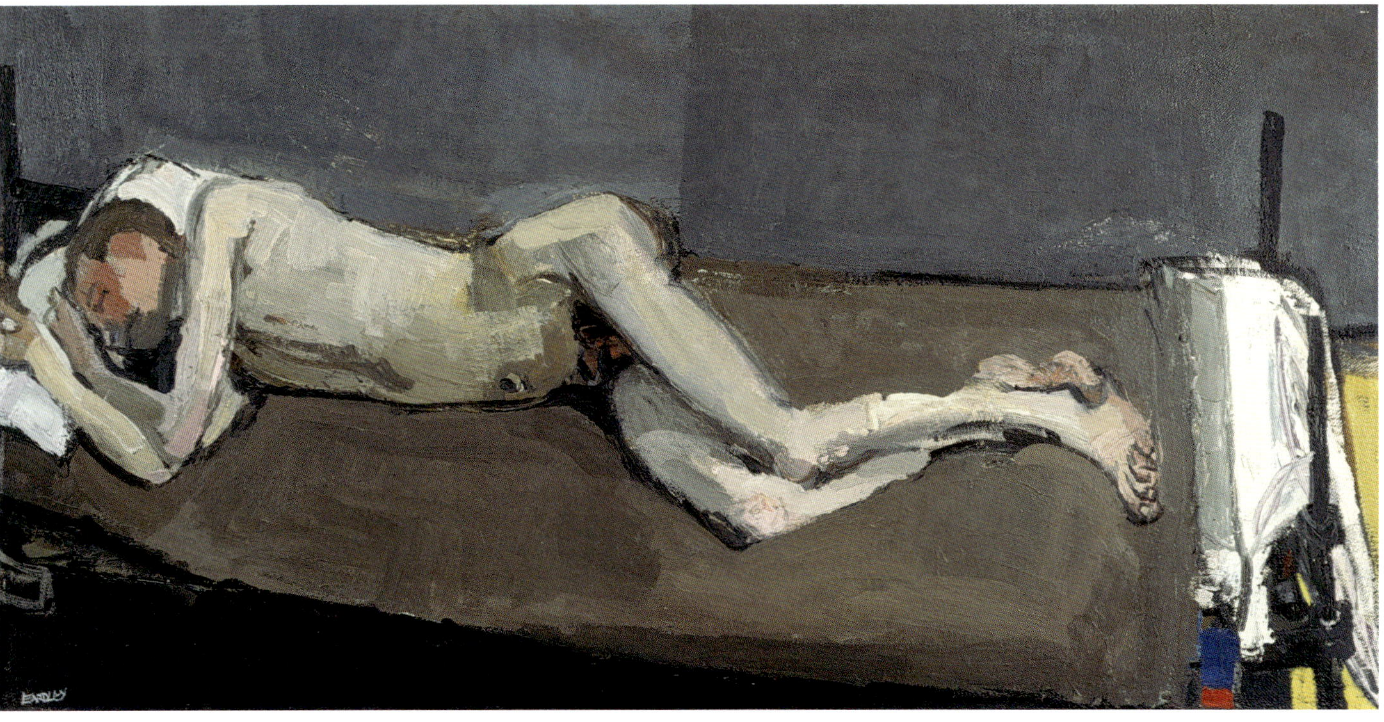

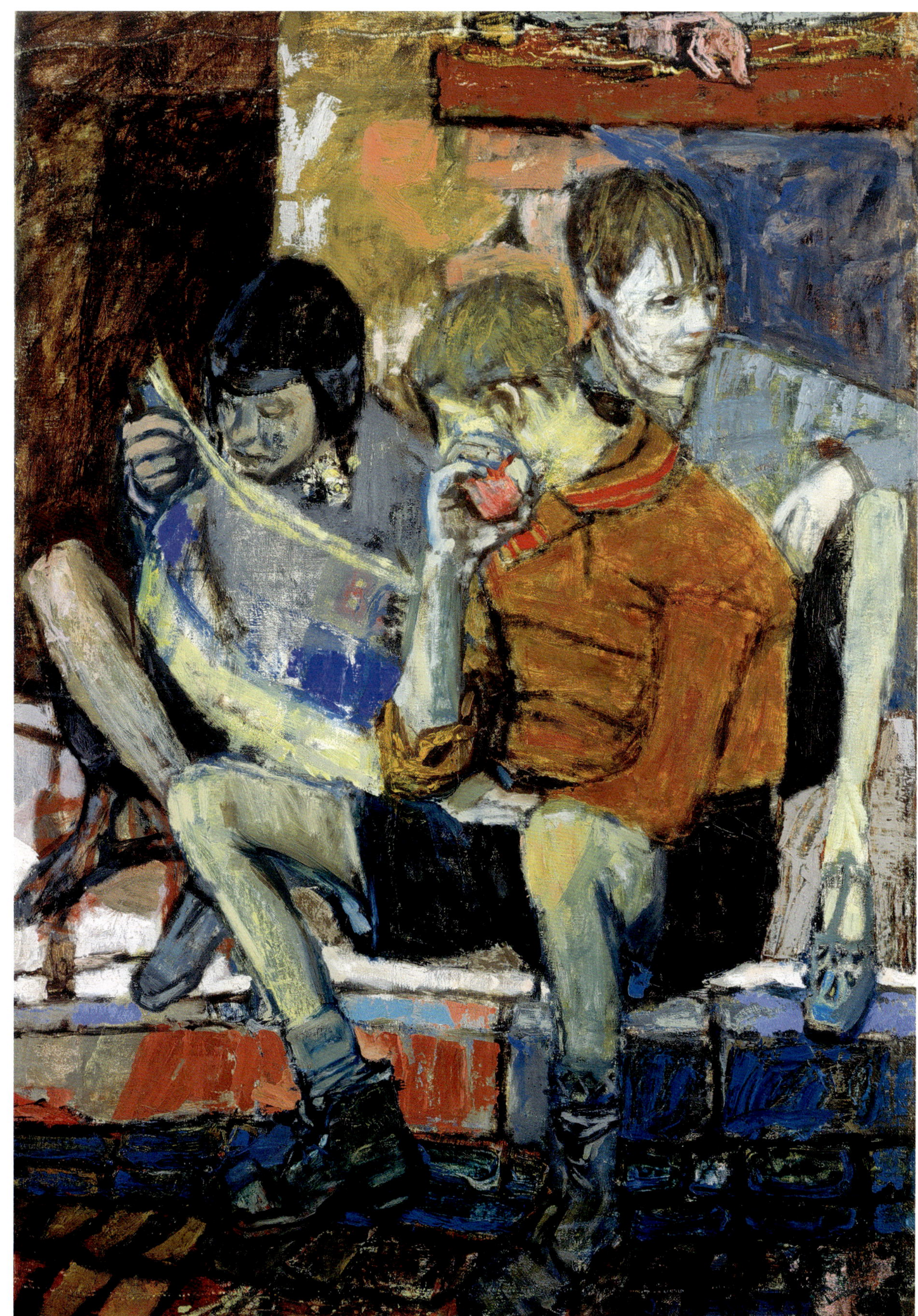

33 | ***The Table***, 1953
Oil on canvas 61 × 91.5cm
The MacLeod Collection

34 | ***Sleeping Nude***, 1955
Oil on canvas 76 × 155.2cm
Scottish National Gallery of Modern Art, Edinburgh

35 | ***Street Kids***, c.1949–51
Oil on canvas 102.9 × 73.7cm
Scottish National Gallery of Modern Art, Edinburgh

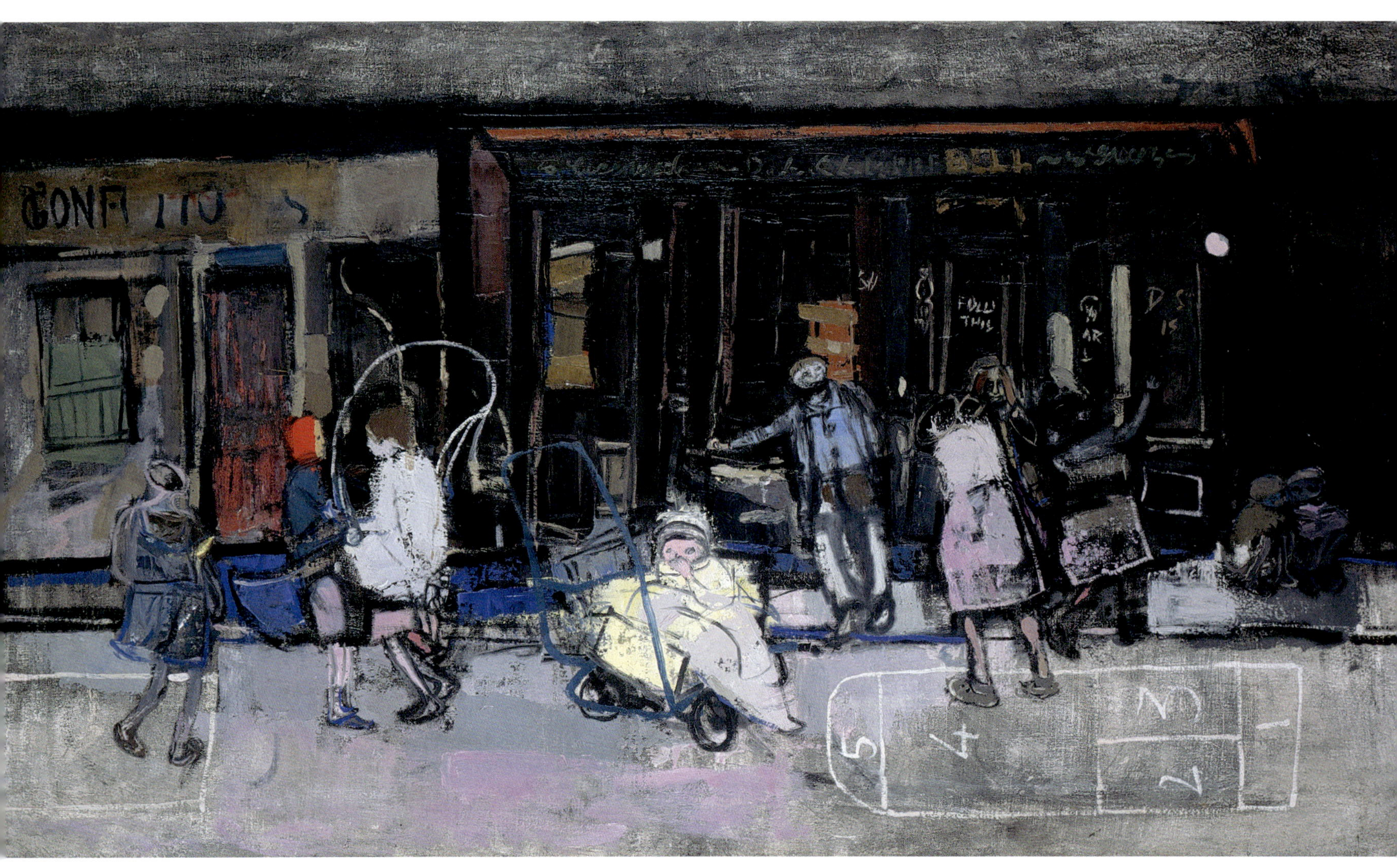

36 | *Rottenrow*, 1956
Oil on canvas 94 × 164cm
Private Collection

37 | *Three Children at a Tenement Window*, 1961
Gouache on paper 45.8 × 37.2cm
The Eardley Family

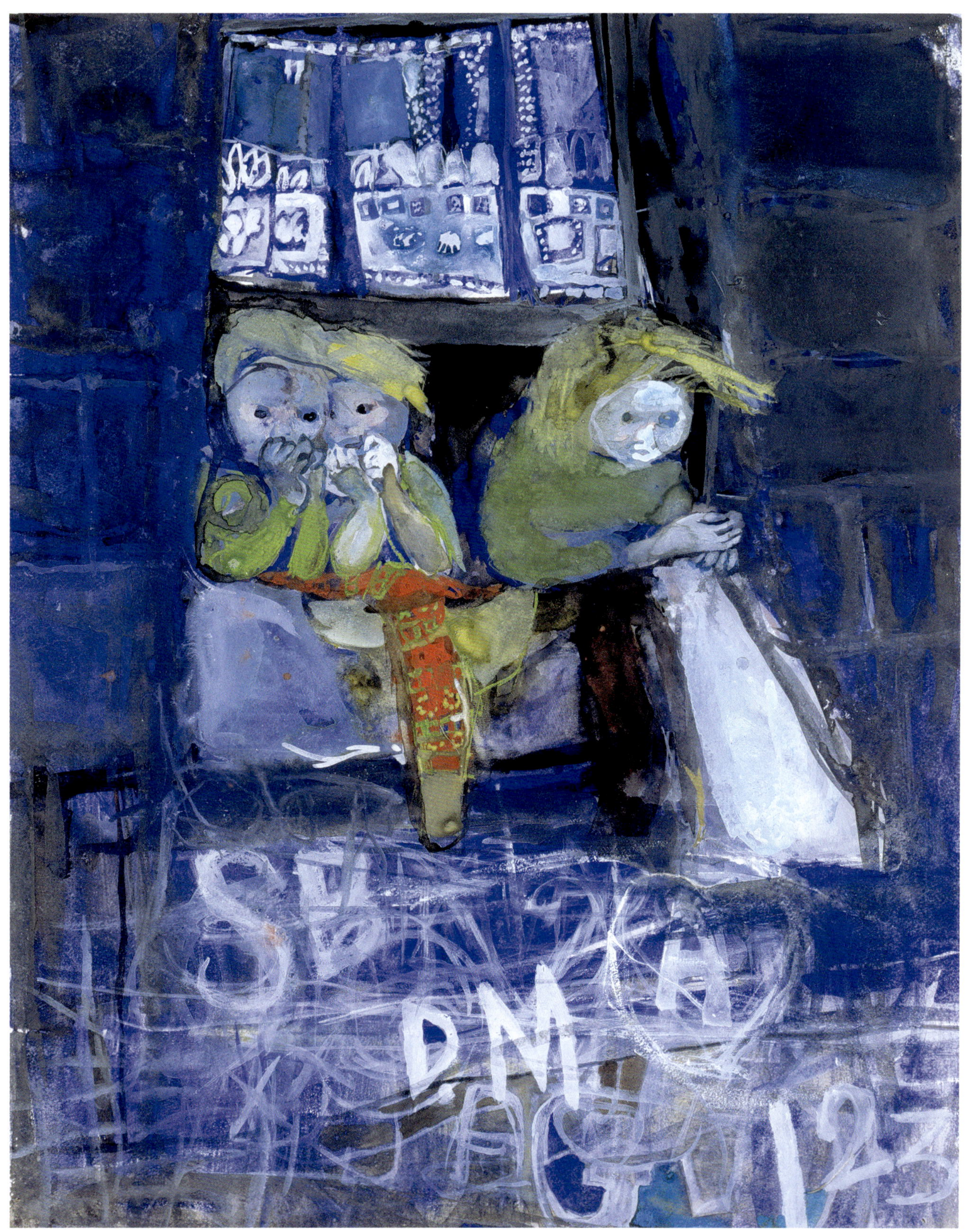
DM
123

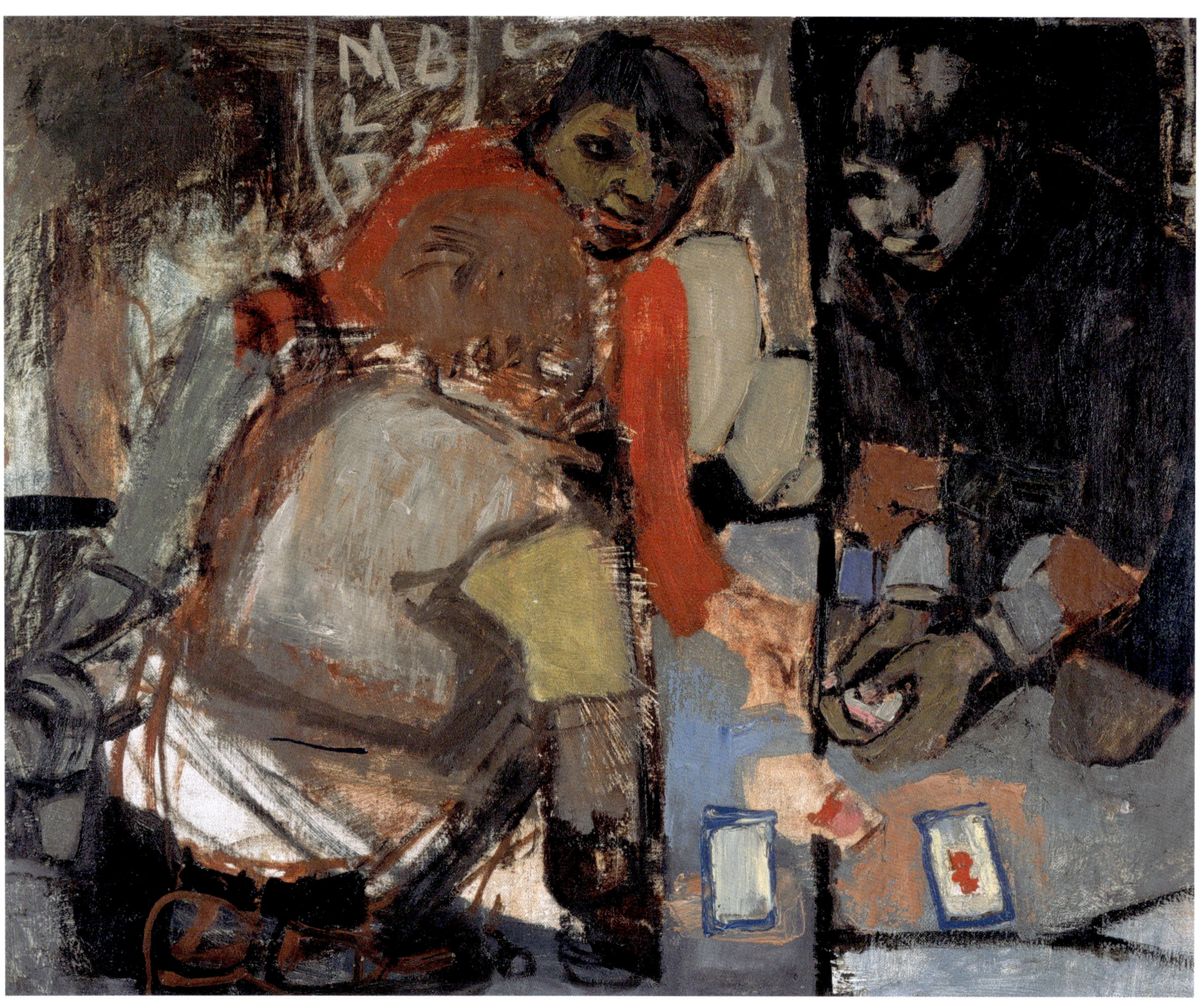

38 | *Children Playing*, c.1955
Oil on canvas 81 × 101.5cm
Private Collection

39 | *Glasgow Children*, 1958
Oil on canvas 91.4 × 71.1cm
Private Collection

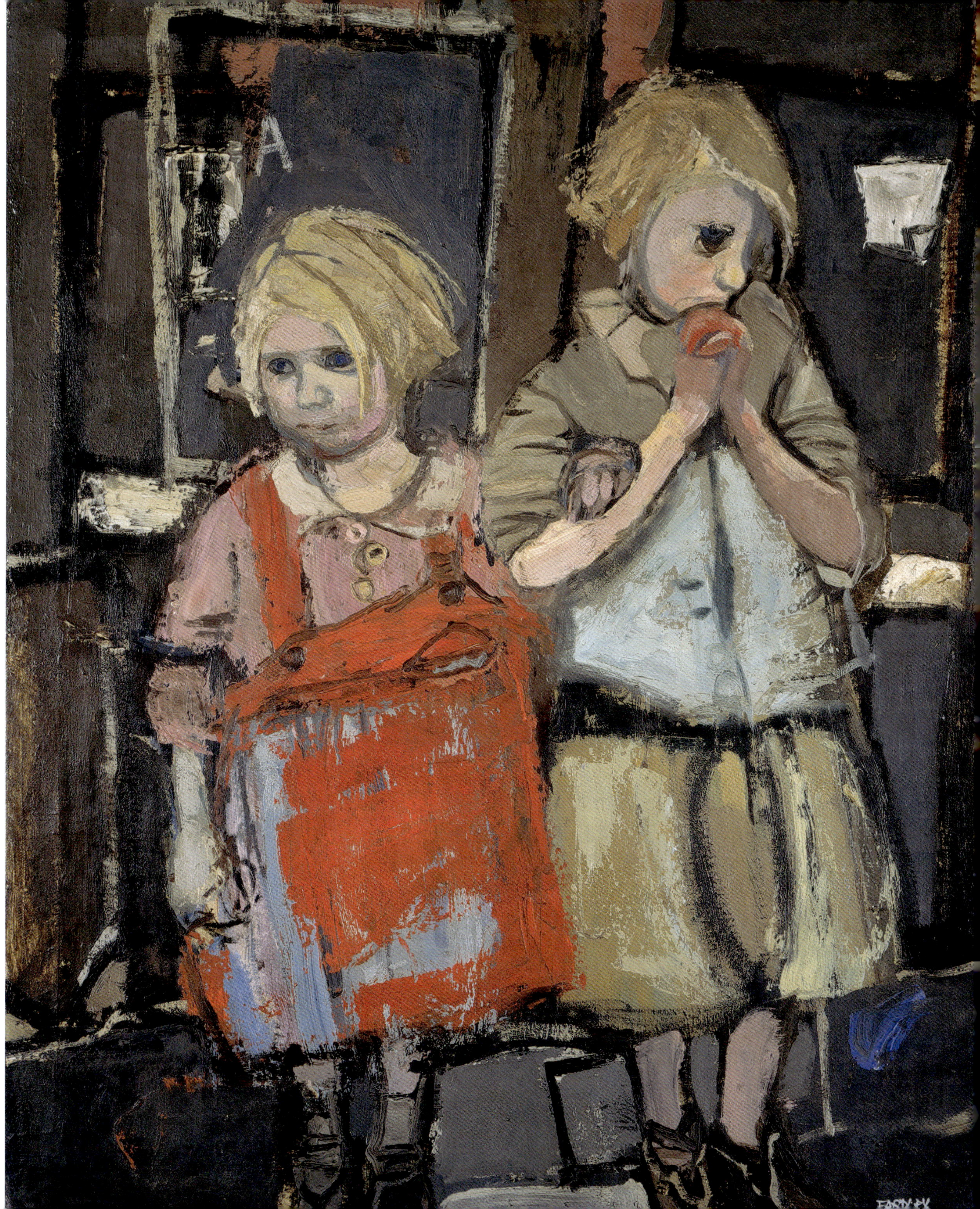

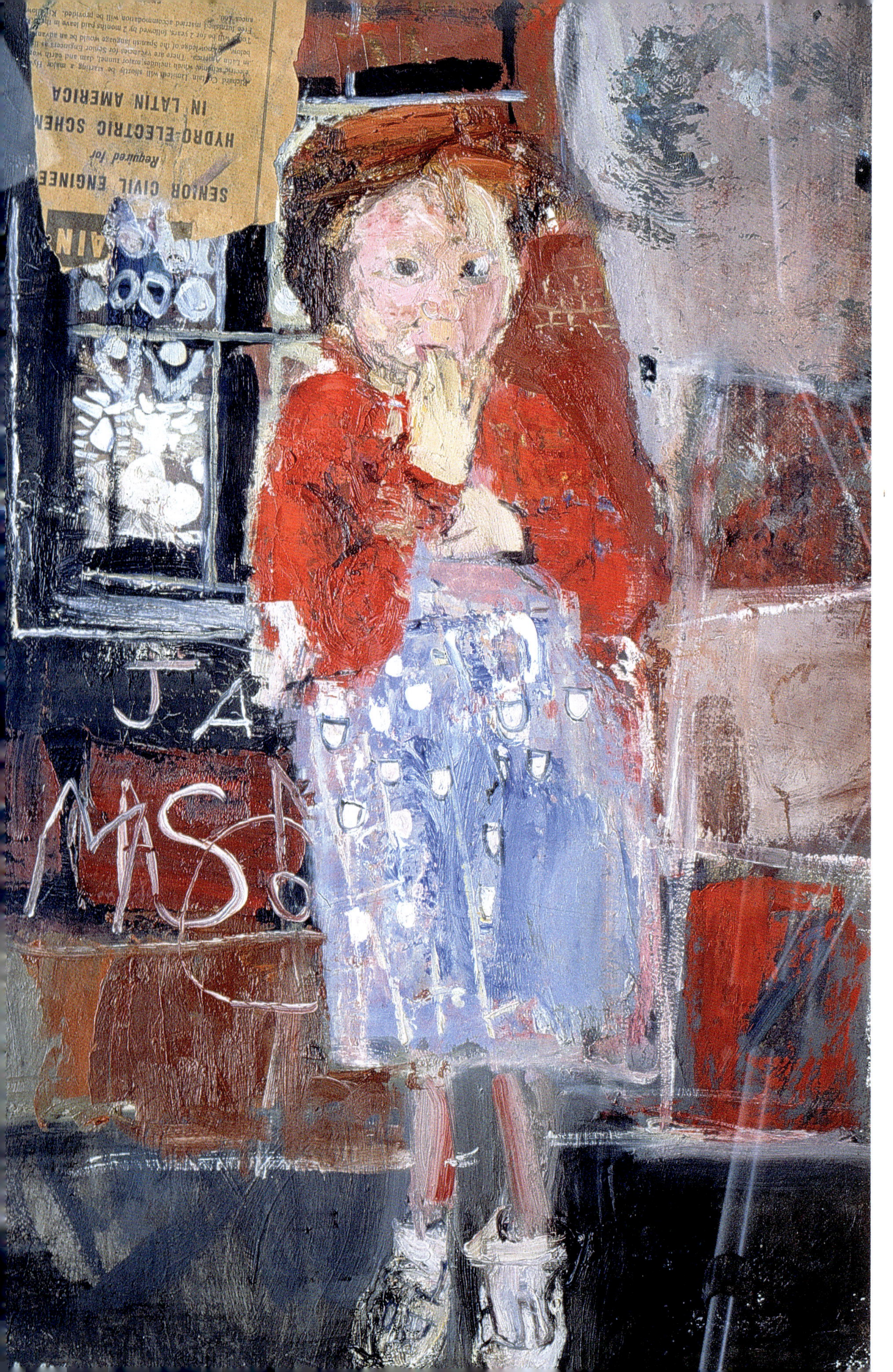
SENIOR CIVIL ENGINEE
Required for
HYDRO-ELECTRIC SCHEM
IN LATIN AMERICA
J A

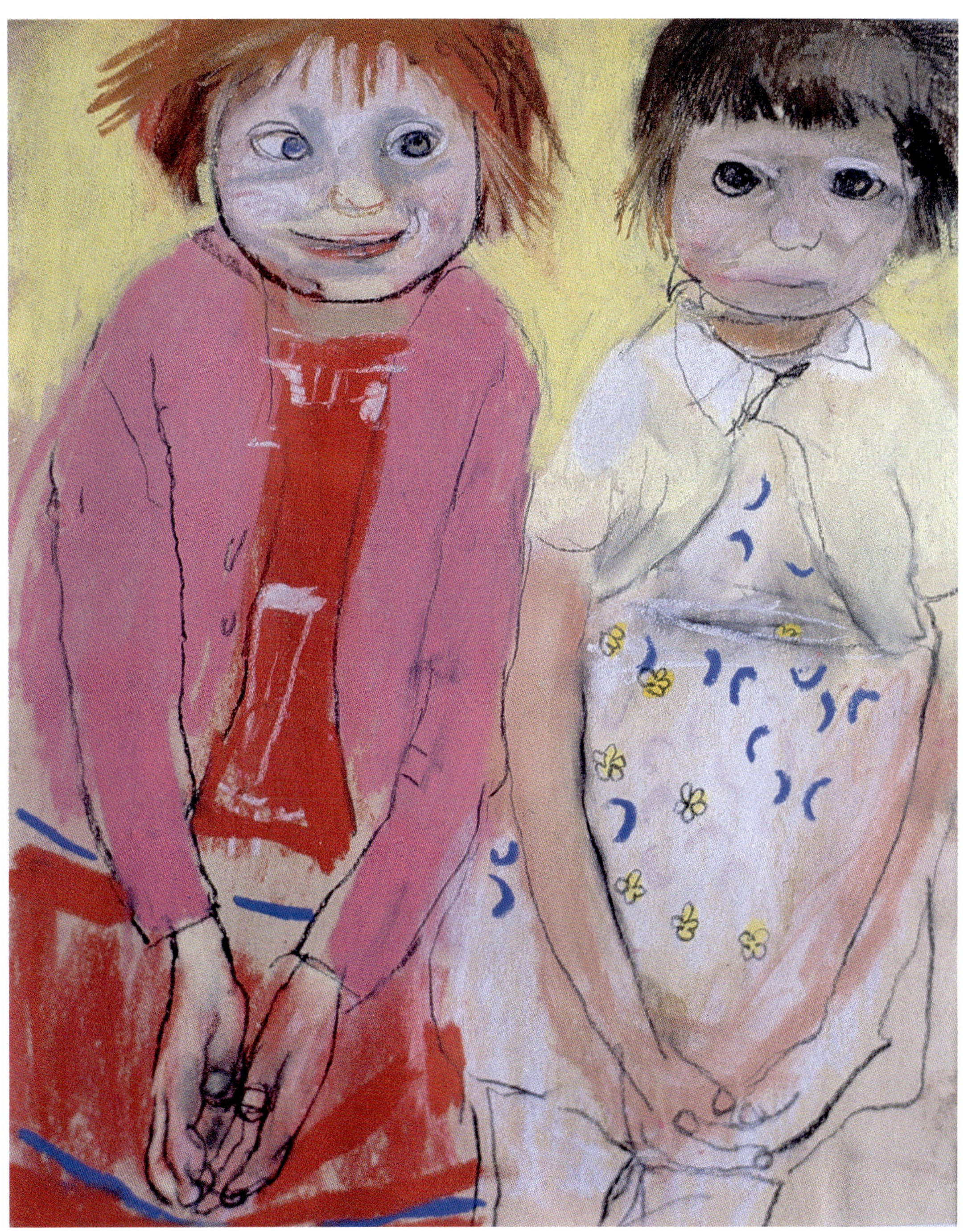

40 | ***Little Girl with a Squint***, 1962
Oil on canvas 75 × 49.5cm
Dumfriesshire Educational Trust, Gracefield Arts Centre, Dumfries

41 | **Pat and Anne Samson**
Chalk on paper 25.5 × 22.9cm
Private Collection

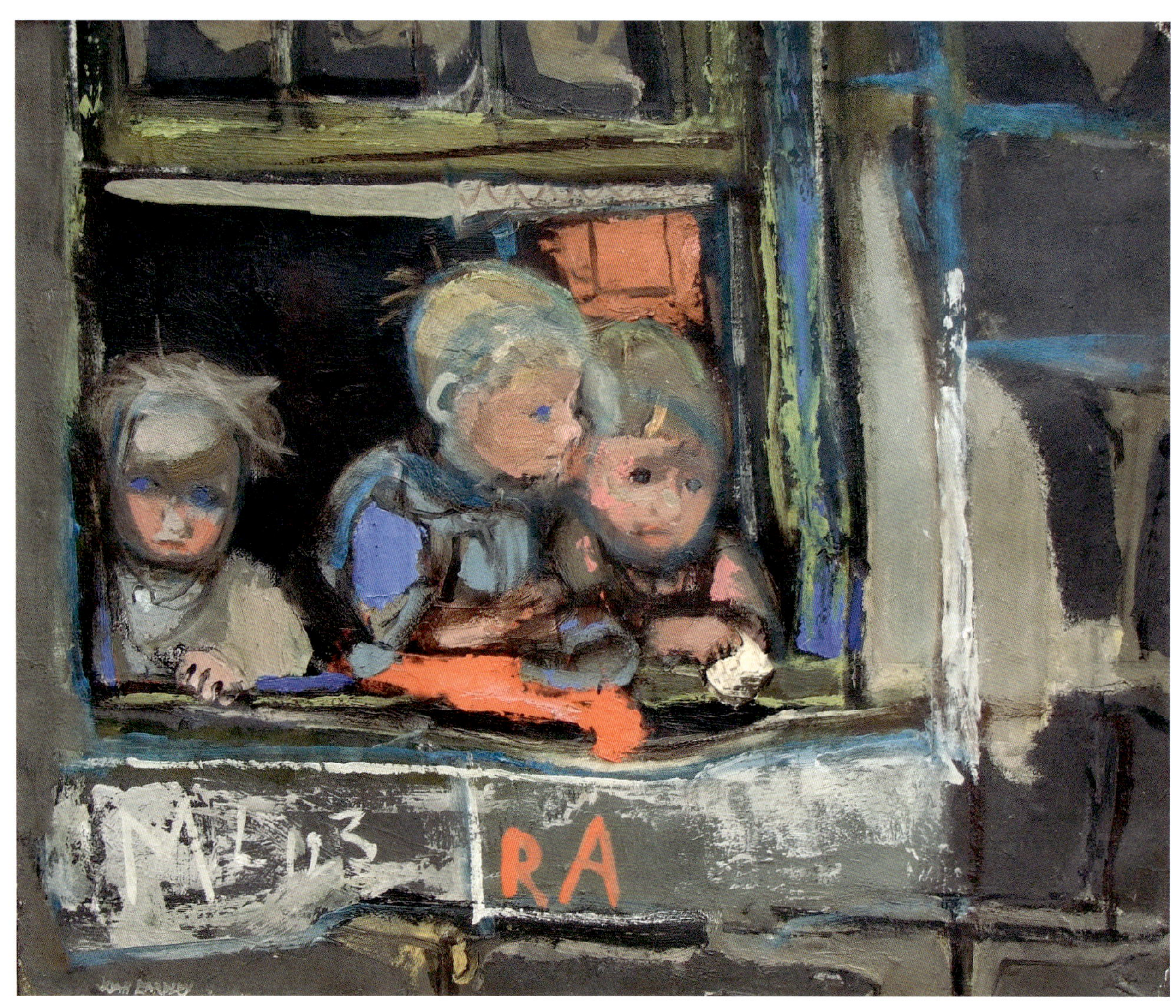

42 | Children at the Window

Oil on canvas 50 × 61cm

Private Collection

43 | *Some of the Samson Family*, 1961

Oil on canvas 105.4 × 108cm

Private Collection

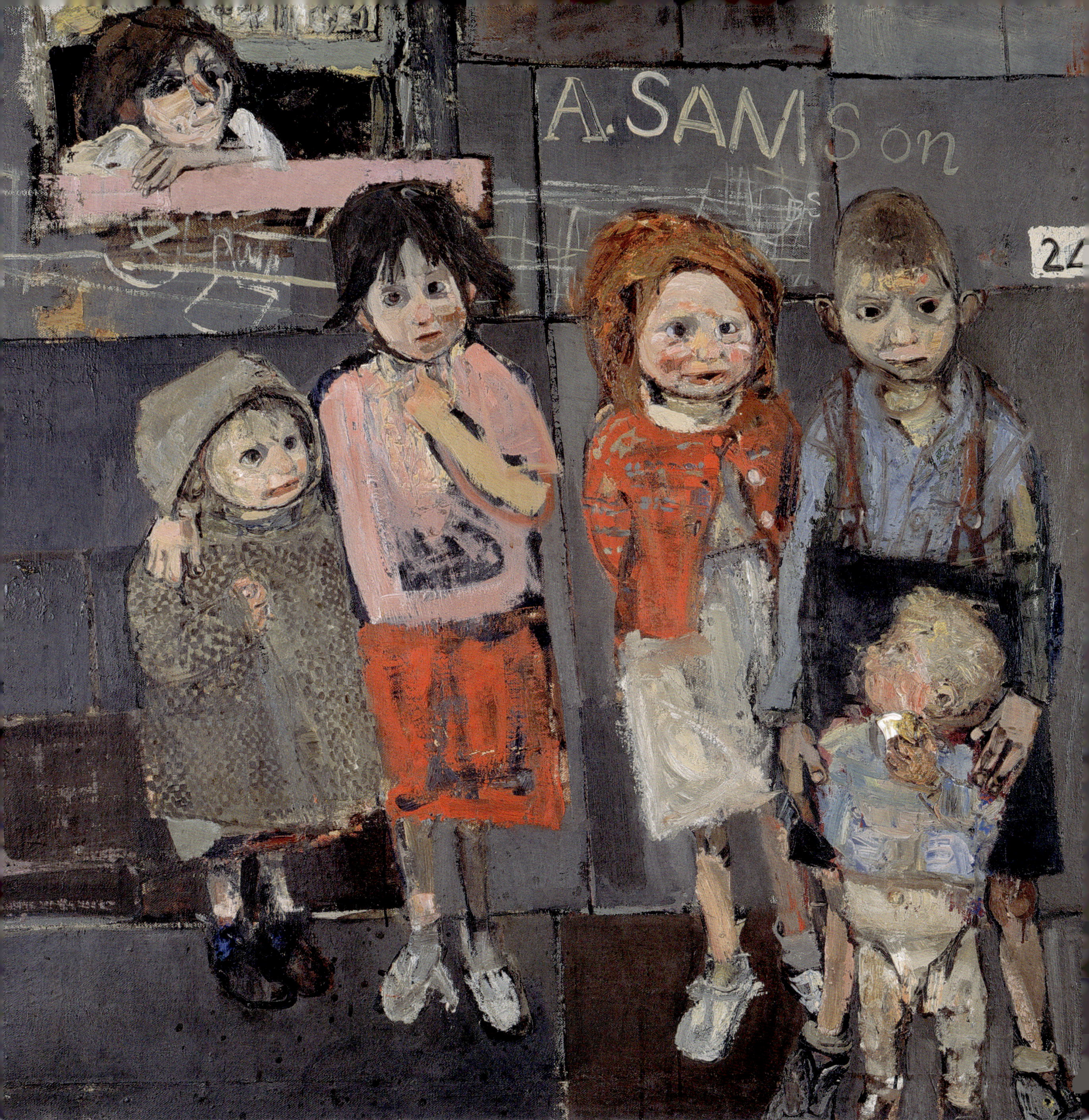
A. SAMSon

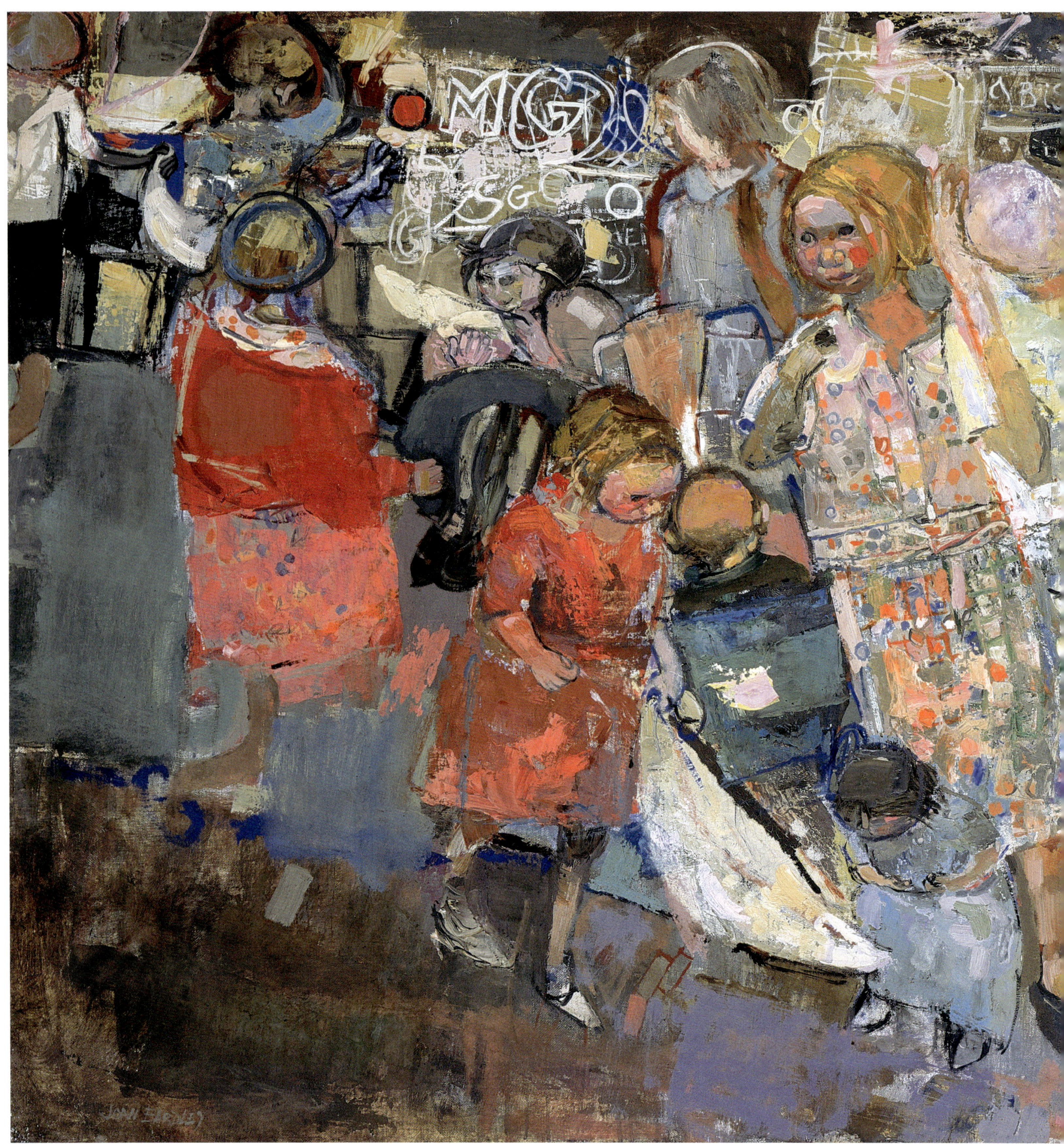

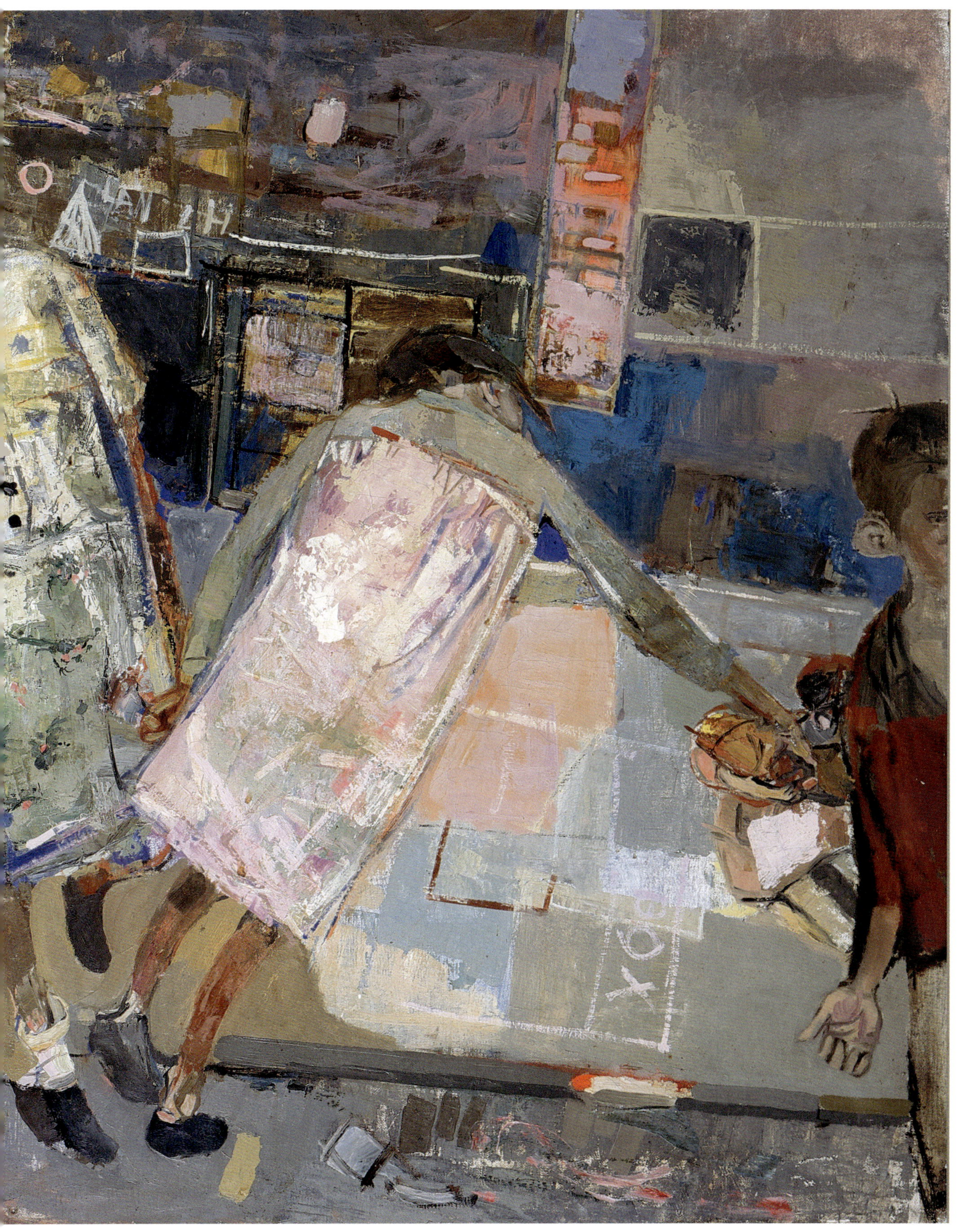

44 | ***Glasgow Back Street with Children Playing***, 1960
Oil on board 101 × 179cm
Private Collection

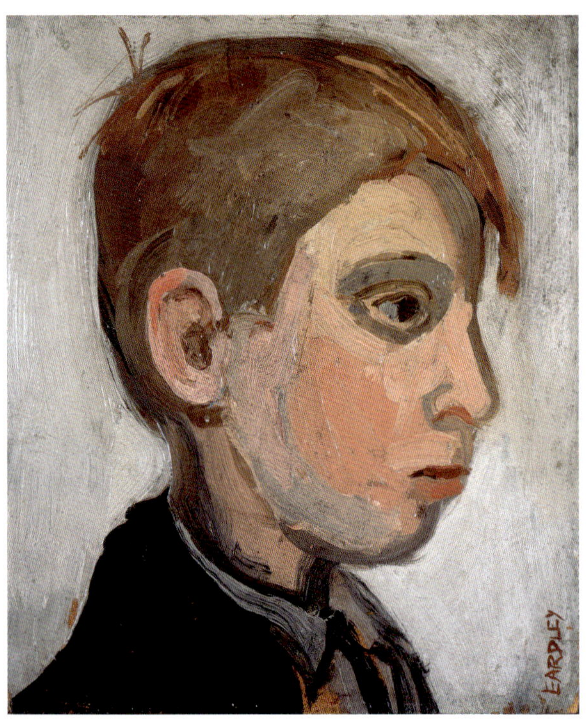

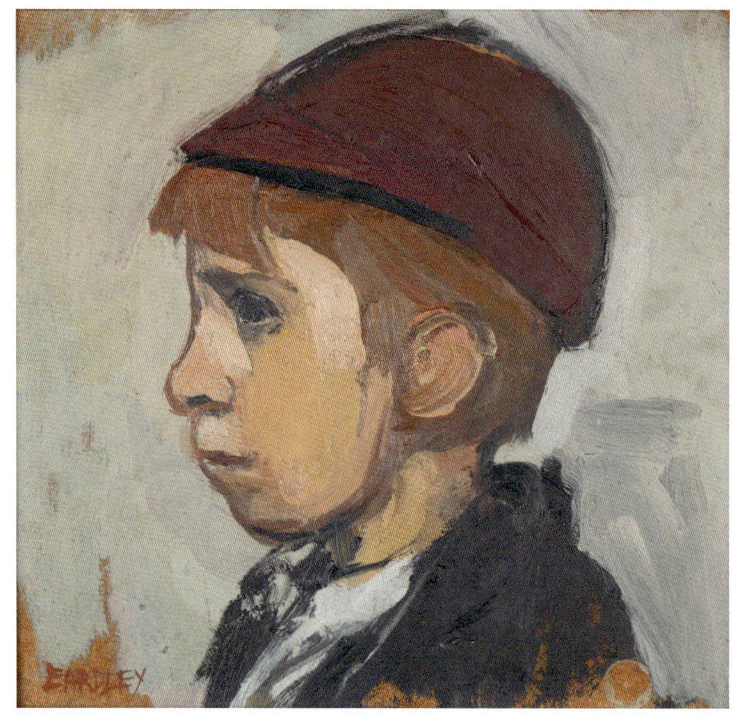

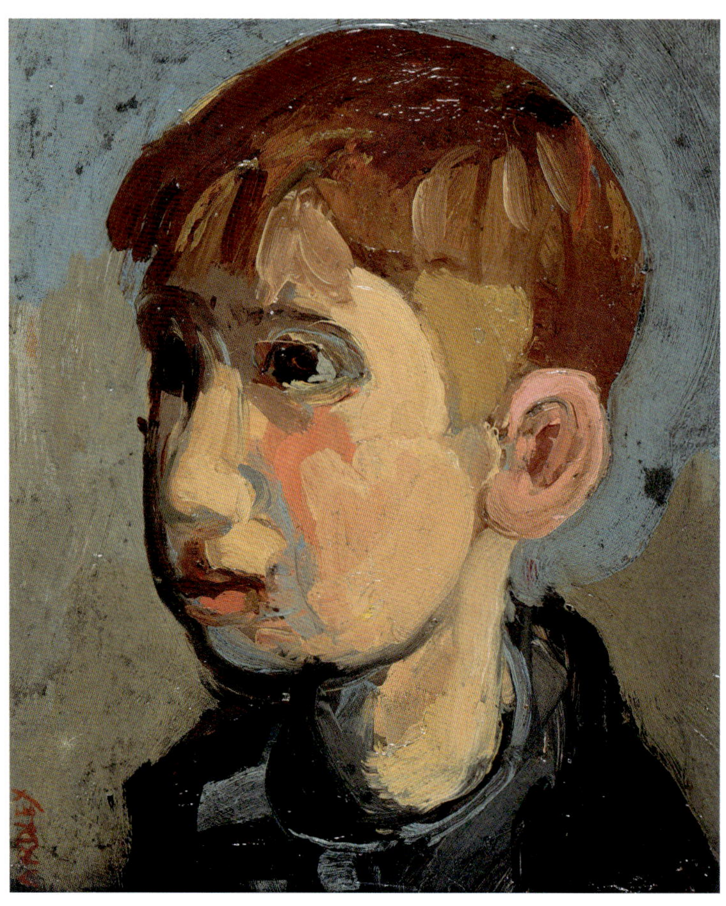

CLOCKWISE

45 | *Boy's Head: A Glasgow Boy*
Oil on board 31.8 × 27.3cm
Collection Henry and Sula Walton

46 | *Boy's Head*
Oil on canvas 25 × 27cm
Government Art Collection

47 | *Head of a Boy*
Oil on canvas 29 × 22.5cm
Private Collection

OPPOSITE

48 | *Andrew with a Comic*, 1955
Oil on canvas 89 × 74cm
Private Collection

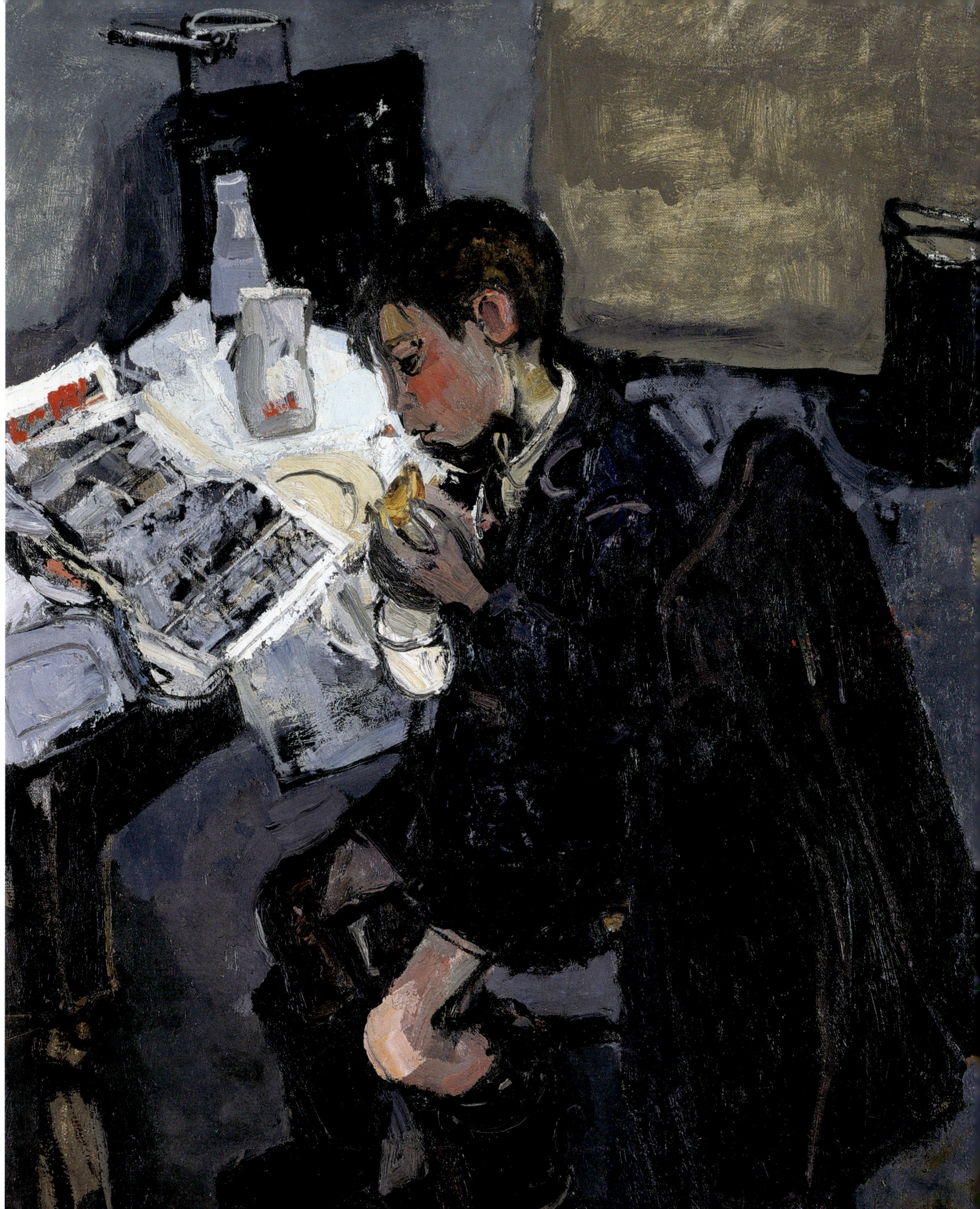

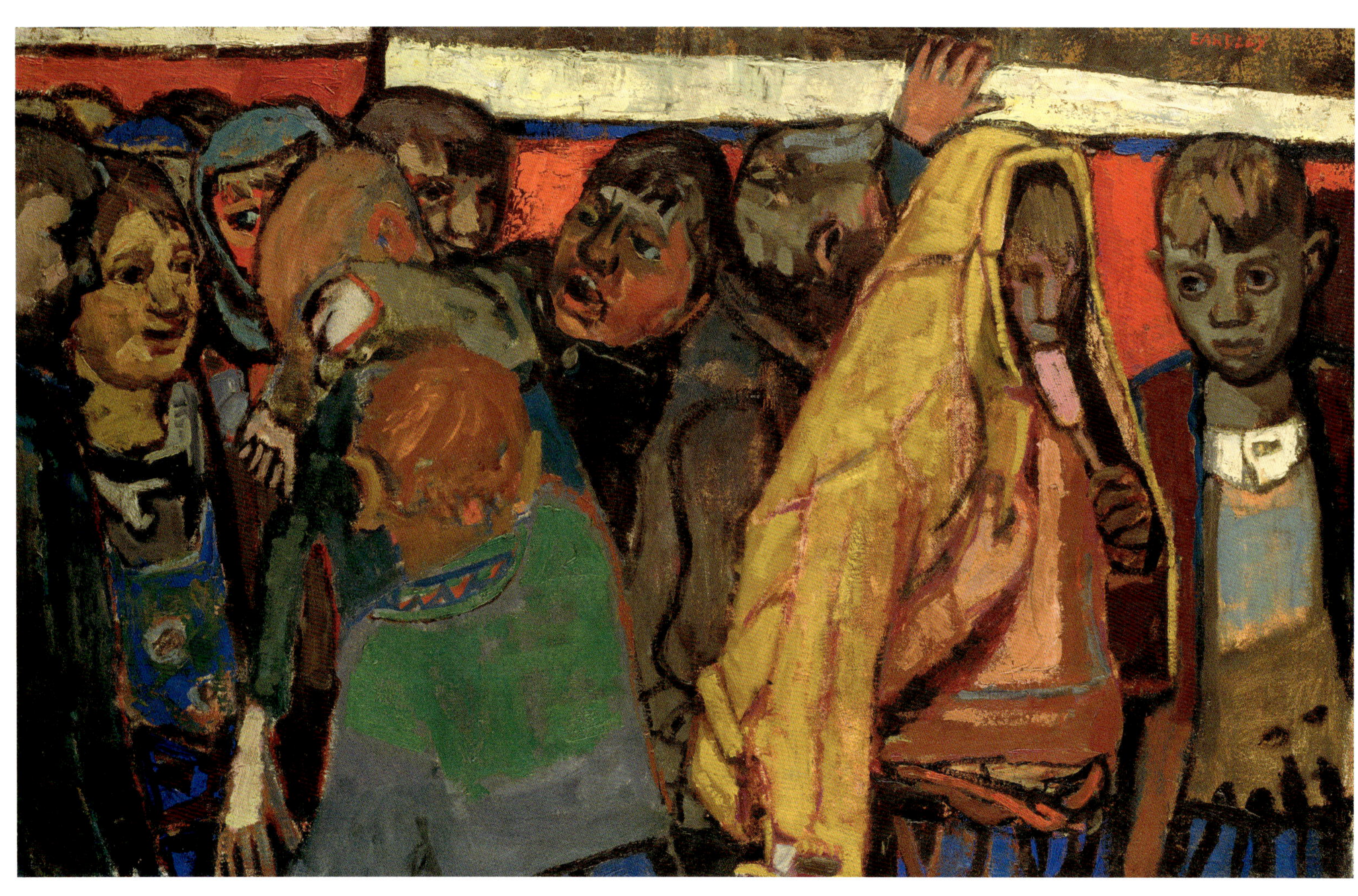

49 | ***Glasgow Kids, A Saturday Matinee Picture Queue***

Oil on canvas 70.8 × 114.5cm

Glasgow City Council (Museums)

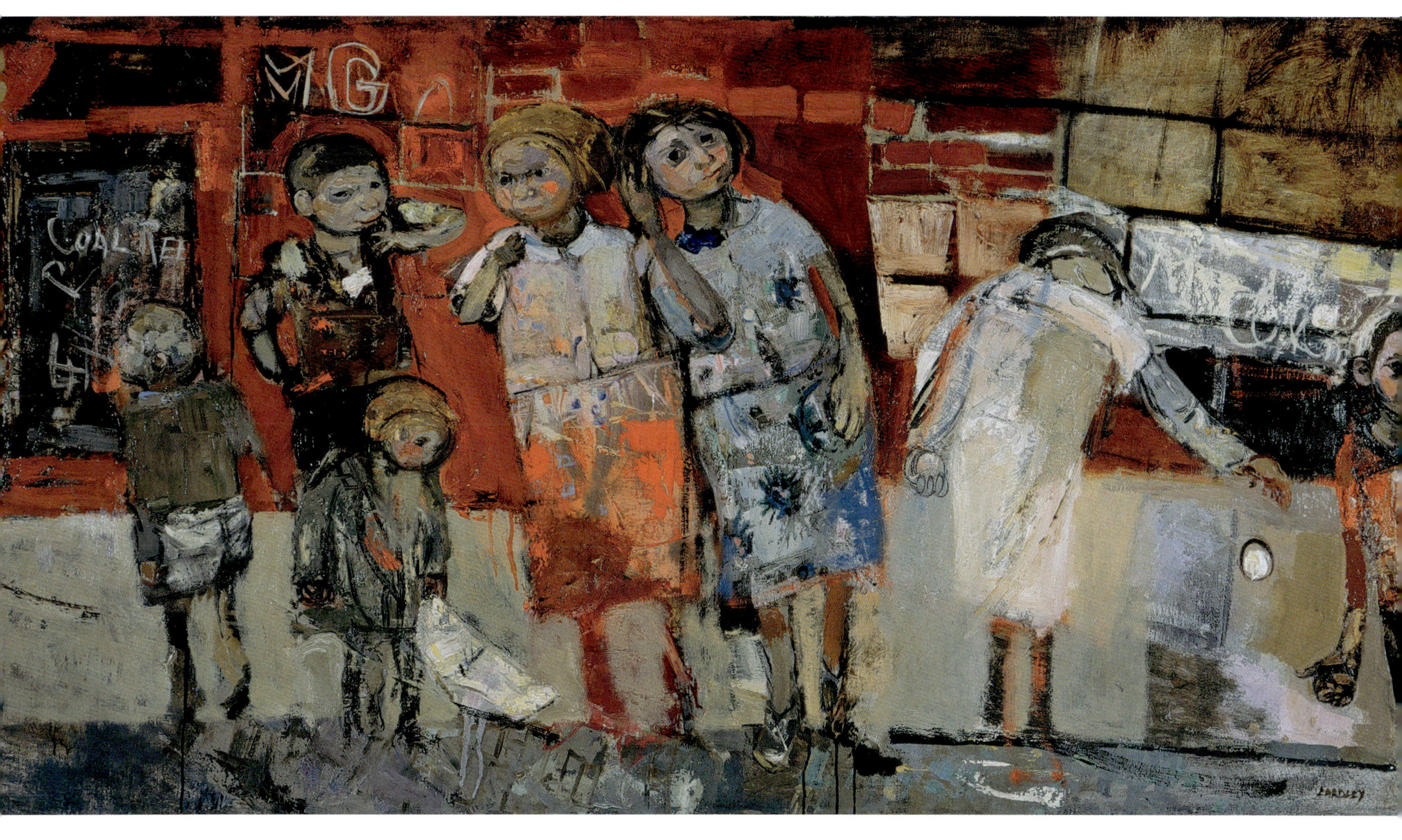

50 | ***Children in a Glasgow Back Street***
Oil on canvas 74 × 140cm
Private Collection

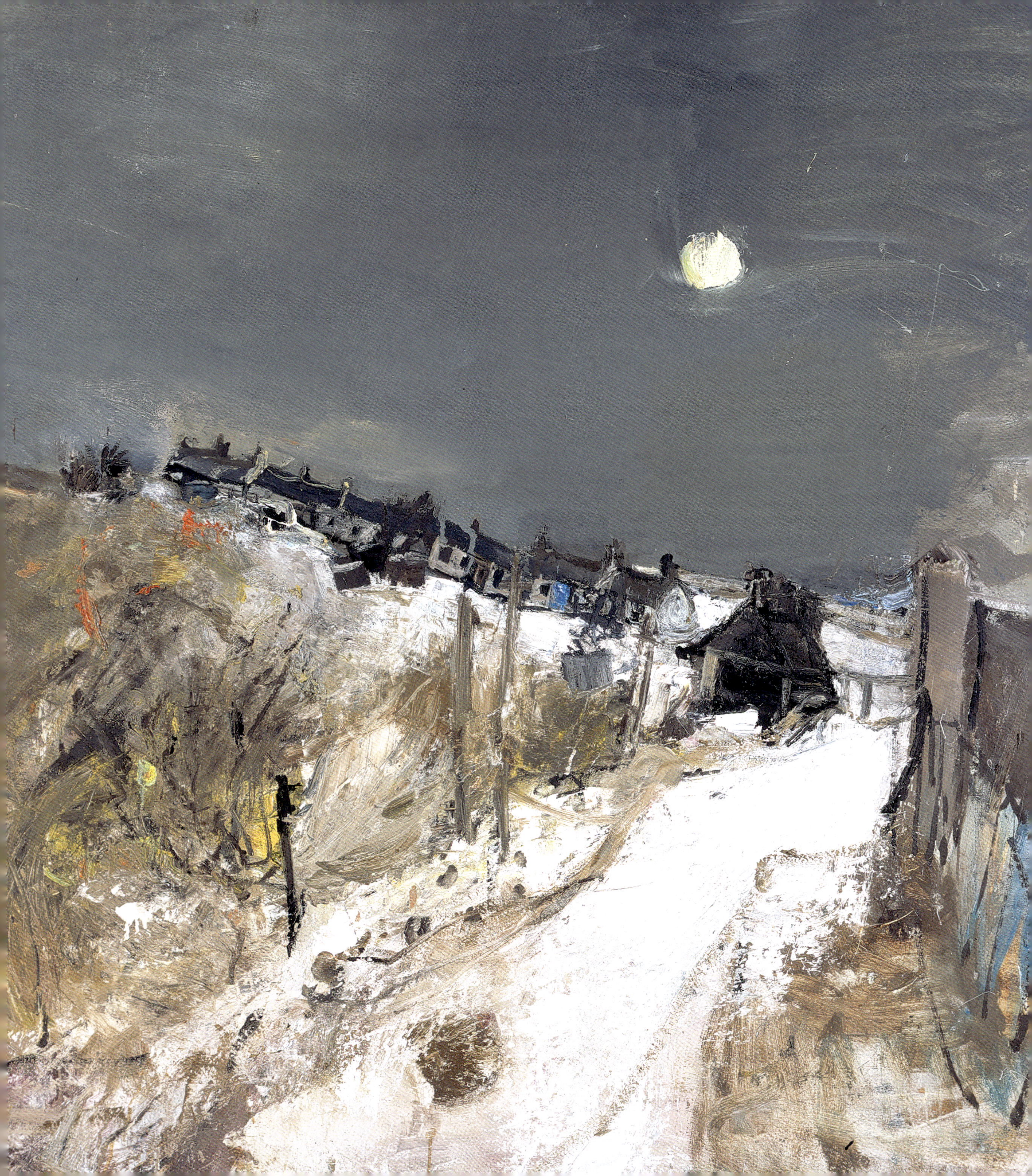

Catterline

51 | *Catterline in Winter*, c.1963 (detail)
Oil on board 120.7 × 130.8cm
Scottish National Gallery of Modern Art, Edinburgh

Eardley's work celebrates two aspects of Scottish identity that are both urban and rural. She also focused on areas of life that were fast disappearing, yet which were tenaciously clinging on. Her works showing poverty-stricken tenement life were balanced by her depictions of the landscape of north-east Scotland. Eardley's journey towards serious landscape painting began in 1951 with a solo exhibition at an exhibition space attached to the Gaumont Cinema in Aberdeen. She showed seventeen works on paper and nineteen paintings, all executed during her student years. They included images of Arran, Lincolnshire, Glasgow, Italy and France. One Aberdeen reviewer commented that Eardley was 'notable among the immediate postwar generation of the (Glasgow) School of Art for the strength and selective quality in her drawings' and that 'her talents have considerably matured in the course of her travels, and one or two of the sketches in this show are of quite exceptional quality'.[43] During this show Eardley contracted mumps and while convalescing she was taken for a drive by a friend and local school teacher Annette Soper who hailed from Stonehaven, just south of Aberdeen. One of the places they visited was the small, isolated fishing village of Catterline, south of Stonehaven. They stayed at the Creel Inn and found that the Watch House, a simple two-room building, set apart from the village on the cliff top, was for sale. Within the year Annette Soper had bought the house and with help from Eardley and Angus Neil, had made it weather-tight. Henceforth, it became the base from which both Annette and Joan would paint, in and around Catterline. In 1952 when Annette married local fisherman Jim Stephen, the couple gave Eardley free use of the Watch House. So began the final decade of Eardley's life, when she commuted back and forth between Glasgow and Catterline.

In order to get an idea of how Eardley responded to the landscape one has to remember that Hugh Adam Crawford had taught his students to feel their painting in their bodies.[44] In response to the huge expanses of sea and sky, Eardley's works became physically larger and more imposing. At the Society of Scottish Artists exhibitions in 1952 and 1953, she showed new landscapes, including *Cornfield at Night*, *Cliffside Cottages*, and *Winter Landscape*. David Irwin, Professor of History of Art at Aberdeen University, who catalogued Eardley's paintings after her death said: 'Joan Eardley was essentially an artist who drew inspiration from subjects in the open air, not in the studio. In Glasgow, slum children played in the streets against a background of scribbled tenement walls and shop windows; in Catterline, human subjects were supplanted by the roar of stormy seas or the hum of the summer fields. From the city she extracted essential characteristics of young and old; on the coast she was interested in neither fisherman nor farmers, but in the sea and the land.'[45]

Eardley was particularly attracted to wild seas and in her letters she speaks of the visual grandeur of storms. The expressive nature of her painting has often been compared with postwar abstract painting in Europe and America, particularly in works such as *Black Sky with Blue Sea* [illustrated on the half-title]. We know from Audrey Walker's notes that Eardley greatly admired the expressive landscapes of Soutine and that they visited London together in 1957 in order to see the great Kandinsky exhibition. Eardley, who was a voracious reader of books and magazines, also had a book on abstract expressionism and talked in an interview with Sydney Goodsir Smith about her interest in European Tachisme, although she stated that she would never go totally abstract.[46] The work of the Tachists, Hans Hartung, Pierre Soulages and Nicolas de Staël all featured in the 1954 Society of Scottish Artists exhibition in Edinburgh, so she could easily have seen their work first-hand.

During the 1950s and up until her death in 1963,

Eardley painted a considerable number of seascapes. She usually painted on hardboard, using not only artist's paint but also boat paint, with newspaper, sand and grasses embedded in the mixture. She used a palette knife to create texture, dribbled paint down the foreground, and used the end of her brush to draw into the wet surface. Big, grey seascapes were enlivened with bold touches of colour. Light on the water or breaking through stormy skies created visual highlights. The mood is brighter in works such as *Foam and Blue Sky* [69], the luscious RSA diploma work *Summer Sea* [1] and the creamy, boiling sea of *Flood Tide* [70]. The dark, winter seas can be seen in *Winter Sea III* [68] and in *The Sea* [67]. In contrast, *Wave Study II* [71] is a gestural semi-abstract composition in yellow and orange that lifts the spirits. But the full majesty of the sea is embodied in *The Wave* [66] with its almost architectural form of a wall of foaming water poised before crashing to the shore. To paint these seacapes, Eardley would have stood on the shoreline in the bay at Catterline. One of Audrey Walker's photographs shows her with her board held down by rocks facing the boiling sea [53]. The only colour photograph of Eardley, also taken by Walker [**frontispiece**], shows her on a summer's day seated on a shooting stick actually in the sea, with her sketchbook facing the shore where the salmon nets, a subject that Eardley returned to in several works, were hung to dry on the makin' green. *Drying Salmon Nets* [56] is a tightly composed work with colours which evoke a winter's day. A later work, the majestic *Salmon Net Posts* [57], is a much larger, semi-abstract composition that looks from the salmon net posts out to sea. Considering the massive size of the biggest seascapes, some were two metres wide, it is amazing that Eardley was able to manhandle these huge boards up and down the steep cliff path. However, thanks to the acquisition of a motor scooter, she could trundle her materials to and fro, and catch the train to Glasgow at Stonehaven [92]. Eardley commuted backwards and forwards between Glasgow

52 | **Eardley painting in a field at Catterline**
Photo: Audrey Walker
Gracefield Art Centre, Dumfries

53 | **Eardley painting facing the sea on the shore at Catterline, c.1950s**
Photo: Audrey Walker
Joan Eardley Archive, Scottish National Gallery of Modern Art, Edinburgh [GMA/A09]

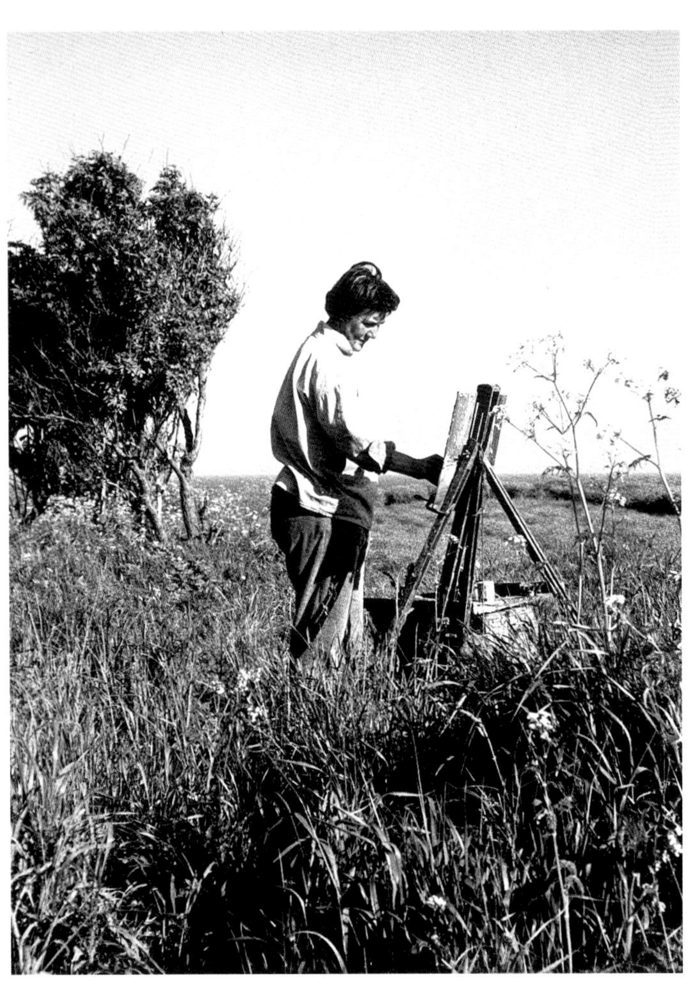

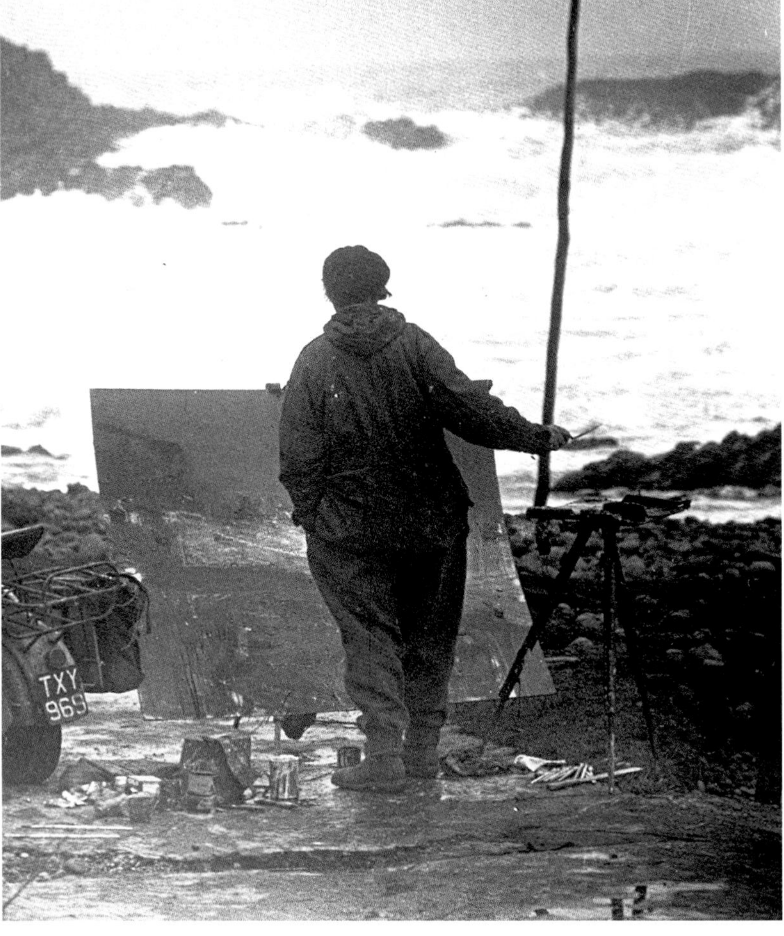

and Catterline and a phone call from a neighbour at Catterline warning of approaching storms would send Eardley racing north again.

In 1955 Eardley bought Number 1 The Row, Catterline [54], which was a shell of a house with no floor, ceiling or sanitation. Eardley and Neil made it weather-tight, laid bark chippings on the floor and pinned up sail-cloths for walls and ceiling. Here, from her own front door, she often painted the shore line, with its jetty and the prominent rock stacks. At some point in the mid-1950s she lived at Sarah's Cottage, named after a previous resident, which was away from the cliff top but then in 1959 came the chance to purchase Number 18, Catterline. This house, which was in good order and had plumbing, faced the sea from the cliff top. A photograph by her friend, the Glasgow photographer, Oscar Marzaroli, shows Eardley, Angus Neil and Eardley's final protégée, the painter Lil Neilson outside Number 18, Catterline [55].

Eardley was greatly attached to the local community and to the countryside around Catterline. Her taped interview is worth quoting at length:

'When I'm painting in the north east – I hardly ever move out of the village. I hardly ever move from one spot. I find the more I know the place, the more I know the particular spot, the more I find to paint in that particular spot ... I do feel the more you know something the more you can get out of it – the more it gives you ... I think I am painting what I feel about scenery – but certainly not scenery with a name because that is the north east – it's just a vast waste, vast seas, vast areas of cliff – all these areas for painting. I very often find I'll take my paints to a certain place that has moved me and I'll begin to paint there and I find perhaps by the end of the summer I haven't moved from that place – my paintings are still there and I've worn a kind of mark in the ground and I leave my paints there overnight and I seem to build up a sort of table and ... a studio seems to have arrived outside and that seems to be how I work. Once I start in a

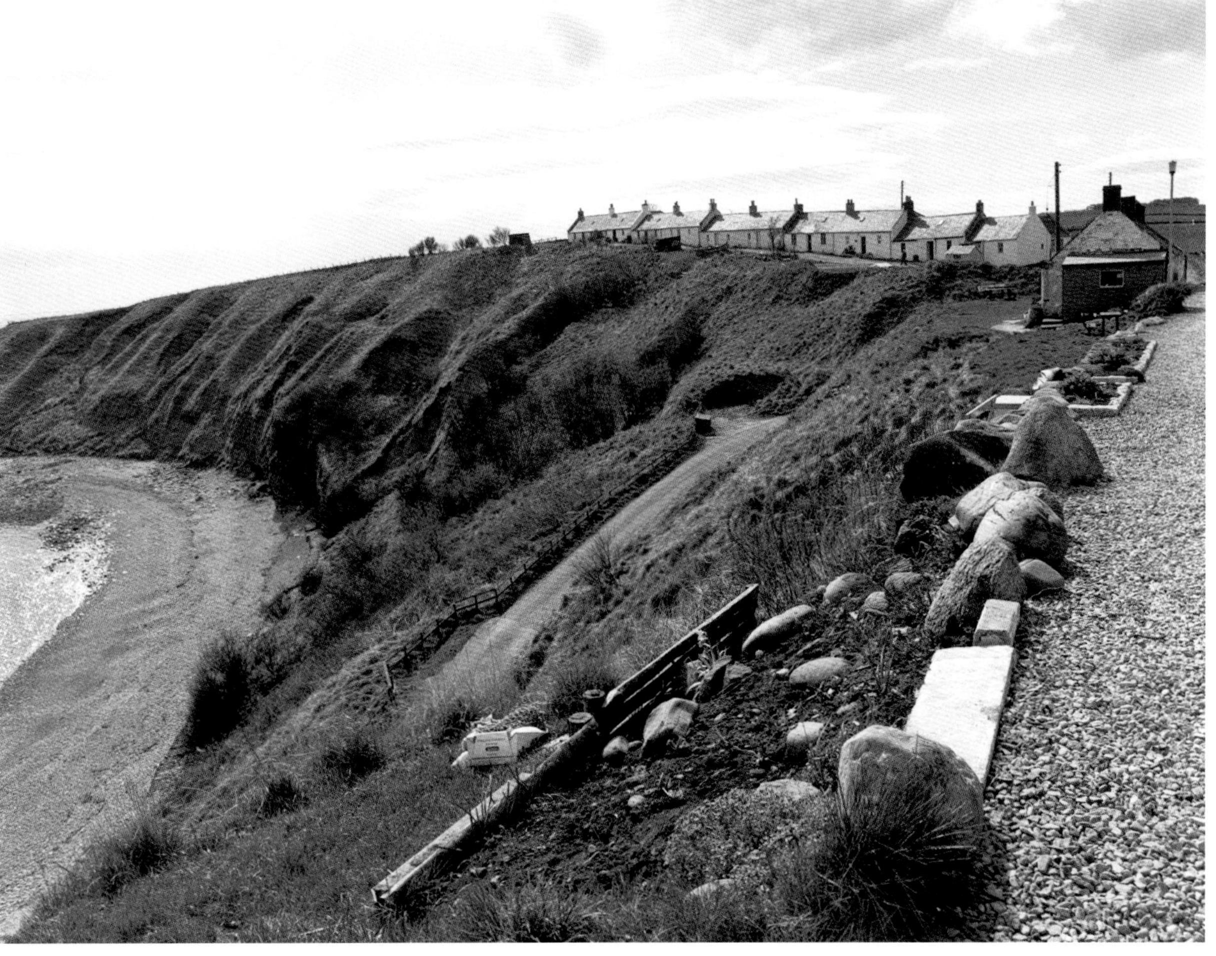

54 | **The Row, Catterline (Number 1 is on the far left) Photo: George Oliver**
Scottish National Gallery of Modern Art, Edinburgh

place I find I don't want to move because I'm trying to do something and you are never really satisfied with what you're doing and so you keep on trying and the more you try the more you think of new ways to do this particular subject so you just go on and on or you might just turn round in the middle of doing a certain painting and you see something else and you run back and get another canvas and try and do that but its still the same spot really and obviously the feeling you are trying to grasp has such terrific clarity and light … I think you've got to know something before you paint it …'[47]

Another popular subject was the beehives in the back garden area on the edge of the cliff at Number 1, which Eardley painted during different seasons, in various weathers and at different times of the day [58, 88]. This sort of serial painting had something in common with Monet, and like Monet she also produced a series of paintings of haystacks, probably in the fields behind The Row [52]. The fields behind The Row became the setting for many lyrical paintings, for example *Summer Fields* [60], *Harvest* [61], *Seeded Grasses and Daisies, September* [62], which incorporated a collage of real grasses and daisies set against a sombre sky, and *Field and Birds* [59]. She also recorded the fields behind The Row in winter, in paintings such as *Snow* [63] and the leaden-skied view of the front of The Row in one of her best-loved works, *Catterline in Winter* [51].

The small community at Catterline was periodically expanded by Eardley's friends, including Angus Neil. In 1960 when teaching at Hospitalfield, Eardley met the young painter Lil Neilson, a graduate of Duncan of Jordanstone College of Art in Dundee. Neilson came to live in Catterline in September 1962 but left in December in order to work in the theatre. Neilson and Eardley maintained contact and at the beginning of 1963 Eardley managed to secure the use of Number 6 The Row, Catterline for Neilson.

Although spending most of her time after 1956 painting seascapes and landscapes at Catterline, Eardley remained in touch with Margot Sandeman. Their friendship gave them the opportunity to discuss the many issues they both faced as professional artists. Every two years they went to London to stay with Eardley's aunt, Sybil Morrison, to see exhibitions and visit museums. Sandeman was married to the potter James Robson, and had two children. She stopped painting while the children were small but resumed in the 1970s. Eardley's other main confidante was Audrey Walker whom she had met in 1952. She also had a family to bring up, as well as supporting her husband Sheriff Allan Walker in his life as a public official in Glasgow and Lanarkshire. The couple's invitations to Eardley to stay at their country home at Caverslea in Selkirkshire led to a series of drawings and paintings of sheep-shearing. Walker was a gifted violinist as well as a photographer. Eardley herself liked classical music – by composers such as Bach, Britten and Bartok – and latterly the jazz music of John Coltrane.[48] After art, music was her principal love.

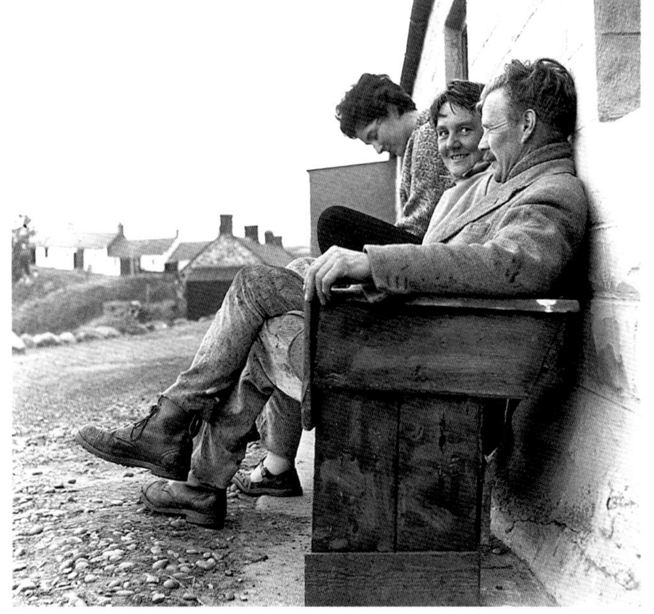

55 | **Anne Marzaroli, Joan Eardley and Angus Neil Number 18, Catterline, c.1963**
Photo: Oscar Marzaroli
Joan Eardley Archive, Scottish National Gallery of Modern Art, Edinburgh [GMA/A09]

56 | ***Drying Salmon Nets*, 1956**
Oil on canvas 71.1 × 154.9cm
The Eardley Family

57 | ***Salmon Net Posts*, 1962**
Oil on board 118.5 × 217.5cm
Tate, Presented by the Friends of the Tate Gallery 1986

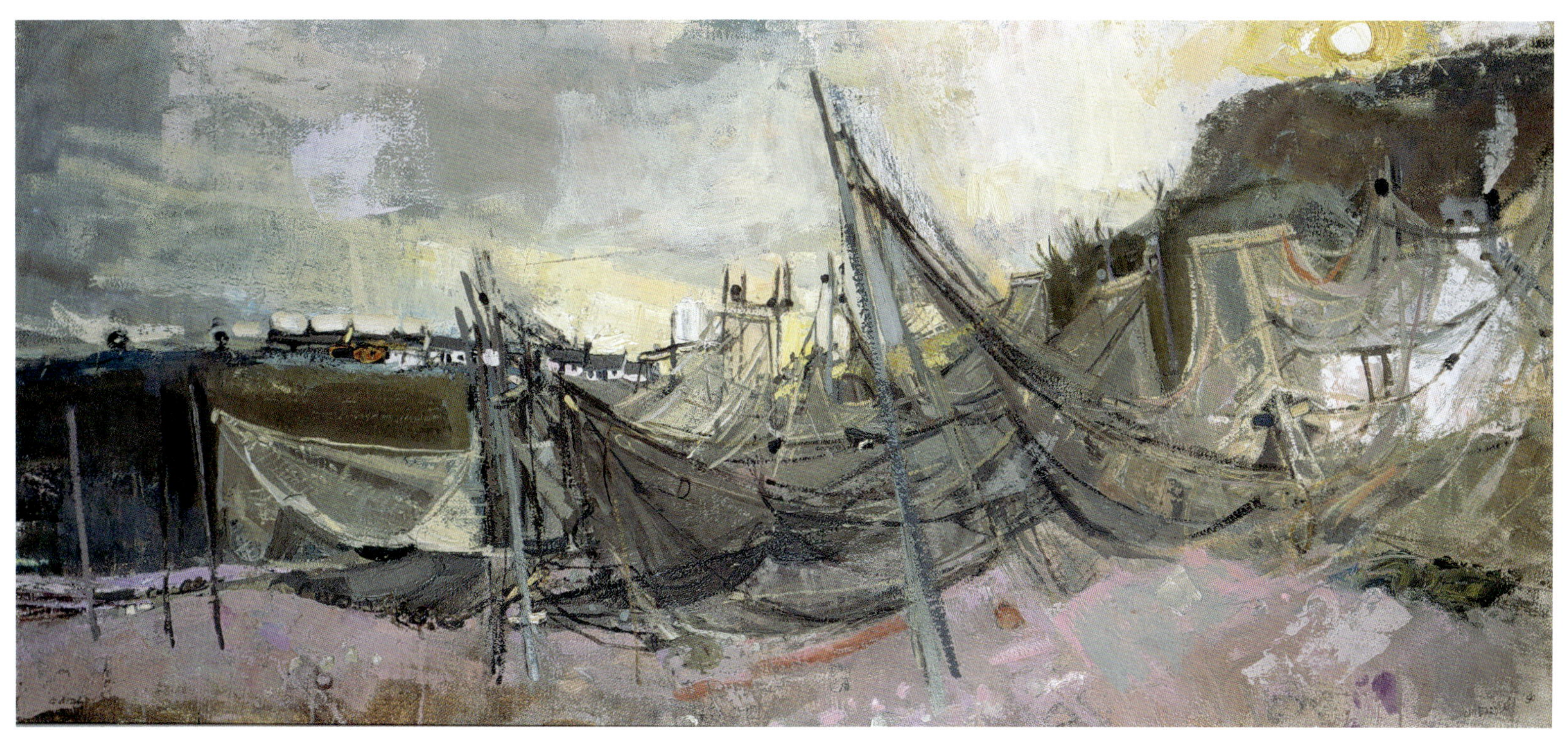

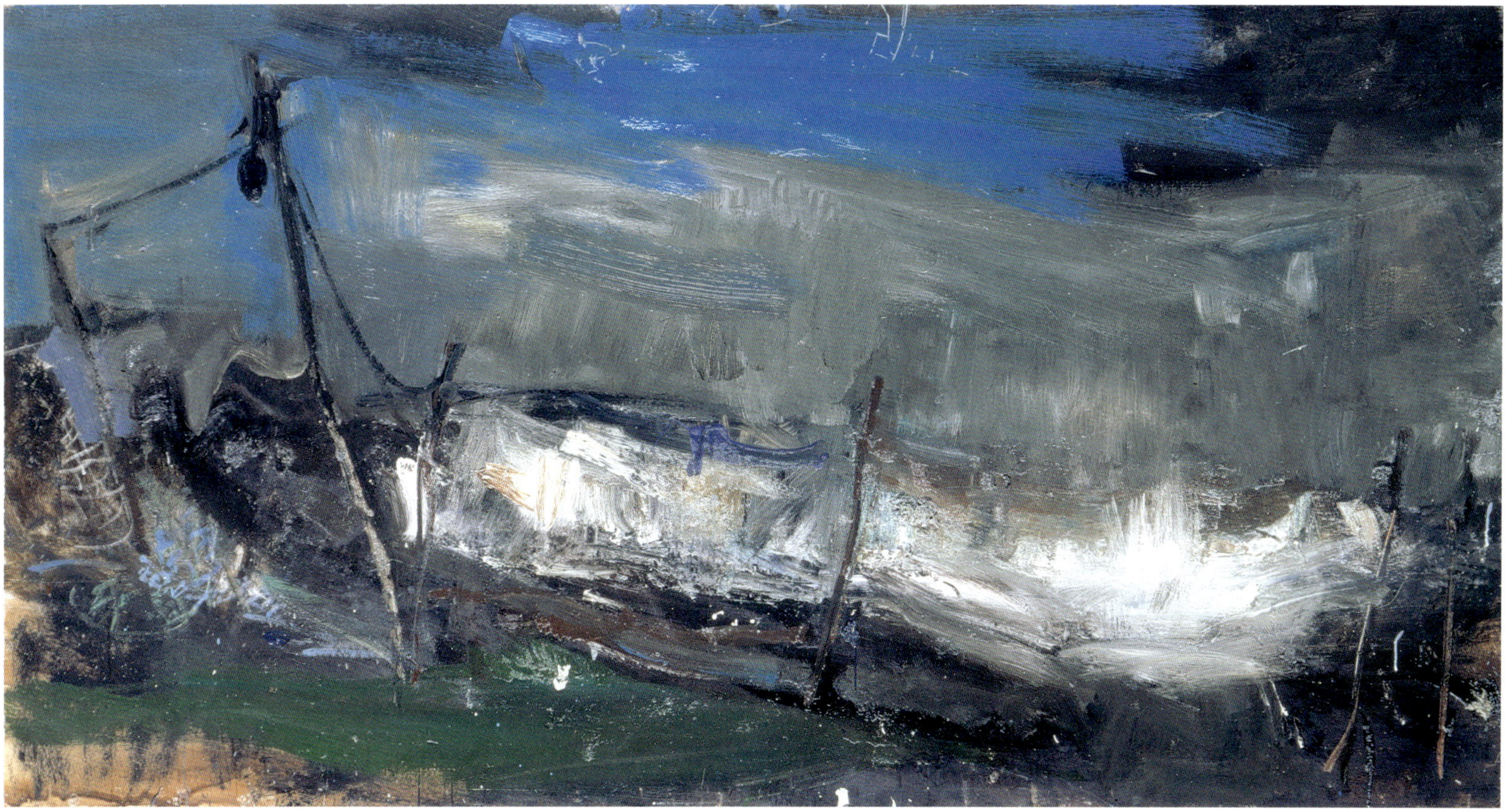

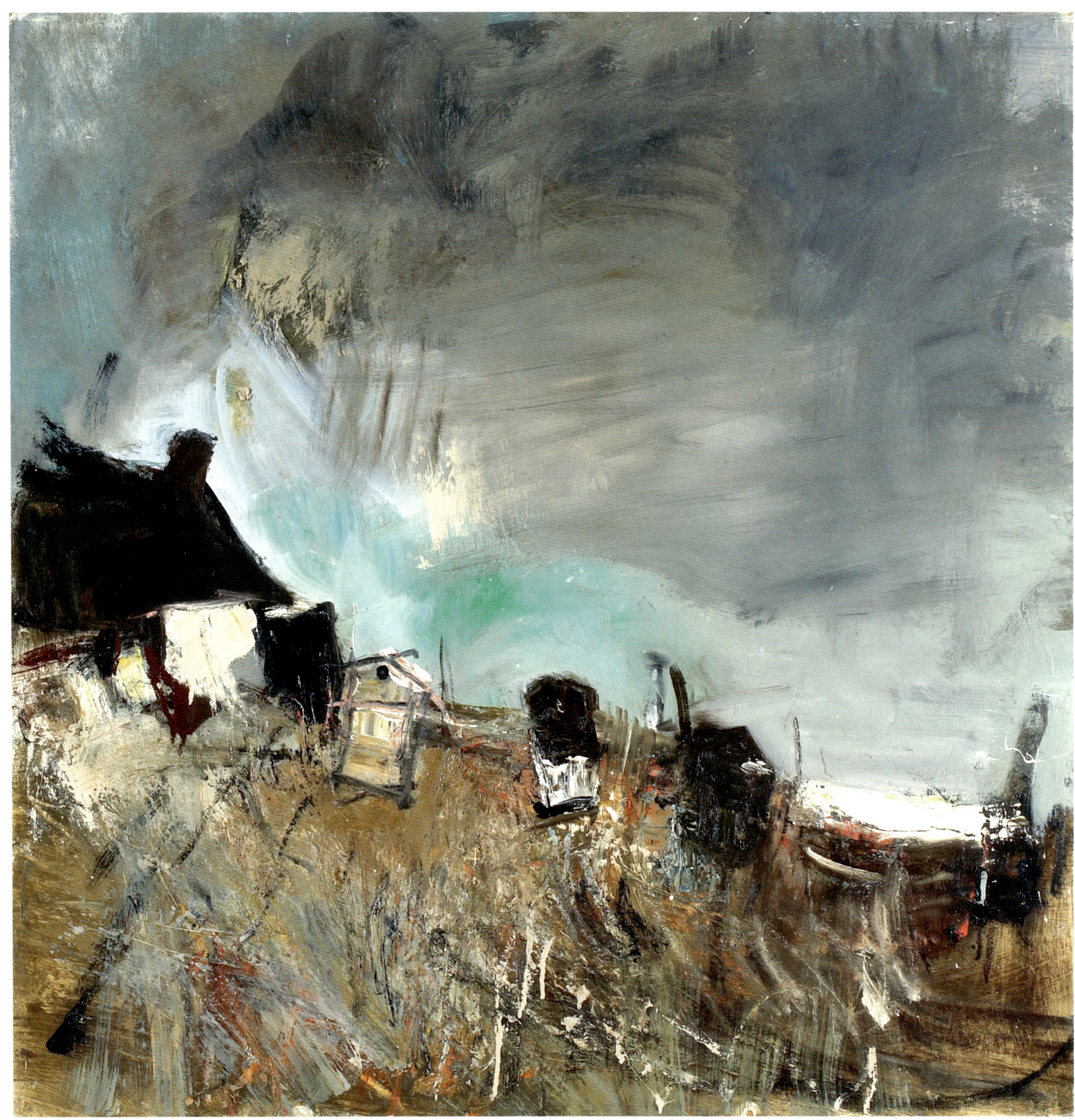

58 | ***Beehives, Approaching Storm, c.1950s***
Oil on board 96.5 × 76.2cm
By kind permission of The Royal Bank of Scotland, Edinburgh

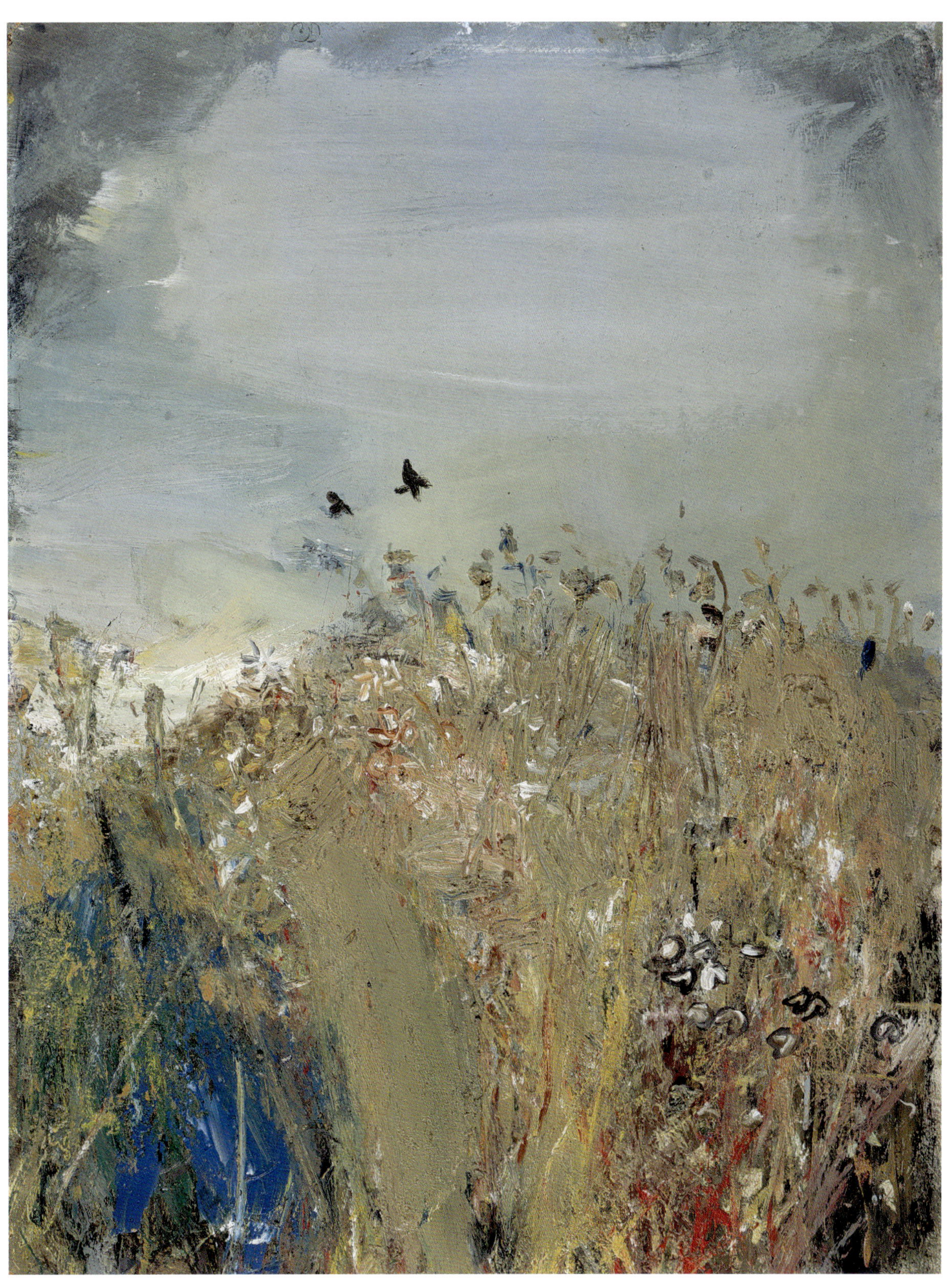

59 | **Field and Birds**
Oil on board 91.5 × 71cm
Cyril Gerber Fine Art, Glasgow

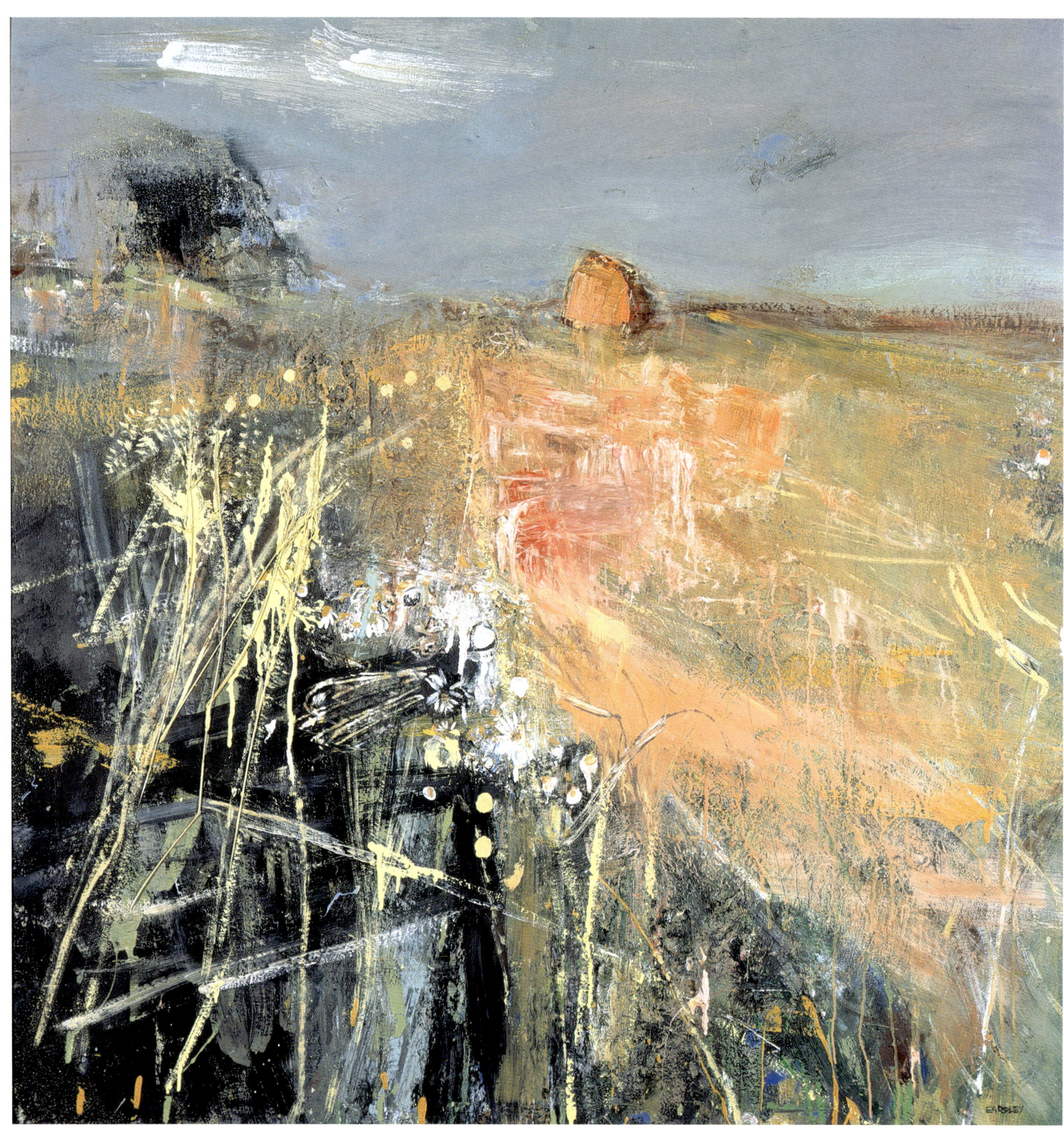

60 | ***Summer Fields*, c.1961**

Oil and grasses on board 106 × 105cm

Scottish National Gallery of Modern Art, Edinburgh

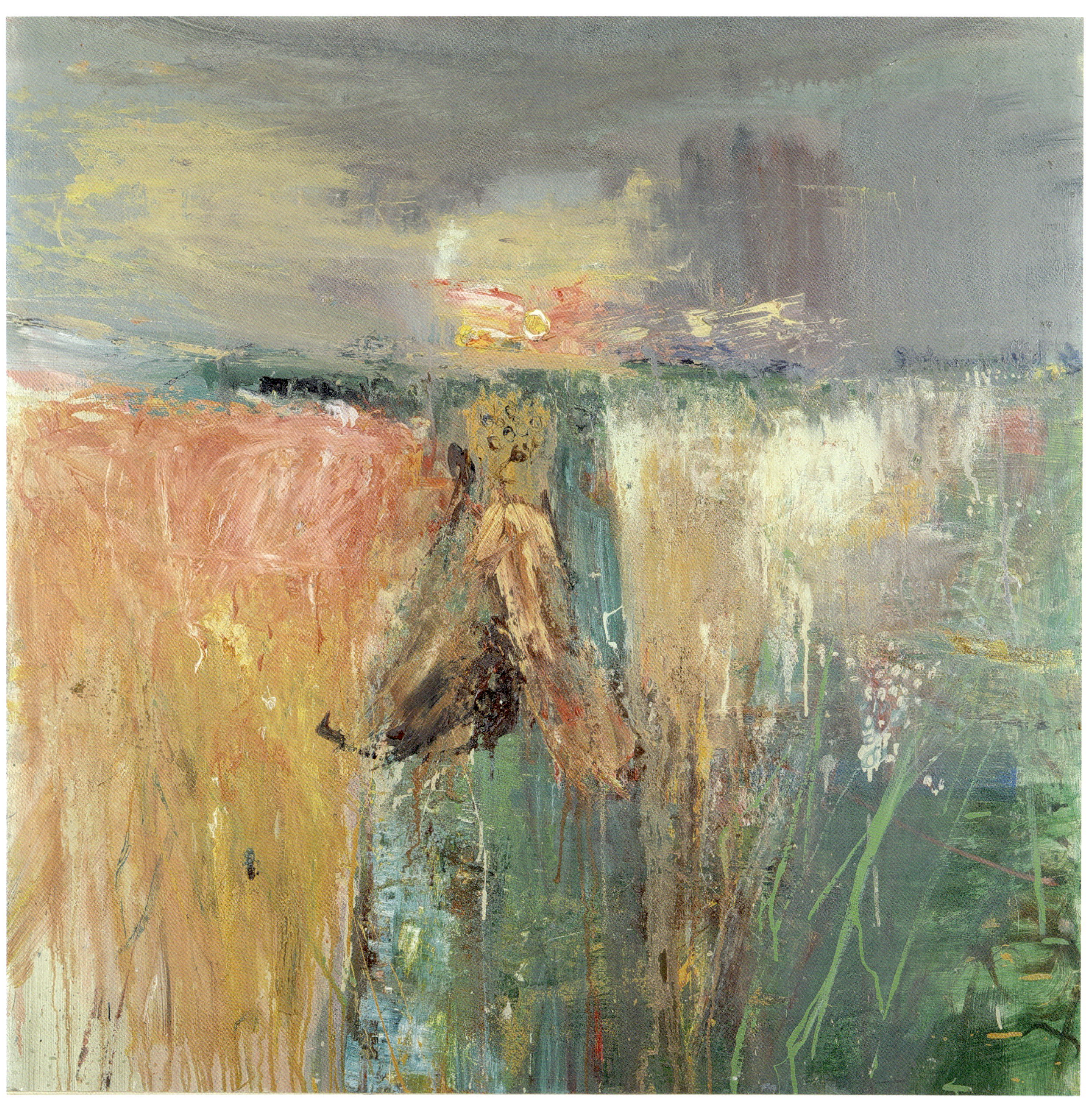

61 | ***Harvest***, 1960-1

Oil and grit on board 118.1 × 118.1cm

Scottish National Gallery of Modern Art, Edinburgh

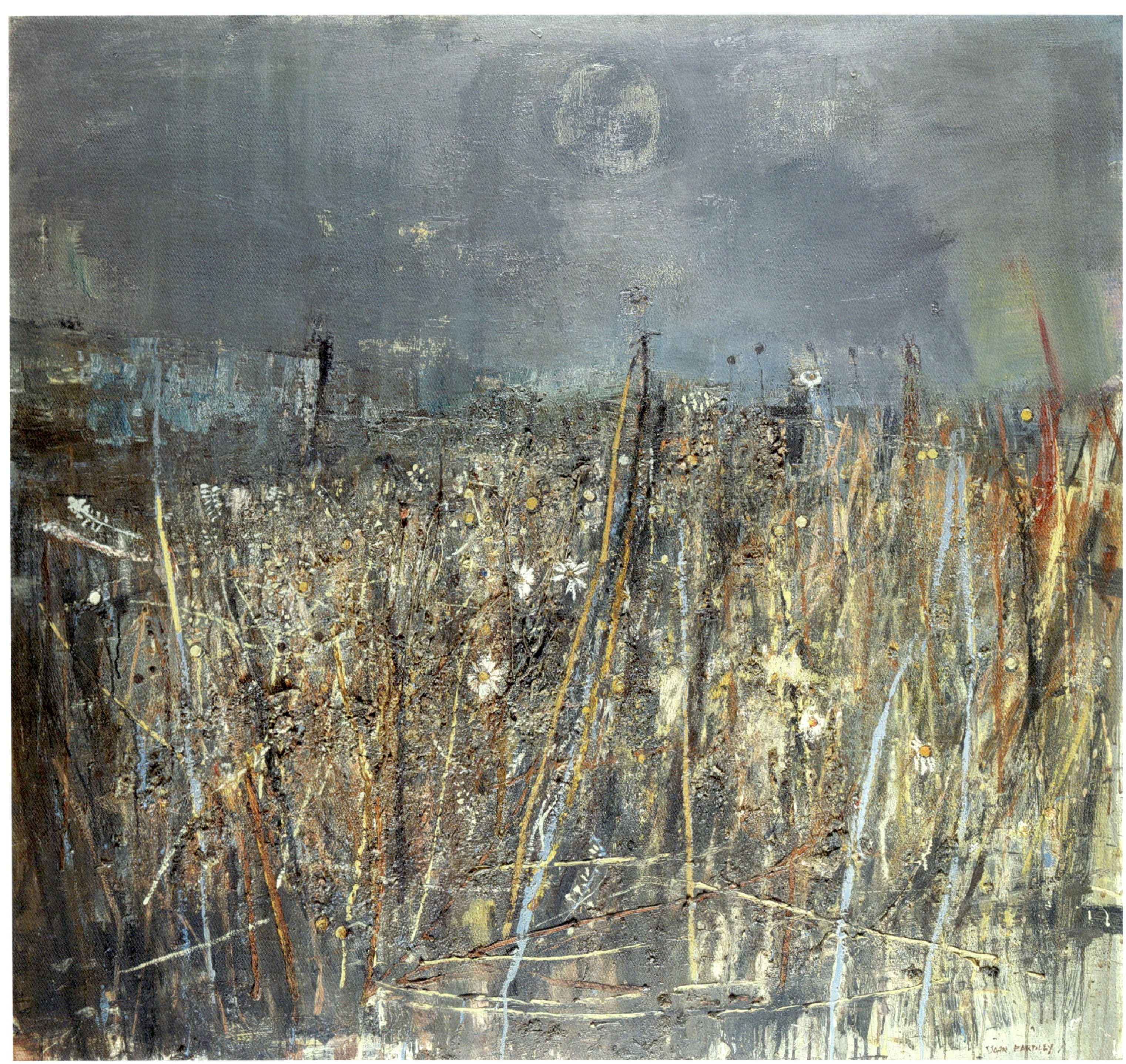

62 | *Seeded Grasses and Daisies, September*, 1960
Oil, grasses and seedheads on board 121.9 × 133.3cm
Scottish National Gallery of Modern Art, Edinburgh

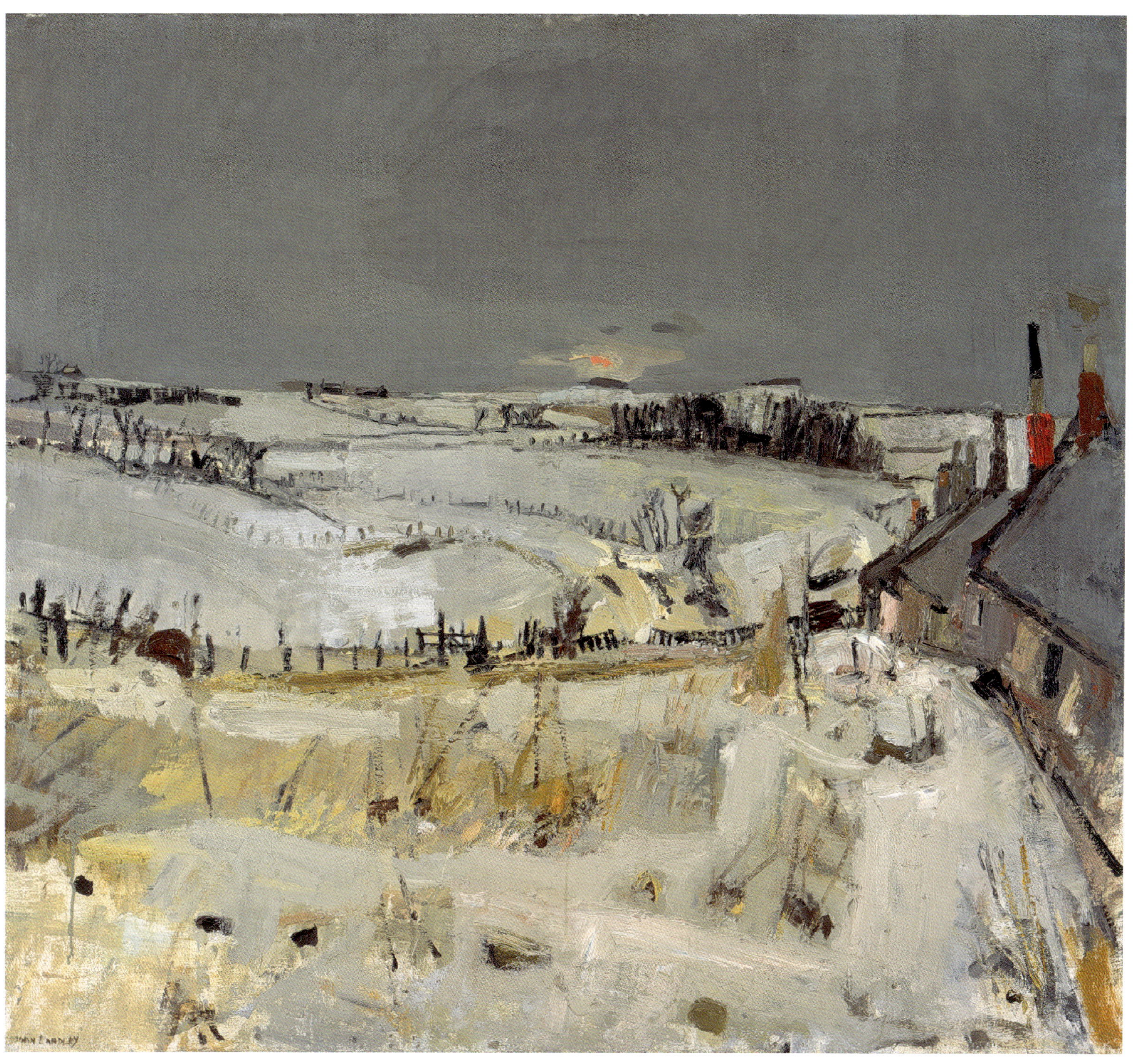

63 | ***Snow*, c.1958**

Oil on board 101.5 × 113.5cm

Scottish National Gallery of Modern Art, Edinburgh

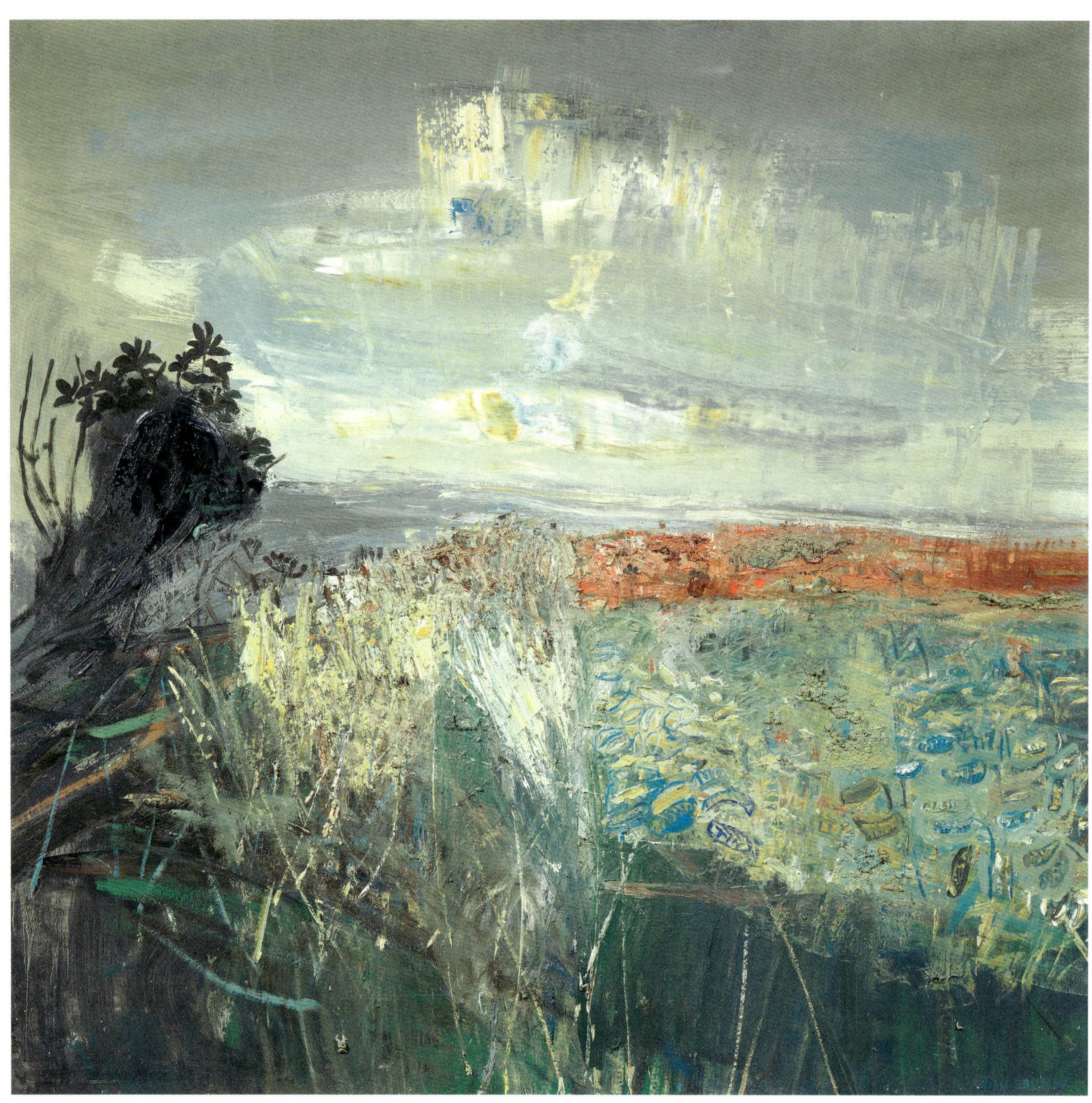

64 | **Field of Barley by the Sea**

Oil on board 107 × 102cm

The Fleming-Wyfold Art Foundation, London

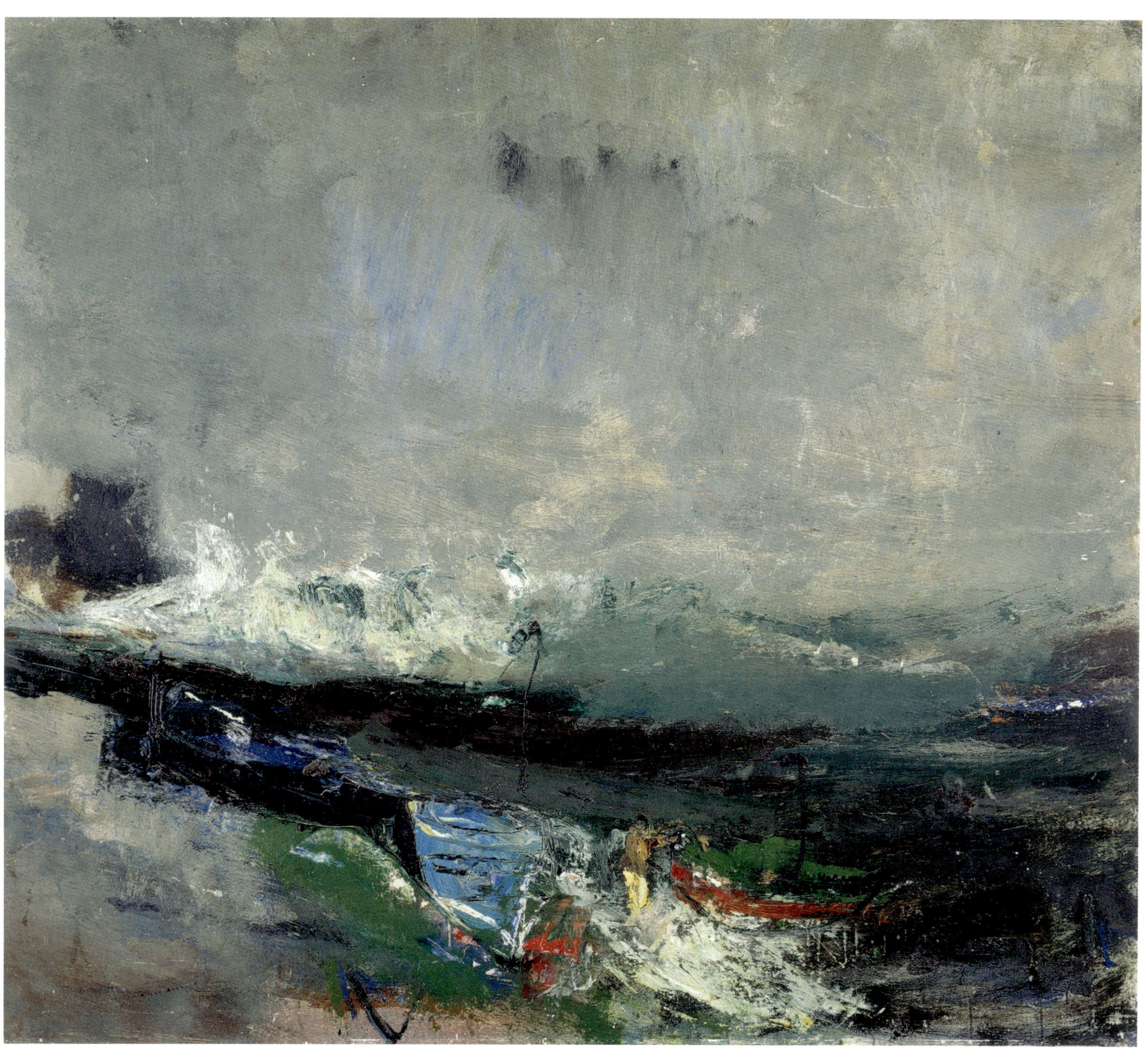

65 | ***Boats on the Shore*, c.1963**
Oil on board 101.6 × 115.6cm
Scottish National Gallery of Modern Art, Edinburgh

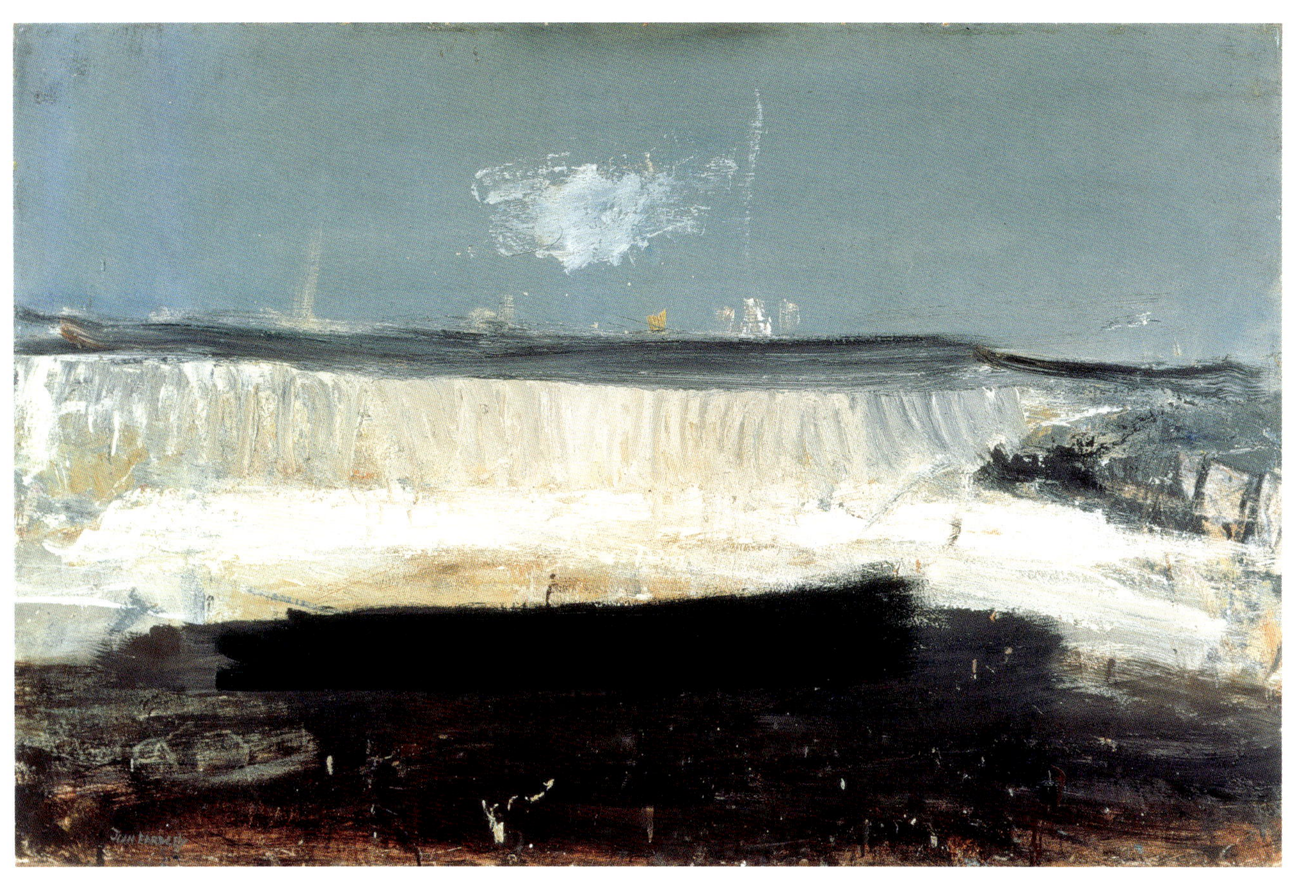

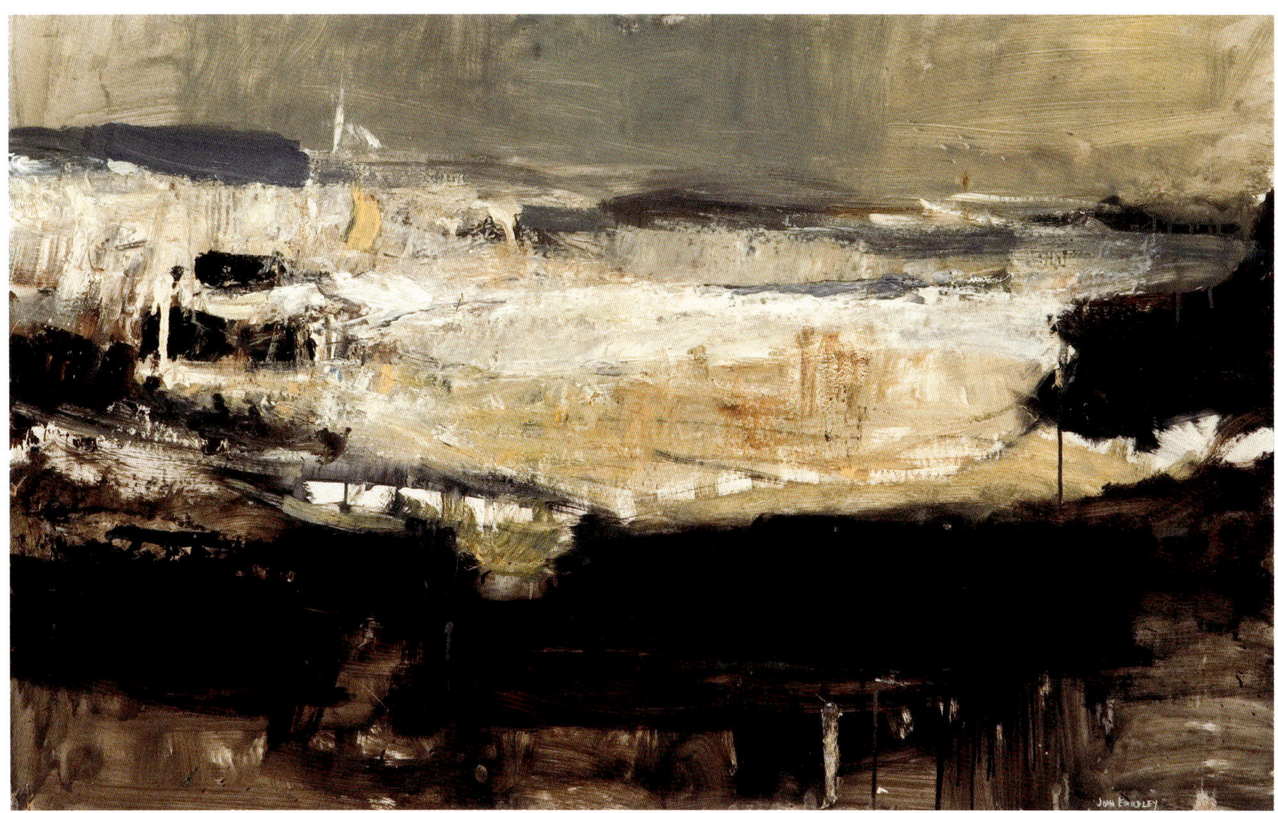

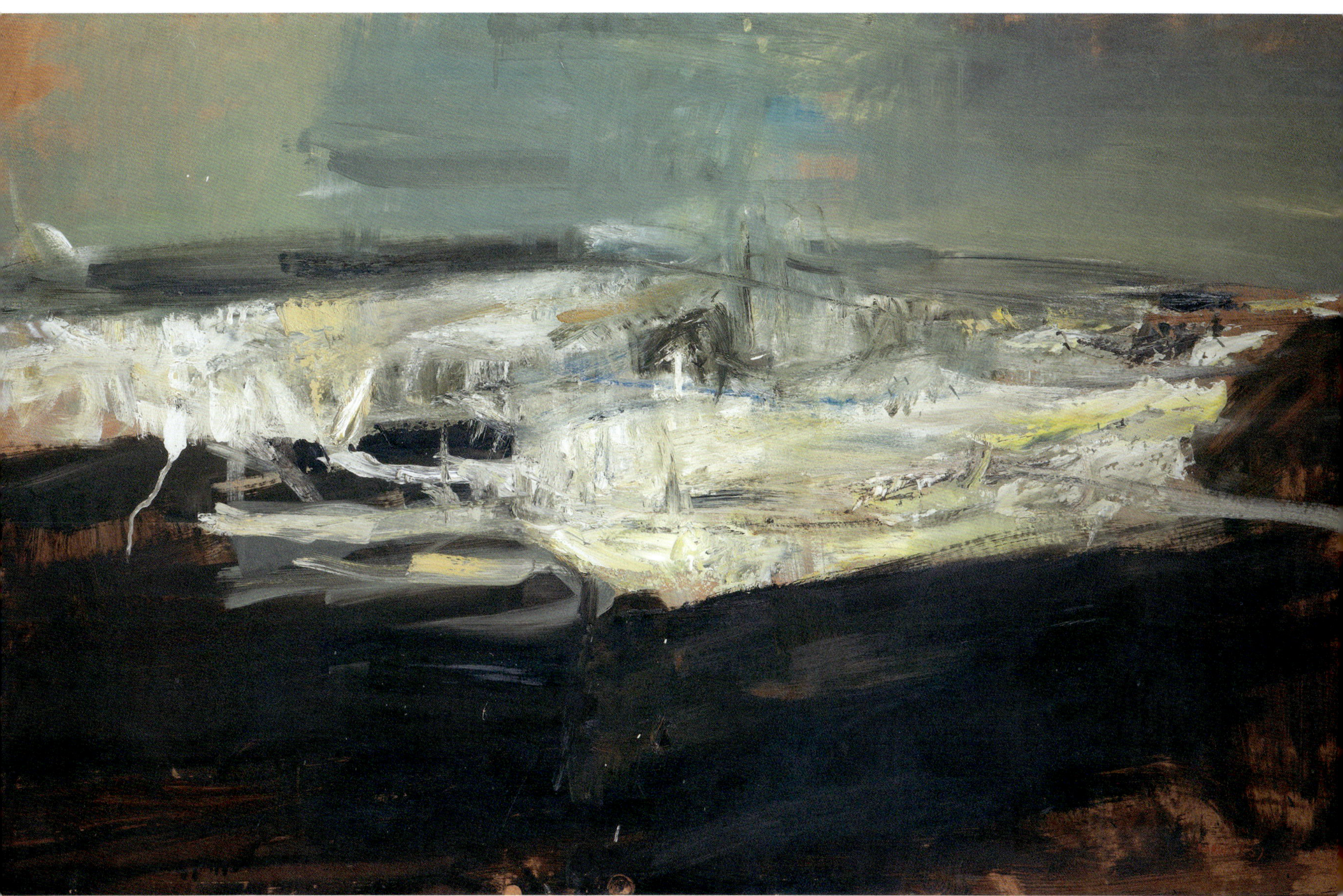

66 | ***The Wave***, 1961
Oil and grit on board 118.1 × 188cm
Scottish National Gallery of Modern Art, Edinburgh

67 | ***The Sea***, 1959
Oil on board 96.5 × 154.9cm
Perth Museum and Art Gallery, Perth & Kinross Council

68 | **Winter Sea III**
Oil on board 94 × 153cm
The Fleming-Wyfold Art Foundation, London

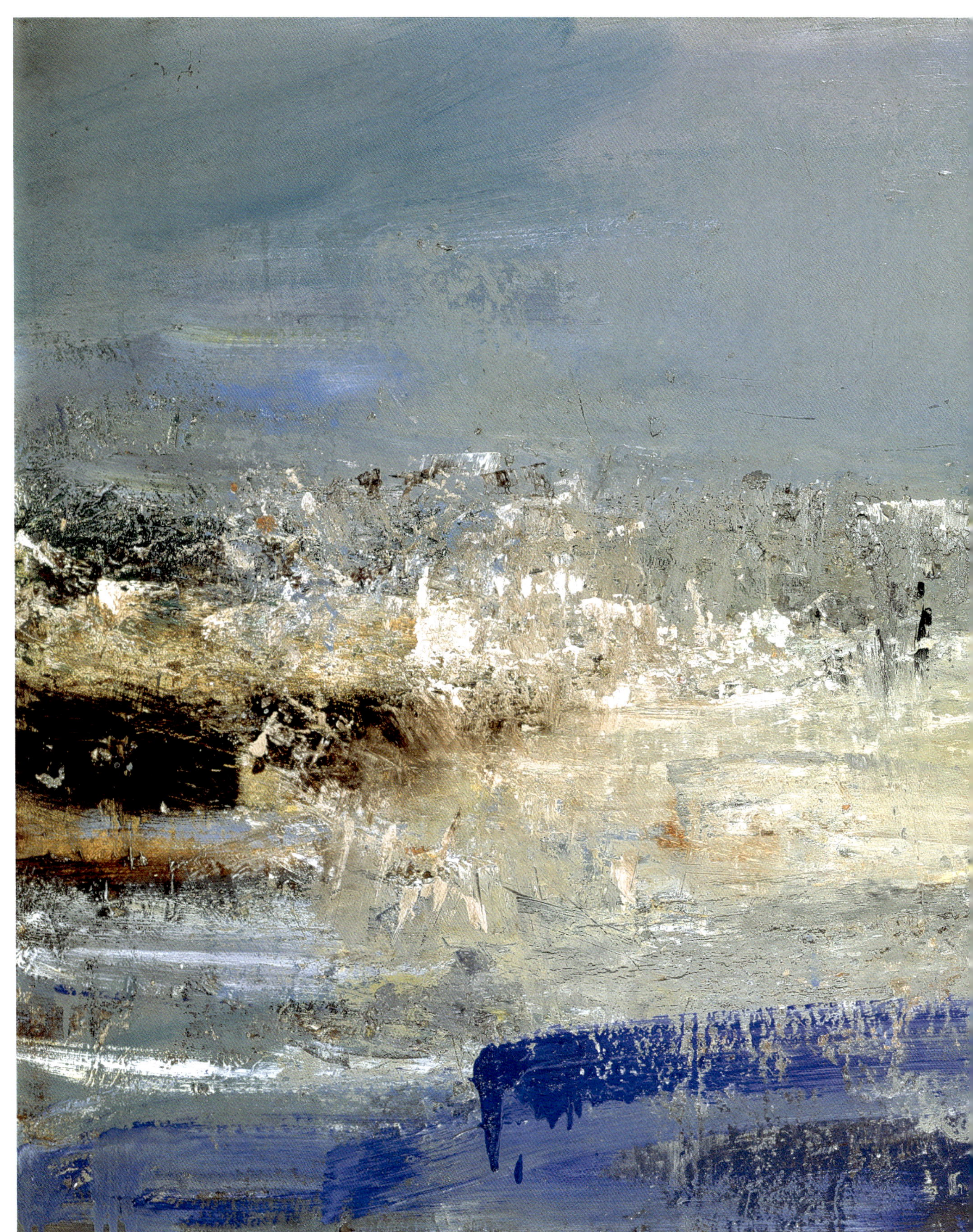

69 | ***Foam and Blue Sky***, 1962
Oil on board
95.2 × 167.6cm
Collection Henry and Sula Walton

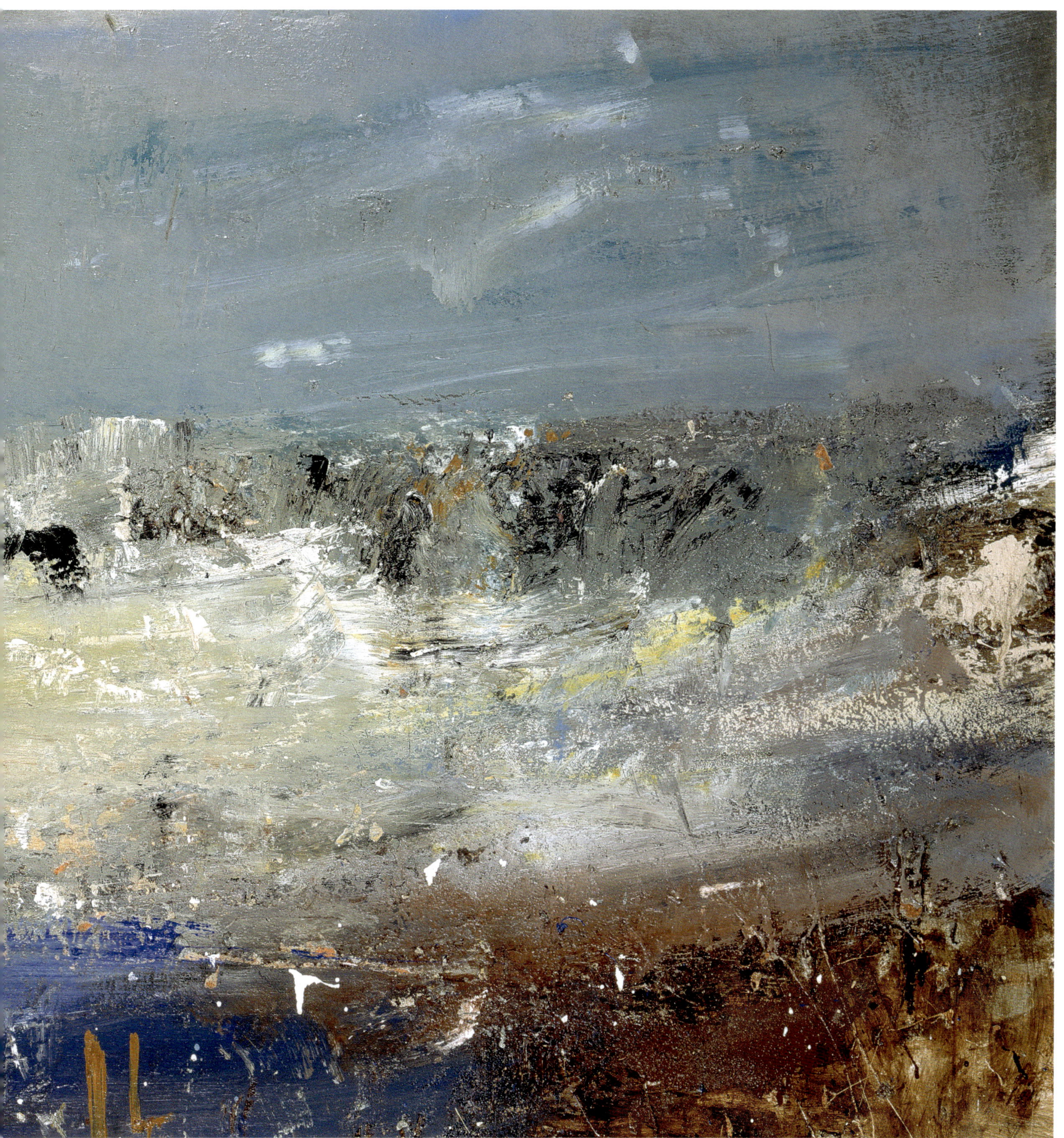

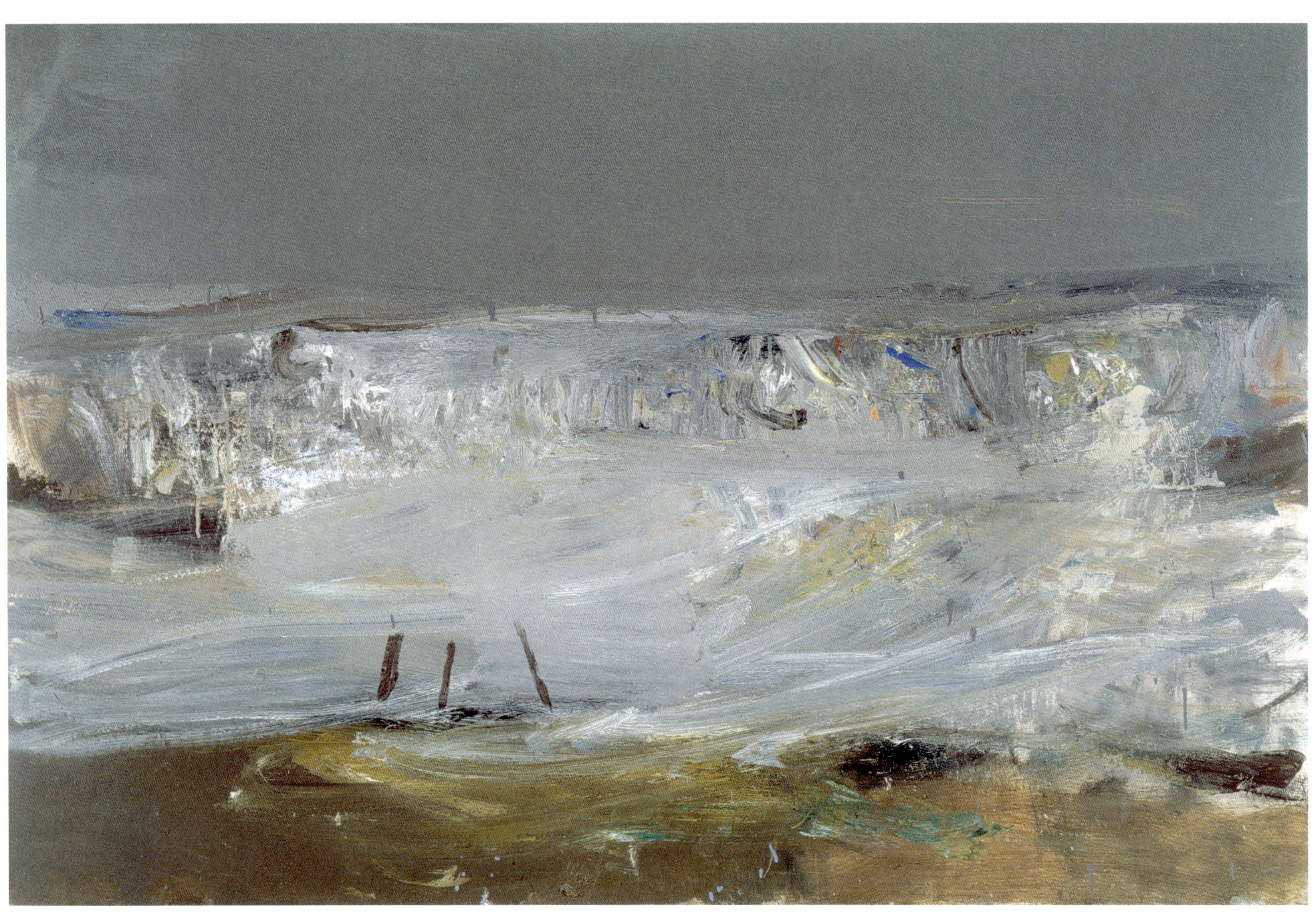

70 | ***Flood Tide***, 1962
Oil on board 120.5 × 183cm
Lillie Art Gallery, East Dumbartonshire Council

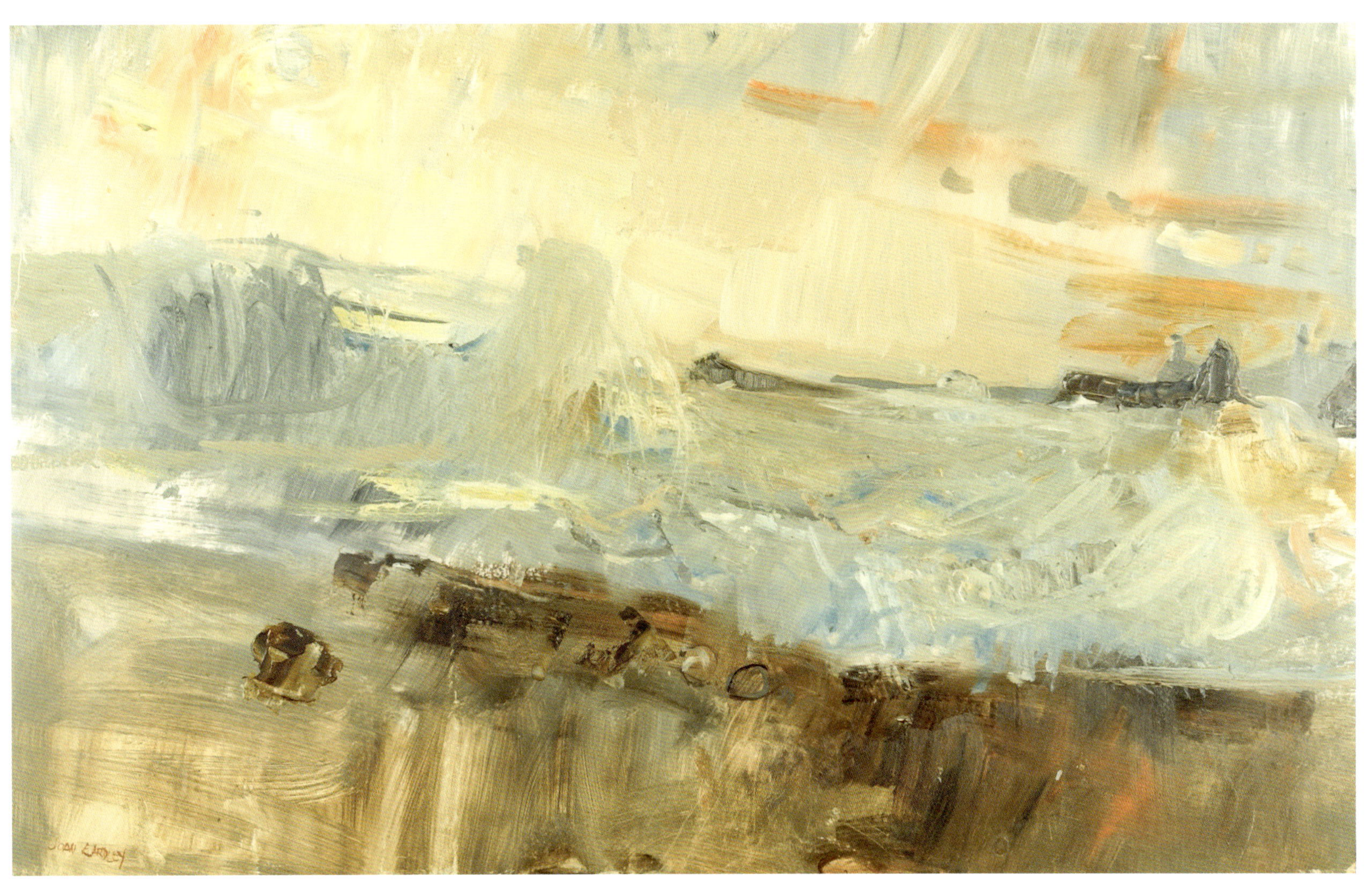

71 | ***Wave Study II***, 1958
Oil on board 55 × 90cm
University of Stirling, Art Collection

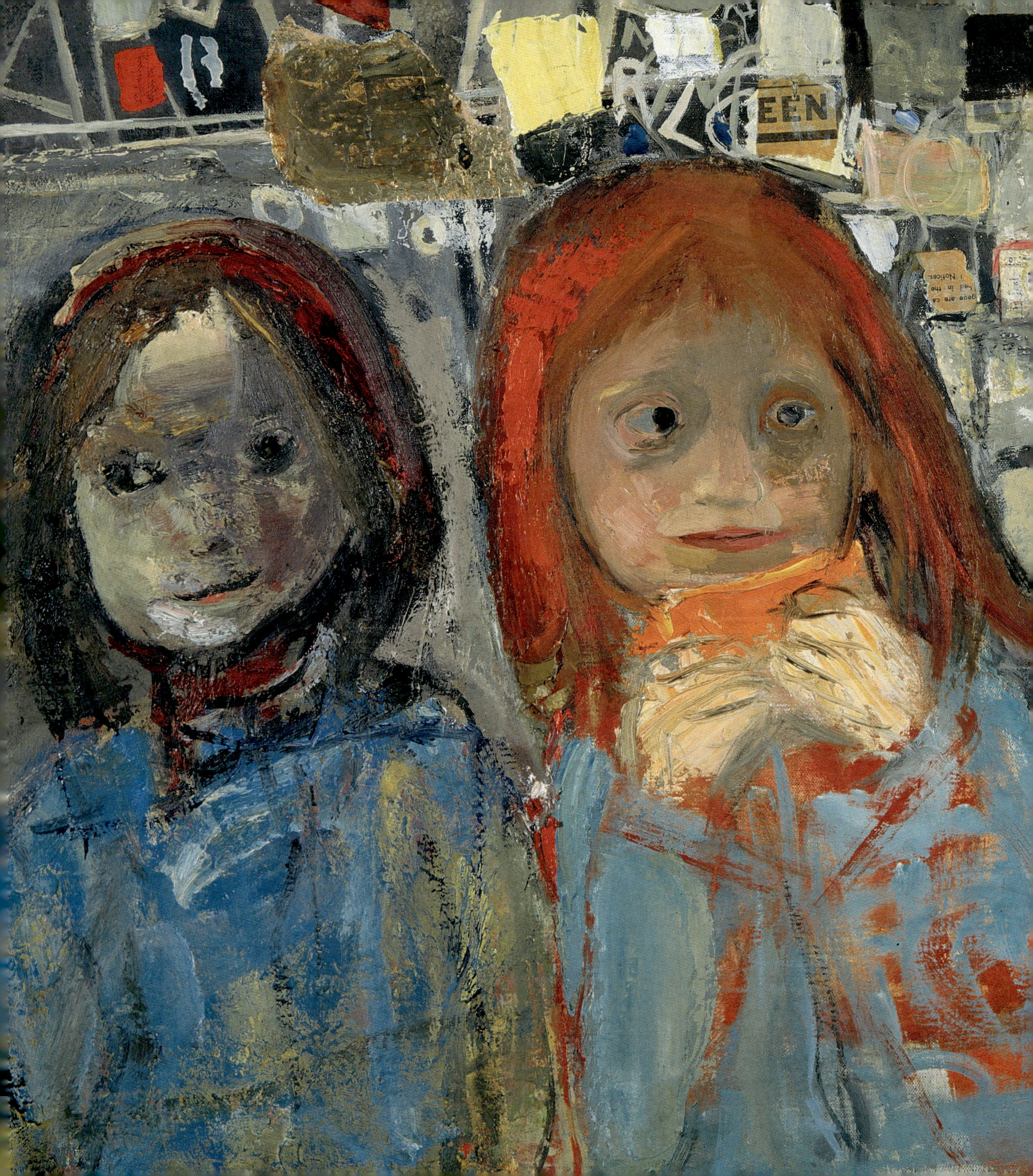
EEN

The Late Work

72 | ***Children and Chalked Wall No.2***, **1963 (detail)**
Oil and collage on canvas
81 × 86.2cm
Abbot Hall Art Gallery, Kendal, Cumbria

Eardley's final Glasgow works were of the children in the heart of Glasgow. On her easel in the Townhead studio, at 204 St James Road, Eardley had a huge oil painting, *Two Children*, which remained unfinished when she died. This painting, now in Kelvingrove Art Gallery and Museum in Glasgow [76], contains all the key themes in Eardley's figurative work. The bright orange ground is studded with a collage of sweet-paper wrappers, foil from cigarette packets, and newspaper scraps. The worn lettering of the boarded-up shop-fronts has been stencilled on. The oddly patterned clothes speak of the hand-me-down items we see in Eardley's own photographs and sketches of the children and create an intense visual texture. The apparent naivety of the figures parallels the work of the young David Hockney.

Eardley had suffered from ill-health from the late fifties including the neck pain, which had necessitated the wearing of a neck brace. She was diagnosed with breast cancer in 1963. She wrote to her dealer, Bill Macaulay of The Scottish Gallery, after a London trip, telling him that the cancer treatment and the drugs she had to take were making it difficult to think clearly. She asked Macaulay to frame all the paintings and drawings intended for her 1963 London show at Roland, Browse and Delbanco in either plain wood baguette moulding or fine Italian gold moulding.[49] The reviews of this show in the *Daily Telegraph* (28 May 1963), *The Times* (7 June 1963) *The Guardian* (29 June 1963), and *Art News and Review* (1 June 1963) refer to her work in the same breath as Turner, Constable and Courbet, and speak of the humanity, honesty and depth of feeling in her paintings of children. Within two days of the show opening, Eardley had sold over half of the thirty-five paintings. One large seascape was bought by the Contemporary Art Society.[50] She saw the London show as a means of preventing herself from being dismissed as provincial and indeed of avoiding becoming provincial in her attitude.

Margot Sandeman has said that Eardley was an agnostic, right until the end.[51] Lil Neilson's friend Rita Guenigault came to Catterline to nurse Eardley in what would prove to be her last months. Eardley was now mortally ill and she was taken by her family from the Aberdeen hospital to die at Killearn Hospital in the countryside north of Glasgow. Friends from Catterline were able to see her on the train as it passed through Stonehaven. She died on 16 August 1963, aged just forty-two, with her mother Irene, sister Pat, and Audrey Walker by her side. Margot Sandeman, who happened to be away from home, raced to Killearn but arrived too late. Eardley was cremated and her ashes scattered on the beach at Catterline. In her memoirs her London dealer Lillian Browse recalled that when Eardley came down for her 1963 show she spent most of the time in the National Gallery in London, studying her favourite masters. On Joan Eardley's death Browse said: '... the art world has lost an outstanding painter and her friends a fine human being ... I count it a privilege to have known this woman who seemed to combine the best in both sexes and who, among the dedicated artists I have met, has not been surpassed by any.'[52]

Eardley's Legacy

It is interesting to compare Eardley with contemporaries such as Eduardo Paolozzi, Alan Davie and William Turnbull, who left Scotland in their twenties and made international reputations. Like Eardley, they all travelled through France and Italy in the late 1940s, but unlike her they plunged head-first into the worlds of Surrealism and Modernism. They met with Peggy Guggenheim, they visited the studios of the leading Paris artists, and they signed up with major London dealers. Had Eardley lived, would she too have developed an international audience and in what ways would her work have changed? It is interesting to note that because she never became an abstract artist, some viewed her work as unsuccessful (Alan Bowness, later to become Director of the Tate Gallery, compared her unfavourably with Peter Lanyon).[53] On the other hand, Eardley's 'felt realism' did not have the visceral effect of Francis Bacon or Lucian Freud, nor did she ever become part of the Kitchen Sink School of British realism, and so she also failed to win support from the realist school of critics, such as John Berger. Indeed, although she has always remained a key figure in Scottish art, south of the border she has become almost invisible.

At the time of her death Eardley was just beginning to reap the rewards of success. In July 1963 she became a Royal Scottish Academician. She was invited to a lunch reception at Buckingham Palace but ill-health prevented her from attending. For the first time in her life, she was financially secure. She died intestate but the records of her estate made by the family solicitors show that although the contents of her house at Catterline were worth just £25, the paintings in the studio were valued at £1000, she had over £2000 in savings and over £4,500 from the proceeds of paintings sold by Roland, Browse and Delbanco and other works sold through the Royal Scottish Academy.[54] The remainder of her estate was made up of the stocks and shares on which she must have survived throughout her working life. The total sum of her estate was £19,881.

In January 1964 a Joan Eardley Memorial Exhibition opened at Glasgow Art Gallery and Museum at Kelvingrove before being shown at the Royal Scottish Academy in Edinburgh. This was the first of several shows organised by Eardley's friend and fellow-student Cordelia Oliver. The exhibition proved a huge success. In just three weeks, the Glasgow venue attracted over 30,000 visitors and 2,000 catalogues were sold. It was officially opened by Eardley's former tutor at Glasgow School of Art, Hugh Adam Crawford, by then Director of Duncan of Jordanstone College of Art in Dundee. In his opening address he declared: 'To many of us this memorial exhibition of Joan Eardley's work is surely one of the saddest, yet, significant experiences of our lives – and what can one say? Of all the painters I know, Joan Eardley is the most directly communicative. Her chief virtue to me lay in the fact that she understood the language of painting better than most, and said things that could only be said in paint ... we are, however, a little surprised and greatly heartened that someone whom we knew and greatly respected had, within less than a quarter of a century, established herself on such a broad front as one of the most distinguished painters of this century.'

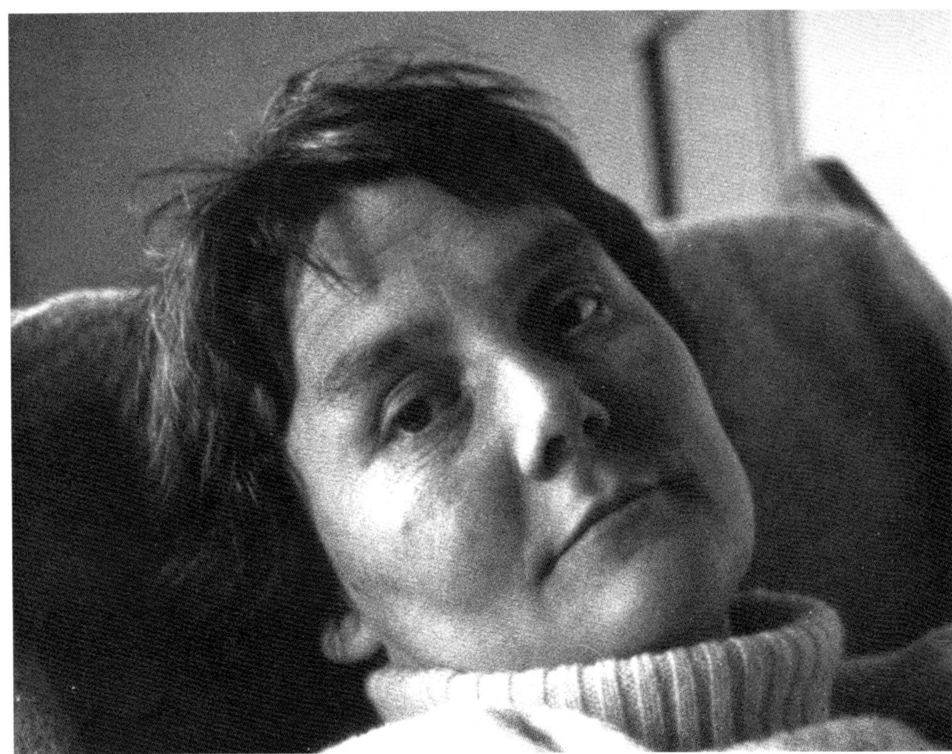

73 | **Joan Eardley**
Photo: Audrey Walker
Gracefield Art Centre, Dumfries

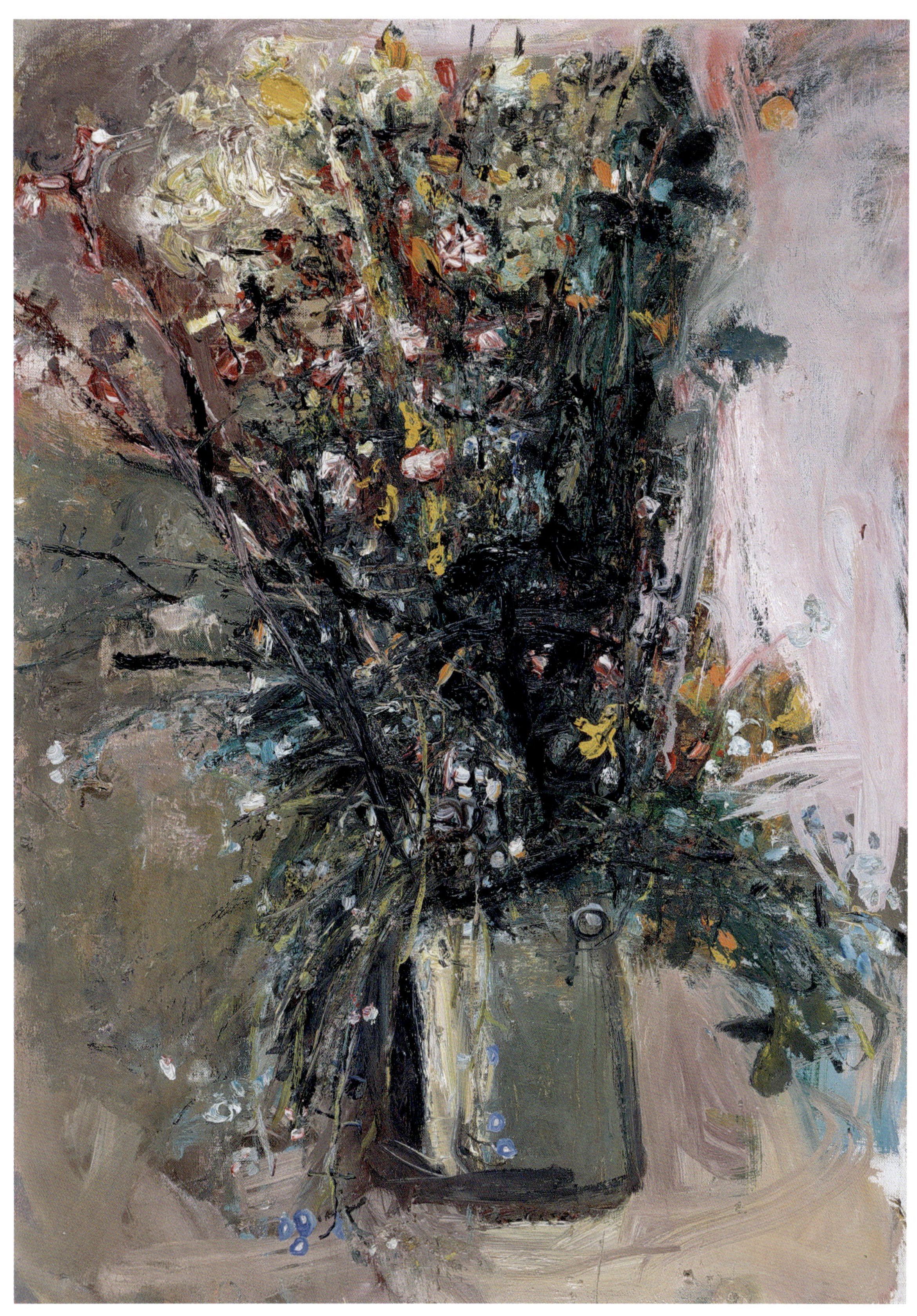

74 | ***Flowers***, 1963
Oil on canvas 69.9 × 49.5cm
Cyril Gerber Fine Art, Glasgow

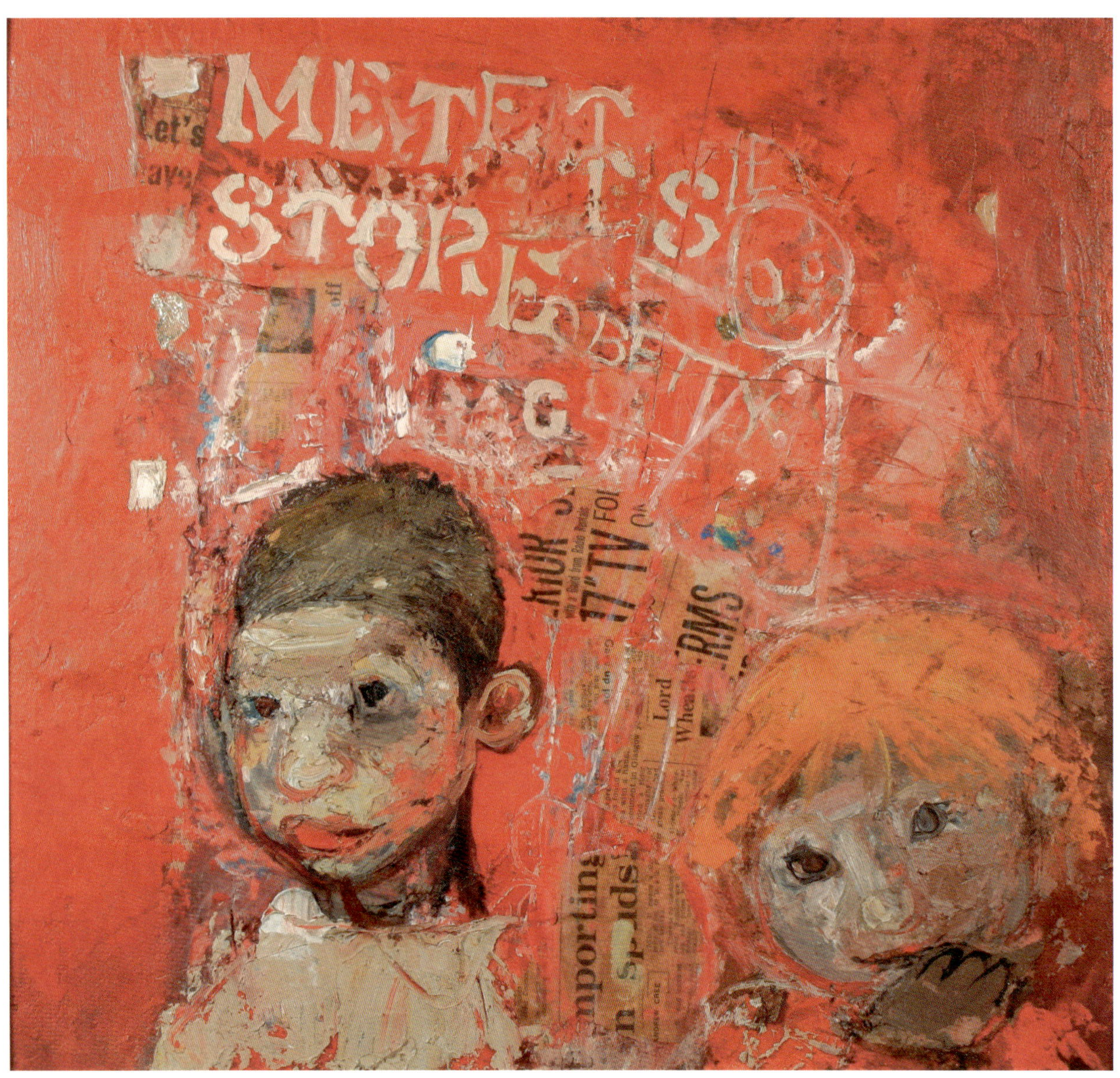

75 | Brian and Pat Samson
Oil on board 43.2 × 45.8cm
Private Collection

76 | *Two Children*, 1963
Oil and collage on canvas (unfinished) 134.7 × 134.7cm
Glasgow City Council (Museums)

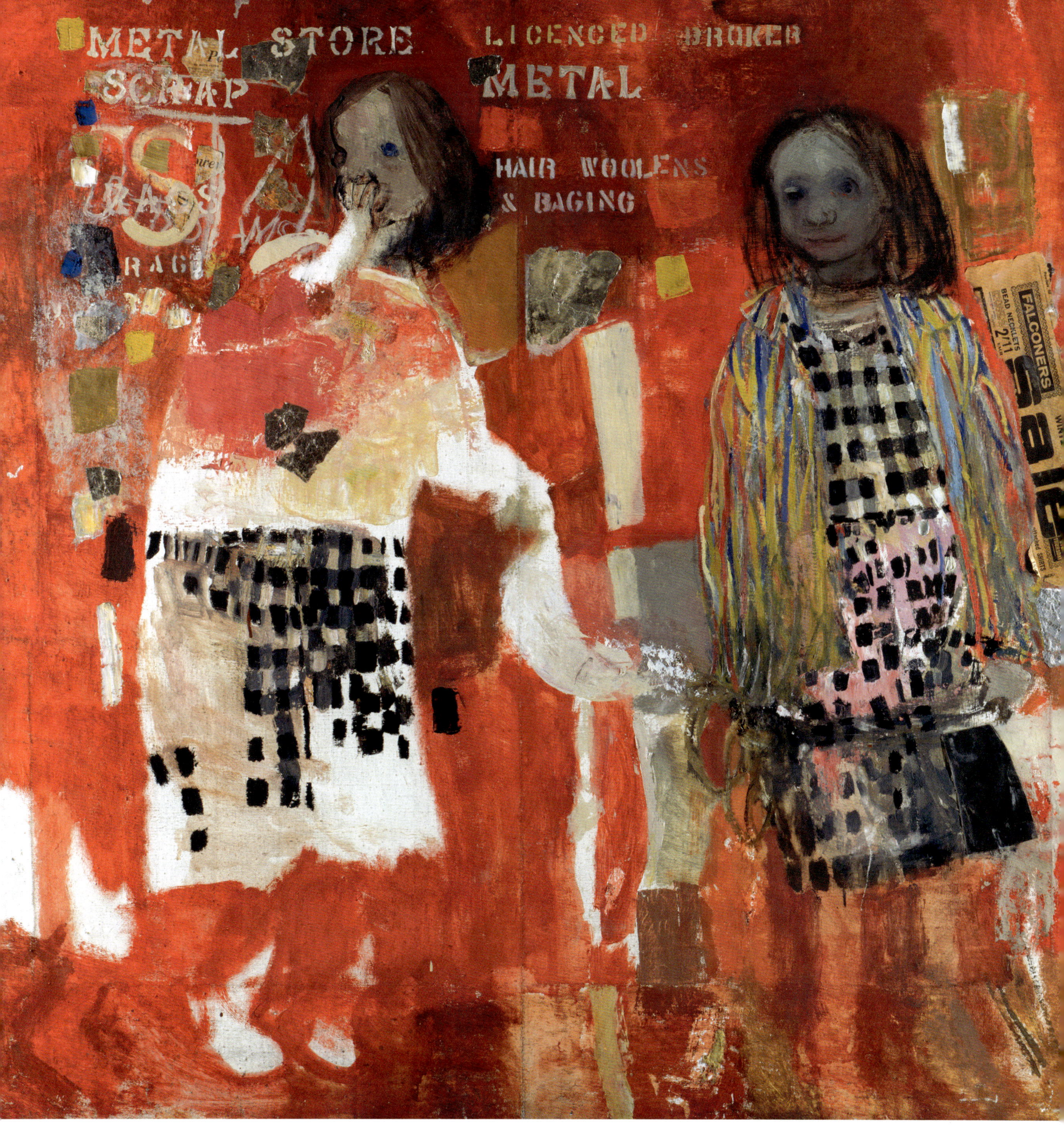
METAL STORE
SCRAP
LICENCED BROKER
METAL
HAIR WOOLENS
& BAGING
RAGS
FALCONERS
Sale

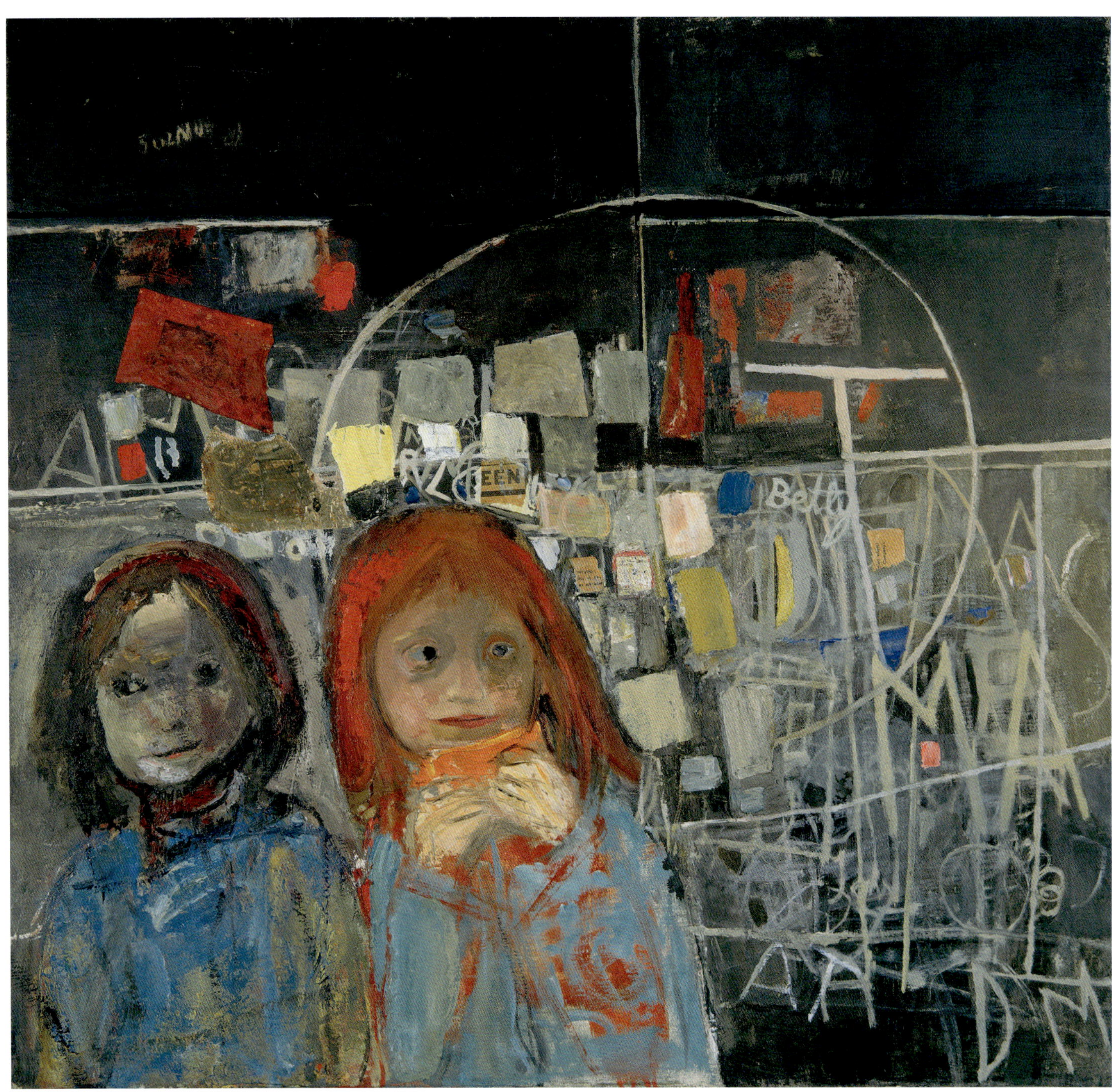

77 | ***Children and Chalked Wall No.2***, 1963
Oil and collage on canvas 81 × 86.2cm
Abbot Hall Art Gallery, Kendal, Cumbria

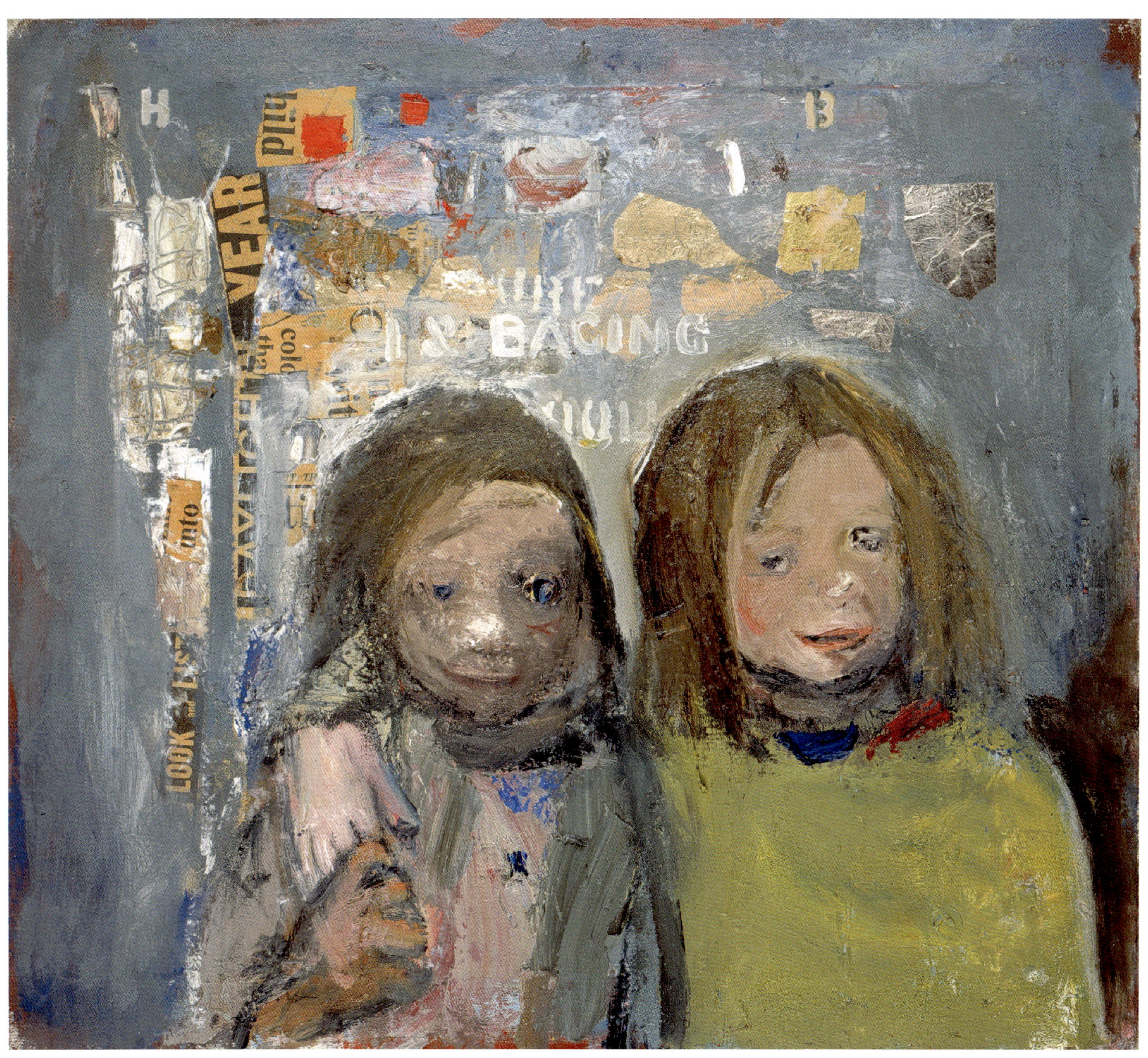

78 | ***Children and Chalked Wall No.3***, 1963
Oil, newspaper and metal foil on canvas 61 × 68.6cm
Scottish National Gallery of Modern Art, Edinburgh

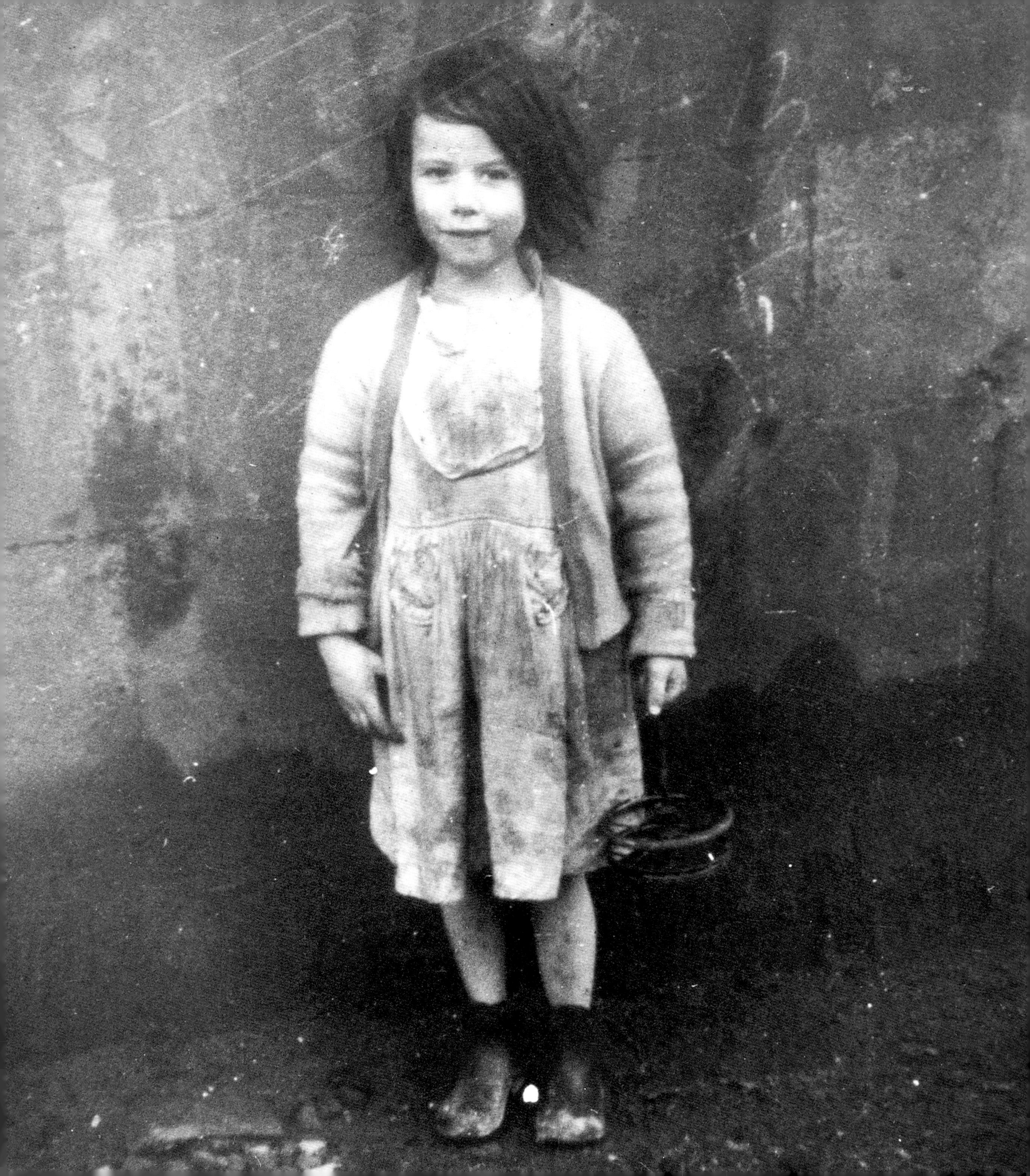

Joan Eardley and Photography

Sara Stevenson

Painters and photographers have engaged in their own conscious ways of looking, using methods and philosophies which do not necessarily mesh. Influences and relationships may be difficult to see, and may only connect through admiration or sympathy. Eardley is evidently connected with a history of the painting of children, but the lively impact of documentary photography in the first half of the twentieth century is also likely to have informed her view of the world. Her interest in actuality, her focus on children in the slums, relate so clearly to concerns central to documentary practice, which she must have known, and she must have been interested in the parallel insights the photographers and the practice of photography offered.

Glasgow itself had a particular relationship to documentary photography. A century beforehand, in 1866, the City of Glasgow succeeded in having an Act of Parliament passed, which enabled them to pull down the worst of the grossly crowded slums around the High Street. Prompted partly by a feeling that they were not just making but destroying history, they commissioned Thomas Annan to photograph the condemned closes. Between 1868 and 1871, he took thirty-one photographs, which express a sense of the architecture and, in a more restricted fashion, of the life lived in these warrens. On some occasions, he was able to arrange a group of people, at other times, the audience emerged unexpectedly from doorways and windows. But children especially, and on one photographic plate a goat, skip past, making a fleeting and touching visual impression [80].

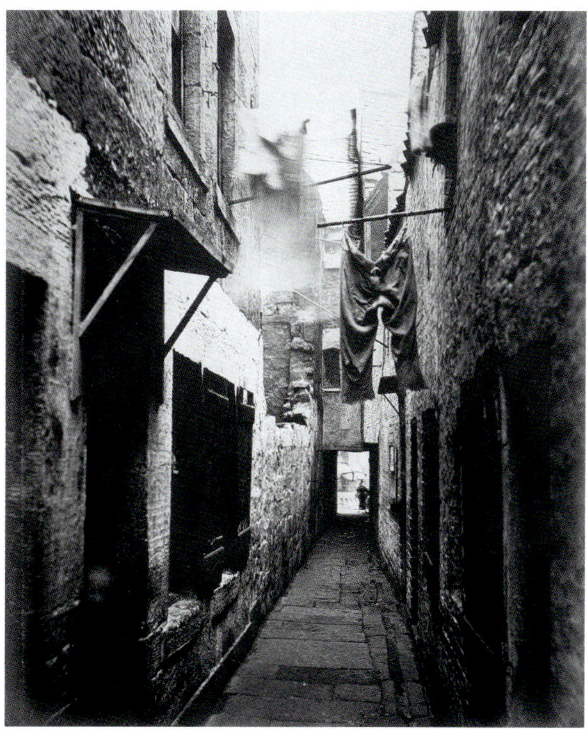

79 | **Unknown child (detail)**
Photo: Joan Eardley
Joan Eardley Archive, Scottish National Gallery of Modern Art, Edinburgh [GMA/A09]

80 | ***Close Number 101 High Street, Glasgow*, 1868–71**
Photo: Thomas Annan
Scottish National Photography Collection at the Scottish National Portrait Gallery, Edinburgh

The connection between Eardley's work and these photographs is debatable – they are not essentially about the people who appear in them. But there is a powerful link between them. For both Annan and Eardley, the two components, the cityscape and the people, were inseparable: two moulds that made a fit. They were dealing with a human landscape. The difference between the two lies partly in the irony that Glasgow's grand and heroic solution – to tear down and rebuild – has turned out to be an unsuccessful solution time and again. Annan's pictures have an unexpected kind of openness and even sometimes a glowing optimism within them – he was an evangelical Christian, and his sense of the picturesque in the Glasgow closes was tempered by his knowledge of their history. Eardley would have known that such simple answers had not worked, and she was more concerned with their present existence than their future improvement. But Annan's photographs and Eardley's paintings have a common understanding that the dominant landscape is a backdrop to the future as well as a mould of the past – the children have a vigour and independence, which liberates them.

The use of photography as an aid to painting is most obvious as a kind of surface anatomy – a photograph may be said to show the outer shell, which the painter can bring to a different kind of life. Eardley apparently used photography in this kind of way, as static notes on graffiti or the way the children wear their clothes – crumpled, grubby, too small, too big, walking around as a disconcerting echo of another child [79]. She wrote about the Samson children: 'They wear each others clothes and sometimes Bobby gets Betty's shoes. You never get them wearing the same clothes even if you ask them. But that doesn't matter, it is part of the thing I feel.'[1] The knowledgeable capture in her snapshots is partly obscured by a technical lack of skill, but this view should be qualified. She evidently experimented with photographic process at some point, trying different papers and making images darker to simplify the picture. Photographs would appear to be a significant part of the painter's method of absorbing visual information. However, Eardley is not, as in Oscar Marzaroli's photograph [85], capturing their smiles and their sympathy to achieve a charming result, she is looking at the differently organised chaos of children, and some of her own snapshots are evidence of her readiness to allow the children to take over the studio itself as a part of their territory [83] and their collaboration with her process of seeing.

In a broader sense, photography may have offered Eardley more than this. It has acted as an impulse both to realism and to surreality – evidence of the extraordinary juxtaposition of the actual brought together on a flat plane; arbitrary gesture or movement within a group; evidence of radical differences in perception of time and space, when the human idea of the moment is disturbed; sequences of images [see 31A–C]; evidence of distortions seen through the non-human vision of the lens.

Eardley's interest in background signs, drawn and scrawled graffiti, has a long photographic history. W.H. Fox Talbot remarked on the accidental character of this capture: 'It frequently happens ... – and this is one of the charms of photography – that the operator himself discovers on examination ... that he has depicted many things he had no notion of at the time. Sometimes inscriptions and dates are found upon the buildings, or printed placards most irrelevant, are discovered upon their walls ...'[2] Signs and notices, whose impact on us should be dominant but is often blanked out by our part-conscious refusal to take an interest, develop an edge when caught within a picture. Time takes out the nagging urgency of posters, letters fall off signs, the picture frame cuts them off in mid-speech, people are caught in strange two-dimensional relations to these gesturing words and symbols. In the twentieth century, Walker Evans's photographs deliberately capture and play with this engaging idea. Joan Eardley asked Audrey Walker to photograph the local graffiti – impossible to invent or remember – to assist in the painting, and even to add a literal extension of the idea of windblown newsprint – stuck to the canvas as part of the work.

Oscar Marzaroli's photographs of Joan Eardley and the Samson children [85], offer us a view of a social working relationship – one characteristic of photography. She was herself a major influence on Marzaroli's photographic practice, and, in the photograph taken in her studio, she beams back at him. The Samson children look both like themselves and like the paintings, in a fascinating three-cornered response – off to the left, looking presumably at Eardley, and straight at Marzaroli, one in doubt, two in unfeigned pleasure, feet neatly lined up, grins anarchic – a whole range of age and emotion. George Oliver noted: 'It is a lovely, cheerful, subtle picture. It is a useful record of the workplace of one of Scotland's significant painters of recent times and it also confirms a fact not too widely understood, that Eardley painted what she saw, not what she imagined she saw.'[3] The children Eardley painted liked being painted, and evidently liked being photographed – they are, like the other children Marzaroli photographed, street kids, looking for entertainment, turning the artist into an audience: they are both subjects and spectators. The underlying idea is a counterbalance to the more melancholy character of much of her painting, and helps to explain the social mechanism which enabled Eardley to paint them so accurately.

In general, Audrey Walker's photographs taken for Eardley's purposes are further back, capturing the fixed elements of the scene as much as the children. But here also there is the same sense of a landscape that belongs to them – the adults stand back and look from doorways – and the children break and overtake the boundaries. They make their own world – barriers are there to be tested, rubbish to be found for archaeological investigation, and a bombsite offers new space to colonise [see 31a–c]. They take over this bizarre and even alarming landscape of tenements, abandoned shops and broken walls. The idea of children – resilient and innocent – playing through broken boundaries, left by war, is forcibly expressed by Henri Cartier-Bresson's picture, taken in

81 | Unknown children
Photo: Joan Eardley
Joan Eardley Archive, Scottish National Gallery of Modern Art, Edinburgh [GMA/A09]

82 | Unknown children playing in the street
Photo: Joan Eardley
Joan Eardley Archive, Scottish National Gallery of Modern Art, Edinburgh [GMA/A09]

83 | Unknown child in Eardley's studio
Photo: Audrey Walker
Joan Eardley Archive, Scottish National Gallery of Modern Art, Edinburgh [GMA/A09]

84 | Unknown children at the entrance to a close
Photo: Joan Eardley
Joan Eardley Archive, Scottish National Gallery of Modern Art, Edinburgh [GMA/A09]

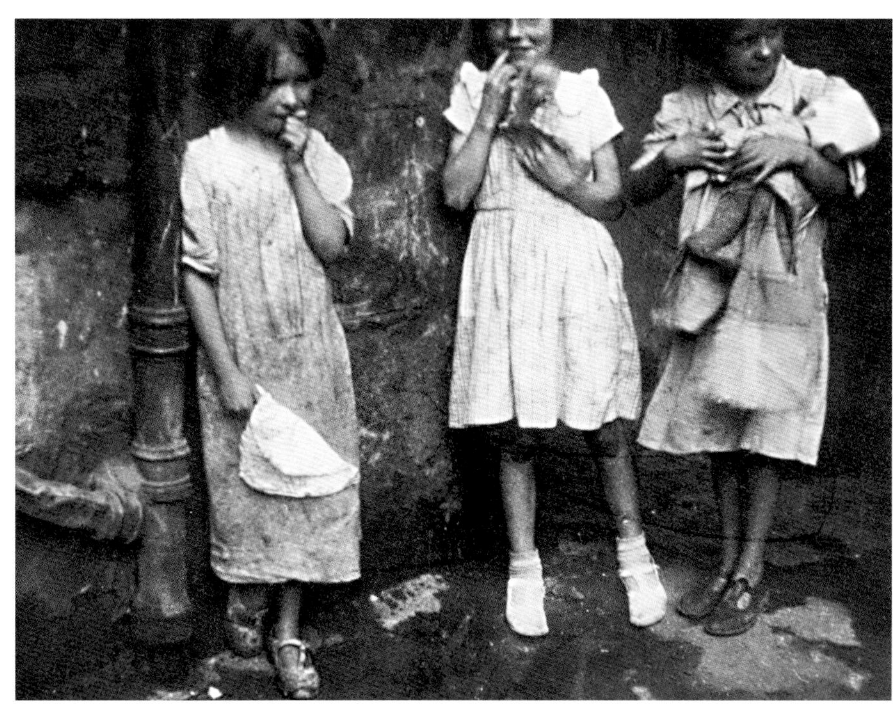
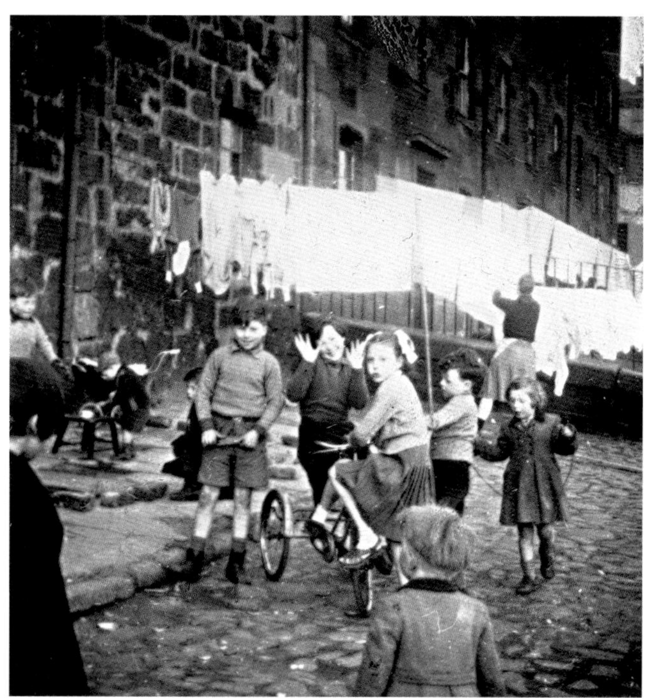
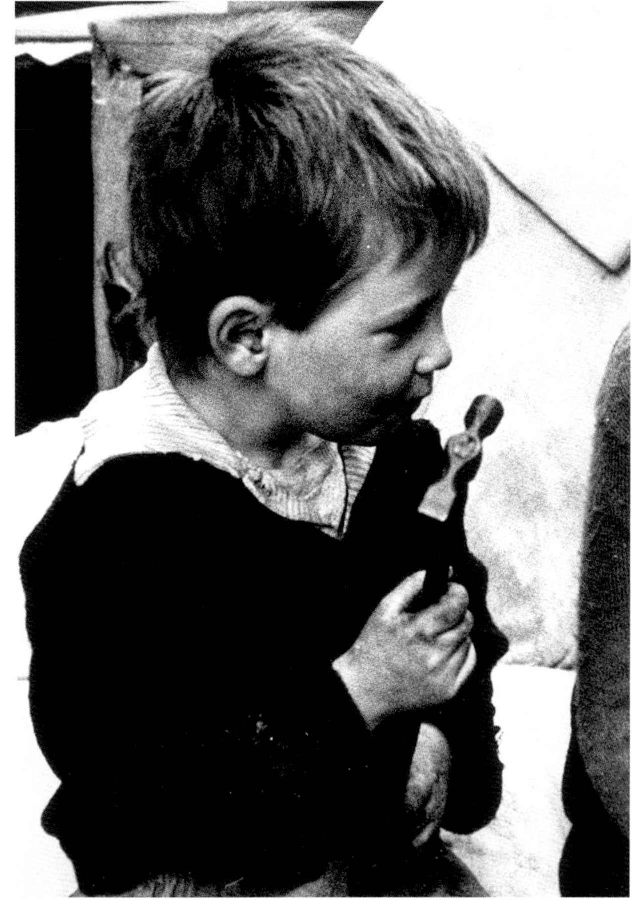
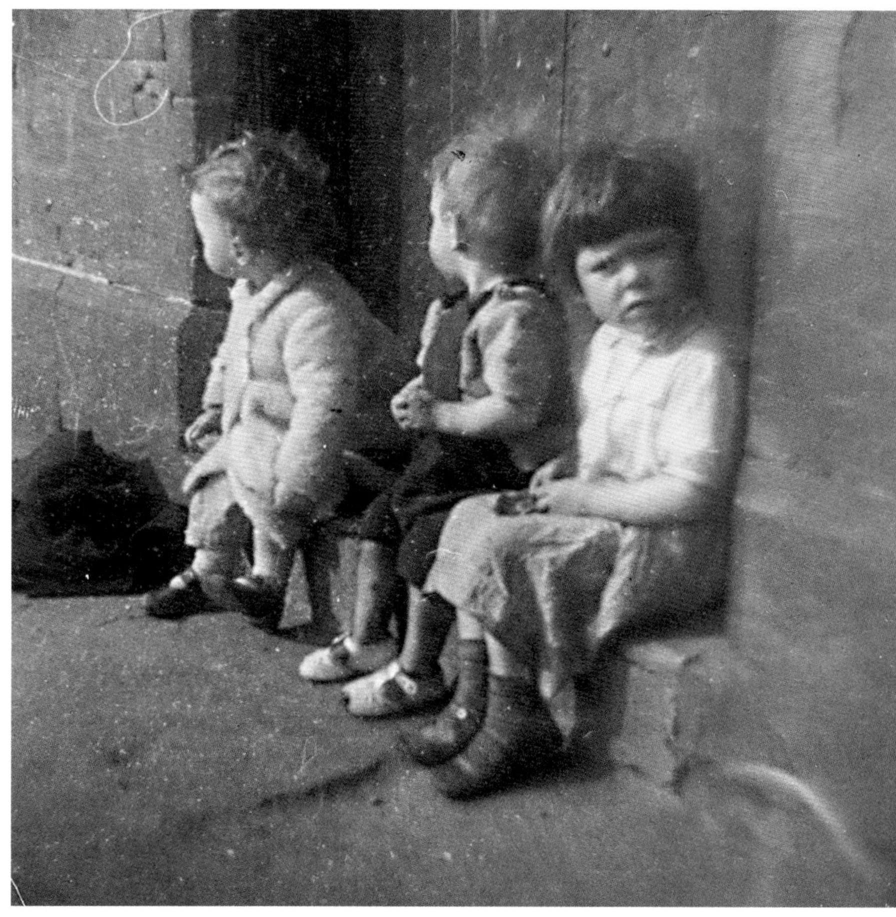

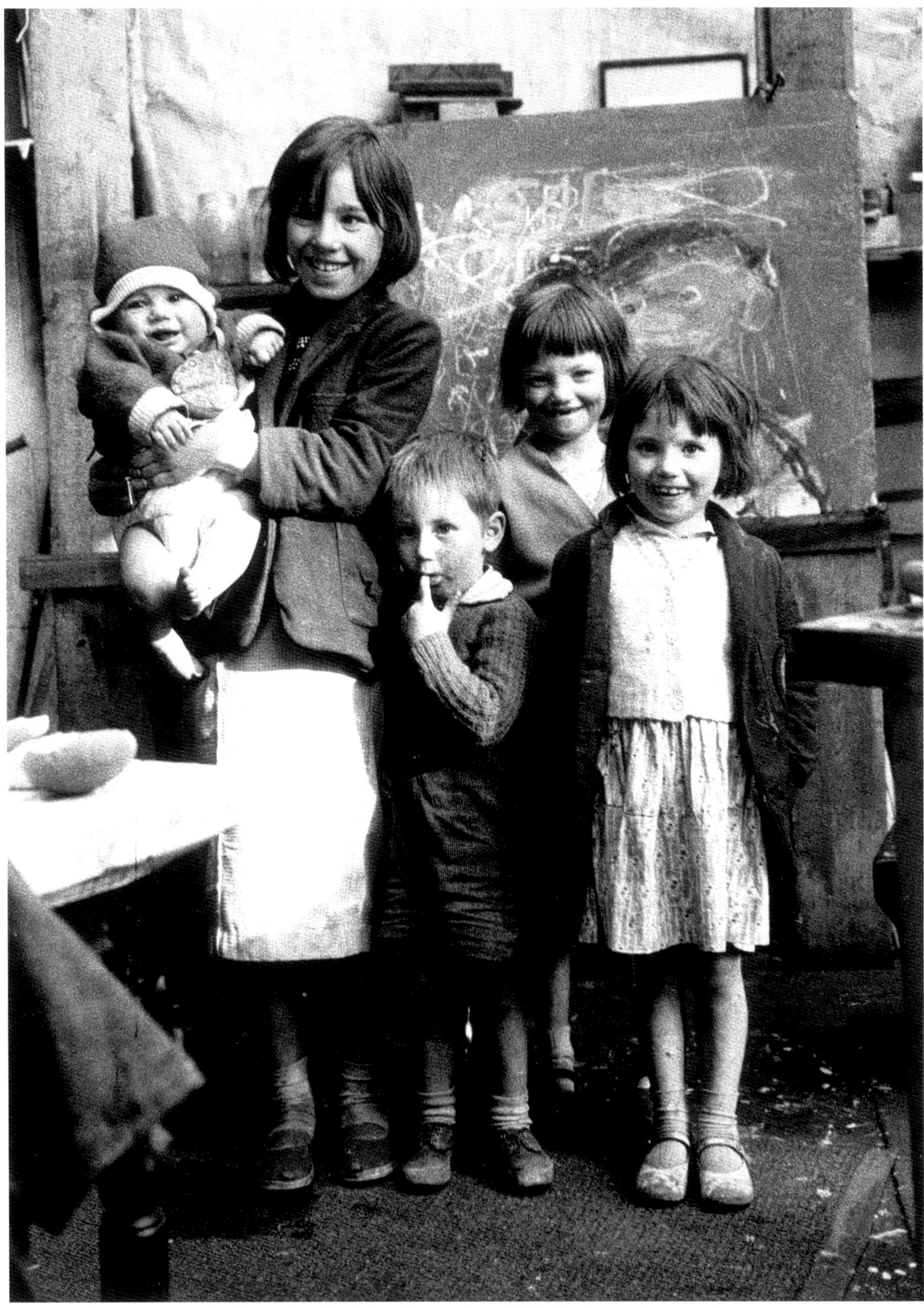

85 | *The Samson Family in Eardley's Studio*
Photo: Oscar Marzaroli
Scottish National Photography Collection at the Scottish National Portrait Gallery, Edinburgh

Seville in 1933, where the children are actively rejoicing in the freedom of a bomb-damaged building. Eardley's and Walker's photographs, taken together, catch something of the seriousness and absorption of the children in their own society. The photographs present a parallel child's landscape, which both illuminates and challenges the paintings.

Early in her career, when talking of drawing, Eardley wrote: 'It is a most satisfying joyful thing. The contact which you get because you are still, and quiet in one place; the things that move, and carry on their daily happenings because they are unconscious of your existence – little mice and bird[s], and even the sun and wind too become part of you.'[4] In her affection for the idea of place, Eardley was able to achieve a realist understanding of her subjects – a deep knowledge. In Glasgow, it was the children's place she found, and it was their world in which she lived. There are two photographic comparisons which might helpfully be made. The first, 'Lewis Carroll' (the Revd Charles Lutwidge Dodgson) seems initially unlikely. He photographed more privileged and arguably constrained children in the context of mid-nineteenth-century England. The formal and emotional impact of his work is by no means the same as that of Eardley's. However, he shares with her an interest in the child's mind – not simply a virtuous idea of innocent childhood, held up as a moral contrast to the weary cynicism of adults, but something more truly energetic and individual. It is perhaps problematic that his photographs are sometimes stiff and a little posed, and this has led to an assumption that his sitters might be victims of a dubious gaze – especially in relation to his nude or part-dressed figures. But this implies that he had a passive and uncommunicative relationship with the children which is not borne out by the history – his rooms and studio at Christ Church contained cupboards with such engaging objects as musical boxes or mechanical bats, and the chemical development could be watched after the photograph was taken. It was a new territory in the same way that Eardley's studio was to become one for the Townhead children.

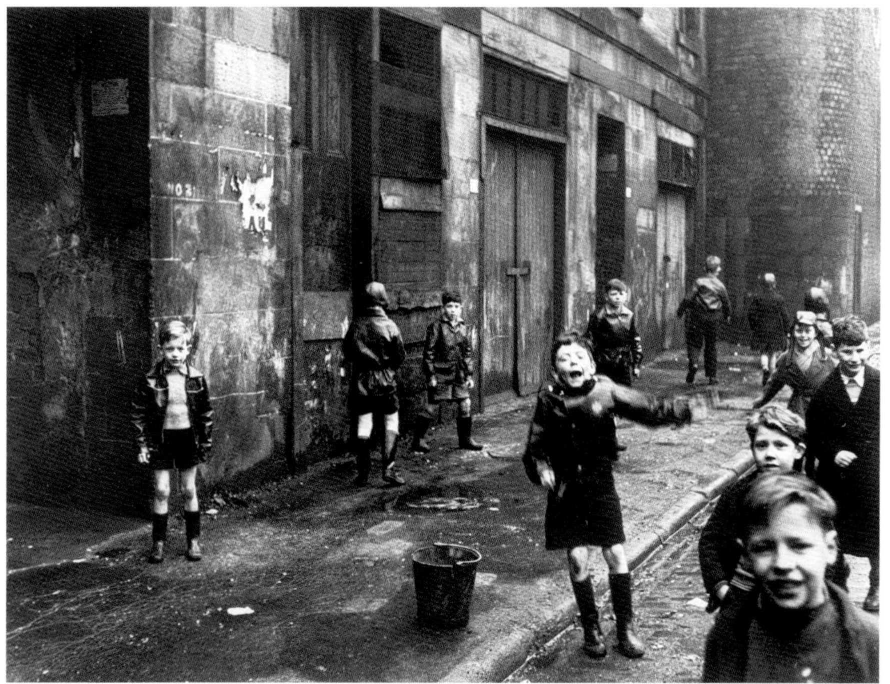

86 | *Children in the Gorbals, Glasgow*, 1958
Photo: Roger Mayne
Scottish National Photography Collection at the Scottish National Portrait Gallery, Edinburgh

This sense of occupying a territory of the mind also offers a parallel between Eardley and a nearer contemporary. Albeit different in intellectual or philosophical approach, her interests and working practice resembled that of the New York painter/photographer, Ben Shahn, who worked closely during the Depression in the distressed areas of the city. Both worked in response to a disastrous disruption to society. Moreover, Shahn was described by the American poet, Archibald MacLeish, who was astonished to find that his studio, deliberately and respectfully isolated on a university campus, had become part of the world: 'It was a room at the top of the building protected from intrusion by back stairs and crooked corridors where the painter was to paint secure from trespass and I approached it with a sense of guilt ... When I came to the door it was wide open and the room was full of the winter smell of undergraduates. There was hardly a square foot of the floor left free to walk on and as for Ben, though he was painting it was not in lonely silence ... I saw then how it was with him: how he found himself in the world and worked in it. ... It would have placed him where he wanted to be placed – where he belonged – not only in the ruined city but among the human throngs who still can hope there and still live.'[5]

In simpler terms, the social documentary photographers developed a similar role as a part of society. Children assisted in the process; they are curious and energetic, they seek entertainment, and the photographer may take pictures showing them responding to him or herself. But the artist who stays put becomes a familiar part of the landscape, and the children will return to their own concerns. Roger Mayne succeeded in this kind of acceptance and periodic invisibility, particularly in his extended essay in Southam Street in London.

He came north to Scotland in 1948, where he took comparable street pictures in Edinburgh and Glasgow, and the children built him into their game [86]. 'The back streets,' wrote Eardley, 'mean almost entirely screaming, playing children – all over the streets.'[6]

Photography, ironically, is not by necessity realist or objective in character, partly because the photographer interferes by being there, and life changes round the focal point of the camera. Evidently, his or her knowledge and conscious decisions affect and change the results. In 1948, Bert Hardy took a series of photographs for a polemic article for *Picture Post* on the slums of Glasgow, called 'The Forgotten Gorbals', demanding the 'destruction of the old Gorbals and the building of a better one'.[7] In the short time Hardy spent there with the author of the article, he succeeded in capturing a distressing reality. Hardy wrote that Bill Brandt had been sent north first: 'Bill returned with his usual contrasty pictures of the backs of policemen standing at the ends of streets, but nothing which really showed the human side of poverty.'[8] His own understanding was informed by his upbringing in the East End of London, which gives the pictures an element of self-portraiture. He said that the picture of the two boys [87] was, 'My favourite picture: this reminds me of what I was like when I was a kid. In this story I concentrated on the children, and how they kept their spirits up in conditions which were often dreadful.'[9] This notably self-confident and cheering picture was not published with the article – Eardley may not have known it, but the children have a similar vigour to that of her own friends. It had for Hardy, as it still does for us, the power of its inherent idea – these children do not evoke pity, they engage our interest. Like Eardley's children, they inhabit a troubling world, and deal with it in an eccentric or anarchic way but with their own personal sense of possession and control – it is their own.

87 | *Two Glasgow Boys*, 1948. Photo: Bert Hardy
Scottish National Photography Collection at the Scottish National Portrait Gallery, Edinburgh

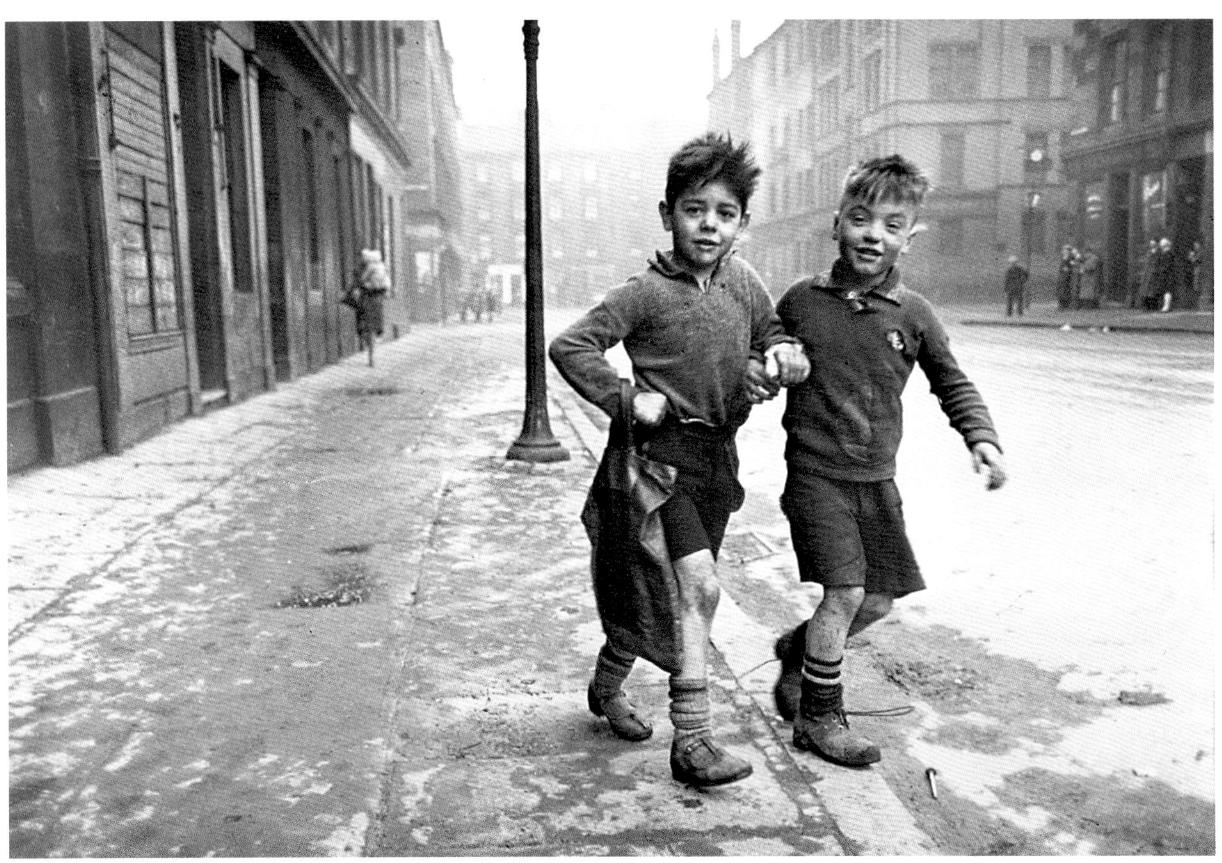

Postscript

Joan Eardley's archive has been given by her sister Pat Black to the Scottish National Gallery of Modern Art. Audrey Walker's letters and papers are with the National Library of Scotland. The Watch House where Eardley began her Catterline paintings was bequeathed by Annette Stephen to Lil Neilson and by Neilson to Ann Steed of Aberdeen Art Gallery who has restored it as a studio for young artists. Eardley's work is held in both public and private collections. A full list of public collections is in Cordelia Oliver's book, *Joan Eardley*, pp.113–14.

Eardley's books remain with her family, they include: Albert Camus, *The Outsider*; Sir James Caw, *Biography of Sir James Guthrie* (her Guthrie Prize from Glasgow School of Art); books on Giotto's frescoes in the Upper Church at Assisi (with a colour supplement insert on mosaics in Christian churches); books on the drawings of Leonardo and Rembrandt; Hans Feibusch, *Mural Painting* (presented to Eardley at Christmas 1946 by Sybil Morrison); *Pencil Drawings of William Blake*; *Lights of Canopus* (an illustrated Indian manuscript in Boston Museum); *Masterpieces in Colour by Sir Joshua Reynolds*; R.H. Wilenski, *Modern French Painters*; Myfanwy Evans, *The Painter's Object* (signed, pencil notes and marks, pictures cut out and page missing); *Modern Drawings in the Museum of Modern Art* (a present from Margot Sandeman and husband James Robson); *Augustus John Drawings*; John Baur, *New Art in America*; Marcel Brian, *Venice*; *Stanley Spencer-Resurrection Pictures 1945–50*; *Henri Rousseau*; *Sunday Times* colour section dated 13 May 1962 which includes a homage to Braque; *The Bayeux Tapestry*; and books on Chagall, Renoir, Miró, and Daumier. Eardley's copy of Burton's *Anatomy of Melancholy* remains with Margot Sandeman.

In planning the 1961 show at The Scottish Gallery in Edinburgh Eardley supplied the following list of works which were available to the exhibition organiser, Bill Macaulay. The list is of interest for the number of serial paintings it includes: *The Sea (1–4)*; *Boats and the Sea (1–2)*; *Winter Sea and Nets*; *Salmon Nets and the Sea*; *Between Fields of Barley*; *Flowers Between Fields*; *Fever-Few July*; *Seeded Grasses and Daisies September*; *A Stook of Oats*; *Harvest Time*; *Stacks (1–3)*; *Bagged Potatoes (1–2)*; *Snow (1–2)*; *Flowers by the Wayside*; *A Stormy Sea (1–5)*; *A Small Line Boat (1–2)*; *The Corner of a Field at Sundown (1–2)*; *The Old Plough*; *Salmon Nets (1–2)*; *Salmon Nets on the Shore (1–2)*; *A Field of Wheat*; *The Sea and the Harbour (1–2)*; *Beehives (1–2)*; *Cottages and a Storm*; *Some of the Samson Family*; *Children Playing and Boarded Up Shops*; *Children and Chalked Wall (1–3)*; *Text Over the Mantelpiece*; *Sunset*; *Stacks at Sunset*; and *A Sweetshop Rotten Row*.

Lil Neilson's library of pre-1963 books includes the works of Jean Paul Sartre, Simone de Beauvoir, Bertolt Brecht, D.H. Lawrence, Herman Hesse, Henry Miller, John Osborne, Nelson Algren, Albert Camus, Baudelaire, Jean Genet, T.S. Eliot, Ezra Pound, John Berger, Walt Whitman, Alice B. Toklas, the letters of Van Gogh and a book on Basil Spence's Coventry Cathedral.

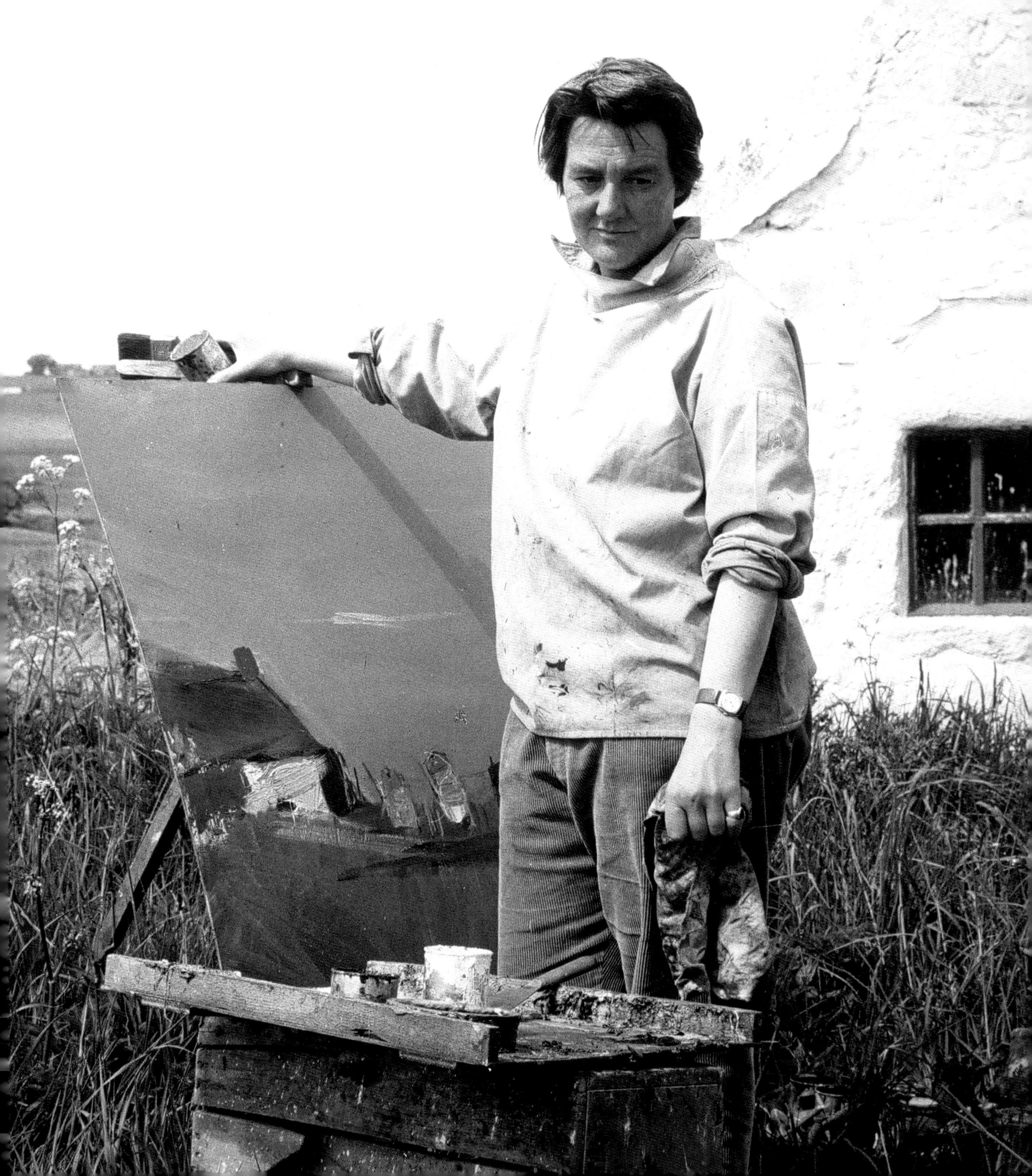

Chronology

1921 Joan Eardley born on 18 May at Bailing Hill Farm, Warnham, Sussex to Irene (née Morrison) and Captain William Eardley.

1922 Younger sister Pat born.

1926 Family home, a dairy farm in Sussex, sold due to father's breakdown. Irene Eardley and her two daughters move to 128 Coleraine Road, Blackheath, London and stay with Joan's maternal grandmother Ellen Morrison (née Fawcett) and Sybil Morrison, Irene's sister. (Ellen Morrison had married twice; her first husband was George Morrison, an Aberdonian, and the second a Glaswegian named Parker.)

1929 Captain Eardley commits suicide.

1938 Joan Eardley leaves school and studies at the local art school in Blackheath for two terms, then enrolls in September at, Goldsmiths College, London, where she also stays two terms.

1939 In April goes on skiing holiday to Val d'Isère, Savoie, in the French Alps with a school friend, Joan Fabricius. Irene Eardley, Ellen Morrison, Joan and Pat move to Scotland to escape the threat of bombing in London and stay with a relative in Auchterarder.

1940 In January family settles at Glenholm, 170 Drymen Road, Bearsden, on the outskirts of Glasgow. Eardley has access to Sybil Morrison's library, which she reads assiduously. Enrolls at Glasgow School of Art as a day student, number 2047, on the General Course. Is taught by Hugh Adam Crawford and supervised for the first two years by Henry Y. Alison. Course includes modelling, anatomy, painting and composition, pattern design, geometry and perspective, and, later, architecture, lettering and lectures on the history of art. Guest lecturers include R.H. Wilenski, Rebecca Crompton, Thomas Bodkin and Nikolaus Pevsner. At Glasgow School of Art meets Margot Sandeman, a fellow resident of Bearsden, who becomes her best friend for the rest of her life.

1942 Eardley spends summer at Corrie on Isle of Arran with Margot Sandeman. Many trips follow during the 40s. Draws Jeannie Kelso. Shows *Woman with a Shawl* at Society of Scottish Artists; subject may be Mrs Kelso from Corrie.

1942-3 Takes the diploma drawing and painting course. Among Eardley's teachers were Hugh Adam Crawford, George Houston, Henry Y. Alison and J. Alix Dick.

1943 Awarded diploma in drawing and painting and wins Sir James Guthrie prize for portraiture with her self-portrait. Enrolls at Jordanhill Teacher Training College but stays only one term. Becomes joiner's labourer as reserved occupation until the end of the war, doing camouflage painting on landing craft. Attends evening classes at Glasgow School of Art in 1943-4 and 1945-6 specialising in life-drawing and painting.

1946 Receives a commission, through family friends in Lincolnshire, to paint a mural in a secondary school in Lincoln, since lost.

1947 Lives in London for a short while. From April to September attends Patrick Allan-Fraser College of Art at Hospitalifield near Arbroath under tutelage of James Cowie. Meets Angus Neil, painter and joiner, who is to be an ally in her future painting developments.

1947-8 Post-diploma studies at Glasgow School of Art. Meets Dorothy Steel. In February elected professional member of the Society of Scottish Artists. Receives diploma (highly commended). Wins two scholarships, the Carnegie scholarship from the Royal Scottish Academy and a travelling scholarship from Glasgow School of Art.

88 | Eardley with a painting of beehives in the garden at the back of Number 1 The Row, Catterline
Photo: Audrey Walker
Joan Eardley Archive, Scottish National Gallery of Modern Art, Edinburgh [GMA/A09]

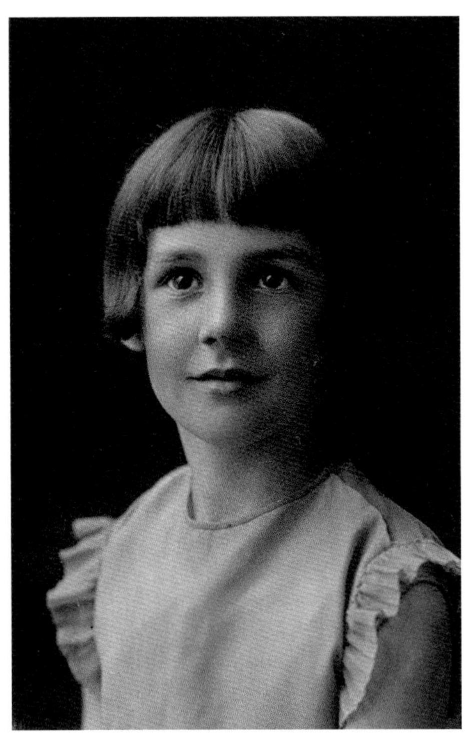

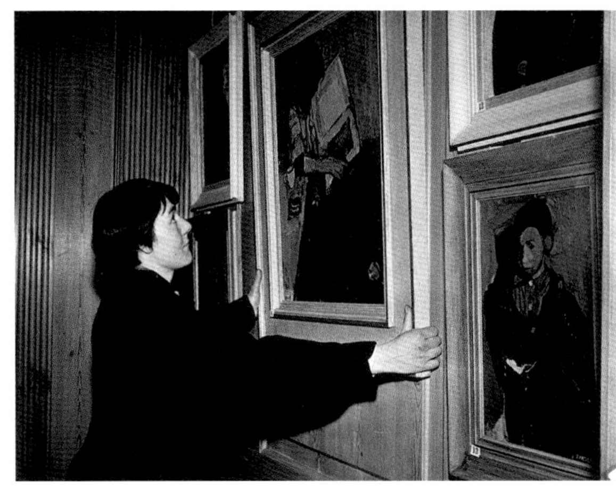

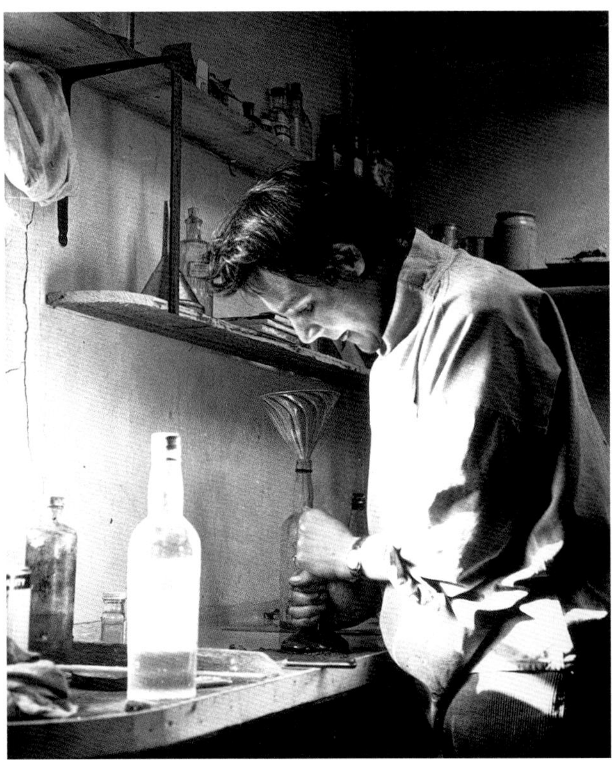

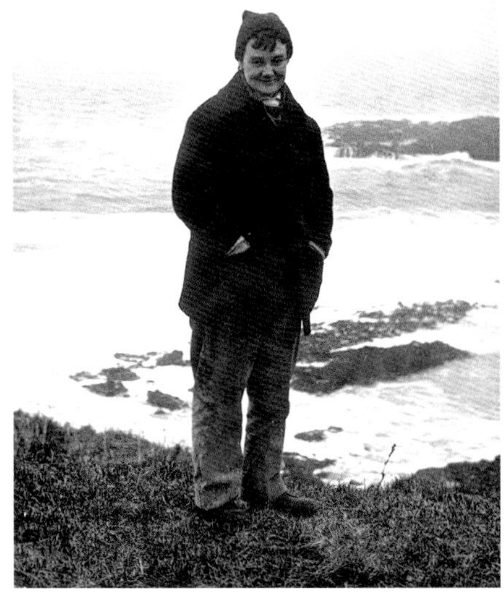

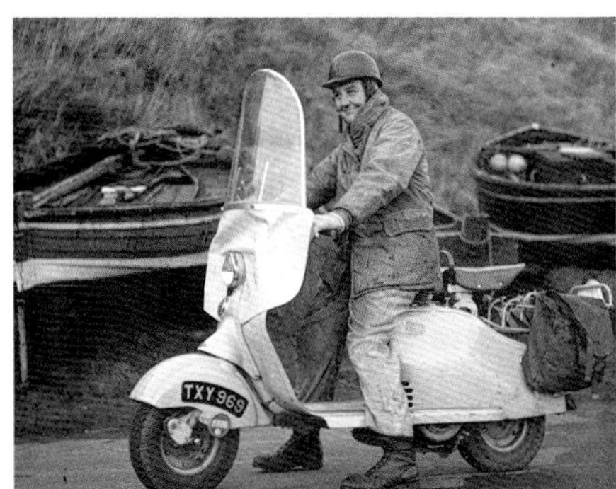

89 | A young Joan Eardley, c.1928
Photographer unknown
Joan Eardley Archive, Scottish National Gallery of Modern Art, Edinburgh [GMA/A09]

90 | Eardley hanging her works at Parsons Gallery, London, 1954
Photo: George Outram & Co.
Joan Eardley Archive, Scottish National Gallery of Modern Art, Edinburgh [GMA/A09]

91 | Joan Eardley at Catterline
Photo: Audrey Walker
Gracefield Art Centre, Dumfries

92 | Eardley on her motor scooter at Catterline, late 1950s
Photo: Audrey Walker

93 | Joan Eardley grinding colours
Photo: Audrey Walker

1948-9 Spends six months travelling in France and Italy, visiting Florence, Venice, Assisi, Ravenna, Padua, Forte dei Marmi, Arezzo, Milan, and Paris. Works by Giotto and Masaccio make biggest impact. Begins painting the disenfranchised in town and country. Asks her mother to send a copy of T.S. Eliot's 'The Waste Land'. Finds colour and shape key to her experience of Italy. Destroys most of her works before leaving Italy. On her return to Glasgow starts drawing and painting children.

1949 Rents a room as a studio at the top of 21 Cochrane Street near to the City Chambers in the centre of Glasgow. Has one-woman show at Glasgow School of Art entitled Drawings of Italy, from which Glasgow School of Art purchases a chalk, ink, and gouache drawing, *Barn and Plough*.

1950 Visits Dorothy Steel in Gourock from 1950-3 and is introduced to Port Glasgow.

1951 Has one-woman show in Aberdeen in an exhibition space attached to the Gaumont Cinema. Falls ill with mumps and during convalescence is taken by Annette Soper to Catterline, a small fishing village south of Aberdeen. They stay at the Creel Inn. First Catterline painting, *Drying Salmon Nets*, shown at the Society of Scottish Artists. Holidays at Cologne du Gers in France with Dorothy Steel, visiting Pyrenees and Lascaux. The Watch House bought by Annette Soper.

1952 Annette Soper marries Catterline fisherman, Jim Stephen, and they let Eardley use the Watch House as a base. Meets Audrey Walker, a photographer, a gifted musician and wife of Sherriff Allan Walker in Glasgow, who becomes a lifelong friend. Walker documents Eardley working in Glasgow and Catterline. She also photographs street graffiti for Eardley to use in her chalked wall paintings. Eardley moves Glasgow studio to 204 St James Road in Townhead, just north of George Square.

1954 Exhibits with Alastair Flattely, Lewin Bassingthwaite, Albert Irvin, Patrick Symons, and Jeffrey Nuttall in Group Show at Parson's Gallery in London.

1955 Eardley buys Number 1 The Row, Catterline. She is elected an Associate of Royal Scottish Academy. Has one-woman shows at St George's Gallery, Cork Street, London, and at The Scottish Gallery, Edinburgh, during Edinburgh International Festival. Visits Walker family home at Caverslea in Borders. Elected Associate of the Royal Scottish Academy.

1956 As a result of a slipped disk suffers neck pain for the rest of her life and needs to wear a surgical collar. Increasingly spends time at Catterline.

1957 Visits London with Audrey Walker to see big Kandinsky exhibition.

1958 Has exhibition in Cosmo Cinema, Glasgow. Shares a show with W.G. Gillies at The Scottish Gallery, Edinburgh, during the Edinburgh International Festival, which includes twenty-five oils and pastels.

1959 Buys Number 18, Catterline and keeps Number 1 as a studio. Has a show with Ann Henderson at the 1957 Gallery in Edinburgh and shows at Arthur Tooth Gallery in London. Critic's Choice exhibition features her work. Visits Marion Finlay, wife of Ian Hamilton Finlay at Comrie, Perthshire.

1960 Eardley is guest tutor at Hospitalfield mid-August to end of September and meets Lil Neilson whom she invites to stay at Catterline.

1961 Has one-woman show at The Scottish Gallery, Edinburgh.

1962 Begins painting flower studies. Shows first signs of serious illness. Has brief holiday at Mentone in December with Dorothy Steel.

1963 Elected Royal Scottish Academician in February and made Honorary Member of Glasgow Society of Lady Artists' Club in March. Holds one-woman show at Roland, Browse and Delbanco, London. Rita Guenigault, a friend of Lil Neilson, nurses Eardley prior to her being hospitalised in Aberdeen. Family suspect a brain tumour with a secondary cancer in her breast and move her to Killearn Hospital. Joan Eardley dies on 16 August 1963 at Killearn Hospital, north of Glasgow. Her ashes are scattered on the beach at Catterline.

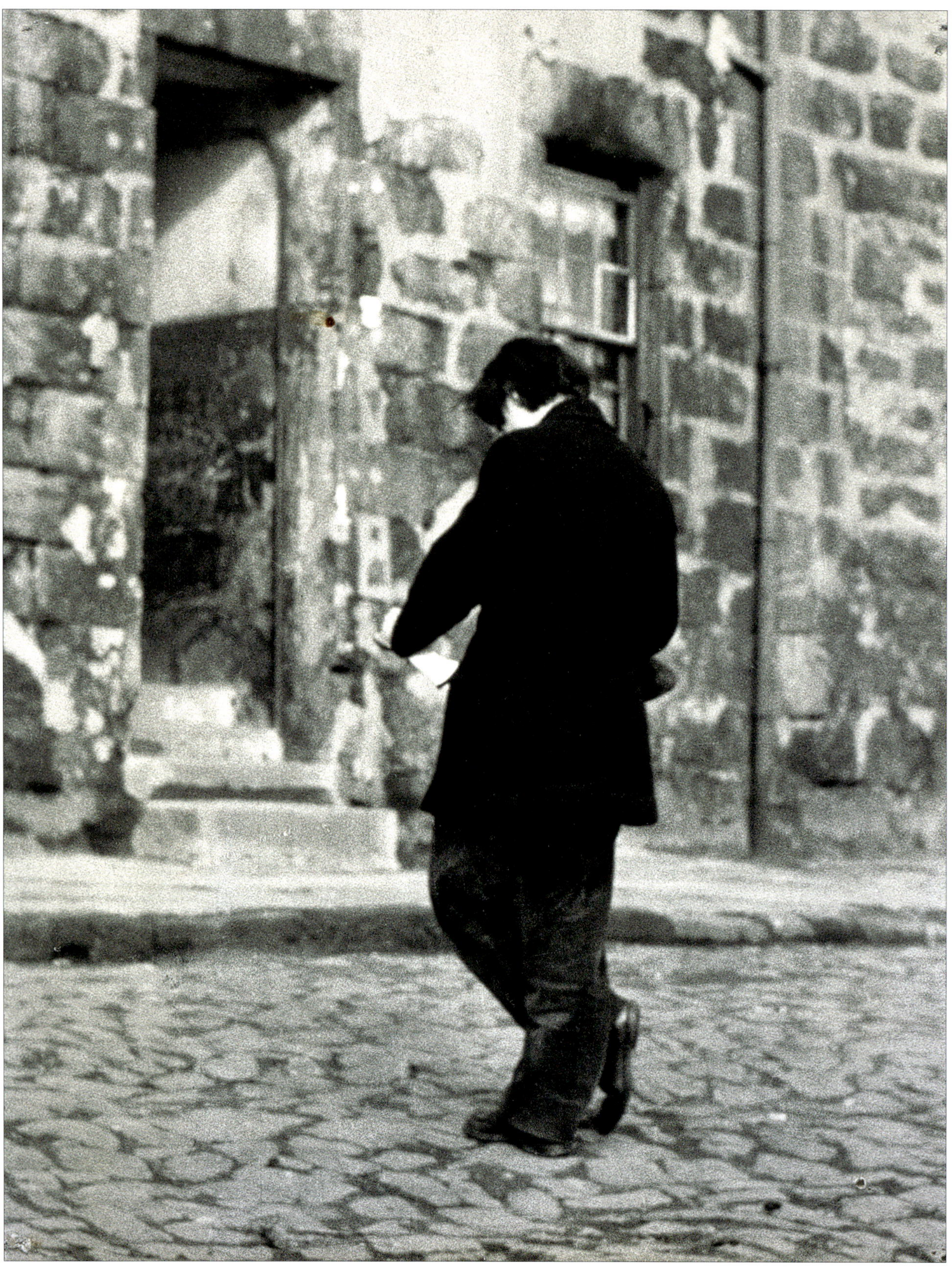

94 | Joan Eardley sketching in front of a Glasgow tenement
Photo: Audrey Walker

Author's Acknowledgements

This book is published on the occasion of a major retrospective exhibition on the life and work of Joan Eardley (1921–1963). Eardley's surviving friends and relatives have been unstinting in their support of this project. I am especially grateful to Joan Eardley's sister Mrs Pat Black and her daughter Anne Morrison for all their help and advice over a number of decades and for their enormous goodwill in presenting the National Galleries of Scotland with a huge body of drawings and archive material. Eardley's fellow students, Cordelia Oliver and Margot Sandeman, have also given a great deal of support with the research, which has brought the subject alive. Ann Steed, a Catterline resident and executor of the estate of Lil Neilson, has given invaluable insights into the role of Catterline in Eardley's life. Bill Buchanan, who, like Cordelia Oliver, has written on Eardley, gave much help and advice. It was also vital to have the first-hand experience of Douglas Hall, former Keeper of the Scottish National Gallery of Modern Art and a great champion of Eardley, and Matilda Mitchell who together with David Irwin catalogued the artist's estate after her death. John G. Walker, the son of Eardley's friend, the photographer Audrey Walker, has kindly made available for our use a large body of photographs of Eardley taken by his mother.

The following organisations have generously agreed important loans to the exhibition: Aberdeen Art Gallery and Museums Collection (Jennifer Melville and Ann Steed); Aberdeen Asset Management PLC Collection (David Watt and Margaret Cottam); The Herbert Art Gallery, Coventry (Ron Clarke); Dumfriesshire Educational Trust, Gracefield Arts Centre (Dawn Henderby); The Royal Bank of Scotland (Frank McGarry); City of Edinburgh Museums and Galleries: City Art Centre (David Patterson); The University of Edinburgh (Jacky MacBeath and Dr John Scally); Royal Scottish Academy (Dr Ian McKenzie Smith and Joanna Soden); Scottish National Portrait Gallery (James Holloway); Henry and Sula Walton Collection; the Eardley Family; Lillie Art Gallery, East Dumbartonshire Council (Hildegard Berwick); Marlene Fairley Collection; Cyril Gerber Fine Art, Glasgow; Glasgow City Council: Kelvingrove Art Gallery and Museum (Mark O'Neill, Hugh Stevenson and Jeff Dunn); Ewan Mundy Fine Art, Glasgow; The Hunterian Museum and Art Gallery (Anne Dulau); Huddersfield Art Gallery (Robert Hall); Abbot Hall Art Gallery, Kendal, Cumbria (Hannah Neale); The Fleming-Wyfold Art Foundation Collection, London (Selina Skipwith); The Government Art Collection (Robert Jones and Jules Breeze); Tate Gallery and Friends of Tate Gallery (Alex Beard and Catherine Clement); Perth Museum and Art Gallery, Perth and Kinross Council (Maria Devaney); University of Stirling Art Collection (Jane Cameron); Derwent College, University of York (Dr Ron Weir); and numerous private collectors who prefer to remain anonymous.

Other colleagues who have been most generous with their time are Cyril and Jill Gerber of Cyril Gerber Fine Art; Guy Peploe of The Scottish Gallery; Emily Walsh and Fiona McAulay of Bourne Fine Art; Duncan Miller of Duncan Miller Fine Art; Chris Brickley of Bonhams, Edinburgh; Nick Curnow of Lyon & Turnbull; Willie Payne of Hospitalfield; and André Zlattinger of Sotheby's. Professor Henry Walton and Bill Buchanan kindly looked at text drafts. The final text was elegantly edited by Patrick Elliott. Personal thanks also go to Anne Davies, Keith Hartley, Daniel Herrmann, Susan Martin, Sara Stevenson, and colleagues in the National Galleries of Scotland for their help and support.

FIONA PEARSON

Senior Curator, Scottish National Gallery of Modern Art

Bibliography

Books and Articles

David Anfam, *Abstract Expressionism*, London, 1990

Philippe Aries, *Centuries of Childhood*, London, 1962

Martin Baillie, 'Joan Eardley RSA', *The Glasgow Review*, summer 1964, vol.1, no.2, pp.23–31

Martin Baillie, *Glasgow Herald*, 20 May 1975

Iain Barnet and Guy Peploe, *150 Years of Aitken Dott, The Scottish Gallery*, Edinburgh, 1992

Oliver Bevan, 'Difficult Children', in *Artists and Illustrators*, no.139, April 1998, pp.18–19, 21

Andrew Blaikie, 'Photography, Childhood and Urban Poverty; Remembering "The Forgotten Gorbals"', in *Visual Culture in Britain*, vol.7, no.2, 2006, pp.47–68

O. Blakeston, 'Joan Eardley (Browse and Darby London exhibition review)', *Arts Review*, vol.32, no.9–10, 23 May 1980, p.18

Douglas Percy Bliss, 'Art in Scotland Now', in *The Studio*, vol.156, no.726, September 1953, pp.65–73

Thomas Bodkin, *The Approach to Painting*, London, 1945

Alan Bowness, 'Reflections on Scottish Painting Today', in *New Saltire*, summer 1961 pp.64–7

Alan Bowness, 'The "Provincial" Painters', in *Arts Magazine*, November 1961

Lillian Browse, *Duchess of Cork Street*, London, 2000

William Buchanan, 'The Gallery at Langholm', in *Scottish Art Review*, vol.x, no.1, pp.1–3

William Buchanan, 'Painting the richness of Glasgow', in *The Listener*, 5 March 1964, pp.394–5

William Buchanan, *Joan Eardley*, Modern Scottish Painters no.5, Edinburgh, 1976

Keith Clements, 'Artists and Places no.11: Joan Eardley', in *Artist*, vol.101, no.12, December 1986, pp.27–9

Emilio Coia, 'Art', *Scottish Field*, September 1964, p.75

Emilio Coia, 'Joan Eardley', in *Scottish Art Review*, vol.9, no.3, 1964, pp.2–7

Emilio Coia, 'Exhibitions', *Scottish Field*, December 1965

Christopher Connell, unpublished thesis on the life of Joan Eardley, Gray's School of Art, Aberdeen, October 1975, Scottish National Gallery of Modern Art Archive

J.D. Fergusson, *Modern Scottish Painting*, Glasgow, 1943

Christopher Finch, *Image as Language: Aspects of British Art 1950–68*, London, 1969

Ian Finlay, *Art in Scotland*, London, 1948

Richard Finlay, *Modern Scotland 1914–2000*, London, 2004

Margaret Garlake, *New Art New World*, New Haven and London, 1998

James Grassie, *Oscar Marzaroli: Shades of Scotland*, Edinburgh, 1989

Henry Guy, 'Angus Neil: The Quiet Man', unpublished typescript, Glasgow School of Art Archive, 1995. Copy held in the Scottish National Gallery of Modern Art Library

Douglas Hall, 'Drawings by Joan Eardley RSA (1921–63)', in *The Connoisseur*, July 1965, pp.178–82

Douglas Hall, *Joan Eardley 1921–1963*, Scottish Artists in the Scottish National Gallery of Modern Art 3, Edinburgh, 1979

H. Forsyth Hardy, 'New Films of Scotland', in *Scottish Field*, May 1963, pp.42–3

Josef Herman, *Related Twilights: Notes from an Artist's Diary*, London, 1975

Robert Hewison, *In Anger: Culture in the Cold War 1945–60*, London, 1981

Derek Hill, *New Statesman*, 29 August 1959

T.J. Honeyman, 'Art in Scotland', in *The Studio*, vol.126, no.606, September 1943, pp.65–77

James Hyman, *The Battle for Realism*, London, 2001

David Irwin, 'The work of Joan Eardley', in *New Saltire*, no.11, April 1964, pp.21–4

David Irwin and Douglas Hall, *Joan Eardley Estate Lists of Paintings and Drawings*, unpublished typescript, Scottish National Gallery of Modern Art Archive

Ian Jeffrey, *The British Landscape 1920–1950*, London, 1984

William Johnstone, *Child Art to Man Art*, London, 1941

Pierre Lavalle, 'Artists', in *Scottish Field*, June 1963, pp.23–5

James Macaulay, Kathy Chambers and Susannah Thompson, *Art Booms with the Guns: The War Years and Glasgow School of Art*, Glasgow, 2001

Nigel McIsaac, 'II Private Patrons View of RSA' in *The Studio*, vol.154, no.773, August 1957, p.56

William McLellan, *The New Scottish Group*, Glasgow, 1947

Duncan Macmillan, *Scottish Art in the Twentieth Century*, Edinburgh, 1994

Terence Mullaly, 'The Tate à la Mode', in *The Daily Telegraph*, 9 December 1965

Eric Newton, *The Penguin Modern Painters: Stanley Spencer*, London, 1947

Eric Newton, *The Guardian*, 29 June 1963

Cordelia Oliver, 'Joan Eardley and Glasgow', in *Scottish Art Review*, vol.14, no.3, 1974, pp.16–19

Cordelia Oliver, 'Joan Eardley and Catterline', in *The Scots Magazine*, vol.112, no.2, November 1979, pp.133–41

Cordelia Oliver, *The Guardian*, 27 May 1975

Cordelia Oliver, *Joan Eardley*, Edinburgh, 1988

Cordelia Oliver, 'Joan Eardley RSA' in *The Green Book*, vol.2, no.4, 1986

Cordelia Oliver, 'Through Women's Eyes: Women Painters in Scotland', in *Modern Painters*, vol.12, no.4, winter 1999, pp.93–4

Fiona Pearson, *Joan Eardley 1921–1963*, Edinburgh, 1988

Bronwen Pulsford, 'A Reminiscence of Joan Eardley', unpublished typescript, Scottish National Gallery of Modern Art Archive, 1983

Robert Rosenblum, *The Romantic Child from Runge to Sendak*, London, 1988

Scottish Artists, 'Joan Eardley Archive Information Paper No.3', unpublished typescript, 1987, Scottish National Gallery of Modern Art Archive

Scottish Artists, 'Joan Eardley Archive Paper No.2 Addendum', unpublished typescript, n.d., Scottish National Gallery of Modern Art Archive

Ben Shahn, *The Shape of Content*, Cambridge, Mass., 1957

Dawn Sidoli, 'Out of the Dark', in *Artists and Illustrators*, no.120, September 1996 pp.12–15

Sydney Goodsir Smith, 'Portrait of the Artist 7: Joan Eardley', *The Scotsman*, 19 August 1961, p.5

Sara Stevenson, *Photographing Children*, Edinburgh, 1993

Neville Wallis, *The Spectator*, 30 August 1963

Victoria Walsh, *Nigel Henderson: Parallel of Life and Art*, London, 2001

R.H. Westwater, 'Joan Eardley' in *Scottish Art Review*, vol.6, no.2, 1957, pp.2–6

R.H. Wilenski, *Modern French Painters*, London, 1940

R.H. Wilenski, *The Modern Movement*, London, 1927 (4th ed. 1947)

H. Harvey Wood, 'Contemporary Scottish Art', in *Scottish Art Review*, vol.III, no.1, 1950, pp.18–26

Malcolm Yorke, *The Spirit of Place, Nine Neo-Romantic Artists and Their Times*, London, 1988

Exhibition Catalogues

in chronological order

Eight Young Contemporary British Painters, Arts Council – Scottish Committee, Edinburgh, 1952

An Exhibition of Paintings by Six Young Artists: Joan Eardley, Alastair Flattely, Lewin Bassingthwaite, Albert Irvin, Patrick Symons, Jeffrey Nuttall, Parsons Gallery, London, 1954

Robert Henriques (introduction), *Eardley*, St George's Gallery, London, 1955

Terence Mullaly (introduction), *Critic's Choice*, Arthur Tooth & Sons Ltd., London, 1959

Lillian Browse, *Joan Eardley*, Roland, Browse and Delbanco, London, 1963

Lilian Browse (introduction), *Joan Eardley, Recent Paintings*, Roland, Browse and Delbanco, London, 1963

Cordelia Oliver, *Joan Eardley* RSA (1921–1963), the Scottish Committee of the Arts Council of Great Britain, 1964

Cordelia Oliver (introduction), *Joan Eardley Memorial Exhibition*, The Scottish Gallery, Edinburgh, 1964

Lilian Browse, *Joan Eardley*, Roland, Browse and Delbanco, London, 1965

Mainly Children: Pastels by Joan Eardley, Roland, Browse and Delbanco, London, 1968

Douglas Hall (introduction), 'Exhibition of Paintings by Joan Eardley', unpublished typescript,, University of Stirling, 1969

Cordelia Oliver (introduction), *Joan Eardley*, Third Eye Centre, Glasgow, 1975

Four Contemporary Scottish painters: Eardley, Haig, Philipson, Pulsford, Ashmolean Museum, Oxford, 1977

Joan Eardley, Royal Scottish Academy, Edinburgh, 1977

Cordelia Oliver, *Painters in Parallel*, Edinburgh College of Art, Scottish Arts Council, 1978

Aftermath: France 1945–54: New Images of Man, Barbican Art Gallery, London, 1982

Elizabeth Dent, *Joan Eardley* RSA 1921–1963, Lillie Art Gallery, Milngavie, 1982

Landscape in Britain 1850–1950, Hayward Gallery, Arts Council of Great Britain, London, 1983

Joan Eardley RSA, The Scottish Gallery, Edinburgh, 1984

David Mellor, *A Paradise Lost: The Neo-Romantic Imagination in Britain 1935–55*, Barbican Art Gallery, London, 1987

Joan Eardley RSA, The Scottish Gallery, Edinburgh, 1988

Cordelia Oliver, *Joan Eardley* RSA, Talbot Rice Gallery, University of Edinburgh, in association with the Royal Scottish Academy, 1988

Nerys Johnson, *Moments of Being*, South Bank Centre, London, 1988

Keith Hartley, *Scottish Art since 1900*, Scottish National Gallery of Modern Art, Edinburgh, 1989

When We Were Young: Childhood in British Art 1880–1989, City Art Centre, Edinburgh, 1989

Joan Eardley, The Scottish Gallery, London, 1990

Old and New Scottish Colourists, Kirkcaldy Museum and Art Gallery, 1991

Sara Holdsworth and Joan Crossley, *Innocence and Experience: Images of Children in British Art from 1600 to the Present*, Manchester City Art Galleries, 1992

Cordelia Oliver, *Angus Neil 1924–1992: paintings and pastels*, foreword by Ian McKenzie Smith, City of Aberdeen District Council, 1994

Certain Days and Other Seasons: Lil Neilson, The Seagate Gallery, Dundee, 1996

Lil Neilson, *Into the Light: The Art of Lil Neilson*, Aberdeen Art Gallery, 1999

Martin Harrison, *Transition: The London Art Scene in the Fifties*, Barbican Art Gallery, London, 2002

Joan Eardley RSA, The Scottish Gallery, Edinburgh, 2003

Tempests and Romantic Visionaries: Images of Storms in European and American Art, Oklahoma City Museum of Art, 2006

Obituaries

Hugh Stewart, *Evening Express*, 31 August 1963

Glasgow Herald, 17 August 1963

J.F.T. Morrison, *The Mearns Leader*, 23 August 1963, p.2

Milngavie and Bearsden Herald, 22 August 1963

The Scotsman, 19 August 1963

Hugh Adam Crawford, SATA *Scottish Art Teacher's Association Bulletin*, September 1963

Neville Wallis, 'Joan Eardley', *The Spectator*, 30 August 1963

Film

Three Scottish Painters (Maxwell, Eardley, Philipson), Templar Film Studios, Scottish Committee of the Arts Council, and British Council, 1963

Radio

Street Kids and Stormy Skies, compiled and produced by Vivian Devlin. First broadcast on BBC Radio Scotland 18 August 1983 to commemorate twentieth anniversary of Eardley's death.

Joan Eardley, presented and produced by Vivian Devlin for broadcast on BBC Radio Scotland 29 March 1988. Review of twenty-fifth anniversary exhibitions planned for 1988 at Talbot Rice Art Centre and Royal Scottish Academy.

BBC taped interview with Eardley, recorded 14 January 1963, Scottish National Gallery of Modern Art Archive.

Photographic & Copyright Credits

All works in the collection of the National Galleries of Scotland and numbers 1, 12, 13, 14, 17, 25, 26, 32, 36, 37, 38, 39, 43, 44, 45, 47, 48, 50, 56, 59, 69 and 74 were photographed by Antonia Reeve and are © the Trustees of the National Galleries of Scotland. The frontispiece and numbers 27, 28, 29, 31a–c, 52, 53, 73, 83, 88, 91, 92, 93 and 94 are courtesy The Walker Estate; numbers 7 and 8 are © Margot Sandeman Estate; numbers 21 and 54 were photographed by and are © the estate of George Oliver; numbers 55 and 85 are © the estate of Oscar Marzaroli; number 57 is photo: Tate; numbers 64 and 68 are courtesy the Fleming Collection; number 86 is the Roger Mayne Archive; number 87 is Bert Hardy / Picture Post via Getty Images; and numbers 92 and 94 are courtesy The Scottish Gallery. Other photographic material was kindly supplied by the lenders.

Notes and References

Notes to pages 11-79

1 See chronology for family history. Irene was Scottish and had herself had some art training.
2 Margot Sandeman interviews with the author on 12 January 2006; 5 December 2006; 18 April 2007; 30 April 2007; and 23 June 2007.
3 See chronology for details of the courses, teachers and register numbers. All this material has been taken from the records held in the Glasgow School of Art Archive.
4 See the *Annual Report* for 1942-3, p.10, in Glasgow School of Art Archive.
5 *Glasgow Herald*, 11 May 1940.
6 Both the Crawford self-portrait and the painting by Eardley are now in the collection of the Scottish National Portrait Gallery in Edinburgh.
7 In 1948 there was a Van Gogh exhibition at Kelvingrove Art Gallery in Glasgow. Also in 1948, Vuillard and Bonnard were shown at the Edinburgh International Festival. The intimate domestic scenes which they painted were a forerunner of Eardley's interiors.
8 Josef Herman, *Related Twilights: Notes from an Artist's Diary*, London 1975.
9 Sandeman correspondence (private collection). Most of the letters are undated. Adler's work was illustrated in the book by Herbert Read, *Art Now*, published in London in 1932.
10 Eardley's correspondence with her mother is in the Joan Eardley Archive, Scottish National Gallery of Modern Art, Edinburgh [GMA/A09].
11 Sandeman correspondence (private collection).
12 Sandeman correspondence (private collection).
13 Joan Eardley Archive, Scottish National Gallery of Modern Art, Edinburgh [GMA/A09].
14 2 January 1947, Eardley to Sandeman from Shepherds Bush, Sandeman correspondence (private collection).
15 Undated letter from Eardley to Sandeman from 136 Coleraine Road, Blackheath SE3, Sandeman correspondence (private collection).
16 26 January 1947 letter from Eardley to Sandeman from Great Missenden, Bucks. Sandeman correspondence (private collection).
17 Undated letter from Eardley to Sandeman from Hospitalfield, Sandeman correspondence (private collection).
18 Henry Guy, 'Angus Neil: The Quiet Man', unpublished typescript dated 10 November 1995 in the Glasgow School of Art Archive. There is a copy in the Scottish National Gallery of Modern Art Library. Guy is the son of Neil's fellow diploma student, Carole Gibbons.
19 Undated letter from Eardley to Sandeman from Hospitalfield, Sandeman correspondence (private collection).
20 A number of Joan Eardley's press cuttings, many undated and from unknown sources, are in the Joan Eardley Archive, Scottish National Gallery of Modern Art, Edinburgh [GMA/A09].
21 Eardley's letters to her mother are in the Joan Eardley Archive, Scottish National Gallery of Modern Art, Edinburgh [GMA/A09].
22 Ibid.
23 From Eardley's Italian notebook, which was gifted by Audrey Walker to Gracefield Art Centre, Dumfries.
24 Ibid.
25 Undated letters in the Joan Eardley Archive, Scottish National Gallery of Modern Art, Edinburgh [GMA/A09].
26 Undated letter from Eardley to her mother, Sandeman correspondence (private collection).
27 Letter from Eardley to her mother in the Joan Eardley Archive, Scottish National Gallery of Modern Art, Edinburgh [GMA/A09].
28 From Eardley's Italian notebook, which was gifted by Audrey Walker to Gracefield Art Centre, Dumfries.
29 Sandeman correspondence (private collection).
30 From Eardley's Italian notebook, which was gifted by Audrey Walker to Gracefield Art Centre, Dumfries.
31 Press clipping from the *Glasgow Herald*, 1949, in the Joan Eardley Archive, Scottish National Gallery of Modern Art, Edinburgh [GMA/A09].
32 *The Scotsman*, 15 October 1949.
33 *Glasgow Herald*, 15 October 1949.
34 William Buchanan, *Joan Eardley*, Edinburgh 1976, p.23.
35 Eardley writes to Sandeman at Forte dei Marmi at the end of 1948 that her mother is sending her the *New Statesman*. Undated letter, Sandeman correspondence (private collection).
36 Extract from a tape recording in the Joan Eardley Archive, Scottish National Gallery of Modern Art, Edinburgh [GMA/A09].
37 In 1947 the Hogarth Press published a book of Scottish nursery rhymes. Eardley gave a copy of the *Oxford Book of Nursery Rhymes* by Peter and Iona Opie to Margot Sandeman when her first child was born.
38 Letters from 22 July to 22 October 1951, Sandeman correspondence (private collection).
39 Sandeman correspondence (private collection).
40 From Eardley's Italian notebook, which was gifted by Audrey Walker to Gracefield Art Centre, Dumfries.
41 Margot Sandeman interviewed by the author, 30 April 2007.
42 *Glasgow Herald*, 24 February 1954, clipping in the Joan Eardley Archive, Scottish National Gallery of Modern Art, Edinburgh [GMA/A09].
43 *The Bon Accord and Northern Pictorial*, Aberdeen, undated clipping in the Joan Eardley Archive at the Scottish National Gallery of Modern Art, Edinburgh [GMA/A09].
44 This was mentioned in a paper given by Cordelia Oliver at the seminar, 'Writing Scottish Art' held at Dundee Contemporary Arts, 8 September 2006.
45 David Irwin, 'The Work of Joan Eardley', in *New Saltire*, no.11, April 1964, pp.21-4.
46 *The Scotsman*, 19 August 1961.
47 Extract from a tape recording in the Joan Eardley Archive, Scottish National Gallery of Modern Art, Edinburgh [GMA/A09].
48 Margot Sandeman remembers Eardley being drawn to the songs of Benjamin Britten as sung by Peter Pears, most notably 'O Rose, Thou Art Sick' after the William Blake poem.
49 Undated correspondence in the archive of The Scottish Gallery, Edinburgh.
50 Now in the Alfred East Art Gallery, Kettering.
51 Margot Sandeman interviewed by the author, 5 December 2006.
52 Lillian Browse, *The Duchess of Cork Street*, London 2000.
53 Alan Bowness, *Arts Magazine*, November 1961.
54 See Kincardine Register Office records held at the National Archives of Scotland, Edinburgh.

Notes to pages 81-6

1 William Buchanan, *Joan Eardley*, Edinburgh 1976, p.36.
2 W.H. Fox Talbot, *The Pencil of Nature*, first published 1845, reprinted in Henry Fox Talbot, *Selected Texts and Bibliography* (ed. Mike Weaver), Oxford 1992, p.94.
3 George Oliver, 'Oscar Marzaroli', in *One Man's World: Oscar Marzaroli Photographs 1955-84*, exhibition catalogue, Third Eye Centre, Glasgow, 1984, p.6.
4 Quoted in William Buchanan, *Joan Eardley*, Edinburgh 1976, p.15.
5 Foreword by Archibald MacLeish in *The Photographic Eye of Ben Shahn* (ed. Davis Pratt), Cambridge Mass. 1975, quoted in Deborah Martin Kao, Laura Katzman and Jenna Webster, *Ben Shahn's New York. The Photography of Modern Times*, exhibition catalogue, Harvard University Art Museums, 2000, p.317.
6 Quoted in Buchanan, p.27.
7 A.L. Lloyd, 'The Forgotten Gorbals' in *Picture Post*, 31 January 1948, pp.11-16.
8 Bert Hardy, *My Life*, London 1985, p.104. For a criticism of this photograph, see Andrew Blaikie, 'Photography, Childhood and Urban Poverty: Remembering "The Forgotten Gorbals"' in *Visual Culture in Britain*, vol. 7 no. 2, 2006, pp.47-68.
9 Ibid., p.107.